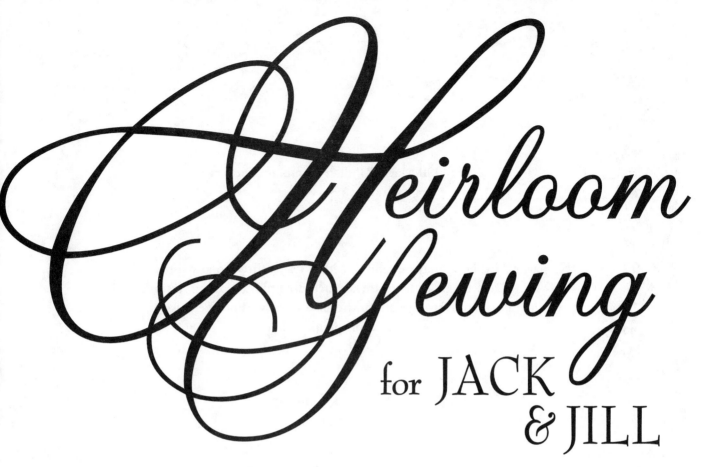

# Heirloom Sewing for JACK & JILL

*May God Bless You*
*Martha Pullen*

*Martha Campbell Pullen, Ph.D.*

Printed By The C. J. Krehbiel Company
Cincinnati, Ohio

Published and Distributed by
Martha Pullen Company
518 Madison Street Huntsville, AL 35801

256-533-9586

ISBN 1-878048-22-8

www.marthapullen.com

# Book Team

## *Heirloom Sewing for Jack and Jill*

by *Martha Campbell Pullen, Ph.D.*

Book Design and Layout by *Kelly Chambers*

Chief Book Engineers: *Charlotte Potter, Patty Smith and Kathy McMakin*

Illustrations by *Angela Cataldo Pullen, Kris Broom, Suzy Peterson,*
*Charlotte Potter, Cynthia Quintela, Diane Bradshaw* and *Julie McMakin*

Photography by *Jennifer & Company* and *Saint Portrait Designers*

Photo Styling by *Charlotte Potter, Claudia Newton, Hilda Wright,*
*Patty Smith, Leighann Simmons, Kathy Baggett, Sue Johnson*

Writing and Editing by *Charlotte Potter, Patty Smith, Louise Baird, Kris Broom, Amelia Johanson,*
*Meredith Miller, Jo Paoletti, Ph.D., Joanna Pullen Hammett* and *Kathy McMakin*

Garment Design and Sewing Contributors: *Sue Pennington, Charlotte Potter,*
*Louise Baird, Donna Marcum, Janice Stewart, Mary Madison Railey, Starlette Picket,*
*Isabelle Lott, Lynda Delallo, Pam Schneider, Sandra Glenn, Charlotte Gallagher,*
*Gail Settle, Marie Hendon, Maggie Hillard, Laura Jenkins Thompson, Edie Townsend,*
*Susan York, Patti Jo Larson* and *Lynne Holyoake*

Smocking Contributors: *Suzy Peterson, Stephanie Self, Beth Gault, Jennifer Roemen,*
*Janice Stewart, Julie Wickland* and *Donna Marcum*

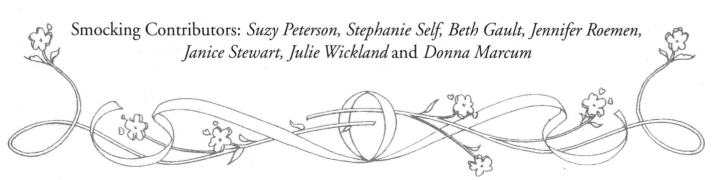

# Dedication

*This book is dedicated with love to our ten grandchildren.*

*Mark 10:13-16*

*13 People were bringing little children to him in order that he might touch them; and the disciples spoke sternly to them.*

*14 But when Jesus saw this, he was indignant and said to them, "Truly I tell you, whoever does not receive the kingdom of God as a little child will never enter it."*

*16 And he took them up in his arms, laid his hands on them, and blessed them.*

Photo by Jennifer and Company

*Sarah Joy Crocker*, my beautiful granddaughter, who loves to sew and who pushes the larger people out of the way so she can bring the little children to see the puppets when we are on mission in Africa.

*Rebekah Anne Crocker*, my beautiful granddaughter, who loves to sew and who memorized a scripture from 1st Peter and said she had learned a verse from "First Rabbit."

*Christopher Alexander Crocker* who loves to laugh and who rolls over and hollers "Everybody pray, pray, pray" when he falls down and hurts his knee.

Sarah Joy, Rebekah and Christopher are the children of Suzanne and John Crocker.

*William Campbell Crocker, jr.* who has impeccable manners and who asked me to pray with him to ask Jesus into his heart at the Dairy Queen.

*James Marshall Wynn Crocker* whose smiles light up my life and who replied when asked if he would like to go get ice cream, "Yes, sir, Granny."

Campbell and Marshall are the sons of Charisse and Camp Crocker.

Photo by Jennifer and Company

*Morgan Ross Pullen*, my beautiful granddaughter, who loves to sew and who is extraordinarily kind, patient and attentive to caring for her little sister Bradley and her baby brother, Ward.

*Amanda Bradley Pullen*, my beautiful granddaughter who loves to sew and who dreams of becoming a "home mommy."

*Mark Edward Pullen, jr. (Ward)* who is our little laughing man who brings such joy to everybody with his smiles, giggles and hugs.

Morgan Ross, Bradley and Ward are the children of Sherry Ann and Mark Pullen.

*Emma Ross Pullen*, my beautiful granddaughter who could talk while she was still sitting in the infant seat. She alternates calling her dog "Willoughby" or "Bubba."

Emma is the daughter of Angela and Jeff Pullen

*Cecil Elizabeth Hammett*, my beautiful granddaughter who is named for me. Her big beautiful blue eyes just dance when she smiles at all who come near.

Cecil is the daughter of Joanna and Chase Hammett.

# Acknowledgments

*The first month of the new millennium, January, 2000 AD.*

*Lamentations 3: 21-24*
*21 But this I call to mind, and therefore I have hope;*
*22 The steadfast love of the Lord never ceases, his mercies never come to an end;*
*23 they are new every morning; great is your faithfulness.*
*24 "The Lord is my portion," says my soul, "therefore I will hope in him."*

As Jeremiah looked at the precious hope in everything surrounding him, he saw that God's steadfast love was never ceasing, his mercies never come to an end, and those mercies are new every morning. How comforting to know of God's love and grace. God has never abandoned me. God has never failed to forgive my many transgressions. The wonderful power of God never ceases to overwhelm me. I have done nothing to deserve the many blessings he has showered upon me, my family and my business. I trust God every day to lead my life in the way He would have me lead it. I flounder miserably but I know He is there to pick up the pieces. I thank God for the privilege of writing this book and for the goodness and strength He has provided for all the people who helped. I ask His special blessings on all who worked diligently to produce this book and on all who read and enjoy this book for many generations to come. God alone gets the credit for our business and for all products developed therein; without Him this book would not have been possible.

Producing a book this complicated, this deep, this long, this detailed, and this complex requires the help of many individuals over a period of several years. I could have never produced this book by myself and I am grateful to each individual who helped in any way. I have always said my greatest business talent God granted to me was the insight to hire wonderful people. A great team has sewn, drafted, written, drawn, edited and edited some more. Their philosophy is somewhat like Mark Twain's who wrote "The difference between the right word and the almost right word is the difference between lightning and the lightning bug." We hope we have written and edited where lightning is on every page. You, of course, will be the judge of that.

Even after several years of sewing for, writing and compiling this book, my group has massive enthusiasm concerning the project. I am reminded of Norman Vincent Peale's statement, "So we must learn how to utilize enthusiasm in order to move into that exciting and creative segment of the human race-the achievers. You will find among them total agreement that enthusiasm is a priceless ingredient of personality that helps to achieve happiness and self-fulfillment." You may remember Dr. Peale's book, *The Power*

*of Positive Thinking.* Our team has never had anything but positive thinking concerning this book even when it became larger and larger and larger and had more and more details added almost daily, it seemed.

Even though my name appears on the cover, I would like to give thanks to the many people who helped me make this book become a reality. The sewing, writing, drafting, encouragement, photography, book design and layout, drawing, printing, inspiration and love of a lot of people always will be a cornerstone of any book produced by Martha Pullen Company. To the following people, I will be eternally gratefully. My love and thanks go to each one of them.

My mother and father, Anna Ruth Dicus Campbell and the late Paul Jones Campbell are the world's greatest parents. The most important lessons they taught me were that God was to be first in my life and that He is never failing. I was taken to church every Sunday of my life and the church was the center of our lives. My family kept the Sabbath holy and we were not allowed to go to the movies or even to go fishing on Sunday. They taught me that nothing replaces hard work and that I should never expect hand outs but rather should work hard for everything in this life. They were always there to encourage me and to demand excellence in my work. I was taught to obey them and to follow the rules of life. Being lazy was not tolerated and they set the first example of this principle themselves. I was taught that this is the best country in the world and that we must respect the laws of the land. They taught me that being kind to those less fortunate was one of my greatest responsibilities since I had been given so much. My parents provided a wonderful education for me through their working very hard and doing without to save for my college expenses. I had a mother and a father in the home who taught me what a home and a family should be. In their later years they taught me that God is still perfect even when very bad things happen to one's health. Both my mother, now, and my father when he was in horrid health, daily have said how good God is to them and how they have been blessed. In short, they have taught me how to accept whatever health problems and great indignities of life should be in front of me.

My late grandmother and grandfather, Martha Isabelle Baker Dicus and Leonard Houston Dicus were among the most influential people in my life and I love them very much. Nannie loved education more than anyone I ever knew and she pushed me for excellence and for achievement. Nannie began teaching in the state of Alabama in 1915 and taught for 3 years during the great depression for no money at all, only promissory notes from the state of Alabama. When I was getting my Ph.D. in education, I asked my Nannie, "Nannie why did you teach for three years for no money?" She replied in a very stern voice, "Why young lady what do you mean? The state of Alabama had no money and the children had to have an education." End of subject. Granddaddy taught me how to climb trees and how to drive a car. Their financial sacrifices for my education and for anything else I needed were tremendous. Nannie's sugar cookies were the world's best comfort food. I also loved her boxes of neatly sliced sour cream pound cake delivered to my mail box when I was at the University of Alabama.

My late mother and father-in-law, Dr. Joyce Buren Pullen and Emma Eileen Hodges Pullen contributed so much love to Joe and me and our children. Mom spent countless hours cooking and baby sitting so I could start this business.

My cousin, the late Christine Finch Jenkins, taught me the joy of sewing when I was a very little girl. We made doll clothes and Christmas stockings with a needle, thread and glue. What fun!

My high school home economics teacher, Sarah Betty Ingram, led me to believe that I could sew anything, design anything and cook anything. I loved my four years of high school home economics classes.

My sister and brother-in-law, Mary Campbell Nixon and Rick Nixon have always been there for me. Mary worked for me in the business for a couple of years and always brought Anna and David for the photo shoots. Mary's son, Alex Walter Jackson, Jr. was also in all of our publications before he was murdered by a drunk driver when he was seven years old. I would like to thank *Mother's Against Drunk Driving* for their efforts in removing drunk drivers from the roads. If you are reading this book please realize that the children that you love more than anything else in this world could be killed by drunk drivers today. Little Al was getting on his bicycle to ride a couple of blocks home on a Friday afternoon in one of the nicest neighborhoods in Montgomery.

My sister, Dottie Campbell Tatum, and my brothers Paul Keith Campbell and Dr. Clifford Ward Campbell for loving me and for always being proud of my business. I love them and their spouses, Joanne Campbell, Millie Campbell and the late Bob Tatum, Also I would like to acknowledge their precious children, Paula, Bonnell, Keith, David, Jon, Carole, Diane, Bonnie and their families.

Our children, Camp, John, Mark, Jeff and Joanna will be mentioned individually; however, each of them had fewer home cooked meals, less time to be hovered over by Mom, less baby sitting time with their children by Grandmother, and less time for me just to be at home because of my building this business. They have been so supportive and they seem very proud of what we have been able to accomplish. I have chosen a special verse of scripture to "send" to each of our children rather than write pages about the wonderful things they have done for me and for my business. I love each of them and their families more than words could ever express.

Our son, William Campbell Crocker and his wife Charisse Fuentes Crocker for working with me in this business and for helping us be where we are today. Their excitement and enthusiasm about sewing and people who sew helped this business grow and thrive

when they were in Huntsville working with me. Both the television show and the subscriber video were Camp's ideas; I still remember the day the two of us went to Tuscaloosa to see if the University of Alabama wanted to be our "partners" in developing *Martha's Sewing Room*. They brought the boys to many photo shoots while they were still small enough to wear the clothing. Although they are living and working in Scottsdale, Arizona today, the ideas they initiated for growth of Martha Pullen Company will always be appreciated. I love them and appreciate them. My scripture for Camp and Charisse is Romans 8:28 "We know that all things work together for good for those who love God, who are called according to his purpose."

Our son, John Houston Crocker and his wife Suzanne Laramore Crocker for loving our Lord so much that they followed His leading and serve him as missionaries with the Southern Baptist International Mission Board in Togo, West Africa. Suzanne has sewn many beautiful garments and quilts for the magazine and for several of our books. Suzanne is teaching the girls how to sew. I love them and I appreciate them. My scripture for John and Suzanne is Matthew 28:18-20 "And Jesus came and said to them, 'All authority in heaven and on earth has been given to me. 19 Go therefore and make disciples of all nations, baptizing them in the name of the Father, and of the Son and of the Holy Spirit, 20 and teaching them to obey everything that I have commanded you. And remember, I am with you always, to the end of the age.'"

Our son, Mark Edward Pullen and his wife Sherry Ann Green Pullen for always encouraging me in my business endeavors and for bringing the children to massive photo shoots. Mark's joining Joe in the dental practice has freed Joe's time substantially so he has been able to work more in the management of my business. Sherry Ann is a wonderful needle woman and she is encouraging the girls to love sewing. I love them and appreciate them. My scripture for Mark and Sherry Ann is Philippians 4: 4-6 "4 Rejoice in the Lord always; again I will say, Rejoice. 5 Let your gentleness be known to everyone. The Lord is near. 6 Do not worry about anything, but in everything by prayer and supplication with thanksgiving let your requests be made known to God."

Our son, Jeffery David Pullen and his wife Angela Cataldo Pullen for always encouraging me in my business endeavors. Angela has been one of our main artists since before they were married. Her art literally lives and breaths the essence of heirloom sewing. I also appreciate her creativity and excitement in working with me in designing machine embroidery disks for many different companies including Martha Pullen Company. I appreciate their moving back to Huntsville for Jeff to start his real estate and construction business. Many thanks, also, for bringing Emma to photo shoots. I love them and appreciate them. My scripture for Jeff and Angela is Psalm 24:1 "The earth is the Lord's and all that is in it, the world, and those who live in it."

Our daughter, Joanna Emma Joyce Pullen Hammett and her husband, Robert Chase Hammett for always being there for me in all of my business endeavors. Joanna is the reason I started this business and it is such a joy to have her and Chase working with me in the business. Imagine my delight the day Joanna told me she was changing her major to fashion merchandising and design. I do so appreciate Chase and Joanna's decision to move back to Huntsville to help me further build this business. From hauling merchandise to Washington State in a big white truck to planning and overseeing the building of our new building Chase has added so much to this business in the short time he has been back in Huntsville. With Joanna and Chase's coming back to Huntsville to join me in this business, I am ready to begin my second 25 years. I figure I'll maybe retire when I am 80 years old, or maybe 85. Thanks for bringing Cecil Elizabeth to photo shoots almost from the first week she was born. I love them and I appreciate them. My scripture for Joanna and Chase is 1 Corinthians 15:58 "Therefore, my beloved, be stedfast, immovable, always excelling in the work of the Lord, because you know that in the Lord your labor is not in vain."

To other family members who love me and always support me, I thank you and I love you! Aunt Elizabeth Dicus; Ann, Steve, Georgia and Molly Kennamer; Jim Dicus; Beryl Parker, Aunt Bessie Campbell; Don and June Campbell, Dean and the late Condon Campbell; Jim and Nancy Campbell, Lucy and Doug Henry; All of their children; Bill Crocker, Granny and PaPa Crocker (Willie and Bill); Scottie and Megan Roland; Jennifer, Rob, Corey and Emma Ann Parker; Pauline Dimitroff and Bob Rosson.

My high school friends are precious to me especially the "gang." They are still among my very best friends and they have been since the third grade. They are sources of great strength and help to me. Thanks to Frances Boyd, Mary Ann Holland, Linda Powers, and Barbara Strain ( in alphabetical order!) Thanks for making the time for all of us to get together every summer and for being my e-mail and prayer partners.

Another high school friend has always been there for me and has always been one of my number one fans. Thanks to Barbara Derrick Spratling.

I would like to thank every student and every teacher who has ever been here to our *Schools of Art Fashion* in Huntsville. Over 10,000 students have arrived here for fun and sewing over the last 16 years. We have the world's best students and the world's best teachers.

I would like to thank every person who has ever bought a Martha Pullen product! Without you we would not have the opportunity to write books like this, produce schools, travel and teach, send catalogues, produce *Sew Beautiful* magazine, produce *Martha's Sewing Room* PBS television series, produce *Martha's Sewing Market* (consumer shows in Arlington, Orlando and Los Angeles), or produce dolls from Germany which make everyone happy.

I appreciate every subscriber to *Sew Beautiful* magazine! This year has seen the largest subscriber base since we started in 1987! We also have wonderful shops who sell the magazine and who host my traveling schools many times a year!

I would like to thank every sewing machine company! I have the great privilege of working for all of the companies! That is a privilege which I do not take lightly. I have lovingly said "If you give me ten minutes, I will sell you one of each."

I would like to thank every person who has contributed garments to both our magazine and to our books. We could never have afforded to have hired all of these gorgeous clothes to be made.

Each of our designers is appreciated not only by me and my staff but by the whole world.

Many individuals have run the business while others have written and produced this book. They are joys in my life and hard work is the backbone of this organization. It has been said that in a small business everyone does fifteen jobs including cleaning up the kitchen and running the vacuum. Each of these individuals has been willing to do anything necessary to keep the business running. I would like to thank Angie Daniel, Chase Hammett, Joanna Hammett, Kathy Pearce, Toni Duggar, Patsy Vaughn, Hilda Wright, Leighann Simmons, Kathy Baggett, Claudia Newton, Jonathan Scull, Beth Bruer, Wendy Brazelton, Jesse McClain, Aritta York, Norma Colbath, Marie Hendon, Cindy Brooks, LaTonya King, Carlotta Boyette, Diane Bradshaw, Rosie Stewart and Amy Duggar.

To the people who physically worked on this book in any capacity, I send my love, congratulations and thanks. In order not to say more about one person than another, Kathy McMakin suggested that we put them all on the book team page and not write about each one individually. Since Kathy is Executive Vice-President of Martha Pullen Company and the chief engineer of this book, I agreed to follow her advice.

There is one person to whom I am especially grateful not only for contributions to this book but for the whole business success we have had. My husband, Joe Ross Pullen, was the reason I was able to start the business and run it through the years when we made no money. He paid all of our family's bills while I worked on expanding and creating. Last year, I convinced him to slow down a little at the dental office and come on over to my business to take over the management. He is now working at both businesses and doing a fabulous job. He developed *Dr. Joe's Pleater* over the last two years and he is officially the "top dog" around here. Everybody loves Joe and thinks he is the best boss ever. He is a wonderful Christian and has traveled for over 15 years with our church, Whitesburg Baptist Church, to do missionary dental work for poor people all over the world. He has done dentistry underneath a tree in the bush in Africa and in a makeshift dental chair in Jamaica. He has stood in the heat of third world countries extracting lowers and has knelt on the ground to work on uppers. His patients sat in a folding chair and his assistant used a flashlight to illuminate the mouth. His statement has been simply, "I come in the name of Jesus to relieve you of your pain." He is faithful to God's work, to his family's needs, to his patient's needs, and to the needs of this business. He is a great visionary and his creativity has helped us expand many avenues of this business. He is a wonderful husband and father. He is my best friend and my forever partner. I love him and I thank him.

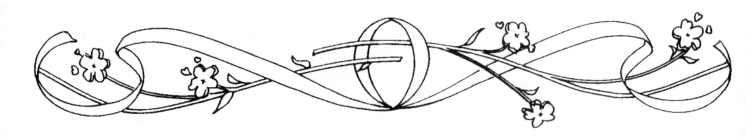

# Table of Contents

A Look Back - Martha's Private Collection     11

Patterns and Pages from the Past     34

Vintage Photographs     63

Looking Back     86

Heirloom Sewing for Jack     107

Heirloom Sewing for Jack or Jill     178

Heirloom Sewing for Jill     211

Duplicate Stitch Graphs     290

Smocking Plate Directions     295

Home Decorating, Crafts & Quilts     303

New Techniques     330

Magic Madeira Technique     339

Australian Madeira Appliqué     349

Classic Techniques     362

Embroidery Techniques     401

Shadowwork Embroidery     409

Smocking Plates     C-36

# Introduction

*Colossians 3: 17*
*17 And whatever you, in word or deed, do everything in the*
*name of the Lord Jesus, giving thanks to God the Father through him.*

This book has been seven years in the making. Writing a "boy's comprehensive book" was orginally to be my next coffee table book with the 500-plus pages and pattern envelope devoted entirely to sewing for our favorite little fellows. As the project began to evolve, we thought heirloom sewing enthusiasts might be better served by a children's book, which included clothing for boys and girls. Woven into its every page, pattern, picture, design, technique and drawing is a stream of consciousness that extends back in my mind to the time I first became a mother in 1965. From the minute William Campbell Crocker was born, I loved to sew adorable clothing for him. After that came John Houston Crocker, Mark Edward Pullen, Jeffery David Pullen, and Joanna Emma Joyce Pullen—I took great joy in sewing for all of them to the extent of embroidering shirts in the mid '70s. With the birth of our grandchildren, these nurturing desires to once again dress my little boys and girls came shouting with a deep resonance.

There is something incredibly magical about the year 2000. It could be because it heralds so many possibilities for a new beginning. That means for us, who love heirloom clothing, going back about a hundred years to the beginning of classic children's clothing for boys and girls. In previous books, we have explored historical boy's clothing; however, boy's patterns have not been featured with their beautifully tailored details. My staff and I have searched high and low for traditional and tailored boy's clothing; we believe we have collected a prized medley of patterns and designs suited for the young man in your family. While planning the little girl's patterns, I couldn't help but let my imagination run wild with truly spectacular, almost fairy tale garments. Half the fun of dressing your Jack or Jill is in finding the perfect combination of historical and modern. Particularly for boys, that means clothes that are "father-friendly."

The history and origin of today's classic boy's and girl's clothing is recorded with photographs, which I have collected from hamlets and cities around the United States. From Bridgeport, Alabama to New York City, the photographs will tell their own stories of mothers and grandmothers who have loved dressing their children. Since photographs cannot actually speak, we have theorized about them just a little for you. Gathering inspiration from old magazines and pattern books has been a passion of mine for over 25 years. Perusing flea markets and antique stores in the United States, England, Canada, France, Australia, and New Zealand for Victorian clothing has

become my favorite hobby next to sewing.

The older I get, the more nostalgic I become. I love to reminisce about my own childhood, my children's childhoods, and times past about which my parents and grandparents told stories. Tender memories of my childhood and my Mama's and Aunt Chris's sewing for me have partly made me into the person that I am today, a person devoted to ensuring this age-old artform is not lost. There is such a special bond between those who are on both the giving and receiving ends of a sewing relationship. Many of my precious family ties were indeed stitched up in the nature of sewing.

My nostalgia about elegant turn-of-the-last-century clothing has become not only a hobby but also my business about which I am so passionate. I love teaching sewing, writing books about sewing, producing Martha's Sewing Room television series for PBS and publishing Sew Beautiful magazine. My staff is comprised of fabulous individuals, and their collective efforts are what make this book outstanding. My staff includes my full-time employees, my designer friends from all over the world, and my sewers who make the designs of others a reality. This book holds special memories for each of us who worked gathering the harvest, so to speak, to collect and present it to you. My worldwide staff has created completely new ways to simplify techniques from the Victorian Age, designed and refined classic styles for today's world, and created some new magic for you, our friend. In closing this introduction I would praise my staff and tell them that two presidents spoke to the issue of hard and worthwhile work, which all of them have done. Harry S. Truman said, "I come to the office each morning and stay for long hours doing what has to be done to the best of my ability. And when you've done the best you can, you can't do any better. So when I go to sleep I turn everything over to the Lord and forget it." And Abraham Lincoln said, "The man who does not do more work than he's paid for isn't worth what he gets."

All of my precious staff who have contributed in any way to this book have certainly deserved every penny he or she has earned and much, much more. A once-in-a-lifetime group of individuals has created this book and pattern envelope for you. We hope you will find cherished patterns and exciting techniques. On the whole, I hope this book will bring you great joy, deepen your understanding of classic children's clothing, help hone your sewing skills, and provide you with new ideas and challenges.

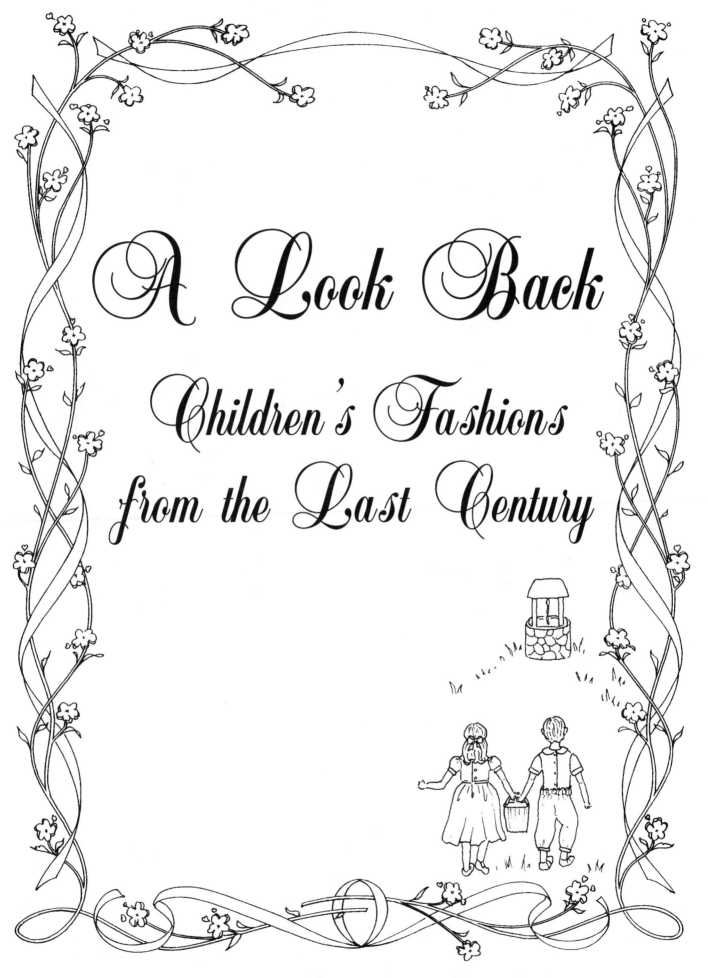

# A Look Back

## Children's Fashions
## from the Last Century

# Martha's Private Collection

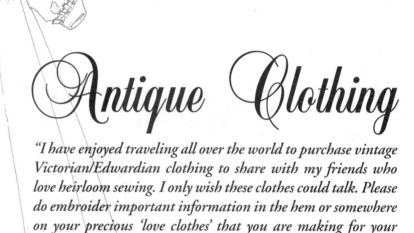

## Antique Clothing

*"I have enjoyed traveling all over the world to purchase vintage Victorian/Edwardian clothing to share with my friends who love heirloom sewing. I only wish these clothes could talk. Please do embroider important information in the hem or somewhere on your precious 'love clothes' that you are making for your family and friends."*

*Martha Pullen*
2000

*There are babies in the high lands and babies in the low, there are pale ones wrapped in furry-skins on the margin for the snow, and brown ones naked in the isles where all the spices grow.*

excerpt from *A Blessing for the Blessed* by L. Alma Tadema

## Baby Underwear

For modern infants, a disposable diaper topped with a cotton T-shirt or onesie serves as adequate underpinnings, but there was a time when the clothing worn underneath a daygown was equally beautiful. This white broadcloth underwear would have fit an average size baby at 3 months old. The neckline formed from Swiss entredeux beading was mitered in front and back to create a square opening. Slightly gathered edging embellishes the neck edge and was used again to trim the armholes. Ten released tucks bridle the front fullness below the neckline. The legs were finished with fancy bands comprised of Swiss entredeux beading and a wide ruffle; the ruffle was further enhanced with 1/4-inch tucks and French lace stitched flat around the circumference. The underwear buttons down the back and across the upper part of the seat. All of the seams are flat felled, and the buttons are pearl.

## Ecru Dotted Swiss Dress

Dresses that are sweet and simple are really all baby girls have ever needed in their closets, no matter from what century they've hailed. A fine example is this ecru dotted Swiss yoke dress with a round collar. Aside from the medium brown bias tape that trims the edge of the collar, and a self-fabric ruffle, embellishment is limited. The self-fabric belt loops at either side on the front apparently were carriers for a sash or perhaps a length of satin ribbon, which was missing when the dress was purchased. A placket with pearl buttons and fabric loops secures the dress in back. The deep hem was stitched with a yellow chain stitch, which I can only assume was originally medium brown and faded to yellow over time.

## White Suit with Coral Embroidery

Little boys tend to be slighted when it comes to the use of color in their finery, but this garment looks perfectly suited for an heir apparent with touches of coral embroidery. Made of a heavy white fabric, almost linen in texture, the design is typical of a little boy's suit - front tucks and a belt - but the collar work and use of color is a departure from the norm. The embroidery, centered between four released 1/4" tucks, is floral in design. Satin stitched dots were worked between the second and third tuck on either side. Embroidery continues around the collar, which was further enhanced with decorative bias binding hand faggoted around the exterior. The cuffs on each sleeve have been illustrated to show that there was a second cuff piece inserted in the sleeve, not just a fold over. The tailored belt fastens in the back with one button and buttonhole; the back placket buttons twice. The crotch is secured with three buttons.

## Tabard Pinafore

Mothers who take the time to sew special garments for their children understandably want them to be worn as much as possible before they're outgrown. A single dress can be worn more often just by adding or removing a pinafore. This design was originally constructed from almost sheer white Swiss batiste. Flat lace outlines the entire garment including the mitered square neckline and side tabs. These tabs connect the front and the back for the ultimate in simple construction.

## Bunny Romper

Large novelty details like the bunny face embroidery on the front of this little romper are relatively rare in antique garments. Typically embellishments were delicate like the children wearing them. Once committed to an oversized motif on the straight front piece, the designer incorporated a geometric grid or windowpane effect into the romper body. The grid — outline stitched by hand in coral thread — provided balance and created the illusion of a cape for the bunny. The single row of the grid was repeated around the sleeves. The bunny face was outline stitched in black embroidery with coral stitches on the ears, eyes, and nose. The romper was purchased in Massachusetts, and the fabric is almost like a modern day-weight poplin. The back placket and crotch close with snaps.

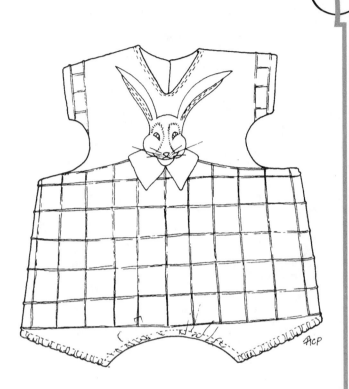

"Snips and snails, and puppy-dogs' tails;
That's what little boys are made of."

## Blue and White Linen Suit

Scallops are a subtle way to decorate a boy's garment without making it look feminine. Here the technique was used for the white cuffs and collar which quietly contrast the blue linen suit. Two released $3/8$" tucks flank the white embroidery on the romper front. Conversely blue embroidery trims the collar. Pearl buttons secure the tailored belt and closures - two on the belt in back, one on the back placket, and three at the crotch of the suit.

## Baby Slips with Tucks

A white baby slip is one of the simplest and sweetest of heirlooms to make. This one features four tucks on the bottom and a machine hem. It ties with fabric tubes, which were run through casings around the neck and waistline. Tying a baby slip as opposed to buttoning it made it possible for a baby to wear it for several months. The neckline was cut low to further accommodate growth - a mother could draw up the ties when the baby was small and let them out as the baby grew. Quite practical for then as well as now.

*"Sugar and spice, and all that's nice;*
*And that's what little girls are made of."*

## Baby Slip with Lace

Much like the previous garment, this white baby slip closes at the waist and neckline with ribbons run through casings. Because the neckline is high, however, the wearing time would not have been as long. Flat lace trims the neckline and sleeves; entredeux and flat lace finishes the skirt bottom. This type of simple slip is just as classic and wearable today as it was one hundred years ago. All little girls need classic white slips, I believe.

## Bow and Daisy Dress

This white Swiss batiste dress appears to have been "pre-manufactured" in origin; it would have come in a kit with embroidery stamped on the fabric. The only seams are underneath the arms; they are French, which is to be expected of most white clothing of the era. The hem was hand pin stitched; only the side seams and the pocket attachment were sewn by machine. The white-on-white embroidery consists of little bows, eyelet daisies, and stem stitches. Two buttonholes were hand worked on each side. Traditionally these were used for a sassy bow tied for embellishment, one on each side. A wide sash on the back was embroidered with a matching design and hand scalloped around four sides. (The back view illustrates this elegant treatment.) These same delicate, hand-buttonholed scallops finish the neckline, sleeves, and pocket top. Additional embroidery trims the sleeves and pocket.

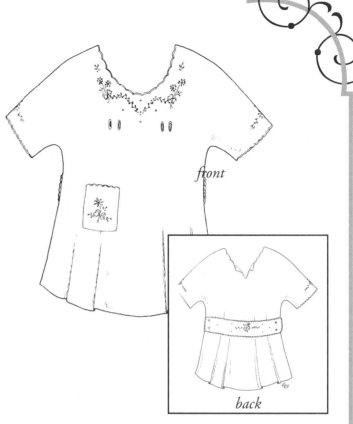

*front*

*back*

## Baby Slip with Tucks and Lace

Full baby slips were a necessity a century ago when inadequate heat sources were not enough to keep houses warm. For this particular design, a square neckline trimmed in lace includes a casing to tighten or loosen depending on the size of the baby wearing it. The same gathered lace trims the armscyes. Six tucks trim the bottom of the skirt. The fabric of this slip, as most, is reasonably heavy. Batistes or broadcloths of this nature were used for durability as well as added warmth. When making slips for your little girls, it is a very practical idea to add a couple of grow tucks which can be released for added length and more wear.

## White Embroidered Middy

"Pre-manufactured" dresses made it that much easier for hard-working mothers of the day to construct beautiful clothing for their little ones. Because the embroidery design would have been stamped directly on the fabric before it was purchased, half of the creative work was already complete. As with most "kit" garments, the only seams on this white batiste dress are at the sides. The hem, neckline, and sleeve were finished with a delicate hand scallop. The front treatment was stitched like a buttonhole so that pretty satin ribbon could be run through to hold in the fullness. Delicate posies flutter down the front. Scalloped triangles draw attention to the neckline and thus to the cherubic face of the child who wore the dress.

*If I were oh, so very small, I'd hide myself away, And creep into a peony cup, To spend the summer's day.*

excerpt from *If* by P. A. Ropes

## Lily of the Valley Coat

It's a pity spring dress coats have become a thing of the past. Vintage versions are among the more prized children's garments in my collections. This particular coat in white piqué was probably made for Easter. The hand embroidery in white-on-white is a trailing ribbon dressed up with lily of the valley flowers and bouquets. Edges of the shawl collar and turned-back cuffs were hand scalloped. A wide band defines the waist, where the coat was secured with two buttons and buttonholes to accommodate added stress in that area. The gathered skirt was finished with a wide plain hem.

## Lily of the Valley Boy Dress

Even into the early 20th century pants were reserved for the older boy. This belted coat dress is a typical garment for the younger child. It is a heavy, striped piqué with extended front pieces, which lap off center. The buttonholes were worked on a placket down the interior edge of the dress so that the button closure was completely hidden. The dress was constructed by machine including the hem - a machine hem being very unusual on a dress of its origin. All of the embroidery, which was worked by hand, was very delicately scalloped on the sleeves, pocket, and down the front. The same scallops outline the collar. Sprays of lily of the valley flowers trim the collar and cuffs. A belt is run around the dress through plain belt loops, creating a slightly dropped waist. The belt was secured in front with a single hidden button and buttonhole.

## Pink Organdy Dress

So many of the antique children's garments in my collection are dated by the silhouette, but this pink organdy yoke dress, is absolutely timeless. Where I am conditioned to expect white-on-white, this dress might be best described as pink on pink - pink lace on pink organdy. It is, in fact, the only dress this old, on which I have seen the use of colored lace. The lace was shaped in a triangle on the yoke, trims the edge of the gathered, short sleeves. and was drawn up into two circles to decorate the front of the skirt. A string of hand embroidery was swaged between the two circles and a tiny blue bow was centered in each. Embroidery, which introduced additional color to the dress - green leaves and stem stitches with yellow bullion flowers - was also worked in the center of the lace triangle. The back of the dress is closed with snaps; the hem was sewn by hand.

## Scalloped Christening Coat

When a child is being christened or presented to a church family, first thoughts turn to the gown, but doesn't an event this important merit a special coat as well? This scalloped christening coat is beautiful enough to serve as the main garment with an ornate slip underneath, or it could be removed to reveal an equally magnificent gown. Six released tucks bridle the fullness at the shoulders on either side of the front opening. The cuffs at the end of the long sleeves were finished with beading and gathered lace edging trim. The front edges of the coat are scalloped and the bottom edge is straight. Beading and gathered lace outline the edges from the neck opening, down the front, and around the bottom. Two lace medallion motifs were inserted at the lower edges in the front. A ribbon run through the neckline closes the coat.

## Linen Smocked Dress

Smocking doesn't always have to be the focal point as on a basic yoke dress, it can work in tandem with an interesting collar treatment, for a more subtle pairing. This long-sleeve antique was constructed from heavy ecru linen. The braided trim on the petal collar was hand stitched and is darker than the linen of the dress. The smocking, on the skirt below the yoke, echoes the darker shade. Two tucks were stitched in at the bottom of the dress. Generally these tucks are referred to as grow tucks because they can be let to out to lengthen the dress as a child grows. A reproduction pattern of this dress was featured in *Sew Beautiful* magazine, #65 (Fall, 1999). The pattern is sized 2-8 and is call "Primrose."

## Swiss Trim Embroidered Dress

The beauty of a basic bodice dress is that it is a classic palette to decorate any way the designer chooses. This white batiste version makes use of tucks and colorful Swiss insertion. Tucks run vertically down the raised yoke - three on either side of the center - and horizontally around the hem - three growth tucks. Swiss insertion in a pink, green, and yellow floral pattern create pointed tabs over the shoulders and in the center of the yoke. Two longer columns of insertion, again ending in points, embellish the skirt. The cuffs and the neck treatment are plain batiste, which complement rather than compete with the decorative work.

## White Angel Sleeves Pinafore

Every once in a while I come upon a garment that looks as if it were fit for an angel. This white batiste pinafore is an example. White Swiss embroidery was used to create the slightly curved V-yoke as well as the angel sleeves. Beading outlines the top and bottom of the yoke with a little gathered lace finishing the neckline. Beautiful pink bows accent both of the shoulders. Beading was applied around the skirt a few inches above the plain hem. This little pinafore could be worn alone in the summer months or over a dress of almost any fabric year round. What a practical garment to have on hand for all seasons!

## Sprays of Flowers Dress

There are so many sweet details on this white, high yoke dress, I can just imagine a grandmother or mother taking extra care to plan out each stitch. Delicate floral sprays were embroidered on the yoke, cuffs, and skirt. French knots form the crisscrosses on the skirt, the little lines around the cuffs, and the center design on the yoke. Swiss beading joins the bodice and skirt; ribbon, run through the beading ties in a bow in back. Gathered lace edging trims the neckline and sleeve cuffs. The hem was secured with hemstitching. A reproduction down to the last bullion would result in a beautiful heirloom dress for today's child.

## Fancy Slip

It is amazing to me how the Victorians and Edwardians put almost as much time and love into the stitching of undergarments as they did the overgarments. This adorable little, white batiste slip has rows of tucks in increments of four all the way down the skirt; the bottom was treated with a beautiful Swiss embroidered edging. The neckline and armscye were finished with gathered lace. This slip is pretty enough to be worn as a dress or pinafore. The skirt would be relatively inexpensive to reproduce, since tucks rather than costly laces serve as the primary embellishment. What a perfectly sweet heirloom to pass from one generation to the next.

## Puffing Christening Dress

So many times christening gowns are generously trimmed from neckline to hem, almost as if the mother believed the more she added the more the infant would sense her love. In reality, it is the simple touch that begets elegance. The designer of this white Swiss batiste gown reserved the use of puffing and lace for the bodice and sleeves. The scooped neckline was outlined in a bias trim, enhanced with a trail of tiny white French knots. Gathered lace was used to complete the neckline treatment. Two narrow puffing strips trim the sleeves at the shoulders; a wider puffing strip was added to the center front, secured with a bias strip of batiste across the middle. The edges of the puffing insert are concealed beneath another strip of bias, upon which white rosebuds were embroidered. Gathered lace was added around the outside edge of the bias trim. Three little belt loops decorated with rosebud embroidery guide the fabric sash. Rosebuds also trim the circumference of the narrow cuffs, which have gathered edging on both top and bottom. The only embellishment on the skirt is a section of three tucks sewn above the plain hem.

## White Pique Pleated Dress

This child's dress appears simple enough, but what I find most interesting about it is the use of pleats to hold the fullness of the skirt. Very few of my vintage pieces were pleated in this manner. I spotted it an at an auction at Christie's in London and couldn't resist its' clean lines. Very simple Swiss trim was gathered around the collar and cuffs; featherstitching was worked on the collar, the cuffs, and around the bottom of the bodice. The dress closes in back with three buttons and buttonholes. When embellishment is spared to this degree, our interests shift to the fabric and construction; both would be of utmost importance when reproducing this yoke dress.

## Scalloped White Coat

Scallops seemed to have been the theme for this white child's dress coat. Not only were they hand made with a buttonhole stitch around the collar and cuffs, but the collar and cuffs were also cut in a scalloped design. White sprays of embroidery with French knots and stem stitching trim the interior of the collar and the cuffs. The coat closes with buttons and buttonholes. Little coats are just as beautiful today as they were many years ago. Personally, I remember having a dress up coat for spring and a separate one for winter to wear to church. This particular design could have very well been made for a child to wear over her Easter finery.

## Simple Older Girl's Dress

The older a child gets, the fewer ruffles she'll wear; this has held true for centuries as evidenced by this child's dress. Trim on this waisted dress was limited to narrow bands of Swiss edging around the collar and cuffs and a waistband of Swiss insertion. Cut wide from neckline to armscye, the design creates somewhat of a dropped shoulder. A single tuck gives the impression of a double hemline at the skirt edge. The dress was constructed from white batiste, which was certainly the most popular fabric around the turn of the last century.

# Boy's Suits

## Circa 1930

While at the Brimfield Market in Brimfield, Massachusetts, I noticed a dealer who had several bags of what appeared to be antique clothing. Upon entering her tent, I asked her about Victorian white clothing. "Well, I have a few things," she replied. "But if you love antique clothing, you might want to see this collection of 1930-ish boy suits I have just acquired." Of course, I was interested. She rummaged through several bags of antiques, pulled out a black garbage sack, and dumped the contents on the table. I was astounded to see so many tailored boys' designs in the same place. After negotiating the price, I purchased the whole collection.

When I brought them home to show Joe, he pointed out that many of these suits resembled clothing he had worn as a boy in the latter part of the '30s. Old pictures of him confirmed the similarities. All of these suits put forth construction ideas that lend authenticity to the suits we make today.

The fabric used most on these suits was a cotton shantung. I have not seen this fabric in many years, although I remember using it in high school home economics. (I believe I made a pair of shorts and a top out of it.)

In addition to the New England suits, I've included one suit I found in London, evidence that little boys here and abroad dressed very similarly during this time period. I hope you enjoy this collection as much as I have enjoyed bringing it to you. Ultimately, I hope to see my readers make little boys' suits inspired by this collection.

## Military Theme Suit

Suits with a military influence are traditionally navy and white, and this version is no exception. The shirt is white with navy and white embroidery. The pants are navy with a navy belt. Broadcloth was the fabric of choice. The attached front panel provides the perfect canvas for machine embroidery, although the mother who made this particular suit hand embroidered the anchor and stripes. The buttons on the suit are pearl and the belt closes with a pearl buckle.

## Salmon Shantung Suit With Ducks

What makes this salmon-colored shantung suit unique is the pieced shirt front, which I assume was designed to give it a closer fit. Standard treatments include the belted waist and cuffed sleeves; piping trims the collar, cuffs, and front placket. The white ducks embroidered on the pocket were detailed in navy blue. The closures are an ecru buckle and buttons on the pants, white buttons down the front of the shirt, and three buttons and buttonholes at the crotch.

## Blue and White Duck Suit

In my collection of 1930s suits, this is one of the few with suspender straps, which I found rather unusual, as it is a style we still use in baby clothing today. The pants and straps are a deep baby blue cotton shantung. Just below each button on the points of the pant front is an embroidered yellow duck with orange feet. The white cotton shantung shirt is relatively plain save for the blue bias trim and narrow white ruffle around the collar. Whenever a child's outfit calls for suspenders or straps, it is a good idea to stitch fabric loops at the shoulder seams of the shirt to keep the straps from slipping. The buttons on both the pants and the shirt are white pearl. The crotch is closed with two snaps.

## Blue Topstitched Suit

Rows of contrast stitching serve as straightforward embellishment, tracing the line of the collar, the sleeves, and the shirt yoke. The shirt and button-on pants are blue cotton shantung with seven rows of white stitching across the yoke. The collar and cuffs are white with blue contrast stitching — four rows on the collar and three rows on the cuffs. Practicality and maybe a little frugality inspires such threadwork, and demonstrates that fussy details aren't necessary on a classic. The buttons are white pearl on both the pants and the shirt. The crotch closes with two buttons and buttonholes.

## Burgundy Anchor Suit

This mother didn't let tradition keep her from using burgundy instead of blue for her son's nautical suit. Most likely it is the color fabric she had, and clearly she put it to good use. The shirt is white cotton shantung; the pants and back section of the collar are burgundy. The belt is burgundy with a silver buckle. The buttons are off-white pearl. As was common on older boys' suits of the time, the pants have an opening in the seam instead of a zipper fly. The crotch is stitched shut. Three strips of burgundy braid trim the collar, which is white in the front and burgundy on the back. The welt pocket was trimmed with an authentic-looking anchor motif.

## Royal Blue and White Cross Stitch Suit

Tailoring isn't restricted to tucks and piping, touches of embroidery can give just as clean a finish when the design is carefully chosen and placed. On this garment, the work is a geometric cross-stitch, but there are countless embroidery designs suitable for little boys' attire whether working by hand or machine. The pants of this suit, as well as the cuffs and tabs on the collar are a royal blue broadcloth. Matching royal blue thread was used for the cross-stitch. So as not to detract from the embroidery design, a button closure was hidden under the collar and again at the bottom of the shirt. Buttons were also used to attach the shirt and shorts beneath the royal blue belt.

## Blue Lamb Suit

This suit with its straps and center insert reminds me of Swiss lederhosen. It is mostly blue cotton shantung with the exception of the red piping across the top of the insert and white trim around the collar. The embroidered leaping lambs are white with tan ears and a black outline stitch. Anytime a garment has a panel or insert of this nature, I imagine the possibilities an embroidery machine has to offer. White pearl buttons were used to close the shirt and the crotch is stitched shut.

## Black Velvet Suit with Cream Silk Shirt

The beauty of this particular romper/suit lies in its simplicity. It required no embellishment, only the richness of black velvet to make it special. It is unlined; the neckline and armholes were finished with a cotton twill bias binding stitched by hand. The leg holes were simply turned under and hemmed. Two large pearl buttons secure the suit at the shoulder. The cream-colored silk shirt was designed with a soft V opening in the front. Two clues lead me to believe there was once a sailor-type dickey bridging the opening; first, the V is rather deep for a child, and second, there is a button on the inside of the opening. The cuffs close with pearl buttons and button loops. Unlike the suit, the shirt is in poor condition, because silk does not hold up like cotton and other natural fibers. When I purchased the suit on Portobello Road in London, I thought immediately it must have been made for a special occasion primarily due to the fabrication.

## Red, White and Blue Oval Front Suit

Perhaps this mother celebrated the Fourth of July as we do Christmas and Easter by making finery for her little ones. She obviously mustered up her creativity to combine red, white, and blue into an adorable button-on suit. The body of the shirt and pants were cut from a type of shantung in royal blue. The center insert of white shantung was outlined in tiny red piping. White shantung was also used for the cuffs and collar, the latter of which was pleated and hemstitched around the very edge. The entire suit was double stitched with white thread, and it closes at the crotch with three buttons and buttonholes.

## Red Scalloped Trim Suit

The red scalloped trim on this white shirt collar was satin stitched by hand, but it would be simple to reproduce using a zigzag machine. My main caution would be to test the colorfastness of the red thread; after concentrating your effort on a child's suit, you wouldn't want the thread to bleed onto the white fabric during laundering. The shaped edge on the shirt front as well as the collar edge were piped in a medium blue to match the blue pants. White pearl buttons close the shirt in three places, one showing and two hidden. White pearl buttons were also used on the pants; however, they have been stitched down with red thread, most likely the same thread that was used for the satin stitching on the collar.

## Ecru and Brown Double Breasted Sailor Suit

Touches of military detailing have always been common on boys' apparel, and suits made in the '30s were no exception. However, the star and stripes motif is one of the few things that is typical about this shirt design. The softly turned collar was trimmed in a relatively wide band of cocoa fabric, which matches the shorts. On the right side, the trim was divided into two pieces to resemble the lapel on a man's suit; the lower piece provided a foundation for the three ecru stripes; a star was hand embroidered on the remaining trim. Down the front of the shirt, a tiny pleat makes it appear as if a separate panel were added to extend the right front; it closes with three pearl buttons. The sleeve cuffs were cut from the brown fabric, but trimmed with a bias strip of ecru fabric applied near the top of the cuff. The belt around the pants is brown, but the buckle is ecru.

## Welt Pockets Blue Suit

Using two shades of blue this suit is masterfully tailored. Baby blue is used for the broadcloth shirt and navy blue for the pants. Navy blue buttons are on the shirt and white buttons on the pants. A silver buckle fastens the pants; however, I believe that a white buckle might have been used originally, lost and replaced with this silver one. Four folded tucks are found on each side of the shirt and two beautifully tailored welt pockets are found on each side of the shirt. This is a larger suit and it has an opening in the front so bathroom activities can take place without taking the pants off completely. Instead of a zipper in little boys pants, early suits just had a discreet opening. Aren't we glad zippers were invented?

## Melon, Royal Blue and Ecru Suit

Color play combined with a notched collar and a touch of bias trim are the only elements required to make this little suit uniquely individual. The suit, cuffs, and bias strip are a melon-colored linen; the collar is ecru linen outlined in royal blue. Flat pearl buttons close the shirt and fasten the two pieces at the waist. Linen - wrinkles and all - has always been one of my favorite fabrics for little boy clothing.

## Faggoting Suit

Fathers who are hesitant to allow their little boys to wear lace or fancy trimmings, might yield if the effect is created by thread work. On this particular suit, a bias tube has been attached to the asymmetrical collar and cuffs with hand faggoting. Approximately every inch along the bias tube, a stitch was taken and left loosely enough to form a series of loops. The results is a scalloped edge. The suit is a cotton blue shantung; the cuffs and collar are white broadcloth. White pearl buttons were used to close the shirt and to attach the pants. White topstitching finishes the armholes and secures the pant hem. Three buttons and buttonholes close the crotch.

## Tailored Appliqué Suit

Tiny appliqués, applied by hand, were common on children's apparel of this era and were most often in the form of animals. Here, however, the art of appliqué furnishes this suit with a delicate geometric design starting at the neck edge and trailing down the front panel. Blue cotton shantung was used for the appliqué on the collar tips and down the front panel. This same fabric was used for the pants and for the piping around the sleeves. The shirt is made of white cotton shantung. White pearl buttons close the shirt and attach the button-on pants. The crotch was simply stitched together.

## Burgundy and White Double Breasted Suit

The sharp contrast of burgundy and white is conversely softened by tatting trim around the collar. The fabric is cotton shantung — burgundy for the pants and piping, white for the shirt. Details that make use of the contrast in color include burgundy buttons and piping against the pristine white fabric, and a white buckle and white piping at the edges of the burgundy belt. The crotch opening on the pants is one of the more interesting details, if for no other reason than it exemplifies a mother's ingenuity. The pants were originally finished with buttons and buttonholes; presumably when the child grew too big for that style, his industrious mother simply lengthened the crotch, sewed shut the buttonholes, removed the buttons, and stitched the two sides together. Perhaps her little one got a few more months wear that way.

# Patterns and Pages from the Past

## A Summer Morn By June Grahame

McCall's Magazine, June, 1912

God kissed the earth, and lo! the glint
Of gold starred all the meadows thick
With dandelions. And clad in tint
Of humble flower, each yellow chick

Obeys my little maiden's call,
And culls the grains of golden corn
That from the tiny fingers fall
In dewy flush of Summer morn.

Oh, little maid, the happy years
That spread before your tender feet,
Are checkered with the smiles and tears
Of morrow-lands. But keep, my sweet,

The Vision, now within your breast
Enfolded like the budding Spring,
And Life will yield its golden best
Though only modest gifts you bring.

STIFF corsets are unknown in France. Paris corsets are always supple and bendable, and this accounts for the ease of French figures, which are never tightened excepting at the waist, leaving the bust and hips quite free.

Over here the figure is usually tightened in too much at the bust and hips, which gives too straight a look to the body and makes it stiff and uncomfortable, movement being rendered ungraceful by this stiffness. Let any girl try to lace her corsets only at the waist, and let her select them as soft and light as possible, and then see if her figure be not as graceful in shape and as elastic as the most graceful and elastic French figure.

No tight, straight-down, even lacing will ever make a pretty figure. If the corset cannot be made expressly to suit the figure, then let it only be laced in the middle at the waist. Even then no real corset should be worn by girls until they are well into their teens. Remember, the softer the corset is the easier it will be, and the tighter it may be laced at the waist without feeling uncomfortable. This is the only way to mould the figure, it is said, without injuring the health.

### GIRLS' CAPE, No. 6000.

Dark blue broadcloth trimmed with black satin strapping stitched with white, made this jaunty and stylish cape. It is cut in circular shape and has its back fullness laid in a fashionable double-box pleat. A rolling collar, adorned with a narrow band of the stitched satin strapping, completes the neck. The fronts are fastened under shaped satin strapping, completes the neck. The fronts are fastened under shaped satin tabs ornamented by tiny buttons. Blue taffeta silk was used as a lining. Heavy English tweed, in shades of brown and white, with straps and tabs of golden brown velvet, stitched with white, would be another pretty combination of materials for this design, but covert, serge, double-faced cloth, or almost any popular coaking can be substituted if desired.

McCall Bazar Pattern No. 5984
Cut in sizes 6, 7, 8, 9, 10 and 11 years

appropriate materials for its manufacture. The straight double-breasted front is adorned with four big white pearl buttons. The neck is cut out in a V shape and completed by a jaunty sailor collar, plainly finished by rows of stitching. Tiny pockets, furnished with stitched flaps are placed on each side of the front just below the waist line. The back is in one piece and hangs almost straight from the neck in the most approved fashion. The sleeves have very little fulness at the shoulders and are plainly completed at the wrists by rows of stitching. Taffeta silk is used as a lining. This coat would also be very stylish and pretty for summer made up of heavy-ribbed white pique, or heavy duck. It could be fastened with four big white pearl buttons and finished by rows of heavy stitiching. If it was thought desirable to introduce color, the stitchings could be of red or navy blue cotton, or the coat could be trimmed with stitched straps of pique or duck according to the material from which it was manufactured. Of course, coats of heavy wash fabrics are unlined.

### GIRL'S BOX COAT, No. 5984.

requires for medium size, 2 1/4 yards material 36 inches wide, 2 1/8 yards 40 inches wide, or 1 1/2 yards 52 inches wide. Silk lining required, 2 3/4 yards; buttons, 4. Cut in 6 sizes, 6, 7, 8, 9, 10 and 11 years.

### CHILD'S CLOAK, No. 5997.

White silk was used to make this sweet little cloak, but cashmere, flannel, serge, nuns' veiling, duck, pique, etc., could be substituted for its development if desired. The pattern is cut with a full skirt gathered on to a short body or yoke, back and front. The bottom is finished by a deep hem. A rolling collar, to which is attatched a remarkably pretty cape, finishes the neck. This cape is tucked for a short distance from the top and then the fulness is left free to flare out like a ruffle. It is scalloped around the bottom and trimmed with the edging and insertion. The sleeves are made with jaunty flaring cuffs trimmed with lace. The collar potion is entirely covered with white all over lace.

### GIRLS' CAPE, No. 6000.

requires for medium size, 1 3/8 yards material 36 inches wide, or 1 1/8 yards 40 inches wide. Silk lining required, 2 yards; silk represented. 3/4 yard; buttons, 6. Cut in 4 sizes, 6, 8, 10 and 12 years.

### GIRLS' BOX COAT. No. 5984.

This smart box coat will be found one of the most serviceable and stylish of outer garments for little girls. A very light shade of tan covert cloth was used for our model, but cheviot, broadcloth, serge, tweed, flannel, duck, pique or heavy linen are all

### CHILD'S CLOAK, NO. 5997.

requires for medium size, 5 1/2 yards material 22 inches wide, 3 1/4 yards 36 inches wide, or 3 yards 40 inches wide. Lace edging represented 6 3/4 yards; insertion, 5 yards. Cut in 6 sizes, 6 months, 1, 2, 3, 4 and 5 years.

McCall Bazar Pattern No. 6000
Cut in 4 sizes 6, 8, 10 and 12 years

McCall Bazar Pattern No. 5997
Cut in 6 sizes 6 months, 1, 2, 3, 4 and 5 years

CHILDREN'S jackets and cloaks are especially smart this spring. Some of the prettiest examples just cover the bottom of the dress, and are mostly adorned with ten or more rows of stitching above the broad hem. Few are seen cut in one piece, as the majority are constructed starting in a 2 1/2 inch broad folds from a rather deep yoke which covers the shoulders, and from which the sleeves also start. The popular material for these garmets is a light-weight weave of cloth in very pale shades of gray and brown, also ecru and ivory white.

The natty little short jackets are anotehr popular out-door garment for children. The fronts are loose, while the back fits almost closely. They are fashioned in all the light cloths, also in dark blue, green, and bright scarlet. They also have velvet or silk collars and cuffs, and the darker shades are brightened up by small, round, gilt buttons on the sleeves and pockets, and in clusters of three or four at intervals down the front.

There are two sorts of sleeves used in children's coats and jackets this year, wither close-fitting, of the same shape as the frock sleeve, but somewhat wider and adorned with rows of stitching at the wrist, or a looser sleeve forming folds on the shoulders and with a deep and very light ruff which is generally of velvet or embroidery.

Little girls' dresses are made very simple this season. The waists blouse slightly in front over a narrow belt. Very few models show flounces, and except for quite young children sashes are not fashionable.

McCall Bazar Pattern No. 5959

McCall Bazar Pattern No. 5959
CHILD'S DRESS.—Green and white striped lawn was used to make this stylish little frock. The pattern is cut with a low round neck, which, if desired, may be filled with a yoke and band collar as shown in the smaller view of the illustration. A lace-trimmed bertha, square in the front and pointed over the shoulders, borders the neck stylishly. The sleeves are gathered in mousquetaire fashion and edged with tiny ruffles of lace. They may be made to reach the elbow or full length. The full straight skirt is sewed onto the waist, the seam being concealed by a dainty belt of insertion. Two rows of insertion also trim the skirt just above the hem. Organdie, swiss, batiste, gingham, chambray, China or taffeta silks, cashmere, challie, etc., are appropriate materials for the development of this design.

No. 5959.—Child's dress (to be made High or Low neck, Long or Short Sleeves), requires for medium size, 4 3/8 yards material 22 inches wide, 2 3/4 yards 36 inches wide, or 2 5/8 yards 40 inches wide. Lining required, 7/8 yard; lace insertion represented, 7 yards; lace edging, 4 yards. Cut in 5 sizes, 2, 3, 4, 5 and 6 years.

## BOYS' SAILOR SUIT,
No. 5985.

Sailor suits are very fashionable at present for little boys' wear. Our model is made with a full blouse, cut out in a V at the neck and filled in by a shield piece and band collar, striped with braid. The big sailor collar is square in the back and pointed in the front. The sleeves are gathered into narrow wristbands at the hands. The kilt skirt is laid in box-pleats back and front and trimmed with two rows of narrow braid. Cadet blue heavy linen trimmed with narrow stitched straps of white linen, the shield piece of the white closely covered with rows of blue stitching, would be very pretty made up by this design, but serge, cheviot, duck, etc. could be used.

Boy's Sailor Suit,
No 5985.
Requires for medium size, 3 3/4 yards material 27 inches wide, 2 5/8 yards 36 inches wide, or 2 1/8 yards 48 inches wide. Soutache braid represented, 9 yards; buttons, 4. Cut in 4 sizes, 1, 2, 3 and 4 years.

McCall Bazar Pattern No. 5985

## CHILD'S GUIMPE DRESS,
No. 5973.

This sweet little frock is made of pale blue and white polka-dotted silk. The cunning bodice is cut with a full front that blouses fashionably at the waist line. The bertha is laid in fine tucks at the top, with the fulness left unconfined for a short distance from the bottom, which makes it stand out like a ruffle. The sleeves are elbow length.

Child's Dress
No.5973.
(to be made High ir Low Neck, Long or Short Sleeves), requires for medium size, 4 3/8 yards material 22 inches wide, 2 3/4 yards 36 inches wide, or 2 5/8 yards 40 inches wide. Lining required 5/8 yard; extra plain material represented, 1 yard; lace edging, 6 yards; velvet ribbon, 1 1/2 yards. Cut in 5 sizes, 2, 3, 4, 5 and 6 years.

McCall Bazar Pattern No. 5973

## GIRL'S SAILOR SUIT, No. 5964.

White flannel with a blue polka dot was used for this smart little suit. The sailor blouse is made with a big collar of navy blue flannel that continues, in the form of a strap, down the front closing to the waist line. The fastening is formed by cord loops and tiny buttons. A shield-piece and stock collar of the plain flannel fills up the V shaped opening left by the big collar. The sleeves have but little fulness at the shoulders and are trimmed at the wrists by bands of stitched blue flannel. The full straight skirt is ornamented, just above the hem, with a band of the plain material.

No. 5964.— Girl's Sailor Suit, requires for medium size, 5 yards material 22 inches wide, 3 1/8 yards 36 inches wide, or 2 3/4 yards 40 inches wide. Lining required, 1 1/4 yards; extra plain material represented, 1 yard; silk cord, 1/2 yard; buttons, 6. Cut in 7 sizes, 6, 7, 8, 9, 10, 11 and 12 years.

McCall Bazar Pattern No. 5964
Cut in sizes 6, 7, 8, 9, 10, 11 and 12 years

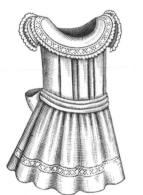

McCall Bazar Pattern No. 6003

No. 6003.—CHILD'S GUIMPE DRESS, requires for medium size, 4 1/2 yards material 22 inches wide, 2 7/8 yards 36 inches wide, or 2 5/8 yards 40 inches wide. Lace insertion represented, 5 1/4 yards; lace edging, 4 1/4 yards. Cut in 6 sizes, 2, 3, 4, 5, 6 and 7 years.

CHILDREN are often worried because their mothers are too attentive, and continually reprove their small ones without reason.

A child should be left alone, and be allowed to play or amuse itself in its own way without the constant direction of a nervous mother.

A boy, for example, enjoys more a few toys, and something which his own ingenuity has worked out, than the most elaborate plaything which has been bought.

In the same way the little girl will lavish her affections on a misshapen doll, probably made at home, while the most artistic production of the toy shop will lie in state, to be taken up on rare occasion.

Keep children well, clothe them sensibly, let them understand they are to amuse themselves, and don't "fuss" at them.

### 5862 - Child's Dress
Cut in 7 sizes, 6 months, 1, 2, 3, 4, 5 and 6 years.

### 5904 - Child's Costume
Cut in 5 sizes, 2, 3, 4, 5 and 6 years.

### 5876 - Child's Cloak
Cut in 6 sizes, 6 months, 1, 2, 3, 4 and 5 years.

### 5829 - Girl's Dress
Cut in 6 sizes, 6, 7, 8, 9, 10 and 11 years.

### 5697 - Boy's Suit
Cut in 5 sizes, 3, 4, 5, 6, and 7 years.

### 5850 - Boy's Blouse and Jacket
Cut in 5 sizes, 2, 3, 4, 5, and 6 years.

### 5333 - Girl's Costume
Cut in 7 sizes, 6, 7, 8, 9, 10, 11, and 12 years.

### 5841 - Boy's Middy Suit
Cut in 4 sizes, 3, 4, 5, and 6 years.

## PATTERN CATALOGUE
### 10 CENTS

**No. 2234.** - Girls' Dress, with Plaited Skirt and a Separate Guimpe, Four sizes, 6 to 12 years. For medium size or a girl of 10 years the dress requires 5 3/8 yards of material 24 inches wide or 3 1/2 yards 36 inches wide; the guimpe needs 1 5/8 yards 36 inches wide.

**No. 2376.** - Girls' Dress with a Separate Guimpe Having High or Low Neck and Long or Three-Quarter Length Sleeves. Four sizes, 6 to 12 years. For medium size or a girl of 10 years the dress requires 4 1/2 yards of material 24 inches wide, or 3 1/4 yards 36 inches wide; the guimpe needs 1 5/8 yards 36 inches wide.

**No. 2393.** - Girls' Dress, Four sizes, 6 to 12 years. For medium size or a girl of 10 years the dress requires 4 yards of material 24 inches wide or 2 3/4 yards 35 inches wide.

**No. 2397.** - Boys' Shirt-Waist, with Separate Turn-Down Collar, Seven sizes, 3 to 15 years. For medium size or a boy of 9 years the waist requires 2 1/2 yards of material 24 inches wide or 1 7/8 yard 36 inches wide.

**No. 2406.** - Ladies' Tailored Shirt or Shirt-waist, with or without Yoke Facing, Six sizes, 32 to 42. For medium size or 36 bust the waist requires 3 5/8 yards of material 24 inches wide, or 2 1/4 yards 36 inches wide.

**No. 2417.** - Girls' Russian Dress, Four sizes, 6 to 12 years. For medium size or a girl of 10 years the dress requires 5 1/2 yards of material 24 inches wide, 3 5/8 yards 36 inches wide.

**No. 2441.** - Girls' Jumper Dress, with Guimpe Having Long or Three-Quarter Length Sleeves, Four sizes, 6 to 12 years. For medium size or a girl of 10 years the dress requires 4 1/8 yards of material 24 inches wide, or 3 yards 36 inches wide; the guimpe needs 1 5/8 yards of material 36 inches wide.

1002          1004          1006          1008

**1002. GIRLS' ONE-PIECE APRON**, 4 sizes, 3 to 9 years; price 10 cents. For 5 years, 1 3/4 yard of material 36 inches wide will be required. Dimity, lawn, gingham or printed wash fabric may be used.

**1004. LITTLE GIRLS' DRESS**, with Princess front panel; 5 sizes, 4 to 12 years; price 10 cents. Transfer pattern for embroidery, No. 1167, price 10 cents. For 8 years, 4 1/8 yards of material 36 inches wide will be required.

**1006. LITTLE BOYS' SUIT**, Consisting of a Blouse with Shield and Standing Collar and Knickerbockers, 3 sizes, 2 to 6 years; price 10 cents. For 4 years, 2 yards of material 44 inches wide will be required.

**1008. GIRLS' DRESS WITH GUIMPE**, 6 sizes, 5 to 10 years; price 10 cents. For 7 years, 3 yards of material 36 inches wide will be required for the dress and 1 1/8 yard for the guimpe.

# Story Hour in the Home

MCCALL'S MAGAZINE, JUNE, 1912

## FOURTH KINDERGARTEN ARTICLE
### by Annie E. Moore
### Teachers College, Columbia University

WAS there ever a child who did not respond to the magic words, Once upon a time? In every language they work a charm, quieting the restless, awakening the listless and enchaining the attention of the most heedless. Pronounce that talisman and children will follow as they did the Piper of Hamelin, rapt, eager, joyous - into the fairy-story world.

Through the schools are doing a great deal in presenting good stories to children, the fairies, after all, do not seem to thrive in the ordinary school atmosphere. The cosy fireside with the intimate family group suits them better for working their spells.

Little children love rhyme and rhythm long before they are able to grasp the thought expressed. While we may no longer actually rock our children to sleep, the sing-song of the voice lulls and quiets by the same rhythmic swing. Let no one be beguiled into thinking that there are better, because newer, rhymes and stories for little children than those of dear old Mother Goose. The child is to be pitied who does not early come to know that goodly and fascinating company surrounding the old dame. Merely pretty sentimental verse and namby-pamby storiettes are no substitute for this sturdy stock of sense and nonsense. The pure fun and wholesome jollity of Mother Goose would alone justify her large place in literature for little children. But notice also what a marvelous introduction she gives to the sights and sounds of this big earth and to the creatures great and small, high and low, that dwell upon it. The procession of animals we meet in Mother Goose is almost as long as that of Noah's Ark. Most of them are friendly domestic creatures of name and fame, as, for example, Tommy Tinker's dog, the pony Dapple-gray and Jack Sprat's pig. Then see what an introduction the children get to the activities and occupations of their elders; for here come peddlers, priests and beggars, farmers, doctors, butchers and smiths, while shepards and milkmaids appear side by side with kings and queens.

There are many poor collections of Mother Goose. Into some have crept doggerel that Mother Goose herself would repudiate, and into others many very sophisticated lines. So, to find a really good edition requires some search.

Children should gradually come to know the fine bits of poetry, truly childlike in subject and spirit, which the great poets have here and there produced. In addition to this, there is much of real merit which has been written especially for children and which may be found in various collections, affording the busy mother an abundance of just what she needs to feed the developing taste for beautiful poetry.

Many grown-ups have serious doubts about the effect of fairy tales. Various objections are heard; that these old tales are full of horrors which fill the minds of children with images causing terror; that they often depict the mean and sordid, suggesting evil quite as much as good; that, while well suited to the primitive people among whom they arose, they do not teach the lessons needed by our present day life. Furthermore, many parents fear if their children hear so much that is purely fanciful they will be dissatisfied with things of everyday life or fail to distinguish between the real and the fact that there are as many different kinds of fairy stories as of any other form of fiction, and that there should be the closest scrutiny of quality and fitness. The mother with her little group has a much easier task in making her selection than the teacher with a large class. Knowing the individuals so well, and watching the after results of the stories, she can easily judge whether any child is over-excited or whether bad dreams result from any of the tales.

Now, as to how and where to find some of the best satisfaction out of it. To the same class belong the old favorites Henny-penny, Little Chick Tuppen and The Gingerbread Boy. There is an excellent collection in which many of these simple little tales having much repetition are found.

The worst features of the old fairy and folk tales are usually presented in the cheap, highly colored toy books offered in such quantities about Christmas time. The horrors of Bluebeard and the Robber Bridegroom are made more hideous by the lurid colors and the bald narrative. Discard all such trash and get one or two standard collections such as Andrew Lang's Blue Fairy Book, Grimm's Fairy Tales or Hamilton Wright Mabie's Fairy Tales Every Child Should Know.

# Ivory Soap in the Laundry - The Washing of Colored Clothes

Although most "wash goods" are now called "fast" color, every house wife, at some time or other, has had a sad experience in washing some particular garment. In other words, many so-called "fast" colors cannot stand ordinary washing methods, so it is safer to use special methods with all of them.

The things which harm colors are: 1st. Boiling the clothes. 2nd. Exposure by sunlight. 3rd. Hard rubbing. 4th. Strong soaps. 5th. Water, itself, in the case of very delicate colors.

The effect of water can be offset, as you know, by setting the colors before washing. When you are sure that water itself will not harm the colors in a garment, the way to wash it thoroughly and safely is to use Ivory Soap as suggested in the following paragraphs. Ivory Soap is pure. It contains no "free" (uncombined) alkali. It will not harm anything that water itself will not harm.

*The Procter & Gamble Co.*

### Ordinary Colored Clothes

Fast color - Make a warm suds of Ivory Soap. Quickly wash, rinse and hang out to dry one garment at a time. If the water is colored by the goods take fresh water for the next garment.

Never rub soap on the goods; nor the goods on the washboard - except wristbands, neckbands and the edges of hems is badly soiled.

When dry, turn garment wrong side out and starch in thin starch. Shake into shape and hang in shade.

When dry, dampen and roll up garment a short time before ironing.

Whenever possible, iron muslins, prints and ginghams on the wrong side.

### Delicate - Hued Muslins, Cambrics, Prints, Etc.

Soak for ten minutes in salt water, a half cupful of common salt to two gallons of cold water. Wring out and wash quickly in Ivory Soap suds. Rinse in blueing water. Starch in boiled starch. Hang in shade.

### Lawns, Organdies, Batistes, Etc.

Wash in warm, weak Ivory Soap suds with salt in suds. Rinse twice in hard water with some salt added. Make smooth, thin starch and put this in last rinse water with a pinch of powdered alum.

### Brown Linens

Pour boiling water over a quarter pound of cheap coffee. Strain through cheese-cloth into two tubs, one for washing, the other for rinsing. Wash with Ivory Soap. Rinse and hang in shade to dry. Iron first on wrong side and then on the right. Do not use blueing.

### Black Goods—Cotton or Silk

Dissolve in a pint of soft water a small cake of Ivory Soap shaved fine. Add $1/2$ oz. ether, $1/2$ oz. Spirits of wine, $1/2$ oz. glycerine, $1 1/2$ oz. ammonia. Put in a bottle and cork tightly. When needed, shake well.

Add a teacupful of above cream to two gallons of water. Use plenty of Ivory Soap and wash the same as other goods. Rinse well in clear water. Iron silk goods on the wrong side, while wet. Dry cotton goods, then dampen.

## Mother's Query Club
### Conducted by Mrs. Charity Brush

*This department is conduced for the great congress of mothers who read McCall's Magazine. We want to help you solve your problems in rearing your children and earnestly invite you to write us about them. Anyone interested in the development of children is also asked to tell us of her experiences. Available contributions will be paid for. No contritions can be returned. Address, Mothers Query Club, McCall's Magazine, New York City.*

CURIOUSLY enough, more than one of the letters received since our last talk has dealt in varying ways with that most important topic, a "double standard." Why some of them ask, do we fairly thrust our boys out, to "see life," as we call it, while we shelter our girls from the knowledge of the very things most essential to the life they will have to live? Why do we condone in the son the most offensive lapses, while the daughter is outcast even from the heart of her mother for the slightest side-stepping from a rigid line of convention? These questions, and others kindred to them, are often uppermost among the problems of the modern mother.

And, indeed, the whole subject is vital to our modern civilization. In the changing industrial conditions of our day, the old-time sheltered life of woman is becoming a thing of the past. It is now the exceptional woman who can be so shielded from the ordinary necessities of existence that she need never even know of them. More and more is it becoming necessary for our girls to go out into the world to fend for themselves, and we are beginning to realize that the security obtained by ignorance is a false one.

On the other hand, in the ever growing fierceness of competition of modern business, the man who suceeds is the man who is physically, mentally, and morally alert—the man whose whole being is keyed to the pitch of effciency. To the mothers of the land is it given to make these men and women who are to replace us in the conduct of affairs, and in their hands rests this whole question of standards. Just as the morals of the boys and girls depend in large measure upon the training of the mothers, so, in the last analysis will the opinion of the world be the opinion of the mothers upon one standard of morality for the girls and another for the boys. One thoughful mother, Mrs. H.H., Arthur, III, has these few words to say of

### YOUR BOY

As a mother, let me advise mothers. There seems to be a widespread impression that mothers must know where their girls are, who their associates are; but very little is said of their brothers. Surely it isn't the lack of love for the boys! No, it's the old tradition that "boys can take care of themselves." What a mistake this is! Boys need mother's advice as much, or even more, than girls. No doubt they would get it, too, if their sins counted the same as their sisters' do in this world. Instead, a man is a privileged being. He must be excused, his faults fortgotten; while for the same offence his sister would be an outcast. Dear mothers, it's only the world which doesn't see your boy as he really is. All human beings are judged the same in the eye of God. All must be pure in heart who enter into the Kingdom of Heaven. So, dear mothers, don't neglect your boys' salvation with the foolish idea that a boy gets along better in the world than a girl. Teach them to treat all girls as they want their sisters treated. Sin is sin no matter where committed, whether by man or woman. God has given man no more right to sin than woman, and each shall be punished according to the sin. Therefore, mothers, look after your boys. When every mother comes to realize this fact there will be less heartache and pain, and not so much need to be looking after your daughters, for the young men, who are their friends and who should be their natural protectors, will do this for you. Be sure, oh, very sure, you know your boy as you do your girl.

# Etiquette and Deportment

ANXIOUS.—I. A bride may have the dresses of her trousseau at any length most becoming and convenient. There need be no difference in the length of the dresses in your trousseau and that of the dresses you wear before you are married. Walking skirts are most convenient when they are ankle length, and dresses for the house or for formal occasions should be longer. 2. The bride's own intial is always used on the bridal linen. 3. It is proper for a bride to shake hands with everyone to whom she is introduced.

BROWN EYES.— Yes, it is proper for a girl thirteen years old to have boy friends, but it is not a good plan to spend too much time with them at ice cream parlors and vaudeville shows, as you say you have been doing. If boys of your age go to school with you, it is perfectly natural for you to walk home together, just as it would be for you to walk home with a girl. You should be able to have your pleasures together in your own home, or in the homes of your schoolmates and friends, and at your age there should be no question of "going with boys." You are far too young. 2. The hair almost invariably comes out after a severe illness. Doctors always recommend, that it be cut, but I think you were wise not to have yours cut. It may not all come out, and what remains will be easier to arrange if it if long than if it is all short. Bring it back from the forehead, not too tightly, but in a soft pompadour effect, without a "rat," of course, and braid it in

one braid to hang down your back. Put a bow near the end, and if it needs a bow on top of the head, to hold it in place, wear one there also.

A VIRGINIA GIRL.— Yes, I think it would be better to wait until the young man has had an opportunity to remove his hat and coat before you enter the room. It might appear to be unseemly haste if you entered the moment he had arrived. 2. When he thanks you for entertaining him, you may say that you are glad he called, and that he enjoyed himself. 3. Yes, when a man and a woman are introduced to each other, the lady's name is mentioned first.

BLUE EYES.—When butter and syrup are served together to be eaten with hot biscuit, do not use your fork any more than you would if you were eating butter alone on the biscuit. Spread a piece with butter, then with syrup, and eat with the fingers. When one is eating ham and eggs or meat and potatoes, it is not necessary to cut them with the knife and fork, then lay the knife down and take the fork in the other hand. It requires constant shifting of knife and fork, and is awkward and inconvenient.

TULIP HOPE.— If there is any purpose in forming your club, why not consider that when you choose a name for it? For instance, if it is a literary club, it might be the Emerson Club, or the Hawthorne Club. If it is a mu-

sical club, call it the Mozart or the Wagner or the Mendelssohn Club. Since there are to be six members, The Sextette would be an appropriate name. It will have more individuality if you choose a name that has some relation to the purpose of the club or to the initials of the members would supply a name.

*Gingham for Girls*

### NO. 6566. GIRL'S RUSSIAN DRESS

The pattern in cut in sizes 6, 8, 10, 12 and 14 years. Bust measure 24, 25, 27, 29 and 31 inches. The eight-year size requires 4 yards of 27 inch material, 3 1/4 yards of 36 inch material or 2 5/8 yards of 44 inch material, and 1/2 yard of contrasting goods. Price of cutting pattern, 10 cents.

PLAIN and check gingham are combined with usual good effect in this stylish Russian dress for girls, the black silk tie adding not a little to the general effectiveness. Simulated straps are embroidered down the front, and serve to trim the closing, which otherwise would be rather plain.

The blouse extends over the skirt far enough to give an impression of a double skirt, but in reality the skirt is merely a circular two-gores model attatched to a sleeveless underwaist which closes at the back. The blouse has a yoke in the back cut in one with the side back, or, to express it a little differently, there is a separate centre back piece set in below yoke depth. There are also two plaits each side of the back.

The sleeve turns back to form the deep cuff and the check facing is set on afterwards, but if preferred the sleeve can be left long and gathered into a wristband. However, the short sleeve is recommended for the season as much from a style view-point as a practical one. Perhaps the real feature of the dress is the belt with pockets, in three sections, the back section is buttoning over the front in strap style. The pockets, made of the plain gingham for contrast, are stitched at each side of the belt and buttoned at the top.

For eight-year size, three yards of plain gingham thirty-two inches wide will be required and one yard of checked gingham thirty-two inches wide will be required and one yard of checked gingham thirty-two or twenty-seven inches wide. Five-eighths of a yard of thirty-six-inch lining will make the underwaist. It is economical to buy one of the made ties.

### CHILD'S YOKE DRESS NO. 486

CHILD's yoke Dress No. 846 is just the thing for very best Sunday wear for the summer. The dress is very simple, easily worked and easily laundered, and owes its beauty entirely to its daintiness. The yoke is charmingly adorned across the front with a garland of forget-me-nots that can be embroidered in a very little while, and the bottom edge and neck are scalloped and finished with a tiny frill of narrow valenciennes lace. The yoke design is shown in detail at the bottom of the page. The little frock is very sweet and lovely, and every mother who likes to have her little daughter look dainty and pretty will want to make the garment. The design comes in one to two year size. Stamped on sheer white lawn of a handsome quality, 60 cents; or stamped on dimity with a fine hairline stripe, 65 cents; or stamped on pure imported linen, 80 cents; with embroidery cotton for working the design, 22 cents extra. Perforated pattern of the design, 12 cents.

### CHILD'S ONE-PIECE DRESS NO. 847

ONE-PIECE dress No. 847, with belt, comes in sizes one to six years. It is a practical, durable garment for hard service, yet it has that distinction which makes it perfectly suitable for dressier wear. The daisy motif for the front is shown in detail at the bottom of the page, and the belt design is similar to it. The embroidery is white. Design stamped on mercerized poplin in either white, pink or blue, on white pique, or on white striped dimity, in size one to three years, 60 cetns; or size four to six years, 80 cents; with embroidery cotton for either size, 22 cents extra. Perforated pattern, 12 cents.

## *Some New Spring Styles*

THE simple little suit No. 7110 has a plain coat blouse, closing in front, with the neck open, and trimmed with a wide collar. There is an inner shield with standing collar which may be made detatchable. The sleeves are tucked at the wrist. The trousers are opened at the sides, and may have a straight lower edge or bloomer finish. The pattern, No. 7110, is cut in three sizes: 2, 4, and 6 years. A medium size requires two yards and $5/8$ of 36-inch material, and $1/2$ yard of 36-inch contrasting goods.

THE ornamental straps, which trim the girls' dress No. 7132 and make it fancy, can be omitted, but this is not advisable. The waist closes in front. The two-piece skirt has a reversed box plait at each side seam. The pattern, No. 7132, is cut in five sizes,: 6, 8, 10, 12 and 14 years. A medium size requires three yards of 36-inch material.

SUIT 7110

DRESS 7132

## CONTRIBUTED BY OUR READERS

*The People's Home Journal, September, 1915*

### EFFECIENCY

*Mother* (at the breakfast table) - "You always ought to use your napkin, George."

*George* - "I am usin' it, mother; I've got the dog tied to the leg of the table with it."

### PUZZLING

*She* - "I wonder where all the pins go."

*He* - "That's a difficult question to answer, because they are all pointed one way and headed the other."

### HAS IT COME TO THIS?

*Niece* - "My husband's so careless; he's always losing his buttons."

*Aunt* - "Perhaps they are not sewn on carefully, dear."

*Niece* - "That's just it; he's awfully slipshod with his sewing."

### OPTIONAL

After the children had partaken of their fruit, Mrs. Blomfield called her son to her. "I noticed your little sister took a very small apple. Did you let her have her choice as I told you to?" "Yes'm, I told her she could take the little one or none, and she chose the little one."

## BON BONS OR CORN PUFFS
# WHICH?

Bubble-Like Tit-Bits are Now Made of Toasted Corn

### TOMMY TUCKER SUIT
### FOR THE LITTLE FELLOW

**No. 4925.** Made of wide wale Kersey pile corduroy. Single breasted coat. Elton collar. Silk cord tie. Outside breast pocket. Wide patent leather belt. Golden or dark brown or Royal blue Plain bottom pants. Full pleateed sleeves, 2½ to 8 years. Price, Delivered Free.

## $1.95

### Girls' Percale School Dress No. 4923

### No. 4922 Boys' Blue Serge Suit

Fastens in back. Pointed collar with inlay of plain percale and bow tie to match. Long waisted. Plain circular skirt, combination pointed peplum piped with plain material to match. 6 to 14 years. Pink and white or blue and white plaids only. Delivered Free.

## $0.39

Extra trousers. Patch pockets, stitched belt. Single breasted style. Coat has bottom facing. Back yoke style with four pleats. Italian lining. Trousers full peg top. Belt loops. Hip pockets and buckle on bottom. 7 to 16 years. Delivered Free.

## $2.12

# Ideas in Small Clothes

## Children's Box-Plaited Dress

One understands why box plaits have a "big showing" this season when a winning little frock like No. 8117 of offered. It is cut in one piece from shoulder to lower edge, and slips over the head.

The dress-pattern, No. 8117, is cut in sizes for from 4 to 10 years. To make the dress in the 8 year size will require $2\,5/8$ yards of 36-inch material; $5/8$ yard of contrasting goods and 4 yards of braid. In all one material, $3\,1/8$ yards will do.

## Children's Dress

As pretty a little dress as you ever saw for a small girl, is shown by No. 8112. Just adding a tab to the top of each box plait, makes the two-gored skirt one of beauty, and where the waist joins, and embroidered belt proves its worth.

The dress-pattern No. 8112, is cut in sizes for from 4 to 10 years. To make the dress in the 8-year size will require $2\,5/8$ yards of 36-inch material; $1/2$ yard of 36-inch contrasting goods, and 4 yards of braid.

## Boy's Russian Suit

The favorite with mothers and with Fashion is a Russian suit like No. 8133, for the small boy. Decidedly a boy's style is the blouse with smart closing-outline, belted at lowered waist-line, fitted with a pocket, and collared and cuffed with contrasting goods.

The suit-pattern, No. 8133, is cut in sizes for 2, 4 and 6 years. To make the suit in the medium size will require 2 yards of 36-inch material, and $1/4$ yard of 32-inch contrasting goods.

## Children's Night Drawers

Cut on the most advanced lines for children's sleeping garments, the night drawers, No. 7914, will be found very cozy for winter's chilly nights. It may have closing at front or back, bishop or plain sleeves, and be made without or with feet.

The night-drawers-pattern, No. 7914, is cut in sizes for from 1 to 12 years. To make the night-drawers in the medium size will require $2\,5/8$ yards of 36-inch material.

8117    8112    8133    7914    8119    8121

## Girls' Dress

The seperate bolero for this design, No. 8119, proves that Fashion plays fair with the junior girl. It is worn over a simple little waist buttoned at back, and joined to a one- piece gathered skirt.

The dress-pattern, No. 8119, is cut in sizes for from 6 to 12 years. To make the dress in the 8-year size will require $3\,1/8$ yards of 36-inch material, $3\,5/8$ yards of braid, and 2 yards of ribbon.

## Girls' Dress

The stylish and becoming collar with its button-decoration, is a big feature of this dress, No. 8121, but it has another, in the vest of contrasting goods. The frock has a body-lining and the waist-fulness is gathered at the lowest part for blousing over the two-piece gathered skirt. The sleeves may be cuffed to match the vest or collar. Give the pattern a chance to prove its worth, and you will be thoroughtly satisfied.

The dress-pattern, No. 8121, is cut in sizes for from 6 to 14 years. To make the dress in the 10-year size will require $2\,7/8$ yards of 36 inch material; $3/8$ yard of contrasting goods, and $1/2$ yard of 36-inch lining.

## Children's Dress

A one-piece gathered skirt and plain waist are neatly joined at a raised waistline, showing to advantage the comfortable lines of this frock, No. 8180. The pockets are rightful possessions and the cape collar is excellent for this little dress.

The dress-pattern, No. 8180, is cut in sizes for from 2 to 8 years. To make the dress in the 4-year size will require $1^7/_8$ yards of 36 inch material; and $^1/_2$ yard of 18 inch contrasting goods.

## Girls' Dress

To draw praise and suit girlish fancy, this frock, No. 8147, has the body part gathered to deep yokes, and a one-piece skirt in plaited effect with panel-front.

The dress-pattern, No. 8147, is cut in sizes for from 6 to 12 years. To make the dress in the 8-year size will require $2^3/_4$ yards of 36-inch material, $^5/_8$ yard of contrasting goods, and $8^1/_4$ yards of braid.

## Children's Coat

There is a wealth of style in this roomy coat, No. 8158, in which any little girl will look her best.

The coat-pattern, No. 8158, is cut in sizes for from 2 to 12 years. To make the coat in the 12-year old size will require $2^3/_4$ yards of 44-inch material, and $7^1/_2$ yards of braid to trim.

## Girls' Dress

The way of Fashion with a young miss is shown by this design, No. 8162. The waist-fronts overlap a surplice vest and have their fulness gathered where a two-gored plaited skirt with panel-front is joined.

The dress-pattern, No. 8162, is cut in sizes for from 6 to 12 years. To make the dress in the 8-year size will require $3^1/_2$ yards of 36-inch material, $^1/_2$ yard of 36-inch contrasting goods, and $^1/_2$ yard of 22-inch linen or silk for vest.

## Children's Rompers

For the pride of the household, No. 8144 represents fetching little rompers. A two-piece bloomersection is gathered at the sides, where it joins the waist.

The rompers-pattern, No. 8144, is cut in sizes for 6 months, 1, 2 and 3 years. To make the rompers on the 2-year size will require $1^7/_8$ yards of 36-inch goods.

## Girls' Dress

An interesting feature of this design, No. 8174, is: having the deep yoke and panel in one piece. The side belt, holding the fulness neatly, is as decorative as the sailor-collar of contrasting goods and the silk tie. Buttons are used to advantage.

The dress-pattern, No. 8174, is cut in sizes for from 6 to 14 years. To make the dress in the 8-year size will require $2^7/_8$ yards of 36-inch material; $^1/_2$ yard of 36-inch contrasting goods, $3^1/_8$ yards if all of one material, 36 inches wide.

# Crimes We Unknowingly Commit Against Our Children

THE MODERN PRISCILLA 1917

Thousands of loving parents are daily unconsciously using methods in bringing up their children which can be easily destroy for life their chance of happiness and success. And the pitiful part of it is that these parents do not realize the irreparable harm they are doing.

Character is not born but builded. You as a parent are the architect of your child's character- the constructor of its future career, for upon character depends success. Abraham Lincoln, perhaps our greatest American, once said: All that I am and all that I ever hope to be I owe to my mother. Great men before and since Lincoln Lincoln have said the same thing- and how truly they spoke!

The trouble has always been that we have never given any real scientific study to the question of child training-we have not searched for the cause of disobedience, the cause of wilfulness, the cause of untruthfulness, and of other symptoms which, if not treated in the right way may lead to dire consequences. Instead, we punish the child for exhibiting the bad trait, or else let it go. As a result, we do the child an actual wrong instead of helping it. What we should do is attack the trouble at its source.

The new system of child training is founded upon the principle that confidence is the basis of control. And the five fundamental principles involved are: suggestion, substitution in choice, parental initiative in cooperation, parental expectation and parental approval.

Under this new system children who have been well-nigh unmangeable become obedient and willing, and such traits as bashfulness, jealousy, fear, bragging, etc., are overcome. But the system goes deeper than that, for it instills high ideals and builds character, which is, of course, the goal of all parents efforts in child training.

Physical punishment, shouted commands and other barbarious relics of the old system have no place in this modern school. Children have made comrades, not slaves; are helped not punished. And the results are nothing short of marvelous.

Instead of a hardship, child training becomes a genuine pleasure, as the parent shares every confidence, every joy, and every sorrow of the child, and at the same time has its unqualified respect. This is a situation rarely possible under old training methods.

And what a source of pride now as well as in after years: To have children whose every action shows culture and refinement, perfect little gentlemen and gentlewoman, yet full of childish enthusiasm and spontaneity with all!

To put in practice these new ideas in child training, strange as it may seem, takes less time than the old method. It is simply a question of applying principles founded on a scientific study of human nature, going at it in such a way as to get immediate results without friction.

The founder of this new system is Professor Ray C. Berry, A.B., M.A (Harvard and Columbia), who has written a complete course in Practical Child Training. This course is based on Professor Berry's extensive investigations and wide practical experience, and provides a well-worked-out plan which the parent can easily follow. The Parents Association, a national organization devoted to improving the methods of child training, has adopted the Berry system, and is teaching its course to its members by mail.

## An Invitation to Join

At this time an invitation is being extended to earnest fathers and mothers who would like to join the association and learn the methods which are providing so universally successful with children of all ages from babyhood to man and woman hood.

### DO YOU KNOW HOW -

to encourage child talk?
to always obtain cheerful obedience?
to eliminate all forms of viciousness?
to correct mistakes of early training?
to replace disinclination for bathing with delight?
to win confidence of children?
to teach punctuality?
to keep child from crying?
Perserverance?
Carefulness?
to develop initiative in child?
teach child to comply with command?
to teach personal courage and self reliance?
to inculcate respect for elders?
to suppress temper in children without punishment?
to overcome obstinacy?
to overcome objectionable habits in children?
to cure habit of coaxing?
to succeed with a child of any age without any authority?
to teach value of money?
to make firmness unobtrusive?
to correct wrong habit of thought?
to discourage the "why" habit in regard to commands?
to prevent round shoulders?
to direct children discreetly in their amusements?
to cultivate mental concentration?
to wisely guide child's choice of companions?
to engender interest in work or study?
to prevent worry in child?
to develop sense of responsibility?
to train child in neatness and order?
to prevent quarreling and fighting?
to cultivate ideal temperament?
to deal with super sensitive child?
to instruct children in the delicate matters of sex?
to cure impertinence?
Discourtesy?
Vulgarity?
to deal with boy who is a bully? A braggart?
to remove fear of darkness?
fear of thunder and lightning and fear of harmless animals?

# Childish Modes Follow
## the Prescribed Straight Lines

No 8517

No. 8495

### No 8517

Obviously the merest amateur could make this smart little coat. The yoke is fitted first and then the skirt portion can be hung from this without difficulty. They are really truly pockets on the side, but that need not be alarming, because the braiding around the edging will cover slight imperfections of workmanship. The wide sailor collar is braided to match, and a cap of black satin braided in the same design completes the costume.

### No. 8495

The youngest son of the family may not join the army, but he can show his patriotism by donning a suit of blue chambray, with red, white, and blue chain-stitch around the belt and white stars outlined with a single stitch for each side and filled in with French knots, embroidered on the front. Other color combinations are just as good, but the belt is always lined with red, white, and blue, and stars may be in either color that contrasts best with the material. No. 8517, sizes 4 to 14; and No. 8495, 1 and 2 years. Price 15 cents each.

# Practical Midwinter Styles for All Ages

Patterns of No. 7422 - Children's Dress. Cut in sizes 2, 4 and 6 years. No. 7589 - Boys' Suit, sizes 2, 4 and 6. No. 8456, sizes 6 to 14 years. No. 8431, Sizes 4 to 10, and No. 8292, sizes 6 to 14 years.

No 7422

No 7589

No 8456

No 8431

No 8292

Careful mothers are giving thoughtful consideration to the clothing of their children this year more than ever before, and the woman who has learned that quality is the very foundation of conservation is looking carefully at material, style, and make.

The rapidity with which American women are grasping the lesson of thrift is one of the big encouraging elements of the war. Thrift is not meaning, to the women of this country, simply going without. It has its root in that much abused and, until now, hardly used word efficiency. What will be the most useful, the most durable, and the best-looking thing I can make, and how shall I achieve this thing with the least possible waste of time, strength, and money are questions that every woman asks herself before she undertakes a task of any sort to-day. She asks these questions particularly in connection with the care and clothing of her family.

Every mother wants her children to be well dressed and she knows that the hall-mark of attractive clothes for both grownups and children, but especially for the little people, is hand-work. And yet, how can I spend the time embroidering when there is such need in the world? is the very next thought. But that difficulty is quickly settled by choosing either garments that are made up all ready to put on when the hand-work has been done, or by taking the utmost advantage of the simplicity that now marks fashionable attire for big and little people. Few seams, straight lines, frank and simple closings all conspire to take the dread out of dressmaking.

Another element of efficiency and hence of thrift is to be found in anticipating our needs. If summer sewing is started early enough there need be no rush just when we should be packing for a trip to cooler climates.

*No. 18-3-52. A piqué shade hat can be worn by little girls of almost any age.*

No. 18-3-52. Hat. Sizes 17 and 20 inches, head measure. Either size stamped on white pique, 50 cents. White embroidery cotton, 12 cents extra. Size, 22-inch. Stamped pique, 60 cents. Embroidery cotton, 15 cents extra. Perforated pattern, any one size, 40 cents.

No. 18-3-55. Stamped made-up bib of fine cotton huckback, 25 cents. Embroidery cotton, 3 cents extra; or embroidery silk, 5 cents extra. Perforated embroidery pattern, 15 cents.

No. 18-3-56. Tray Cloth. Size, 16x20 inches. Stamped made-up cloth of fine cotton huckback, 3 cents. Embroidery cotton, 3 cents extra; or embroidery silk, 5 cents extra. Perforated embroidery pattern, 30 cents.

No. 18-3-58. Carriage Pillow. Size, 13x19 inches. Stamped on white pique, same material for back, 50 cents. White embroidery cotton, 20 cents extra. Perforated embroidery pattern, 35 cents.

No.18-3-59. Carriage Strap. Stamped on white pique, 15 cents. White embroidery cotton, 13 cents extra. Perforated embroidery pattern, 20 cents; or transfer pattern, 10 cents.

*No. 18-3-54. No one need be coaxed to wear this apron of colored chambray with binding and small dogs in white. Four-year size stamped on pink, blue, or tan with dogs stamped on white poplin, 55 cents; eight-year size, 65 cents. White bias binding, 35 cents; black embroidery cotton for outlining dog's and lettering, and red for dogs' tongues, 6 cents. Perforated pattern, either size, 35 cents.*

No. 18-3-53. One would always feel well dressed in a thin white frock of India linon. It is made up and needs only to be scalloped with white and embroidered in pink. Size 1 to 2 years, 75 cents; 4-year size, $1.00. Embroidery cotton, 12 cents.

No. 18-3-57. To toss about a clown's head would make one feel quite a pirate. The face is stamped in red and blue on a made-up bean-bag which costs 15 cents. Embroidery cotton for outlining, 6 cents.

*Bib, No. 18-3-55, and tray cloth, No. 18-3-56, are made up ready to embroider in blue.*

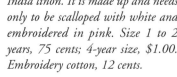

## Street Dresses for Older Girls

The embroidery on this dress is so placed that it will not interfere with any devices that you may have for lengthening a dress to meet any requirements. The hem can be turned down, the skirt slipped down on the waist to give more length from the shoulder to belt or the sleeves lengthened and still the embroidery can remain unchanged. Two shades of one color are used for the embroidery which is an interesting, semi-conventional pattern, effective and easily worked. This would be an attractive dress for poplin if made of white and should satisfy so young a girl for any summer parties or afternoon entertainments.

No.8666. Sizes 10, 12 and 14 years. Stamped on white, rose, blue or tan poplin, $3.25; or on white linen, $4.00. Embroidery cotton, all white or two shades of a color, 27 cents extra. Perforated embroidery pattern, 40 cents.

## A Play Garment for Little Tots

A single yard of material is required for this new and practical over-all romper. For real out-of-doors play it should be made of dark serviceable material; chambray is good, and of course there is gingham and galatea. For less strenuous requirement it could be made of white or light-colored poplin. The ducks worked in outline will delight the youngsters. If color is used for the garment, embroidery should be white and vice versa. If you wish, the lower edge of the legs can be gathered in with elastic, but the small boy will surely prefer it as it appears here.

## ...And a Coat for Little Sister

A charming coat of white pique with collar and cuffs of pink or blue linen is shown at the lower right. A child of only a year could wear this coat and if she is as old as seven or eight she could still wear the same model without feeling any sacrifice of childish dignity. The collar and cuffs could be of white also. In either case they are trimmed with a simple pattern in white soutache braid. Collar and cuffs stamped on pink or blue linen, and white pique not stamped to complete coat. Sizes 1, 2 and 4 years, $1.60. Sizes, 6 and 8 years, $2.20. White soutache braid, 27 cents extra. Perforated braiding pattern, 35 cents; or transfer pattern, 15 cents.

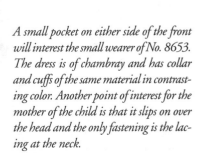

*A small pocket on either side of the front will interest the small wearer of No. 8653. The dress is of chambray and has collar and cuffs of the same material in contrasting color. Another point of interest for the mother of the child is that it slips on over the head and the only fastening is the lacing at the neck.*

# A Mother is Known by Her Children's Clothes

If daughter's thin dresses are ready mother may not need to stop canning and sew up a muslin slip when the scorching weather arrives. Haven't you seen those mothers who sew frantically for two weeks before vacation and stay up until the morning to finish packing, only to arrive in the country or at the shore, tired, cross, and secretly worried about the condition of the houses they have left? We aren't going to be like that very much longer, for we are learning that everything depends on health, and health depends on happiness on keeping up with our job, whether it be clothing and feeding a family or running a nation.

It is with all of these principles in mind that your editors and artists, here in the *PRISCILLA* establishment, plan and think and work to help you. And each little garment and article shown here has passed upon by several experts, to be sure that you are getting something that is practical, worth while, and of good quality. Aren't they all nice? Don't you like them?

All of the embroidery is in simple and familiar style, and the garments that require to be made up are easily handled. The little pique hat, No. 18-3-52, for instance, has a double brim, but there is nothing difficult about it, just embroider the design, then baste the two pieces together, buttonhole the scallops through both and bind the inner edge with a straight fold one inch wide, for a head band. The crown is a flat round piece with a drawstring run into a casting at the edge. Tack the crown on so that it can be removed easily for laundering.

*No. 18-3-62. Girls' Dress. Size, 6 years. Stamped on white pique, $1.75. Size, 10 years. Stamped on white pique, $2.15. White embroidery cotton, 21 cents extra. Perforated embroidery pattern, either size, 40 cents.*

If you are two or four, you may wear this linen hat. No. 18-3-63. Hat. Sizes, 17 and 20 inches head measure. Either size stamped on white poplin, 45 cents. Embroidery cotton, 9 cents extra. Perforated embroidery pattern, either size, 35 cents; or transfer pattern, 15 cents.

18-3-63

No. 18-3-60. Boy's Rompers. Collar, cuffs, and pockets stamped on white poplin, and pink, blue, or tan chambray to complete rompers, 85 cents. Embroidery cotton, 3 cents extra. Perforated embroidery pattern, 35 cents; or transfer pattern, 15 cents. Paper cutting pattern No. 3895, 50 cents. Sizes, 2 and 4 years.

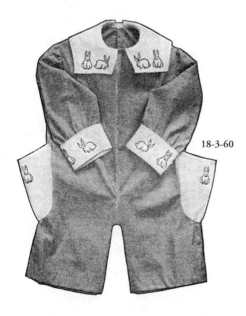

18-3-60

No. 18-3-52. The Pique Frock above for a girl of two years has excellent lines and tubs well. Mothers who are Hooverizing their time will find the little coat and hat at the right helpful when planning the summer wardrobe of small daughter. They come all made in a very good-looking wide ribbed pique and need only to be embroidered. The pockets are an attractive feature.

BATHROBE AND SLIPPERS
1957

1957

1977

COAT 1977
CAP 1940

# COSTUMES TO PLEASE THE TEMPERAMENTAL BOY

**1957** - A new bathrobe of terry cloth gives a touch of comfort and ease to the absorbed reader of the "Life of Buffalo Bill." It is cut on new, very simple lines that are particularly good for a garment of this type in eider-down, terry cloth and blanketing. It can be finished with a hood instead of the collar, and the slipper is made with a sole.

10 years requires 3 1/8 yards terry cloth 36 inches wide for bathrobe and slippers.

This bathrobe is splendid for boys of 2 to 12 years.

**1977-1940** - A cap and overcoat to match of cloth mixture are prime importance when one starts out for hockey. This is an extremely simple overcoat with a single-breasted front and adjustable collar. Use cheviot, mixed coatings, chinchilla or tweeds with a cap of woolens, checks or serge.

12 years requires 2 1/2 yards cloth mixture coating 54 inches wide, including cap in 7 hat size or 22 1/4 head measure.

This coat, 1977, is for boys of 4 to 16 years; the cap, 1940, is for boys 6 1/4 to 7 1/2 cap size or 20 to 20 3/4 head measure.

TAM-O'-SHANTER
1477 SET 2010

HAT 1945
COLLAR 2010

DRESS 2003
BRAID DESIGN 10697

HAT 1945
SET 2010

BATHROBE OR
WRAPPER 1999

DRESS 2009

DRESS 2011
SMOCKING DESIGN
10744

# DESIGNED FOR THE NEEDS OF IMPORTANT PEOPLE

**1999** - A new bathrobe or wrapper is cut on very simple lines and could be made from a kindergarten blanket. The lower edge is straight, and an inverted plait under the arm gives a suitable width. The slipper is made with a sole. You could use a blanket, eiderdown, toweling or flannelet.

4 years requires a blanket not less than 60 inches wide and 76 inches long.

This bathrobe is for children and girls, $1/2$ to 14 years.

**2010-1945-1477** - A new set of collar and muffs completes the costume with hat or tam.

View 1, 10-year size requires $3/8$ yard fur cloth 54 inches wide for collar and under section of brim, 1.2 yard velvet 35 or 36 wide; view 2, $5/8$ yard 54 inches wide for collar, muff, upper section of brim and top knot, $5/8$ yard velvet 35 or 36 inches wide. View 3, 8 year-size, $3/4$ yard fur cloth 54 inches wide.

Set 2010, is for girls of 2 to 14 years; Tam-oí-shanter, 1477, for girls, misses and children. Hat, 1945, is for girls of 2 to 12 years.

**2009** - Velours and wool plaid are combined in a splendid frock for the schoolgirl. The Dress slips on over the head and the long kimono body is graceful and becoming. The skirt is straight. You could use velveteen, taffeta, plaid silks or checks, serge, gingham, chambray, cotton poplin or linen, or gingham combined with chambray for school.

10 years requires 1 yard velour 35 or more inches wide for front, back and sleeves, $1 1/8$ yard wool plaid 44 inches wide for skirt.

Dress, 2009, for girls of 8 to 15 years.

**2003** - Dark cotton poplin competes equally well in the class-room or at home. The sleeve is made with one seam, the skirt is straight, and the dress has a particularly pretty closing. You could make it of gingham, chambray, linen, cotton poplin, serge, plaids, checks or velveteen.

12 years requires $2 1/2$ yards cotton poplin 35 or 36 inches wide, $1/2$ yard 27 or more inches wide for collar, cuffs and pocket-laps. Braid design 10697 trims the dress.

Dress, 2003, for girls of 8 to 15 years.

**2011** - Georgette smocked in color makes an adorable dress for the small person. The Empire yoke follows a particularly pretty out line in front and ends in a sash behind. The sleeve is made with one seam, and the straight skirt is gathered. You could use chambray, serge, linen, batiste, cottonvoile or any plain cotton material, or gingham without the smocking.

4 years requires $1 5/8$ yard Georgette 39 or 40 inches wide. Smocking design 10744 trims dress.

This dress is for little girls of 2 to 10 years.

## For Folks, Little Folks and Dolls

**415** - A doll from Paris, France, will insist on the Dutch-hip silhouette in her Christmas frock, a new cape vested with a contrasting color, a petticoat, combination and Billy Burke pajamas. She has an extremely chic little Rue de la Paix hat for the street.

24-inch requires 5/8 yard flowered voile 39 or 40 inches wide, 1/4 yard contrasting 39 or 40 inches wide.

The girl dolls' set is for dolls 14 to 30 inches high.

**413** - Under an adorable cape this 1920 model doll wears a dress with the new short sleeve - distinctly French. Her hat is nice for motoring and quite stylish enough for afternoon tea. For lingerie she has an envelope chemise and pajamas.

24-inch requires 7/8 yard satin 35 or 36 inches wide for hat and cape, 1/2 yard velvet 35 or 36 inches wide for outside of brim and inside of yoke.

This girl dolls' set is for dolls 14 to 30 inches high.

**414** - This doll has been brought up by the Montessori method, has had her adenoids removed, and her wardrobe will fill a young mother with Christmas joy. It consists of a delightful cape, a flirtatious hat and a perfect duck of a dress made with a jumper. She also has a petticoat, combination and a nightgown.

24-inch requires 1 batiste 35 or 36 inches wide, 7 yards lace edging.

This dolls' set is for dolls 14 to 30 inches high.

**2058** - You aren't quite sure whether this is a doll or a baby, and that is just the way your own three-year-old will look in these Dutch-silhouette rompers. They are in one piece and slip over the head, fastening at the bottom. They are easy to make,

DRESS OF GIRL DOLLS' SET **415**

CAPE, HAT AND DRESS OF GIRL DOLLS' SET **413**

ROMPERS **2058**

DRESS OF DOLLS' SET **414**

SUIT **2068**

DRESSING-GOWN **2029**

for the sleeve is kimono. Use chambray, cotton crepe, cotton poplin or seersucker.

3 years requires 2 yards gingham 32 inches wide.

These rompers are for children 1 to 5 years.

**2068** - The woman who likes something distinctive for her small son will welcome this suit. The shape of the yoke and the box plaits are smart and the cuff hem at the bottom of the blouse makes pockets. The trousers are straight. Use homespun, khaki, galatea, chambray, woolen mixtures, linen, serge, gabardine or corduroy.

5 years requires 3/4 yard serge 44 inches wide, 3/8 yard flannel 27 inches wide, 3 1/2 yards braid.

This suit is for little boys 2 to 7 years.

**2029** - A handsome dressing-gown is a Christmas gift that only has to be seen to be appreciated. It is a luxurious thing for any man from six to sixty or beyond. These gowns are made of silk faille, silk repp, shauntung, satin, flannel or doublefaced material.

34-inch breast or 16 or 17 years requires 4 1/4 yards velveteen 35 or 36 inches wide, 3/4 yard satin 35 or 36 inches wide.

This dressing-gown is for boys 24 to 34 inches breast; also for men.

## New Fashions in Their Infancy

**2049** - A delightful little play and school dress eliminates the problem of petticoats by means of a particularly nice pair of bloomers. The body is cut in one with its sleeves and the skirt is straight. For the younger children you would make the dress without the skirt and straps and have a nice pair of Empire rompers. Gingham, chambray, cotton poplin, linen and serge are the best materials. A contrasting body gives a guimpe effect.

4 years requires 2 yards plain gingham 32 inches wide, 1⅝ yard checked gingham 32 inches wide. This dress is for little girls of 2 to10 years.

**2031** - The separate skirt and tub blouses are very practical for school, though if you prefer to keep your girl in an all-wool dress you can attach the skirt to a blouse of the same material. The dress slips on over the head and the sleeve is made with one seam. You can make the whole dress of gingham, chambray, cotton poplin, serge or checks, or you can use wash blouses with a serge, check or plaid skirt.

12 years requires 1¾ yard plain chambray 32 inches wide including plaitings, 2⅛ yards plaid gingham 32 inches wide. This dress is for juniors and girls of 8 to 15 years.

**2019** - A white linen vestee makes a commendable break in the front of a navy-blue cotton poplin frock. The plaits at the front and back of the straight skirt are smart, but a mother might prefer to gather the skirt all the way around. It has the regulation waistline and is set on the kimono waist to give a one-piece dress effect. Use gingham, chambray, linen, serge, checks, etc. "Odile" is a delightful embroidered rag doll from Alsace-Lorraine.

10 years requires 2¼ yards of cotton poplin 35 or 36 inches wide, ⅝ yard linen 35 or 36 inches wide. The doll is 10780. The dress is for juniors and girls of 6 to 15 years.

**2022** - A dress that will make a child want to stay in the Never-never-grow-up side of the nursery has the French short sleeve

DRESS 2031

DRESS 2049

DRESS 2022

DRESS 2019
DOLL 10780

DRESS 2042
SMOCKING
DESIGN
10744

DRESS 2017
SMOCKING
DESIGN
10744

and a ruffled neck. The Empire body is cut in one with the panels and the tucked side skirt is straight. It slips over the head and can be made of crepe de Chine, silk crepe, taffeta, cotton voile, batiste, organdy or lawn. This is an exceptionally dainty dress for parties, dancing school, etc.

6 years requires 2 yards Georgette 39 or 40 inches wide, ⅜ yard dotted net 39 or 40 inches wide for plaitings, 2 yards ribbon. This dress is for girls of 4 to 12 years.

**2017** - The English use smocking on their children's clothes and one understands why when you see it on a little dress of nainsook, lawn, cotton voile, dimity, handkerchief linen, crepe de Chine or chambray. The sleeve is made with one seam and if you use the inverted plaited fulness under the arm you get a straight lower edge. Or you can have a gored underarm seam. 3 years requires 1⅝ yard linen 35 or 36 inches wide, ⅜ yard contrasting linen 35 or 36 inches wide. Smocking design 10744 trims the dress. This dress is for little girls of 1 to 6 years.

**2042** - You couldn't find a daintier dress for a little girl than this one made with a square yoke, smocking and a charming collar. The sash arrangement is unusual, though for a simple straight dress you can omit both the sash and smocking. The fulness under the arm is laid in an inverted plait and the lower edge is straight. Use cotton voile, batiste, dimity, nainsook, crepe de Chine or Georgette crepe. The sleeve has one seam.

5 years requires 1⅞ yard crepe de Chine 39 or 40 inches wide. Smocking design 10744 trims the dress. This dress is for little girls of 2 to 10 years.

PUBLISHED ON THE
10TH OF THE MONTH.

PRICE
FOURPENCE.

M. 2241
4 TO 10 YEARS

M. 2259
2 TO 8 YEARS

62337
6 TO 12 YEARS

62336
2 TO 8 YEARS

**M. 2241** - For dressy occasions is this really smart little model, covered with straw and the brim faced with satin of a contrasting shade. Daisies and buttercrups are wreathed round the crown, and narrow velvet ribbon is tied at right side. Materials: 27-inch millinery net, 2 yard; 3-inch wide straw, 2 yards; 22-inch satin, 1 yard; two dozen each of buttercups and daisies.

**No. 62336** - The daintiest and sweetest little Frock imaginable for the lovely summer fabrics - cotton, voile, georgette, fine zephyr, or Japanese silk in white or colours - Of 40-inch material, 2¹/₂, 2³/₄, or 3 yards; insertion, 2 yards.

**M. 2259** - A picturesque and becoming poke of soft satin. Tiny roses or other small flowers outline the brim, and picot-edged ribbon bands and bows the crown. Materials: 27-inch buckram, ¹/₂ yard; 22-inch material, 1 ¹/₄ yards; 2-inch wide ribbon, 1¹/₂ yards; three dozen small flowers. Flat paper pattern, with full description, quantity of material required, etc., price 1s. each post free.

**No. 62337** - A stylish Frock for serge, tussore, gingham, sponge cloth, or poplin, with sash of Oriental ribbon, and collar and cuffs, which may be made detachable. - Of 32-inch material, for dress, 2, 2¹/₄, or 2¹/₂ yards; 40-inch trimming material, ¹/₄ yard; ribbon, 2³/₄ yards; edging, 3 yards.

62563
6 TO 14 YEARS

62564
6 TO 14 YEARS

62562
4 TO 12 YEARS

62565
12 TO 18 YEARS

**No. 62562** - Daintiness it self is this tucked frock for plain or printed voile. - Of 27-inch material, $2^1/_4$, $2^1/_2$, $2^3/_4$, or 3 yards; 40-inch trimming material, $^3/_8$ yard; edging, $3^1/_2$ yards; ribbon, 2 yards.

**No. 62563** - Just a simple but most attractive Magyar Frock, finished with needle-running in coarse silk or mercerised cotton. - Of 40-inch material, $2^1/_2$, $2^3/_4$, 3 or $3^1/_4$ yards; ribbon, 3 yards.

**No. 62564** - This Frock is cut in bolero fashion; zephyr, fine print, sponge cloth, or tussore will look well. - Of 40-inch material, $2^1/_4$, $2^1/_2$, $2^3/_4$, or 3 yards.

**No. 62565** - An attractive Frock, with new yoke and fashionable loose sleeve. - Of 36-inch material, $4^1/_4$, $4^1/_2$, or $4^3/_4$ yards.

62593

62594

62595

*These Patterns are in sizes 1 to 4 years, price 1s. each set, post free.*

**No. 62594** - A most attractive Set of Coat, Frock and Hat, which is certain to please both the maker and the wearer. The fashionable mushroom hat matches the coat, which is just the thing to be worn over a summer dress of washing silk, zephyr, voile, or cotton crepe. - Of 34-inch material, for coat and hat, 3 or 3$\frac{1}{4}$ yards; 36-inch material, for dress, 1$\frac{5}{8}$ or 1$\frac{7}{8}$ yards.

**No. 62593** - This Set of Knickers, Coat, Hat and Blouse equips a little boy for any occasion. The square-necked blouse can be of zephyr, tussore, poplin, or Viyella, and the coat and knickers of fine serge, Shantung, pique, or drill, with hat to match. - Of 40-inch material, for hat, tunic and knickers, 2$\frac{3}{4}$ to 3 yards; 31-inch material, for blouse, $\frac{7}{8}$ to 1 yard.

**No. 62595** - A dainty Magyar Frock for voile or silk, a Petticoat and very useful Pinafore of new smart shape make up this delightful Set. The pinafore looks attractive made in fine print, casement cloth, zephyr, or spotted muslin. - Of 27-inch material, for pinafore, 1$\frac{7}{8}$ or 2 yards; 27-inch material, for dress, 1$\frac{1}{2}$ or 1$\frac{3}{4}$ yards; 40-inch material, for petticoat, $\frac{1}{2}$ to $\frac{5}{8}$ yard; 3-inch lace, 1$\frac{3}{4}$ yards; edging 2$\frac{1}{4}$ yards.

*Let their clothes be comfortable and well built*

59090
6 TO 12 YEARS

60914
6 TO 14 YEARS

61152
4 TO 10 YEARS

62039 - 2 TO 8 YEARS

60951 - 2 TO 8 YEARS

61285 - 2 TO 8 YEARS

60707 - 4 TO 12 YEARS

59524
2 TO 10 YEARS

No. 60914 - Shirt and Knickers for sports wear. - Of 30-inch material, 2¼, 2½, 2¾, or 3 yards; 40-inch material, for knickers, ¾, 1, 1¼, or 1½ yards.

No. 59090 Boy's Blazer. For flannel, bound with braid or ribbon of the school colours. - Of 29-inch material, 2¾, 2⅞, or 3 yards; braid, 4¼ yards.

No. 60707 - Knickers and flannel Blzaer are easy to make. Of 29-inch material, for coat, 2, 2¼, 2½, or 2¾ yards; 29-inch material, for knickers, 1¼, 1½, 1⅝, or 1¾ yards.

No. 61285 - A smart Tunic Suit for serge or washing fabrics. - Of 42-inch material, 1¾, 2, or 2¼ yards.

No. 61152 - The slip-on Coat, with cap to match, in rainproofed twill, covert coating, or serge is always in good style. - Of 50-inch material, 1¾, 1⅞, or 2⅛ yards; 27-inch canvas, for cap, ½ yard; 27-inch lining, ⅛ yard.

No. 62039 - Flannel, serge, or drill will make this simple Suit for a small boy. - Of 42-inch material, 1¾, 1⅞, or 2 yards.

No. 60951 - Knickers buttoned over a frilled shirt make a picturesque first Suit. - Of 40-inch material, for blouse, 1⅓, 1¼, or 1⅜ yards; 40-inch material, for knickers, ⅝, ¾, or ⅞ yard.

No. 59524 - A Shirt and Combinations are very much less expensive made at home than bought ready to wear. - Of 30-inch material, 1½, 1⅝, 1¾, or 2 yards; 32-inch material, for shirt, 1¾, 1⅞, 2, or 2⅛ yards.

# The First School Clothes

Woman's Home Companion, August, 1931

DRAWING BY
*Clara Ernst*

The first lesson in school often means a big change in the child's wardrobe. It is the beginning of a new order, of woolens with a grown up air.

For the boy who goes to school in the city nothing is smarter than an English jacket suit. It consists of shorts and a collarless in tweed or flannel and a broadcloth shirt with a turn-over Eton collar. An Eton cap and a mannish tie are also part of the costume.

For the boy whose school clothes need not to be at all formal there is the double sweater outfit. In the sketch you can see only the top layer but underneath the light blue jersey cardigan is a matching pull-on sweater and that in turn goes over a white broadcloth vest- a vest with the popular Eton collar, no sleeves, and buttons to fasten it to the dark blue wool shorts.

This same sleeveless vest with its turn-over collar is also a good idea for the small girl when she wears a sweater and skirt. It fills out the plain V-neck and gives the protection of a wash material under the knitted wool.

In the illustration this six-year-old wears her vest with a dark blue pull on sweater, a red and blue plaid skirt and a red leather jacket- all very like her sister at boarding school. Her companion has a lemon-yellow two-piece jersey and a stitched hat in brown felt, turned up on the side in the new grown-up style now in Vogue.

Accessories for the child at school vary little from year to year. There are always long socks and berets; ghillie oxfords and brogues. Coats too keep to the same lines and for either boys or girls nothing it seems can ever take the place of the double-breasted topcoat in dark blue reefer cloth or smooth tan woolen.

For rainy weather, however, Miss six-year- old has an advantage over her brother. She can appear in a sleeveless cape coat of water-proofed sudanette in white, green, blue, and brown with a hat and umbrella to match-an unusually practical outfit because it can be worn over a coat of any weight.

# Vintage Photographs

The Perell Studio
SHARON, PENNSYLVANIA

I have to believe that this mother is extremely proud of her three children as they sit and browse through a book during their portrait session. The mother is holding her youngest daughter, yet all three children look to be very close in age. She is wearing a beautiful blouse. Her hair is twirled on top of her head and is fastened by combs and clips. The son is wearing a corduroy blazer with a startched white shirt and a dark colored tie. He doesn't seem to mind that he is the only boy with three lovely ladies. The younger of the two girls looks over her sister's arm to catch a glance at the book. The older sister is matching in almost the same dress as her sister. Her dimple is a sure sign that she is happy to be with her family.

Oh, my, what a fortunate little girl! It is almost hard to believe what a playroom of this type must have meant for this little girl and her friends! The doll house reminds me of the ones in the Bethnal Green Museum of Childhood in London with its marvelous size, its elaborate front entrance and its beautiful curtains at the windows. I can only imagine what kinds of dolls, furniture and other accessories are found inside the doll house. Her doll appears to be a German or French porcelain doll which she is lovingly rocking. Don't you just love the huge bow in her hair? Her pretty white dress and shoes probably have been chosen carefully for this picture which appears to be in her house. Don't you just love the little stove, cupboard with dishes, and dresser found underneath the window sill? Even the printed curtains seems to spell out "precious little girl's room" in my mind. I love her white stockings and shoes with bows on the toes. One can almost wonder what the titles of the books on the table beside her are. There are two stuffed animals on this table also which I think are teddy bears.

Looking at this little girl's face, I can sense that she is being very quiet so her baby can go to sleep. Having porcelain dolls dressed in these white clothes was so common during this late Victorian-early Edwardian period that it is no wonder that her dress is very similar to her "mama's." Probably the doll's shoes were boots with little buttons on the side. The doll's hair seems to be dark with a braid of some sort wrapped around her head; her mouth is open with her teeth showing. This is one of the most precious pictures that I have ever purchased. It was purchased in Dallas.

I love this picture and I am amazed how it looks like any picture of little girls today. Her haircut is the a type of the popular "bob" style, almost the same as haircuts today for little girls. Her mother has taught her good manners and she has no problems sitting straight up and looking directly into the camera. Her beautiful dress is ordained with incredible sewing details and ribbon. Her matching white satin bow in her hair is the perfect addition to create a beautiful portrait of a beautiful little girl.

*Studios*
PHILADELPHIA, PA
WASHINGTON, D.C.
ATLANTIC CITY, NJ

These three precious sisters might be the best of friends! Their demeanor toward each other gives me the feeling they are loving and sweet children. No protesting, no tears, or arguing lead's me to believe these girls are nothing more than a joy to be around. They are all wearing matching bonnets that seem to be made of special Swiss eyelet. They also are wearing white dresses, adorned with lace, eyelet and ribbon. This picture shows how loving and kind sisters can be with each other even at this age. They are leaning against a chair arm on the left hand side and look angelic in their all-white outfits.

It seems interesting how a photographer would juxtapose such an adorable clean cut little boy in such a desolate background! Notice the attention to detail on this small child's beautiful sailor suit. It wasn't uncommon for boys to wear a skirt and a lace collar. The outfit looks to be navy blue or black and the three stripes of ribbon appear to be gold due to the way they look in the photograph. Notice the tiny buttons down the front of the top and the boy's dark tights and shiny black lace-up boots. Although the little boy doesn't seem to be overzealous about having his picture made, I would guess that he knows he is looking great for his photo shoot!

Doris May Safford - 1 year, 2 months, 10 days

BOSTON

Can't you just see this "engineering-mind mathmatical" mother writing on the back of her beloved daughter's picture, "age 1 year, 2 months, 10 days." Upon close examination of this photo, I belive this dress is an "antique dress" from about circa 1880. The square, low neck is not typical for 1908 when the picture is dated from Purdy of Boston. I also believe the elbow length puffed sleeves have been added to the original scooped neck dress since short sleeves traditionally went with this type of baby dress. These type dresses, if indeed this is the case, were called "conversion dresses" and were commonly found with christening dresses. There seems to be a beauty pin on the sleeve which I have never seen before. Look at the sweet locket around her neck and the big, marvelous bow in her gorgeous curly hair. I also love her long white socks with the ankle shoes and the little bows. What fun this mother must have had dressing her baby for this photograph!

M. Pomeranetz

NEW YORK

This adorable little boy doesn't look thrilled to be having his picture made with his tricycle, but he still looks like a million dollars in his suit. His blouse has a white collar which is trimmed in an eyelet type edging. The jacket and pants look like they were made out of linen. The jacket sleeves have cuffs made of the same material and edging as the blouse. A large satin bow closes the front of the jacket. Notice the three gold buttons at the bottom of each pants leg. He also has on black tights and black leather button-up boots. His hair is long for a boy and his bangs are cut in an interesting V-shape. His soft curls lay gently on his shoulders and his innocence is quite apparent.

These three children are probably two brothers and a sister. The boy on the right and the girl seem to be very similar in age and could very well be twins. The background is a painting of a building on the water. The background seems to be very majestic when compared to the foreground of straw, a burlap sack, and a rock. The older sister's outfit is a sailor suit with white stripes and some type of horizontal striped shirt and dark tights underneath. She also has on button-up black boots. The two boys are matching in their adorable striped shirts and black pants. The shirts button up the front and have a "sailor-type" collar. The collars are piped in the same striped material the bodice of the shirt is made from. The point of the collar is tied in a bow with two medallions that hang down. One brother has on black leather zip-up boots while the younger brother is wearing his dress-up shoes with bows on top.

Ernest Spencer Roche - March 21, 1890
Austin Summerfield Roche - July 8, 1895

BROOKLYN, NEW YORK

Earnest and Austin are wearing beautiful smiles for the photographer. Smiling children are very unusual in photographs made around the turn of the last century. I love their big eyes and don't they look just alike? The little bow ties are so adorable on Earnest's "tuxedo shirt" and on Austin's round portrait collar shirt. I like Austin's striped ribbon tie with this plaid suit and Swiss embroidered shirt and collar. It appears that his collar is detachable just by looking at the neckline of his shirt. Notice the white cuffs on Austin's suit with the little Swiss ruffle. It appears that the trim on Earnest's suit jacket is narrow pintucks and that he has wider tucks on his dark shirt. I love the covered buttons running down the front of his shirt. The collar of Earnest's suit is darker than his suit and my best guess would be that the collar makes a deep sailor dip in the back. What an adorable picture!

## Louis L. Driggs, Jr.

### HARTFORD, CONNECTICUT

There isn't a date on the back of this photograph but I chose to put it right after Ernest and Austin because the large sailor collar appears to be very simiar to the one in the previous picture. It appears that braid is stitched on this large sailor collar top with the middly bottom. The pants are straight legged and come to the knee. This young man wears dark stockings and I would guess the whole outfit is navy blue including the socks and the wonderful large sailor tie. The shirt has a high neckline and there is a white handkerchief in the pocket. His shiny shoes complete the outfit.

Henry

This picture makes me laugh when I think about how this child must have been acting. It is apparent by Henry's hair that he must have been a handful. It is obvious that getting his picture made was not something he really wanted to do. Notice his mother crouched down behind him and her hand on his left arm! He obviously was not about to sit still! Poor Henry didn't want his picture made! Although his hair is disheveled and his demeanor is frazzled, he still looks as cute as can be in his dress. The ruffled collar and lace petticoat make this outfit complete. I would guess he didn't like his shoes, so his mother didn't make him put them on. He is sitting on a beautifully embroidered cloth and there is an ornate lamp and table in the background. I hope for his sake that he behaved the rest of the photo shoot!

Gubelman Studio
JERSEY CITY

Don't you adore this photgraph of two brothers and a sister or three brothers? A baby boy could have worn a white dress like this one so why do I think this is a sister? There appears to be a little bow on the shoe and the dress is closed with beauty pins. It just seems like the baby is a girl to me. I think this picture was made around 1900 since I have found a boy pattern in the October, 1900 *McCall's Magazine* which is very similar to the sailor suit the little boy is wearing. This type suit is called a *Boys' Russian Blouse Suit* and the description of a similar suit in the magazine has such an interesting description. "Russian blouse suits are at present the very height of fashion for little boys' wear. Our model is made of dark blue serge with collar facing and shielf-piece of bright red, but cheviot, broadcloth, flannel, galatea, etc., can be substituted for its development if desired. The front of the blouse crosses diagonally from left to right and fastens invisibly under a fly. The big sailor collar is cut quare in the back and has ointed ends in the front. The knickerbockers, which complete this smart suit, are cut in the most up-to-date tailor style."

The older boy's suit is double breasted and he wears a traditional shirt and tie. His pants are straight and come right below the knee and are embellished with three buttons. Don't you just love his high top shoes and dark stockings?

## Natalie Eddy Driggs - 3 years old

WASHINGTON, D.C.

(Above, left) - In this first picture of the set, little Natalie appears to be on the roof of a building leaned against a stone retaining wall. Her sweet haircut has left her bangs blunt cut, while her adorable curls are peeping out from the lace ruffle that lines the inside of her hat.  The large satin ribbon is tied under her neck as a means to keep her hat in place. Her overcoat is a dark color and has been embellished by lace cutwork on the sleeves and collar. Notice the tiny ring and the cute dimples on her left hand. I think the expression on her face is priceless. She looks as though she really doesn't want to have her picture taken, yet she has no problem striking a pose!

## Natalie Eddy Driggs - 4 years old

WASHINGTON, D.C.

(Above, right) - In this next picture, Natalie is four; a year older but none the less more excited about her portrait session! She is wearing almost the same style of coat that she had on the year before. Her mother must have enjoyed making this pattern immensely. Natalie doesn't seem to have changed much and she still wears the same ring as the year before. She is standing on a mat in front of a stone wall and still bears the same expression.  She still has a head full of curls and sweet gentle eyes.

## *Houston Hale Driggs - 1895*

### WASHINGTON, D.C.

Houston, yes this is a boy, could easily be mistaken for a little girl! Since he is Natalie's brother, it is no surprise he also has lots of curls. This picture was taken in 1895 which is probably after both of his sister's portraits were taken because of the change in the use of the type of film and the print on the portraits themselves. His seems to be more recent than Natalie's, but not by more than two or three years. His hair is much longer than Natalie's. His "dress" is made of horizontal pin-stripe fabric and has three buttons at the top. The collar is split in front and is composed of a double layer of lace ruffles. His expression well exceeds his years, for he almost gives the facial expressions of a grown man. His Aunt Roberta must have been so proud to see what a fine young man her nephew was becoming!

This family portrait is interesting because it was probably taken during WW I. The father's uniform and type of hat indicate this time period. I think the children are six and three and they seem to feel comfortable about having their pictures made. The little girl is wearing a light colored dress which has a drop waist with large ribbon rosettes on the waistline. I think her hair bow is amusing since it is almost as big as her entire head! She is also wearing white tights and black boots. The little boy on the other hand, has on a sailor suit which has a smaller collar than suits seen in earlier years. He too is wearing white tights, but he has on ankle strap black dress shoes. The mother is wearing a two-piece dark suit that has a jacket and an ankle length skirt. She is dressed very plainly and conservatively and has on a minimal amount of jewelry.

This little boy is enjoying himself even though I think his mother was the one who wanted this portrait done. He is sporting a sailor suit that has a square V-neck collar and laces up the front. The toy rubber ball that he is holding has the alphabet and numbers on it. He is sitting on a table and his pose is very playful and youthful. His short haircut resembles the typical style for boys of this era. His black stockings and black leather lace-up boots make the perfect addition to his outfit. By his expression, it is clear that he is a happy little boy with a light heart and insatiable appetite for fun! When Camp and John were little boys, the photographer had a ball in the studio for them to hold. Joe, my husband, was also photographed with a ball in his hands when he was little. I think a ball makes a cute prop.

J. D. Toloff
EVANSTON, ILLINOIS

Jannie Nocholl
MEXIA, TEXAS

This little girl is so happy to be having her picture made and her beautiful dress is complimented by her beautiful expression. Her dark brown eyes and dark brown curls make you want to just hug her! She is wearing a white dress that has a large round collar with eyelet around the edges. The skirt is pleated and falls just below her knees. It is typical of the period how she is wearing black tights and black shoes with such a dainty white dress. I am sure her Uncle Charlie was thrilled to receive such a wonderful photograph of his exquisite niece. The words on the back of the photo read, "To Uncle Charlie."

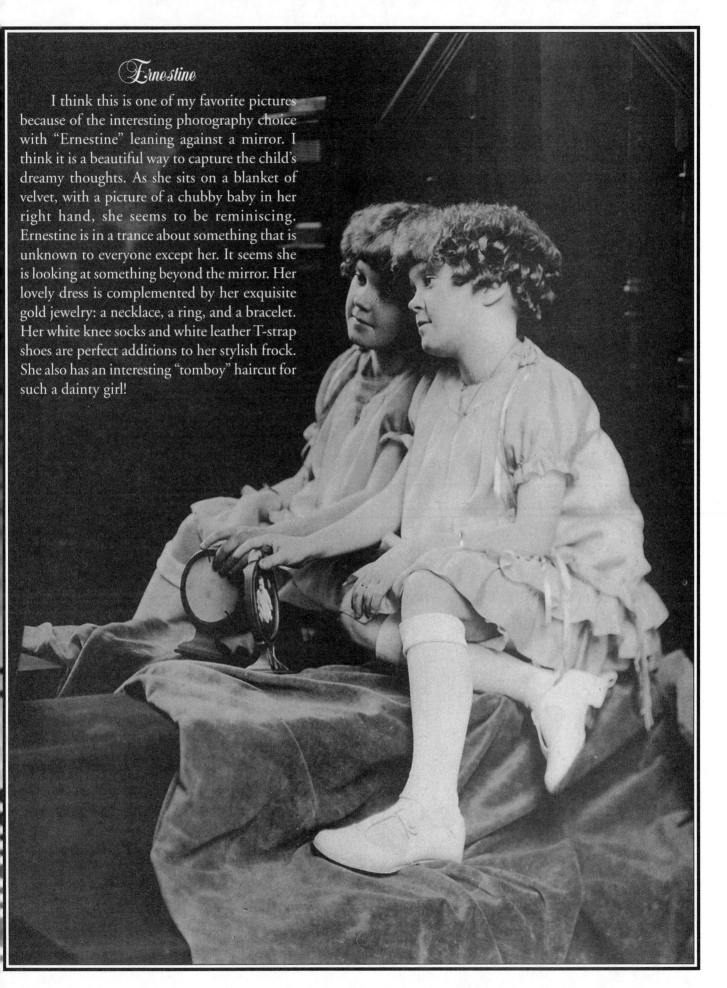

## Ernestine

I think this is one of my favorite pictures because of the interesting photography choice with "Ernestine" leaning against a mirror. I think it is a beautiful way to capture the child's dreamy thoughts. As she sits on a blanket of velvet, with a picture of a chubby baby in her right hand, she seems to be reminiscing. Ernestine is in a trance about something that is unknown to everyone except her. It seems she is looking at something beyond the mirror. Her lovely dress is complemented by her exquisite gold jewelry: a necklace, a ring, and a bracelet. Her white knee socks and white leather T-strap shoes are perfect additions to her stylish frock. She also has an interesting "tomboy" haircut for such a dainty girl!

Ettlin's Portraits
NEW YORK

What a wonderful fake tree stump and rustic fence in the background! The little boy is wearing one of those "Russian Blouse Suits" so once again I think this portrait was taken around 1900. The little girl is beautifully dressed in her white dress with necklaces and she carries a little purse. There is an armband of some sort on her long sleeve and just look at that wonderful bow in her hair. Her little short haircut is very stylish today among little girls. Isn't it amazing how styles always come round again? I love their boots which button on the sides. The little black stockings and shorter dress are very interesting. The baby has on a traditional 1900 white baby dress with the neckline which really comes to the neckline. The little boy seems to be much happier about having his picture made than his big sister. Maybe she is worried that the baby will fall off of the stump!

I think this picture is older than most of the other pictures. This little boy is wearing a gingham dress with a large collar. It also has a dark belt and a large bow at the neck. His ringlets must have taken forever to fix and finally get to stay in place all over his head. He has a very serious look on his face and he seems very intense for such a small child. He is holding a gold pocket watch in his right hand that is hanging from his neck by a matching gold chain. My guess would be that this watch belonged to his father or grandfather and it was to belong, now, to this little boy. It is a precious idea to photograph a child with a family heirloom which has been given to the child.

It is very unusual to find a picture of a child which also includes a doll or a toy. I love this tiny picture which I purchased in Massachusettes. I love her short hair with her sausage curls and large bow. My best guess for the year of this photo would be circa 1900 based on her French or German doll and her clothing. Don't you just love her little locket around her neck? Please do photograph your little ones with a favorite toy and precious jewelry. One of my favorite pictures of Joanna when she was little had her holding her Madame Alexander's "Mary" in her arms. She slept with this doll until she went to college and I do so treasure the picture of her and the doll when she was a little girl.

This trio is enough to make anyone smile. These three are obviously related because of the apparent resemblance to each other. Both of the boys are wearing sailor suits made from linen and the large collars are interesting. Each of the boys also has on black tights and black boots. All three have on the same pin. The boy's pin is on the right side of the collars and their sister's is on the left. The younger of the two boys, on the left, holds his hat timidly in his hands, while the eldest brother has obviously done away with his since it can be seen thrown behind him in the background. The little girl, who is the youngest, sits proudly in between

her two brothers on a chair. She is wearing a white dress with a V-neck collar and the collar seems to be trimmed in eylet. There are roses strewn around her as she sits innocently, and I can only imagine how cute she would be if she would only put on the hat in her left hand. These are children from a wealthy family because all three of them have silver rings on their middle fingers. I would guess these children were having their portrait made for some type of occasion during the spring because of the fabrics that they are wearing and the freshness of the roses.

This picture is truly worth a thousand words. It could be anything - a birthday party, a family get-together, an Easter celebration, or a number of other occasions. The gentleman on the left is obviously enjoying being surrounded by six youths. They could very well be his grandchildren or his great-grandchildren. It is a spring afternoon because of the sunlight and the light clothing the children are wearing. The children are also enjoying themselves by the smiles that are present on their faces. The baby in the highchair looks so sweet in her ruffled dress and tiny tie-up boots. Notice the sailor suit the little boy in the front is wearing. It looks to be made of linen and it is clear that hi

mother had a tough time keeping him clean because of the napkin tied around his neck. The little girl to the righ didn't let taking pictures stop her from snacking on what ever the children are eating. Her dainty dress and match ing hair bow seem perfect for the occasion and the weather My favorite child in the picture is the little girl that i seen in between the baby and the little boy. Her expres sion seems to show how off guard she has been caught i this moment of photography. All together, you can jus hear the laughter and the conversations that are going o at this table and the excitement that is radiating from this unforgettable meal.

Wolfe
LEBANON, PENNSYLVANIA

These three have to be brothers from looking at th resemblance not only of physical characteristics, but also fa cial expressions. They look as if they are pained to have thi picture made. The two younger boys have on matching outfits of white sailor type tops and shorts. The tops have sailor collar and tie in the front. You can see these outfits ar two separate pieces, while the middle child is wearing a one piece sailor suit. His top looks the same as the other tw boys, but his pants are buttoned to his shirt at his waist. H looks the most disgruntled to be having his picture mad and if I had to guess it is probably because he has had to d it more times than his younger brothers!

If this picture can't bring a smile to your face, I don't know what will! Such a happy child! I can just imagine this little tyke laughing from the time he gets up in the morning until he goes to bed at night. This adorable little boy doesn't mind that his mother has him in a beautiful lace dress that looks as though it should belong to his sister by today's standards. He seems to be enjoying himself immensely and he likes having his picture taken. I think it is sweet how his boots look too tight on his chubby calves!

Dana Studios
NEW YORK, BROOKLYN

The expression on this little boy's face is astounding! He looks as if he is just about to smile at something, but the photographer was seconds too early! He is standing on a black wooden chair in front of a gray faded backdrop and he obviously doesn't mind this set-up! He is wearing a tan and white checked top (indicated on the back of the picture) that crosses over and is secured by three toggle buttons. The top is also kept on by a small belt that is fastened by a white gold buckle. He is also wearing bloomers made from the same material with black tights. His shoes are black lace-up boots with thick white shoe laces. Notice his cute blunt bowl hairstyle and the lightness of his hair probably means he had VERY light blonde hair as a little boy.

Johanne Hesbeek
ESTERSVEU HOLTE

Finding pictures of children holding toys is very unusual. These two adorable boys have the cutest staring expressions. Look at the precious bowed legs on the little brother. Don't you just love the soup bowl haircut on the older brother and his white big tied bow tie? Little brother seems to have gotten the curls in the family but look at that stark white hair. At first I thought this toy was a doll but realizing that the suit was a boy suit, I didn't think they would have photographed a little boy carrying a doll. The toy is a mouse or animal of some sort with clothing on. Very unusual toy. Did you notice the knee length pants on the older boy closed with three buttons? Although the writing on the back is in another language one child seems to be 4 years old and another 14 months old.

Ernest

BROOKLYN, NEW YORK

This little boy looks so happy to be having his picture made! He is smiling and seems to have no trouble looking directly into the camera and saying "CHEESE!" He is proud to be donning his sailor suit with the white handkerchief in his breast pocket. He makes striking a pose look easy with his hat in his right hand and his other hand in his pocket. His black stockings and black button-up boots look broken in. His hair is neatly combed and cut and he seems to know that he is looking great! On second thought, I bet he is wearing his older brother's "hand me down" shoes. They look a little too big.

Bridgeport, Alabama is a tiny town today. I cannot imagine how small it must have been around the turn of the century when this professional photograph was taken. I love this outside picture taken with the little girl in front of a crudly made wicker chair and the rural fence. Notice the leaves on the ground and the dirt yard which was very typical of southern homes of this period. Such a cute little hairdo with the crooked part in the middle. This little miss looks a little leary of the photographer and does not seem too happy about having her picture made at all. Her little black shoes appear to be tied with white shoe laces and she appears to have on black stockings. My mother tells about wearing black stockings and black shoes when she was a little girl.

Rapier

BRIDGEPORT, ALABAMA

This little girl is stylish in her lace dress with a satin sash. As she sits on a small table, the flower she is holding adds to the loveliness of the overall femininity of this little girl. Her mother put her hair in rollers for the occasion and gave her a white satin ribbon to tie in her hair. Notice the delicate lace work on every inch of this dress. The dress was probably white lace and the sash more than likely a pastel color by the way it appears in this photograph. She also has on white tights and socks that look as if they were crocheted. Her shoes tie with large white bows. She seems to be very confident in her ability to look ravishing!

*Eberhardt Rommel*
WILLIAMSBRIDGE, NEW YORK

This priceless picture of a father and his child is the epitome of a heartfelt bond between fathers and children. This little child is dressed in a beautiful white gown that has vertical rows of lace at the top and then is finished with alternating tucks and strips of lace at the bottom. Notice her tiny cross around her neck. This could have very easily been a christening dress. The child's father looks at his child with adoring affection. This type of picture of father and child is rare for the time in which it was taken. Please have some of your children and grandchildren photographed with Dad in the picture. The first formal pictures of Cecil Elizabeth were made with Cecil, Joanna and Chase.

# Looking Back:
## Infant's Clothing in the 19th Century

*by Jo Paoletti*

Though the styling of infants' clothing changed very little throughout the nineteenth century, its' quantities changed considerably. Mass-production of textiles made it possible for even the tiniest Americans to have larger wardrobes than their eighteenth century counterparts. Otherwise, the traditional pattern of wearing white dresses until the age of one or two persisted. Women's magazines and household manuals did provide more information than had been available earlier, a boon to those who had moved far from their own mothers before becoming mothers themselves. For the most part, this information was extremely consistent from one generation to the next, until the very end of the century.

Suggested layettes appearing in *Godey's* in 1852 and in an 1886 book entitled *Our Baby* are remarkably similar. Flannel abdominal binders were listed by both, as were undershirts, dresses, underskirts, slips and, of course, diapers. Those formed the basic wardrobe for most babies born during this century. In the winter time the infant wore all of them at once, layered for warmth. First came the binder, a long strip of soft wool flannel wrapped around the baby's abdomen. These were deemed necessary to protect the navel until it healed and also to prevent umbilical ruptures throughout the first year. Mothers were constantly advised not to wrap these too tightly, as they would then do more harm than good. Binders could be pinned shut or could have long strings attached, which were then tied around the child. Then came the diaper, usually of linen, though cotton was increasingly used, and some mothers used cotton flannel diapers inside linen ones for extra absorbency. Until the invention of the safety pin in the late 19th century straight pins were used to close both diapers and binders.

Over the binder and the diaper went a shirt, either knitted or cut from silk and wool flannel. The shirt was usually long-sleeved and often had tabs, buttons or garters at the hem for attaching to the baby's stockings. Next the waist-blanket went on. Also called a pinning blanket or barrow coat, this was a flannel petticoat with a three-or four-inch waistband, which was pinned, tied or buttoned around the baby's midsection. Caller, in 1886, suggested that her readers not bother making any, as they would be provided by "elderly female friends," who still believed they were a necessity. By then they were being discarded in favor of "skirts on a waist," sleeveless cotton bodices with wool or cotton flannel skirts sewn, buttoned or pinned onto the hem. These flannel skirts were used earlier in the century as a layer over the pinning blanket.

Even after all this turning, rolling, pinning and tying, the baby was only half-dressed. The next layer was a long-sleeved cotton "slip," so called because it was slipped on over the head and fastened in the back, usually with ties, buttons or, in the latter half of the century, snaps. Stockings were drawn on and attached to the undershirt, followed by soft cloth or leather shoes. Finally came the dress: long-sleeved, white cotton, often styled with a yoke, and the most elaborate piece of the ensemble. If the baby were to go out, there were bonnets, cloaks and shawls to add as well. In the summertime, lighter fabrics were used and some layers were omitted. A slip worn over the shirt, band and diaper was considered sufficient by many authors, and even the undershirt was optional in extremely hot weather.

Most authors recommended that the layette include four to six of each garment, plus three or four dozen diapers. Baby laundry was supposed to be done more frequently than the rest of the family wash, though the constant reminders to wash wet diapers before reusing them indicate that some mothers looked for short-cuts. Before the introduction of waterproof pants around the turn of the century, wet clothing was a constant problem, aggravated by the many layers of clothing being worn. Mothers were sometimes advised to leave baby clothes open from hem to above the waist or to pull up the layers underneath the baby so only the diaper would have to be changed.

Throughout the century, an infant's first clothes were quite long, to protect the baby's feet and legs from cold drafts. Many families today may possess a long white dress that has come down through the family as a christening dress, but which originally was worn for everyday. *Godey's* suggested that baby's dresses be one yard long for daily wear, and a yard and a half or two yards long for visiting and christening. If a mother did provide a long, elaborate dress for her child, chances are that it was worn for a variety of dressy occasions. The tradition of having a special outfit worn only for christening is a recent one, like its counterpart, the white wedding dress, both of which became more common among middle-class families in the twentieth century.

When the baby was beginning to creep, between four and eight months of age, a mother could expect to spend considerable time shortening all of his skirts, slips and dresses to just about floor-length. In this way, the newborn's layette could be worn throughout most of the first year, if cleverly made to allow for growth. This practice, together with the small size of most recommended layettes, may have limited the extent to which baby clothes, particularly everyday garments, were handed down to younger siblings. This is one of the reasons traditionally given for dressing both male and female infants in dresses. A more likely explanation is that gendered dress was considered inappropriate for young children, whose asexual innocence was so often cited as one of their greatest charms.

Infants' clothing was not immune to fashion changes, and trends in the styling of women's dresses were reflected in those for babies. In the 1820s, when women's sleeves were still short and puffed, baby dresses sported the same style. As women's clothing became more voluminous, so did baby dresses, though not to the extent that would have required numerous petticoats or a cage crinoline. The trend toward more concealing dress was felt in both women's and infants' clothing, resulting in longer sleeves and higher necklines after 1830. Trim for baby clothes was lighter and smaller in scale, though reflecting current tastes in pattern, such as the interest in Greek key borders in the 1860s. Women who adopted Jaeger's system of woolen underwear for themselves in the 1870s could very well have used all-wool underwear (including diapers) for their babies as well.

Other trends seen in nineteenth-century baby clothes are uniquely theirs. In the 1850s small, close-fitting caps, often sewn-on, fell out of favor, replaced by larger bonnets, which framed the face. A variety of materials were used, depending on the season. Calico, muslin and straw were popular in the summer or in warm climates, while quilted silk or satin-lined velvet were preferred for winter. Also in mid-century, the bracelets once used to control excess sleeve fabric were replaced by ribbons through which the sleeves could be looped and tied. The introduction of pastel trimming for baby clothes dates to the 1860s, when pink or blue sashes were added to the traditional white dress. These colors were rarely used to signify gender, as they reportedly were in France at the time. More often, they were used as "nursery colors," appearing in many of the clothes and furnishings found in the baby's room.

The biggest change in babies' lives during this period was that they became more involved in their parents' social activities. In the first half of the century, the youngest babies in middle and upper-class homes rarely left the nursery, and babies under one year rarely left the house. A writer in *Godey's* describes a dress for a baby several months old, "old enough to be called for to show to company." The introduction, in 1848, of the first baby carriage by a New York inventor, eventually made babies' lives more public by making them more portable. Infants' fashions found in magazines from the second half of the century are more elaborate and include many styles for "visiting" or "walking," once occupations of the fashionable lady, which now included her children as well.

# Looking Back:
# 19th Century Clothing for Little Children

*by Jo Paoletti*

In the eighteenth century, styles distinctly for children had been introduced, bridging the years between infancy and adulthood. In the nineteenth century, children's fashion were further subdivided into two groups: styles for school-age children and a new category for younger children. These new styles appeared gradually over the first half of the century, and were commonplace by the 1850s. In the second half of the century, women's magazines featured fashions for this age group much more often than styles for infants or for older children. This was largely because infants' costume changed so slowly and older children's clothing was usually a shorter, simpler version of adult dress. In contrast, fashions for small children, especially boys, combined trends in women's clothing with a strong element of fantasy that resulted in styles that were distinctly childlike and picturesque.

Until the very end of the nineteenth century, both boys and girls wore skirts until the age of five or six. The practical reasons given for this practice (ease of dressing and toileting, a larger supply of hand-me-downs) were probably much less important than traditional attitudes toward childhood and gender. Children were not supposed to think about gender differences, and clearly distinctive clothing would have made such differences more apparent. To nineteenth-century parents, a newborn boy was male but not masculine; at three years his gender might be revealed in fleeting moments of play. He would be more masculine at eight and even more "manly" at fourteen. In their view, it was appropriate to let a child's masculine or feminine nature emerge naturally and let the clothing reflect those changes, not foreshadow them. Accordingly, fashions for little boys and girls were very similar, with occasional subtle gender differences not found in infants' clothing.

From 1820 through the 1840s, fashions for little children were very much miniature versions of women's clothing, with the main distinctions found in the fit of the bodice, length of the skirt and choice of fabric. For women, the bodice gradually lengthened and became more tapered, extending to a deep V-shape by the late 1840s. The waistline for young children conformed to the natural waistline or fell just slightly above it, conforming to their more pear-shaped torsos. Light stays were used for little girls, to help shape their figures, and there is some evidence that boys' dresses also, featured boning or were worn with corsets. A slightly looser fit allowed for both movement and growth. In the 1820s, children's dresses became much shorter than women's, usually reaching to a point between the calf and the knee. This revealed the white cotton drawers, or pantalettes, which had been worn by children since around 1800. They became longer and more elaborate, filling the gap between hem and boot-top; some illustrations show their decorative edges extending a good six to eight inches below the skirt. Both boys and girls wore pantalettes: a short story in *Godey's* refers to a well-educated young man having started school when he was still "a little fellow in his pantalettes." These were essentially two separate legs gathered into a flat waistband but with a completely open crotch from front to back. "Closed drawers," with a completely sewn crotch seam, were not commonly used until the 1870s or 80s.

The fabrics chosen for little children's clothing were somewhat different from those used for older children and women. In the first place, many of the prints and patterns popular for women's fashions were too large to be used for children. Modish styles for women could be adapted for children by using small-scale designs if they were available; plaids, checks and tiny calico prints were often used. But very often the best choice was a solid-color fabric. Similarly, trims had to be scaled down, and *Godey's* recommended omitting the trim altogether rather than applying machine-made trimming that was too large for the child's body. In the 1840s, there was some indication that manufacturers were beginning to produce fabrics scaled specifically for children: tiny floral prints went out of style for women, but remained on the market as a perennial favorite for children's clothing.

It is very hard to distinguish between boys and girls in illustrations or portraits dating before 1850. The cut of their clothing was virtually identical. Lace, ribbon and braided trim was used for both boys and girls. Girls' dresses were made up in floral fabric more often than were boys' styles, and both *Godey's* and *Peterson's* recommended dark neutral colors (brown, black, gray) more often for boys. But outside of these few not-very-firm rules, most dresses for little children give no clue to the sex of the wearer. Accessories help a little. Girls' hair is sometimes longer, even long enough to be styled in a simple version of women's hairstyles, with long love-locks at either side of the face. But most little children in portraits or fashion plates have hair that is about chin-length and very simply parted and combed. Sandals were more often worn by girls, and boots by boys, though that is not a consistent pattern. Sometimes the artist may give additional clues to the child's identity: a drum or a toy whip for a little boy, a doll for a girl. But a modern curator in a museum, faced with an unaccessorized dress and not a scrap of information, must describe the garment just as *Godey's* would have - a child's dress.

Late in the 1840s a few styles specifically for boys made their appearance, marking the beginning of a very gradual trend toward gender-specific dress for small children. From the middle of the century to the 1890s, most boys under the age of six would continue to wear skirted styles, but there were distinctions between those styles and styles for girls. The primary influence behind this trend was Queen Victoria of England, much admired in America as a model wife and mother. In 1846, she commissioned Wintherhalter to paint a portrait of the Prince of Wales dressed in a child-sized replica of the uniform of a sailor in the Royal Navy. Engravings of the suit appeared in women's magazines within months of the portrait's unveiling, and the sailor suit became enormously popular for big and little

boys alike. Unlike Prince Edward's suit, which had long trousers, most adaptations for little boys had kilts, or pleated skirts, mingling traditional boys' costume with military dress. Similarly, descriptions of the Highland dress worn by the royal family on their visits of Balmoral Castle inspired plaid kilt suits for little boys, as well as tartan dresses for both boys and girls.

In the 1840s dresses gave way slightly in popularity to tunics and coatdresses worn over skirts, particularly for little boys. Other military styles were favored, in addition to sailor suits; the most common was the Zouave suit, which featured a short, unfitted, collarless jacket usually trimmed with braid. This same jacket was a vogue for women from the late 1840s through the early 1860s. Whether dresses or suits, fashions for little children had the same full skirts seen on women's dresses, shaped with layers of stiff petticoats or (less often) hoops.

The introduction of the sailor suit and Highland costume accompanied a trend which further divided clothing for little boys into styles for two age groups that we today call toddlers and preschoolers. Boys from one to three years wore dresses and skirts very similar to those worn by girls. From three to about six years they wore kilts or wide short trousers either gathered at the knee or left ungathered, almost like today's baggy surfing shorts. The ungathered version was referred to as Garibaldi trousers and often worn with the Garibaldi blouse, with its full sleeves and stand-up collar. The gathered style, called knickerbockers, first appeared in the 1860s, paired with a variety of jackets and tunics. These were fuller than twentieth century knickers, looking more like Dutchman's breeches, which may have inspired them. Another possible explanation is that they were derived from the trousers worn by the New York Knickerbockers, a very popular baseball team. Certainly the sports connotation didn't hurt their popularity with little boys eager to be out of skirts. As Garibaldi's and knickerbockers began to be worn more, pantalettes were left for girls and smaller boys.

While boys were adopting knickerbockers and Garibaldi pants, little girls continued to dress like their mothers. Fashionable dress for women was becoming more complex and elaborate, and styles for girls were no less intricate. *Godey's* offered this admiring description of a walking suit for a little girl of four or five: "Made of lilac satin, with narrow pinked flounces, black grenadine overskirt, trimmed and fringed with guipure and insertion. The lilac bodice is trimmed with drapery and has a cape covering the shoulders." A black lace bonnet, lilac gloves and parasol completed the outfit.

Clothing for both girls and boys became more elaborately trimmed, primarily due to the availability of inexpensive trimmings and the ease with which it could be applied with the sewing machine. Colors were deep and highly saturated, and heavy plushy fabrics such as velvet and velveteen were favored for clothing and trimmings. Texture was important, whether in the form of pique for a simple, washable dress or, as in an 1865 description in *Godey's*, as steel-button-studded leather trim on a little girl's brown merino dress.

The 1870s and 1880s marked the high point of elaborate dress for children (or the low point, according to its critics). Closely reflecting trends in women's fashions, a single outfit might be made up in two or three fabrics and trimmed in as many different trims. Every possible historical, literary and fantastic source was exploited for design inspiration, particularly for little boys, who appeared as sailors, cavaliers, highlanders and numerous other guises. Gender distinctions became more blurred in the late seventies and eighties, between a vogue for short "garcon" haircuts for girls and long, curly locks for boys. (The garcon style aside, most children had long hair, and mothers were advised not cut girls' or boys' hair before the age of six or seven, as cutting would make their hair coarser and darker.)

Multi-piece costumes were much more popular than one-piece dresses, to the point that most dresses for two - to - four-year-olds were designed to look like suits, with bodices, vests, overskirts and underskirts all sewn into one garment. Waistlines dropped to the hip or lower in the late 1870s, freeing the child's torso but sometimes hobbling the upper legs instead. Despite growing criticism from advocates of children's dress reform, the tight, low-waisted silhouette persisted for little children through the first part of the twentieth century, even though it went out of fashion for women and older children in the 1880s.

Fashionable American mothers were in no mood to reform their own dress or that of their children in the 1880s, the decade which saw fantastic dress for children reach its height with the Lord Fauntleroy craze. Frances Hodgeson Burnett, the English-born author of both the original 1885 story and the enormously

successful play, did not invent the Fauntleroy style. Illustrator Reginald Burch based little Cedric's black velvet knickers suit with the lace-trimmed Van Dyke collar on a suit worn by Burnett's youngest son, Vivian, for a photographic portrait a few years earlier. It was, in fact, a style already in its decline when the story was published in 1885, a perfect choice for little Cedric Errol, living with his widowed mother in a poor section of New York City. Like Scarlett O'Hara's finery, Cedric's was a homemade attempt at gentility, cut from one of his mother's old black velvet dresses.

*Little Lord Fauntleroy* was one of the most successful books of the century, and the play - claimed to be the first produced for a children's audience - was a hit on both sides of the Atlantic. In 1889, there were more than a dozen companies touring America, bringing the tale of Cedric, his bitter grandfather and "Dearest" mother to practically every town that had a hall to play in. It was as much a play for mothers as for children, since Cedric's eventual winning of his grandfather's love and respect is owed entirely to his moral training by his mother. Cedric was a mother's ideal son - chivalrous, loving and brave. Small wonder then that Little Lord Fauntleroy's shabby cavalier suit inspired millions of imitations, none of them humble or shabby. If a boy's mother wanted him to have one, there was no escape. Fauntleroy suits were available ready-made in stores or by mail, and patterns were featured in every women's magazine and pattern book.

The Fauntleroy craze faded in the 1890s, but boys' memories of it did not. Thanks to photography, their ignominy was made permanently visible on the family mantle or parlor table, continuing to inflict shame long after the suit was outgrown and the love-locks were cut. After Frances Hodgson Burnett's death in 1924, the City of New York proposed a statue honoring her, to be placed in Central Park. The response from men in their forties and fifties was a barrage of letters pouring out their pent-up resentment of Burnett, her little hero and, most of all, those awful velvet suits.

# Looking Back:
## Baby Clothing 1890 - 1919

*by Jo Paoletti*

We might think of the turn of the last century as charming and old-fashioned, but for someone living at that time, nothing could be further from the truth! Between 1890 and 1919, clothing for infants changed noticeably, as child-rearing became more modern. Babies were more lightly dressed and were able to move their arms and legs more freely. Their previously all-white wardrobes became more colorful. Even more dramatic changes in infants' clothing were to come much later, with the introduction of stretch fabrics in the 1950s, but the movement toward more practical baby clothes had its roots in the turn of the century.

Many of these changes were prompted by studies conducted by doctors, giving them a basis in science. This helped young women convince their own mothers that the new ways were preferable to the old ones. The traditional practice of dressing the baby in many layers of clothing, for instance, was intended to protect the child from "bad air," as well as harmful drafts. Advances in microbiology proved that germs in the air, not the air itself, were the culprits, and doctors were quick to point out that over-heated babies were more prone to rashes, nausea and fussiness, than those who were less heavily dressed. The result was fewer layers of clothes, more open windows and walks in the fresh air, and the brief addition of fine-woven veils to the traditional layette. Many people believed that these veils would screen out germs and bacteria, even though doctors pointed out that even a very fine mesh would admit microbes through easily.

Dr. John Rice Griffith's book, *The Care of the Baby*, gives a fairly thorough account of existing practices in the mid-1890s, as well as his own advice. The abdominal binder (usually a long woven or knitted rectangle) was used too tightly and for too long a time, he wrote. Skirts were too long and dressing the baby was too time-consuming and tiresome for the baby. Some of his advice seems appallingly obvious. Apparently, many mothers were reusing wet diapers without washing them; Griffith pointed out that air-drying was not sufficient to kill bacteria that caused odors and rashes.

Dr. Griffith described three styles of baby clothes in use at the time. The "oldest" style consisted of a diaper, shirt, barrow coat, petticoat, slip and dress - too many items, in his opinion. The most popular style omitted the barrow coat (which resembled a petticoat with a wide waistband) and substituted a princess-style petticoat (one with no waistline seam) for the yoke-style petticoat. This was a slight improvement, but still was cumbersome to put on and to wear. Griffith pointed out that the outfit as described involved four layers of sleeves (shirt, petticoat, slip and dress), which restricted the baby's arms considerably and still made dressing a difficult task.

The "newest" style of dress for babies, and the one Griffith recommended, omitted both the shirt and the barrow coat, and reduced the remaining layers to three princess-style garments. The innermost layer was a sleeved flannel petticoat, then a sleeveless one, topped with a single cotton long-sleeved dress. Together, these three garments comprised a "Gertrude suit," with each layer opening with a row of buttons that went from neck to hem. The three pieces could be nestled into each other and the whole suit put on at once. Concern about ease of dressing was based not only on the amount of time and effort it involved, but also on the new belief, promoted that many doctors, that babies could be "spoiled" by too much handling.

The usual length for the dress was thirty inches, which Griffith would have liked to have seen reduced to twenty-five. (Remembering that the average newborn is about twenty inches long, even the shortest dress would fall a good twelve inches below the child's feet.) In 1910, the longest dresses in the Sears, Roebuck catalog were twenty-seven inches, and a new "demi-long" style (twenty-four inches) was introduced in 1917. This shortening of babies' dresses made stockings and booties more popular as a means of keeping the child's feet warm.

Griffith also recommended that mothers make "creeping aprons" (loose-fitting coveralls with elasticized leg holes) for children just learning to crawl. Though similar in appearance to today's creepers, creeping aprons were worn over the baby's dress, not instead of it. According to Griffith, they could not yet be purchased ready-to-wear, though patterns were available. By 1913, Sears was offering snap-crotch creepers sized as small as six months which were intended to be worn simply over a child's underwear.

The introduction of creepers brought about one important change: the introduction of a bifurcated style of clothing for babies (that is, a style with legs or leg openings). They originally were designed for boys and girls, with no gender differences. Distinctive masculine and feminine creeper styles did not appear in the mail-order catalogs until the 1920s. In the meantime, creepers remained gender neutral, just as baby dresses traditionally had been.

Griffith and other writers on child care were less enthusiastic about one modern invention: waterproof diaper covers and pants. Usually made of rubberized silk, these were claimed to cause chafing and diaper rash. The suggested alternatives included double-diapering and disposable, "paper" diaper linens, available through mail-order catalogues early in 1911. But the problem of keeping a child's bedding and clothes dry (as well as protecting Mother's and Father's laps) was best solved with waterproof pants, the experts' objections notwithstanding. Toilet-training was the ultimate solution, of course, and the child care books abounded with advice as to how and when to train a baby. Modern parents find these descriptions puzzling, since they often recommend starting bowel training very early in the first year (even "as soon as the umbilical has healed," or about three or four weeks old). Today's wisdom is that most children achieve control between two and three years, and few parents even think of introducing the potty before their child is eighteen months old. The usual explanation is that our ancestors' apparent success in toilet training was a combination of the parents being trained to anticipate their children's needs and the practice of strapping babies onto potties for fifteen minutes or half an hour a day until they complied. Certainly this was partially true, but the role of waterproof pants should also be taken into account. These permitted older babies to wear thick cotton underpants so they were literally "no longer in diapers" but made accidents less of a disaster. Tellingly, mail-order houses carried waterproof pants in sizes from six months to four years. It is comforting to suspect that tales of early training may not be entirely accurate!

It is not uncommon to find long infant gowns from this period in antique stores labeled "christening gowns," but in reality few babies had a special dress made just for that occasion and worn only once. With extremely long dresses still popular for small babies right up to around 1920, the antique store gowns - no matter how elaborate - are probably not christening gowns. Nor was the handwork necessarily done by the mother or another relative. Embroidered pieces from the Philippines, including fabric with the motifs in situ as well as finished dresses, were plentiful and very reasonably priced.

# Children's Fashions
## at the Turn of the 19th Century *by Jo Paoletti*

elongated cocoon or cigar shape in the 1910s. Women wore lighter underwear and less of it. They bobbed their hair in imitation of dancing star Irene Castle. In short, women moved into the twentieth century shedding the trappings of nineteenth-century dress as they went, emerging in clothing that was lighter in weight, easier to make or purchase, and less restrictive.

Likewise, dresses for girls and little boys of the period lost most of the upholstered look found in the clothing of the late 1870s and 80s. For little girls, and for boys still in skirts, dresses in deep yokes were favored, the dress falling in gathers or pleats from the yoke to the hem. The yokes could be decorated with lace, embroidery, tucks or smocking, with the same trim sometimes being used at the wrist, as well. Dresses for very little girls and boys (one or two years) usually had no discernable waistline; slightly older boys and girls from three to thirteen or fourteen wore dresses with belts or sashes at about hip-level.

For very little children, there was hardly any distinction made between boys' and girls' dresses. Pink, blue, gray and tan were given as suitable colors for either sex, and the main differences seem to have been that extremely elaborately trimmed dresses were just for girls, though plain styles could be worn by either. Sailor styles were very popular, available with pleated skirts for little boys and girls, or with shorts or bloomers for slightly older boys. Boys and girls had similar hairstyles, a simple "Buster Brown" bob with bangs, inspired by the popular cartoon character. Rompers and overalls were introduced in the 1890s and became overwhelmingly popular for pre-schooler's playclothes. In general, little children's dresses were simple, refreshingly practical and distinctively child-like.

Since girls and little boys dressed so much like their mamas at the turn of the century, the reforms on women's fashions from 1890 to 1910 were bound to affect children as well. For women, the changes were dramatic. The fitted bodice, made of the same fabric as the skirt, was giving way in popularity to shirtwaists and other lightweight, washable tops. Beginning in the 1890s, lingerie dresses (ready-to-wear, cotton dresses trimmed with lace insertion) offered women comfortable yet fashionable clothing in hot weather. Active sports, including swimming, golf, tennis and bicycling, enjoyed growing popularity, stimulating changes in the clothing appropriate to each sport and everyday dress, as well. Sweaters, for example, once considered athletic clothing, were adapted for casual wear and became especially popular among high-school and college students.

A few hesitant steps were also made toward liberating women's bodies from the restrictions of traditional clothing. Hemlines were raised as high as the lower part of the calf during the First World War. The shape of clothing went from the smoothly corseted S-shape of the turn of the century to an

The importance of outdoor play for children had been promoted by the leaders of the playground movement since the mid 1880s. In schoolyards and city parks, jungle gyms and see-saws and swings were installed to provide boys and girls with safe places to exercise. By the 1890s clothes specifically desired for play were becoming popular. Overalls of denim or some other sturdy, washable fabric were worn by both boys and girls as early as 1900. Warm snowsuits and knitted overtrousers permitted children to romp outdoors in the winter, as well. This was an important consideration, since part of the new philosophy was that exercise should be a daily, year-round activity, except for the severest weather.

Boys' clothing evolved most rapidly during this period. Creepers and rompers were offering parents an alternative to dresses for very little boys, and boys over the age of three were sometimes put into short trousers, rather than kilts. This change began in the 1890s and was well-established by 1910. Fashion writers in the mid-nineties generally agreed that boys of two or three could wear kilts and blouses instead of one-piece dresses, but discouraged mothers from putting them in trousers until at least age five. At least, that was what they wrote in their general articles; in the advice columns, where they responded to questions from individuals, they allowed more leeway. One mother wrote and described her four-year old boy, giving his height and asking whether he should wear kilts or trousers. The answer was "Dress the boy ... in knee trousers, blouses and short jackets, as he is as large as most boys at six years and must be dressed according to his size, not his age." Given parents' usual objectivity, the suggestion that large, "manly-looking" boys could be put into trousers early undoubtedly helped fuel the trend away from dresses for pre-school boys.

By 1900, suits that combined long tunics with short, full trousers were gaining in popularity for the three-to-five-year-old boy. *Vogue* outlined the stages of boy-dressing very specifically: long dresses until six months, then short dresses until age three, then either Russian blouses with knickers or kilt suits up to the age of five or six. A Russian blouse was a style of tunic with an asymmetrical, collarless banded neck opening, similar to the Dr. Zhivago shirts of the 1960s. Some kilt suits even came with matching knickers, to be worn underneath the skirt or instead of it. Sailor suits were the best style for boys from age five to six until they reached nine or ten years, according to *Vogue's* authority.

Within the next decade, the Russian blouse and sailor suit, worn with full knickers, dominated fashion for little boys. *Harper's Bazar* noted that boys were usually put into trousers as soon as they were too old for baby frocks, at about three years. (*Ladies' Home Journal* even showed a Russian blouse suit for a two-year old boy, provided he be "a sturdy little fellow and not too babyish"). Overalls and rompers were frequently recommended for play clothes, suggesting that two-piece costumes may have been considered dressier. An article in *The Delineator* suggests that the trend toward more masculine dress for little boys was due to pressure from fathers, who objected to styles that were too feminine-looking. Given the twenty-year time span since the "Lord Fauntleroy plague," this very well could be the survivors of that fancy-dress style having their say at last.

Certainly the costume styles of the 1880s had fallen from favor. Though still seen fairly regularly in magazines and catalogs in the 1890s and early 1900s, by 1906 *Harper's Bazaar's* Cristine Terhune Herrick was declaring them gone from fashion. Fauntleroy suits and Highland kilt styles still appeared occasionally as late as the nineteen twenties, but were rarely worn, except for formal portraits and very dressy occasions. Most of the time they were mentioned in print, it was with a disdainful tone. By 1920, the modern boy had definitely made his appearance!

# "I thank you, modern mother mine..."
## Baby Clothing 1919 - 1945 *by Jo Paoletti*

Infants' clothing changed dramatically during the years between the wars (1919-1941). Dresses became shorter, rompers more popular (especially for boys) and babies were covered with fewer layers. Mary Brooks Pickens' 1921 textbook, *Maternity and Infants' Garment*, reflected older, more traditional ways of dressing babies. Her suggested layette for newborns included slips (pull-on dresses), night dresses, belly bands, undershirts, pinning blankets, underskirts, kimonos, stockings and booties. She did subscribe to contemporary principles of simplicity, however, calling fancy, handmade dresses "inadvisable and unnecessary" and heirloom christening gowns "unjustifiable" because of the care they required and the microbes they might harbor. Her dress patterns feature "short" dresses -- 27 inches from neck to hem, though yardage for 36-inch dresses were also provided. Louise Zabriskie, in a 1930 article in *Parents*, recommended that sleeveless knitted undershirts replace the long belly band wrapped around the body. If old-style bands were used, they should be worn only for the first few weeks, just until the cord was healed. The undershirt had the additional function of helping to support the diaper, to which it was pinned front and back. The shirt and diaper could be worn alone in hot weather, and extra layers could be added on cooler days: a long-sleeved shirt or dress (with or without a sleeveless slip underneath). Stockings and booties were optional, even at night, when nightgowns with drawstrings at the bottom could be worn to prevent chilling.

Kay Hardy, in *Sewing for the Baby* (1944), made no mention of the band at all. Her layette list included knitted wool soaker pants (to replace rubber pants, which were virtually impossible to get during the war), nightgowns, wrappers (robes), dresses and sleeveless slips and a christening gown (then becoming more traditional). Undershirts, bonnets, booties and bibs were also mentioned, but stockings were specifically noted as "not needed for the young baby."

Layettes such as these comprised the wardrobe for infants up to the age of about six months, or until the crawling stage was reached. At that point creepers were introduced to the baby's wardrobe, either substituted for the dress or worn over it. In the summertime, low-cut sunsuits exposed the baby's arms, shoulders, neck and chest to the sun's "beneficial" rays. Light clothing, already the norm for women's everyday dress, had become acceptable for babies. *The Ladies' Home Journal* pediatrician - columnist Josephine Baker observed in 1928 that "our own emancipation from long and heavy clothing has been passed on to our babies." Her advice has a very modern ring to it: babies should wear the same amount of clothing winter and summer, with extra wraps for going outside, if needed. Dresses should be no longer than 22 inches. Old-fashioned woolen underwear caused the baby to become overheated, which was just as bad as being too cold. A Johnson's baby powder ad in the same issue neatly summed up the new philosophy: "Bless him! Your baby isn't cluttered up with clothes, as you were! He's free to kick...and romp...and play! And every thriving little muscle says, 'I thank you, modern mother mine...'"

To dress one's child in long, heavy, elaborate dresses, or swaddle him in layers of flannel and muslin, was to ignore the findings of modern science. Doing so would endanger the child's physical and psychological development, experts warned. Parents, especially mothers, were increasingly being held accountable for their children's healthy development. They turned for advice, not to their own parents, but to pediatricians and home economists and others who could tell them the best, most modern ways to raise their children. Forget the generation gap between adolescents and their parents; the generation gap between parents and grandparents can be just as wide.

For all the improvements in infants' clothing, there were some practices that might appear strange to the modern parent. One of the reasons for reducing the number of garments a baby wore was to minimize the amount of handling the child received. Rocking, holding and other touches and caresses - beyond what was involved in feeding, dressing or bathing - was considered by many experts to be detrimental. They believed that babies could be "spoiled" by too much handling and become nervous and demanding. Too much rocking interfered with digestion and prevented babies from falling asleep, it was maintained, and mothers were advised to handle their babies as little as possible.

Another odd innovation of this period was the "slumberguard," basically a fitted sheet with a hole in the center for the baby's head. Its purpose to prevent active infants from throwing their covers off. Perhaps it was a reaction to the trend towards lighter clothing for children, designed to comfort parents who worried that their babies would become chilled at night. A similar idea was seen in the "sleeping bag," which was made like the drawstring-closure nightgown but with a hem long enough that the ties could be attached to the rails of the crib. Both of these items disappeared from the marketplace during the 1940s, as heavy, footed "blanket sleepers" became more popular.

Compared with earlier infants' clothing, baby clothes of this period generally allowed freer movement and were simpler to make and to care for. It also was more individualized, with the increasing use of colorful fabrics and of creepers in addition to dresses. There seemed to be a growing desire to dress babies in styles that were fun to look at and to wear, decorated with nursery-rhyme characters, baby animals and other juvenile motifs. Infant styles were developing a fashion of their own, though it did not emerge full-blown until after the Depression and the Second World War.

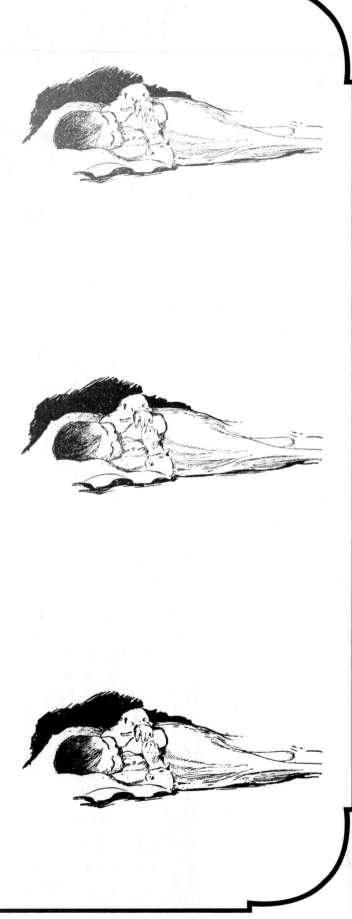

# Looking Back: Girls' Fashions, 1919 - 1945

*by Jo Paoletti*

Like their mothers, girls of this period enjoyed a new freedom in dress. Unstructured lightweight dresses, simple underwear and short, uncomplicated hair styles were popular throughout the twenties, thirties and forties. The cult of the sun triumphed over Victorian discomfort at the sight of bare legs, and short white or pastel anklets replaced long cotton stockings. Sleeveless and short-sleeved dresses gained in popularity over long sleeves, which tended to look awkward as the girl outgrew her clothes. Instead, mothers were advised to add long-sleeved sweaters, with easily-rolled cuffs, over short-sleeved winter dresses. The slender silhouette so fashionable for women in the 1920s was perfect for little girls, especially the youngest ones, whose silhouettes tend to be pear-shaped rather than hour-glass.

Waistlines returned to women's fashions in the nineteen-thirties but little girls' styles continued to fall loosely from the shoulders or a yoke on the bodice. For all the bleakness of adult clothing of the Depression years, girls' clothing contained increasing elements of fun and whimsy, thanks in large part to the styles made popular by Shirley Temple. The red-and-white polka-dot dress she wore in *Stand Up and Sing* (1934) was the first of many children's fashions she inspired. It sold millions of copies on both sides of the Atlantic, making Shirley Temple a fashion leader as well as the best-paid star in Hollywood at the tender age of six. Shirley Temple's mop of curls introduced an entire generation to the Saturday night hair-curling routine.

Great Britain had its own stars who influenced girls' clothing. Instead of actresses, however, these were royalty: Princesses Elizabeth and Margaret Rose. Their simply-tailored, appealing clothing was unglamorous enough to be copied by ordinary people, a far cry from the elaborate toilettes of many nineteenth-century royal children.

While girls wore dresses most of the time, all kinds of bifurcated garments were accepted for play clothes. From dresses with matching panties to denim overalls and dungarees, American girls were wearing pants in some form more and more often. Pajamas enjoyed increasing popularity, although most girls still wore nightgowns. In the 1940s, playsuits consisting of a one-piece romper with a separate skirt were worn by school-age girls and by women. Bifurcated did not equate "masculine," however; girls' styles were feminized in color, style or decoration. In a college textbook on children's clothing, students were given a hypothetical case in wardrobe planning for a three-year-old girl and her four-year-old brother. One of the objectives of the exercise was to teach the students that, while boys and girls might wear similar styles for play, gender-appropriate clothing could "contribute to mental development at a very early age."

Many novel styles were introduced during the nineteen-forties, even during the years of wartime restrictions. Little girls could be one-half of brother - sister, mother - daughter or big - and - little - sister pairs, in the coordinated outfits so popular throughout the decade. A related style was an ensemble consisting of a dress and a doll in an identical costume. After decades of boys-only cowboy outfits, the first cowgirl styles made their appearance. Separates (skirts, blouses and jumpers) multiplied the wardrobe options of school-age girls beyond the limits of one-a-day dresses. Sears, Roebuck and Company even offered reversible two-piece outfits that combined to provide enough different looks for nearly the whole school week .

The war in Europe influenced girls' fashions even before the United States entered the conflict late in 1941. Dirndl skirts, inspired by the folk costumes of occupied countries, were immensely popular, and tulips and "Dutch girl" caps honored the well-publicized resistance fighters in the Netherlands. As aunts and older sisters joined the war effort, military-style uniforms could transform a second-grader into a miniature WAC or WAVE. The emergence of a strong teenage market during the war years provided an important new source of fashion influence for younger girls. Where once little girls had dressed like their mothers, more and more of the trends for grade-school girls were set by high school and college students. This was especially true of girls in the "pre-teen" age group, who wore girls' sizes ten through fourteen and were anxious to distance themselves from their younger sisters.

Looking back on girls' styles of this period, some of them still look fresh and fashionable. Small wonder! Simple, playful and practical, it seems they were destined to be instant classics.

# Sewing & Shopping
## in the 19th Century  *by Jo Paoletti*

Much more is known about how adult's clothing was made during the nineteenth century than about sources of children's clothing. Since so few references to mass-produced children's clothing can be found, it seems likely that much of it was handmade, mostly at home, for most of the period. Ready-to-wear clothing for boys past the age of three or four was available as early as the 1840s, an off-shoot of the growing menswear industry. But the rest - babies, little boys and girls of all ages - were dressed by their female relatives or by professional dressmakers until well after the Civil War.

This work of making clothes was made faster by the adoption of the sewing machine for home use in the 1850s. The additional speed of the sewing machine did not lighten women's burdens, ironically, since at the same time fashion was decreeing more and fancier trimmings, all of which could be created using the new machines. Cutting garments was still difficult; old clothes could be taken apart and used as models for new dresses and suits, though this method did not solve the problem of sizing. Alternatively, a dressmaker could make a pattern that could then be used for several garments, a costlier method that ensured a better fit. The earliest instance of children's clothing patterns being sold by mail-order appears in *Godey's* in 1854, which notes that Mrs. H. G. Suplee of Chestnut Street in New York would sell patterns for children's clothes up to age eight on a subscription basis (probably to dressmakers) or singly. Ebenezer Butterick also offered a few patterns for infants' dresses in the 1860s and McCall's showed a variety of children's styles in his first catalog in the 1870s.

By the 1880s mothers were rebelling against the tyranny of the sewing machine, urged on by authors such as Stella Gilman (1884), who argued that women should "spend time with the children, not on the children." Instead, the sewing was delegated to the swelling numbers of immigrants plying the needle trades in New York's garment district. Mass-produced ready-to-wear clothing freed mothers from sewing for their children and greatly reduced the demand for seamstresses, though baby clothing continued to be predominantly hand-made until the nineteen-twenties.

Throughout the second half of the nineteenth century, women spent increasing amounts of time shopping for clothing or clothing materials. Long before the advent of ready-to-wear clothing, dry goods houses offered vast assortments of stylish fabrics and trimmings. Materials could then be made up at home or taken to dressmakers to be made into fashionable garments. In large cities, some dressmakers were able to specialize in children's styles; *Godey's* cited two such establishments, Bradbrooks in New York and Mrs. Edwards in Philadelphia, as being the leaders in children's fashions in the early eighteen fifties. In 1852, these were eclipsed by the opening of Genin's Bazaar in New York, a store — possibly the first — devoted exclusively to children's furnishings. Materials could be purchased there and taken elsewhere to be made up, or Genin's own seamstresses could produce custom-made garments in the store. Evidently some ready-made styles were also available, as were hats, shoes and other accessories. *Godey's* description of Genin's sounds like a perfect nineteenth-century consumers' palace in miniature, with its life-like wax models in display cases, and its ornate interior, complete with a cut-glass fountain stocked with goldfish dominating the center of the store. After Genin's, many children's specialty shops opened in major cities, and the department stores also featured special sections for children. The advent of mail-order companies such as Montgomery Ward and Sears, Roebuck and Company, toward the end of the century, made fashionable ready-made clothing available even to the most remote rural areas.

# Pink & Blue: The True Story
*by Jo Paoletti*

Like an actor's costume, the clothing we wear every day "proclaims the man" - and the woman. This is as true in our own culture as it is in others, and in our own times as it was long ago. The differences may vary, but there have always been distinctions between male and female dress. Children in our society begin to learn these patterns long before they start school. Even in infancy, before the child can begin to comprehend the meaning of such signals, clothing is used to communicate the baby's gender to all observers. You may think that the gender distinctions used in modern children's dress are firmly-established cultural patterns of fairly long-standing use. You may also believe that such distinctions are powerful influences on young children. In either case, you are probably mistaken!

In European cultures, the differences between men's and women's clothing have changed considerably over time. In central and southern Europe, both men and women wore skirts; in northern areas such as Scandinavia, men also wore leggings or breeches. From the 14th through the 18th centuries, men's clothing was usually more elaborate than women's; rich fabrics, furs, elaborate hats and heavy jewelry were signs of manliness and success. Only at the very end of the 18th century did the women begin to overtake men as fancy and stylish dressers, as women's clothing became more elaborate and men's fashions were toned down in color and ornament.

At the end of the nineteenth century, both men's and women's costumes underwent important changes again, reflecting adjustments in the definition of masculinity and femininity. Women's clothing became more practical and less confining, borrowing characteristics from men's costume. The tucked-in shirtwaist, which replaced the boned bodice, is one example. Another is the use of trousers or knickerbockers for sports. Men's clothing simultaneously became less varied and expressive than it had been. The business suit became a uniform for American men, and coats and jackets became boxier and less fitted to the body.

Since clothing is an important means by which gender rules are learned by young children, we might expect these changes in adult costume were also seen in children's clothing. Indeed, parallel changes did occur in girls' clothing, which became more practical and varied, just as women's fashion's had. But boys' clothing underwent even more dramatic changes than men's. Unlike men's clothing, which were conservatively masculine to begin with and proceeded to become more so, boys' fashions had been quite similar to styles worn by girls and women. For them to become more like adult male dress required shifting from one pole to the opposite. The changes which have occurred in the last century are so fundamental that only a few shadows of the old patterns of children's dress remain. One is the christening robe, the only style of "dress" still worn by modern American boys

Clothing for toddlers and young children was the first to become more gender-specific, beginning in the late 1890s. Before that, most clothing for young children was based on that of adult women and made little distinction between boys and girls. To nineteenth century parents, the happy process of their children's growing-up also entailed a lamentable loss of innocence. Infancy and toddlerhood were years of "bliss... before consciousness begins...", the prelude to "that blank wall of foregone conclusions which shuts out fairyland." To the Victorian parent, sexual awareness would come soon enough; there was no need to hurry it by dressing babies like little men and women.

Accordingly, children's clothing throughout most of the nineteenth century worked to obscure gender differences for as long as possible, as well as postpone adult clothing until the early teens. Toddler boys and girls wore short loose-fitting dresses until they were two or three years of age. From then until the age of five or six, children wore dresses or suits with short skirts. Both boys' and girls' skirted styles bore a strong resemblance to women's dress of the period, usually reflecting current fashions in sleeve, neckline and so on. However, that is not to say that the boys were dressed exactly like girls. Descriptions of toddlers' clothing in fashion magazines indicate that there could be subtle differences between male and female styles:

"For boys of a year or a year and a half the blouse dress is worn, for morning wear confined at the waist with a belt. But little difference is noticed in the general style of their dress except the hat and less elaborate trimming on their dresses."

"...little boys' dresses button up the front, those of their sisters fasten in back..."

Generally speaking, however, an outfit that made a baby look like a little man would have been considered in poor taste. A modern parallel would be a strapless party dress for a three-year-old girl.

For boys, the transition from childhood to adulthood was achieved in a series of distinct stages. Three stood out as milestones: his first short haircut, breeching (when dresses were replaced by short trousers) and his first pair of long pants. A boy's first haircut and trousers were both described in the popular literature as traumatic for a mother, foreshadowing the day when she would lose her son to the world outside the home. "It was the trousers that did it, Mary," one mother complained in 1901 *Harper's Magazine* story, "From the moment he put on trousers he objected to being kissed."

Ostensibly, it was the mother who decided when her son was old enough to wear short trousers or knickerbockers instead of dresses. But this decision was not necessarily an easy one, or even one made without pressure from the father, relatives and friends, or the boy himself. The actual age at which this happened was extremely flexible; the usual guidance offered by fashion advisors was that the decision be based on the boy's size and appearance, not his age. A small, delicate six-year old might still be wearing skirts, while his sturdy, big-for-his-age neighbor could already have graduated to knickerbockers at five. Whatever the effect of this practice on individuals, the overall result was that acquiring masculine clothing was not merely a matter of being old enough, but also of looking and behaving in a masculine manner.

"Her disposition, with her natural feminine tastes and tenderness, is always inclining her to deck her child with the gewgaws of finery and coddle him with the delicate appliances of luxury. The timely check from the manly boy may therefore prevent her from persisting in an effeminating process which would be sure, if continued, to deprive him of his best characteristics."

Throughout the nineteenth century, the process of growing up for the little boy was accompanied by the gradual "de-feminization" of his clothing. For girls, it was a much simpler process. In contrast to the distinct stages found in boys' costume - infant dress, toddler dress, pre-schooler's skirted suit, and schoolboy's knickerbockers - girls' clothing changed much less dramatically between infancy and age six. Once she had outgrown the simple frocks of toddlerhood, a girl's clothing gradually conformed more and more to adult women's styles.

Around the turn of the century, clothing styles for children underwent several important changes. Adult gender conventions were being transformed. Also, increasingly casual American lifestyles and a new emphasis on active play and organized sports for children encouraged the adoption of more practical and comfortable children's clothing. For girls, "practical" often meant "masculine" styling - shirts, knickers for sports dress and play clothes, and simpler everyday clothing. As girls appropriated costume features once exclusively masculine, boys' clothing began to lose its resemblance to female dress. This trend began in the 1890s, when elaborate, "costume styles," such as the Little Lord Fauntleroy suit, fell out of favor. One author of the 1890s wrote, disapprovingly:

"I saw a boy with a predestinate idiot of a mother, wearing a silk hat, ruffled shirt, silver-buckled shoes, kid gloves, cane, and a velvet suit with one two-inch pocket which is an insult to his sex."

These costume styles had been popular since the 1860s for boys between the ages of four and six. Most were based on antique styles for men - Lord Fauntleroy, for instance was depicted by illustrator Reginald Birch wearing a velvet "cavalier" suit, inspired by seventeenth-century men's dress. In the 1890s, costume styles were replaced by plainer styles, particularly the Russian tunic and the sailor suit. The sailor suit, in fact, became so ubiquitous that it could be considered the juvenile equivalent of the business suit - the uniform of the new boy of the twentieth century.

Another change that began in the 1890s was the earlier substitution of trousers for dresses for little boys. By the turn of the century, boys wore dresses only until the age of two or three years, rather than until five or six as before. It is very clear that these changes were not intended to "hurry" the boy towards adulthood. For adolescent boys, the age of transition from short pants to long trousers had not changed, but continued to occur around the age of twelve. The transformation in little boys' clothing was meant to differentiate boys from girls at an earlier age than before. What had happened? Two things. First, girls were being permitted more freedom to be physically active - in popular terms, to look and act more like boys. This would not have mattered to an eighteenth-century parent, who believed that masculinity and femininity were innate qualities which would emerge naturally as the child grew. But the parent of the late nineteenth century lived in a different world - a world where eminent child psychologists were writing in popular magazines that gender distinctions could and must be taught, and the earlier the better. The eighteenth century parent believed that boys grew into men as acorns grew into oak trees; late nineteenth-century parents believed that their little acorns might turn into willow trees without parental intervention.

After the turn of the century, clothing for small children continued to become progressively more gender-specific. The changes which had begun in the clothing of two-to-six-year-olds began to influence infants' costume, as well. For centuries, American costume had made no distinction between male and female infants. White was the color of infancy, perhaps because of its connotation of purity, and also as visible proof of the conscientiousness of the mother in keeping her child clean. Equally important was the practical matter of fading or bleeding colors, which made white a better choice for garments which were laundered frequently. But by the earlier part of the twentieth century, important changes had occurred in the popular view of infants, as psychologists began to discover the extent to which babies were aware of and affected by their surroundings. The same forces that had altered the clothing styles of pre-schoolers - anxiety about shifting gender roles and the emerging belief that gender could be taught - also transformed infantswear.

The first change in clothes for children under the age of three appeared early in the twentieth century, with the introduction of rompers or creepers - one-piece garments with gathered leg openings and buttons or snaps closing the crotch. Originally introduced in the 1890s for older children's playclothes, within a short time rompers and creepers were available for toddlers and, eventually, for babies as well. They were a significant departure from traditional infants' clothing on two counts. First, they were bifurcated (i.e., had leg openings or legs.). Second, creepers were usually made of colored fabrics - solid blues and reds, gingham checks in pink, red, and blue, and blue or gray ticking

Priscilla Poister

stripes were all popular - in vibrant contrast to the white traditionally used for dresses. Both of these characteristics allowed parents to dress their babies in costumes regarded as "appropriate" to each child's personality and activities. One of the results of these parental choices was the creation of a system of gender symbolism where none had previously existed.

This is not to say that the introduction of creepers resulted in an immediate end to centuries of genderless costumes for children under three. Until the rules of gender coding evolved completely, most rompers were essentially unisex, since not all parents - or manufacturers - agreed on the appropriate styles, colors and decoration for boys and girls. Even bifurcation was not uniformly perceived as "masculine" styling. On the one hand, creepers were worn by little boys whose parents thought that dresses were too "unmanly" for their sons, but creepers also offered progressive parents of daughters a practical alternative to dresses for playclothes. Until clearly distinctive styles were available for each sex, a baby boy and a baby girl could both wear the same style romper, although they might be wearing them for different reasons.

To see how long the introduction of this gender symbolism actually took, consider the conventions of modern children's clothes. Pink is for girls; blue is for boys. Pastels are feminine. Only girls may wear dresses. Even trim materials and pictorial motifs (trains, flowers, baseballs, butterflies) are selected according to the sex of the intended wearer. (This may seem to ignore the "unisex" styles sold in gift boxes and intended as shower gifts, but these are notable for their conscious avoidance of any gender symbolism.) None of these conventions was true of most childrens' clothing prior to World War I, and some of them did not become "traditional" until the post-war baby boom.

The most surprising example is the common practice of dressing girls in pink and boys in blue. Many exceptions to this rule can be found as late as the nineteen-forties. In fact, in the beginning the rule was just the opposite. A writer in a trade magazine for the babywear industry wrote, in 1918:

"There has been a great diversity of opinion on the subject, but the generally accepted rule is pink for the boy and blue for the girl. The reason is that pink being a more decided and stronger color is more suitable for the boy; while blue, which is more delicate and dainty is prettier for the girl."

Twenty years later, *Parents Magazine* was still engaged in the debate: "There seem to be more reasons for choosing blue for girls, than the customary pink...red symbolizes zeal and courage, while blue is symbolic of faith and constancy..All these points lead to blue for girls."

Note that by then, pink was "customary," though still not universal; the same article reported a poll conducted by a New York department store revealed that, while 78% of their customers preferred pink for baby girls, 22% still favored blue for girls and pink for boys. Between 1900 and 1940 both colors were often used interchangeably, even while the modern pattern was gradually emerging. A set of twin paper dolls (boy and girl) published in the late nineteen thirties shows identical blue buntings as well as matching pink bathrobes, although the boy holds a blue rattle and the girl's rattle is pink. Since pre-packaged layette sets are intended to be purchased before the baby's arrival, it is interesting to note that Sears, Roebuck and Company did not offer its layettes in a "neutral" color (yellow) until the nineteen-fifties. Before that time, layettes were offered only with a choice of pink or blue trim, despite the fact that this was long before medical technology made it possible to know the baby's sex in advance. It would appear that it took forty or fifty years of colored baby clothes for our present "pink and blue" symbolism to evolve completely. The first generation to be systematically color-coded was the postwar Baby Boom.

Nor did boys suddenly stop wearing baby dresses with the introduction of rompers. Dresses remained a staple item in infants' wardrobes well into the twentieth century. As late as the early nineteen-fifties, some baby boys still wore white dresses, even though rompers, overalls and footed sleepers were far more common by then. In fact, Sears included white dresses in their unisex layettes until 1958. But for the most part, the infants' white dress, traditional for centuries, went out of fashion after the Second World War.

Today, no one would think of putting a kindergarten-age boy in a dress. Except for plain jeans, little boys' and girls' pants are distinguished by color and design, so that a little girl is not wearing masculine clothing when she wears trousers. Infantswear is not only color-coded but differentiated by motifs (flowers and butterflies versus airplanes and footballs) or other details (ruffles for girls, mock fly openings for boys). Even as adult gender roles have supposedly become less distinct, boys and girls are dressed as if they were players on two different teams. Does this have any effect on children?

The changes which occurred in children's clothing were the result of parents' conviction that gender roles could be taught through dress. But can they? Is there any evidence in the historical record or the psychological literature that this is true? Most children are unaware of sexual distinctions or their meaning until the second or even third year of life, so gender distinctions in the clothing of a month-old infant can have little direct effect on the child's training. It is highly effective in molding the expectations and behavior of the parents and others who hold, speak to and play with the baby. This has been repeatedly shown by psychologists who have observed adult behavior when confronted with babies dressed in a variety of outfits. These test subjects reacted differently when they thought the child was a girl than when they were led to believe the baby was a boy. The most interesting reaction, however, was when they were confronted with a baby of unknown sex. Some responded by choosing neutral toys to offer the baby or by guessing the chid's sex - usually erroneously - based on the baby's size, appearance, or behavior. A few, clearly frustrated by an ambiguous social situation, peeked into the child's diapers to see for themselves. It is clear from these studies that the primary function of gender-specific infants' clothing is to enable others (especially strangers) to make appropriate social responses to the baby.

It seems likely, however, that a nineteenth-century baby boy in a long white gown was probably treated differently from an identically-dressed baby girl simply because the people around him knew he was a boy and didn't need clothing cues to be reminded. Modern infants lead more public lives than did babies of a century ago or more, who spent most of their first year or more at home surrounded by family and friends. The sex of a child is probably no more important today than it was a hundred years age. The immediate symbolic communication of child's sex, however, is expected, even demanded, in American today. Accordingly, today's parents often admit to dressing their babies for outings conscious of the need to provide strangers with clues to the baby's gender. Modern baby clothes reflect babies' larger social lives and our fascination with their individuality, not any change in the treatment of boy and girl infants.

Even if more gender-specific clothing had little effect on infants, might not changes in clothing for older children be expected to have resulted in different patterns of gender identity in their later childhood and adult lives? Perhaps, but the simple fact is that they apparently have had very little effect. Boys have worn an amazing range of styles in the last three centuries, yet show no evidence of growing up into dramatically different styles of manhood from generation to generation; boys in kilts, boys in velvet cavalier suits and boys in denim overalls grew up to be American men in all the usual varieties. And the first pink-and-blue generation, the Baby Boomers, grew up to challenge traditional gender roles and dress their own children in unisex styles. If clothes make the man, they do it in a very round-about way!

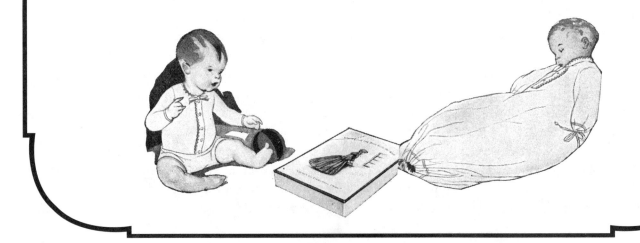

# Mother Love and Baby Booties: The Saga of Ready-made Baby Clothes

by Jo Paoletti

Picture this: a young husband, returning home from a day at the office, finds his wife sitting in a rocking chair, knitting a tiny pair of booties. No words are necessary; we know she is expecting a baby. By preparing a layette for her unborn child, she is preparing herself for motherhood in a time-honored way. Even in our fast-paced, high-tech world, there is something about a baby that awakens the sleeping crafter in many of us.

We all know that clothes are powerful and important in shaping our identities from the very beginning. But the impact of baby clothing, especially clothing acquired before the baby's arrival is even greater, especially on the parents and their close relatives. These tiny garments are invested with tremendous emotional meeting as expressions of love and hope. Whether it is an heirloom christening gown made by a doting soon-to-be aunt, or a Harvard sweatshirt that Grandpop orders online, that very first wardrobe is very special! It should come as no surprise, then, that infants' wear was the form of clothing most resistant to mass-production and, even today, one of the most likely to be handmade. Ready-made baby clothes faced an uphill battle for acceptance a century ago, because they posed a direct challenge to the existing notion of a "good mother."

Unlike other kinds of mass-produced ready-to-wear clothing, which were, for the most part, quickly recognized and accepted for the labor-saving they represented, ready-made baby clothes met with a cool initial reception. It was not a matter of quality; no one argued that Sears' booties were not as warm as the ones Mama hand-knit. There was also no question that preparing a layette (the newborn's trousseau, a complete wardrobe for the first few months) was time-consuming and placed enormous demands on the skill and patience of the mother-to-be. But to many turn-of-the-century women, the home-made layette represented an investment of time and emotion that was a necessary part of motherhood. At a time when both infant and maternal mortality was high, a carefully-stitched dress might be a mother's last gift to her child, or her only remembrance of its existence. Preparing the layette was also considered a natural way to channel the young wife's thoughts toward motherhood, and well-meaning friends and relatives were advised not to do the task for her. Even if her sewing skills were poor, the simple, flawed garments from her own hand would be better than the most elaborate dresses and robes provided by someone else. Small wonder that ready-made, pre-assembled layettes were greeted with less-than-universal approval when they were introduced in the 1890s!

"...many a loving, hopeful thought does the young mother-that -is-to-be stitch into the dainty little garments that are destined to enwrap her newly-acquired treasure. It is preeminently the mother whose pleasure it is to make all such garments with her own skillful fingers that we have in mind; she who procures her layette all ready-made, misses half the sweetness and blessing of her privilege of motherhood."
— "For the Autocrat of the Family," *The Standard Designer*, 1896

The expectant mother who believed that mail-order bibs might be the emotional equivalent of hand-made might still hesitate under the threat of disease-bearing microbes:

"If any baby clothes are bought ready-made, it is advisable to sterilize them before they are used, unless you know they have been made under sanitary conditions."
— *McCall's Magazine*, December, 1916

There were also voices speaking in favor of purchasing layettes - the progressive advocates of "modern" homemaking. These new experts, notably home economists and doctors, argued against the investment of so much time and effort in handsewing clothes which would be worn for so short a time, particularly when so many inexpensive ready-made items were available. This was especially true after 1920, as baby clothes became more simple in cut and ornamentation. According to a 1929 report in the *Journal of Home Economics*, it was probably not economical to make flannel kimonos, simple dresses and nightgowns, or the cut and hem diapers, unless the housewife set an extremely low value on her time. Home economics extension agents tried to teach homemakers to consider both time and money when planning their babies' wardrobes, and to spend less time adorning their children and more time teaching them.

Their message was not entirely an appeal to cold practicality, however. Instead they conjured up the image of the modern housewife, using new technology to improve her family's everyday life. Eventually, practicality won out: by the nineteen-forties, ready-made baby clothes had been widely accepted, and expectant mothers were being encouraged to make a few small things because it was "fun to make a few yourself." Today, no one thinks twice about dressing their baby in ready-mades.

But did handmade baby clothes become extinct, victims of Efficiency and Economy — the twin demons of modern life? Hardly. If anything, today's passion for heirloom sewing has raised handsewing to new heights. The same women who carry cell phones and keep in touch with far-flung friends and relatives by E-mail can be found browsing the dainty trimmings in their local fabric store (or on the Internet) and carefully stitching French seams on a batiste christening gown. There's no conflict between the Old Ways and the New Ways, just the urge each of us feels to find our personal balance point. Can today's efficient manager and homemaker find satisfaction in old-fashioned craftsmanship? You bet your baby booties.

# Heirloom Sewing

## for

## Jack

# Marshall's Scalloped Shirt

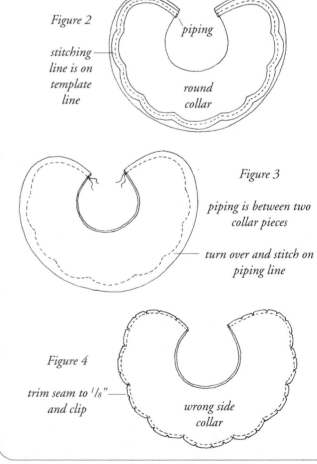

Using yellow poly-cotton batiste this shirt has a very unique and tailored collar. It is piped in tiny piping made of the same plaid as the knicker pants to accompany the shirt. The scalloped and piped cuffs turn up in a very tailored style. This suit closes in the back with buttons and buttonholes and can be used to button on with any of the pants from this book. In using dark piping with a lighter colored shirt, I think it is advisable to use either a poly-cotton batiste or broadcloth simply because they are thicker than Swiss batiste.

Pants shown in the illustration
are the V-waist Button-on Knickers.

## Fabric Requirements

|  | Sizes 1-2 | Sizes 3-4 | Sizes 6-8 |
|---|---|---|---|
| Fabric 45" | $1^{1}/_{4}$ yds | $1^{3}/_{8}$ yds | $1^{1}/_{2}$ yds |
| $^{1}/_{2}$" buttons | 5 | 5 | 5 |

$^{1}/_{3}$ yard of fabric for piping or 2 yards of purchased piping
2 yards of cording if making piping

## Pattern Pieces

All pattern pieces are found in the pattern envelope.
Round collar, shirt short sleeve, shirt front, shirt button back.
Templates: Marshall's Scalloped Collar template and Marshall's Scalloped Sleeve template
All seams $^{1}/_{4}$". Finish seams with a zigzag or serger.

## Cutting

Cut the following: Two round collars, two shirt sleeves cut on fold line #2, one shirt front with center front on the fold, two backs on the selvage, two cuff facings $2^{1}/_{4}$" by width of sleeve bottom, one bias neck facing 1" wide by the neck measurement.

## Construction

1. Trace the Marshall's scalloped collar template on the outer edge of the collar (fig. 1).
2. Refer to the technique "Making Piping" and make enough piping to go around the collar and sleeves. Sew the piping on the traced lines with raw edges of the piping toward the outer edge

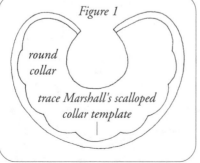

Figure 1

round collar

trace Marshall's scalloped collar template

of the collar (fig. 2). Lay the collars with right sides together. Piping will be sandwiched in-between the collars.

Figure 2

stitching line is on template line

piping

round collar

Figure 3

piping is between two collar pieces

turn over and stitch on piping line

Figure 4

trim seam to $^{1}/_{8}$" and clip

wrong side collar

Sew the collars together following the stitching line of the piping (fig. 3). Trim and clip the seam (fig. 4).

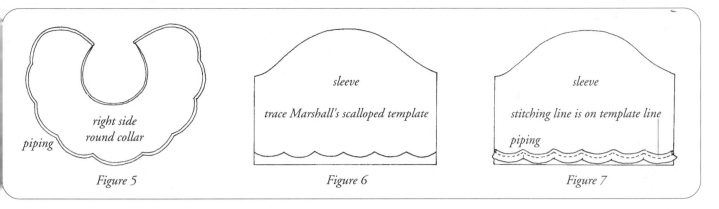

right side
round collar

piping

Figure 5

sleeve

trace Marshall's scalloped template

Figure 6

sleeve

stitching line is on template line

piping

Figure 7

Turn right side out and press (fig. 5).

3. Trace the Marshall's scalloped sleeve template on the bottom of the sleeve (fig. 6). Sew piping on the right side of the sleeve on the traced lines with the raw edges of the piping toward the

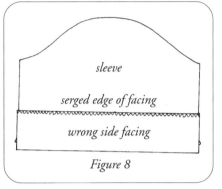

sleeve

serged edge of facing

wrong side facing

Figure 8

raw edge of the sleeve (fig. 7). Finish one edge of the sleeve facing. Place the sleeve facing on the bottom of the right side of the sleeve with right sides together (fig. 8). Using the stitching line of the scalloped piping, sew the facing to the sleeve bottom (fig. 9). Trim and clip seam (fig. 10). Flip the facing down and sew the sleeve and cuff side seam by matching the piping seam using ¹/₄" (fig. 11).

4. Turn up the facing and hem the sleeve by hand or machine (fig. 12). Turn 1¹/₄" of the cuff to the right side and tack in place at the underarm seam (fig. 13).

5. Place the front and backs right sides together and stitch the shoulder seams with a ¹/₄" seam (fig. 14).

6. Place the wrong side of the collar to the right side of the neck of the shirt. Pin in place (fig. 15). Fold the shirt back facing on the fold line to the right side of the bodice (collar will be between the back and the facing) (fig. 16).

7. Cut a bias strip 1" wide by the neck measurement. Fold the bias strip in half and press. Place the cut edges of the strip to the neck of the collar/shirt. The bias strip starts and stops ¹/₂" from the back edge. Cut off any excess bias (fig. 16).

8. Stitch the bias strip to the neck edge using a ¹/₄" seam, starting at the fold lines on the back edges of the shirt.

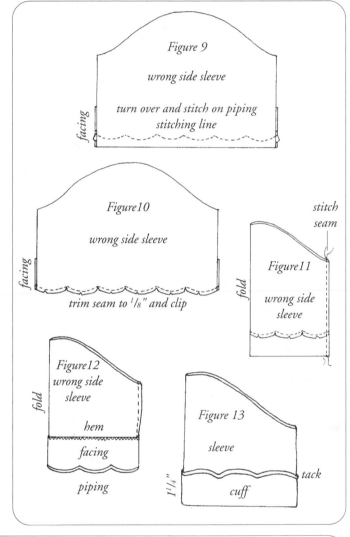

Figure 9

wrong side sleeve

turn over and stitch on piping stitching line

facing

Figure 10

wrong side sleeve

facing

trim seam to ¹/₈" and clip

stitch seam

Figure 11

fold

wrong side sleeve

Figure 12
wrong side sleeve

fold

hem

facing

piping

Figure 13

sleeve

1¹/₄"

cuff

tack

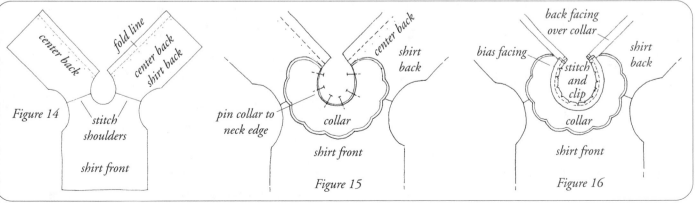

center back

fold line

center back
shirt back

Figure 14

stitch shoulders

shirt front

center back

shirt back

pin collar to neck edge

collar

shirt front

Figure 15

back facing over collar

bias facing

stitch and clip

shirt back

collar

shirt front

Figure 16

9. Trim the seam to ⅛". Clip the neck edge and understitch the bias band. Understitching is done by stitching through the bias band and the trimmed seam (fig. 17).

10. Holding the collar away from the shirt, stitch the facing to the shirt (fig. 18).

11. With the right sides together sew the side seams of the shirt with a ¼" seam (fig. 19).

12. Fit the sleeves to the armholes and sew the sleeves to armholes (fig. 20).

13. Finish the bottom edge of the shirt as follows: with the facings open, fold up ¼" and press. Fold up ¼" again and press, creating a narrow hem (fig. 21). Fold the facings along the fold line and stitch the hem in place (fig. 22).

14. Position the buttonholes on the left hand side by placing a dot ½" from the top fabric edge of the neckline and ½" over from the fold line (fig. 23).

15. Place a dot every 3" down the back of the shirt ½" from the fold.

16. Stitch a ½" buttonhole beginning at the dot and placing the buttonholes horizontally. Continue the buttonholes down the back of the shirt. Cut the buttonholes open with a buttonhole cutter or seam ripper (fig. 23).

17. Lap the left side of the blouse over the right side and mark the placement for the buttons.

18. Attach the buttons along the marks on the right side of the shirt (fig. 23).

19. Fit garment to the child and mark placement for buttons at waist. If child is not available, refer to the waistline marking on the pattern and the buttonhole placement on the pants to determine the button placement. Make a ½" pleat behind the buttons placement line. Sew buttons in place (fig. 24). A piece of twill tape may be placed on the wrong side behind the button for more stability.

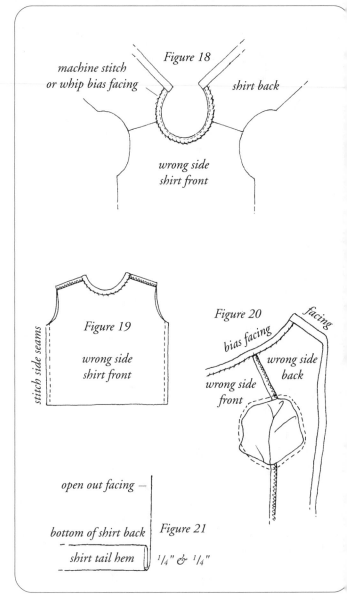

Figure 17

understitch

Figure 18

machine stitch or whip bias facing

shirt back

wrong side shirt front

Figure 19

wrong side shirt front

stitch side seams

Figure 20

facing

bias facing

wrong side back

wrong side front

open out facing —

bottom of shirt back

shirt tail hem

Figure 21

¼" & ¼"

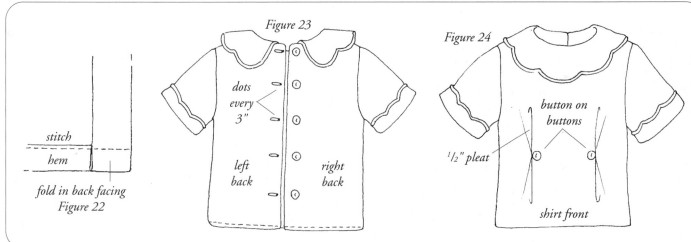

stitch

hem

fold in back facing
Figure 22

Figure 23

dots every 3"

left back

right back

Figure 24

button on buttons

½" pleat

shirt front

# Christopher's Double Piping Shirt

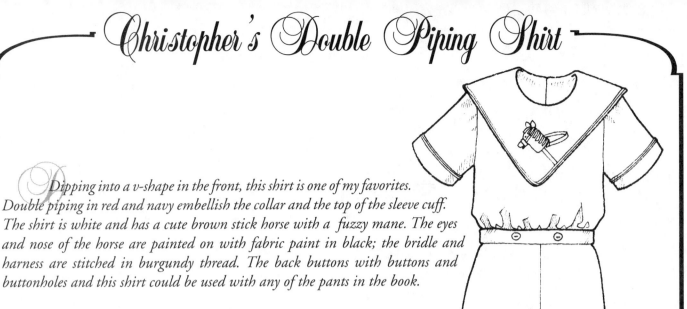

$\mathscr{D}$ipping into a v-shape in the front, this shirt is one of my favorites. Double piping in red and navy embellish the collar and the top of the sleeve cuff. The shirt is white and has a cute brown stick horse with a fuzzy mane. The eyes and nose of the horse are painted on with fabric paint in black; the bridle and harness are stitched in burgundy thread. The back buttons with buttons and buttonholes and this shirt could be used with any of the pants in the book.

Pants shown in the illustration are the Straight Front Knee Pants.

## Fabric Requirements

|                        | Sizes 1-2 | Sizes 3-4 | Sizes 6-8 |
|------------------------|-----------|-----------|-----------|
| Fabric 45"             | 1 1/4 yds | 1 3/8 yds | 1 1/2 yds |
| (for long sleeves, add 1/4 yd) |   |           |           |
| Buttons 1/2"           | 5         | 5         | 5         |

Small pieces of brown and dark brown fabric
Thread to match both browns, burgundy thread for harness
Yarn for mane
Fabric for Double piping: 1/4 yd of two different colors
Permanent marker for eyes and nose

## Pattern Pieces

All pattern pieces are found in the pattern envelope.
Pointed collar, shirt front, shirt button back, shirt short sleeve
Templates: horse appliqué template found at the end of these directions
All seams 1/4". Finish all seams with a zigzag or serger.

## Cut Out

Two pointed collars, one shirt front with center front on the fold, two shirt backs on the selvage, two sleeves cut on fold line #2, one bias neck facing 1" wide by neck measurement

## Construction

1. Trace the appliqué design onto one of the collars. Refer to the technique, Machine Appliqué and appliqué the design onto the collar (fig. 1).

2. Refer to the technique for double piping and make enough piping to go around the collar and sleeves. Sew double piping around the outer edge of the collar matching the raw edge of the piping with the raw edge of the collar (fig. 2).

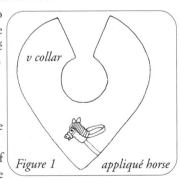

v collar

Figure 1          appliqué horse

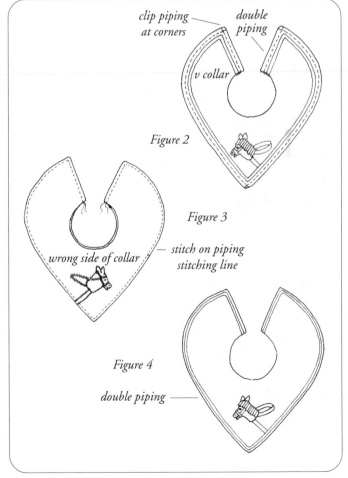

clip piping at corners

double piping

v collar

Figure 2

Figure 3

wrong side of collar

stitch on piping stitching line

Figure 4

double piping

3. Place the collars with the right sides together and sew the collars together using the piping stitching line as a guide (fig. 3). Trim and clip the seam. Turn right side out and press (fig. 4).

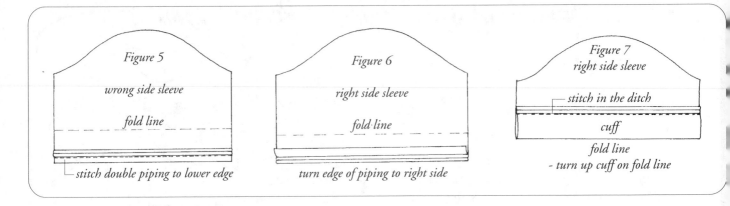

Figure 5

wrong side sleeve

fold line

stitch double piping to lower edge

Figure 6

right side sleeve

fold line

turn edge of piping to right side

Figure 7
right side sleeve

stitch in the ditch

cuff

fold line
- turn up cuff on fold line

4. Sew double piping to the bottom edge of the wrong side of the sleeve by matching the raw edges of the piping with the raw edge of the sleeve (fig. 5).

5. Turn the raw edges to the right side with the double piping on the bottom edge (fig. 6). Press seam in place.

6. Fold the cuff to the right side on the fold line. (fig. 7). Stitch the cuff in place by stitching in the ditch where the piping was attached.

7. Place the right side of the front to the right side of the backs at the shoulders. Sew ¹/₄" shoulder seams (fig. 8).

8. Place the wrong side of the collar to the right side of the shirt. The back edges of the collar should not extend beyond the center back lines of the back shirt (fig. 9). Fold the back edges of the shirt to the right side along the fold lines (fig. 10). The back edges of the collar will be sandwiched between the back folded edges of the facing and the shirt.

9. Fold the bias neck facing in half lengthwise, with the long cut edges even. Press.

10. Place the bias strip to the right side of the bodice with both long edges of the strip even with the neck edge. The strip will be placed over the collar and the folded back facings (fig. 10).

11. Stitch all layers together using a ¹/₄" seam. Trim and clip the seam allowance (fig. 10).

12. Press the bias strip away from the shirt, toward the seam allowance. Understitch the bias facing (fig. 11).

13. Flip the back facings to the inside of the shirt. Fold the bias strip to the inside of the shirt creating a facing (fig. 12). The bias strip will not show on the right side of the shirt. Press.

14. With the collar away from the shirt, stitch the binding to the bodice by hand or machine (fig. 12).

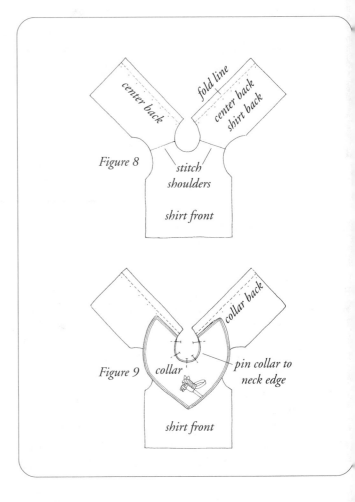

Figure 8

center back

fold line

center back
shirt back

stitch
shoulders

shirt front

Figure 9

collar back

collar

pin collar to
neck edge

shirt front

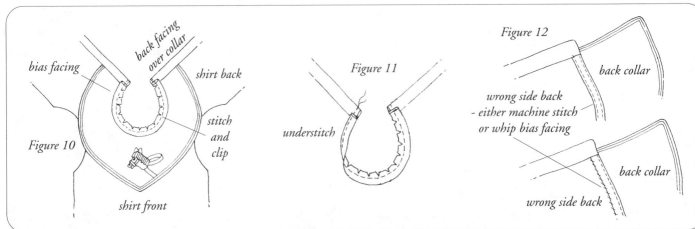

bias facing

back facing
over collar

shirt back

Figure 10

stitch
and
clip

shirt front

Figure 11

understitch

Figure 12

back collar

wrong side back
- either machine stitch
or whip bias facing

back collar

wrong side back

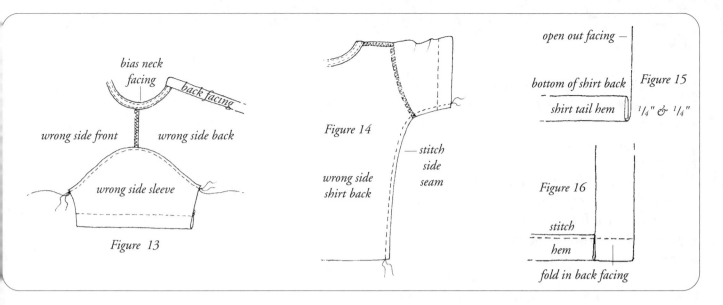

Figure 13

Figure 14

wrong side shirt back

stitch side seam

open out facing —

bottom of shirt back — Figure 15

shirt tail hem — $^1/_4$" & $^1/_4$"

Figure 16

stitch

hem

fold in back facing

bias neck facing

back facing

wrong side front

wrong side back

wrong side sleeve

15. Fit the sleeve to the armhole and stitch in place (fig. 13).

16. Place right sides together at the sides and sleeves matching underarm seams. Sew side seams from bottom of sleeve to the bottom of the shirt (fig. 14).

17. Finish the bottom edge of the shirt with a shirt tail hem. With the facings open, fold up $^1/_4$" and press. Fold up $^1/_4$" again and press, creating a narrow hem (fig. 15). Fold the facings along the fold line and stitch the hem in place (fig. 16).

18. Position the buttonholes on the left hand side by placing a dot $^1/_2$" from the top fabric edge of the neckline and $^1/_2$" over from the fold line (fig. 17).

19. Place a dot every 3" down the back of the shirt $^1/_2$" from the fold (fig. 17).

20. Stitch a $^1/_2$" buttonhole beginning at the dot and placing the buttonholes horizontally. Continue the buttonholes down the back of the shirt. Cut the buttonholes open with a buttonhole cutter or seam ripper (fig. 17).

21. Lap the left side of the blouse over the right side and mark the placement for the buttons.

22. Attach the buttons along the marks on the right side of the shirt (fig. 17).

23. Mark placement for the buttons on the shirt front. Make a $^1/_2$" pleat behind the button placement line. Sew buttons in place (fig. 18). A piece of twill tape may also be placed on the wrong side behind the button for more stability.

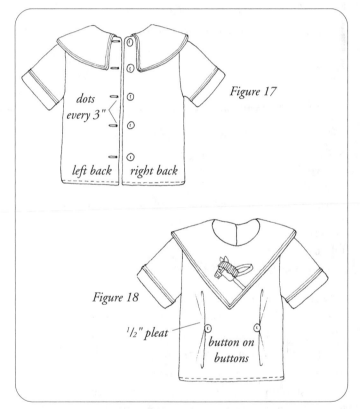

dots every 3"

left back    right back

Figure 17

Figure 18

$^1/_2$" pleat

button on buttons

## Directions for Horse Appliqué

1. Let stick run off collar.

2. Use cord or yarn for mane.

3. Ribbon or trim can be used for the bridle and reins.

4. The head could be padded slightly beneath the appliqué.

Horse Appliqué Template

# Campbell's Jabot Shirt

Using antique Irish crocheted edging on a double jabot, this ecru handkerchief linen shirt is a beautiful heirloom to be treasured for many generations to come. The long sleeved shirt has cuffs which button with antique pearl buttons. The same antique pearl buttons are used down the back of the shirt. A lined Peter Pan collar has the double jabot neatly tucked underneath in the front. The top jabot has two sets of seven folded tucks with the antique crochet on the first layer; the second jabot piece is plain except for the antique crochet around the edges. This is the perfect portrait suit or ring bearer suit. It can be worn with any of the pants in the book. I would love to see ecru linen matching pants for a ring bearer's suit, possibly black velveteen for Christmas and certainly blue linen for Easter. This shirt can be worn with many different pants for year round use.

Pants shown in the illustration
are the Button-on Suit Pants.

## Fabric Requirements

**SHIRT**

| | Sizes 1-2 | Sizes 3-4 | Sizes 6-8 |
|---|---|---|---|
| Linen 45" | 1 1/4 yds | 1 3/8 yds | 1 1/2 yds |
| Buttons 1/2" | 7 | 7 | 7 |

Directions for Jabot are given at end of shirt construction

**JABOT**
Fabric 1/4 yd for all sizes
1" Lace Edging 1 3/4 yds for all sizes

All seams are 1/4". Finish seams with a zigzag or serger.

## Pattern Pieces

All pattern pieces are found in the pattern envelope.
Shirt front, shirt button back, long sleeve, Peter Pan collar, long sleeve cuff

## Cutting

Cut one shirt front on the fold, two shirt button backs on the selvage, four Peter Pan collars, two long sleeves, two long sleeve cuffs and one bias neck facing 1" wide by neck measurement

## Construction

1. Place the collars with the right sides together and stitch together (fig. 1). Trim and clip seam. Turn to the right side and press.
2. Place the right side of the front to the right side of the backs at the shoulders. Sew the shoulder seams using 1/4" seams (fig. 2).
3. Place the wrong side of the collar to the right side of the shirt. The back edges of the collar should not extend beyond the center back lines of the back shirt. Fold the back edges of the shirt to the right side along the fold lines. The back edges of the collar will be sandwiched between the back folded edges of the facing and the shirt (fig. 3).
4. Fold the bias in half lengthwise, with the long cut edges even. Press.

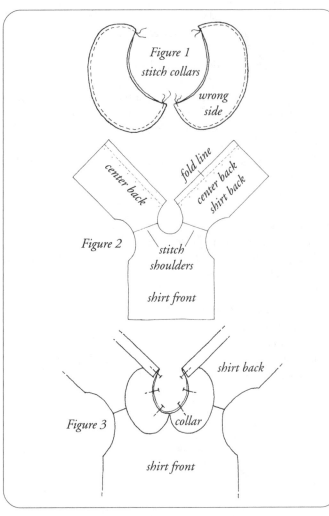

Figure 1
stitch collars
wrong side

center back | fold line | center back shirt back

Figure 2
stitch shoulders
shirt front

shirt back

Figure 3
collar
shirt front

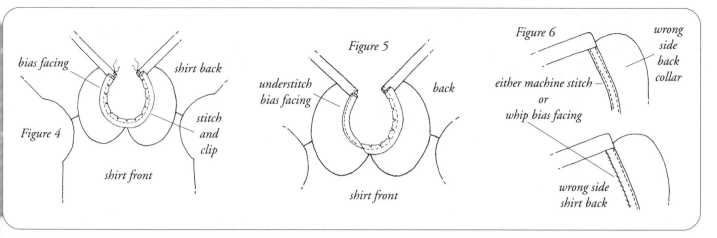

Figure 4 — bias facing, shirt back, stitch and clip, shirt front

Figure 5 — understitch bias facing, back, shirt front

Figure 6 — either machine stitch or whip bias facing, wrong side back collar, wrong side shirt back

5. Place the bias strip to the right side of the bodice with both long edges of the strip even with the neck edge. The strip will be placed over the collar and the folded back facings (fig. 4).

6. Stitch all layers together using a $^1/_4$" seam. Trim and clip the seam allowance (fig. 4).

7. Press the bias strip away from the shirt, toward the seam allowance. Understitch (fig. 5).

8. Flip the back facings to the inside of the shirt. Fold the bias strip to the inside of the shirt creating a facing. The bias strip will not show on the right side of the shirt. Press.

9. With the collar away from the shirt, stitch the binding to the bodice by hand or machine (fig. 6).

10. Fit the sleeve to the armhole and stitch in place (fig. 7).

11. Place the sides of the shirt together matching the underarm seam and the bottom of the sleeve. Sew the side shirt and the sleeve seam stopping the sleeve seam at the dot. This opening will form the placket for the sleeve (fig. 8). Finish the sleeve seam edges for the placket by turning in $^1/_4$" and $^1/_4$" again and stitching the seams to the inside by hand or machine (fig. 9).

12. Fit the bottom of the sleeve to the cuff. Place two folds in the bottom of the sleeve to make the sleeve fit the cuff. The cuff will extend $^1/_4$" on each side of the cuff. Stitch the cuff in place (fig. 10).

13. Turn under $^1/_4$" along the unfinished edge of the cuff and press. Turn the cuff to the outside folding it in half with the right sides together and sew sides of the cuff. The sides will be flush with the sleeve placket (fig. 11).

14. Flip the cuff to the wrong side. The folded edge of the cuff will meet the stitching line for the cuff. Hand-whip the cuff in place (fig. 12).

15. Make buttonholes in the cuffs and sew on buttons (fig. 13).

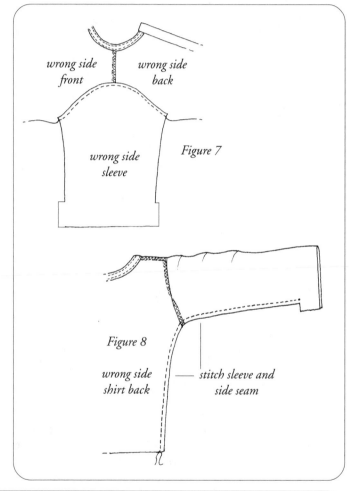

Figure 7 — wrong side front, wrong side back, wrong side sleeve

Figure 8 — wrong side shirt back, stitch sleeve and side seam

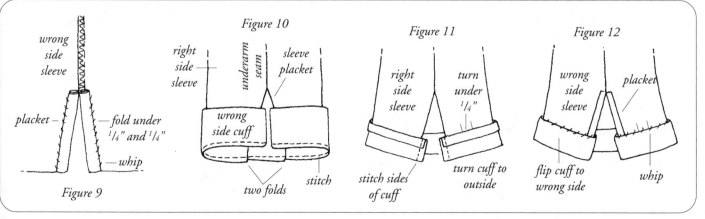

Figure 9 — wrong side sleeve, placket, fold under $^1/_4$" and $^1/_4$", whip

Figure 10 — right side sleeve, underarm seam, sleeve placket, wrong side cuff, two folds, stitch

Figure 11 — right side sleeve, turn under $^1/_4$", stitch sides of cuff, turn cuff to outside

Figure 12 — wrong side sleeve, placket, flip cuff to wrong side, whip

16. Finish the bottom edge of the shirt as follows: with the facings open, fold up $^1/_4$" and press. Fold up $^1/_4$" again and press, creating a narrow hem (fig. 14). Fold the facings along the fold line and stitch the hem in place (fig. 15).

17. Position the buttonholes on the left hand side by placing a dot $^1/_2$" from the top fabric edge of the neckline and $^1/_2$" over from the fold line.

18. Place a dot every 3" down the back of the shirt $^1/_2$" from the fold (fig. 16).

19. Stitch a $^1/_2$" buttonhole beginning at the dot and placing the buttonholes horizontally. Continue the buttonholes down the back of the shirt. Cut the buttonholes open with a buttonhole cutter or seam ripper (fig. 16).

20. Lap the left side of the shirt over the right side and mark the placement for the buttons.

21. Attach the buttons along the marks on the right side of the shirt (fig. 16).

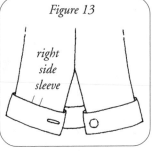

Figure 13

right side sleeve

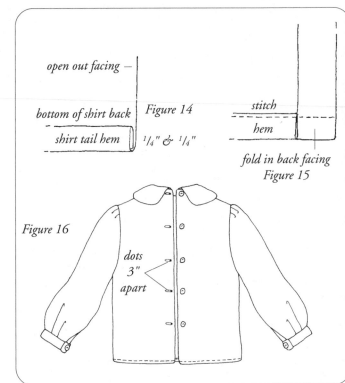

open out facing —

bottom of shirt back    Figure 14    stitch

shirt tail hem    $^1/_4$" & $^1/_4$"    hem

fold in back facing
Figure 15

Figure 16

dots 3" apart

## Fabric Requirements - Jabot

Fabric Requirements For All Sizes:  Fabric $^1/_4$ yd; 1" Lace Edging 1$^3/_4$ yds

Finished Measurements: 6$^3/_4$" by 9$^1/_2$" top piece; 8" by 11" bottom piece

Cut a piece of fabric 5$^3/_4$" by 13$^1/_2$", one piece 6$^3/_4$" by 9$^1/_4$" and a bias strip 5$^1/_2$" by 1$^1/_2$"

## Construction

1. Find the center of the 5$^3/_4$" by 13$^1/_2$". Measure out from the center on both sides $^1/_2$" and make a fold line for a tuck on each side, $^3/_4$" from this fold line make another, $^3/_4$" from this line make another and continue this until there are 7 lines on each side of the center. A total of 14 lines across, 7 on each side of center (fig. 1).

2. Make $^3/_8$" tucks on each fold line. Total of 14 tucks. Press the tucks from the center toward the outer edge (fig. 2).

3. Attach the lace edging to three sides using the technique Lace to Fabric. Lace will have to be gathered at the corner. Be sure to put enough fullness to make the lace lay flat (fig. 3).

4. Attach the lace edging to three sides of 6$^3/_4$" by 9$^1/_4$"(two short sides and one long side) (fig. 4).

5. Lay the tucked piece on top of the plain piece, centering the tucked piece and matching the raw edges.

6. Treating the two pieces as one, run gathering threads in the top at $^1/_8$" and $^1/_4$" (fig. 5).

7. Cut a bias strip 5$^1/_2$" by 1$^1/_2$". Press in half to make the strip 5$^1/_2$" by $^3/_4$". Gather the jabot to fit the band leaving $^1/_4$" extended on each side the of band. Place the bias strip on the top of the right side of the Jabot matching the raw edges, Sew the band to the Jabot with a $^1/_4$" seam (fig. 6). Flip the bias up and fold the $^1/_4$" ends of the bias strips toward the strip over the fabric (fig. 7). Fold the bias band to wrong side enclosing the seam and whip to the seam line to finish (fig. 8).

8. Place the center of the jabot to the center front neckline under the collar. Whip the jabot in place following the neckline curve (fig. 9).

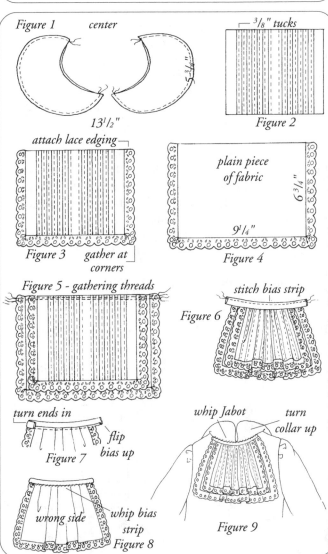

Figure 1    center

13$^1/_2$"

— $^3/_8$" tucks

Figure 2

attach lace edging —

Figure 3    gather at corners

plain piece of fabric

6$^3/_4$"

9$^1/_4$"

Figure 4

Figure 5 - gathering threads

stitch bias strip

Figure 6

turn ends in

flip bias up

Figure 7

whip Jabot    turn collar up

wrong side    whip bias strip

Figure 8

Figure 9

# David's Shirt

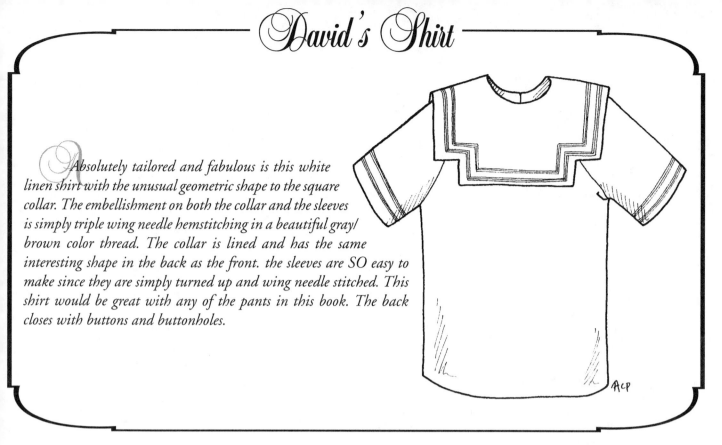

*Absolutely tailored and fabulous is this white linen shirt with the unusual geometric shape to the square collar. The embellishment on both the collar and the sleeves is simply triple wing needle hemstitching in a beautiful gray/brown color thread. The collar is lined and has the same interesting shape in the back as the front. the sleeves are SO easy to make since they are simply turned up and wing needle stitched. This shirt would be great with any of the pants in this book. The back closes with buttons and buttonholes.*

## Fabric Requirements

|  | Sizes 1-2 | Sizes 3-4 | Sizes 6-8 |
|---|---|---|---|
| White linen 45" | 1¼ yds | 1⅜ yds | 1½ yds |
| (for long sleeves, add ¼ yd) | | | |
| Buttons ½" | 5 | 5 | 5 |

Gray machine embroidery thread
Wing needle 100/16
All seams are ¼". Finish seams with a zigzag stitch or serger.

## Pattern Pieces

All pattern pieces are found in the pattern envelope.
Shirt front, shirt button back, square collar, shirt short sleeve
Template: Square Corner Collar template found on this page

## Cutting

Cut one shirt front on the fold, two shirt button backs on the selvage, two square collars (remove the fabric from each corner using the square corner template so that collar looks like fig. 1), two short sleeves on fold line #2 and bias neck facing 1" by neck measurement.

## Construction

1. Place the collars with right sides together and stitch together (fig. 1). Trim and clip seam. Turn to the right side and press.
2. A triple entredeux stitch using a wing needle is done ½" from the finished edge following the outline of the collar. A second row is done ½" from first row of stitching (fig. 2).
3. Place the right side of the front to the right side of the backs at the shoulders. Sew shoulder seams with a ¼" seam (fig. 3).
4. Place the wrong side of the collar to the right side of the shirt. The back edges of the collar should not extend beyond the center back lines of the back shirt. Fold the back edges of the shirt to the right side along the fold lines. The back edges of the collar will be sandwiched between the back folded edges of the facing and the shirt (fig. 4).

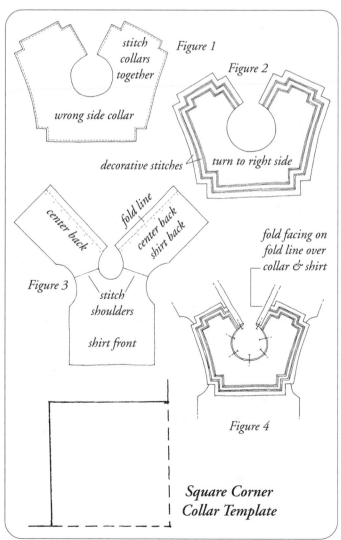

stitch collars together

*Figure 1*

wrong side collar

*Figure 2*

decorative stitches

turn to right side

center back

fold line

center back shirt back

*Figure 3*

stitch shoulders

shirt front

fold facing on fold line over collar & shirt

*Figure 4*

*Square Corner Collar Template*

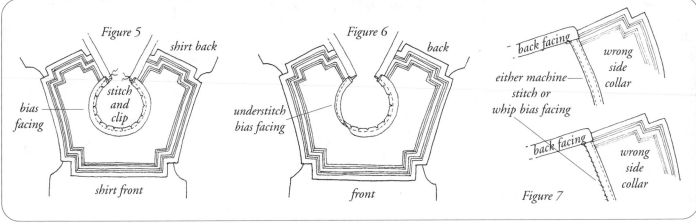

Figure 5 — stitch and clip — shirt back — bias facing — shirt front

Figure 6 — understitch bias facing — back — front

Figure 7 — back facing — wrong side collar — either machine stitch or whip bias facing — back facing — wrong side collar

5. Fold the bias neck facing in half lengthwise, with the long cut edges even. Press.

6. Place the bias strip to the right side of the bodice with both long edges of the strip even with the neck edge. The strip will be placed over the collar and the folded back facings (fig. 5).

7. Stitch all layers together using a $1/4$" seam. Trim and clip the seam allowance (fig. 5).

8. Press the bias strip away from the shirt, toward the seam allowance. Understitch (fig. 6)

9. Flip the back facings to the inside of the shirt. Fold the bias strip to the inside of the shirt creating a facing. The bias strip will not show on the right side of the shirt. Press

10. With the collar away from the shirt, stitch the binding to the bodice by hand or machine (fig. 7).

11. Fold the hem of the sleeve to inside with wrong sides together (fig. 8). Press.

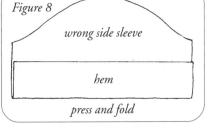

Figure 8 — wrong side sleeve — hem — press and fold

12. Decorative stitching is done on the right side of the sleeve $1/2$" from the folded cuff edge and a second row $3/8$" above the previous row. Trim extra hem fabric from above the last row of decorative stitching (fig. 9).

13. Fit the sleeve to the armhole and stitch in place (fig. 10).

14. Place the sides of shirt together matching the underarm seam and the bottom of sleeve. Sew the side shirt and the sleeve seam (fig. 11).

15. Finish the bottom edge of the shirt as follows: with the facings open, fold up $1/4$" and press. Fold up $1/4$" again and press, creating a narrow hem. Fold the facings along the fold line and stitch the hem in place (fig. 12 & 13).

16. Position the buttonholes on the left hand side by placing a dot $1/2$" from the top fabric edge of the neckline and $1/2$" over from the fold line (fig. 14).

17. Place a dot every 3" down the back of the shirt $1/2$" from the fold.

18. Stitch a $1/2$" buttonhole beginning at the dot and placing the buttonholes horizontally (fig. 14). Continue the buttonholes down the back of the shirt. Cut the buttonholes open with a buttonhole cutter or seam ripper.

19. Lap the left side of the blouse over the right side and mark the placement for the buttons (fig. 14).

20. Attach the buttons along the marks on the right side of the shirt.

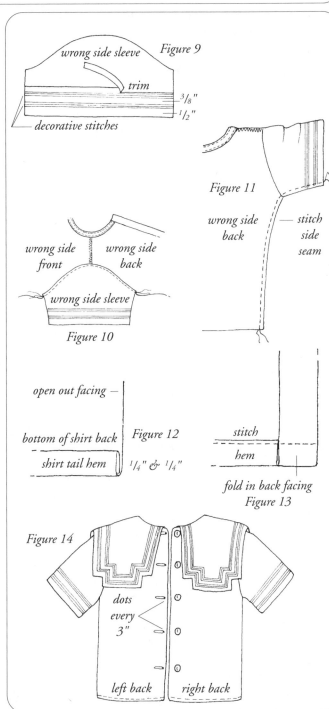

Figure 9 — wrong side sleeve — trim — $3/8$" — $1/2$" — decorative stitches

Figure 11 — wrong side back — stitch side seam

Figure 10 — wrong side front — wrong side back — wrong side sleeve

Figure 12 — open out facing — bottom of shirt back — shirt tail hem — $1/4$" & $1/4$"

Figure 13 — stitch — hem — fold in back facing

Figure 14 — dots every 3" — left back — right back

# Ward's Bias Trim Shirt

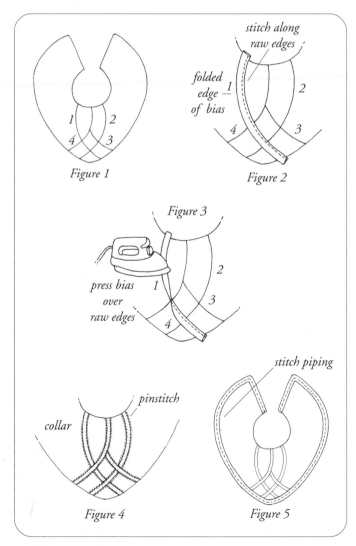

$\mathscr{B}$lack has long been one of my favorite colors for older children. This adorable little shirt has a wonderful rounded v-collar with bias piping in a tan and black gingham fabric around the collar. The bias trim embellishing the front of the collar is made with the same tan and black gingham fabric. This piping is also used at the top of the cuff on the sleeves. The bias trim on the front of the collar almost looks like Celtic shaping since one piece goes under and the next piece over the other strips of bias. The bias trim on the collar has been stitched down with a tiny pinstitch although a little zigzag would be acceptable also. The back of the shirt is trimmed with buttons and buttonholes and this shirt would be great with any of the pants in this book.

Pants shown in the illustration
are the Pleated Front Knickers.

## Fabric Requirements

|  | Sizes 1-2 | Sizes 3-4 | Sizes 6-8 |
|---|---|---|---|
| Black Fabric 45" | 1¼ yds | 1³⁄₈ yds | 1½ yds |
| (for long sleeves, add ¼" yd) | | | |
| ½ yard Check Fabric | | | |
| Cording | 2 yds | 2 yds | 2 yds |
| Black Buttons | 5 | 5 | 5 |

All seams are ¼". Finish seams with a zigzag stitch or serger.

## Pattern Pieces

All pattern pieces are found in the pattern envelope.
Shirt front, shirt button back, pointed collar, shirt short sleeve
Template: Bias collar template found at the end of these instructions

## Cutting

Cut one shirt front on the fold, two shirt backs on the selvage, two short sleeves on second fold line, two pointed collars and a bias neck strip 1" by neck measurement. Cut 3½ yards of ¾" bias from the check fabric. Make two yards of piping to be used around the collar and the sleeves. Fold the remaining bias in half and press.

## Construction

1. Trace the template design of the bias on the right side of one of the collars (fig. 1). Shape the folded bias on the template lines in the order that the lines are numbered. Bias is shaped with the raw edges extended ⅛" over the template line. Sew the bias in place ⅛" from the raw edge (fig. 2). After the strip is stitched in place the bias is pressed over the raw edges (fig. 3). Both folded edges are then stitched down with a pinstitch (fig. 4).
2. Shape piping around the outer edge of the collar ¼" from the edge. Stitch in place (fig. 5).
3. Place the collars with the right sides together, the piping will be sandwiched between the collars, and stitch together using the seam in step 2 as a guide and stitching just inside. Trim and clip the seam (fig. 6). Turn to the right side and press.

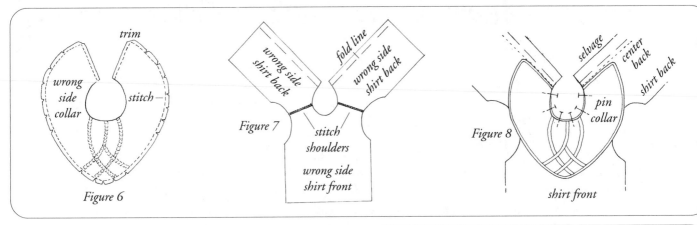

Figure 6

Figure 7

Figure 8

4. Place the right side of the front to the right side of the backs at the shoulders. Sew shoulder seams (fig. 7).

5. Place the wrong side of the collar to the right side of the shirt. The back edges of the collar should not extend beyond the center back lines of the back shirt (fig. 8). Fold the back edges of the shirt to the right side along the fold lines. The back edges of the collar will be sandwiched between the back folded edges of the facing and the shirt (fig. 9).

6. Fold the bias in half lengthwise, with the long cut edges even. Press.

7. Place the bias strip to the right side of the bodice with both long edges of the strip even with the neck edge. The strip will be placed over the collar and the folded back facings (fig. 9).

8. Stitch all layers together using a 1/4" seam. Trim and clip the seam allowance (fig. 9).

9. Press the bias strip away from the shirt, toward the seam allowance. Understitch (fig. 10).

10. Flip the back facings to the inside of the shirt. Fold the bias strip to the inside of the shirt creating a facing. The bias strip will not show on the right side of the shirt. Press.

11. With the collar away from the shirt, stitch the binding to the bodice by hand or machine (fig. 11).

12. Sew piping to the bottom edge of the wrong side of the sleeve by matching the raw edges of the piping with the raw edge of the sleeve (fig. 12).

13. Turn the raw edges to the right side with the piping on the bottom edge (fig. 13). Press seam in place.

14. Fold the cuff to the right side on the fold line. (fig. 14). Stitch the cuff in place by stitching in the ditch where the piping was attached.

15. Fit the sleeve to the armhole and stitch in place (fig. 15).

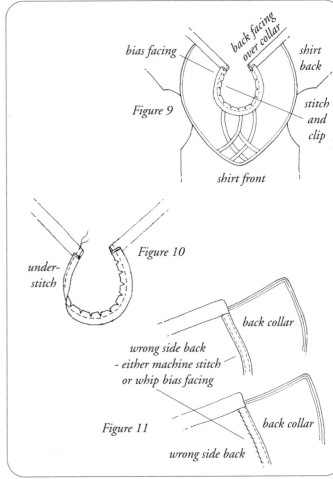

Figure 9

Figure 10

Figure 11

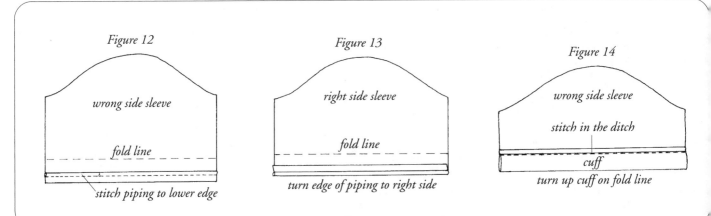

Figure 12

wrong side sleeve

fold line

stitch piping to lower edge

Figure 13

right side sleeve

fold line

turn edge of piping to right side

Figure 14

wrong side sleeve

stitch in the ditch

cuff

turn up cuff on fold line

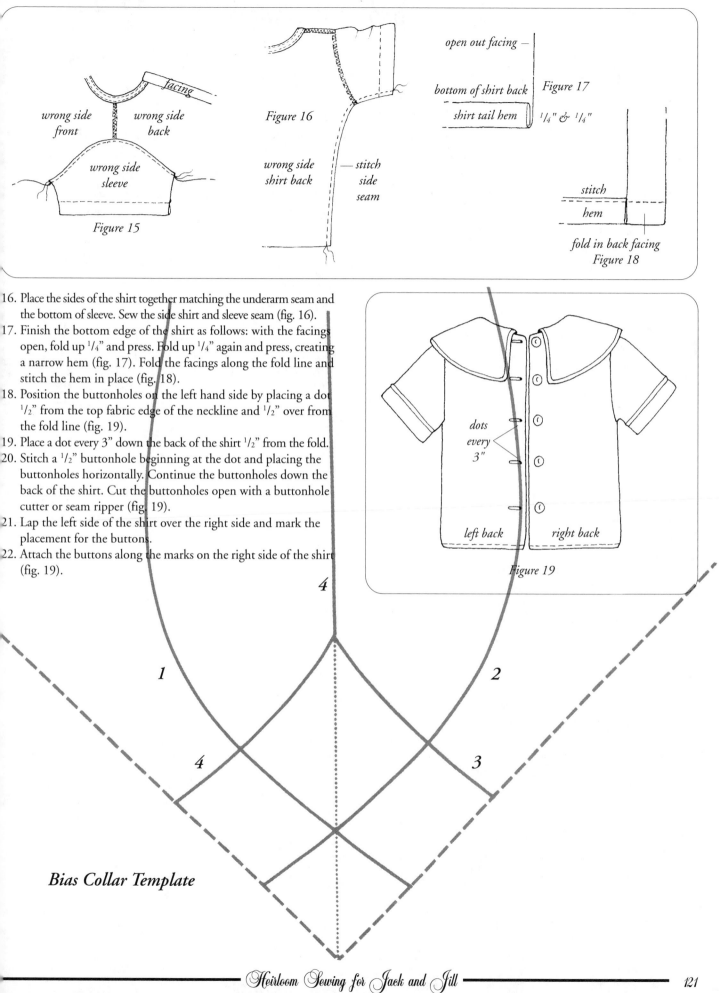

wrong side front

wrong side back

facing

wrong side sleeve

Figure 15

Figure 16

wrong side shirt back

— stitch side seam

open out facing —

bottom of shirt back

shirt tail hem

Figure 17

$^1/_4$" & $^1/_4$"

stitch

hem

fold in back facing
Figure 18

16. Place the sides of the shirt together matching the underarm seam and the bottom of sleeve. Sew the side shirt and sleeve seam (fig. 16).

17. Finish the bottom edge of the shirt as follows: with the facings open, fold up $^1/_4$" and press. Fold up $^1/_4$" again and press, creating a narrow hem (fig. 17). Fold the facings along the fold line and stitch the hem in place (fig. 18).

18. Position the buttonholes on the left hand side by placing a dot $^1/_2$" from the top fabric edge of the neckline and $^1/_2$" over from the fold line (fig. 19).

19. Place a dot every 3" down the back of the shirt $^1/_2$" from the fold.

20. Stitch a $^1/_2$" buttonhole beginning at the dot and placing the buttonholes horizontally. Continue the buttonholes down the back of the shirt. Cut the buttonholes open with a buttonhole cutter or seam ripper (fig. 19).

21. Lap the left side of the shirt over the right side and mark the placement for the buttons.

22. Attach the buttons along the marks on the right side of the shirt (fig. 19).

dots every 3"

left back          right back

Figure 19

Bias Collar Template

1    4    2    3

4

# Tied Sailor Collar Shirt

Designed after one of my antique boy sailor suits, this navy blue linen shirt has a very unusual collar. It has built in ties which indeed tie in a scout knot on the front. The shirt is a slip over shirt rather than one which closes with buttons and buttonholes. The beautiful red and navy plaid bias trim strips make Celtic loops around the sailor collar. The front closes with a hook and eye in the front right under the place where the ties are tied. The sleeves are simply turned up and the bias plaid trim is stitched on top. All of the bias plaid strips are stitched down using a pin-stitch; however, a zigzag stitch would be acceptable if you do not have a pin-stitch on your machine. What a magnificent shirt to be worn either tucked in or on the outside. The antique suit from my collection intended for the shirt to be worn on the outside. The sailor look has been in fashion since the mid 1800s and I believe it will always be worn in high fashion. This shirt would be just as cute for little girls as it is for boys.

Pants shown in the illustration are the Straight Front Knee Pants.

## Fabric Requirements

|  | Sizes 1-2 | Sizes 3-4 | Sizes 5-6 |
|---|---|---|---|
| Navy Linen 45" | 1$^1$/$_4$ yds. | 1$^3$/$_8$ yds. | 1$^1$/$_2$ yds. |

(Add 1/4 yd. to all sizes for long sleeves.)

| | | | |
|---|---|---|---|
| Plaid for Bias | $^1$/$_2$ yd. | $^1$/$_2$ yd. | $^1$/$_2$ yd. |

$^1$/$_4$" bias tape maker
Hook and eye

## Pattern Pieces

All pattern pieces are found in the pattern envelope.
Sailor shirt pull-over front, shirt back, shirt short sleeve, pull-over shirt sailor collar.
Template: Sailor bias template found in pattern envelope
All seams $^1$/$_4$". Finish seams with a zigzag stitch or serger.

## Cutting

Cut one pull-over shirt back placing center back on fold line, one pull-over shirt front on fold line, two shirt sleeves on fold line #2, 2 pull-over shirt sailor collars, one bias neck band 1" wide by neck measurement plus 1", from the selvage a strip $^3$/$_4$" wide by 5" for the placket. Cut 3$^1$/$_2$ yards of $^1$/$_2$" bias from the plaid fabric.

## Construction

1. Trace the template design for the bias on the right side of one of the collars starting from the back corners and repeating the design to the front edge. Adjust the template as needed. (fig. 1).

2. Sew the bias strips together to create one long strip with a $^1$/$_4$" seam (fig. 2). Feed the bias strip into the wide end of the $^1$/$_4$" bias tape maker. Secure the end of the bias tape to the ironing board with a pin. Pull the tape maker and press the bias tape as it comes through the opening (fig. 3).

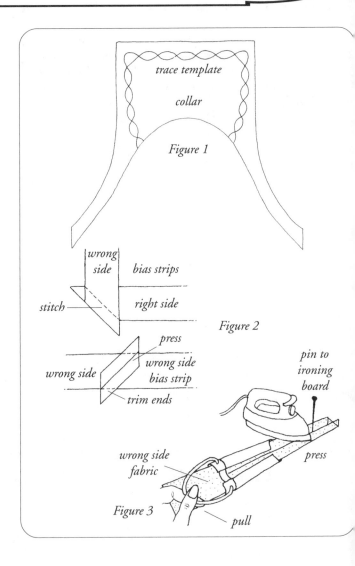

*trace template*

*collar*

*Figure 1*

wrong side — bias strips

stitch — right side

*Figure 2*

press

wrong side bias strip

wrong side

trim ends

pin to ironing board

wrong side fabric

press

*Figure 3*

pull

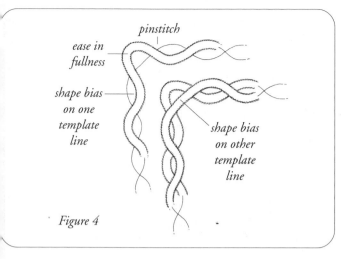

Figure 4

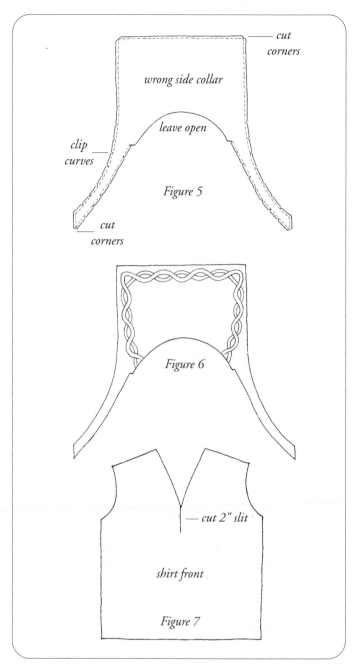

Figure 5

Figure 6

— cut 2" slit

shirt front

Figure 7

3. Shape the folded bias on the template lines by centering the bias strip over the template lines. Shape one line at a time as shown. (fig. 4). The folded edge is then stitched down on the edge with a pinstitch on both sides of the bias (fig. 4). Complete all of the bias shaping.

4. Place the collars with right sides together and stitch around the collar and ties leaving open between the dots at the neck edge. Trim and clip the seam (fig. 5). Turn the collar right side out and press (fig. 6).

5. To make the placket in the center front, cut a 2" slit down the center front of the shirt (fig. 7). Cut a strip of fabric from the selvage 5" by $^3/_4$". Pull the slit in the shirt apart to form a "V". Place the right side of the strip to the right side of the shirt slit, cut edge to cut edge (fig. 8). The stitching will be done from the wrong side with the shirt on top and the placket strip on the bottom. The placket strip will be straight and the shirt will form a "V" with the point of the "V" $^1/_4$" from the edge of the placket. Stitch, using a $^1/_4$" seam. It is important to catch a few fibers in the seam at the point of the "V" (fig. 8). Press the seam allowance toward the selvage edge of the placket strip. Turn the selvage edge to the inside of the shirt, enclosing the seam allowance. Stitch in place by hand or machine (fig. 9). Fold the right side of the placket to the inside of the shirt and pin. Leave the left side of the placket open (fig. 10). On the inside of the placket, stitch the placket at

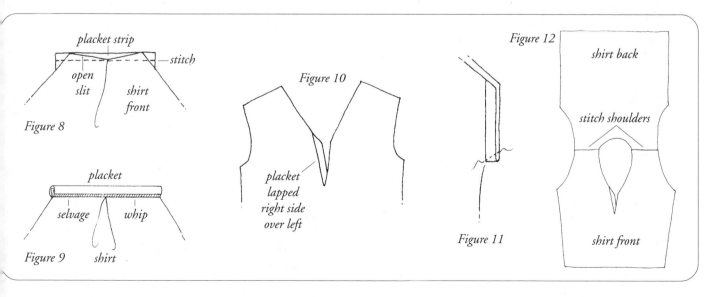

Figure 8

Figure 9

Figure 10

Figure 11

Figure 12

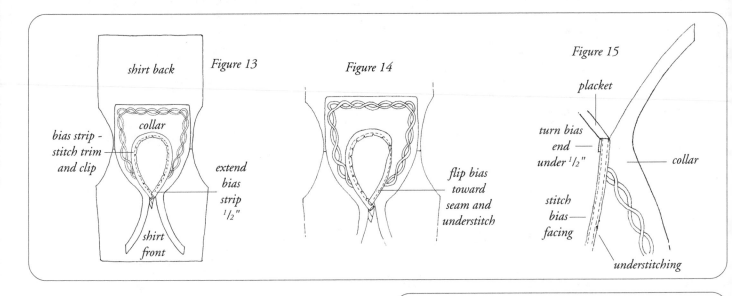

Figure 13

Figure 14

Figure 15

shirt back

collar

bias strip -
stitch trim
and clip

extend
bias
strip
½"

shirt
front

flip bias
toward
seam and
understitch

placket

turn bias
end
under ½"

collar

stitch
bias
facing

understitching

an angle from the lower inside edge to the folded edges (fig. 11).

6. Sew the back to the front at the shoulder seams (fig. 12).

7. Place the collar to the neck opening with the wrong side of the collar to the right side of the shirt. The left side of the placket will be extended and the right side folded back (fig. 13).

8. Fold the bias neck strip in half and press. Place the cut edges of the strip to the neck of the collar/bodice extending the bias strip ½" at the slit edge (fig. 13).

9. Stitch the bias strip to the neck edge using a ¼" seam.

10. Trim the seam to ⅛". Clip the neck edge and understitch the bias band. Understitching is done by stitching through the bias band and the trimmed seams (fig. 14).

11. Fold the ½" of bias under. Holding the collar away from the bodice, stitch the facing to the bodice (fig. 15).

12. Fold the hem on the sleeve to right side and stitch in place (fig. 16). Cover the raw edge of the sleeve hem with the bias tape. (fig. 17). Pinstitch the bias over the seam stitching on both sides of the tape (fig. 17).

13. Fit the sleeve to the armhole and stitch in place (fig. 18).

14. Place the right sides together at the sides and the sleeves matching the underarm seams. Sew the side seams from the bottom of the sleeve to the bottom of the shirt (fig. 19).

15. Finish the bottom edge of the shirt as follows: with the facing open, fold up ¼" and press. Fold up ¼" again and press, creating a narrow hem (fig. 20). Fold the facings along the fold line and stitch the hem in place (fig. 21).

16. Sew a hook and eye at the top of the placket opening (fig. 22).

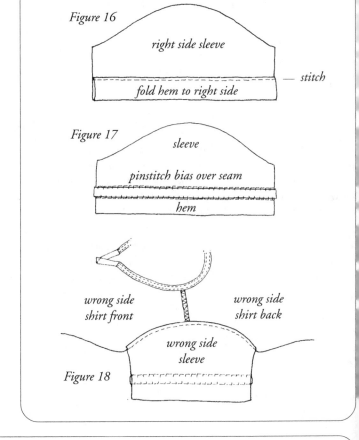

Figure 16

right side sleeve

stitch

fold hem to right side

Figure 17

sleeve

pinstitch bias over seam

hem

wrong side
shirt front

wrong side
shirt back

wrong side
shirt front

wrong side
shirt back

wrong side
sleeve

Figure 18

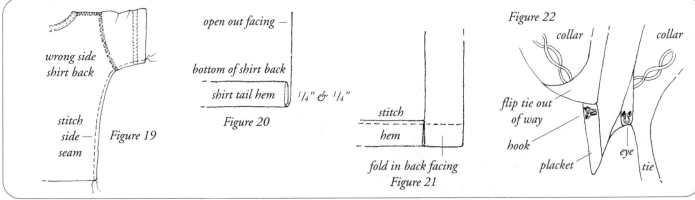

wrong side
shirt back

stitch
side
seam

Figure 19

open out facing

bottom of shirt back

shirt tail hem

¼" & ¼"

Figure 20

stitch

hem

fold in back facing

Figure 21

Figure 22

collar

collar

flip tie out
of way

hook

placket

eye

tie

# White Shirt with Plaid Madeira Border

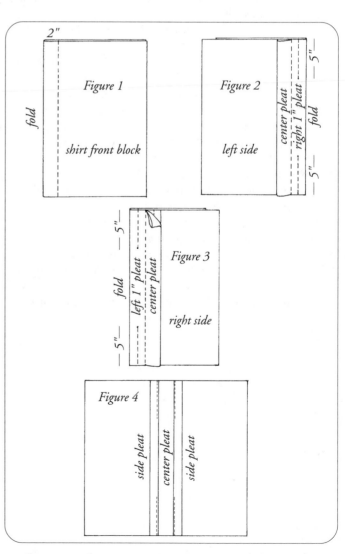

*This has to be one of my favorite shirts in the whole Jack and Jill book. I adore Madeira borders for men, women, girls and boys. This collar is simply fabulous. The shirt is made of white Victorian batiste (cotton broadcloth); the plaid Madeira border is made of plaid featuring marine blue, light blue, pink and yellow. This suit just speaks, "Make me for Easter." The front of the shirt has three wonderful pleats and there is a machine embroidered monogram on the center of the shirt in a marine blue. Long sleeves make this a wonderful shirt for year round wear unless you live in Arizona or South Florida! The back closes with buttons and buttonholes and the shirt can be worn with any of the pants in this book.*

Pants shown in the illustration
are the Pleated Front Knickers.

## Fabric Requirements

|  | Sizes 1-2 | Sizes 3-4 | Sizes 6-8 |
|---|---|---|---|
| Cotton fabric 45" | 1¹/₂ yds. | 1³/₄yds. | 1³/₄yds. |
| Plaid fabric | ¹/₃ yd. | ¹/₃ yd. | ¹/₃ yd. |

Thread for monogram to match fabric

6) - ⁵/₈" buttons

2) - ³/₄" buttons

2) - ³/₈" buttons

Wash-away basting thread

## Pattern Pieces

All pattern pieces are found in the pattern envelope.

Button back shirt, shirt front, long sleeve, long sleeve cuff, square collar

Templates: Madeira appliqué template found in the pattern envelope, curved collar corner template found at the end of these directions, Monogram found in Million Different Variations Shirt instructions.

All seams ¹/₄". Finish seams with zigzag stitch or serger.

## Cutting

From the white cotton, cut: a block of fabric 7" wider than the shirt front pattern and 1" longer, fold in half and mark the fold indicating the center front. Cut a square of fabric 2" larger than the collar pattern. Cut two long sleeves, two long sleeve cuffs, 2 shirt backs on the selvage and one bias strip 1" wide by the neck measurement.

## Construction

Fold the width of the shirt front block in half along the fold. Stitch a seam 2" from the folded edge down the fabric. This will make the center pleat (fig. 1).

On the right side of the fabric make another fold 2" from the stitching line of the first fold. Press this fold in place. Secure the fold in place 1" from the folded edge by stitching 5" down from the top and 5" up from the bottom (fig. 2). Make another fold on the left side following the same directions (fig. 3).

Lay the block out flat and press the center pleat in the middle so that it is evenly spaced between the two side pleats (fig. 4). Refold

Figure 1
fold
shirt front block
2"

Figure 2
left side
center pleat
right 1" pleat
fold
5"
5"

Figure 3
fold
left 1" pleat
center pleat
right side
5"
5"

Figure 4
side pleat
center pleat
side pleat

the block in half and place the shirt front pattern on the fold (fig. 5). Cut out the shirt front.

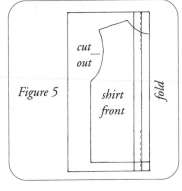

*Figure 5*

4. Press the facing to the wrong side on each of the back pieces. Place the backs to the front at the shoulder seam with right sides together and sew the shoulder seams with a ¹/₄" seam (fig. 6).

5. Place the curved collar corner template on the outer front and outer back corners of the square collar pattern (fig. 7a). Trace creating a shaped square collar. Trace a line 1¹/₂" inside the collar edge for the Madeira border (fig. 7b). (Trace the shaped square collar on the collar fabric.) Mark the center front of the collar and stitch the monogram by hand or machine. Cut out the collar.

6. Refer to the techniques, Magic Madeira Appliqué and stitch the Madeira appliqué border on the collar.

7. Hem the back edges of the collar with a small hem (fig. 8).

8. Place the wrong side of the collar to the right side of the shirt. The back edges of the collar should not extend beyond the center back lines of the shirt back. Fold the back edges of the shirt to the right side along the fold lines. The back edges of the collar will be sandwiched between the back folded edges of the facing and the shirt (fig. 9).

9. Fold the bias neck strip in half lengthwise, with the long cut edges even. Press.

10. Place the bias strip to the right side of the bodice with both long edges of the strip even with the neck edge. The strip will be placed over the collar and the folded back facings (fig. 9).

11. Stitch all layers together using a ¹/₄" seam. Trim and clip the seam allowance (fig. 9).

12. Press the bias strip away from the shirt, toward the seam allowance, and understitch (fig. 10).

13. Flip the back facings to the inside of the shirt. Fold the bias strip to the inside of the shirt creating a facing. The bias strip will not show on the right side of the shirt. Press

14. With the collar away from the shirt, stitch the bias binding to the bodice by hand or machine (fig. 11).

15. Fit the sleeves to the armholes and sew the sleeves in place (fig. 12).

16. Place the sides of the shirt together matching the underarm seam and the bottom of the sleeve. Sew the side shirt and the sleeve seam stopping the sleeve seam at the dot. This opening will form

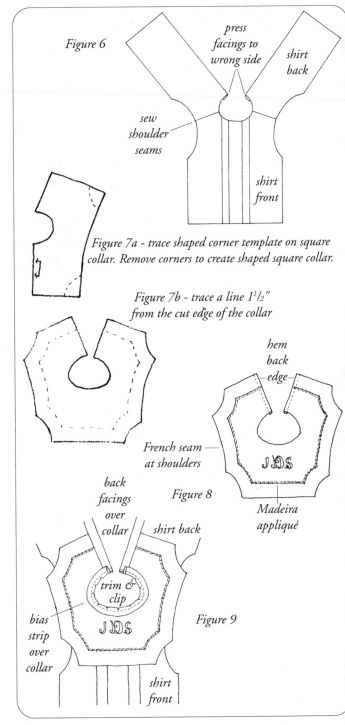

*Figure 6*

press facings to wrong side

shirt back

sew shoulder seams

shirt front

*Figure 7a - trace shaped corner template on square collar. Remove corners to create shaped square collar.*

*Figure 7b - trace a line 1¹/₂" from the cut edge of the collar*

hem back edge

French seam at shoulders

*Figure 8*

Madeira appliqué

back facings over collar

shirt back

trim & clip

bias strip over collar

*Figure 9*

shirt front

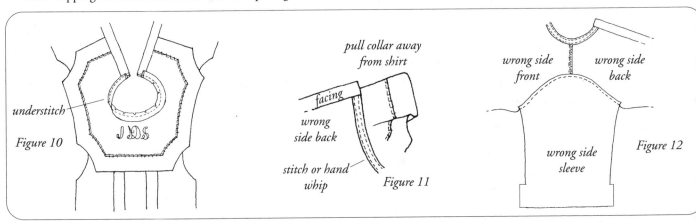

understitch

*Figure 10*

pull collar away from shirt

facing

wrong side back

stitch or hand whip

*Figure 11*

wrong side front

wrong side back

wrong side sleeve

*Figure 12*

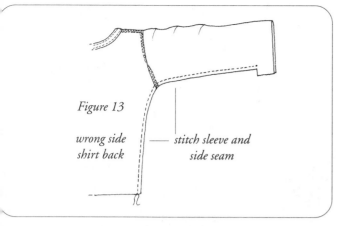

Figure 13

*wrong side shirt back* — *stitch sleeve and side seam*

the placket for the sleeve (fig. 13). Finish the sleeve seam edges for the placket by turning in ¹/₄" and press and ¹/₄" again and stitching the seams to the inside by hand or machine (fig. 14 ).

7. Fit the bottom of the sleeve to the cuff. Place two folds in the bottom of the sleeve to make the sleeve fit the cuff. The cuff will extend ¹/₄" on each side of the cuff. Stitch the cuff in place (fig. 15).

8. Turn under ¹/₄" along the unfinished edge of the cuff to the wrong side and press. Turn the cuff to the outside folding it in half with the right sides together and sew the sides of the cuff. The sides will be flush with the sleeve placket. (fig. 16 ).

9. Flip the cuff to the wrong side. The folded edge of the cuff will meet the stitching line for the cuff. Hand-whip the cuff in place (fig. 17).

10. Make buttonholes in the cuffs and sew on buttons (fig. 18).

11. Finish the bottom edge of the shirt as follows: with the facings open, fold up ¹/₄" and press. Fold up ¹/₄" again and press, creating a narrow hem (fig. 19). Fold the facings along the fold line and stitch the hem in place (fig. 20).

12. Position the buttonholes on the left hand side by placing a dot ¹/₂" from the top fabric edge of the neckline and ¹/₂" over from the fold line.

13. Place a dot every 3" down the back of the shirt ¹/₂" from the fold (fig. 21).

14. Stitch a ¹/₂" buttonhole beginning at the dot and placing the buttonholes horizontally. Continue the buttonholes down the back of the shirt. Cut the buttonholes open with a buttonhole cutter or seam ripper (fig. 21).

15. Lap the left side of the shirt over the right side and mark the placement for the buttons.

16. Attach the buttons along the marks on the right side of the shirt.

17. Fit the garment to the child and mark placement for buttons at the waist. If the child is not available, refer to the waistline marking on the pattern and the buttonhole placement on the pants to determine the button placement. Make a ¹/₂" pleat behind the button placement mark. Sew buttons in place. A piece of twill tape may be placed on the wrong side behind the button for more stability.

**Curved Corner Collar Template**

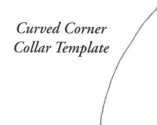

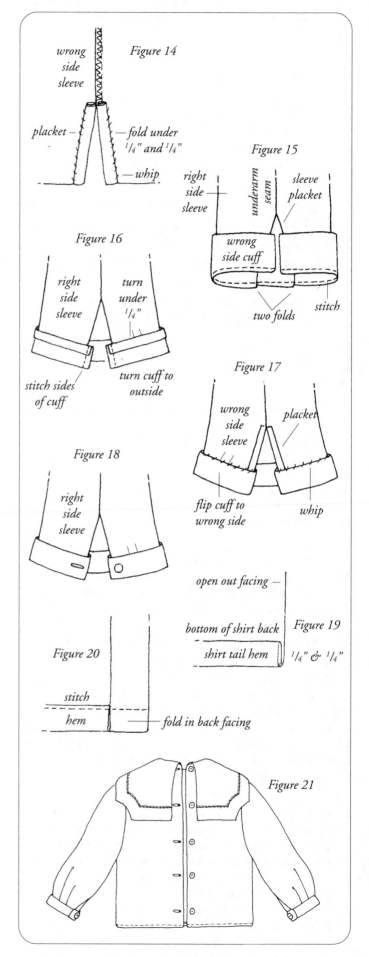

Figure 14

*wrong side sleeve*

*placket* — *fold under ¹/₄" and ¹/₄"* — *whip*

Figure 15

*right side sleeve* *underarm seam* *sleeve placket*

*wrong side cuff*

*two folds* *stitch*

Figure 16

*right side sleeve* *turn under ¹/₄"*

*stitch sides of cuff* *turn cuff to outside*

Figure 17

*wrong side sleeve* *placket*

*flip cuff to wrong side* *whip*

Figure 18

*right side sleeve*

Figure 19

*open out facing* — *bottom of shirt back* *shirt tail hem* ¹/₄" & ¹/₄"

Figure 20

*stitch* *hem* *fold in back facing*

Figure 21

# Tucked Panel Lapel Shirt

*Folded tucks ³/₈" wide are found in the panel of this white linen lapel shirt. The lapels are of a black and white gingham and have wonderful stitching done in red thread. The shirt sleeves cuffs are black and white gingham with the same red machine stitching. The look of black, white and red is very crisp and very tailored since there is no lace on this shirt. The back of the collar is shaped like a sailor collar. It buttons in the back with black buttons and buttonholes. This shirt could be used with any of the pants in this book. Note: ¹/₂" ribbon can be used to embellish the collar and sleeves instead of machine embroidery. Three yards will be needed.*

## Fabric Requirements

|  | Sizes 1-2 | Sizes 3-4 | Sizes 6-8 |
|---|---|---|---|
| White Fabric 45" | 1¹/₄ yd | 1¹/₂ yd | 1⁵/₈ yd |
| (Add ¹/₄ yd to all sizes for long sleeves) | | | |
| Black check fabric | ¹/₂ yd | ¹/₂ yd | ¹/₂ yd |
| Red embroidery thread | | | |
| Buttons ¹/₂" | 5 | 5 | 5 |

## Pattern Pieces

All pattern pieces are found in the pattern envelope.
Lapel collar center front panel, lapel collar, lapel collar side front, shirt button back, short shirt sleeve, short sleeve cuff.

All seams ¹/₄". Finish all seams with a zigzag stitch or serger.

## Cutting

Cut a piece of fabric 2" wider and 14" longer than the lapel collar center front panel. Cut out two collars from the black check fabric and two collars from the white for collar lining. Cut out two short sleeve cuffs from the black check 3¹/₂" by the bottom cuff measurement. Cut out two short sleeves on fold line #1, two side fronts and two backs on the selvage from the white, and one bias neck facing 1" wide by the neck measurement.

## Construction

1. On the piece of fabric cut for the front panel, make the first tuck by measuring 4" down from the top edge of the fabric and press a fold in the fabric. Measure 1¹/₂" down from the fold line and press in another fold. Measure 1¹/₂" down from this fold line and press in another fold. Continue this until there are 14 fold lines pressed in the fabric (fig. 1).

2. Sew a tuck at each fold line ³/₈" from the folded edge. Make fourteen tucks (fig. 2).

3. Place the pattern for the lapel collar center front panel on the tucked fabric with the center front neck edge 2¹/₂" down from

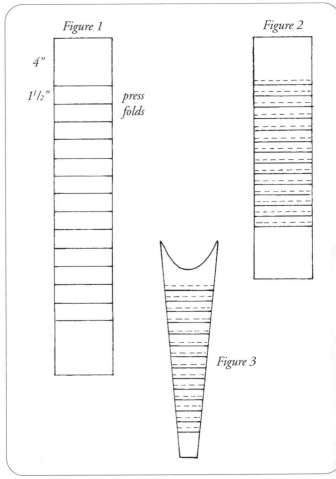

Figure 1

4"

1¹/₂"

press folds

Figure 2

Figure 3

the top edge of the fabric and cut out panel (fig. 3).

4. Place the right side of the check collar to the right side of the white collar fabric. Sew together with a ¹/₄" seam. Trim and cli

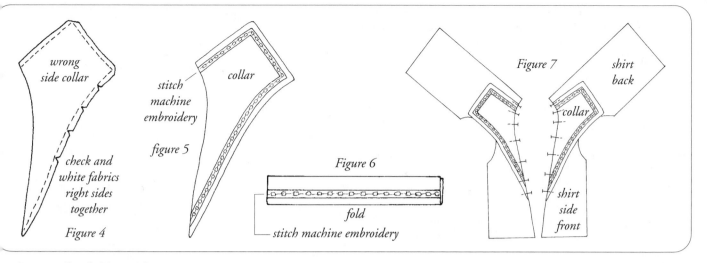

wrong side collar

check and white fabrics right sides together

Figure 4

stitch machine embroidery

collar

figure 5

Figure 6

fold

stitch machine embroidery

Figure 7

shirt back

collar

shirt side front

the seam (fig. 4). Turn and press.

The machine embroidery consists of two rows of satin stitching with a row of satin stitched dots between the rows. Practice on a scrap piece of fabric to determine the width and length of the satin stitch desired. The outside line of the satin stitch is done $^1/_2$" to the inside for the finished edge of the collar. The design should cover approximately $^1/_2$" (fig. 5).

Fold the cuffs in half with the wrong sides together along the long side. Press.

The machine embroidery is done $^3/_8$" to inside of the folded edge (fig. 6).

Place the right side of the shirt back to the right side of the shirt side front. Sew the shoulder seams with a $^1/_4$" seam allowance.

Place the finished collar to the shirt with the wrong side of the collar to the right side of the shirt. Pin the collar onto each side (fig. 7).

0. Place the front panel to one side of the shirt/collar with the right sides together and stitch in place with a $^1/_4$" seam. Sew other shirt/collar to the other side of the front panel (fig. 8).

1. Fold the bias neck strip in half lengthwise, with the long cut edges even. Press.

2. With the back folds folded to the outside of the bodice, place the cut edges of the bias strip to the cut edge of the neck. Trim the ends of the bias so that the folds of the back bodice extend $^1/_4$" beyond the edges of the bias facing. Stitch the bias strip facing in place using a $^1/_4$" seam. Trim the seam to $^1/_8$". Clip along the seam allowance (fig. 9). Press the facing toward the seam allowance and understitch (fig. 10). Fold the facing completely to the inside of the shirt, folding the back folds to the inside of the shirt. Stitch the facing in place by hand (fig. 11).

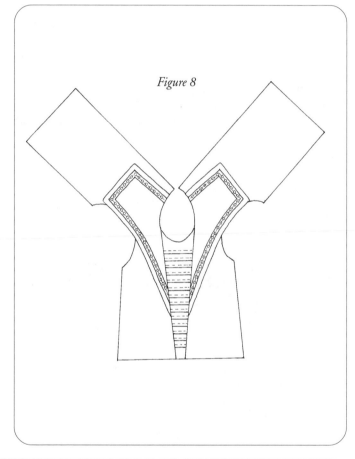

Figure 8

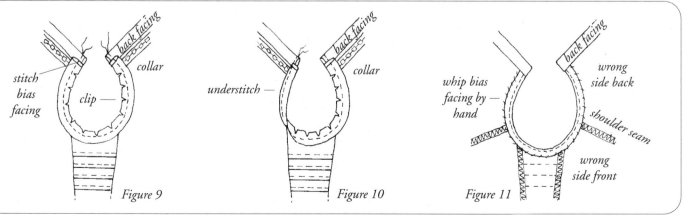

stitch bias facing

back facing

collar

clip

Figure 9

understitch

back facing

collar

Figure 10

whip bias facing by hand

back facing

wrong side back

shoulder seam

wrong side front

Figure 11

13. Place the right side of the cuff to the wrong side of the sleeve bottom matching the raw edges of the cuff to the bottom edge of the sleeve. Sew the cuff to the sleeve with a ¼" seam (fig. 12). Finish the seam. Fold the cuff to the right side enclosing the seam and press in place (fig. 13).

14. Fit the sleeve to the armhole and stitch in place (fig. 14).

15. Place the sides of shirt together matching the underarm seam and the bottom of the cuff. Sew the side shirt and sleeve seam (fig. 15).

16. Finish the bottom edge of the shirt as follows: with the facings open, fold up ¼" and press. Fold up ¼" again and press, creating a narrow hem (fig. 16). Fold the facings along the fold line and stitch the hem in place (fig. 17).

17. Position the buttonholes on the left hand side by placing a dot ½" from the top fabric edge of the neckline and ½" over from the fold line.

18. Place a dot every 3" down the back of the shirt ½" from the fold (fig. 18).

19. Stitch a ½" buttonhole beginning at the dot and placing the buttonholes horizontally. Continue the buttonholes down the back of the shirt. Cut the buttonholes open with a buttonhole cutter or seam ripper.

20. Lap the left side of the blouse over the right side and mark the placement for the buttons.

21. Attach the buttons along the marks on the right side of the shirt (fig. 18).

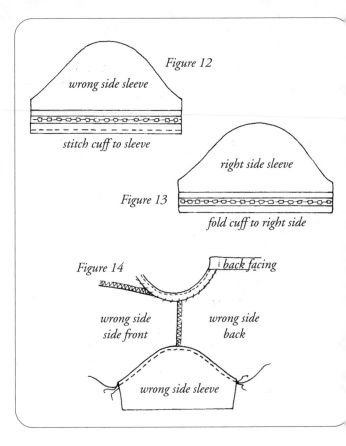

Figure 12
wrong side sleeve
stitch cuff to sleeve

Figure 13
right side sleeve
fold cuff to right side

Figure 14
back facing
wrong side side front
wrong side back
wrong side sleeve

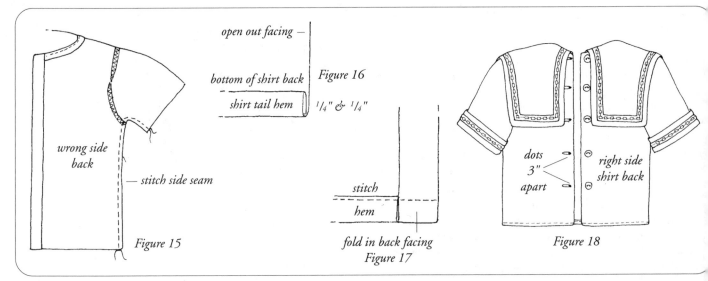

wrong side back
— stitch side seam
Figure 15

open out facing —
bottom of shirt back
shirt tail hem
Figure 16
¼" & ¼"

stitch
hem
fold in back facing
Figure 17

dots 3" apart
right side shirt back
Figure 18

# Ecru Batiste and Linen Shirt

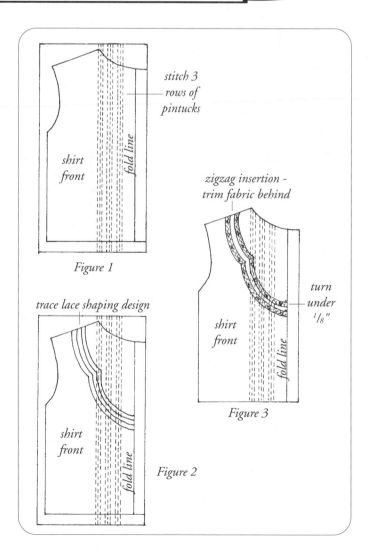

$\mathcal{M}$ade of Swiss batiste, Nelona, this ecru shirt has many fabulous details which are very interesting. The collar is made of ecru handkerchief linen. The collar has three double needle pintucks with the ecru French insertion shaped all the way around. Each side of the shirt has three sets of three double needle pintucks. Two rows of ecru French lace insertion is shaped on both sides of the front only. A very interesting use of ecru Swiss entredeux is found on this shirt. The purchased entredeux is used for the finish around the collar as well as down both sides of the front placket. This purchased ecru Swiss entredeux is also used to join the cuffs of the shirt with the sleeves. Trimmed entredeux is very masculine and this is a wonderful way to use it especially on boy's clothing. The cuffs close with two buttonholes and buttons. The shirt has buttonholes and buttons down the front and ecru pearl buttons are used down the front and on the sleeves. The fabric has been cut away from behind the laces on both the collar and the lace shaping on the shirt front.

Pants shown in the illustration are the Pleated Front Pants
(refer to the directions for the Pleated Front Knickers).

## Fabric Requirements

|  | Sizes 1-2 | Sizes 3-4 | Sizes 6-8 |
|---|---|---|---|
| Batiste 45" | $1^1/_4$ yds. | $1^3/_8$ yds. | $1^1/_2$ yds. |
| Linen | $^3/_8$ yd. | $^3/_8$ yd. | $^3/_8$ yd. |
| Insertion lace $^3/_8$" | 3 yds. | $3^1/_8$ yds. | $3^1/_4$ yds. |
| Entredeux | $2^1/_4$ yds. | $2^1/_4$ yds. | $2^1/_3$ yds. |
| Buttons - $^3/_8$" | 9 | 9 | 9 |

## Pattern Pieces

All patterns are found in the pattern envelope.
Shirt button front, shirt back, button front collar, long sleeve, long sleeve cuff
Templates: Ecru batiste lace front, Ecru batiste collar
All seams $^1/_4$". Finish seams with zigzag or serger.

## Cutting

Draw two fronts on the fabric, use the selvage edge for the facing finish, mark fold line, cut out the blocks that the fronts were drawn in larger than the drawn pattern. Embellishment will be done to fabric then the pattern will be retraced and cut out. Cut one back on the fold, two long sleeves, two cuffs, and a bias band 19" by 1" for the neck facing. Cut out one collar on the fold line from the linen.

## Embellishing Fronts and Collar

Refer to the fold line on the fronts and begin the first row of pintucks $1^1/_2$" from the fold line. Make three rows of pintucks spacing them $^1/_4$" apart. Skip over $^1/_2$" and make three more rows of pintucks. This will make the second set of pintucks. Skip over $^1/_2$" and make three rows of pintucks. This will make the third set of pintucks (fig. 1). Place the pattern on the front with the pintucks. Retrace the pattern if needed. Trace the lace shaping design onto the fronts (fig. 2). Shape the lace on the lace shaping lines. Turn under $^1/_8$" of lace where the lace shaping stops at the front fold line. Stitch the lace to the fabric using a small zigzag stitch. Trim the fabric from behind the lace. Cut out the fronts (fig. 3).

stitch 3 rows of pintucks

shirt front

fold line

*Figure 1*

trace lace shaping design

shirt front

fold line

*Figure 2*

zigzag insertion - trim fabric behind

shirt front

fold line

turn under $^1/_8$"

*Figure 3*

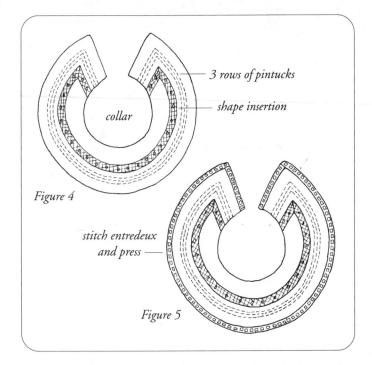

Figure 4

3 rows of pintucks

shape insertion

collar

stitch entredeux
and press

Figure 5

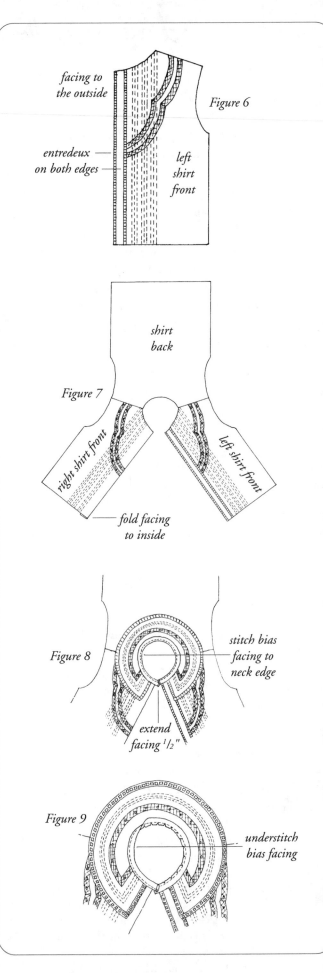

facing to
the outside

Figure 6

entredeux
on both edges

left
shirt
front

shirt
back

Figure 7

right shirt front

left shirt front

fold facing
to inside

Figure 8

stitch bias
facing to
neck edge

extend
facing ¹/₂"

Figure 9

understitch
bias facing

3. Trace the collar template onto the collar. Shape the lace on the template line. Stitch the lace to the collar using a small zigzag stitch. Stitch shaped pintucks. (fig. 4).

4. Measure around the outer edge of the collar and cut a piece of entredeux to this measurement. Stitch the entredeux to the collar on the seam line with right sides together. Refer to the technique, Entredeux to Fabric to attach the entredeux. Press the entredeux out from the collar. Trim the fabric from the outer edge of the entredeux (fig. 5).

## Construction

1. The right and left side facings are done differently. The left front facing is folded to the right side and embellished with entredeux. Place the entredeux to the outside edge of the facing, just inside the selvage edge of the facing, with right sides together. Stitch the entredeux to the fabric using the technique, Entredeux to Fabric. Press the entredeux to the right side and trim the outer edge of the fabric from the entredeux.

2. Measure the folded edge of the facing and cut a piece of entredeux to this measurement. Trim the fabric edge from one side of the entredeux. Butt the trimmed edge of the entredeux to the folded edge of the facing and stitch the entredeux to the fabric with a small zigzag stitch. Trim the outer fabric edge of the entredeux (fig. 6).

3. On the front right side, turn the facing to the wrong side on the fold line and press (fig. 7).

4. With the right sides together sew the shoulder seams.

5. Fit the collar to the neckline, pin in place. Fold the bias neck facing in half with the wrong sides together and press. Place the cut edges of the strip to the neck of the collar/bodice. Let ¹/₂" of bias strip extend from the facing line.

6. Stitch the bias strip to the neck edge using a ¹/₄" seam, starting at the fold lines on the front edges of the neckline (fig. 8).

7. Trim the seam to ¹/₈". Clip the neck edge and understitch the bias band. Understitching is done by stitching through the bias band and the trimmed seams (fig. 9).

8. Fold the extended bias strip to the inside enclosing the seam.

Holding the collar away from the shirt, stitch the facing to the shirt (fig. 10).

Fit the sleeve to the armhole and stitch in place (fig. 11).

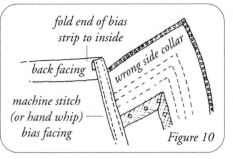

fold end of bias strip to inside

wrong side collar

back facing

machine stitch (or hand whip) bias facing

Figure 10

0. Place the sides of the shirt together matching the underarm seam and the bottom of the sleeve. Sew the side shirt and the sleeve seam stopping the sleeve seam at the dot. This opening will form the placket for the sleeve (fig. 12). Finish the sleeve seam edges for the placket by turning in ¼" and press and ¼" again and stitching the seams to the inside by hand or machine (fig. 13 ).

1. Fold the cuff in half with right sides together and stitch the ends of the cuff with a ¼" seam (fig. 14). Fold right side out and press.

2. Place entredeux to the top of the cuff with right sides together and stitch to the top of the cuff using the seam line as a guide and the technique, entredeux to fabric. Press the entredeux out (fig. 15).

3. Fit the entredeux/cuff to the bottom of the sleeve, adjusting the folds if necessary. Using the technique, entredeux to fabric, stitch the cuff to the sleeve (fig. 16).

4. Finish the bottom of the shirt with a shirttail hem.

5. Space 5 buttonholes down the front of the shirt 3" apart. Make buttonholes and sew on the buttons. The left front facing is held in place with the buttonholes (fig. 17).

6. Space 2 buttonholes on the top of the cuff. Make buttonholes and sew the button on the opposite side of the cuff (fig. 17).

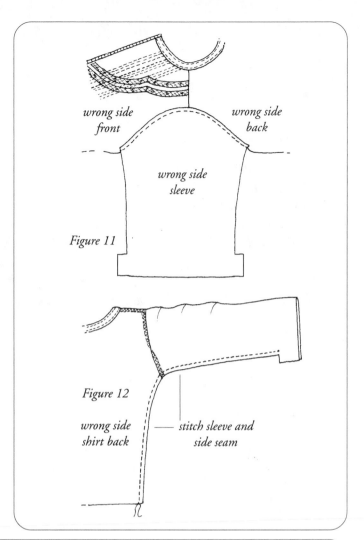

wrong side front

wrong side back

wrong side sleeve

Figure 11

Figure 12

wrong side shirt back

stitch sleeve and side seam

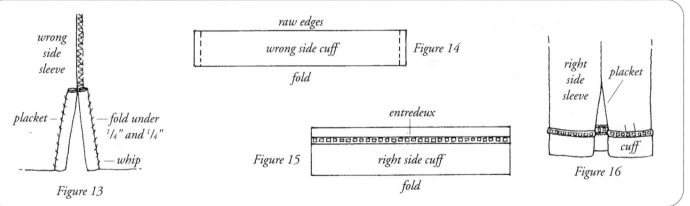

wrong side sleeve

placket

fold under ¼" and ¼"

whip

Figure 13

raw edges

wrong side cuff

Figure 14

fold

entredeux

right side cuff

Figure 15

fold

right side sleeve

placket

cuff

Figure 16

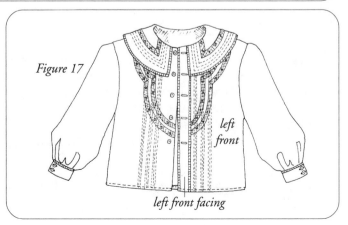

Figure 17

left front

left front facing

# Silk and Blue Linen Shirt

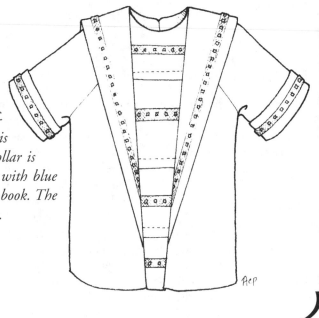

A beautiful creamy white silk batiste is the fabric for the shirt; pale blue handkerchief linen is used for the lapels and the cuffs of the shirt. The front panel has 3/8" tucks and off-white lace in-between these tucks. This off-white French lace is used to embellish the collar and the cuffs. The back of the collar is shaped like a sailor collar. This suit would be especially nice with blue linen pants and this shirt could be used with any pants in the book. The back buttons with creamy white pearl buttons and buttonholes.

## Fabric Requirements

|  | Sizes 1-2 | Sizes 3-4 | Sizes 6-8 |
|---|---|---|---|
| White Silk fabric 45" | $1^1/_8$ yds | $1^1/_4$ yds | $1^3/_8$ yds |
| (Add $1/_4$ yd to all sizes for long sleeves) | | | |
| Blue Linen fabric | $1/_2$ yd | $1/_2$ yd | $5/_8$ yd |
| Lace insertion $5/_8$" | 3 yds | 3 yds | $3^1/_8$ yds |
| Buttons $1/_2$" | 5 | 5 | 5 |

## Pattern Pieces

All pattern pieces can be found in the pattern envelope.
Lapel collar center front panel, lapel collar side shirt front, shirt button back, lapel collar, short shirt sleeve, short sleeve cuff.

All seams $1/_4$". Finish seams with a zigzag stitch or serger.

## Cut Out

Cut a piece of fabric 2" wide by 5" longer than the center panel. Cut two collars from the blue linen and two collars from the white silk for the collar lining. Cut two short sleeve cuffs from the blue linen. Cut two short sleeves from the silk on fold line #1, two side fronts, two backs on the selvage and a bias neck facing 1" wide by the neck measurement from the silk.

## Construction

1. Make the first tuck in the fabric cut for the front panel by measuring 5" down from the top edge of the fabric and press a fold in the fabric. Measure 4" down from the fold line and press in another fold. Measure 4" down from this fold line and press in another fold. There are now 3 fold lines pressed in the fabric (fig. 1).

2. Sew a tuck at each fold line $3/_8$" from folded edge. Make three tucks (fig. 2).

3. Draw a line for the lace insertion placement 1" above the stitching line for each tuck. Draw a line 1" below the fold in the bottom tuck.

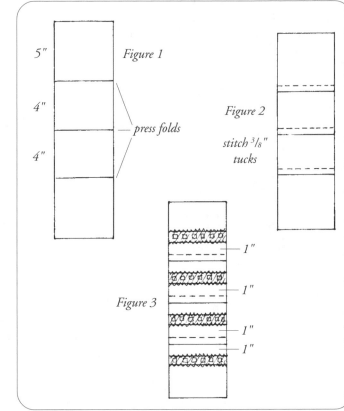

Figure 1

press folds

5"
4"
4"

Figure 2

stitch $3/_8$" tucks

Figure 3

1"
1"
1"
1"

4. Place the lace insertion with the bottom edge on the drawn lines. Place the lace insertion with the top edge on the bottom drawn line. Stitch the lace in place on both sides of the lace insertion with a small zigzag stitch (fig. 3).

5. Trim the fabric from behind the lace insertion.

6. Place the lapel collar center front panel on the embellished fabric

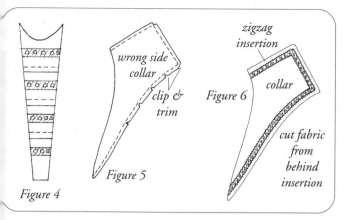

Figure 4

wrong side collar

clip & trim

Figure 5

zigzag insertion

collar

Figure 6

cut fabric from behind insertion

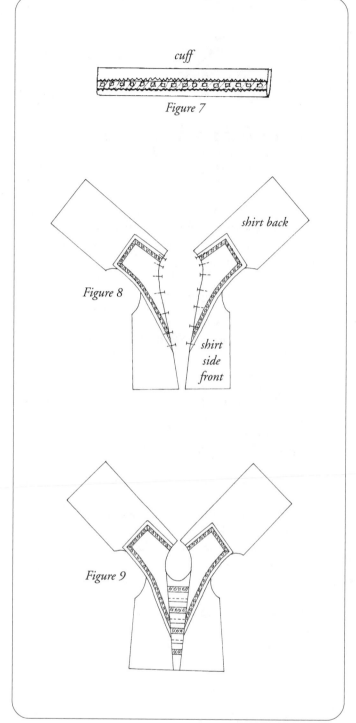

cuff

Figure 7

shirt back

Figure 8

shirt side front

Figure 9

with the center front neck edge 2" down from the top edge of the fabric and cut out (fig. 4).

7. Place the right side of the linen collar to the right side of the silk collar. Sew together with a ¼" seam. Trim and clip seam (fig. 5). Turn and press.

8. Shape the insertion lace ½" from the finished edge on the right side of the blue linen around the collar, mitering the lace at the back corners. Stitch in place on both sides of the lace insertion with a small zigzag stitch. Trim the fabric from behind the lace insertion (fig. 6).

9. Fold the cuff in half with the wrong sides together along the long side. Press.

10. Place the lace on the cuff ⅜" from the folded edge. Stitch the lace to the cuff along both sides of the lace with a small zigzag stitch. Trim the fabric from behind the lace insertion (fig. 7).

11. Place the right side of the shirt back to the right side of the shirt side front. Sew the shoulder seams with a ¼" seam allowance.

12. Place the finished collar to the shirt with the wrong side of the collar to the right side of the shirt. Pin the collar onto each side (fig. 8).

13. Place the center front to one side of the shirt/collar with the right sides together and stitch in place with a ¼" seam. Sew other shirt/collar to the other side of the center panel (fig. 9).

14. Fold the bias neck strip in half lengthwise, with the long cut edges even. Press.

15. With the back folds folded to the outside of the bodice, place the cut edges of the bias strip to the cut edge of the neck. Trim the ends of the bias so that the folds of the back bodice extend ¼" beyond the edges of the bias facing. Stitch the bias strip facing in place using a ¼" seam. Trim the seam to ⅛". Place clips along the seam allowance (fig. 10). Press the bias toward the seam allowance and understitch (fig. 11). Fold the facing completely to the inside of the shirt, folding the back folds to the inside of the shirt. Stitch the facing in place by hand (fig. 12).

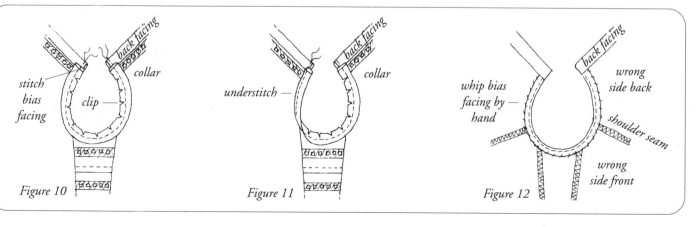

back facing

collar

stitch bias facing

clip

Figure 10

understitch

back facing

collar

Figure 11

whip bias facing by hand

back facing

wrong side back

shoulder seam

wrong side front

Figure 12

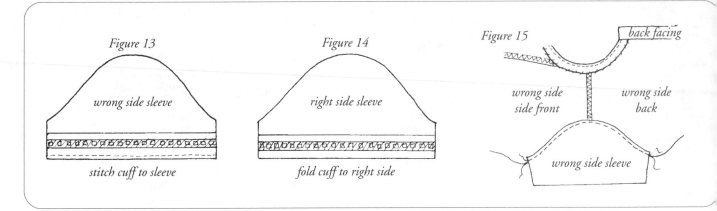

Figure 13 — *wrong side sleeve* / *stitch cuff to sleeve*

Figure 14 — *right side sleeve* / *fold cuff to right side*

Figure 15 — *back facing* / *wrong side side front* / *wrong side back* / *wrong side sleeve*

16. Place the right side of the cuff to the wrong side of the sleeve bottom matching the raw edges of the cuff to the bottom edge of the sleeve. Sew the cuff to the sleeve with a $^1/_4$" seam (fig. 13). Finish the seam. Fold the cuff to the right side enclosing the seam and press in place (fig. 14).

17. Fit the sleeve to the armhole and stitch in place (fig. 15).

18. Place the sides of shirt together matching the underarm seam and the bottom of the cuff. Sew the side shirt and sleeve seam (fig. 16).

19. Finish the bottom edge of the shirt as follows: with the facings open, fold up $^1/_4$" and press. Fold up $^1/_4$" again and press, creating a narrow hem (fig. 17). Fold the facings along the fold line and stitch the hem in place (fig. 18).

20. Position the buttonholes on the left hand side by placing a dot $^1/_2$" from the top fabric edge of the neckline and $^1/_2$" over from the fold line.

21. Place a dot every 3" down the back of the shirt $^1/_2$" from the fold (fig. 19).

22. Stitch a $^1/_2$" buttonhole beginning at the dot and placing the buttonholes horizontally. Continue the buttonholes down the back of the shirt. Cut the buttonholes open with a buttonhole cutter or seam ripper.

23. Lap the left side of the blouse over the right side and mark the placement for the buttons.

24. Attach the buttons along the marks on the right side of the shirt (fig. 19).

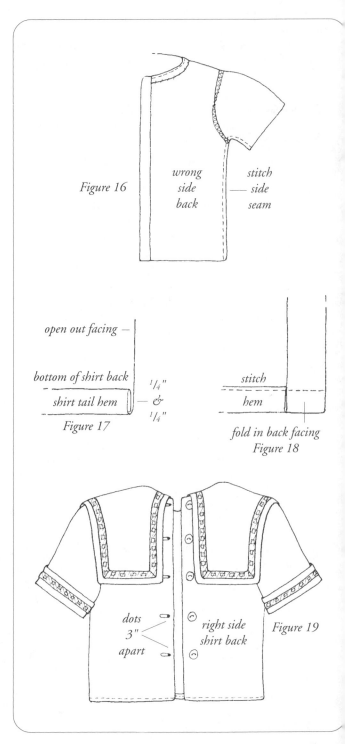

Figure 16 — *wrong side back* / *stitch side seam*

Figure 17 — *open out facing* / *bottom of shirt back* / *shirt tail hem* / $^1/_4$" & $^1/_4$"

Figure 18 — *stitch hem* / *fold in back facing*

Figure 19 — *dots 3" apart* / *right side shirt back*

# White Linen Lapel Collar Shirt

Wonderfully tailored this white linen shirt has many interesting details. The center panel consists of folded tucks and very tailored white French lace insertion. Swiss entredeux travels down each side of this panel. The interesting collar is shaped like a sailor collar in the back and feature lapels on the front. Each collar has curved lace insertion with blue machine embroidered dots on either side. The sleeves feature the lace insertion with a row of the blue dots embroidered on each side. The shirt closes in the back with buttons and buttonholes. This shirt could be used with any of the pants in the book.

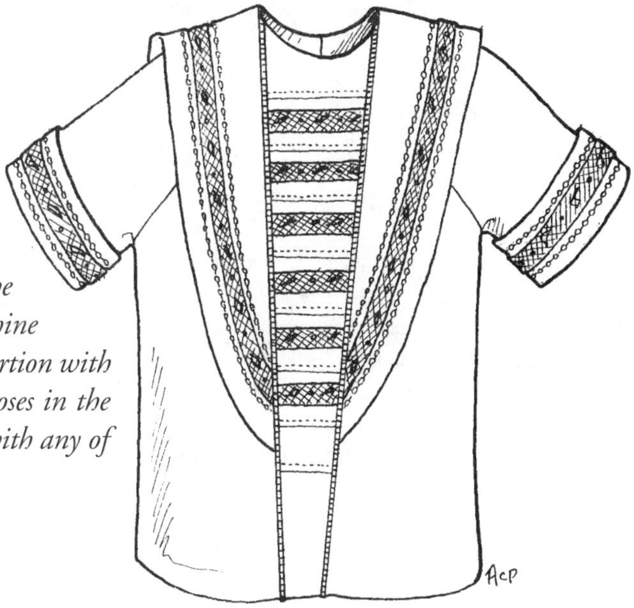

## Fabric Requirements

|  | Sizes 1-2 | Sizes 3-4 | Sizes 6-8 |
|---|---|---|---|
| White Fabric 45" | 1¼ yds. | 1½ yds. | 1½ yds. |
| (Add ¼ yd to all sizes for long sleeves) | | | |
| Entredeux | 1⅛ yds. | 1¼ yds. | 1⅜ yds. |
| Lace insertion | 3 yds. | 3½ yds. | 3¾ yds. |
| Blue Thread | | | |
| Buttons ½" | 5 | 5 | 5 |

## Pattern Pieces

All pattern pieces are found in the pattern envelope.
Lapel collar center front panel, lapel collar side front, shirt back, lapel collar, short shirt sleeve, short sleeve cuff.

All seams ¼". Finish seams with zigzag stich or serger.

## Cutting

Cut two sleeves on fold line #1, two side fronts and two backs on the selvage from the linen. Cut two sleeve cuffs. Cut a piece of fabric 2" wider by 6" longer than the pattern measurement for the center front panel. Cut four collars from the white linen, one bias neck band 1" wide by the neck measurement.

## Construction

1. On the fabric rectangle, cut for the center front panel, make the first tuck by measuring 5" down from the top edge of the fabric and press a fold in the fabric. Measure 2" down from the fold line and press in another fold. Measure 2" down from this fold line and press in another fold. Continue pressing fold lines until there are 8 fold lines pressed in the fabric (fig. 1).

2. Sew a tuck at each fold line ¼" from the folded edge. Make eight tucks (fig. 2).

3. Draw a line for the lace insertion placement ⅜" above the stitching line for each tuck except for the last tuck.

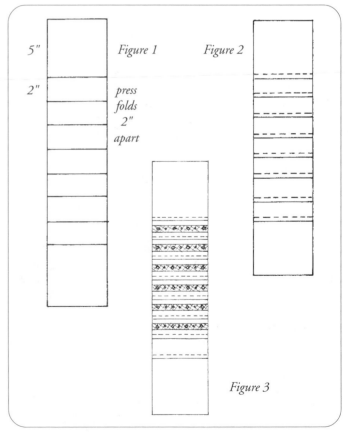

5"

2"

*Figure 1*

press folds 2" apart

*Figure 2*

*Figure 3*

4. Place the lace insertion with the bottom edge on the drawn line. Stitch the lace in place on both sides of the lace insertion with a small zigzag stitch. Note: The lace insertion will be centered between the fold of the tuck above it and the stitching line of the tuck below it. (fig. 3).

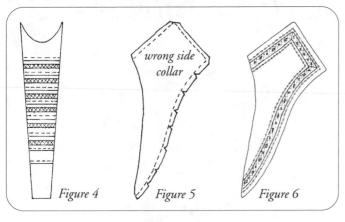

Figure 4    Figure 5    Figure 6

*wrong side collar* (Figure 5)

5. Trim the fabric from behind the lace insertion.

6. Place the pattern for the lapel collar center front panel on the embellished fabric with the center front neck edge 3$^1/_2$" down from the top edge of the fabric and cut out (fig. 4).

7. Place the right sides of the linen together for the two collars. Sew together with a $^1/_4$" seam. Trim and clip seam (fig. 5). Turn and press.

8. Shape the insertion lace $^3/_4$" from the finished edge around the collar, mitering the lace at back corners. Stitch in place on both sides of the lace insertion with a small zigzag stitch. Trim the double layer of fabric from behind the lace insertion (fig. 6).

9. Decorative stitches are done $^1/_4$" from the lace on both sides of the lace insertion (fig. 6). The decorative stitching will be $^1/_2$" from the outside edge of the collar.

10. Fold the cuff in half with the wrong sides together along the long side. Press.

11. Shape the lace on the cuff $^3/_8$" from the folded edge. Stitch the lace to the cuff along both sides of the lace with a small zigzag stitch. Trim the fabric from behind the lace insertion. Decorative stitches are done $^1/_4$" from the lace on both sides of the lace insertion (fig. 7).

12. Place entredeux on the outside edges of the center panel. Stitch the entredeux to the fabric with a $^1/_4$" seam using the technique, Entredeux to Flat Fabric (fig. 8).

13. Place the right side of the shirt back to the right side of the shirt side front. Sew the shoulder seams with a $^1/_4$" seam allowance.

14. Place the finished collar to the shirt with the wrong side of the collar to the right side of the shirt. Pin the collar onto each side (fig. 9).

15. Place the center panel to one side of the shirt/collar with the right sides together and stitch in place using the technique, Entredeux to Flat Fabric. Sew other shirt/collar to the other side of the center panel (fig. 10).

16. Fold the bias strip in half lengthwise, with the long cut edges even. Press.

17. With the back folds folded to the outside of the bodice, place the cut edges of the bias strip to the cut edge of the neck. Trim the ends of the bias so that the folds of the back bodice extend $^1/_4$" beyond the edges of the bias facing. Stitch the bias strip facing in place using a $^1/_4$" seam. Trim the seam to $^1/_8$".

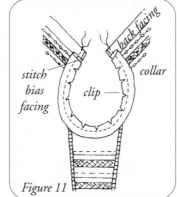

*stitch bias facing*    *clip*    *collar*    *back facing*

Figure 11

Place clips along the seam allowance (fig. 11). Press the facing toward the seam allowance

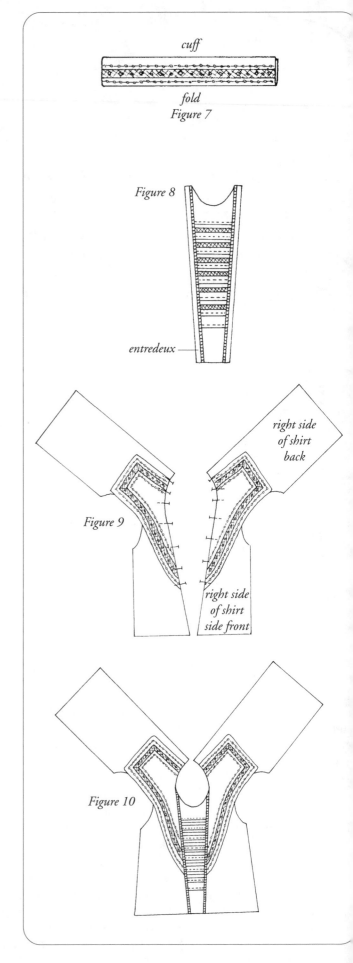

*cuff*

*fold*

Figure 7

Figure 8

*entredeux*

Figure 9

*right side of shirt back*

*right side of shirt side front*

Figure 10

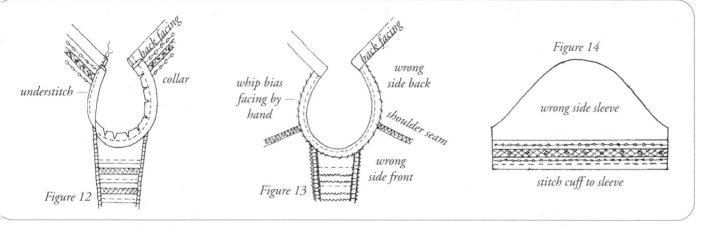

*underststitch* — *collar*

*Figure 12*

*whip bias facing by hand* — *back facing* · *wrong side back* · *shoulder seam* · *wrong side front*

*Figure 13*

*Figure 14*

*wrong side sleeve*

*stitch cuff to sleeve*

and understitch (fig. 12). Fold the facing completely to the inside of the shirt, folding the back folds to the inside of the shirt. Stitch the bias facing in place by hand (fig. 13).

8. Place the right side of the cuff to the wrong side of the sleeve bottom matching the raw edges of the cuff to the bottom edge of the sleeve. Sew the cuff to the sleeve with a $^1/_4$" seam (fig. 14). Finish the seam. Fold the cuff to the right side enclosing the seam and press in place (fig. 15).

9. Fit the sleeve to the armhole and stitch in place (fig. 16).

10. Place the sides of shirt together matching the underarm seam and the bottom of the cuff. Sew the side shirt and sleeve seam (fig. 17).

11. Finish the bottom edge of the shirt as follows: with the facings open, fold up $^1/_4$" and press. Fold up $^1/_4$" again and press, creating a narrow hem (fig. 18). Fold the facings along the fold line and stitch the hem in place (fig. 19).

12. Position the buttonholes on the left hand side by placing a dot $^1/_2$" from the top fabric edge of the neckline and $^1/_2$" over from the fold line.

13. Place a dot every 3" down the back of the shirt $^1/_2$" from the fold (fig. 20).

14. Stitch a $^1/_2$" buttonhole beginning at the dot and placing the buttonholes horizontally. Continue the buttonholes down the back of the shirt. Cut the buttonholes open with a buttonhole cutter or seam ripper.

15. Lap the left side of the blouse over the right side and mark the placement for the buttons.

16. Attach the buttons along the marks on the right side of the shirt (fig. 20).

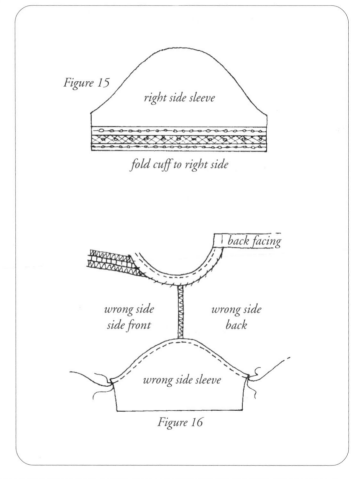

*Figure 15*

*right side sleeve*

*fold cuff to right side*

*back facing*

*wrong side side front* · *wrong side back*

*wrong side sleeve*

*Figure 16*

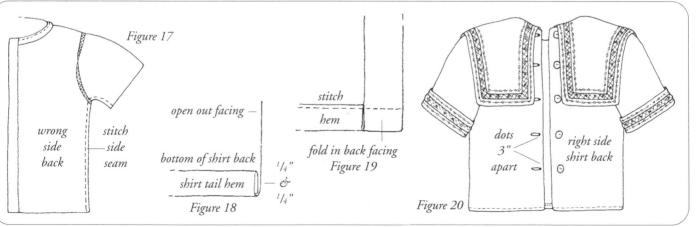

*Figure 17*

*wrong side back* · *stitch side seam*

*open out facing* — *bottom of shirt back* · *shirt tail hem* · $^1/_4$" & $^1/_4$"

*Figure 18*

*stitch* · *hem* · *fold in back facing*

*Figure 19*

*dots 3" apart* · *right side shirt back*

*Figure 20*

# Gingham Linen Lapel Collar Shirt

Very tailored would be my descriptive phrase to describe this wonderful white linen shirt with the gingham (tan and white) linen lapel collar. The center panel is of white linen with machine embroidery at the top. The lapel collar is made of tan and white gingham linen with two rows of very tailored off-white French lace insertion. The back of the collar is shaped like a sailor collar. The cuffs are made of the tan and white gingham linen with the off-white French insertion in the middle. The back closes with buttons and buttonholes. This shirt could be used with any of the pants in the book.

Pants shown in the illustration are the Front Buttoned Pants.

## Fabric Requirements

|  | Sizes 1-2 | Sizes 3-4 | Sizes 6-8 |
|---|---|---|---|
| Fabric 45" white | 1 yd. | $1^1/_4$" yds. | $1^3/_8$ yds. |
| Beige check fabric 45" | $5/_8$ yd. | $5/_8$ yd. | $3/_4$ yd. |
| $3/_8$" Lace insertion | $4^1/_8$ yd. | $4^3/_8$ yds. | $4^3/_4$ yds. |
| Machine embroidery thread |  |  |  |
| $1/_2$" Buttons | 5 | 5 | 5 |

## Pattern Pieces

All pattern pieces are found in the pattern envelope.
Lapel collar center front panel, lapel collar side front, lapel collar, shirt button back, long shirt sleeve, long sleeve cuff.
All seams $1/_4$". Finish seams with a zigzag stitch or serger.

## Cut Out

Cut a piece of fabric 2" wider and 4" longer than the center panel. Cut four collars from the beige check linen. Cut two long sleeve cuffs from the beige check linen. Cut two long sleeves, two side fronts and two backs on the selvage from the white linen, one bias neck facing 1" wide by the neck measurement.

## Construction

1. Select a design $2^1/_2$" wide by 2" and machine or hand embroider a design centering the design 5" from the top edge on the fabric piece for the center panel. (fig. 1).
2. Place the pattern for the center panel on the embellished fabric with the center front neck edge $2^1/_2$" down from the top edge of fabric and cut out (fig. 2).
3. Place the right sides of the linen together for the two collars. Sew together with a $1/_4$" seam. Trim and clip seam (fig. 3). Turn and press.
4. Shape the insertion lace $1/_2$" from the finished edge on the right

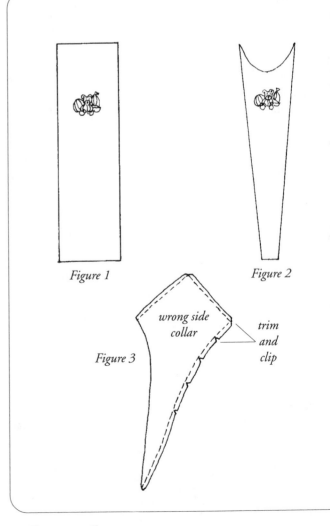

*Figure 1*

*Figure 2*

wrong side collar

trim and clip

*Figure 3*

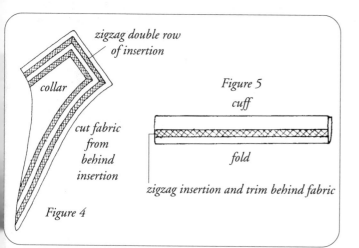

Figure 4

*zigzag double row of insertion*

*collar*

*cut fabric from behind insertion*

Figure 5

*cuff*

*fold*

*zigzag insertion and trim behind fabric*

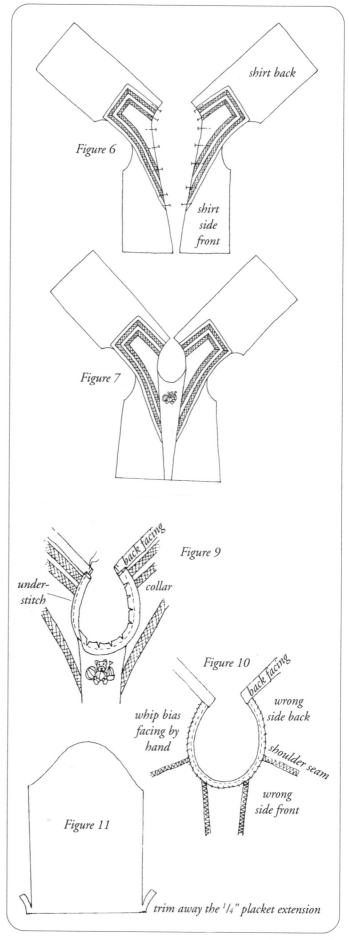

Figure 6

*shirt back*

*shirt side front*

Figure 7

Figure 9

*under-stitch*

*back facing*

*collar*

Figure 10

*whip bias facing by hand*

*back facing*

*wrong side back*

*shoulder seam*

*wrong side front*

Figure 11

*trim away the 1/4" placket extension*

side of the linen around the collar, mitering the lace at the back corners. Stitch in place on both sides of the lace insertion with a small zigzag stitch. Shape a second row of lace insertion $3/8$" to the inside edge of the above insertion. Stitch in place on both sides of the lace insertion with a small zigzag stitch. Trim the fabric from behind the lace insertion (fig. 4).

5. Fold the cuff in half with the wrong sides together along the long side. Press.

6. Shape the lace on the cuff $3/8$" from the folded edge. Stitch the lace to the cuff along both sides of the lace with a small zigzag stitch. Trim the fabric from behind the lace insertion (fig. 5).

7. Place the right side of the shirt back to the right side of the shirt side front. Sew the shoulder seams with a $1/4$" seam allowance.

8. Place finished collar to the shirt with the wrong side of the collar to the right side of the shirt. Pin the collar onto each side (fig. 6).

9. Place the center panel to one side of the shirt/collar with the right sides together and stitch in place with a $1/4$" seam. Sew other shirt/collar to the other side of the center panel (fig. 7).

10. Measure around the neck with the back facings folded to the inside of the shirt. Cut a bias strip 1" wide by the length around the neck.

11. Fold the bias neck strip in half lengthwise, with the long cut edges even. Press.

12. With the back folds folded to the outside of the bodice, place the cut edges of the bias strip to the cut edge of the neck. Trim the ends of the bias so that the folds of the back bodice extend $1/4$" beyond the edges of the bias facing. Stitch the bias strip facing in place using a $1/4$" seam. Trim the seam to $1/8$". Place clips along the seam allowance (fig. 8). Press the facing toward the seam allowance and understitch. (fig. 9). Fold the facing completely to the inside of the shirt, folding the back folds to the inside of the shirt. Stitch the facing in place by hand (fig. 10).

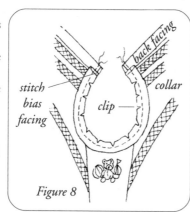

*stitch bias facing*

*back facing*

*collar*

*clip*

Figure 8

13. Trim the $1/4$" placket edges from the side of the sleeve (fig. 11). Place pleats in the bottom of the sleeve. Place the right side of

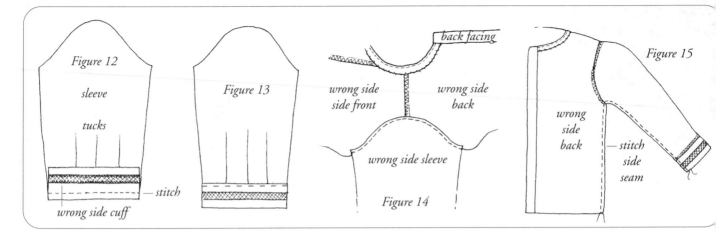

Figure 12
sleeve
tucks
stitch
wrong side cuff

Figure 13

back facing
wrong side side front
wrong side back
wrong side sleeve
Figure 14

Figure 15
wrong side back
stitch side seam

the cuff to the right side of the sleeve bottom matching the raw edges of the cuff to the bottom edge of the sleeve. Adjust the pleats in the sleeve if needed. Sew the cuff to the sleeve with a $^1/_4$" seam. Finish the seam (fig. 12). Press the cuff to the right side with the seam toward the sleeve and top stitch the seam in place about $^1/_8$" from the seam (fig. 13).

14. Fit the sleeve to the armhole and stitch in place (fig. 14).

15. Place the sides of shirt together matching the underarm seam and the bottom of the cuff. Sew the side shirt and sleeve seam (fig. 15). Take a larger seam on the cuff if needed.

16. Finish the bottom edge of the shirt as follows: with the facings open, fold up $^1/_4$" and press. Fold up $^1/_4$" again and press, creating a narrow hem (fig. 16). Fold the facings along the fold line and stitch the hem in place (fig. 17).

17. Position the buttonholes on the left hand side by placing a dot $^1/_2$" from the top fabric edge of the neckline and $^1/_2$" over from the fold line.

18. Place a dot every 3" down the back of the shirt $^1/_2$" from the fold (fig. 18).

19. Stitch a $^1/_2$" buttonhole beginning at the dot and placing the buttonholes horizontally. Continue the buttonholes down the back of the shirt. Cut the buttonholes open with a buttonhole cutter or seam ripper.

20. Lap the left side of the shirt over the right side and mark the placement for the buttons.

21. Attach the buttons along the marks on the right side of the shirt (fig. 18).

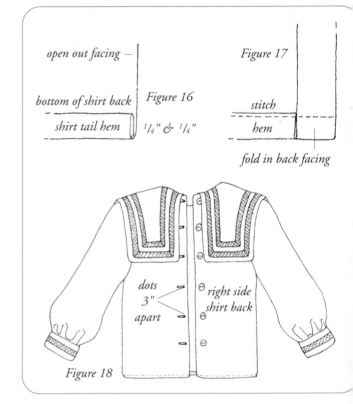

open out facing
bottom of shirt back
shirt tail hem
Figure 16
$^1/_4$" & $^1/_4$"

Figure 17
stitch
hem
fold in back facing

dots 3" apart
right side shirt back
Figure 18

# Greyson's Shirt

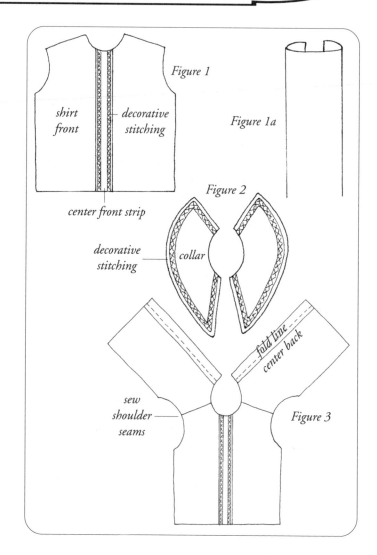

This adorable little white striped broadcloth shirt appears to be buttoned up the front but the front button placket is for embellishment only; it buttons up the back. The measurement for the separate front panel is one and five eighths inches wide; there is green decorative stitching which looks like little cross stitches with straight stitching on each side. This separate shirt panel is attached to the front of the shirt with this decorative machine cross stitching. Three green buttons are stitched on this panel for fun. The lined collar has this same decorative green machine cross stitch design all the way around it. The tops of the cuffs are stitched to the shirt using this same adorable green machine cross stitching. The back buttons with white pearl buttons and buttonholes.

Pants shown in the illustration
are the V-front Button-On Suit Pants.

## Fabric Requirements

| | Sizes 1-2 | Sizes 3-4 | Sizes 5-6 | Sizes 7-8 |
|---|---|---|---|---|
| Fabric | $1^{1}/_{4}$ yds. | $1^{1}/_{4}$ yds. | $1^{1}/_{4}$ yds. | $1^{1}/_{4}$ yds. |
| Decorative Buttons $^{1}/_{2}$" | 3 | 3 | 3 | 3 |
| Buttons $^{7}/_{8}$" | 5 | 5 | 5 | 5 |
| Decorative stitching thread | | | | |

## Pattern Pieces

All patterns are found in the pattern envelope.
Shirt front, shirt button back, shirt short sleeve, flat collar.
All seams $^{1}/_{4}$". Finish seams with a zigzag stitch or serger.

## Cutting

Cut one shirt front on the fold, two shirt button backs on the selvage, four flat collars, two shirt short sleeves on fold line #2, one bias neck facing 1" wide by the neck measurement, and a strip for the front 2-5/8" wide by the length of the shirt front.

## Construction

1. Press under $^{1}/_{2}$" on each long side of the strip for the center front (fig. 1a). Position the strip in the center front of the shirt front. Pin in place. Stitch decorative stitching down each side of the strip $^{1}/_{8}$" from the folded edge. Trim the neck curve from the front panel using the shirt neckline as a guide (fig. 1).
2. Place the shirt collars with right sides together and stitch together using a $^{1}/_{4}$" seam. Turn right side out and press. Stitch decorative stitching $^{1}/_{8}$" from the outer edge of each collar (fig. 2).
3. Place the right side of the front to the right side of the backs at the shoulders. Sew the shoulder seams using a $^{1}/_{4}$" seam (fig. 3).
4. Place the wrong side of the collar to the right side of the shirt. The back edges of the collar should not extend beyond the center back lines of the shirt back. Fold the back edges of the shirt to the right side along the fold lines. The back edges of the collar

Figure 1

Figure 1a

shirt front — decorative stitching

center front strip

Figure 2

decorative stitching — collar

fold line center back

sew shoulder seams

Figure 3

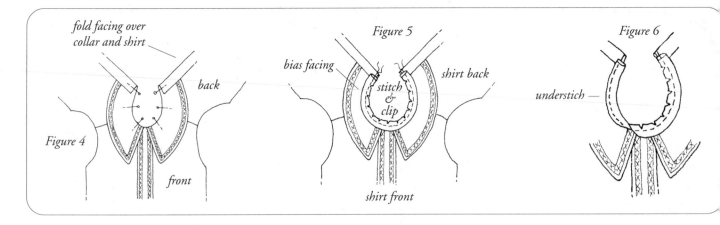

fold facing over collar and shirt

back

Figure 4

front

Figure 5

bias facing

stitch & clip

shirt back

shirt front

Figure 6

understich

will be sandwiched between the back folded edges of the facing and the shirt (fig. 4).

5. Fold the bias in half lengthwise, with the long cut edges even. Press.

6. Place the bias strip to the right side of the bodice with both long edges of the strip even with the neck edge. The strip will be placed over the collar and the folded back facing.

7. Stitch all layers together using a $1/4$" seam. Trim and clip the seam allowance (fig. 5).

8. Press the bias strip away front the shirt, toward the seam allowance. Understitch (fig. 6).

9. Flip the back facings to the inside of the shirt. Fold the bias strip to the inside of the shirt creating a facing. The bias strip will not show on the right side of the shirt. Press.

10. With the collar away front the shirt, stitch the binding to the bodice by hand or machine (fig. 7).

11. On the bottom edge of each sleeve, fold $1/4$" up to the right side and press in place. Fold the cuff to the right side on the fold line (fig. 8). Stitch the cuff in place using the decorative stitch and stitching $1/8$" from the folded edge (fig. 9).

12. Fit the sleeve to the armhole and stitch in place (fig. 10). Place the sides of the shirt together matching the underarm seam and the bottom of the sleeve. Sew the side shirt and sleeve seam (fig. 11).

13. Finish the bottom edge of the shirt as follows: With the facing open, fold up $1/4$" and press. Fold up $1/4$" again and press, creating a narrow hem (fig. 12). Fold the facings along the fold line and stitch the hem in place (fig. 13).

14. Position the buttonholes on the left hand side by placing a dot $1/2$" from the top fabric edge of the neckline and $1/2$" over from the fold line. Place a dot every 3" down the back of the shirt $1/2$" from the fold (fig. 14).

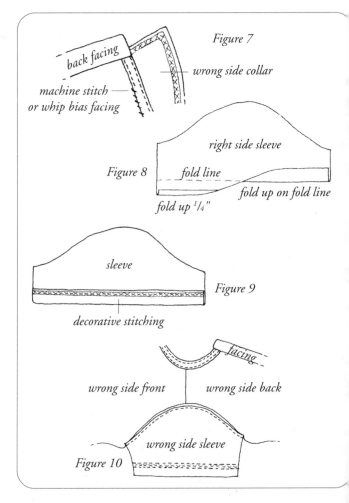

Figure 7

back facing

machine stitch or whip bias facing

wrong side collar

Figure 8

right side sleeve

fold line

fold up on fold line

fold up $1/4$"

Figure 9

sleeve

decorative stitching

wrong side front

wrong side back

Figure 10

wrong side sleeve

facing

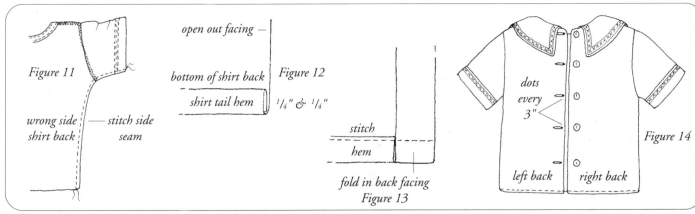

Figure 11

wrong side shirt back

stitch side seam

open out facing

bottom of shirt back

shirt tail hem

Figure 12

$1/4$" & $1/4$"

stitch

hem

fold in back facing

Figure 13

dots every 3"

left back

right back

Figure 14

15. Stitch a ¹/₂" buttonhole beginning at the dot and placing the buttonholes horizontally. Continue the buttonholes down the back of the shirt. Cut the buttonholes open with a buttonhole cutter or seam ripper.
16. Lap the left side of the shirt over the right side and mark the placement for the buttons.
17. Attach the buttons along the marks on the right side of the shirt (fig. 14).
18. Fit the garment to the child and mark placement for the buttons at the waist. If the child is not available, refer to the waistline markings on the pattern and the buttonhole placement on the pants to determine the button placement. Make a ¹/₄" pleat behind the button placement line in the front and the back. Sew the buttons in place (figs. 14 & 15). A piece of twill tape may be placed on the wrong side behind the button for more stability.
19. Sew 3 buttons down the center front spacing the first button 1" down from the finished neck edge, at 2¹/₂" and 4" (fig. 15).

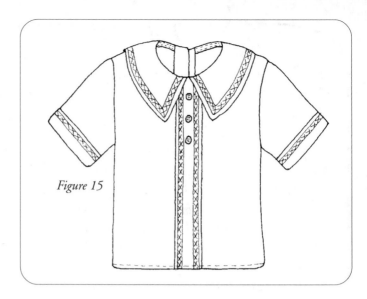

Figure 15

# Logan's Madeira Appliqué Shirt

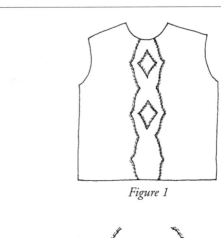

Designed especially for the cover of this book, this classic white shirt is fabulous. Made of white and blue linen the easy technique for Windowpane Madeira appliqué was used for embellishing the front. The Madeira treatment on the front is in the same blue linen as the pants. Two gorgeous pearl buttons are found inside the white windowpane; French knots of silk ribbon are on all four sides of these buttons; three French knots of blue silk ribbon are on the outside joints of both windowpanes. The lined Peter Pan collar has entredeux around the edge with white tatting attached to the edge of the entredeux. Silk ribbon has been run through every two holes of the entredeux on both the trim around the collar as well as the same trim at the top of the cuff of the sleeves. Extra special detailing on this shirt also includes the sewing on of the buttons with silk ribbon on both the decorative buttons in the center of the windowpane Madeira as well as the back of the suit. The buttons on the pants have also been attached with blue silk ribbon rather than thread. A pinstitch was used to attach the Windowpane Madeira to the shirt.

Pants shown in the illustration are the Button-on Suit Pants.

## Fabric Requirements

|  | Sizes 1-2 | Sizes 3-4 | Sizes 6-8 |
|---|---|---|---|
| White linen 45" | $7/8$ yd. | 1 yd. | 1 yd. |
| Blue linen 45" | $1/6$ yd. | $1/6$ yd. | $1/6$ yd. |
| Entredeux | $1^1/2$ yd. | $1^5/8$ yd. | $1^3/4$ yd. |
| Tatted edging | $1^1/2$ yd. | $1^5/8$ yd. | $1^3/4$ yd. |
| Silk ribbon 2mm | 2 yds. | 2 yds. | 2 yds. |
| $3/4$" buttons | 8 | 8 | 8 |
| $3/8$" buttons | 5 | 5 | 5 |

## Pattern Pieces

All patterns are found in the pattern envelope.
Shirt front, shirt button back, shirt short sleeve, Peter Pan collar.
Template: Logan's Madeira Appliqué Shirt Template
All seams $1/4$". Finish seams with a zigzag stitch or serger.

## Cutting

Cut one shirt front on the fold, two shirt button backs on the selvage, four Peter Pan collars, two shirt short sleeves cutting on fold line #2 and one bias neck facing 1" wide by neck measurement.

## Construction

1. Embellish the shirt front (referring to Bradley's Madeira Appliqué Dress) using the template and the technique for Madeira Appliqué - Panels and Windows and referring to Bradley's Madeira Appliqué Dress Bodice, steps 1-5 (fig. 1).

2. To complete the front embellishment: The buttons are sewn on with 2 mm silk ribbon. The French knots are hand embroidered with silk ribbon (fig. 2).

3. Trim $1/4$" from the outer edge of the collars, this will allow for the trim. Place the collars with the right sides together and stitch together (fig. 3). Trim and clip seam. Turn right side out and press.

4. Embellish the outer edge of the collar with entredeux and tatting. Measure around the outer edge of the collar and cut two pieces of entredeux to this measurements. Trim one fabric edge from

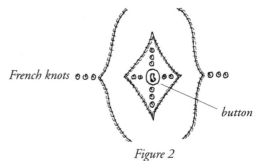

French knots

button

*Figure 1*

*Figure 2*

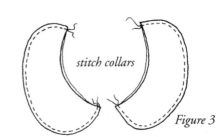

stitch collars

*Figure 3*

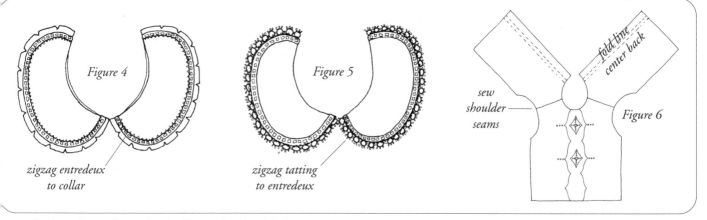

Figure 4

zigzag entredeux
to collar

Figure 5

zigzag tatting
to entredeux

sew
shoulder
seams

fold line
center back

Figure 6

each piece of entredeux, clip the fabric edge that is left on the entredeux. Shape the entredeux around the outer edge of both collars and zigzag the edge of the entredeux to the finished collar (fig. 4). Trim the outer fabric edge from the entredeux and zigzag tatted edging to the entredeux using the technique, lace to entredeux (fig. 5). Thread silk ribbon through the entredeux.

5. Place the right side of the embellished front to the right side of the backs at the shoulders. Sew the shoulder seams using a 1/4" seam (fig. 6).

6. Place the wrong side of the collar to the right side of the shirt. The back edges of the collar should not extend beyond the center back lines of the back shirt. Fold the back edges of the shirt to the right side along the fold lines. The back edges of the collar will be sandwiched between the back folded edges of the facing and the shirt (fig. 7).

7. Fold the bias in half lengthwise, with the long cut edges even. Press.

8. Place the bias strip to the right side of the bodice with both long edges of the strip even with the neck edge. The strip will be placed over the collar and the folded back facing.

9. Stitch all layers together using a 1/4" seam. Trim and clip the seam allowance (fig. 8).

10. Press the bias strip away from the shirt, toward the seam allowance. Understitch (fig. 9).

11. Flip the back facings to the inside of the shirt. Fold the bias strip to the inside of the shirt creating a facing. The bias strip will not show on the right side of the shirt. Press.

12. With the collar away from the shirt, stitch the binding to the bodice by hand or machine (fig. 10).

13. Measure across the bottom of the sleeve and cut two strips of entredeux to this measurement. Trim the fabric on one side of the entredeux to 1/8". Sew the entredeux to the bottom edge of the wrong side of the sleeve matching the trimmed edge of the entredeux to the bottom edge of the sleeve. Refer to the technique, entredeux to flat fabric.

14. Turn the finished edge to the right side with the entredeux on the bottom edge. Press in place. Trim the remaining fabric edge from the entredeux (fig. 11). Attach tatting to the entredeux

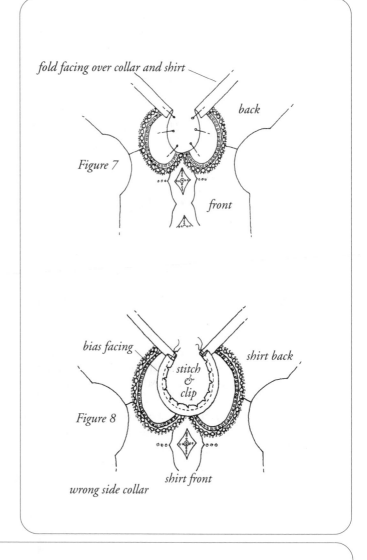

fold facing over collar and shirt

back

Figure 7

front

bias facing

shirt back

stitch
&
clip

Figure 8

shirt front

wrong side collar

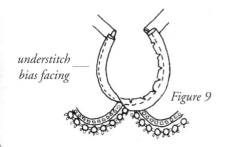

understitch
bias facing

Figure 9

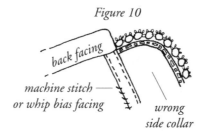

Figure 10

back facing

machine stitch
or whip bias facing

wrong
side collar

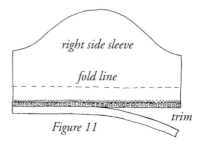

right side sleeve

fold line

Figure 11

trim

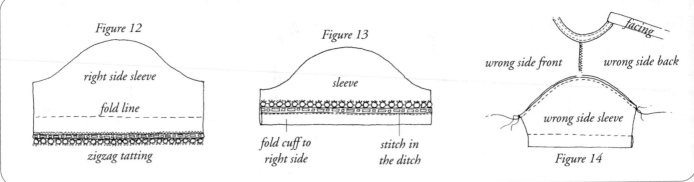

Figure 12

right side sleeve

fold line

zigzag tatting

Figure 13

sleeve

fold cuff to
right side

stitch in
the ditch

facing

wrong side front          wrong side back

wrong side sleeve

Figure 14

using the technique, lace to entredeux. Thread silk ribbon
through the entredeux (fig. 12).

15. Fold the cuff to the right side on the fold line. Stitch the cuff in
place by stitching in the ditch where the entredeux was attached
(fig. 13).

16. Fit the sleeve to the armhole and stitch in place (fig. 14). Place the
sides of the shirt together matching the underarm seam and the
bottom of the sleeve. Sew the side shirt and sleeve seam (fig. 15).

17. Finish the bottom edge of the shirt as follows: With the facing
open, fold up $1/4$" and press. Fold up $1/4$" again and press, creating
a narrow hem (fig. 16). Fold the facings along the fold line and
stitch the hem in place (fig. 17).

18. Position the buttonholes on the left hand side by placing a dot $1/2$"
from the top fabric edge of the neckline and $1/2$" over from the
fold line. Place a dot every 3" down the back of the shirt $1/2$"
from the fold (fig. 18).

19. Stitch a $1/2$" buttonhole beginning at the dot and placing the
buttonholes horizontally. Continue the buttonholes down the
back of the shirt. Cut the buttonholes open with a buttonhole
cutter or seam ripper.

20. Lap the left side of the shirt over the right side and mark the
placement for the buttons.

21. Attach the buttons along the marks on the right side of the shirt
(fig. 18).

22. Fit garment to child and mark placement for buttons at waist. If
child is not available, refer to the waistline marking on the pattern
and the buttonhole placement on the pants to determine the
button placement. Make a $1/2$" pleat behind the button placement
line in the front and the back (fig. 18). Sew buttons in place
with silk ribbon. A piece of twill tape may be placed on the
wrong side behind the button for more stability.

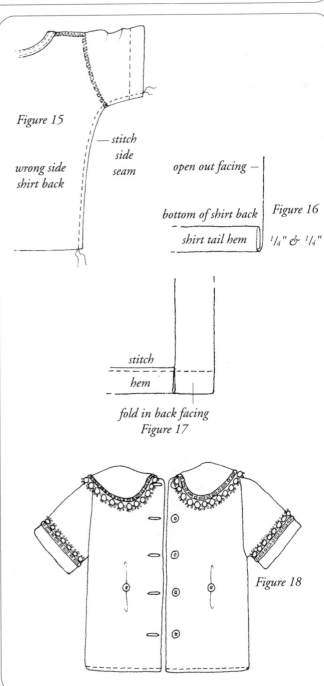

Figure 15

stitch
side
seam

wrong side
shirt back

open out facing —

bottom of shirt back          Figure 16

shirt tail hem          $1/4$" & $1/4$"

stitch

hem

fold in back facing
Figure 17

Figure 18

# Sailor Collar with Tie

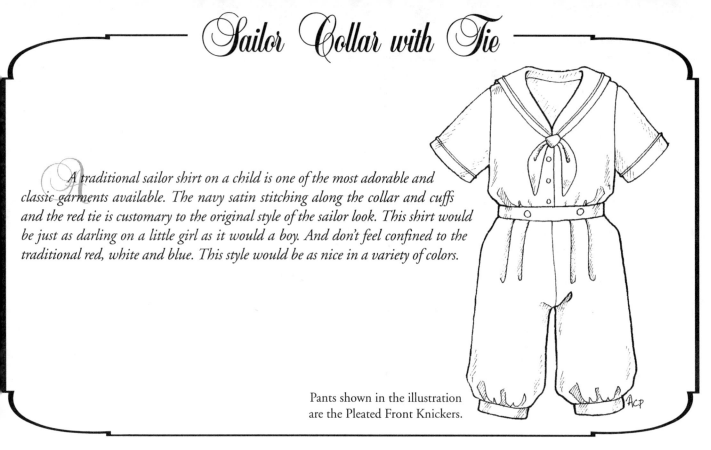

A traditional sailor shirt on a child is one of the most adorable and classic garments available. The navy satin stitching along the collar and cuffs and the red tie is customary to the original style of the sailor look. This shirt would be just as darling on a little girl as it would a boy. And don't feel confined to the traditional red, white and blue. This style would be as nice in a variety of colors.

Pants shown in the illustration are the Pleated Front Knickers.

## Fabric Requirements

|  | Sizes 2 | Sizes 3 | Sizes 4 |
|---|---|---|---|
| Broadcloth 45" | 1 yd. | 1¼ yds. | 1¼ yds. |
| (For long sleeves add ¼ yd.) | | | |
| Navy thread | | | |
| Small piece of red fabric 30" by 4½" | | | |
| ³/₈" Buttons | 5 | 5 | 5 |

## Pattern Pieces

All pattern pieces are found in the pattern envelope. Sailor collar for button front, sailor button front, shirt back, back neck facing, short sleeve. All seams ¼". Finish seams with a zigzag stitch or serger.

## Cutting

Two sailor collars, two sailor button fronts, one shirt back placing center back on the fold, one back neck facing on the fold, two sleeves using fold line #2 as the cutting line, from red cut out a piece 30" by 4½".

## Construction

1. Place the collars with right sides together and stitch around the collar (fig. 1a). Trim and clip seam. Turn the collar right side out and press.
2. Satin stitch the collar ½" from the finished edge (fig. 1b).
3. With right sides together place the shoulders of the front shirt and back shirt together and stitch in place with a ¼" seam.
4. Press the facing on the shirt fronts to the wrong side on the fold line. Place the back facing to the front facings at the shoulder and stitch in place with right sides together (fig. 2). Finish the outer edge of the front and the back facings by serging the edge of the facing or turn under ¼" to the wrong side of the facing and stitch.
5. Place the wrong side of the collar to right side of the shirt. Pin the collar in place. Fold the facing to the right side over the collar and pin to the collar around the neck edge. Stitch the facing to the shirt at the neck edge with a ¼" seam (fig. 3).
6. Finish the bottom edge of the sleeve with a serger or turn under

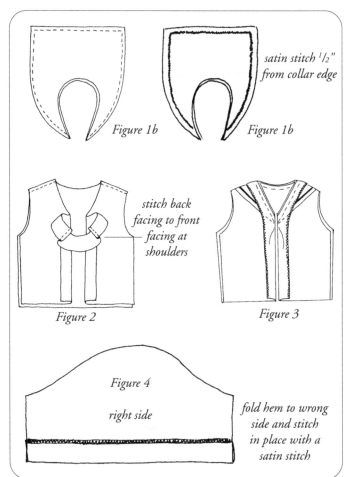

satin stitch ½" from collar edge

Figure 1b    Figure 1b

stitch back facing to front facing at shoulders

Figure 2    Figure 3

Figure 4

right side

fold hem to wrong side and stitch in place with a satin stitch

⅛" and stitch in place. Press the hem in the sleeve along fold line #1 to the wrong side at the bottom of the sleeve. Satin stitch with the navy thread to hold the hem in place (fig. 4).

7. Fit the sleeves to the armhole and stitch in place.

8. Place the sides of the shirt with right sides together, matching the underarm seam and sew the shirt side and sleeve seam (fig. 5).

9. With the facings open, fold up $\frac{1}{4}$" and press. Fold up $\frac{1}{4}$" again and press, creating a narrow hem (fig. 6a). Fold the facings along the fold line and stitch the hem in place (fig. 6b).

10. Fold the red strip with right sides together and stitch along the side with a $\frac{1}{4}$" seam (fig. 7a). Turn right side out. Tuck raw end back into tube. Whip together by hand (fig. 7b). Mark the center of the tie and match the center back beneath the collar. Pin the tie to the back. Bring the tie to the front underneath the collar. Tie into a square knot. (Refer to finished drawing.)

11. Position the buttonholes on the left-hand side of the shirt front by placing a dot $\frac{1}{4}$" over from the fold line and $\frac{1}{2}$ down from the neck edge.

12. Place a dot every 2" down the front of the shirt and $\frac{1}{2}$" over from the fold line.

13. Stitch a $\frac{1}{2}$" buttonhole beginning at the dot and placing the buttonholes horizontally. Continue the buttonholes down the shirt front. Cut the buttonholes down the shirt front. Cut the buttonholes open with a buttonhole cutter or seam ripper.

14. Lap the left side of the shirt over the right side and mark the placement for the buttons.

15. Attach the buttons along the mark on the right side of the shirt.

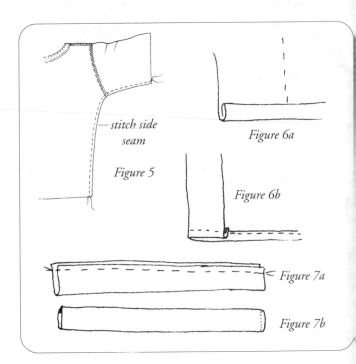

stitch side seam

Figure 5

Figure 6a

Figure 6b

Figure 7a

Figure 7b

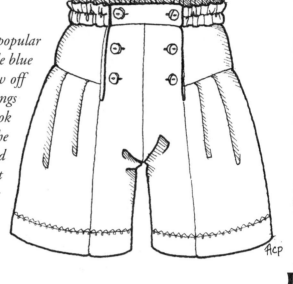

*These pants are almost identical to the sailor suit pants popular around the turn of the century (1900). These pants are made of pale blue handkerchief linen. The gorgeous antique pearl buttons really show off the style of the pants. They have wonderful pockets just right for things like Match Box cars and frogs. The front pleats add fullness and look just like Daddy's pleated pants. The yoke of the pants goes from the front to the back. Wing needle machine hemstitching actually is used to hem the pants. Elastic is found in the waistband to insure a perfect fit even on skinny waists. What a perfect and classic pair of pants for your little ones.*

## Fabric Requirements

|  | Sizes 4 | Size 6 | Size 8 |
|---|---|---|---|
| 45" Fabric - Shorts | 1 yd. | 1 yd. | 1 yd. |
| 45" Fabric - Pants | 1 1/2 yds. | 1 5/8 yds. | 1 3/4 yds. |
| Elastic (1/4") | 1 yd. | 1 yd. | 1 yd. |
| Buttons (1/2" to 3/4") - six are needed for all sizes | | | |

All seams are 1/4". Finish all seam allowances with a zigzag or serger.

## Pattern Pieces

All pattern pieces are found in the pattern envelope.
Front Pants Yoke, Back Pants Yoke, Pants Waistband, Front Flap Waistband, Side Pocket, Side Pocket Lining, Pants Placket, Pants Front Flap Facing, Center Front Pants, Side Front Pants, Back Pants.

## Cut Out

Two back pants yokes, one waistband, two pants backs, one front flap waistband, two side front pants, two center front pants, two front pants yokes, two side pockets, two side pocket linings, one front flap facing and two plackets.

## Construction

1. Place the back pants yoke to the pants back with right sides together, matching the raw edges. Stitch with a 1/4" seam. Press the seam toward the yoke (fig. 1).

2. Place the pants backs, right sides together matching the yoke seams and the back crotch. Stitch the center back crotch seam using a 1/4" seam (fig. 2).

3. Mark the pleats on the side front pants. Fold in place and stitch 1/8" from the top edge of the pants to hold in place (fig. 3).

4. Place the side pocket lining to the pants front, right sides together and stitch in place (fig. 4). Press the side pocket lining to the wrong side on the seam line.

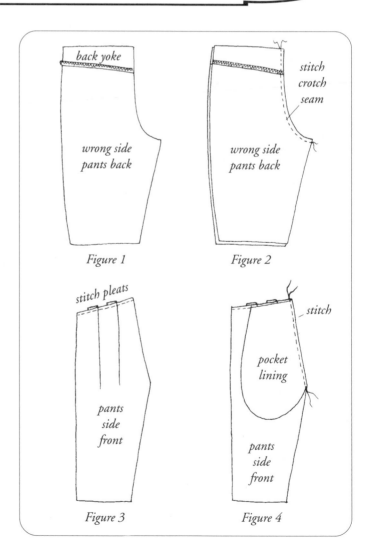

*Figure 1*

*Figure 2*

*Figure 3*

*Figure 4*

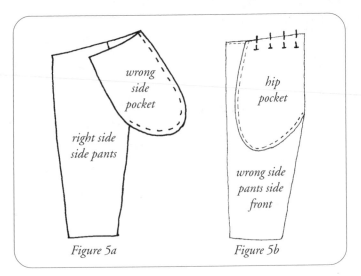

*Figure 5a*

*wrong side pocket*

*right side side pants*

*hip pocket*

*wrong side pants side front*

*Figure 5b*

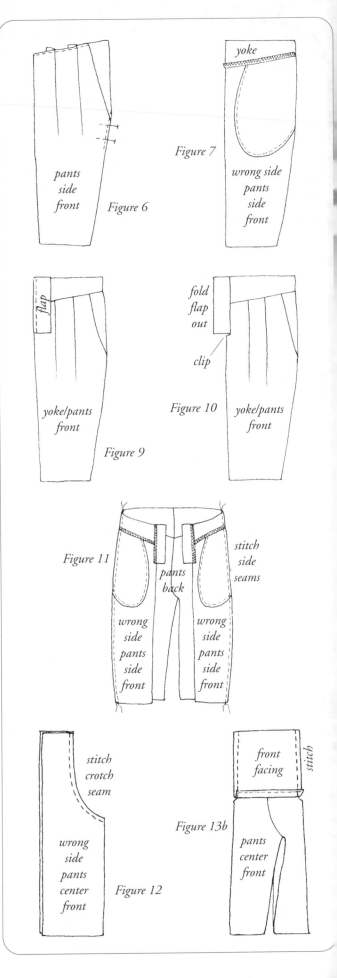

*pants side front*  *Figure 6*

*yoke*

*Figure 7*

*wrong side pants side front*

*flap*

*fold flap out*

*clip*

*yoke/pants front*

*Figure 10*

*yoke/pants front*

*Figure 9*

*Figure 11*

*pants back*

*stitch side seams*

*wrong side pants side front*

*wrong side pants side front*

*stitch crotch seam*

*front facing*

*stitch*

*wrong side pants center front*

*Figure 12*

*Figure 13b*

*pants center front*

5. With the side pocket lining pulled away from the pants, place the side pocket on top of the side pocket lining, right sides together and stitch the pocket to the pocket lining along the outside curved edge of the pockets (fig. 5a). Fold the pocket to the wrong side of the pants front along the pants and pocket lining seam. Pin the pocket to the top edge of the pants (fig 5b).

6. Pin the pocket to the pants side front and stitch in place ⅛" from the raw edge (fig. 6).

7. Pin the front yoke to the side front with the right sides together and stitch in place. Press the seam toward yoke (fig. 7). Repeat steps 3 - 7 for other side of pants front.

8. Fold the placket piece in half, right sides together, forming a long rectangle. Sew one short side of the placket together. Turn right side out and press (fig. 8). Repeat for other placket piece.

*Figure 8*

*stitch flap and turn*

9. Place the placket to the top front edge of the yoke/pants front with the raw edge of the placket top even with the top edge of the yoke and the long raw edges of the placket matching the edge of the pants. Stitch the placket to the pants with a ¼" seam along the long side of placket (fig. 9). Clip the seam allowance even with the lower edge of the placket. Flip the placket away from the pants and press (fig. 10). Attach the remaining placket to the other yoke/pants piece in the same manner.

10. Place the side front pants to the back pants, right sides together at the side seam, matching the yoke seams. Stitch, using a ¼" seam (fig. 11).

11. Place the center front pants, right sides together and sew the crotch seam using a ¼" seam (fig. 12).

12. Finish the bottom edge of the front flap facing by turning up ¼" to the wrong side and stitch in place (fig. 13a).

13. Place front facing with right sides together to the pants center front matching the top and side edges (fig. 13b). Stitch the facing to the pants on each side. Clip the seam allowance below the facing (fig. 13b). Flip the facing to the wrong side and press.

*Figure 13a*

*front flap facing*

14. Place the front flap waistband to the top edge of the center front

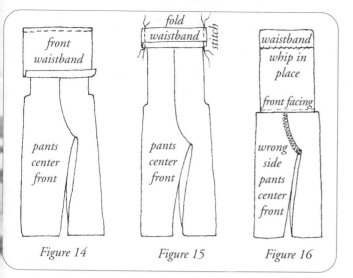

Figure 14     Figure 15     Figure 16

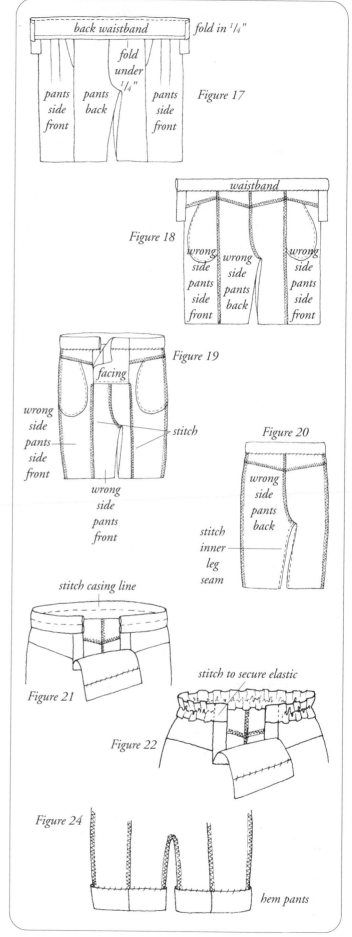

Figure 17

Figure 18

Figure 19

Figure 20

Figure 21

Figure 22

stitch to secure elastic

Figure 24

hem pants

pants with right sides together. The waistband will extend ¹/₄" on each side of pants. Stitch the waist band to the pants with a ¹/₄" seam. Fold ¹/₄" to the wrong side along the long unfinished side of the waistband (fig. 14). Flip the waistband away from the pants and fold in half with the right sides together. Stitch sides of the waistband with ¹/₄" seam (fig. 15). Flip the band to the inside enclosing the seam and stitch in place by hand or machine (fig. 16).

15. Place the pants waistband to the top edge of the pants side/back with the right sides together. The waistband will extend ¹/₄" on each side of the pants. Stitch the waistband to the pants with a ¹/₄" seam. Fold ¹/₄" to the wrong side along the long unfinished side of the waistband. Fold ¹/₄" to the wrong side on each short end of the band. Press (fig. 17). Flip the waistband away from the pants and fold in half with the wrong sides together, enclosing the seam. Stitch the bottom of the band in place by hand or machine. The ends of the band were left unstitched to allow elastic to be inserted in the band (fig. 18).

16. Place the center front pants to the pants side/back with right sides together. Pin the seams together matching the clipped seams. Stitch with a ¹/₄" seam (fig. 19). Stitch the inner leg seam matching the front and back crotch seams (fig. 20).

17. Stitch a line down the middle of the back waist band to form two casings in the band (fig. 21). Cut two piece of elastic to the following measurement: Size 4 - 13¹/₂"; Size 6 - 14"; Size 8 - 15".

18. Thread elastic through the casings securing the ends of the elastic 1¹/₄" from the edge of the waistband (fig. 22).(Note: ¹/₄" to ¹/₂" of the elastic should extend beyond the stitching lines to make sure the elastic does not pull away from the stitching.)

19. Mark three evenly spaced buttonholes on each side of the front opening with one buttonhole in the center of the waistband, one buttonhole 1" from the lower edge of the opening and one buttonhole in the center of these two. Stitch buttonholes to fit the button size. Sew buttons in the corresponding location on the placket and waistband. Refer to finished drawing (fig. 23).

20. Finish the bottom edge of the pants legs with a zigzag, serger or fold ¹/₄" to the inside and press.

21. Turn up the hem to the wrong side 1" or to the desired length. Stitch in place by hand or machine (fig. 24).

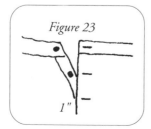

Figure 23

1"

# V - Waist Button-On Knickers

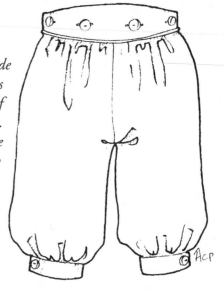

*These have to be my all time favorite pants for little boys or girls. Made in the knicker length, they are so classic and cute. The bottom of the knickers has a cuff which closes with a button and buttonhole. We have made lots of versions using piping around the front waistband which has the cute v-shape. It is not necessary to pipe this front waistband; however, it is so cute. There are four buttonholes on the front waistband and two on the back waistband which also has elastic. It is not necessary to put any buttonholes in the back since there is elastic. The choice is yours. Make lots of these pants to go with the shirts for either a boy or a girl. Nearly every fabric would be wonderful in this cute pair of knickers.*

## Fabric Requirements

| Fabric 45" | Sizes 1-2 | Sizes 3-4 | Sizes 5-6 |
|---|---|---|---|
| Fabric 45" | 7/8 yd. | 1 1/8 yds. | 1 1/4 yds. |
| 1" elastic | 1/4 yd | 1/3 yd | 1/3 yd |
| 1/2" Buttons | 4 | 4 | 4 |
| Optional: Piping | | | |

## Pattern Pieces

All patterns are found in the pattern envelope.
Button-on knickers front, button-on knickers back, button-on knickers cuff and button-on knickers waistband.

All seams are 1/4". Seams finished with a zigzag stitch or serger.

## Cutting

Cut two button-on knicker fronts, two button-on knicker backs, two button-on knicker cuffs and one button-on knicker waistband from the fabric.

OPTIONAL: suspenders - Cut two fabric strips 2 1/2" wide by the following lengths: Size 5-6 to 28", sizes 3-4 to 26" and sizes 1-2 to 25".

## Construction

1. Mark the indicated fold lines, dots, buttonhole placement and other markings on the fabric pieces with a wash-out marker.
2. Turn in 1/4" on the edge of the upper extensions of the back and front knickers pieces. Stitch close to the edge (fig. 1a). Turn the back extension to the inside along the fold line and pin (fig. 1b).
3. On both the front and back pieces turn in 1/4" of the lower leg extension. Stitch in place (fig. 1a).
4. Place the front and back knickers right sides together at the side seams and stitch between the dots marked at the upper and lower extensions. Clip to the dot at the extensions. Finish the leg seam and press (fig. 2).

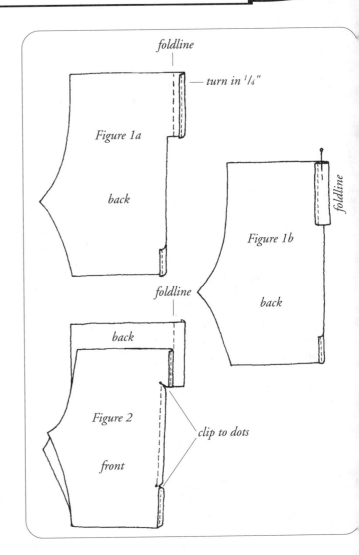

foldline
turn in 1/4"
Figure 1a
back
foldline
Figure 1b
back
foldline
back
Figure 2
front
clip to dots

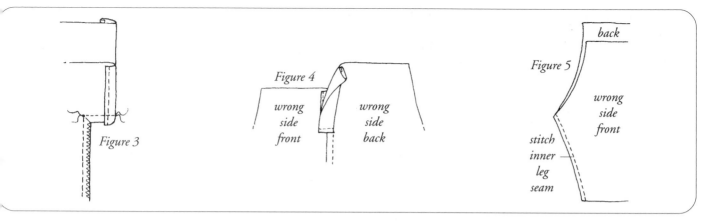

Figure 3

Figure 4

wrong side front    wrong side back

Figure 5

back

front

wrong side front

stitch inner leg seam

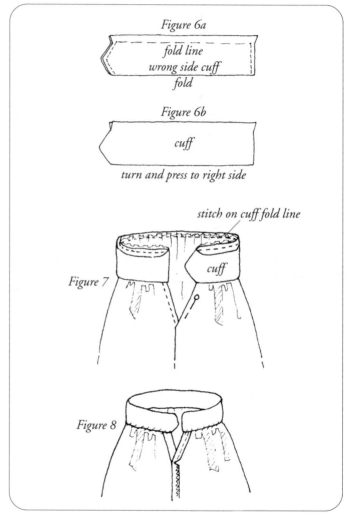

Figure 6a

fold line
wrong side cuff
fold

Figure 6b

cuff

turn and press to right side

stitch on cuff fold line

Figure 7

cuff

Figure 8

. With the extensions right sides together, stitch across the bottom edge of the extension from the dot to the outside edge (fig. 3).

. Fold the extension toward the front of the knickers, pressing at the front fold line. Pin the front fold in place (fig. 4).

. With right sides together, stitch the inner leg seams (fig. 5).

. Press under ¼" on each long edge of each cuff piece. With right sides together, fold the cuff pieces in half along the fold line and stitch both ends to the pressed folds (fig. 6a). Clip the corners, turn right side out and press (fig. 6b).

. Fold the lower front extension to the inside ¼", press and pin. The back extension will remain extended. This creates a mock placket.

0. Run two gathering rows around the bottom of the legs, ⅜" and ¼". Gather the legs to fit the cuffs. Place the right side of the cuff to the right side of the leg. The pointed side of the cuff should line up with the folded side of the leg opening. The straight side of the cuff should line up with the extended side of the leg opening. Stitch (fig. 7).

1. Trim the seam and press it toward the cuff. Hand whip the remaining edge of the cuff to the inside at the seam line (fig. 8).

2. Place one leg inside of the other leg, right sides together, and line up the center front and back seams. Stitch the seam from the top center front around to the top center back. Trim the seam and clip notches in the curve (fig. 9).

3. Place gathering rows along the top edge of the knickers front ½" and ¼" from the edge. Gather the front to fit the waistband.

4. Piping Option: Make a piece of piping (refer to "Making Piping" if needed) 1" longer than the measurement of the short sides plus one "v" side. Stitch the piping to the right side of the waistband starting at the fold, clipping the corners, and continuing to the opposite fold (fig. 10a).

5. Place the waistband right sides together to the front edge, with the fold line of the extensions meeting the seam allowance of the

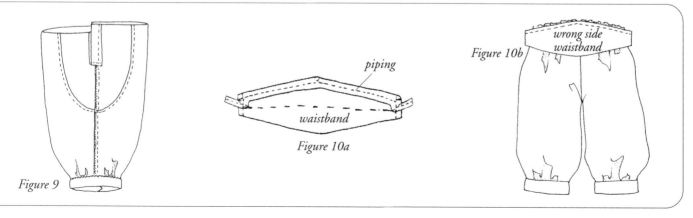

Figure 9

piping

waistband

Figure 10a

Figure 10b

wrong side waistband

band. Stitch, pivoting at the point in the center (fig. 10b).

16. Trim the seam and the corner. Turn the waistband up and press the seam toward the band. Fold the waistband in half along the fold line, right sides together. Stitch the ends, being careful not to catch the pants in the seam and securing well at the bottom edge (fig. 11).

17. Trim the seams and turn the waistband right side out and to the inside. Turn under ¼" to the wrong side at the bottom of the waistband and hand whip the edge of the band to the inside at the seam line. Work the four buttonholes in the front waistband at the markings (fig. 12).

18. Turn in ¼" along the top edge of the back of the knickers. Fold the casing to the inside along the fold line, wrong sides together, making sure that the top front of the knickers and the top back are even. Stitch close to both top and bottom long edges.

19. Cut a piece of elastic to the following measurement:

Size 1-2      6" to 6½"
Size 3-4      7" to 8"
Size 5-6      9" to 10"

Run the elastic through the casing, leaving ½" free from elastic at each end. Secure with several rows of straight stitching. Sew buttons on the back extensions opposite the buttonholes (fig. 13). Option: Buttonholes can be sewn through the elastic in the pants back half-way between the center back and the side openings.

20. Optional - Suspenders. Fold each suspender in half lengthwise. Stitch along the long side using a ¼" seam. Turn each suspender to the right side, press. Finish the short ends of the suspenders by turning the cut edges to the inside and hand or machine stitching in place. Hand whip the backs of the suspenders to the inside of the back waistband. The suspenders can crisscross in the back (fig. 14).

21. Try the knickers on the child. Mark and sew the buttons on the front ends of the suspenders.

22. Work the buttonholes on the pointed ends of the cuffs, line up and sew buttons on the other ends of the cuffs (fig. 15).

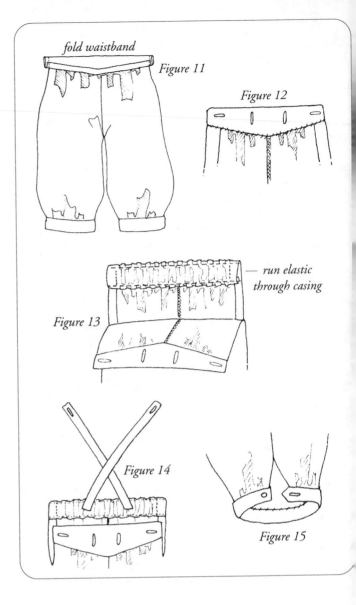

fold waistband

*Figure 11*

*Figure 12*

*Figure 13*

— run elastic through casing

*Figure 14*

*Figure 15*

# V - Front Button-on Pants

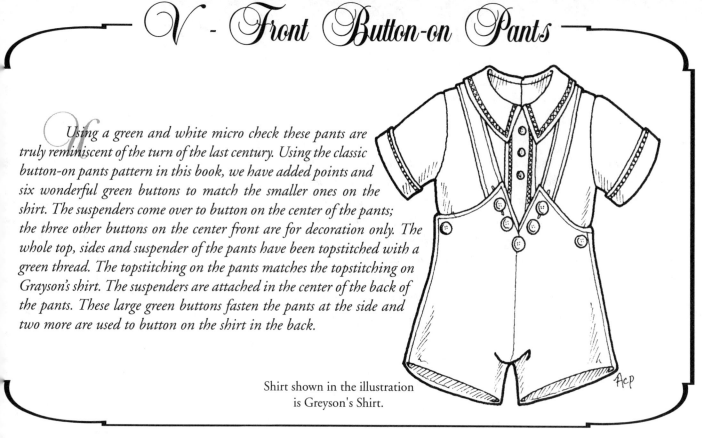

*Using a green and white micro check these pants are truly reminiscent of the turn of the last century. Using the classic button-on pants pattern in this book, we have added points and six wonderful green buttons to match the smaller ones on the shirt. The suspenders come over to button on the center of the pants; the three other buttons on the center front are for decoration only. The whole top, sides and suspender of the pants have been topstitched with a green thread. The topstitching on the pants matches the topstitching on Grayson's shirt. The suspenders are attached in the center of the back of the pants. These large green buttons fasten the pants at the side and two more are used to button on the shirt in the back.*

Shirt shown in the illustration
is Greyson's Shirt.

## Fabric Requirements

|  | Sizes 1-2 | Sizes 3-4 | Sizes 5-6 |
|---|---|---|---|
| Fabric 45" (pants and lining) | $1^1/_4$ yds | $1^1/_4$ yds | $1^1/_4$ yds |
| Buttons $^1/_2$" to $^7/_8$" | 9 | 9 | 9 |

## Pattern Pieces

All patterns are found in the pattern envelope.
Button-on pants front, button-on pants back
Template: V button-on template (found in the pattern envelope)
All seams $^1/_4$". Finish seams with a zigzag stitch or serger.

## Cutting

Place the V-front button template on the top of the button-on pants front pattern (fig. 1). Tape template in place. Cut four pants fronts (two will be for the lining) and four pants backs (two will be for the lining), two strips 3" wide by 25" long for the suspenders. Transfer the dot on the side placket to all pieces. Mark placement for decorative buttons on the front.

## Construction

. Follow the constructions steps 1-11 for Button-On Suit Pants (pgs. 158-159).
. Stitch decorative topstitching $^1/_4$" from the edge on both the front and back. When topstitching around the pants front carry the topstitching down the side to the hem line $^1/_4$" from the side seam.

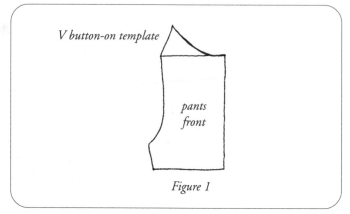

*V button-on template*

*pants front*

*Figure 1*

## Suspenders

1. Place the fabric with right sides together and sew down the long side with a $^1/_4$" seam.
2. Turn right side out and press with the seam in the middle of the suspender. Stitch decorative topstitching down each side of the suspender $^1/_4$" from the edge.
3. Finish one end of the suspender by serging or turning under and stitching. Make a buttonhole (the size to fit the buttons) 1/2" from the finished edge of each suspender. Fit the suspenders to the child and pin in place along the pants back. Cut off the excess on each suspender. Serge the suspender ends and stitch in place along the pants back.

# Button-On Suit Pants

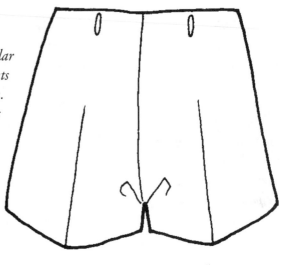

From the 1920s up until today, this style has been so popular and beloved by little boys and their mothers alike. These lined pants were worn on the cover of this book made in pale blue linen. Buttonholes are found all the way around the pants; antique buttons are sewn onto the shirt to complete this outfit. These pants are fabulous made in almost any fabric. I have pictures of my husband wearing pants like these when he was a little boy and my boys wore button-on pants also. All of my grandsons have worn button-on pants and hopefully their sons will also. I adore these pants for little boys.

## Fabric Requirements

Sizes 1-5

Fabric 45"          1 yd. for pants and lining

## Pattern Pieces

All pattern pieces are found in the pattern envelope.
Suit pants front, suit pants back
All seams ¹/₄". Seams may be finished with a zigzag stitch or serger.

## Cutting

Two front pants and two back pants. From the lining fabric cut the following: two front pants and two back pants. Transfer the dot on the side placket to all back pieces.

## Construction

1. Place the outer front pieces right sides together and stitch using a ¹/₄" seam. Clip the curve. Repeat for the lining front pieces.

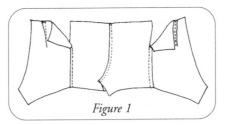

*Figure 1*

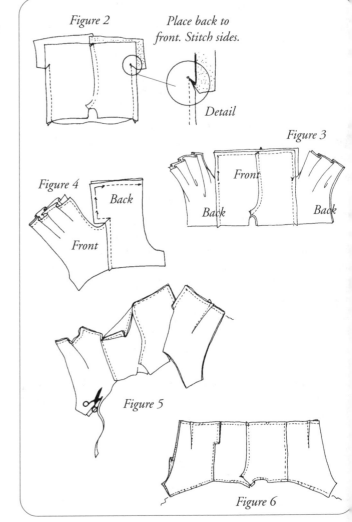

2. Place the back to each side of the front, right sides together. Using a ¹/₄" seam, stitch starting at the bottom of the pants and stopping at the dot. Repeat for the lining (fig. 1 and 2).

3. Place the lining to the outer pants, right sides together, pin along the top, plackets and hem. If there are darts, stitch them now.

4. Starting at the placket dot of the front, stitch from the dot up the placket, across the top of the pants, down the placket and to the dot (fig. 3).

5. Along the back pants, stitch from the dot along the outer edge of the placket and across the top. Repeat for the other side (fig. 4).

6. Trim away ¹/₈" of the lining at the hems (fig. 5).

7. Stitch the lining to the outer pants at the hems. This creates a tube. Clip corners and hem curves (fig. 6).

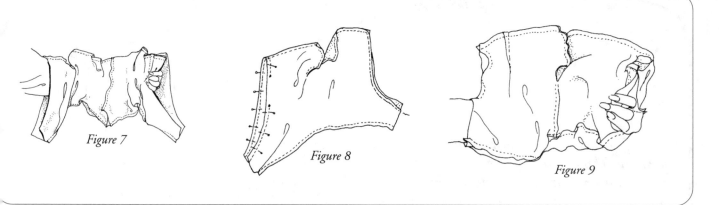

Figure 7

Figure 8

Figure 9

Place your hand between the lining and the outer pants, pull the back through to meet the back, lining to lining and outer fabric to outer fabric (fig. 7). Pin in place.

Starting at the crotch, stitch the back seam in place leaving a 3″ opening in the lining seam (fig. 8). Clip the curves. This creates another tube at the crotch.

10. Reach through the crotch and pull one through to the other (fig. 9). Pin together, lining to lining and outer fabric to outer fabric. Stitch in place. You will be stitching in a circle (fig. 10).

11. Turn the pants to the right side through the 3″ opening. Close the opening by hand (fig. 11). Press well.

12. Refer to the buttonhole placement on the pattern. Add buttonholes, fit the garment to the child and sew buttons on shirt where needed.

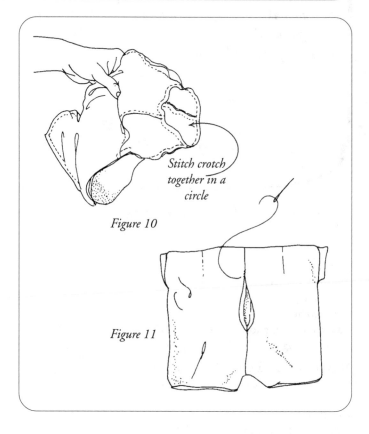

Stitch crotch together in a circle

Figure 10

Figure 11

# Pleated Front Knickers

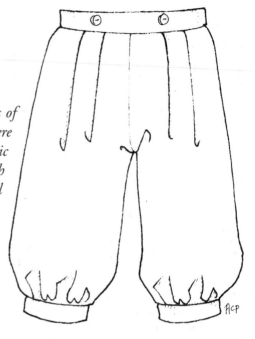

*E*asy, super easy to make would be one of my first descriptions of these pants. This is such a classic pair of pants for a little boy or girl. There are two pleats on the front with a plain waistband. The back has an elastic waistband and there are no buttons, zippers or anything which takes much time to make. The legs have a simple cuff. We have also shown in several pictures in this book, these easy pants made in a knicker length with a simple cuff on the bottom.

## Fabric Requirements

|  | Sizes 1-2 | Sizes 3-4 | Sizes 5-6 |
|---|---|---|---|
| Fabric 45" |  |  |  |
| Knickers | $^7/_8$ yd. | $1^1/_8$ yds. | $1^1/_4$ yds. |
| Pants | 1 yd. | $1^1/_2$ yds. | $1^5/_8$ yds. |

$^3/_4$" elastic $^1/_3$ yd
two decorative $^3/_4$" buttons
fusible interfacing for waistband

## Pattern Pieces

All pattern pieces are found in the pattern envelope.
Pleated front, pleated back, pleated waistband
Cuff:
1 = $10^1/_4$" by 3"
2 and 3 = $10^3/_4$" by 3
4 and 8 = 11" by 3"
Knickers may be made without a cuff. Measure child for finished length and cut knickers to this length plus $1^1/_2$".
All seams $^1/_4$". Finish seams with a zigzag stitch or serger.

## Cutting

Two fronts, two backs, one waistband, two cuffs. Knickers may be made without a cuff. Measure child for finished length and cut knickers to this length plus $1^1/_2$".

## Construction

1.  Sew the center back seam with a $^1/_4$" seam. Press the seam to one side.
2.  Turn under and press $^1/_4$" to the wrong side along the top edge of the knickers/pants back. Turn under and press another 1" to the inside ((fig. 1). Stitch close to the bottom edge to form a casing. Measure the child to determine the amount of elastic to cut for the casing, or refer to these measurements:

| | |
|---|---|
| Size 1-2  = $9^1/_4$" | Sizes 3-4  = $9^3/_4$" |
| Sizes 5-6 =  $10^3/_4$" | Sizes 7-8 = 11" |

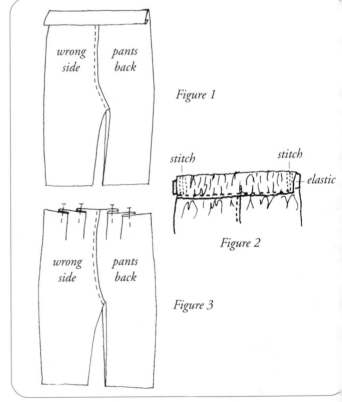

*wrong side*   *pants back*

*Figure 1*

stitch   stitch

elastic

*Figure 2*

*wrong side*   *pants back*

*Figure 3*

Cut a piece of $^3/_4$" elastic to the correct size, and run it through the casing. Stitch the elastic in place at both ends of the casing. To keep the elastic from twisting inside the casing, you may stitch through all layers "in the ditch" of the center back seam (fig. 2)

3.  Sew the center front seam. Press the seam to one side. Pin and baste the pleats in place, with the pleats folded toward the side seams (fig. 3).

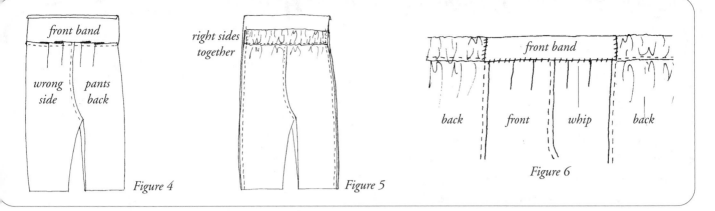

Figure 4

Figure 5

Figure 6

Press the fusible side of the interfacing to the wrong side of the waistband piece. Fold the waistband in half lengthwise and press a crease along the fold; open the waistband out flat.

Stitch the long edge of the waistband to the knickers front top edge, matching centers and side edges. Press the seam toward the waistband. Press $1/4$" to the wrong side on the other long edge of the waistband (fig. 4).

Pin the knickers front and back with right sides together at the side seams, having the crease in the waistband even with the top edge of the back casing. Stitch the side seams (fig. 5). Press the seams toward the front, including the side seam allowances of the waistband. fold the waistband to the inside and stitch in place by hand (fig. 6).

For knickers run two rows of gathering stitches along the bottom edges of the legs at $1/4$" and $1/8$" (fig. 7). Gather the bottom leg edge to fit the long edge of one cuff. Pin and stitch. Press the seam toward the cuff. Press $1/4$" to the wrong side of the other long edge (fig. 8).

Open out the $1/4$" turned-under edge of the cuff. Sew the inner leg seam, starting at one cuff edge, sewing all the way up one leg and down the other leg to the other cuff edge (fig. 9). Press the seam to the back.

Refold the $1/4$" edge to the wrong side of the cuff. Fold the cuffs to the inside, letting the folded edge meet the seam line. Stitch in place by hand.

On the waistband front, make a mark on each side of the center front at the following distances, and make a vertical buttonhole at each of the two marks:
Size 1 = $2^1/2$"       Sizes 2 - 3 = $2^3/4$"
Size 4 = $2^7/8$"       Size 5 = 3"
Size 6 = $3^1/4$"

Pants are hemmed by fitting the pants on the child and mark the hem. Turn under $1/4$" to the wrong side on the bottom edge. Turn hem up to the wrong side and hem by hand.

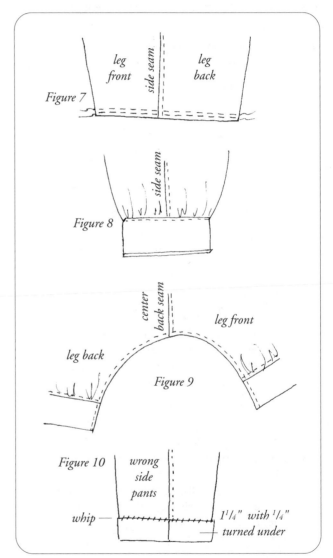

Figure 7

Figure 8

Figure 9

Figure 10

# Straight Front Knee Pants

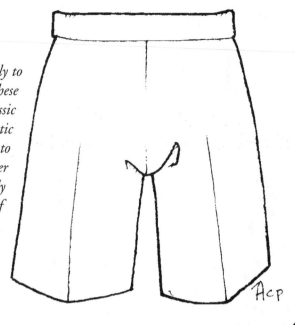

From 1900 to 1915 pants styles for little boys were usually to the knee and straight or below the knee and gathered (knickers). These easy to make pants are very classic. The straight front has a classic waistband and the pants end just above the knee. The back has elastic for a wonderful fit. A button is found on each side of the pant leg to give the illusion of being buttoned. You might put three buttons rather than one if you want the pants to look exactly as they did in the early part of this century. If you look in the historic photograph section of this book, you will have fun seeing pants like this and most of the other styles in this book.

## Fabric Requirements

|  | Sizes 1-3 | Sizes 4-6 |
|---|---|---|
| Fabric 45" | $^1/_2$ yd. | $^5/_8$ yd. |
| 1" elastic | 8" | 10" |
| $^3/_4$" buttons | 2 | 2 |
| $^1/_2$" buttons for pants leg | 2 | 2 |

## Pattern Pieces

All pattern pieces are found in the pattern envelope.
Knee pants front , knee pants back, knee pants waistband.
All seams $^1/_4$". Finish seams with a zigzag stitch or serger.

## Cutting

Cut two knee pants fronts, two knee pants backs, one knee pants waistband.

## Construction

1. Mark the indicated fold lines, dots, buttonhole placement and other markings on the fabric pieces with a wash-out marker.
2. Turn in $^1/_4$" on the edge of the upper extensions of the back and front pieces. Stitch close to the edge (fig. 1). Turn the back extension to the inside along the fold line and pin (fig. 2).
3. Place the front and back knee pants right sides together at the side seams and stitch from the dot at the extensions to the bottom. Clip to the dot at the extensions (fig. 3).
4. With the extensions right sides together, stitch across the bottom edge of the extension

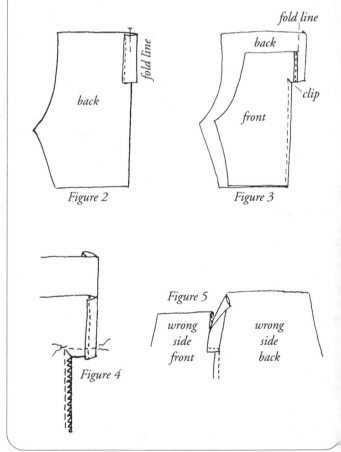

Figure 2

Figure 3

Figure 5

wrong side front

wrong side back

Figure 4

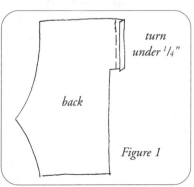

turn under $^1/_4$"

back

Figure 1

from the dot to the outside edge (fig. 4).

5. Fold the extension toward the front of the knee pants, pressing at the front fold line. Pin the front fold in place (fig. 5).

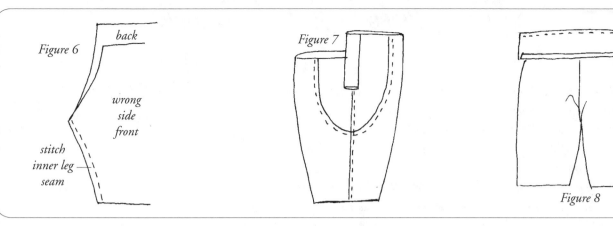

Figure 6  
back  
wrong side front  
stitch inner leg seam  

Figure 7

Figure 8

5. With right sides together, stitch the inner leg seams (fig. 6).
7. Place one leg inside of the other leg, right sides together, and line up the center front and back seams. Stitch the seam from the top center front around to the top center back (fig. 7).
8. Place the waistband with right sides together to the front edge, with the fold line of the extensions meeting the seam allowance of the band (fig. 8).
9. Turn under ¹/₄" to the wrong side on the unfinished edge of the waistband. Fold the waistband in half along the fold line with right sides together. Stitch the ends, being careful not to catch the pants in the seam and securing well at the bottom edge (fig. 9). Turn the waistband right side out and to the inside. Hand whip the edge of the band to the inside at the seam line. Work two buttonholes in the front waistband at the markings (fig. 10).
10. Turn under ¹/₄" along the top edge of the back of the knee pants. Fold the casing to the inside along the fold line, wrong sides together, making sure that the top front of the knee pants and the top back are even. Stitch close to both the top and bottom long edges.
11. Cut a piece of elastic to the following measurements:

Sizes 1-2          6" to 6¹/₂"
Sizes 3-4          7" to 8"
Sizes 5-6          9" to 10"

Run the elastic through the casing, leaving ¹/₂" free from elastic at each end. Secure with several rows of straight stitching (fig. 11). Sew buttons on the back extensions opposite the buttonholes.
12. Sew a button on the side of each pants leg to give the illusion of being buttoned.

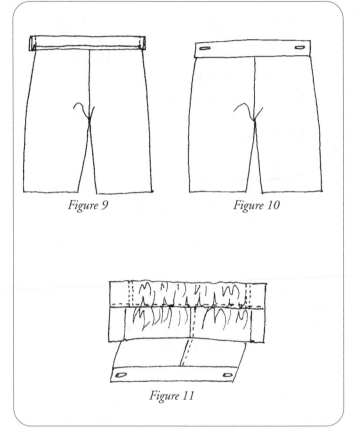

Figure 9          Figure 10

Figure 11

# One Piece Sailor Romper

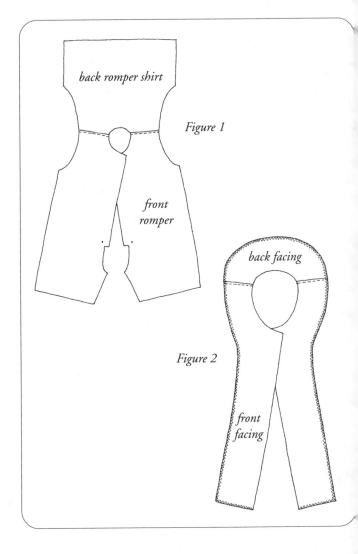

*M*ade of white linen this sailor romper reminiscent of the early 1900s is my absolute favorite little boy's suit ever!! I cannot wait to make one of these for Ward and Christopher, my grandsons small enough to wear this type of suit. The front buttons with five vintage Mother of pearl buttons and buttonholes. The back buttons on with a waistband with five vintage Mother of pearl buttons and buttonholes. The sailor collar is adorable and it is trimmed with a tiny baby blue and white gingham ribbon. It is rounded in the front and square in the back. The top of the turned under cuffs are trimmed with baby blue and white gingham ribbon also. There is a little boat, made with this same gingham ribbon, on the front of the suit— just stitched down with straight stitching on both sides. The bottom of the suit has cuffs. If the father of the family prefers a suit for christening for a boy rather than a dress, this is the perfect christening suit since it goes down to a size one. Most of our babies have worn a size one when they were about three months old!

## Fabric Requirements

| | Sizes 1 | Sizes 2-3 | Sizes 4-5 |
|---|---|---|---|
| Fabric 45" | 1$^1$/$_3$ yds. | 1$^1$/$_2$ yds. | 1$^3$/$_4$ yds. |
| Gingham Ribbon $^3$/$_8$" | 2$^1$/$_2$ yds. | 2$^3$/$_4$ yds. | 2$^3$/$_4$ yds. |
| Buttons ($^1$/$_2$") | 5 | 5 | 5 |
| Buttons ($^5$/$_8$") | 5 | 5 | 5 |
| Lightweight Fusible Interfacing (optional): $^1$/$_2$ yard all sizes. | | | |

## Pattern Pieces

All pattern pieces are found in the pattern envelope.
Front romper, romper front facing, romper back facing, back romper shirt, back romper pants, cuff, romper collar, romper sleeve, romper back waistband.
Templates: Sailboat template found at the end of these directions.
All seams are $^1$/$_2$". Finish all seam allowances with a zigzag or serger.

## Cutting

Two front rompers, one back romper shirt from the fold , two back romper pants, one romper back waistband, two romper front facings, one romper back facing from the fold, two romper collars from the fold, two romper sleeves and two romper cuffs.

## Construction

1. Transfer the dot to each front romper piece. Option: Cut two front facings, one back facing and one back waistband from the interfacing. Fuse the interfacing to the corresponding pieces.
2. Place the front romper pieces to the back romper shirt at the shoulders right sides together. Stitch using a $^1$/$_2$" seam (fig. 1).
3. Place the front facings to each side of the back facing right sides together and stitch in place with a $^1$/$_2$" seam. Finish the outer and lower edges of the facing using a zigzag, serger or fold the edge under $^1$/$_8$" and stitch (fig. 2).
4. Place the collar pieces right sides together and stitch along the outer edges using a $^1$/$_2$" seam. Trim the seam allowance to $^1$/$_4$".

*back romper shirt*

*Figure 1*

*front romper*

*back facing*

*Figure 2*

*front facing*

Turn the collar to the right side and press. Place the ribbon to the collar ½" from the finished edge. Miter the ribbon at the corners. Stitch in place along each side of the ribbon using a straight stitch (fig. 3).

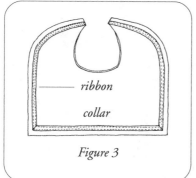

Figure 3

5. Place the wrong side of the collar on the right side of the romper. Center the collar on the romper. Pin in place.

6. Place the facing to the collar/romper right sides together. Stitch using a ½" seam. Stitch the lower edge of the facing to the dot of the romper fronts. Trim the seam allowance to ¼". Clip the curves and corners. Place a diagonal clip to the dot (fig. 4).

7. Flip the facing to the inside of the romper and press. Pull the facing and seam allowance away from the romper and collar. Stitch (understitch) the seam allowance to the facing ¹/₁₆" from the seam line around the neck. This stitching should start 1" from the edge of the front opening (fig. 5).

8. Place the front romper pieces right sides together, matching the dots and stitch from the dot to the crouch (fig. 6). Trim the seam allowance to ¼" and clip the curves.

9. Lap the front romper pieces left over right. Press. Top stitch across the lower edge of the front opening (fig. 7).

10. Stitch a buttonhole 2½" from the lower edge of the front opening and ½" from the neck opening. Stitch the remaining three buttonholes evenly spaced between the top and bottom buttonholes. The buttonholes should fit ½" buttons (fig. 7).

11. Trace the sailboat template (fig. 25) along the left side of the romper front. Shape the ribbon along the template line for the sailboat. Pin and straight stitch in place (fig. 8).

12. Turn the lower edge of the shirt back to the inside ⅛" and ⅛" again and press. Stitch in place with a straight stitch.

13. Zigzag or serge across the lower edge of each sleeve. Press the hem to the wrong side of each sleeve (fig. 9). On the right side place the ribbon 1" from the sleeve edge and straight stitch in place along each side of the ribbon. This will hem the sleeves (fig. 10).

14. Place the sleeve to the romper right sides together. Stitch using a ½" seam (fig. 11).

15. Place the back romper pants right sides together at the center back. Stitch in place. Finish the seam allowance with a zigzag

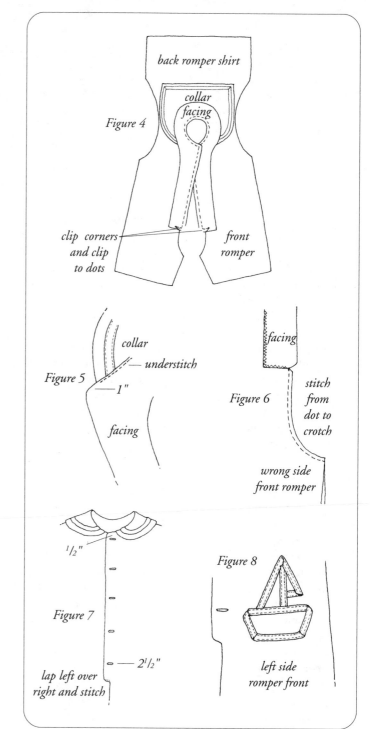

Figure 4

clip corners and clip to dots

back romper shirt

collar facing

front romper

Figure 5

collar

understitch

1"

facing

Figure 6

facing

stitch from dot to crotch

wrong side front romper

½"

Figure 7

lap left over right and stitch

2½"

Figure 8

left side romper front

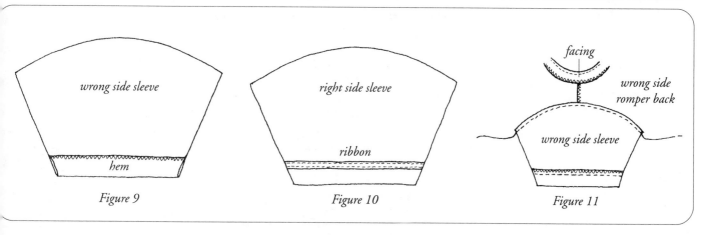

wrong side sleeve

hem

Figure 9

right side sleeve

ribbon

Figure 10

facing

wrong side romper back

wrong side sleeve

Figure 11

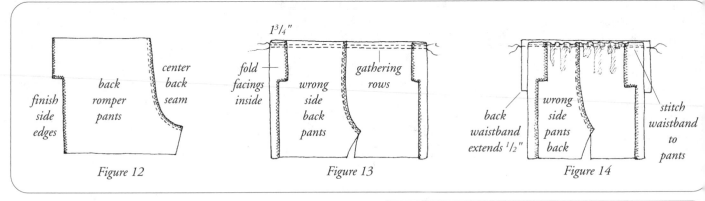

finish side edges    back romper pants    center back seam

*Figure 12*

1³/₄"

fold facings inside    wrong side back pants    gathering rows

*Figure 13*

back waistband extends ¹/₂"    wrong side pants back    stitch waistband to pants

*Figure 14*

or serger. Also finish each side edge of the pants with a zigzag or serger (fig. 12).

16. Fold each side of the pants facing to the inside 1³/₄". Press. The facing will remain folded to the inside of the pants (fig. 13).

17. Run two gathering rows ¹/₄" and ¹/₂" along the waist of the pants back (fig. 13). Gather to fit the back waistband.

18. Place the back waistband to the top edge of the pants with right sides together. The waistband will extend ¹/₂" on each side of pants. Stitch the waistband to the pants with a ¹/₂" seam (fig. 14). Fold ¹/₂" to the wrong side along the long unfinished side of the waistband (fig. 15). Flip the waistband away from the pants and fold in half with the right sides together. Stitch the sides of the waistband with ¹/₂" seam (fig. 16). Flip the band to the inside enclosing the seam allowance and stitch in place by hand or machine (fig. 17).

19. Stitch five evenly spaced buttonholes (to fit ⁵/₈" buttons) in the waistband starting ⁵/₈" from each side (fig. 18).

20. Place the back romper pants to the romper front right sides together matching the lower edges. Stitch in place using a ¹/₂" seam stopping at the dot, backstitch. Matching crouch seam at the inner leg, stitch the inner leg seam (fig. 19).

21. Place the romper back to the romper front, right sides together along the sleeves/sides matching the underarm seams. Stitch using a ¹/₂" seam (fig. 20). Note: The lower edge of the shirt back will extend into the seam of the pants; when stitching the shirt to the seam allowance of the romper front, do not catch the pants back. Finish the seam allowance with a zigzag or serger.

22. Place the short ends of each leg cuff piece right sides together to form a circle. Stitch using a ¹/₂" seam (fig. 21).

23. Run two gathering rows in the lower edge of each pant leg at ¹/₄" and ¹/₂". Place the cuff to the pants right sides together. Gather the pants leg to fit the cuff. Stitch the cuff to each leg using a ¹/₂" seam. Fold the unfinished edge of the cuff ¹/₂" to the wrong side (fig. 22). Fold the cuff, wrong sides together along the center

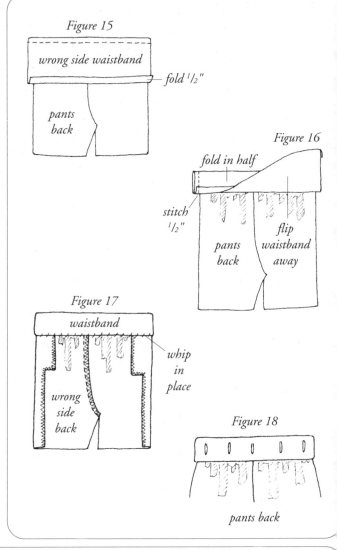

*Figure 15*

wrong side waistband

fold ¹/₂"

pants back

*Figure 16*

fold in half

stitch ¹/₂"

pants back

flip waistband away

*Figure 17*

waistband

whip in place

wrong side back

*Figure 18*

pants back

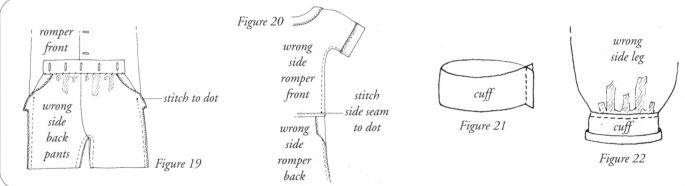

romper front

stitch to dot

wrong side back pants

*Figure 19*

*Figure 20*

wrong side romper front

stitch side seam to dot

wrong side romper back

cuff

*Figure 21*

wrong side leg

cuff

*Figure 22*

line, with the upper part of the cuff enclosing the seam allowance. Stitch the upper edge of the cuff in place by hand or machine (fig. 23).

24. Attach ¹/₂" buttons opposite the buttonholes along the front of the romper (see finished drawing).

25. Lay the romper on a flat surface with the back pants overlapping the back shirttail. Mark five evenly spaced button placement dots along the back of the shirt (fig. 24). Option: Before sewing the buttons to the shirt back, fuse a small ¹/₄" square of interfacing on the wrong side at each button placement mark. This interfacing will keep the button from pulling a hole in the fabric.

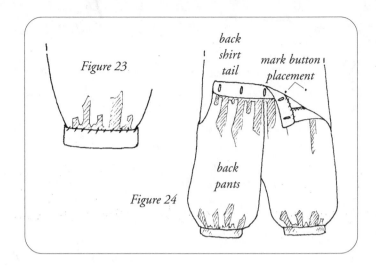

Figure 23

back shirt tail

mark button placement

back pants

Figure 24

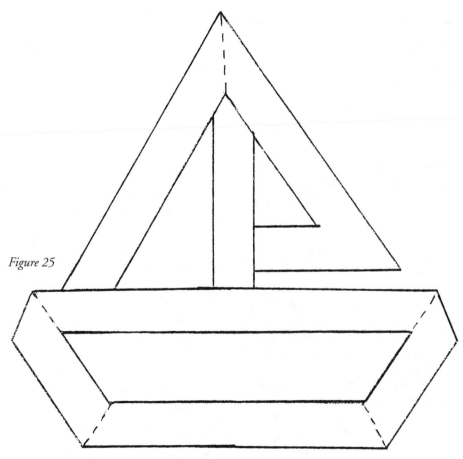

Figure 25

**Gingham Ribbon Sailboat Template**

# Short Lined Pleated Romper

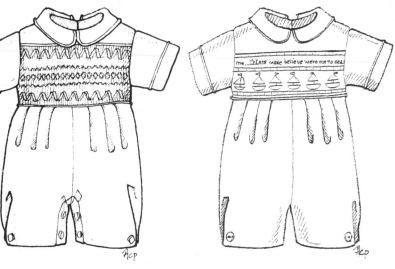

Shown in two different versions, this short little boy's lined romper is fabulous. Having three pleats in both the front and back to hold in the fullness it is very tailored. The pale green broadcloth smocked version has a wonderful smocked inset with tiny piping at the top and bottom. The lined collar has the delicate piping as do the sleeves at the top of the cuff. The bottom closes with four buttons and buttonholes. The lower fullness in the legs is held in with a little pleat secured by a button. The back of the romper has a wide belt with a button and buttonhole; the actual suit closes with three buttons and buttonholes.

One of the versions of this suit was made of a burgundy border print which was used on the bottom of the front bodice. The effect is that an inset of smocking or something similar has been added when in effect it is only border fabric. This is a great idea. The little burgundy romper has also had the extra fullness in the legs pulled in with a small pleat secured with a wooden button. Purchased grippers have been used to fasten the bottom of this suit.

## Fabric Requirements

|  | Sizes 2 | Sizes 3-4 |
|---|---|---|
| 45" wide fabric | 1³/₈ yds. | 2¹/₈ yds. |
| ¹/₂" Buttons | 8 | 8 |
| 2 decorative buttons for legs |  |  |
| Cord for making piping |  |  |
| Thread to match fabric |  |  |

## Pattern Pieces

All pattern pieces are found in the pattern envelope. Pleated romper front bodice, pleated romper back bodice, pleated romper pants front (short length), pleated romper pants back (short length), child's shirt sleeve, Peter Pan or flat collar, belt (optional). Smocking design will also be needed if smocked version is used. All seams ¹/₄". Finish seams with a zigzag stitch or serger.

## Cutting

Cut two pleated romper bodices on the fold, two pleated romper back bodice on the fold, four pleated romper pants front (short length) (two will be for the lining), four pleated romper pants back (short length) (two will be for the lining), two child's shirt sleeve (cut on fold line #1), four cuff strips 1" wide by the length of the sleeve bottom and four collars. Smocking option: one fabric strip for smocking 6" by 45".

NOTE: If using border print as shown on the sailboat romper, the lower edge of the bodice front will need to be placed ¹/₄" below the lower edge of the border portion you would like to have visible on the front of the garment. Illustrations are shown for the smocked version of the romper.

## Piping

Refer to the section on Making Piping and make enough piping to go around the collar and across the lower edge of each sleeve. You will also need enough piping to go across the lower edge of the bodice front and across the lower edge of the bodice back if you are not using a belt. If you are making the smocked version of this outfit, you will also need enough piping to fit across the yoke where it attaches to the smocked piece. Trim the seam allowance of the piping to ¹/₄" before attaching it to the garment.

## Flat Collar

1. Mark the front and back of the collar pieces before removing them from the pattern.
2. Place two collar pieces onto a flat surface right sides up with the center fronts meeting.
3. Place the piping to the collar pieces matching the raw edges.
4. Stitch the piping to the collar.
5. Lay the other collar pieces to the ones just sewn, right sides together sandwiching the piping between the two layers. Flip the collars over and using the stitching line made when attaching the piping, stitch the collar pieces together. Clip the curves. Turn and press.

## Smocked Bodice Version

1. Pleat the strip of fabric. Smock the design given. Suggested number of pleating and smocked rows:

|  | Pleated | Smocked |
|---|---|---|
| Size 2 | 8-10 | 6-8 |
| Size 3 | 10-12 | 8-10 |
| Side 4 | 12-14 | 10-12 |

We have used a shade darker floss than the fabric for the smocking and ¹/₈" ribbon to weave through the smocking in a color close to the fabric.

2. Block the smocking panel to the same width as the lower edge of the bodice front.
3. Cut two pieces of piping the same width as the lower edge of the bodice front.
4. Attach the piping just above the first row of smocking and just below the last row of smocking.
5. Trim away the excess fabric from the smocking panel even with the raw edge of the piping on the top and bottom of the panel.
6. Place the smocking panel on a flat surface (a lace shaping board or padded ironing board would work great) and place the bodice

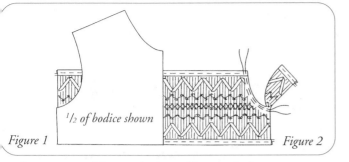

Figure 1

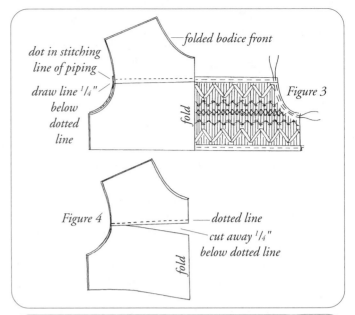

Figure 2

Figure 3

Figure 4

*¹/₂ of bodice shown*

folded bodice front

dot in stitching line of piping

draw line ¹/₄" below dotted line

fold

dotted line
cut away ¹/₄" below dotted line

fold

front on top of the smocked panel having the lower raw edges even (fig. 1). Pin through both layers.

7. Trace the armhole curve onto the smocked piece.

8. Remove the pieces from the board and straight stitch just inside the armhole curve on the smocked piece only. Stitch again just inside the first stitching line (approximately ¹/₁₆") (fig. 2).

9. Trim away the armhole curve along the line drawn (fig. 2).

10. To create the yoke front, fold the front bodice in half and place on top of the smocked insert having the lower edges even. Dot along the bodice on top of the stitching line attaching the piping. Draw a line ¹/₄" below the dotted line (fig. 3). Cut away the lower portion of the bodice along the lower drawn line (fig. 4).

11. Stitch the created yoke to the top of the smocked insert using the stitching line of the piping as a guide.

12. This smocked front bodice will now be treated as one piece during construction and called the bodice front.

13. Lay bodice aside.

## Lined Pants

1. Place a mark 5" from the top edge of the pants back. Place the pant backs right sides together and stitch the center back seam beginning at the mark and stitching towards the crotch. Clip to the seam at the mark.

2. Place the pant fronts right sides together and stitch the center front seam.

3. Place the romper front and back right sides together and stitch the side seams.

4. Repeat step 1, 2, and 3 above for the lining pieces.

5. Place the lining and the pants right sides together and stitch across the lower edge of the pants leaving the crotch open (fig. 5).

6. Turn the pants right side out and press the lower edge of the pants.

7. Measure across the crotch of the pants and cut two rectangles 2" by the crotch width measurement.

8. Place a rectangle right sides together to the pants front crotch treating the lining and the outside fabric as one.

9. Stitch the placket in place (fig. 6).

10. Along the other long side of the placket piece, press under a ¹/₄" seam allowance (fig. 7).

11. Fold the placket right sides together placing the fold of the seam allowance even with the seam of the crotch. Stitch along each end of the placket.

12. Turn the placket right side out and whip the folded edge to the seam line of the crotch.

13. Repeat steps 8 through 12 for the pants back crotch.

14. Sew snaps across the crotch placing one at the center seam and spacing the others on each side of the center. You may use snap tape instead of individual snaps.

15. Pin the top raw edges of the lining and pants together.

16. Cut a strip of fabric 10¹/₂" by 2". Place a continuous lap placket

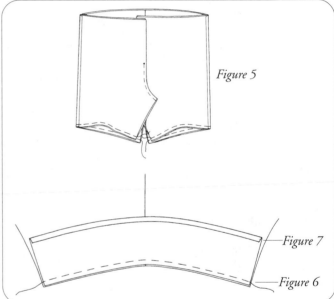

Figure 5

Figure 7

Figure 6

in the center back of the pants treating the lining and outside fabric as one. Fold back the placket on the left side of the pants and pin. Leave the placket extended on the right side of the pants. NOTE: The following pleats are made through both layers of fabric.

17. Place 3 pleats in the pants front and back as indicated on the pattern.

18. Fold a ¹/₂" pleat at at the bottom outside leg side seam and secure in place with a button. See finished drawing.

19. Lay the pants aside.

## Construction

1. Place the front bodice right side up on a flat surface. Place the folded back yokes with wrong sides folded together onto the front yoke, lining up the shoulder seams. Place the other front bodice piece (the lining) right side down onto the back yokes, lining up the shoulder seams.

2. Separate the two layers of the back yoke pieces at the shoulders. Pin one of the back yoke layers to one of the front yoke pieces and the other layer to the other front yoke piece at the shoulders.

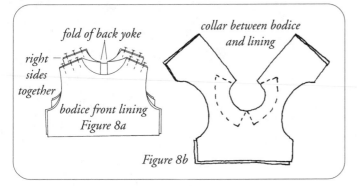

fold of back yoke

right sides together

collar between bodice and lining

bodice front lining
Figure 8a

Figure 8b

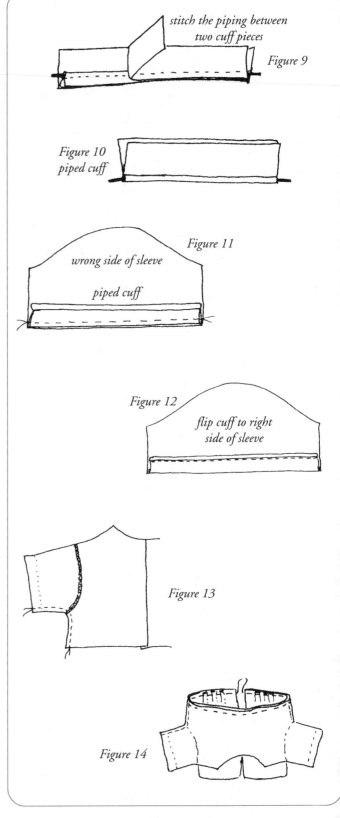

stitch the piping between two cuff pieces
Figure 9

Figure 10
piped cuff

Figure 11
wrong side of sleeve
piped cuff

Figure 12
flip cuff to right side of sleeve

Figure 13

Figure 14

Repeat for the other side of the bodice (fig. 8a).

3. Stitch the shoulder seams together on each shoulder.

4. Open up the bodice pieces and press well pressing the shoulder seams open.

5. Place the collar onto the bodice front, lining up the center of the collar with the center of the bodice front.

6. Flip the "lining" portion of the bodice over sandwiching the collar between the bodice front and backs and the bodice front and backs lining. Pin well (fig. 8b).

7. Stitch through all layers around the neck and clip the seam allowance.

8. Turn and press well. The bodice and lining will now be treated as one layer.

9. Place the piping to one long side of the sleeve cuff right sides together matching the raw edges.

10. Stitch the piping in place. Place the second cuff to the first, right sides together. The piping will be inbetween the layers. Stitch the second cuff in place along the stitching line (fig. 9). Flip the cuff layers, wrong sides together (fig. 10). Press well.

11. Place the sleeve cuff to the lower edge of the wrong side of the sleeve.

12. Stitch the cut edges of the cuff to the sleeve (fig. 11).

13. Fold the cuff to the right side of the sleeve along the seam line and pin in place.

14. Stitch in the ditch between the piping and the cuff to attach the cuff to the sleeve, if desired (fig. 12).

15. Run two rows of machine stitching along the top of each sleeve at $^1/_8$" and $^3/_8$".

16. Place the sleeve to the bodice with right sides together using the gathering lines to ease the sleeve into the bodice. Pin in place.

17. Stitch the sleeves into the bodice.

18. Place the bodice front and the bodice backs right sides together and stitch the side seam of the bodice and the sleeve seam (fig. 13).

19. Pin the top edge of the pants to the lower edge of the bodice front and back. The center back of the pants will stop at the fold of the back bodices.

20. Stitch a $^1/_4$" seam using the stitching line of the piping where available as a guide (fig. 14).

21. Press the seam towards the bodice.

22. Work three evenly spaced horizontal buttonholes $^1/_2$" from the fold on the left side of the back bodice.

23. Sew the buttons on the right side of the back bodice.

## Belt (Optional)

1. Place two belt pieces right sides together and stitch the long sides and curved end with a $^1/_4$" seam. Turn the belt right side out and press well.

2. Repeat step 1 for the other two belt pieces.

3. Work a horizontal buttonhole $^1/_2$" from the curved end of one of the belt pieces. Sew a button $^1/_2$" from the end of the other belt

4. Button the belts together.

5. Lay the romper on a flat surface with the back facing you.

6. Place the belt on the romper back with the bottom edge of the belt even with the armhole seam just below the bodice seam.

7. Mark the belt on each side even with the side seams of the romper

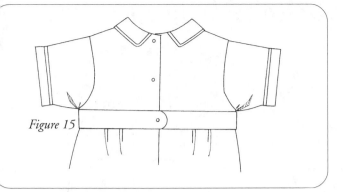
Figure 15

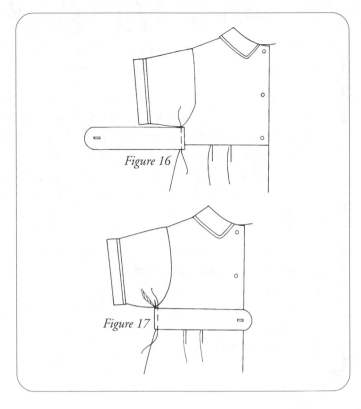
Figure 16

Figure 17

(fig. 15).

. Remove the belt and cut away the excess belt along the mark.

. Unbutton the belt and place the buttonhole side of the belt along the side seam with the raw edge of the belt $^1/_4$" from the side seam. The raw edge of the belt will be towards the back bodice of the romper. NOTE: Be sure the belt laps the same as the romper back.

0. Stitch the belt to the romper along the side seam (fig. 16).

1. Trim the seam allowance to $^1/_8$".

2. Fold the belt towards the back bodice and topstitch $^1/_4$" from the side seam to secure the belt in place (fig. 17).

3. Repeat steps 9 - 12 for the other side of the belt.

# Knicker Length Pleated Romper

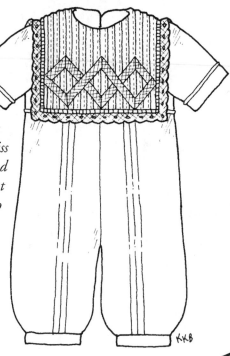

*This white romper would be perfect for a wedding, a portrait, Easter, or in other fabrics for almost any dress up occasion for a boy. Add puffed sleeves and it is just as cute for a little girl. The square collar is magnificent with its double needle pintucks running vertically on both the front and the back. Ecru lace insertion has been shaped into three diamonds on the front; they have been attached with wing needle pinstitching. Ecru Swiss entredeux is found around the collar and flat ecru lace has been stitched around the collar. The corners of the flat ecru French lace have been mitered. The front of the knickers have three pleats on each side of the center seam; the pleats go all the way to the bottom of the knickers. There is a band at the bottom of the knickers. These same three pleats are found on the back of the suit once again ending at the bottom of the knickers. The back closes with buttons and buttonholes. Tiny white broadcloth piping is found at the bottom of the front and back bodice and at the top of the cuffs of the sleeves.*

## Fabric Requirements

|  | Sizes 2 | Sizes 3-4 |
|---|---|---|
| 45" wide fabric | $1^3/_4$ yds. | $2^1/_8$ yds. |
| $^1/_2$" wide insertion lace (ecru) | 2 yds. | $2^1/_4$ yds. |
| $^5/_8$" wide edging lace (ecru) | $1^1/_2$ yds. | $1^7/_8$ yds. |
| Ecru entredeux | $1^1/_2$ yds. | $1^7/_8$ yds. |
| $^1/_2$" buttons | 4 | 4 |

Cord for making piping
Lightweight thread to match material and lace.

## Pattern Pieces

All pattern pieces are found in the pattern envelope.
Pleated romper front bodice, pleated romper back bodice, pleated romper pants front (knicker length), pleated romper pants back (knicker length), child's shirt sleeve, square collar with the following length added to the front and back: size 2 add 1", size 3 add $1^1/_2$", size 4 add $1^3/_4$", belt (optional).
Template: romper diamond.
All seams $^1/_4$". Finish seams with a zigzag stitch or serger.

## Cutting

Cut two pleated romper bodices on the fold, two pleated romper back bodice on the fold, two pleated romper pants front (knicker length), two pleated romper pants back (knicker length), two child's shirt sleeve (cut on fold line #2), two pants cuffs 2" wide by the following length: size 2 = 11", size 3 = $11^1/_2$", size 4 = 12" and one piece of fabric 18" by 45" to be pintucked for the collar.

## Piping

Refer to the section on Making Piping and make enough piping to go across the lower edge of each sleeve. You will also need enough

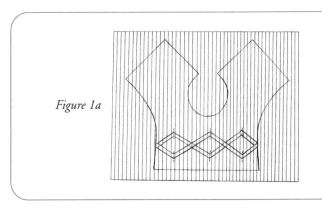

*Figure 1a*

piping to go across the lower edge of the bodice front and across the lower edge of the bodice back. Trim the seam allowance of the piping to $^1/_4$" before attaching it to the garment.

## Square Collar

1. Stitch pintucks parallel to the selvage across the 18" by 45" piece of fabric referring to Basic Pintucking found on page 369. You may not need the entire 45" width of fabric. Place the pattern for the extended square collar onto the pintucked piece to ensure that you have stitched enough pintucks for the size collar you are making.

2. When you have stitched enough pintucks for the collar, press the pintucked piece.

3. Trace the collar and the lace diamonds template lines onto the pintucked piece (fig. 1a).

4. Shape the insertion onto the pintucked piece referring to the section on lace shaping.

5. Stitch the lace insertion to the pintucked piece with a pinstitch or zigzag stitch on both sides of the insertion. Trim away the

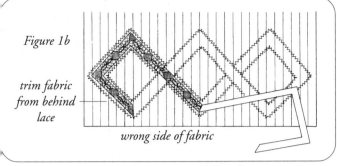

Figure 1b

trim fabric
from behind
lace

wrong side of fabric

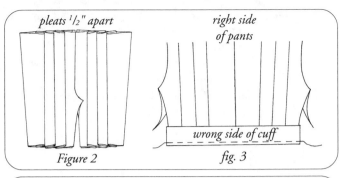

pleats ¹/₂" apart

right side
of pants

wrong side of cuff

Figure 2          fig. 3

pintucked fabric from behind the lace (fig. 1b).

6. Cut out the collar along the drawn lines.
7. Attach the entredeux around all sides of the collar except the neck opening and center back referring to the technique entredeux to fabric.
8. Attach the lace edging flat to the entredeux mitering the corners
9. Finish the back edges of the collar by turning ¹/₈" and ¹/₈" again to the wrong side. Stitch in place.

## Pants

1. Place a mark 5" from the top edge of the pants. Place the pant backs right sides together and stitch the center back seam beginning at the mark and stitching towards the crotch. Clip to the seam at the mark.
2. Place the pant fronts right sides together and stitch the center front seam.
3. Place the romper front and back right sides together and stitch the side seams.
4. Turn the pants right side out and press well.
5. Cut a strip of fabric 10¹/₂" by 2". Place a continuous lap placket in the center back of the pants. Fold back the placket on the left side of the pants and pin. Leave the placket extended on the right side of the pants.
6. Place three pleats in the pants as marked. Pin in place.
7. Place three pleats in the back as marked. Pin in place.
8. Pin pleats in bottom of pants. These pleats will be in line with the pleats below the bodice. Creases will be pressed in the pants to "connect" the pleats (fig. 2).
9. Pin the cuff to the lower edge of each pants leg adjusting the pleats if necessary. Stitch the cuff to the lower edge of the pants (fig. 3).
10. Stitch the inner leg seam.
11. Fold under a ¹/₄" hem along the unfinished edge of each cuff. Fold up the cuff to meet the seam line and whip along the folded edge.
12. Lay the pants aside.

## Construction

1. Place the front bodice right side up on a flat surface. Place the folded back yokes with wrong sides folded together onto the front yoke, lining up the shoulder seams. Place the other front bodice piece (the lining) right side down onto the back yokes, lining up the shoulder seams.
2. Separate the two layers of the back yoke pieces at the shoulders. Pin one of the back yoke layers to one of the front yoke pieces and the other layer to the other front yoke piece at the shoulders. Repeat for the other side of the bodice (fig. 4).
3. Stitch the shoulder seams together on each shoulder.
4. Open up the bodice pieces and press well pressing the shoulder

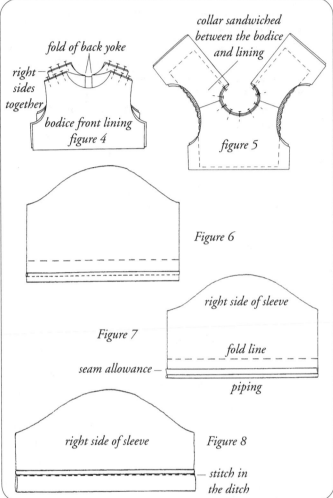

fold of back yoke

right sides together

bodice front lining
figure 4

collar sandwiched between the bodice and lining

figure 5

Figure 6

Figure 7

seam allowance

right side of sleeve

fold line

piping

right side of sleeve          Figure 8

stitch in the ditch

seams open.

5. Place the collar onto the bodice front, lining up the center of the collar with the center of the bodice front.
6. Flip the "lining" portion of the bodice over sandwiching the collar between the bodice front and backs and the bodice front and backs lining (fig. 5). Pin well.
7. Stitch through all layers at the neck and clip the seam allowance. Open up the bodice pieces and understitch the collar seam allowance to the lining around the neck portion of the bodice.
8. Turn completely and press well. The bodice and lining will now be treated as one layer.
9. Sew piping to the wrong side at the bottom edge of each sleeve with a ¹/₄" seam (fig. 6). Press seam toward the sleeve (fig. 7). Fold the cuff to the right side on the fold line. Stitch the cuff in place by stitching in the ditch between the cuff and the piping (fig. 8).
10. Run two rows of machine stitching along the top of each sleeve at ¹/₈" and ³/₈".

11. Place the sleeve to the bodice with right sides together using the gathering lines to ease the sleeve into the bodice. Pin in place.

12. Stitch the sleeves into the bodice.

13. Place the bodice front and the bodice backs right sides together and stitch the side seam of the bodice and the sleeve seam.

14. Pin the top edge of the pants to the lower edge of the bodice front and back. The back of the pants will stop at the fold of the back bodices.

15. Stitch a ¼" seam using the stitching line of the piping where available as a guide (fig. 9).

16. Press the seam towards the bodice (fig. 10).

17. Work three evenly spaced horizontal buttonholes ½" from the fold on the left side of the back bodice.

18. Sew the buttons on the right side of the back bodice.

NOTE: These pants may easily be lined by making a second pair of pants and inserting one inside the other wrong sides together then treating the two layers as one when inserting the placket, adding the cuffs and attaching the pants to the bodice. Additional fabric will need to be purchased if you choose to line the pants.

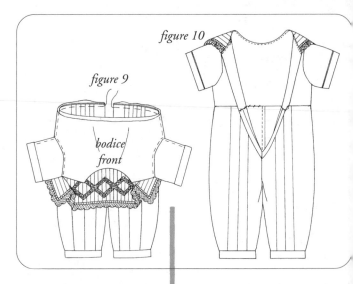

figure 10

figure 9

bodice front

A belt may be added by referring to the optional belt directions listed in the Short Lined Pleated Romper.

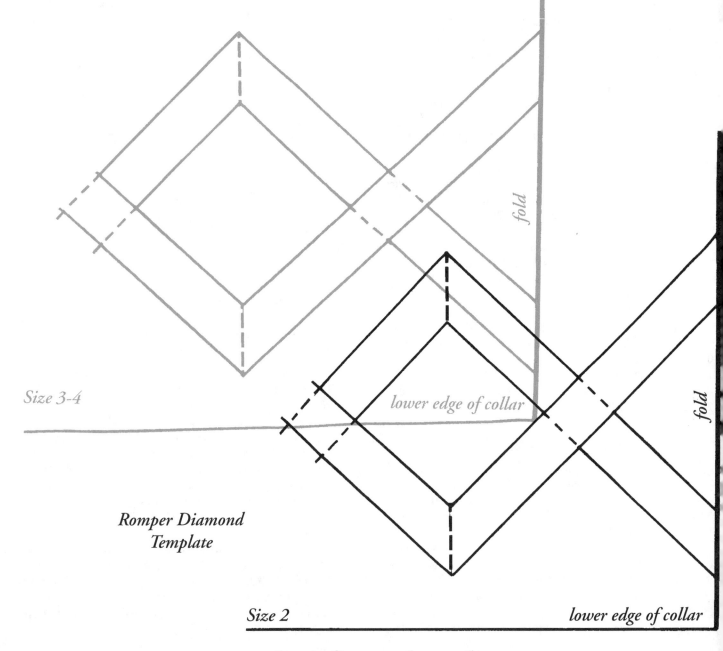

Size 3-4

fold

lower edge of collar

fold

Romper Diamond
Template

Size 2

lower edge of collar

# 1907 Romper

Although this romper originally appeared in Sew Beautiful magazine as a pattern designed by Mary Madison Railey, she has given us permission to publish it in Jack and Jill because I think it is so adorable that a boy/girl collection would not be as perfect without it's being included. This is an actual pattern dated 1907 found in very brittle condition but still usable. After Mary pieced it together for the first time, she found great versatility. It quickly became her favorite pattern for her sons. Try this in red velvet over a sweet shirt from this book for Christmas. In yellow cotton appliquéd with Humpty Dumpty, as we show it, it became a romper for playschool. In white linen, it has been used with a beautiful shirt for Easter finery or for a ring bearer's suit for a wedding. This romper would also be sweet for a little girl with a puff sleeved blouse and a little embroidery with a feminine flavor. The back closes with four buttons and buttonholes. We love the big, beautiful pearl variety. Have fun choosing your favorite Jack and Jill shirt to go with this adorable, authentic 1907 rompers. You can also choose to put the buttonholes on either the waistband of the suit and buttons on the bib; or you can chose to put the buttonholes on the bib and the buttons on the suit. Both ways are cute.

## Fabric Requirements

|  | 1-2 | 3-5 |
|---|---|---|
| Outer fabric | 1 yd | $1^1/_4$ yd |
| Lining | 1 yd | $1^1/_4$ yd |

(5) $^7/_8$" to 1" buttons
Scrap of fusible interfacing for back waistband
Snaps, button or snap tape for crotch
If an applique is used, refer to Humpty Dumpty for supplies.

## Pattern Pieces

All pattern pieces are found in the pattern envelope.
Antique romper front, antique romper top back, antique romper cuff and antique romper back.
All seams $^1/_2$" unless otherwise indicated.

## Preparation

1. Before cutting, place the pattern pieces together and measure the front and the back length from shoulder seam to shoulder seam and compare to your child's torso measurements (fig. 1). Allow 4 inches of extra length for ease in crotch area (2 inches in front and 2 inches in back). This allows for bending, sitting and reaching. Add or subtract by extending or folding front through middle (fig. 2). Add or subtract equal amount to bottom back (fig. 3).

2. Cut the following: two front rompers, two front romper linings, two back rompers, two back romper linings, one top back from the fold, one top back lining from fold (note cutting line for the lining), two cuffs from the fold and one back waistband 4" by the length given on the following chart:

| Size | Length |
|---|---|
| 1 | $11^3/_4$" |
| 18m | $12^1/_2$" |
| 2 | 13" |
| 3 | $13^3/_4$" |
| 4 | 14 " |
| 5 | $14^1/_2$" |

3. Embellish the front before construction if desired.

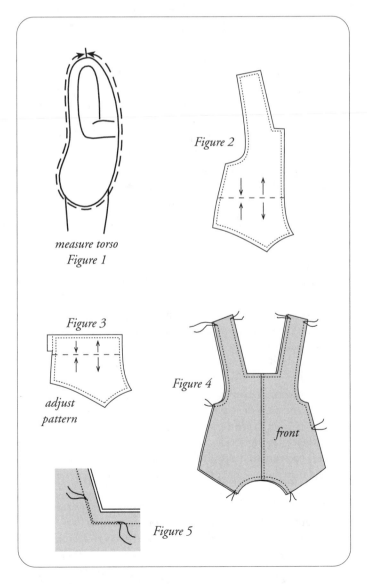

measure torso
Figure 1

Figure 2

Figure 3

adjust
pattern

Figure 4

front

Figure 5

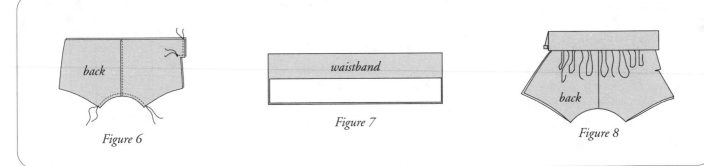

back

waistband

*Figure 7*

back

*Figure 6*

*Figure 8*

## Construction

1. Stitch the center seams of front and back using a $^1/_2$" seam allowance. Repeat for lining.

2. Place the front lining to the front with right sides together and stitch the arm opening and neckline stopping at the $^1/_2$" shoulder seams, backstitch. Stitch the crotch seam and placket edge to the dot indicated on the pattern (fig. 4). Reinforce stitch each corner of neckline. Clip the corner (fig. 5). Turn and press.

3. Place the back lining to the back with right side together and stitch the placket to the dot indicated on the pattern. Also stitch the crotch seam (see fig. 6). Trim the extra placket extentions from the back to look like figure 6. Trim the seam, turn and press the placket.

4. Cut a piece of interfacing to the same length but half the width of the back waistband. Press the band in half to mark the foldline and fuse the interfacing to one half of the band (fig. 7).

5. Run two rows of gathering stitches $^3/_8$" and $^3/_4$" from the top edge of the back romper, catching both layers of fabric. Gather this edge to fit the waistband leaving $^1/_2$" of band extended on placket side. Leave $1^1/_2$" ungathered on each end of back. Stitch a $^1/_2$" seam right sides together (fig. 8). Trim the seam and press.

6. Place the front to the back, right sides together and stitch $^1/_2$" side seams. On placket side, stitch to the dot indicated on the pattern. On the opposite side, the front underarm will end at fold of waistband. Stitch and finish the seams and press toward the back (fig. 9).

7. Press under the raw edge of waistband $^3/_8$". Fold the waistband in half right sides together and stitch the placket side only of the waistband using a $^1/_2$" seam (fig. 10). Trim the seam. Fold the opposite end of the waistband under $^1/_2$" and flip band to back side. Pin in place. Topstitch $^1/_8$" from seam edge on right side, the back edge of the waistband will be caught in the stitching. Hand whip the remaining end together (fig. 11).

8. Topstitch $^3/_4$" from each edge of crotch to create a crotch placket. Run gathering stitches in each leg opening $^3/_8$" and $^3/_4$" from edge.

9. Fold and press the cuffs in half to mark fold. Press one long edge under $^3/_8$". Gather the leg to fit the cuff. Place the cuff to the gathered leg, right sides together. Stitch at a $^1/_2$" seam. Turn the cuff back on itself along foldline and stitch both ends $^1/_2$". Trim and turn the cuff and pin in place. Stitch in the seam ditch from right side to catch cuff inside edge of the cuff.

10. Stitch the buttons and buttonholes or apply snaps or snap tape to crotch at this time. Set aside front and bottom back for now. *NOTE: For an older child, trim $^1/_2$" from the crotch and stitch a seam instead of a placket; apply cuff in a circle instead of flat.*

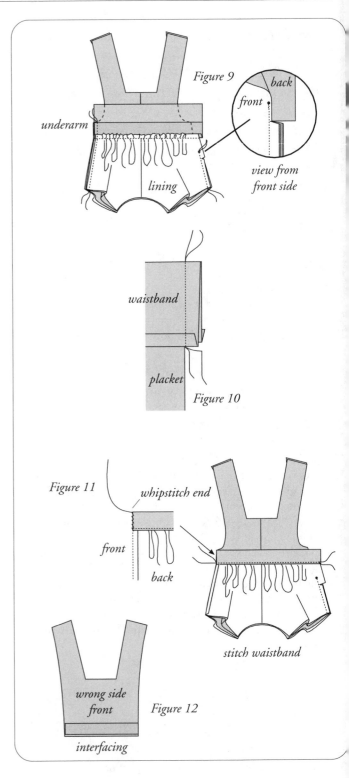

*Figure 9*

underarm

back

front

lining

*view from front side*

waistband

placket

*Figure 10*

*Figure 11*

whipstitch end

front

back

*stitch waistband*

wrong side front

*Figure 12*

interfacing

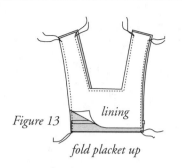

*Figure 13*

lining

fold placket up

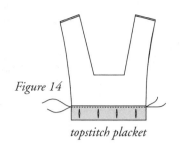

*Figure 14*

topstitch placket

shoulder

flip lining down

front

back

*Figure 15*

11. To construct the top back, fuse a strip of interfacing to the lower back below the foldline on wrong side of fabric (fig. 12). Fold the bottom edge to wrong side ½". Fold the placket along the fold line to right side and pin. Place the lining on top with right sides together, stitch the sides and neckline stopping ½" from shoulder seams; backstitch (fig. 13). Reinforce the stitched corners. Turn inside out and flip the placket to back side over lining.

12. Topstitch across placket edge along fold. Mark and stitch four buttonholes evenly across the lower edge (fig. 14).

13. Place the outer fabric shoulder seams together and stitch (fig. 15). Trim.

14. Trim the lining shoulder seams ¼" and fold inside. Whipstitch the opening by hand (fig. 16).

15. Stitch a buttonhole on the waistband ¾" from the edge of placket end. Stitch a button to the front placket on the inside top corner (fig. 17). Align back flap over back waistband, mark and stitch buttons.

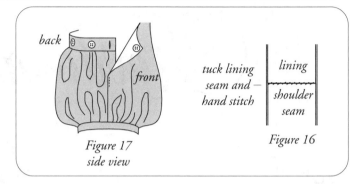

back

front

*Figure 17*
*side view*

tuck lining seam and hand stitch

lining

shoulder seam

*Figure 16*

## Humpty Dumpty Appliqué

1. Embellish the front before constructing using the Humpty Dumpty appliqué design.

Option I - Machine Appliqué (Refer to Machine Appliqué - pg. 385)
   Supplies: scrap fabric, fusible web and thread to match fabric
   For machine appliqué cut on the design line, fuse with fusible web and stitch edges with a satin stitch.

Option II - Magic Madeira Appliqué (Refer to Magic Madeira Motifs - pg. 346)
   Supplies: scrap fabric, water soluable stabilizer and DMC floss for details.

For Madeira appliqué, cut ⅛" outside the template edge. For easy Madeira appliqué, place water-soluble stabilizer on the right side of the appliqué. Stitch on the design line, clip and notch the curves and corners. Slit the stabilizer in the center, turn the piece inside out using a point turner to shape the piece. Place the piece on the garment and hand stitch around the edge. DMC embroidery floss was used for detailing.

DMC six-stranded embroidery floss color as seen in photograph:
   #964 mint green - eyes
   #138 gray - outline of eyes
   #761 pink - nose, mouth, hands, daisies
   #727 yellow - bow tie and daisies
   #407 brown - wall
   #912 green - stems and leaves
   blue to match gingham check for feet and details
   white on collar and button on shirt

appliqué design

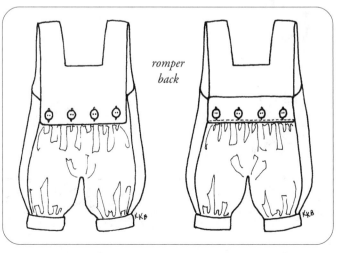

romper back

# Heirloom Sewing for Jack or Jill

# Million Different Variations Shirt

Honestly, in deciding what to name this shirt we thought of how many variations you can "do" to this shirt. It is designed for either a boy or a girl depending on what type of sleeve you choose. Actually girls can wear a straight sleeve; however, I do not suggest the puffed sleeve for a boy. We have loved stitching appliqué on the round and square collars and this shirt can be made to go with any of the pants in the book. Have fun with this shirt and enjoy thinking that you might not ever have to buy another children's shirt pattern for several lifetimes.

The round collar is so nicely tailored and we have finished most of the shirts with fabric piping either to match the shirt or to match the pants. On some of the collars we have added tatting or lace; some are plain. The square collar is equally wonderful and ever so versatile. On our square collars we have added appliqué and piping around the outside edges. For a very tailored look, only the piping is necessary. Many times for boys, Dad will let Mom put a little tatting around the collar; sometimes he will not. We find for family unity, the use of any type of "lace" on a boy should be a family decision.

The cuffs on many of these shirts have piping at the top; some do not. There is one version which simply has the sleeve turned up and hemmed; others have piping and tatting added. Oh the joy of sewing with a basic pattern; all decisions are yours to create and enjoy. We have included many appliqué designs in this Jack and Jill book; your favorite appliqué would be wonderful on these collars as would machine embroidery.

Our granddaughters love to "machine embroider." At a very young age, our granddaughters love to "sew" by doing machine embroidery. As their little hands mature more, they love to sew such things as pillows and simple clothing. For your little boys and girls, they can indeed "sew" these shirts if you let them do the machine embroidery.

Please enjoy this versatile shirt pattern. It is so classic and it is one of the absolutely "must have" patterns we decided would be included when this book was in the planning stages several years ago.

## COLLAR DIRECTIONS INCLUDED:

### Monogrammed Round Collar

### Ginger Bread Boy or Girl Collar

### Christmas Tree Collar

### Angel Collar

### Easter Egg Collar

### Bubble Gum Collar

### Dog and Cat Collar

The Shirt General Directions can be found on pages 194.
All pattern pieces can be found in the pattern envelope.

## Fabric Requirements

These are general requirements for a shirt with short sleeves and a square or round collar, extra fabric will need to be added for long sleeves. Check each specific directions for specific items needed for each shirt.

|  | Sizes 1-2 | Sizes 3-4 | Size 6-8 |
|---|---|---|---|
| Fabric 45" | 1 yd | $1^1/_8$ yds | $1^1/_4$ yds |
| Buttons $^1/_2$" | 5 | 5 | 5 |

## Pattern Pieces

Shirt front, shirt button back, either shirt short sleeve or puffed sleeve, either square or round collar. A long sleeve may also be used with any of the shirts. If using a long sleeve the long sleeve cuff pattern piece will also be needed. Add $^1/_4$ yard to measurements above for long sleeves.

## Cutting

One shirt front on the fold, two shirt buttons backs on the selvage edge, two collars, two sleeves, (two long sleeve cuffs if using the long sleeve or two sleeve bands using the following lengths: Size 1 and 2=7 $^5/_8$", 3 and 4=8$^1/_4$", 6=8 $^3/_4$", 8=9 $^3/_4$", if doing the puff sleeve), one bias neck facing 1" wide by the neck measurement.

All seams are $^1/_4$". Finish seams with a zigzag stitch or serger.

Specific directions are given for each collar and sleeve. General Directions to complete shirt are given at the end of the specific directions.

*smaller letters ca[.]
be found at the
end of this sectio[n]*

# Monogrammed Round Collar

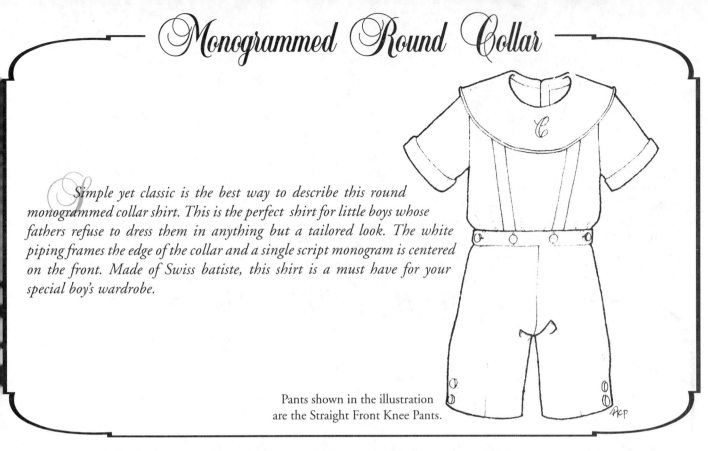

*S*imple yet classic is the best way to describe this round monogrammed collar shirt. This is the perfect shirt for little boys whose fathers refuse to dress them in anything but a tailored look. The white piping frames the edge of the collar and a single script monogram is centered on the front. Made of Swiss batiste, this shirt is a must have for your special boy's wardrobe.

Pants shown in the illustration
are the Straight Front Knee Pants.

## Specific Fabrics or Notions

1½ yds of purchased piping or cording and fabric to make 1½ yds of piping. If making piping refer to the technique section on "Making Piping".

## Specific Pattern Pieces

Round collar, short shirt sleeve, shirt front, shirt button back. Template: Monogram chart.

## Cutting

Cut one shirt front on the fold, two shirt button backs on the selvage, two short sleeves on bottom cutting line, a block of fabric larger than the collar, one round collar on the fold, one bias neck facing 1" wide by the neck measurement.
All seams are ¼". Finish seams with a zigzag stitch or serger.

## Collar and Sleeve Finish

1. Trace the collar on the fabric piece noting the center front. Refer to the machine directions on monogram techniques, and monogram the design onto the collar. If doing monogram by hand, trace the monogram design in the center of the collar, hand embroidery the monogram. Retrace the collar if needed and cut out the collar (fig. 1).

2. Sew the piping around the outer edge of the collar matching the raw edge of

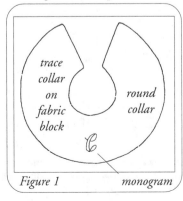

*trace collar on fabric block*

*round collar*

*Figure 1*  *monogram*

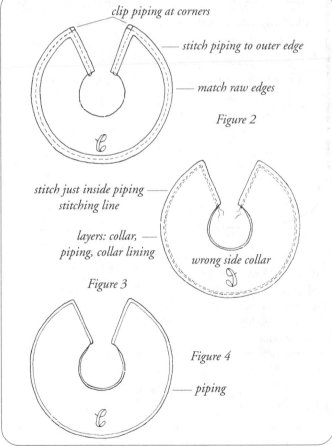

*clip piping at corners*

— *stitch piping to outer edge*

— *match raw edges*

*Figure 2*

*stitch just inside piping stitching line*

*layers: collar, piping, collar lining*

*wrong side collar*

*Figure 3*

*Figure 4*

— *piping*

the piping with the raw edge of the collar (fig. 2).

3. Place the collars with right sides together and sew the collars together using the piping stitching line as a guide (fig. 3). Trim and clip seam. Turn right side out and press (fig. 4).

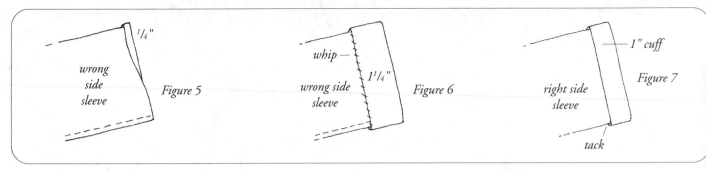

*wrong side sleeve* — ¹/₄" — *Figure 5*

*whip —* *wrong side sleeve* — 1¹/₄" — *Figure 6*

*right side sleeve* — 1" cuff — *Figure 7* — *tack*

4. Refer to Shirt General Directions, steps 1-8.
5. Turn under ¹/₄" on the bottom edge of the sleeve and press (fig. 5). Turn up 1¹/₄" hem and whip in place by hand or hem on the machine (fig. 6) Turn up a 1" cuff to the outside of the sleeve

and tack in place at the seam line (fig. 7).
6. Refer to the Shirt General Directions, steps 9-14 to complete the shirt.

# Angel Collar Shirt

*W*ith a dress made of satin and wings of gold lamé, this blonde appliquéd angel is singing her heart out. Her halo is gold lamé thread and all of her clothing is stitched down with gold lamé thread. Little pieces of lace are gathered for the yoke of her dress and for the skirt. On the blouse where we used this angel, we gathered matching lace edging around the round collar of the blouse. We put gold lamé knickers with this angel blouse.

Pants shown in the illustration are the V-waist Button-on Knickers.

## Specific Fabrics or Notions

3 yds. - ³/₈" Lace edging
Small pieces of white satin, gold, flesh colored, yellow (or to match child's hair) fabric
Thread to match yellow, flesh, and gold for appliqué
Fabric marking pens, blue and red
⁵/₈" buttons four if buttoning the knickers on the shirt.
Buttons for back

## Specific Pattern Pieces

Round collar, shirt front, shirt button back, puffed sleeve.

## Cutting

Cut one shirt front on the fold, two shirt backs on the selvage, two puffed sleeve, two bias strips 1¹/₂" wide by the following lengths: Size 1 and 2=7 ⁵/₈", 3 and 4=8¹/₄", 6=8 ³/₄", 8=9 ³/₄, a block of fabric larger than the collar, one round collar on the fold, one bias neck facing 1" wide by the neck measurement.

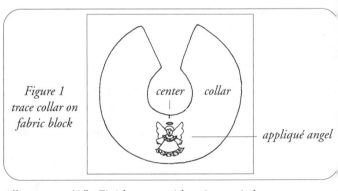

*Figure 1 trace collar on fabric block* — *center* — *collar* — *appliqué angel*

All seams are ¹/₄". Finish seams with a zigzag stitch or serger.

## Collar

1. Trace the collar on the fabric piece noting the center front. Refer to the technique, Fabric Appliqué and appliqué the angel on the right side of the collar in the center of the collar (fig. 1). Cut out the collar

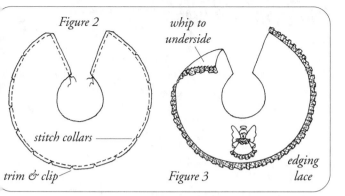

Figure 2

whip to underside

stitch collars

trim & clip

Figure 3

edging lace

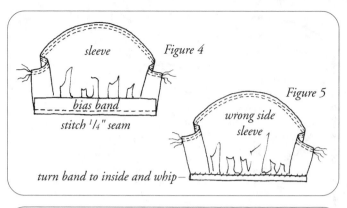

sleeve

Figure 4

bias band

stitch ¼" seam

Figure 5

wrong side sleeve

turn band to inside and whip

Lay the collars with the right sides together. Sew around the collar. Trim and clip the seam (fig. 2). Turn the collar right side out and press.

Measure around the outer edge of the collar. Cut a strip of lace edging twice this measurement. Gather the lace to fit around the collar and whip the lace to the underside of the collar (fig. 3). Refer to the Shirt General Directions, steps 1-6.

## Sleeve

Fold the bias sleeve bands in half and press. Run two gathering rows in the bottom of each sleeve at $^1/_8$" and $^1/_4$". Gather the bottom of the sleeve to fit the bias sleeve band. Place the right side of the bias strip to the right side of the sleeve and stitch using a $^1/_4$" seam (fig. 4).

Fold the remaining edge of the bias strip to the wrong side of the sleeve $^1/_4$". Stitch the folded edge just over the seam allowance on the inside of the sleeve creating a $^1/_4$" bias binding (fig. 5). Run two gathering rows in the top of each sleeve at $^1/_8$" and $^1/_4$". Gather the top of the sleeve to fit the arm opening of the shirt. The gathers should fall about 3" to $3^1/_2$" on each side of the shoulder seam.

Refer to the Shirt General Directions, steps 7-14 to complete the shirt.

Angel Collar Appliqué

# Gingerbread Collar Shirt

*What an adorable gingerbread man done in brown. The candy canes are made of a striped fabric in green and white. His eyes, nose and mouth are stitched on by hand and his pants are a gray striped velveteen. The knickers for the child are also of the gray and white striped velveteen. The gingerbread man and the child match.*

Pants shown in the illustrations are the Pleated Front Knickers.

## Specific Fabrics or Notions

1¹/₂ yds of purchased piping or fabric and cording to make 1¹/₂ yds of piping. Refer to the technique section on "Making Piping." Two novelty buttons for knickers, small pieces of fabric for appliqué, thread for shadowwork embroidery

## Specific Pattern Pieces

Round collar, shirt front, shirt button back, puffed sleeve for girls or shirt short sleeve for boys.

## Cutting

Cut one shirt front on the fold, two shirt backs on the selvage, (for girls, two puffed sleeves, two cuffs 2¹/₂" wide by the following lengths: Size 1 and 2=7⁵/₈", 3 and 4=8¹/₄", 6=8³/₄", 8=9³/₄"), (for boys, two shirt short sleeves on the bottom cutting line), a block of fabric larger than the collar, one round collar on the fold, one bias neck facing 1" wide by the neck measurement.

All seams are ¹/₄". Finish seams with a zigzag stitch or serger.

## Collar

1. Trace the collar on the fabric piece noting the center front. Trace the design onto the collar and work shadow embroidery or complete applique. Retrace the collar if needed and cut out the collar (fig. 1).
2. Sew the piping around the outer edge of the collar matching the raw edge of the piping with the raw edge of the collar (fig. 2).
3. Place the collars with right sides together and sew the collars together using the piping stitching line as a guide(fig. 3). Trim and clip seam. Turn right side out and press (fig. 4).
4. Refer to Shirt General Directions, steps 1-6.

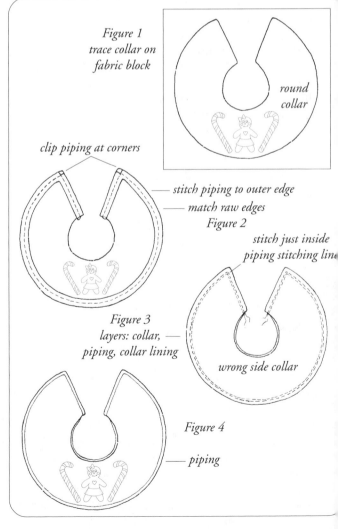

*Figure 1 trace collar on fabric block*

round collar

clip piping at corners

stitch piping to outer edge
match raw edges
*Figure 2*

stitch just inside piping stitching line

*Figure 3 layers: collar, piping, collar lining*

wrong side collar

*Figure 4*

piping

## Girl's Sleeve

Run gathering rows in the top and bottom of each sleeve at ¼"
and ⅛". Gather the bottom of the sleeve to fit the sleeve band.
Sew the bottom of the sleeve to the band with a ¼" seam (fig.
5). Press the seam toward the sleeve band. Gather the top of the
sleeve to fit the arm opening of the shirt. The gathers should fall
about 3" to 3½" on each side of the shoulder seam.
Refer to the Shirt General Directions, steps 7 and 8.
Press under ¼" to the wrong side on the bottom edge of the cuff
(fig. 6). Turn cuff to the wrong side to form a 1" cuff and enclosing
the seam. Whip in place by hand (fig. 7).
Finish the shirt referring to the Shirt General Directions, steps
9-14 to complete the shirt.

## Boy's Sleeve

Sew a stay stitching line along the top of each sleeve at ¼".
Refer to Shirt General Directions, steps 7-8.
Turn under ¼" on the bottom edge of the sleeve and press (fig.
8). Turn up 1¼" hem and whip in place by hand or hem on the
machine (fig. 9) Turn up a 1" cuff to the outside of the sleeve
and tack in place at the seam line (fig. 10).
Refer to the Shirt General Directions, steps 9-14 to complete
the shirt.

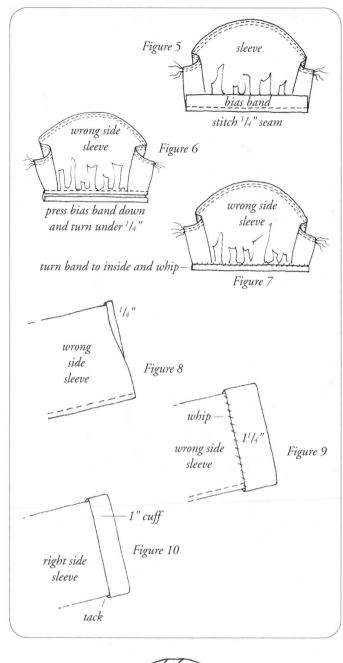

Figure 5  sleeve  bias band  stitch ¼" seam

Figure 6  wrong side sleeve

press bias band down and turn under ¼"

turn band to inside and whip—  wrong side sleeve  Figure 7

wrong side sleeve  ¼"  Figure 8

whip—  wrong side sleeve  1¼"  Figure 9

1" cuff  Figure 10  right side sleeve  tack

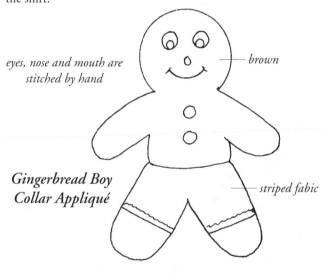

*eyes, nose and mouth are
stitched by hand*

— brown

— striped fabic

**Gingerbread Boy
Collar Appliqué**

**Gingerbread Girl
Collar Appliqué**

purple
pink
red
purple

white
red or green

*designs can be appliqué
or shadow work*

# Christmas Tree Collar Shirt

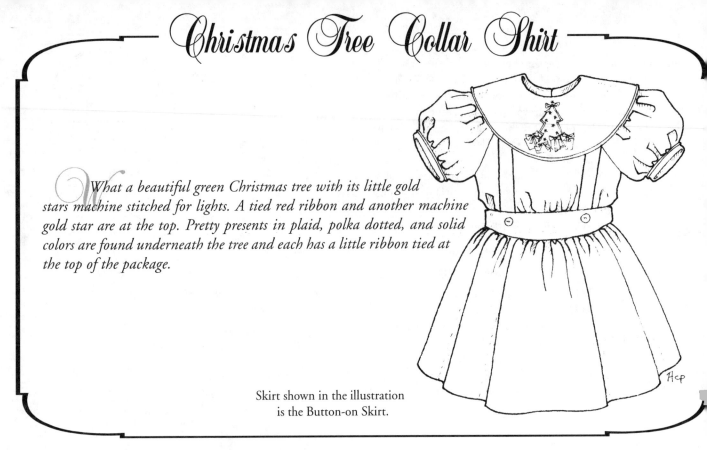

*W*hat a beautiful green Christmas tree with its little gold stars machine stitched for lights. A tied red ribbon and another machine gold star are at the top. Pretty presents in plaid, polka dotted, and solid colors are found underneath the tree and each has a little ribbon tied at the top of the package.

Skirt shown in the illustration
is the Button-on Skirt.

## Specific Fabrics or Notions

$2^{1}/_{2}$ yds of purchased piping or $^{1}/_{3}$ yard of plaid fabric and cording to make piping. Refer to the technique, "Making Piping" and make $2^{1}/_{2}$ yards of piping.

Small pieces of fabric for appliqué, green for tree and four other small pieces of yellow and prints for packages and brown for tree trunk.
Gold metallic thread for stars.
Small pieces of ribbon for packages and tree top.
Four $^{1}/_{2}$" buttons to match the skirt fabric if planning to button the bottom to the shirt.
Buttons for the shirt

## Specific Pattern Pieces

Round collar, shirt front, shirt button back, puffed sleeve.

## Cutting

Cut one shirt front on the fold, two shirt backs on the selvage, two puffed sleeve, two bias strips $1^{1}/_{2}$" wide by the following lengths: Size 1 and 2=7 $^{5}/_{8}$", 3 and 4=8$^{1}/_{4}$", 6=8 $^{3}/_{4}$", 8=9 $^{3}/_{4}$", a block of fabric larger than the collar, one round collar on the fold, one bias neck facing 1" wide by the neck measurement.
All seams are $^{1}/_{4}$". Finish seams with a zigzag stitch or serger.

## Collar and Sleeve Finish

1. Trace the collar on the fabric piece noting the center front. Refer to the technique, "Fabric Appliqué" and appliqué the Christmas tree on the right side of the collar in the center of the collar (fig. 1). Cut out the collar.
2. Sew the piping to the outer edge of the collar matching the raw edges of the piping and the collar with a $^{1}/_{4}$" seam (fig. 2). Lay the collars with right sides together. Sew around the collar just inside the piping stitching line (fig. 3). Trim and clip the seam. Turn the collar right side out and press (fig. 4).

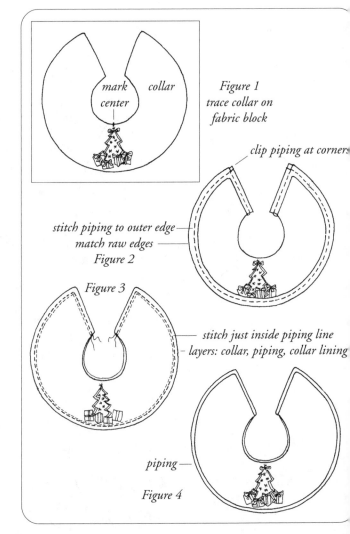

mark center    collar center

*Figure 1*
*trace collar on*
*fabric block*

*clip piping at corners*

*stitch piping to outer edge*
*match raw edges*
*Figure 2*

*Figure 3*

*stitch just inside piping line*
*layers: collar, piping, collar lining*

*piping*

*Figure 4*

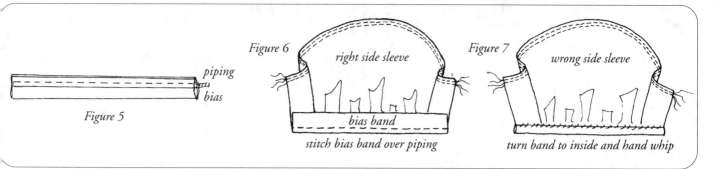

Figure 5

Figure 6  right side sleeve

bias band
stitch bias band over piping

Figure 7  wrong side sleeve

turn band to inside and hand whip

3. Refer to the Shirt General Directions, steps 1-6.

## Sleeve

1. Fold the bias sleeve bands in half with wrong sides together and press. If the edge of the piping is not $\frac{1}{4}$" trim to $\frac{1}{4}$", place the raw edge of the piping to the raw edge of the sleeve bands, and baste the piping in place with a zipper foot or cording foot with a $\frac{1}{4}$" seam allowance (fig. 5).

2. Run two gathering rows in the bottom and top of each sleeve at $\frac{1}{8}$" and $\frac{1}{4}$". Gather the bottom of the sleeve to fit the binding. Place the right side of the bias strip to the right side of the sleeve with the piping sandwiched between the sleeve and the band and stitch using a $\frac{1}{4}$" seam allowance (fig. 6).

3. Fold the bias strip to the wrong side of the sleeve.

4. Stitch the folded edge just over the seam allowance on the inside of the sleeve creating a $\frac{1}{4}$" bias binding (fig. 7). **NOTE:** The gathers should fall about 3" to $3\frac{1}{2}$" on each side of the shoulder seam.

5. Refer to the Shirt General Directions, steps 7-14 to complete the shirt.

*Christmas Tree Appliqué*

# Easter Egg Collar Shirt

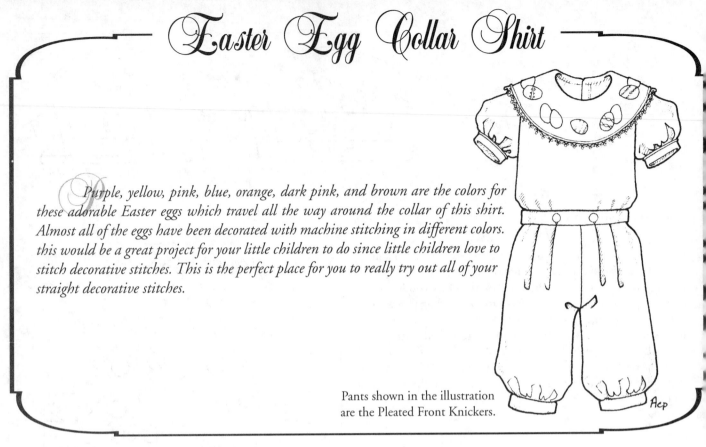

Purple, yellow, pink, blue, orange, dark pink, and brown are the colors for these adorable Easter eggs which travel all the way around the collar of this shirt. Almost all of the eggs have been decorated with machine stitching in different colors. this would be a great project for your little children to do since little children love to stitch decorative stitches. This is the perfect place for you to really try out all of your straight decorative stitches.

Pants shown in the illustration are the Pleated Front Knickers.

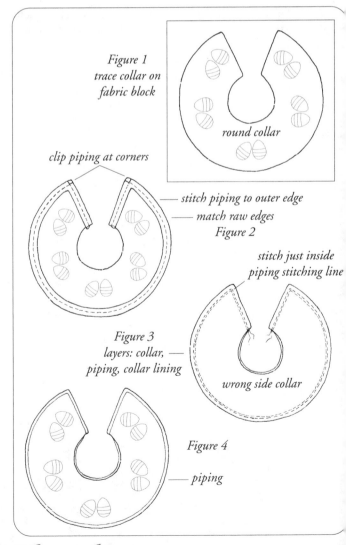

Figure 1
trace collar on fabric block

round collar

clip piping at corners

stitch piping to outer edge
match raw edges
Figure 2

stitch just inside piping stitching line

Figure 3
layers: collar, piping, collar lining

wrong side collar

Figure 4

piping

## Specific Fabrics or Notions

2$^1/_2$ yds of purchased piping or $^1/_3$ yard of plaid fabric and cording to make piping. Refer to the technique, "Making Piping" and make 2$^1/_2$ yards of piping.
1$^1/_2$ yds of $^1/_2$" trim
Small pieces of colorful fabric to blend with piping.
Decorative stitching thread
Two $^1/_2$" button if using button to button on pants.
Buttons for the shirt back

## Specific Pattern Pieces

Round collar, shirt front, shirt button back, puffed sleeve.

## Cutting

Cut one shirt front on the fold, two shirt backs on the selvage, two puffed sleeve, two strips 2" wide by the following lengths: Size 1 and 2=7 $^5/_8$", 3 and 4=8$^1/_4$", 6=8 $^3/_4$", 8=9 $^3/_4$, a block of fabric larger than the collar, one round collar on the fold, one bias neck facing 1" wide by the neck measurement.
All seams are $^1/_4$". Finish seams with a zigzag stitch or serger.

## Collar and Sleeve Finish

1. Trace the collar on the fabric piece noting the center front. Trace again $^1/_2$" (or width of edging) inside of the traced collar to allow for the trim. Refer to the technique, "Fabric Appliqué" and appliqué the Easter Eggs on the right side around the collar and centering one egg at center front (fig. 1). Cut out the collar on the inside traced line. Trim $^1/_2$" from the outer edge of the other round collar.

2. Sew the piping to the outer edge of the collar matching the raw edges of the piping and the collar with a $^1/_4$" seam (fig. 2). Lay the collars with right sides together. Sew around the collar just inside the piping stitching line (fig. 3). Trim and clip the seam. Turn the collar right side out and press (fig. 4).

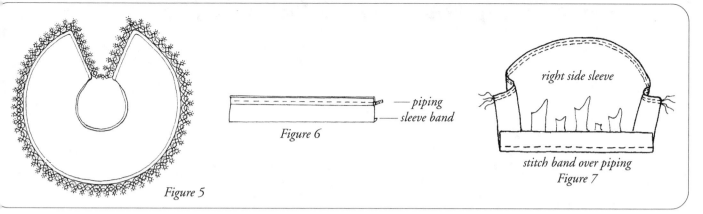

Figure 5

piping
sleeve band

Figure 6

right side sleeve

stitch band over piping
Figure 7

Shape the edging around the other edge of the collar and whip in place by hand just behind the piping (fig. 5).
Refer to the Shirt General Directions, steps 1-6.

## Sleeve

Sew piping to one long side of each band with a $^1/_4$" seam (fig. 6). Run gathering rows in the top and bottom of each sleeve at $^1/_4$" and $^1/_8$". Gather the bottom of the sleeve to fit the sleeve band. Sew the bottom of the sleeve to the band sandwiching the piping between the right side of the sleeve and the sleeve band with a $^1/_4$" seam (fig. 7). Press the seam toward the sleeve band (fig. 8). Gather the top of the sleeve to fit the arm opening of the shirt. The gathers should fall about 3" to $3^1/_2$" on each side of the shoulder seam.
Refer to the Shirt General Directions, steps 7 and 8.
Press under $^1/_4$" to the wrong side on the bottom edge of the sleeve band (fig. 9). Turn sleeve band to the wrong side to form a $^3/_4$" sleeve band and enclosing the seam. Whip in place by hand (fig. 10).
Finish the shirt referring to the Shirt General Directions, steps 9-14 to complete the shirt.

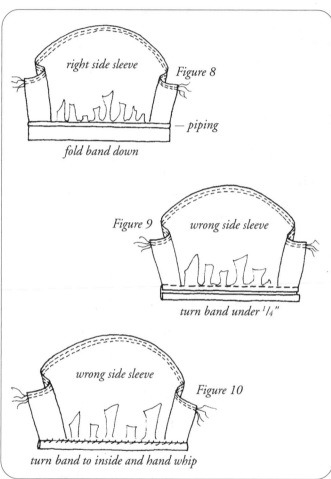

right side sleeve    Figure 8

piping

fold band down

Figure 9    wrong side sleeve

turn band under $^1/_4$"

wrong side sleeve    Figure 10

turn band to inside and hand whip

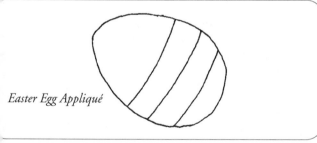

Easter Egg Appliqué

# Bubble Gum Collar Shirt

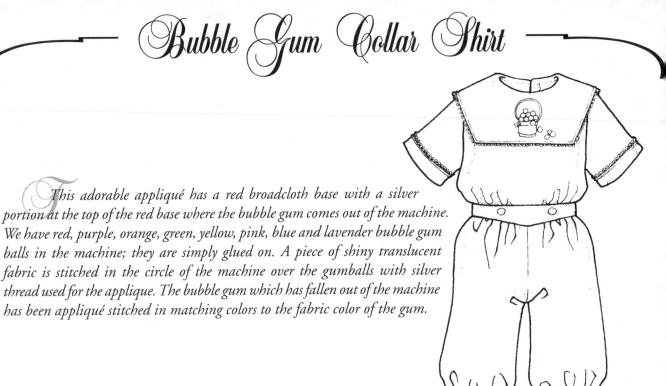

*T*his adorable appliqué has a red broadcloth base with a silver portion at the top of the red base where the bubble gum comes out of the machine. We have red, purple, orange, green, yellow, pink, blue and lavender bubble gum balls in the machine; they are simply glued on. A piece of shiny translucent fabric is stitched in the circle of the machine over the gumballs with silver thread used for the applique. The bubble gum which has fallen out of the machine has been appliqué stitched in matching colors to the fabric color of the gum.

Pants shown in the illustration are the V-waist Button-on Knickers.

## Specific Fabrics or Notions

3 yards of purchased piping or ¹/₃ yards of poka dot fabric and cording to make piping. Refer to the technique "Making Piping" and make 3 yards of piping.

3 yard of ¹/₄" trim

Small pieces of fabric for the bubble gun, a piece of red for the bottom of the machine, a small piece of silver for the machine, and a sheer fabric for the plastic gum container on the machine. Decorative embroidery threads.

## Specific Pattern Pieces

Shirt front, shirt button back, shirt short sleeve, square collar. The collar pictured has been tapered in 1¹/₄" (fig. 1a and 1b).

## Cutting

Cut out a block of fabric larger than the collar, one square collar on the fold (taper collar if desired), one shirt front on the fold, two shirt button backs on the selvage, two shirt short sleeves on fold line #2.

All seams are ¹/₄". Finish seams with a zigzag stitch or serger.

## Collar and Sleeve Finish

1. Trace the collar on the fabric piece noting the center front. Trace again ¹/₄" (or width of edging) inside of the traced collar to allow for the trim. Refer to the technique, "Fabric Appliqué" and appliqué the gum ball machine on the right side of the collar in the center of the collar (fig. 2). Cut out the collar on the inside traced line. Trim ¹/₄" from the outer edge of the other round collar.

2. Sew the piping to the outer edge of the collar matching the raw edges of the piping and the collar with a ¹/₄" seam (fig. 3). Lay the collars with right sides together. Sew around the collar just inside the piping stitching line (fig. 4). Trim and clip the seam.

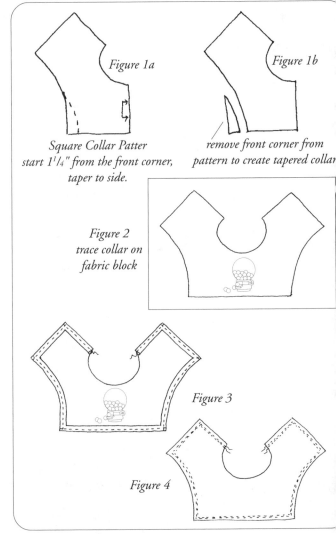

*Figure 1a*

*Figure 1b*

*Square Collar Patter start 1¹/₄" from the front corner, taper to side.*

*remove front corner from pattern to create tapered collar*

*Figure 2 trace collar on fabric block*

*Figure 3*

*Figure 4*

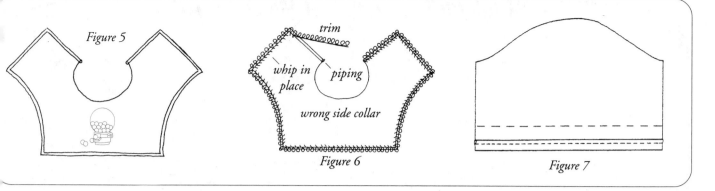

Figure 5

trim
whip in place
piping
wrong side collar

Figure 6

Figure 7

Turn the collar right side out and press (fig. 5).

Shape edging around the outer edge of the collar and whip in place by hand to the underside of the piping (fig. 6).

Refer to the Shirt General Directions, steps 1-6.

Sew piping to the wrong side at the bottom edge of each sleeve with a ¼" seam (fig. 7). Press seam toward the sleeve (fig. 8). Fold the cuff to the right side on the fold line. Stitch the cuff in place by stitching in the ditch between the cuff and the piping (fig. 9). Whip edging to the back side of the piping (fig. 10).

Refer to the Shirt General Directions, steps 7-14 and complete the shirt.

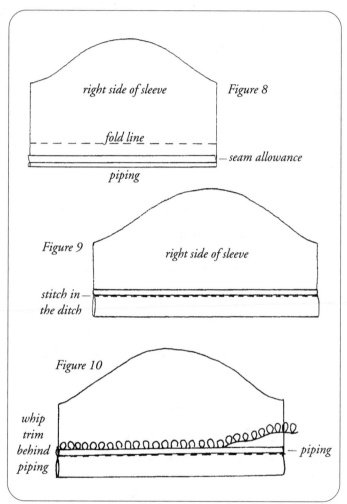

right side of sleeve          Figure 8

fold line

— seam allowance

piping

Figure 9          right side of sleeve

stitch in — the ditch

Figure 10

whip trim behind piping

— piping

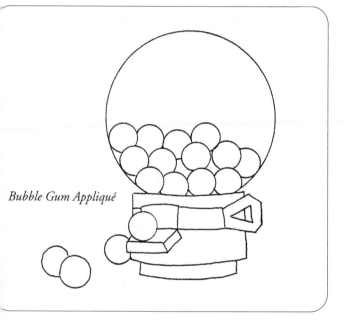

Bubble Gum Appliqué

# Cat and Dog Collar Shirt

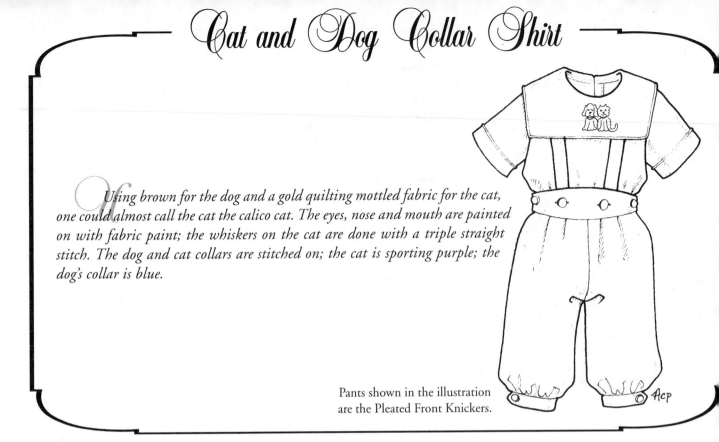

Using brown for the dog and a gold quilting mottled fabric for the cat, one could almost call the cat the calico cat. The eyes, nose and mouth are painted on with fabric paint; the whiskers on the cat are done with a triple straight stitch. The dog and cat collars are stitched on; the cat is sporting purple; the dog's collar is blue.

Pants shown in the illustration are the Pleated Front Knickers.

## Specific Fabrics or Notions

3 yards of purchased piping or 1/3 yards of plaid fabric and cording to make piping. Refer to the technique "Making Piping" and make 3 yards of piping.
Small pieces of fabric for dog and cat. Decorative embroidery threads, black, blue and red fabric markers.

## Specific Pattern Pieces

Shirt front, shirt button back, shirt short sleeve, square collar

## Cutting

Cut out a block of fabric larger than the collar, one square collar on the fold, one shirt front on the fold line, two shirt button backs on the selvage, two shirt short sleeves on fold line #2.
All seams are 1/4". Finish seams with a zigzag stitch or serger.

## Collar and Sleeve Finish

1. Trace the collar on the fabric piece noting the center front. Refer to the technique, "Fabric Appliqué" and appliqué the dog and cat on the right side of the collar in the center of the collar (fig. 1). Cut out the collar.

*Figure 1 trace collar on fabric block*

2. Sew the piping to the outer edge of the collar matching the raw edges of the piping and the collar with a 1/4" seam (fig. 2). Lay the collars with right sides together. Sew around the collar just inside the piping stitching line (fig. 3). Trim and clip the seam.

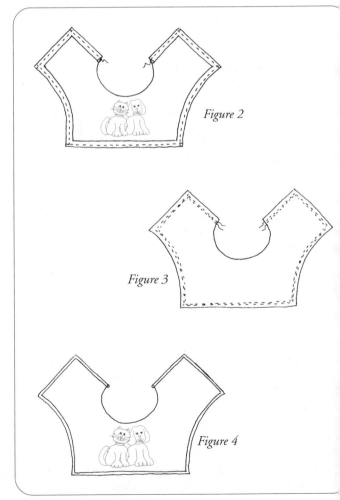

*Figure 2*

*Figure 3*

*Figure 4*

Turn the collar right side out and press (fig. 4).

3. Refer to the Shirt General Directions, steps 1-6.

Detail of Emma's
Peach Nightie

Emma's Peach Nightie

Anna's Cream
Nightie

C-1

*1907 Romper*

*Lace Waves Overskirt Dress*

*Back View of the
Lace Waves Overskirt Dress*

*Silk and Blue Linen Shirt*
*Front Buttoned Pants*

*Black Ribbon Tabbed Dress*

*Ecru Batiste and
Linen Shirt*

*...ort Lined Pleated Romper
(Border Fabric Version)*

*Pleated Front Knickers
"Long Pants Version"*

*Bubble Gum Collar Shirt
V-waist Button-on Knickers*

C-5

*Marshall's Scalloped Shirt*
*V-waist Button-on Knickers*

*Short Lined Pleated Romper*
*(Smocked Version)*

*Pretty in Pink Dress*

*...pbell's Jabot Shirt*
*...ton-on Suit Pants*

*David's Shirt*
*Pleated Front*
*Knickers*

*Tucked Panel*
*Lapel Shirt*

*Pleated Front*
*Knickers*

Q-7

*Robin's Egg Australian Madeira Dress*

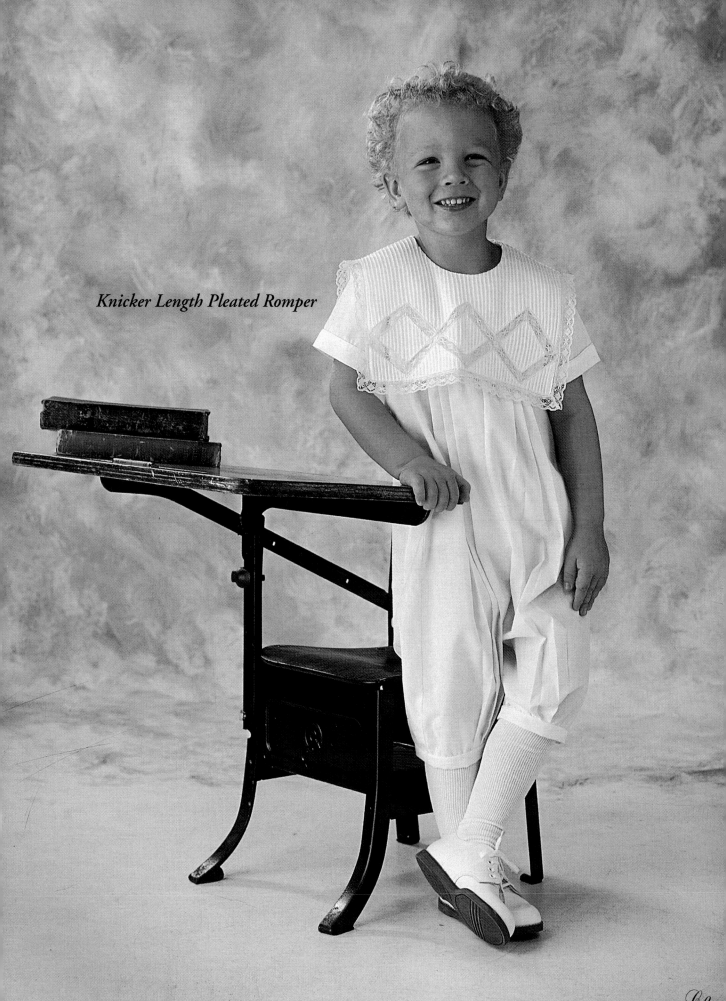

*Knicker Length Pleated Romper*

White Shirt with
Plaid Madeira Border
Pleated Front Knickers

Pink Heart Dress

Detail of Pink Heart Dress

Blue Silk Ribbon Embroidered Dress

Back view of the
Blue Silk Ribbon Embroidered Dress

*Monogrammed Round Collar Shirt*
*Straight Front Knee Pants*

*Rebekah's Butterfly Linen Dress*

*ngham Linen*
*el Collar Shirt*

*Front Buttoned Pants*

*Ward's Bias Trim Shirt*

*V-waist*
*Knickers*

*Let's Go Dutch Dress*

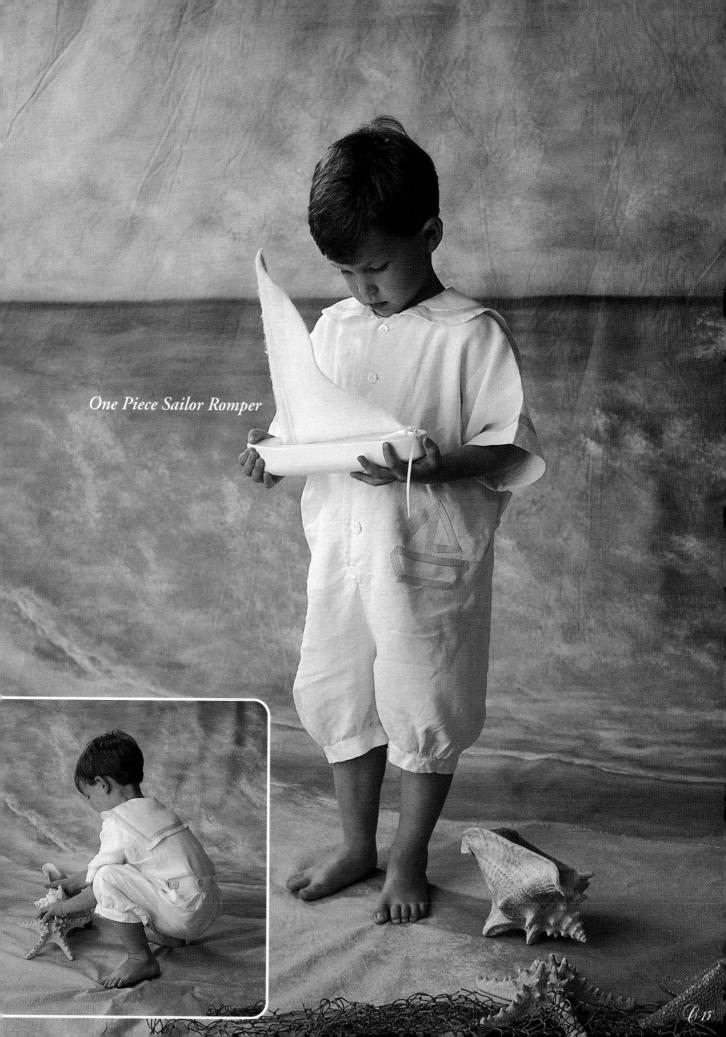

*One Piece Sailor Romper*

C-15

*Baby Cars (Smocking Plate)*
*Bib Front Knickers*

*Woven Ribbon*
*Bib Front Knickers*

*Simple Hearts*
*Bib Front Knickers*

*Simple Diamonds*
*Bib Front Knickers*

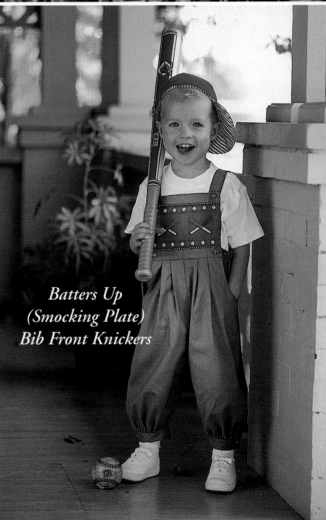

*Batters Up*
*(Smocking Plate)*
*Bib Front Knickers*

*Carousel*

*V-waist Button-on Knickers*

*Bike Ride Dress*

*Prehistoric Play -waist Button-on Knickers*

*Easter Egg Collar Shirt V-waist Button-on Knickers*

*The Tiny Tennies Blue Gingham Dress*

*Logan's Madeira Appliqué Shirt*
*Button-on Suit Pants*

*Bradley's Madeira Appliqué Dress*

*Skirt Close-up of*
*Bradley's Madeira Appliqué Dress*

*Bodice Close-up of*
*Bradley's Madeira Appliqué Dress*

*Silk French Waterfall Dress*

*Dog and Cat Collar Shirt*
*V-waist Button-on Knickers*

*Santa's Ride*

*Pleated Front Knickers*

*Christmas Tree
Plaid Dress*

*Cupid's Heart Dress*

*Baby Blues
Button-on Suit Pants*

19

*Morgan's Embroidery Masterpiece*

*Close-up of Morgan's Embroidery Masterpiece*

*White and Pink Madeira Dress*

*Cecil's Royal Diamond Dress*

C-21

*Close-up of Greyson's Shirt and V Front Button-on Suit Pants*

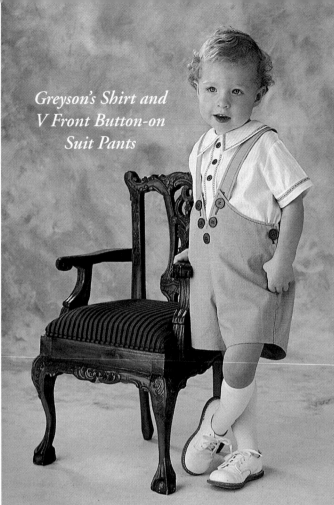

*Greyson's Shirt and V Front Button-on Suit Pants*

*Sailor Collar with Tie Pleated Front Knickers*

*Tied Sailor Collar Shirt Straight Front Knee Pants*

*White Linen Lapel Collar Shirt*
*Front Buttoned Pants*

*Christopher's Double Piping Shirt*
*Straight Front Knee Pants*

*Sarah Joy's Snowman Dress*

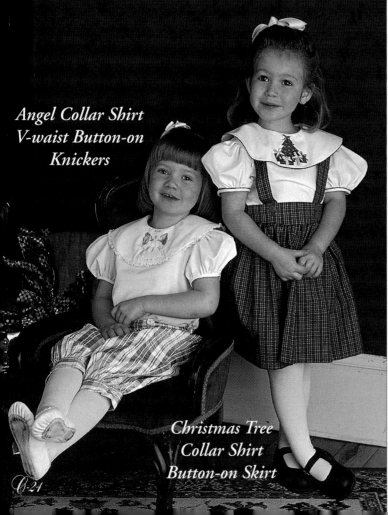

*Angel Collar Shirt*
*V-waist Button-on*
*Knickers*

*Christmas Tree*
*Collar Shirt*
*Button-on Skirt*

*Gingerbread Boy and Girl Collar Shirt*
*Pleated Front Knickers*

Gingerbread Man with Checkerboard Border

Brenda's Ice Cream Cone with Chevron Border

Teddy Bear Hero
Jenk's Football
Lucky Seven

Flipper and Friend with Wave/Sky Border

Apple for the Teacher
School Slate

Beauteous Bow

Hot Air Balloons

Andrew's Airplanes

Capital Chick
Easter Eggs

Pupil's Pencils

Q-25

# Valentine Museum

The Valentine collects, preserves and interprets the materials of the life and history of Richmond. Known for its innovative programming, the museum has established a tradition of reaching out to new and diverse audiences, enhancing the quality of life for all of the city's residents. The Valentine's lively exhibitions explore many aspects of Richmond's history, using a variety of methods, from framed documents to tough-screen interactive. Success in its endeavors has earned the museum a reputation as one of the best urban history museums in the nation.

Visit the Valentine, the Museum of the Life and History of Richmond, for a fun and stimulating experience of history!

Located at 1015 East Clay Street, Richmond, Virginia.
For more information, visit their website www.valentinemuseum.com.

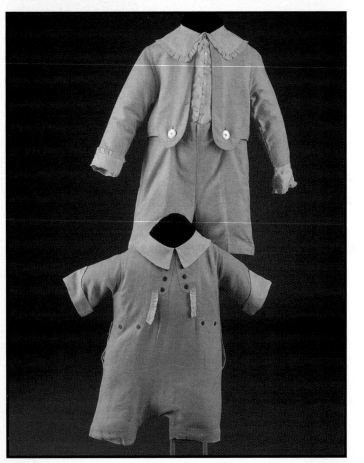

The pink cotton shorts suit has a false shirt of white silk edged self-fabric ruffles; the silk shirt front, collar and cuffs are all p of the suit jacket. This suit was worn by the ring bearer in a 19 wedding.

The 1920 boy's one-piece lavender romper is cleverly cut wi seams and trim giving the effect of a jacket buttoned to sh pants. But the "buttons" are purple thread embroidery. The romp is also trimmed with white linen collar and cuffs and pleat ruffles of white handkerchief linen.

(left) These charming brother and sister outfits were designed and made by a Richmond dressmaker in the early 1940s. The blue linen boy's romper and the girl's dress are trimmed with pleated ruffles of white handkerchief linen edged with a row of faggotting at the double layer hem. Both garments are made in two pieces which button together in the front and back.

(right) The dark pink faille dress and hooded cape ensemble from about 1870 was worn by a little boy. The dress is trimmed in black velvet and black velvet looped ribbons. Both the dress and the cape are decorated with black soutache braid couched in an elaborate pattern.

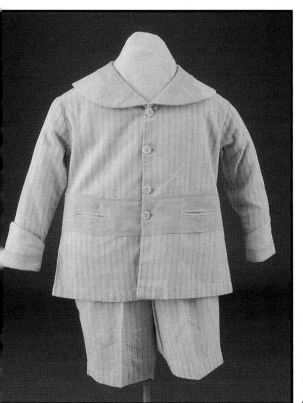

(left) The boy's shorts suit from about 1915 is made of a pink and white woven striped cotton and trimmed with solid pink and white cotton. The top has a wide flat two-tone pink and white collar with white embroidered stars at the front neck. The top's waistband has two practical welt pockets edged in white.

# The Charleston Museum

The Charleston Museum, founded in 1773, is America's first museum. The collection preserves and interprets the social and natural history of Charleston and the South Carolina coastal region. Exhibits focus on early Native Americans, trade and commerce, the plantation system and Civil War memorabilia. An eclectic array of clothing, furniture, photographs, ceramics, tools, silver, pewter, toys and games reveal a portrait of Charlestonians.

Located at 360 Meeting street, across from the Charleston Visitor's Center, the museum is open daily Monday-Saturday 9-5 and Sunday 1-5.

For more information, visit their website www.charlestonmuseum.com.

### Girls' Cashmere and Silk Dress, circa 1880

The dress was made in Paris. It was made for a young girl in the fa
Mrs. Sidney Legendre of Medway Plantation, South Carolina.

The cashmere muted turquoise bodice has narrow, vertical tucks that flair out over the hips, extending partway over the skirt and en
pleated ruffles. The front opening is a pleated and smocked insert green silk satin. The long sleeves of cashmere have rouching arou
cuffs. Inside each cuff and inside the neck opening is pleated gauz
French Valencienne lace edging. Under the second ruffle of the ski
gauze which is box-pleated with three tiny pleats on each side and f
with a wider lace edging is attached to extend beneath the dress he
faux petticoat.

### Boy's Three-piece Cotton Velveteen Suit, circa 187

The suit was made for and worn by Dr. Ellison A. Smyth, Jr. of Cha
when he was seven years old.

The seal brown velvet suit consists of a coat, vest and trousers. The
no collar or laps and fastens down the front with six covered butto
front outer edge is bound with black binding tape. It is lined w
cotton twill and is handmade. The trousers come to just below the kn
the side seams are bound with black binding tape. The jacket is de
with five pairs of black covered buttons that do not fasten. The slee
ture two diagonal bands of the same black binding tape that finishes
edges. The jacket is also lined in tan cotton twill.

The antique advertising cards depicting children and the print
"Cross-Stitch" featured in the photograph are part of Laura
Thompson's personal collection.

### Girls' Two-piece Cotton Pique Dress, circa 1870

The dress was made and embroidered in France. Miss Minnie Reese had the dress made for Miss Alice Reese of Charleston and then gave it to her niece, Miss Caroline Rutledge, who also wore it as a child.

The skirt is attached to a plain, sleeveless bodice which buttons up the back. The skirt is embroidered in white cotton embroidery thread on white cotton pique. Down each side of the buttoned opening are satin stitched flowers and dots bordered by scallops worked in the buttonhole stitch. The dress jacket front opening, bottom edge, collar, and cuffs are embroidered in the same design to match the skirt. Mother of pearl buttons are used to close the skirt and the jacket.

### Boy's Two-piece Cotton Velveteen Suit, circa 1886

The "little Lord Fauntleroy suit" was make in New York by Best and Company for Master Murray Bennet of Charleston. He is featured wearing it in a photograph in the Charleston Museum's collection.

The coat of black velveteen is lined with silk. The bodice is lined in black and the sleeves are lined in white. The coat is edged with braid and is fastened at the collar by two small buttons with a separate triangular piece. The coat is trimmed down both sides of the front with a design made of rickrack and soutache braid. This design is again repeated along the seams of the sleeves and the two seams on the back of the coat. The black velveteen trousers are trimmed around the pockets and down the side seams with black braid. One small button fastens at each side of the waistband.

The antique French children's book, postcard and folder of hat pins featured in the photograph are part of Laura Jenkins Thompson's personal collection.

### Girl's White Lawn Dress, circa 1905

The dress is one of two of a pair in the museum's collection. They were made for sisters in the family of Mrs. Sidney Legendre of Medway Plantation, South Carolina.

The dress is long-waisted with three-quarter length sleeves. It buttons up the back and features a square, ruffled collar. Rows of tucks and inverted ruffles run vertically down the bodice from the square neck to the dropped waist. The sleeves and skirt have two rows of scalloped ruffles at the bottom. Simple, one-row entredeux is featured at the waist while multiple row entredeux joins the ruffles to the collar and to the sleeves and to the skirt. The raw edges of the entredeux and the ruffles are roll and whipped by hand. The feather stitching featured on the collar is also embroidered by hand.

### Boy's Blue and White Cotton Sailor Suit, circa 1915

The suit was called a Tom Sawyer suit and meant to be worn at the beach or for play. It was made by the Washburn-Elder Company and is a size "Age-8". It was worn by the boys of the J.H. Muller family of Charleston.

The boy's short romper of blue cotton denim opens down the front with four mother of pearl buttons. The left breast pocketflap, pin-tucked sailor collar and short sleeve cuffs are of white cotton duck. The back features a flap that opens horizontally at the waist and has three buttons which close it. There is a band in white which buttons on over this and attaches in the front to secure.

The antique needle books depicting nautical and patriotic themes and the print titles "Dolly's Sea Trip" featured in the photograph are part of Laura Jenkins Thompson's personal collection.

Brandon's Quilt

C-50

Close-up of Brandon's Quilt

Close-up of Brandon's Q

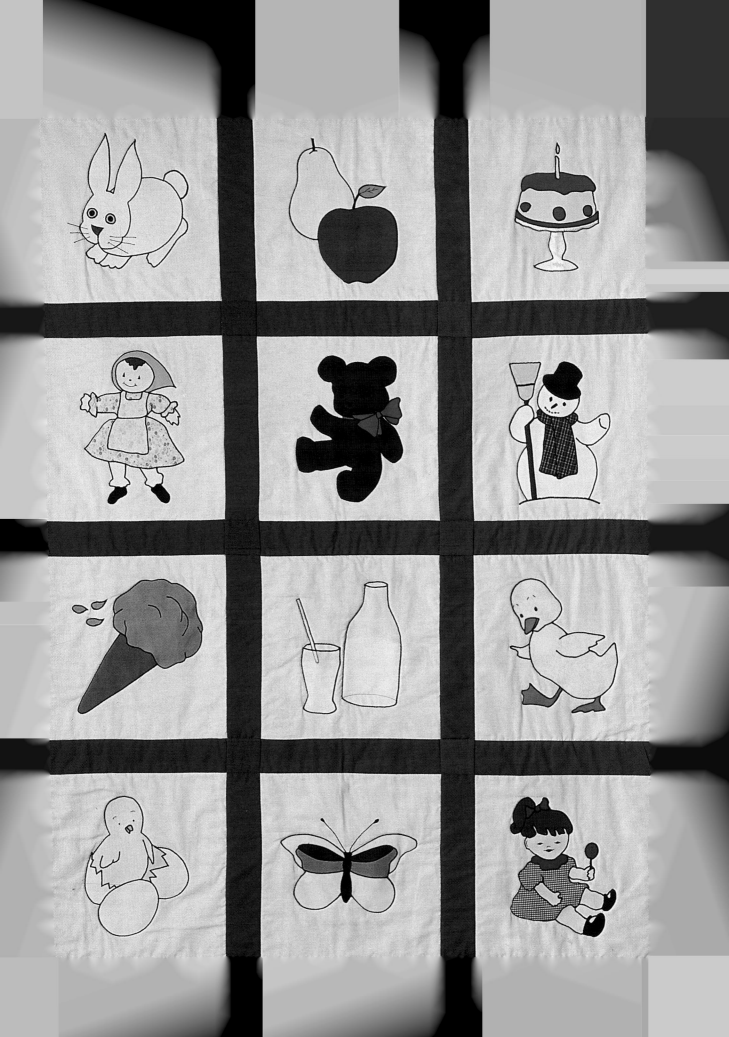

*Memory Fan Pillow*

*Cutwork Flower Calico Bunny*

Ballet Bookends

Baseball Bookends

A STAR SLEEPS HERE

"A Star Sleeps Here"
Door Decoration

"The Princess Sleeps Here"
Door Decoration

The Princess Sleeps Here

Embroidered Teddy Bear

"The Prince Sleeps Here"
Door Decoration

THE PRINCE SLEEPS HERE

Embroidered Teddy Bear

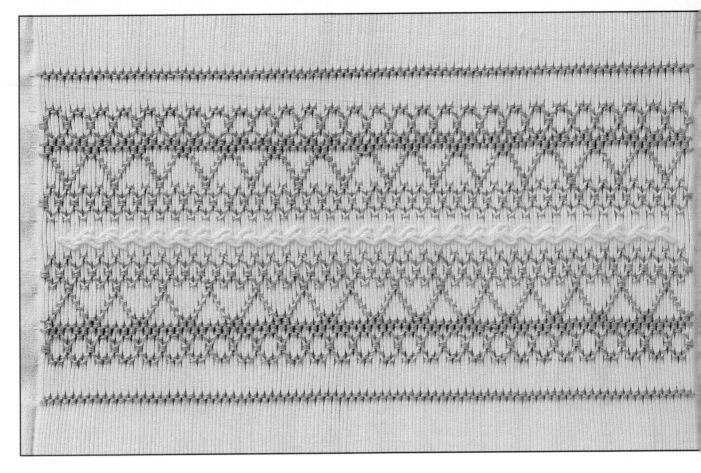

# Baby Blues

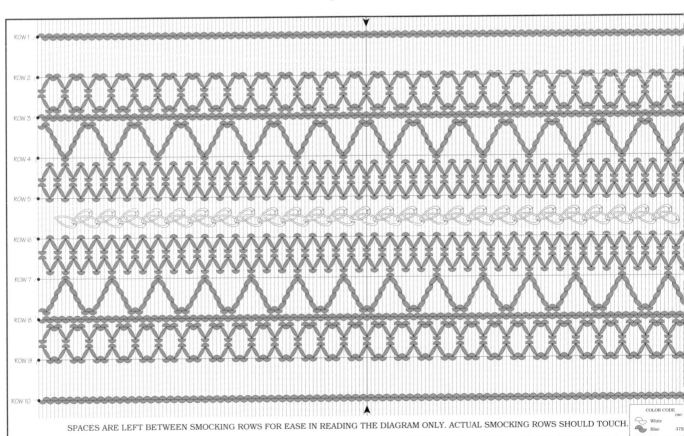

SPACES ARE LEFT BETWEEN SMOCKING ROWS FOR EASE IN READING THE DIAGRAM ONLY. ACTUAL SMOCKING ROWS SHOULD TOUCH.

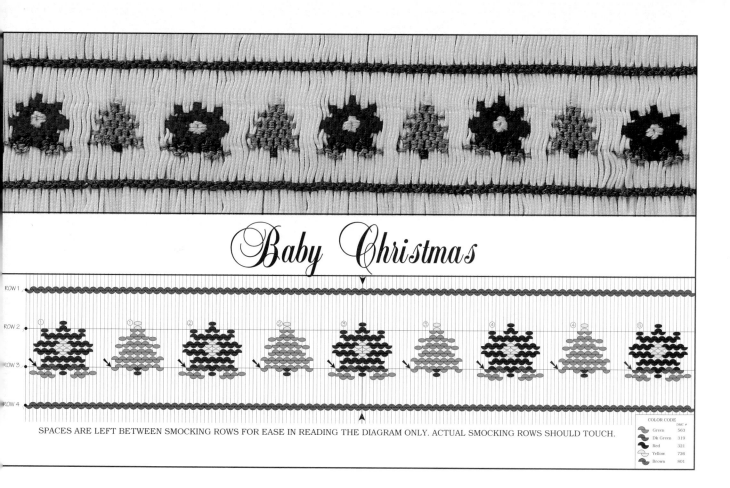

# Baby Christmas

| | |
|---|---|
| ROW 1 | |
| ROW 2 | |
| ROW 3 | |
| ROW 4 | |

SPACES ARE LEFT BETWEEN SMOCKING ROWS FOR EASE IN READING THE DIAGRAM ONLY. ACTUAL SMOCKING ROWS SHOULD TOUCH.

| COLOR CODE | | |
|---|---|---|
| | | DMC # |
| | Green | 563 |
| | Dk Green | 319 |
| | Red | 321 |
| | Yellow | 726 |
| | Brown | 801 |

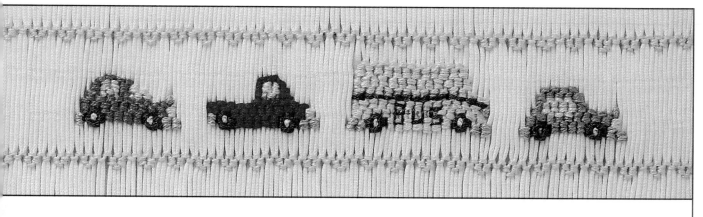

# Baby Cars

| | |
|---|---|
| ROW 1 | |
| ROW 2 | |
| ROW 3 | |
| ROW 4 | |

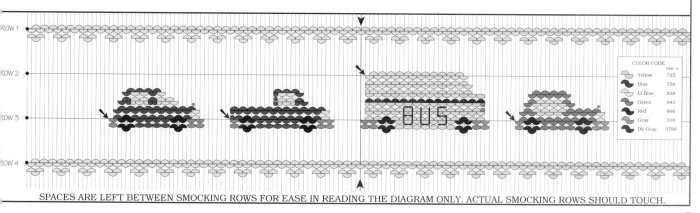

| COLOR CODE | | |
|---|---|---|
| | | DMC # |
| | Yellow | 725 |
| | Blue | 798 |
| | Lt Blue | 828 |
| | Green | 943 |
| | Red | 666 |
| | Gray | 318 |
| | Dk Gray | 3799 |

SPACES ARE LEFT BETWEEN SMOCKING ROWS FOR EASE IN READING THE DIAGRAM ONLY. ACTUAL SMOCKING ROWS SHOULD TOUCH.

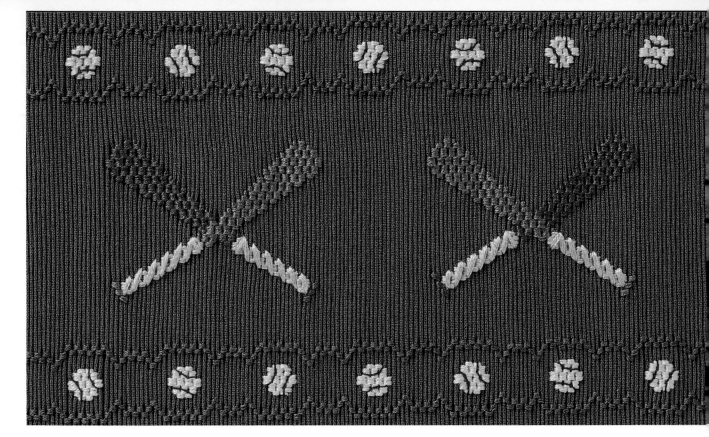

# Batter's Up

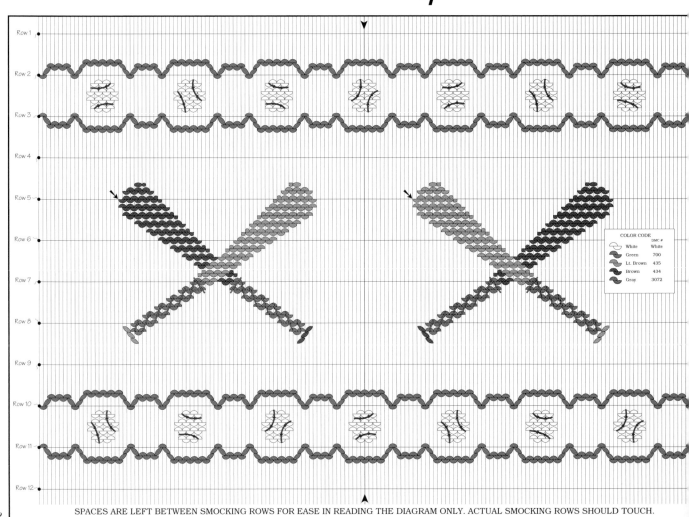

| | COLOR CODE | |
|---|---|---|
| | | DMC # |
| | White | White |
| | Green | 700 |
| | Lt. Brown | 435 |
| | Brown | 434 |
| | Gray | 3072 |

Row 1
Row 2
Row 3
Row 4
Row 5
Row 6
Row 7
Row 8
Row 9
Row 10
Row 11
Row 12

SPACES ARE LEFT BETWEEN SMOCKING ROWS FOR EASE IN READING THE DIAGRAM ONLY. ACTUAL SMOCKING ROWS SHOULD TOUCH.

# Bike Ride

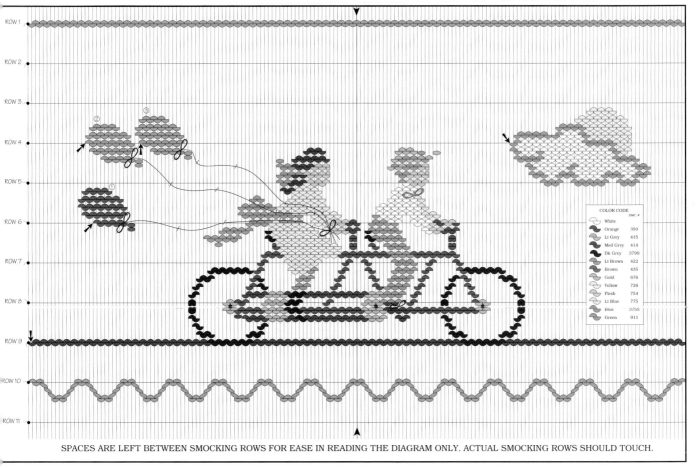

| COLOR CODE | | |
|---|---|---|
| | | DMC # |
| | White | |
| | Orange | 350 |
| | Lt Grey | 415 |
| | Med Grey | 414 |
| | Dk Grey | 3799 |
| | Lt Brown | 422 |
| | Brown | 435 |
| | Gold | 676 |
| | Yellow | 726 |
| | Flesh | 754 |
| | Lt Blue | 775 |
| | Blue | 3755 |
| | Green | 911 |

ROW 1
ROW 2
ROW 3
ROW 4
ROW 5
ROW 6
ROW 7
ROW 8
ROW 9
ROW 10
ROW 11

SPACES ARE LEFT BETWEEN SMOCKING ROWS FOR EASE IN READING THE DIAGRAM ONLY. ACTUAL SMOCKING ROWS SHOULD TOUCH.

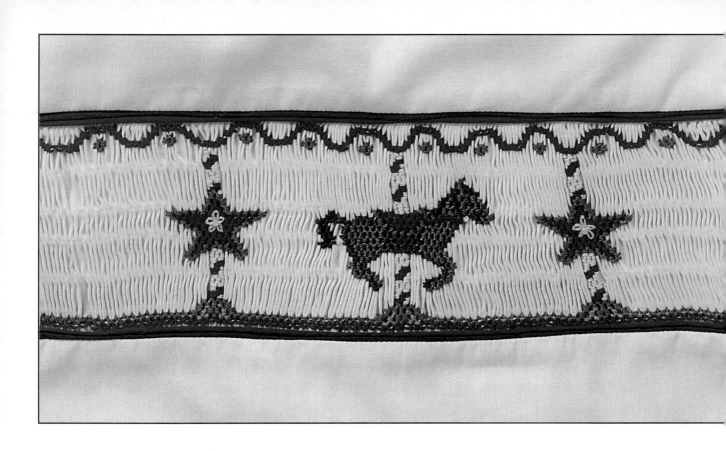

## Carousel

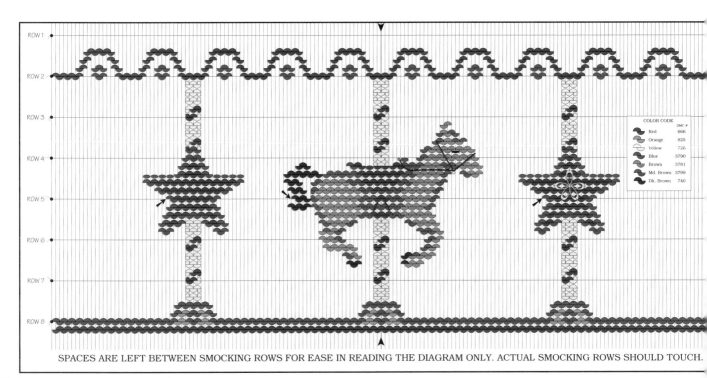

| COLOR CODE | | |
|---|---|---|
| | | DMC # |
| | Red | 666 |
| | Orange | 825 |
| | Yellow | 726 |
| | Blue | 3790 |
| | Brown | 3781 |
| | Md. Brown | 3799 |
| | Dk. Brown | 740 |

SPACES ARE LEFT BETWEEN SMOCKING ROWS FOR EASE IN READING THE DIAGRAM ONLY. ACTUAL SMOCKING ROWS SHOULD TOUCH.

# Christmas Tree

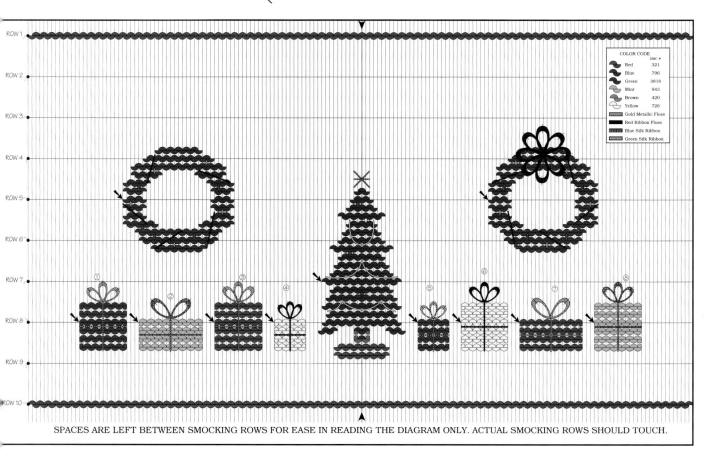

| | COLOR CODE | |
|---|---|---|
| | | DMC # |
| | Red | 321 |
| | Blue | 796 |
| | Green | 3818 |
| | Mint | 943 |
| | Brown | 420 |
| | Yellow | 726 |
| | Gold Metallic Floss | |
| | Red Ribbon Floss | |
| | Blue Silk Ribbon | |
| | Green Silk Ribbon | |

SPACES ARE LEFT BETWEEN SMOCKING ROWS FOR EASE IN READING THE DIAGRAM ONLY. ACTUAL SMOCKING ROWS SHOULD TOUCH.

# *Cupid's Hearts*

| COLOR CODE | | DMC # |
|---|---|---|
| Pink | | 962 |
| Dk. Pink | | 309 |
| Bright Pink | | 776 |
| Grey | | 415 |
| Med. Grey | | 318 |
| Lt. Blue | | 800 |
| Med. Blue | | 334 |
| Lt. Flesh | | 948 |
| Flesh | | 754 |
| Yellow | | 307 |

Row 1
Row 2
Row 3
Row 4
Row 5
Row 6
Row 7
Row 8

SPACES ARE LEFT BETWEEN SMOCKING ROWS FOR EASE IN READING THE DIAGRAM ONLY. ACTUAL SMOCKING ROWS SHOULD TOUCH.

# Flowers and Butterflies

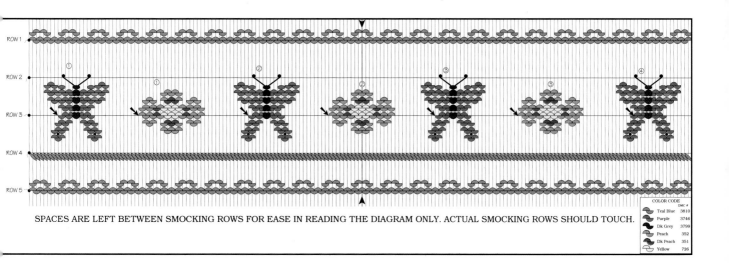

SPACES ARE LEFT BETWEEN SMOCKING ROWS FOR EASE IN READING THE DIAGRAM ONLY. ACTUAL SMOCKING ROWS SHOULD TOUCH.

| COLOR CODE | |
|---|---|
| | DMC # |
| Teal Blue | 3810 |
| Purple | 3746 |
| Dk Grey | 3799 |
| Peach | 352 |
| Dk Peach | 351 |
| Yellow | 726 |

## Let's Go Dutch

| COLOR CODE | | |
| --- | --- | --- |
| | | DMC # |
| | White | |
| | Blue | 809 |
| | Green | 912 |
| | Pink | 961 |
| | Tan | 435 |
| | Gray | 414 |

SPACES ARE LEFT BETWEEN SMOCKING ROWS FOR EASE IN READING THE DIAGRAM ONLY. ACTUAL SMOCKING ROWS SHOULD TOUCH.

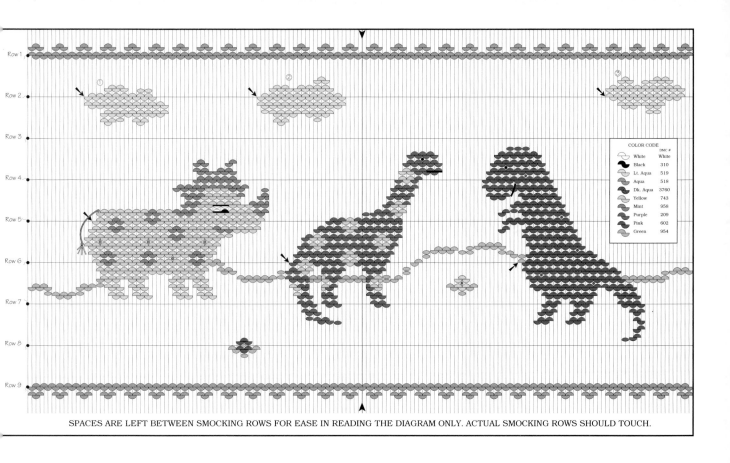

| COLOR CODE | DMC # |
| --- | --- |
| White | White |
| Black | 310 |
| Lt. Aqua | 519 |
| Aqua | 518 |
| Dk. Aqua | 3760 |
| Yellow | 743 |
| Mint | 958 |
| Purple | 209 |
| Pink | 602 |
| Green | 954 |

SPACES ARE LEFT BETWEEN SMOCKING ROWS FOR EASE IN READING THE DIAGRAM ONLY. ACTUAL SMOCKING ROWS SHOULD TOUCH.

# Prehistoric Play

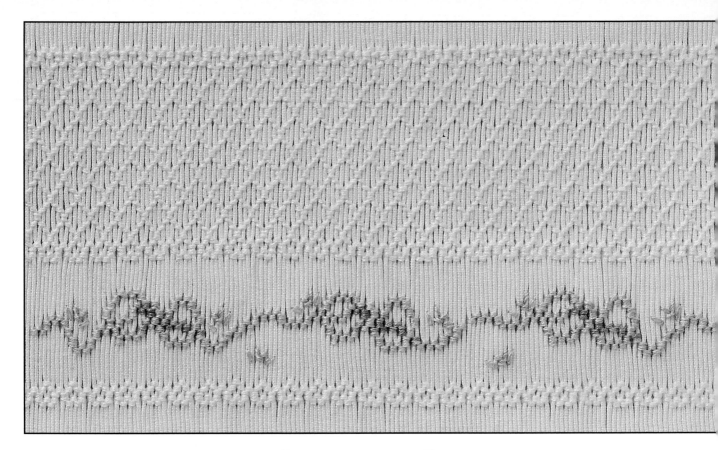

# Pretty in Pinks

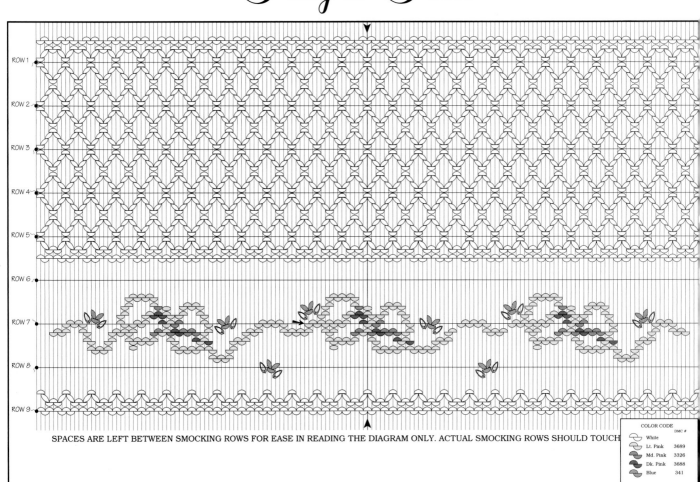

SPACES ARE LEFT BETWEEN SMOCKING ROWS FOR EASE IN READING THE DIAGRAM ONLY. ACTUAL SMOCKING ROWS SHOULD TOUCH

| COLOR CODE | |
|---|---|
| | DMC # |
| White | |
| Lt. Pink | 3689 |
| Md. Pink | 3326 |
| Dk. Pink | 3688 |
| Blue | 341 |

ROW 1
ROW 2
ROW 3
ROW 4
ROW 5
ROW 6
ROW 7
ROW 8
ROW 9

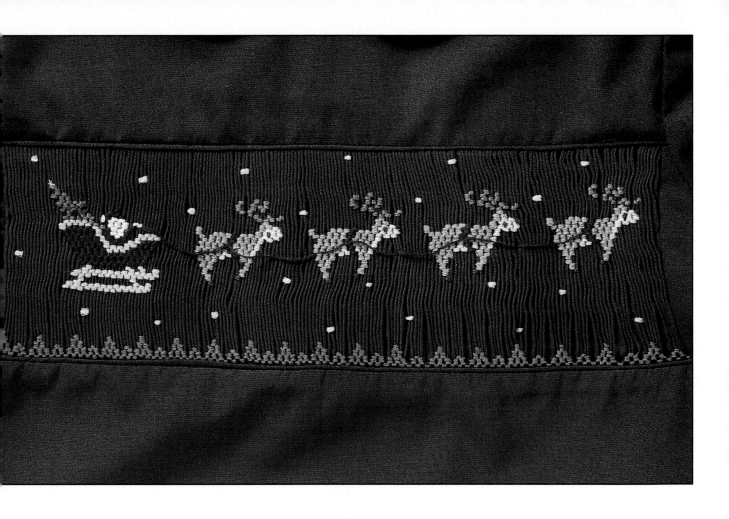

# Santa's Ride

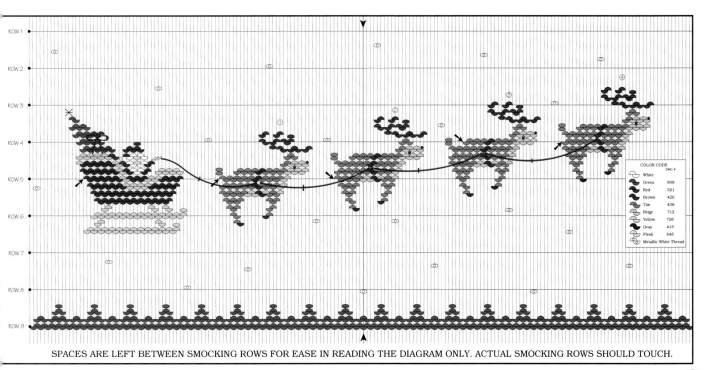

| COLOR CODE | |
|---|---|
| | DMC # |
| White | |
| Green | 909 |
| Red | 321 |
| Brown | 420 |
| Tan | 436 |
| Beige | 712 |
| Yellow | 726 |
| Gray | 413 |
| Flesh | 945 |
| Metallic White Thread | |

SPACES ARE LEFT BETWEEN SMOCKING ROWS FOR EASE IN READING THE DIAGRAM ONLY. ACTUAL SMOCKING ROWS SHOULD TOUCH.

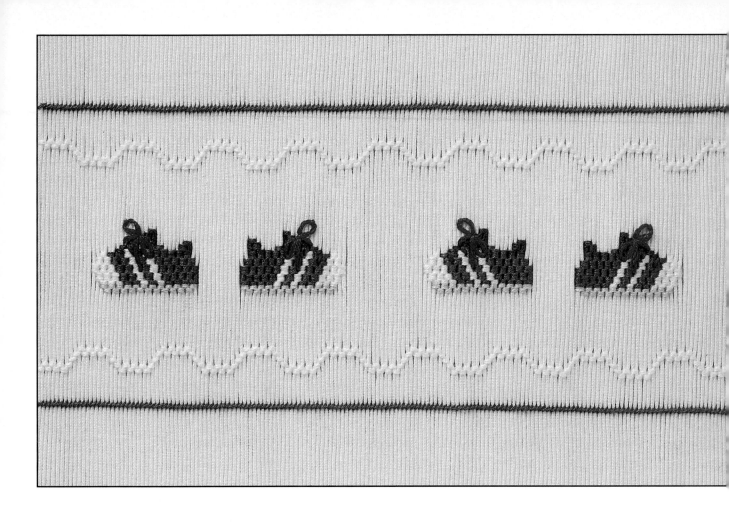

# Tiny Tennies

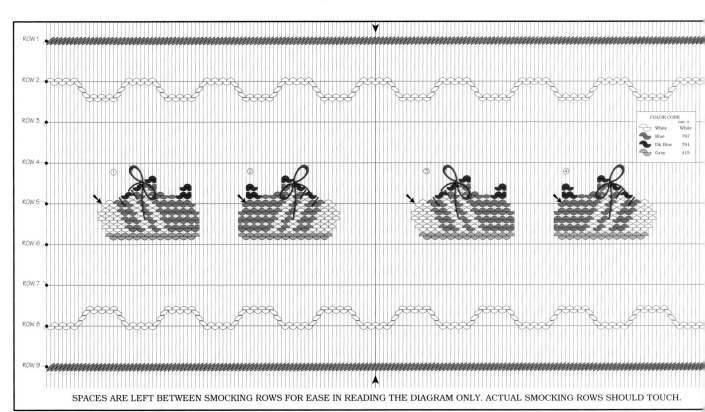

SPACES ARE LEFT BETWEEN SMOCKING ROWS FOR EASE IN READING THE DIAGRAM ONLY. ACTUAL SMOCKING ROWS SHOULD TOUCH.

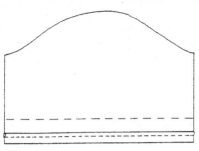

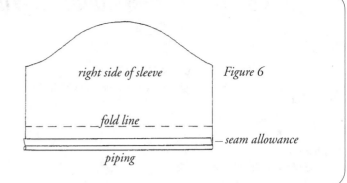

right side of sleeve    Figure 6

*fold line*

— seam allowance

*piping*

*Figure 5*

## — Sleeve —

Sew piping to the wrong side at the bottom edge of each sleeve with a ¼" seam (fig. 5). Press seam toward the sleeve (fig. 6). Fold the cuff to the right side on the fold line. Stitch the cuff in place by stitching in the ditch between the cuff and the piping (fig. 7). Refer to the Shirt General Directions, steps 7-14 to complete the shirt.

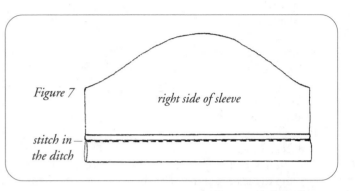

*Figure 7*

right side of sleeve

stitch in — the ditch

*Dog and Cat Appliqué*

# General Shirt Directions

## General Construction

1. Place the front and backs right sides together and stitch the shoulder seams with a ¹/₄" seam (fig. 1).

2. Place the wrong side of the collar to the right side of the neck of the shirt. Pin in place (fig. 2). Fold the shirt back facing on the fold line to the right side of the shirt (collar will be between the back and facing) (fig. 3).

3. Fold the bias neck strip in half and press. Place the cut edges of the strip to the neck of the collar/shirt. The bias strip starts and stops ¹/₂" from the back edge. Cut off any excess bias (fig. 3).

4. Stitch the bias strip to the neck edge using a ¹/₄" seam, starting at the fold lines on the back edges of the shirt (fig. 3).

5. Trim the seam to ¹/₈". Clip the neck edge and understitch the bias band. Understitching is done by stitching through the bias band and the trimmed seam (fig. 4).

6. Holding the collar away from the shirt, stitch the facing to the bodice (fig. 5).

7. Fit the sleeve to the armhole and stitch in place (fig. 6a and fig. 6b).

8. Place the right sides together at the sides and sleeves matching the underarm seams. Sew the side seams from the bottom of the sleeve to the bottom of the shirt (fig. 7a and 7b).

9. Finish the bottom edge of the shirt as follows: With the facings open, fold up ¹/₄" and press. Fold up ¹/₄" again and press, creating

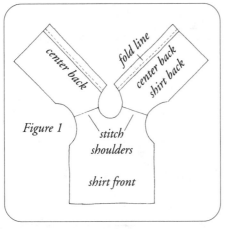

*Figure 1*

center back • fold line • center back • shirt back • stitch shoulders • shirt front

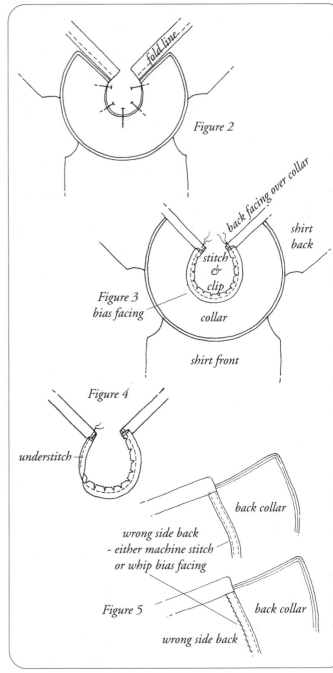

*Figure 2*

fold line

*Figure 3*
*bias facing*

back facing over collar • shirt back • stitch & clip • collar • shirt front

*Figure 4*

understitch

*Figure 5*

back collar • wrong side back – either machine stitch or whip bias facing • back collar • wrong side back

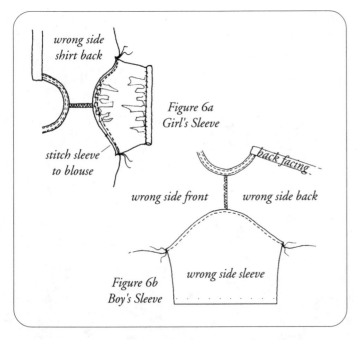

*wrong side shirt back*

*stitch sleeve to blouse*

*Figure 6a*
*Girl's Sleeve*

back facing • wrong side front • wrong side back • wrong side sleeve

*Figure 6b*
*Boy's Sleeve*

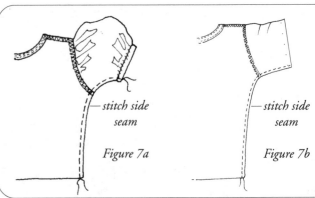

stitch side seam

*Figure 7a*

stitch side seam

*Figure 7b*

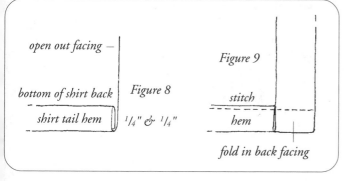

open out facing —

bottom of shirt back    *Figure 8*

shirt tail hem    ¹/₄" & ¹/₄"

*Figure 9*

stitch

hem

fold in back facing

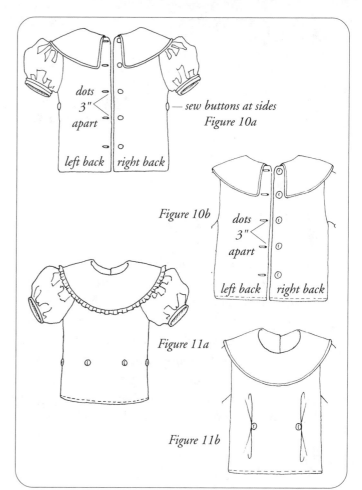

*dots 3" apart*

left back | right back

— sew buttons at sides
*Figure 10a*

*Figure 10b*    *dots 3" apart*

left back | right back

*Figure 11a*

*Figure 11b*

a narrow hem (fig. 8). Fold the facings along the fold line and stitch the hem in place (fig. 9).

10. Position the buttonholes on the left hand side by placing a dot ¹/₂" from the top fabric edge of the neckline and ¹/₂" over from the fold line. Place a dot every 3" down the back of the shirt ¹/₂" from the fold (fig. 10a and 10b).

11. Stitch a ¹/₂" buttonhole beginning at the dot and placing the buttonholes horizontally. Continue the buttonholes down the back of the shirt. Cut the buttonholes open with a buttonhole cutter or seam ripper.

12. Lap the left side of the shirt over the right side and mark the placement for the buttons (fig. 10a and 10b).

13. Attach the buttons along the marks on the right side of the shirt (fig. 10a and 10b).

14. Mark the placement for the buttons on the shirt front referring to the skirt or knicker waistband. Sew buttons in place making a ¹/₂" pleat behind the button and stitching through all layers of the fabric (fig. 11a and 11b).

A B C D E F G
H I J K L M
N O P Q R S T
U V W X Y Z

# Smocked Shirts

### Prehistoric Play Smocked Shirt

Precious for either a boy or a girl this smocked white shirt has many wonderful details. This version was made especially for a little girl with the cute puffed sleeves. The three dinosaurs are pink, yellow and purple. The clouds are blue and the sweet smocked design at the top and at the bottom is blue. All dinosaurs have "spots" stitched in coordinating colors. Green grass travels behind the dinosaurs and perky red and yellow flowers peek through the grass. The white Peter Pan collar is piped in green as are the sleeves. White tatting edges the bottom of the shirt collar and the top of the piping on the sleeve cuffs. The back closes with buttons and buttonholes. Cute little green broadcloth knickers are worn with this button-on shirt.

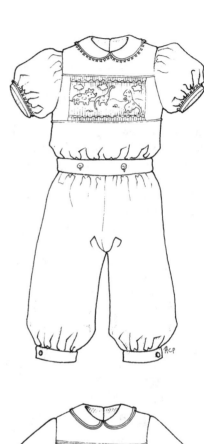

### Carousel Shirt

Made for a little boy with the straight sleeves; put puffed sleeves in, and a little girl would love this outfit as well. The shirt is piped in navy and red double piping; this same double red and navy piping is found at both the top and the bottom of the smocked inset and on the cuffs of the shirt. The horse on the center pole is smocked in brown; stars are on the other carousel poles. The waves are in red and navy and touches of orange are found in the carousel poles. The back closes with button and buttonholes and an adorable plaid fabric is used for the knickers.

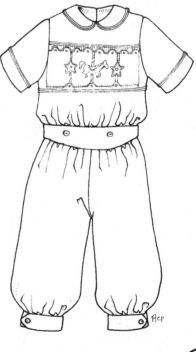

# Smocked Shirts

### Santa's Ride Shirt

Perfect for any little boy or girl for Christmas is this adorable navy outfit piped in red around the Peter Pan collar and the sleeves. Red piping is also used at the top and bottom of the smocked inset. Santa has four reindeers one of whom has a red nose. Guess who that is? Little white metallic snowflakes are sprinkled throughout the night and the smocking on the bottom of the plates looks like tree tops over which Santa is flying. The shirt buttons on any of the pants in this book and the back closes with buttons and buttonholes. The pants were sewn in the same navy broadcloth as the shirt.

### Baby Blues Shirt

The white fabric for this shirt is a reasonably heavy 100% cotton broadcloth. The Peter Pan collar is piped in self piping as are the center tuck, the sleeves and the top and bottom of the smocked inset. Two tucks are found on either side of the center piped tuck of the shirt. The smocking is wonderful done in pastel blue and white only. Pastel blue and white striped fabric was used for the button-on pants; the back of the shirt closes with buttons and buttonholes. This very beautiful smocking design is simple to do because it is geometric. Even a very inexperienced smocker can achieve beautiful results with the Baby Blues smocking graph.

# Smocked Shirts

## Directions for Constructing the Following Smocked Shirts:

*Santa's Ride*

*Prehistoric Play*

*Carousel*

*Baby Blues*

**The General Smocked Shirt Directions can be found on pages 201-202.**

## Fabric Requirements

|            | Sizes 1-2    | Sizes 3-4    | Size 6-8    |
|------------|--------------|--------------|-------------|
| Fabric 45" | 1³/₈ yds.    | 1⁵/₈ yds.    | 1³/₄ yds.   |
| Buttons ¹/₂" | 5          | 5            | 5           |

Decorative Buttons to button on pants or skirts if desired.
Smocking Plate and smocking supplies.
3 yards of purchased piping or fabric to make piping and cording.
1¹/₂ yards of ¹/₄" flat trim for collar and sleeves if desired or  3 yards of ¹/₄" trim if gathering trim.

## Pattern Pieces

All pattern pieces are found in the pattern envelope.

Shirt front (note yoke line on shirt front), shirt button back, Peter Pan collar, shirt short sleeve, or puffed sleeve

## Cutting

Cut four Peter Pan collars, two shirt button backs on the selvage, one yoke on the fold, a 45" strip of fabric large enough to accommodate the smocking plate, and two shirt short sleeve on fold line # 2 or two puffed sleeves on the shirt cutting line, 2 bias strips 1¹/₂" wide by the following lengths: Size 1-2 = 7 ⁵/₈, 3-4 = 8¹/₄", 6 = 8 ³/₄", 8 = 9 ³/₄" for puffed sleeve bands and one bias neck facing 1" wide by the neck measurement.

All seams are ¹/₄".  Finish seams with a zigzag stitch or serger.

## Smocking and Shirt Front Construction

1. Pleat a 45" wide strip of fabric with the number of pleating rows needed for the actual smocking plus an extra pleating row above and below the first and last row of smocking. Remove the pleats ¹/₄" from each short side to allow for seam allowances. Tie off the pleating to the following measurement:
   Size 1 = 8", Size 2 to 6 = 8¹/₂", Size 8 = 9".
   Smock as directed on the smocking design plate.

2. Cut two fabric pieces the length of the smocked panel by the following measurment:
   Size 1 and 2 = 2¹/₂", Size 3 and 4 = 3", Size 6 = 3¹/₂", Size 8 = 4¹/₂".

3. Stitch a fabric piece to each side of the smocked panel using a ¹/₄" seam. Overcast the seam allowance with a zigzag or serger (fig. 1).

4. Create two pieces of piping the width of the smocked panel

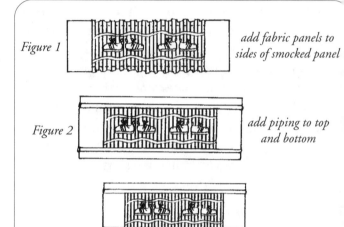

Figure 1 — *add fabric panels to sides of smocked panel*

Figure 2 — *add piping to top and bottom*

*lower shirt panel*

Figure 3

including the side pieces. Refer to "Making Piping" if needed. Place strips of wash-a-way basting tape on each piece of piping and stick the piping to the smocked panel/fabric panel, top and bottom, almost touching the smocking. Baste the piping in place if desired. Set aside (fig. 2).

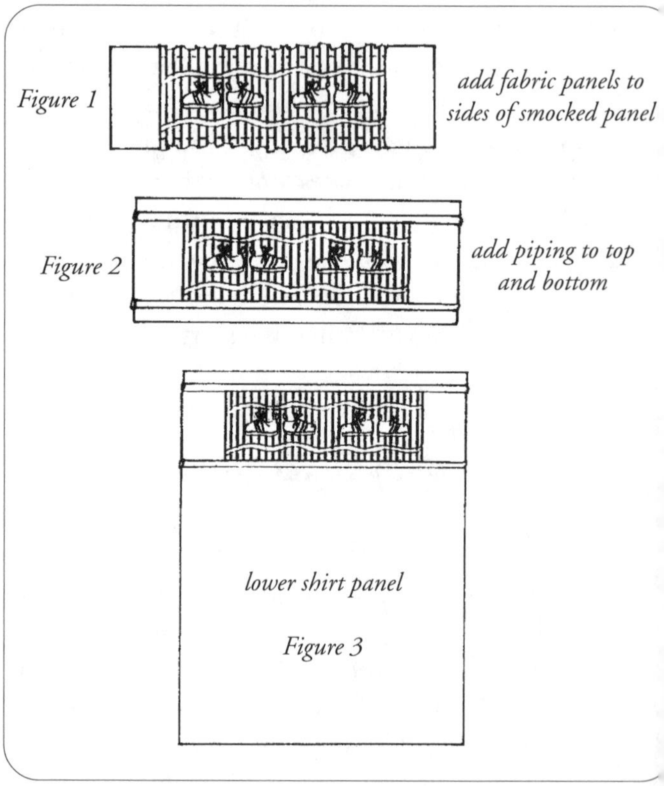

5. Cut a piece of fabric for the lower shirt panel to the width of the piped smocked panel and the following length:
   Size 1 = 8³/₈", Size 2 = 9¹/₄", Size 3 = 10¹/₈", Size 4 = 10¹/₂", Size 6 = 12¹/₄", Size 8 = 13".
   NOTE: Refer to "Decorating the Yoke and Lower Panel" if decoration is desired.

6. Center the lower shirt panel on the bottom of the piped smocked panel, right sides together. Stitch in place along the seam of the piping (fig. 3).

7. Center the yoke on the top of the piped smocked panel, right

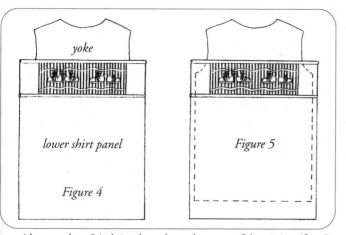

yoke

lower shirt panel

Figure 4

Figure 5

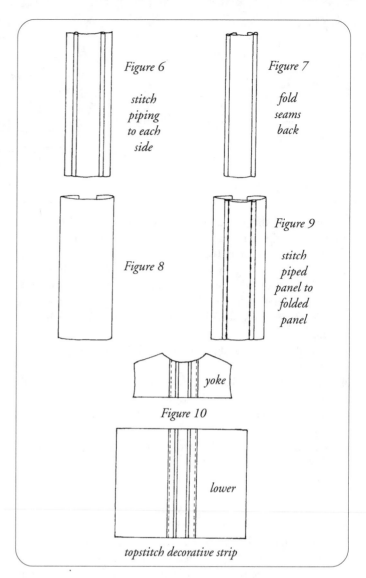

Figure 6

stitch piping to each side

Figure 7

fold seams back

Figure 8

Figure 9

stitch piped panel to folded panel

yoke

Figure 10

lower

topstitch decorative strip

sides together. Stitch in place along the seam of the piping (fig. 4).

8. Place the shirt pattern on the created fabric, matching the shoulders and neck edge. Cut out the shirt (fig. 5).

## Decorating the Yoke and Lower Panel (Optional)

1. Cut a strip of fabric $1^3/4$" wide by the length of the shirt pattern.
2. Create two pieces of piping the length of the fabric strip. Attach a piece of piping to each long side of the fabric strip (fig. 6). Fold the seam allowance of the piping/fabric strip to the wrong side. Press (fig. 7).
3. Cut a strip of fabric $4^3/4$" wide by the length of the shirt pattern. Fold 1" to the wrong side along each long edge (fig. 8).
4. Center the wrong side of the piped strip to the right side of the folded strip. Stitch together along the "ditch" of the piping (fig. 9). Before the yoke is stitched to the smocking strip place a piece of the decorative strip in the center of the yoke and stitch to the yoke $1/8$" from the each folded edge creating the tucked look. Attach the remaining decorative strip in the same manner to the center of the lower shirt/blouse panel before attaching the lower panel to the smocked panel (fig. 10).

## Peter Pan Collar

1. The collar is designed for no trim, if trim is to be added, subtract the finished width of the trim from only the outer edge of the pattern piece. Do not change the neck seam (fig. 11) .
2. Measure around the outer edge of two of the Peter Pan collars. Make enough piping to go around the collar. Refer to the technique "Making Piping."
3. Trim the piping to $1/4$" seam allowance. Sew the piping to the outer edge of two of the collars matching the raw edges of the collar and piping, clipping the piping where needed to fit around the collar (fig. 12).
4. Place the piped collars to the collar facings with right sides together and stitch together using the stitching line of the piping as a guide.
5. Turn right side out and press (fig. 13). If adding tatting whip the tatting to the underside of the piping by hand.

## Creating the Sleeves - Girl or Boy
### Girl Sleeve

Cut two puffed sleeve on the shirt cutting line, two bias strips $1^1/2$" wide by the following length: Size 1 and 2=$7^5/8$", 3 and 4=$8^1/4$", 6=

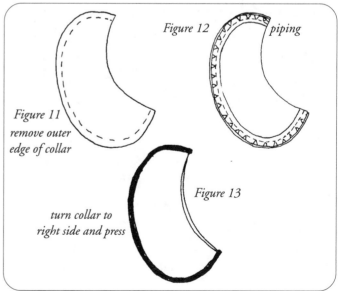

Figure 12

piping

Figure 11
remove outer edge of collar

Figure 13

turn collar to right side and press

$8^3/4$", 8=$9^3/4$.

NOTE: Use the size 2 puffed sleeve for the size 1 shirt and the size 4 puffed sleeve for the size 3 shirt.

1. Fold the bias sleeve bands in half with wrong sides together and press. If the edge on the piping is not $1/4$" trim to $1/4$", place the

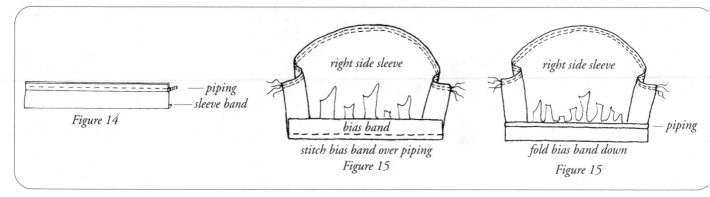

piping
sleeve band

*Figure 14*

right side sleeve

bias band

stitch bias band over piping

*Figure 15*

right side sleeve

piping

fold bias band down

*Figure 15*

raw edge of the piping to the raw edge of the sleeve bands, and baste the piping in place with a zipper foot or cording foot with a ¹/₄" seam allowance (fig. 14).

2. Run two gathering rows in the bottom and top of each sleeve at ¹/₈" and ¹/₄". Gather the bottom of the sleeve to fit the binding. Place the right side of the bias strip to the right side of the sleeve with the piping sandwiched between the sleeve and the band and stitch using a ¹/₄" seam allowance (fig. 15).

3. Fold the remaining edge of the bias strip to the wrong side of the sleeve ¹/₄".

4. Stitch the folded edge just over the seam allowance on the inside of the sleeve creating a ¹/₄" bias binding.

5. Whip edging to the sleeve with the base of the trim behind the piping by hand (fig. 16).

6. Gather the top of the sleeve to fit the arm opening of the shirt. The gathers should fall about 3" to 3¹/₂" on each side of the shoulder seam.

### Boy Sleeve
Cut two shirt short sleeves on fold line #2.

1. Sew piping to the wrong side at the bottom edge of each sleeve with a ¹/₄" seam (fig. 17). Press seam toward the sleeve (fig. 18). Fold the cuff to the right side on the fold line. Stitch the cuff in place by stitching in the ditch between the cuff and the piping (fig. 19).

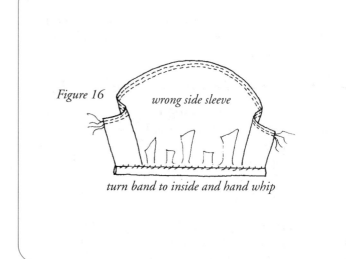

*Figure 16*

wrong side sleeve

*turn band to inside and hand whip*

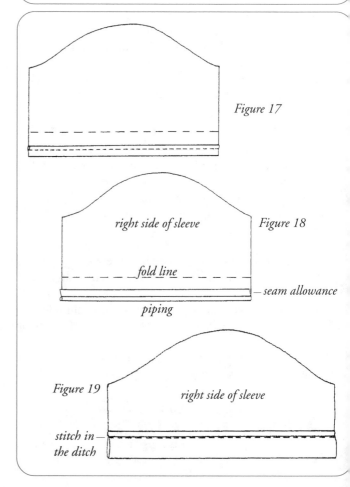

*Figure 17*

right side of sleeve    *Figure 18*

fold line

seam allowance

piping

*Figure 19*

right side of sleeve

stitch in the ditch

# General Smocked Shirt Directions

## General Construction

1. Place the front and backs right sides together and stitch the shoulder seams with a $1/4$" seam (fig. 1).

2. Place the wrong side of the collar to the right side of the neck of the shirt. Pin in place (fig. 2). Fold the shirt back facing on the fold line to the right side of the shirt (collar will be between the back and facing) (fig. 3).

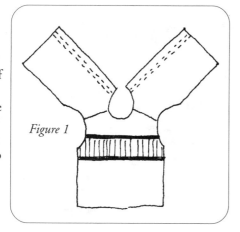

Figure 1

3. Fold the bias neck strip in half and press. Place the cut edges of the strip to the neck of the collar/shirt. The bias strip starts and stops $1/2$" from the back edge. Cut off any excess bias (fig. 3).

4. Stitch the bias strip to the neck edge using a $1/4$" seam, starting at the fold lines on the back edges of the shirt (fig. 3).

5. Trim the seam to $1/8$". Clip the neck edge and understitch the bias band. Understitching is done by stitching through the bias band and the trimmed seam (fig. 4).

6. Holding the collar away from the shirt, stitch the facing to the bodice (fig. 5).

7. Fit the sleeve to the armhole and stitch in place (fig. 6a and fig. 6b).

8. Place the right sides together at the sides and sleeves matching the underarm seams. Sew the side seams from the bottom of the sleeve to the bottom of the shirt (fig. 7a and 7b).

9. Finish the bottom edge of the shirt as follows: With the facings open, fold up $1/4$" and press. Fold up $1/4$" again and press, creating

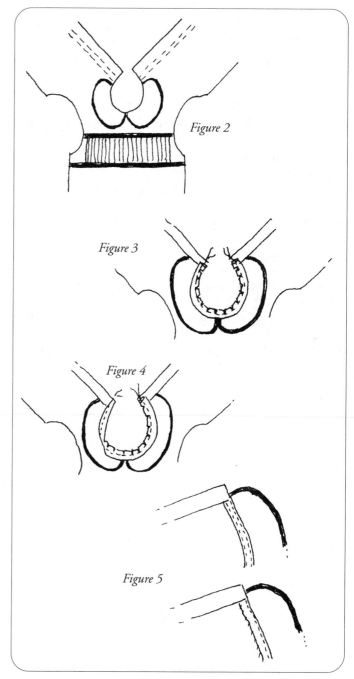

Figure 2

Figure 3

Figure 4

Figure 5

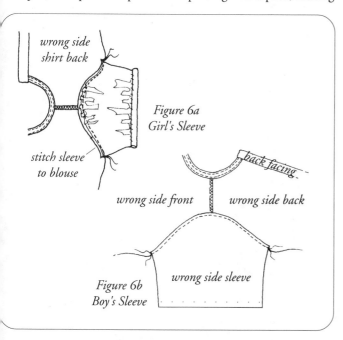

wrong side shirt back

Figure 6a
Girl's Sleeve

stitch sleeve to blouse

back facing

wrong side front

wrong side back

wrong side sleeve

Figure 6b
Boy's Sleeve

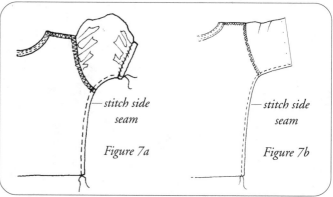

stitch side seam

stitch side seam

Figure 7a

Figure 7b

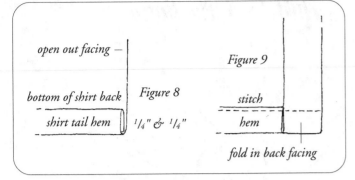

Figure 8

open out facing —

bottom of shirt back

shirt tail hem

$^1/_4$" & $^1/_4$"

Figure 9

stitch

hem

fold in back facing

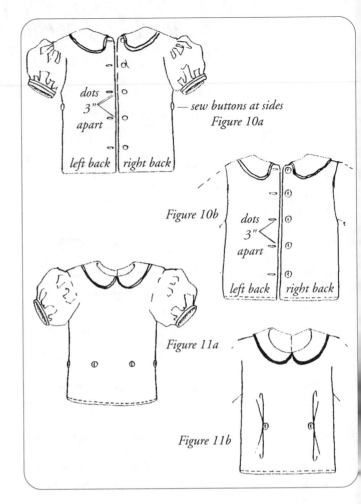

dots
3"
apart

left back | right back

— sew buttons at sides
Figure 10a

Figure 10b

dots
3"
apart

left back | right back

Figure 11a

Figure 11b

a narrow hem (fig. 8). Fold the facings along the fold line and stitch the hem in place (fig. 9).

10. Position the buttonholes on the left hand side by placing a dot $^1/_2$" from the top fabric edge of the neckline and $^1/_2$" over from the fold line. Place a dot every 3" down the back of the shirt $^1/_2$" from the fold (fig. 10a and 10b).

11. Stitch a $^1/_2$" buttonhole beginning at the dot and placing the buttonholes horizontally. Continue the buttonholes down the back of the shirt. Cut the buttonholes open with a buttonhole cutter or seam ripper.

12. Lap the left side of the shirt over the right side and mark the placement for the buttons (fig. 10a and 10b).

13. Attach the buttons along the marks on the right side of the shirt (fig. 10a and 10b).

14. Mark the placement for the buttons on the shirt front referring to the skirt or knicker waistband. Sew buttons in place making a $^1/_2$" pleat behind the button and stitching through all layers of the fabric (fig. 11a and 11b).

# Bib Knickers

When we were deciding on the patterns to include in *Heirloom Sewing for Jack and Jill,* we thought about a pattern which would be cute for a little boy or a little girl. Loving knickers has been a passion of mine for many years. They are cute on both boys and girls and they are appropriate for many occasions. Dress them up or dress them down, they still look precious. Coupled with a bib front, one can use them for smocking designs, woven ribbons, appliqué or lace work. I have seen velveteen knickers with lace shaping or the big, corduroy knickers with appliqué on the bib and cotton knickers with smocking on the bib. We feel that this pattern is so cute and that it will cover a world of clothing ideas for your little boys and girls.

One version has woven ribbons on the bib front. Four have smocking. The woven ribbon version has a white background fabric with tiny little flowers and lady bugs on it. The buttons are bright yellow, making for a festive outfit just right for summer occasions. Since everybody loves pockets, our knickers have two pockets in the front. The buttons do not really open at the waistline; they are just for looks. The buttons on the shoulders do unbutton and that is the way your little ones will come in and out of these knickers. The legs button also. There is elastic at the waistline and a cute high bib panel in the back. The front and back bibs are lined.

The four smocked versions have piping at the top and the bottom of the bib smocked inset. I believe your little ones will love this outfit and don't forget that you can make it as plain or as fancy as you want.

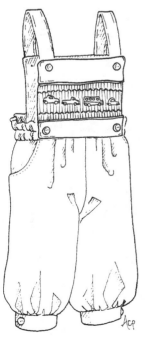

*Ribbon Bib Knicker*

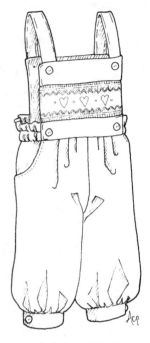

*Smocked Heart Bib Knicker*

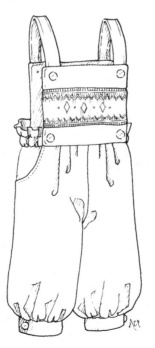

*Smocked Baby Cars Bib Knicker*

*Smocked Diamond Bib Knicker*

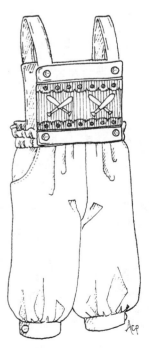

*Smocked Batters Up Bib Knicker*

# Bib Knickers

These knickers are shown in a smocked bib version and a woven ribbon bib version. Following the general directions, you will find directions for each specific bib.

## General Directions

### Fabric Requirements

| Size | Fabric (woven ribbon or smocked) | Smocked Insert (smocked only) | Pleated Rows | Smocked Rows |
|------|------|------|------|------|
| 2 | 1¹/₈ yds. | 6" | 8 - 10 | 6 - 8 |
| 3 | 1¹/₈ yds. | 6" | 8 - 10 | 6 - 8 |
| 4 | 1¹/₄ yds. | 6" | 9 - 11 | 7 - 9 |
| 5 | 1¹/₃ yds. | 6" | 10 - 12 | 8 - 10 |
| 6 | 1¹/₃ yds. | 6" | 12 - 14 | 10 - 12 |

### Other Supplies

¹/₂ yd. of ¹/₂" elastic; six ¹/₂" to ⁵/₈" buttons; 8" x 10" piece of medium weight fusible interfacing; wash-out basting tape, piping; DMC floss for the smocked bib; assorted ribbons for woven bib (see the specific directions for the woven bib yardage requirements); 6" x 9" piece of batiste for woven bib

## Cutting Directions

The pattern is found in the pattern envelope.

All seams are ⁵/₈" unless otherwise indicated.

1. Cut the following pieces: 2 bib pant fronts, 2 bib pant backs, 2 bib pocket facings, 2 bib pocket linings, 2 bib cuffs, 2 straps, 2 front bib pieces, 1 back bib facing.

2. The lining of the bib front will be cut after the bib insert is made.

## Pants Front

1. With right sides together, stitch the pants center front seam. Clip the curves and finish the seam with a zigzag or serger (fig. 1).

2. Baste or pin the pleats in the upper pants front. The pleats will point to the sides (fig. 2).

3. Place the pocket facing to the pants front, with right sides together; stitch along the upper curve. Trim the seam to ¹/₄". Clip curves and turn the facing to the inside of the pants and press (fig. 3). Top stitch along the pressed pocket edge (fig. 4).

4. Place the pocket lining to the pocket facing, with right sides together. The pocket lining will extend above the pocket facing. Stitch only the lining to the facing, starting at the sides and stitching to the dot; backstitch. Clip the seam allowance at the

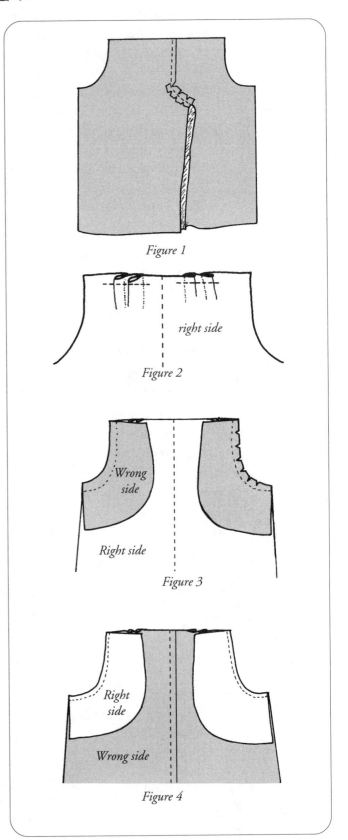

*Figure 1*

*right side*

*Figure 2*

*Wrong side*

*Right side*

*Figure 3*

*Right side*

*Wrong side*

*Figure 4*

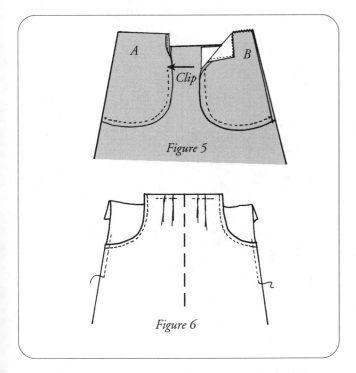

Figure 5

Figure 6

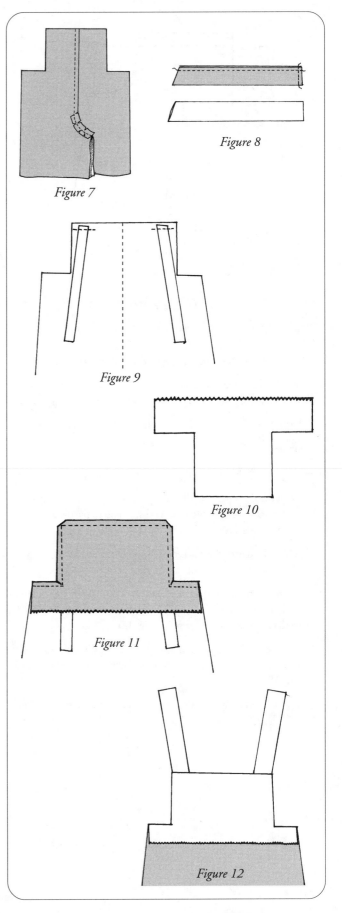

Figure 7

Figure 8

Figure 9

Figure 10

Figure 11

Figure 12

top of the stitching line. Finish the seam edges above the clip. Turn the allowance seam above the clip to the back side to form a facing and stitch. Turn the lining seam above the clip to the inside and stitch (fig. 5a). Zigzag, serge or hem the top edge of the pocket lining (fig. 5b).

5. Pin or baste the pocket in place along the sides of the pants (fig. 6).

## Pants Back

1. With right sides together, stitch the pants center back seam. Clip the curves and finish the seam edges with a zigzag or serger (fig. 7).

2. Straps: Fold the strap in half, right sides together, stitch along the long side and across the short straight side with a ³/₈" seam. Turn the strap to the right side through the pointed end. Press (fig. 8).

3. Pin the straps to the right side of the back bib with the points toward the center back. The edge of the strap should be ⁵/₈" from the side of the bib (fig. 9).

4. Finish the end of the bib facing (the long side) using a machine zigzag, serger or by turning up ¹/₄" to the wrong side, pressing and stitching with a straight stitch (fig. 10).

5. Place the back bib facing to the back bib, with right sides together. The straps will be between these two layers. Stitch as shown in (fig. 11). Clip the corners, turn and press (fig. 12).

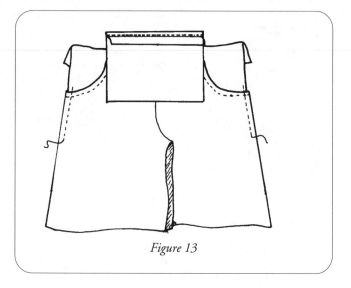

Figure 13

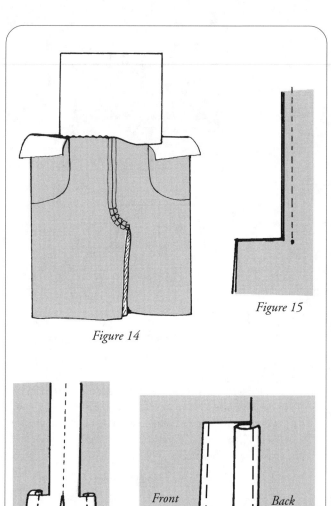

Figure 14

Figure 15

## Bib Front

Follow the directions for each specific bib front.

## Attaching the Bib Front

1. Sew the right side of the bib to the right side of the pants front. Do not stitch through the lining (fig. 13). Trim the seam to ¹/₄".

2. Turn the edge of the lining to the inside of the bib and whip to the seam (fig. 14).

## Finishing the Knickers

1. Stitch the front pants to the back pants along the side seams, starting at the top of the pants and stitching to the placket extension; backstitch (fig. 15).

2. Fold each edge of the placket extension to the inside ¹/₈", then ¹/₈" again. Stitch (fig. 16).

3. The back extension will extend past the side seam by ³/₈". Fold to achieve this and pin in place. The front extension will be folded to the inside along the seam line (fig. 17).

4. Fold the cuff in half with right sides together; stitch the short sides together. Trim the seam and turn the cuff to the right side; press (fig. 18).

5. Run two gathering threads in the bottom of the pants at ¹/₈" and ³/₈" (fig. 19).

Figure 16

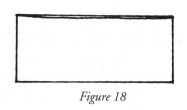

Front          Back

Figure 17

Figure 18

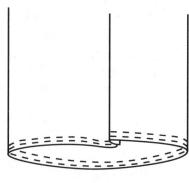

Figure 19

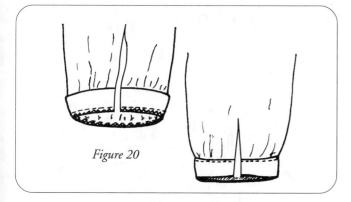

*Figure 20*

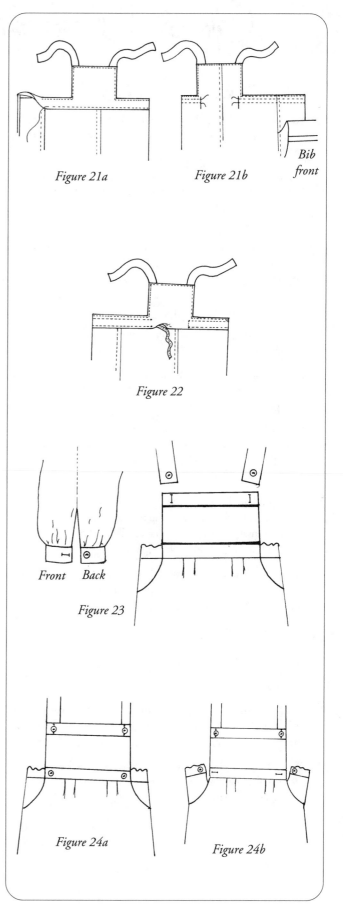

*Figure 21a*    *Figure 21b*    *Bib front*

*Figure 22*

Front    Back

*Figure 23*

*Figure 24a*    *Figure 24b*

6.  Pull the bobbin thread to gather the legs to fit the cuff. Pin the cuff to the pants, right sides together, and stitch, using a $^1/_4$" seam. Finish the seam with a zigzag or serge. Top stitch the seam allowance to the cuff (fig. 20).

7.  Fold the top edge of the pocket lining to the inside even with the back bib facing. Top stitch along the fold and the edges of the back bib (fig. 21a).

    Elastic placement stitching lines:

    Measure $^5/_8$" from the folded edge and straight stitch from the edge of the pocket facing/bib to 1" into the back bib. The second line is the same length as the first, and is $^5/_8$" below the first stitching line (fig. 21b).

8.  Cut two pieces of $^1/_2$" elastic to the following measurements:

    Size 2 = $6^1/_2$" ; size 3 = 7" ; size 4 = $7^1/_2$" ; size 5 = 8" ; size 6 = $8^1/_2$" .

9.  Run the elastic through the casing. Stitch the ends of the elastic in place through the bib and bib lining; this will create a ruffle above the elastic (fig. 22).

## Buttonholes and Buttons

1.  Work buttonholes in the front edge of the leg cuff. The buttonholes are made horizontally about $^1/_4$" to $^1/_2$" from the edge. Buttonholes are also made in the upper bib strip. These buttonholes are made vertically about $^3/_4$" to 1" from the upper edge (fig. 23).

2.  Attach buttons on the straps and back edges of the cuffs. Also attach the bottom bib strip to the pocket lining by sewing on the buttons through the pocket lining and the bib (you will stitch through the elastic) (fig. 24a); or you could make buttonholes in the bottom bib strip. The buttons, in this case, would be sewn on the pocket lining, through the elastic (fig. 24b).

# Specific Directions for Knickers Bibs

## Smocked Insert Bib

1. Tear a strip of fabric 6" for the insert. For geometric smocking designs, the strip should be 36" long; for picture smocking, make the strip 45" long.

2. Use the chart in the general instructions as a guide for the number of pleating rows; remember that you should pleat two rows more than you will smock.

3. Remove the pleating threads from a ⁵/₈" seam allowance at each end of the panel. Pull up the pleating threads and tie off the pleated panel to the measurement for your size: size 2 = 6" ; size 3 = 6¹/₄" ; size 4 = 6¹/₂" ; size 5 = 6³/₄" ; size 6 = 7" (these measurements are for the pleated area only, and do not include the seam allowances) (fig. 1).

4. Smock the design according to the instructions on the graphs found on page 210, 295-302.

5. Block the smocking to fit the bib strips. If the panel has been tied off too short, add strips to the sides of the panel to make it wide enough to fit the top and bottom strips (fig. 2).

6. Using a ⁵/₈" seam allowance, attach corded piping to one long side of each top and bottom bib strip. Press the seam allowances toward the wrong side of the bib strips, exposing the piping along the folded edge (fig. 3).

7. Attach washout basting tape to the seam allowances on the wrong side of the bib strip, above the piping (fig. 4). Press the bib strips onto the inset, allowing the piping to fall between the first smocked row and the extra pleating row (fig. 5).

8. Stitch the bib strips to the top and bottom of the smocked panel; "stitch in the ditch" between the piping and the bib strip (fig. 6). Press the bib well.

9. See section "Lining the Bib" (page 209).

## Woven Ribbon Insert

Refer to "Lace and Ribbon Weaving" found on page 360.

1. Cut a rectangle of batiste 6" x 9" (the 6" side is the vertical, the 9" side is the horizontal). Pin the rectangle to a lace board or foam board, or ironing board.

2. Weave ribbon as directed in the "Lace and Ribbon Weaving" general directions, making sure that the batiste is completely covered with the ribbon.

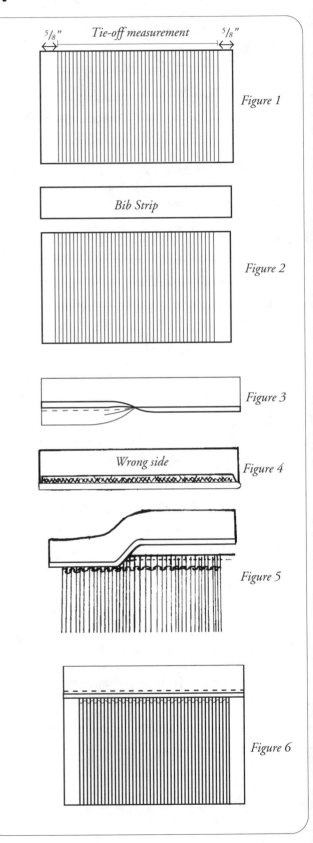

⁵/₈"    Tie-off measurement    ⁵/₈"

Figure 1

Bib Strip

Figure 2

Figure 3

Wrong side

Figure 4

Figure 5

Figure 6

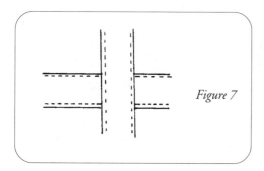

*Figure 7*

3. After all of the weaving is done, remove the pins from the board and flat-pin the ribbons to the batiste. Topstitch the ribbons down, stopping and tying off each time you come to an under lap. A straight stitch or zigzag may be used. You may match the thread color to the ribbons, or use an invisible thread (fig. 7).

4. Turn the panel to the wrong side and press well. Measure and mark the batiste to the correct size (6" x the length of the bib strips). Trim the batiste and ribbons to the correct size (fig. 8).

5. (Optional) To attach piping between the bib strips and the insert, stitch piping to one long edge of each bib strip, using a ⅝" seam (fig. 9). Refer to A. steps 6-8.

6. With right sides together, pin the bib strips to the top and bottom edges of the insert. Stitch with a ⅝" seam allowance. Press the seams toward the bib strips (fig. 10).

7. See section "Lining the Bib."

## Lining the Bib

1. Cut the bib lining the same size as the finished insert panel (fig. 11). Press a piece of fusible interfacing to the wrong side of the lining to add stability to the bib.

2. With right sides together, pin the bib and the bib lining together. Using a ⅝" seam allowance, begin stitching ⅝" from the bottom edge on one side, stitch up the side, across the top and down the other side, stopping the stitching ⅝" from the bottom edge (fig. 12).

3. Clip the corners and turn the bib to the right side; press the bib well (fig. 13).

4. Topstitch "in the ditch" between the piping and the bib strips; if there is no piping, stitch "in the ditch" between the bib strips and the insert. You will be stitching through all layers, to add stability (fig. 14).

5. Refer to pages 204-207 of the general directions to finish the knickers.

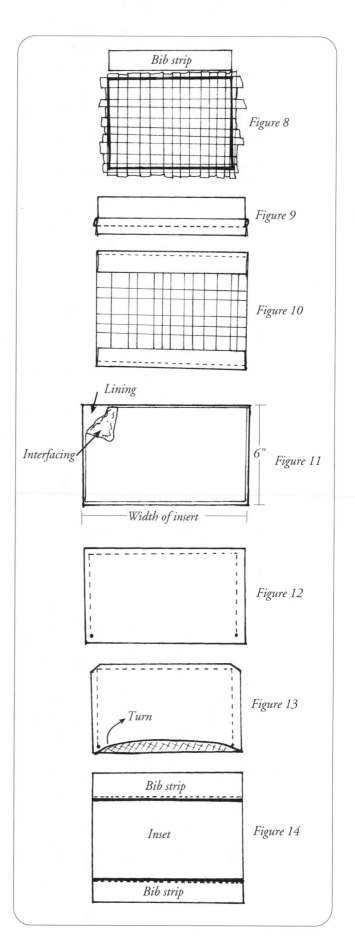

*Figure 8*

*Figure 9*

*Figure 10*

Lining

Interfacing

6" *Figure 11*

Width of insert

*Figure 12*

Turn

*Figure 13*

Bib strip

Inset

Bib strip

*Figure 14*

# Knickers Bibs

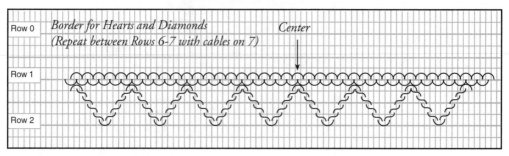

Row 0 — Border for Hearts and Diamonds
(Repeat between Rows 6-7 with cables on 7)    Center

Row 1

Row 2

## Top and Bottom Borders for Hearts and Diamonds

Pleat 8 rows. Smock the top and bottom holding rows on the right side with a stem or outline stitch (this replaces backsmocking). Use 3 strands of DMC floss for borders, 4 strands for hearts and diamonds.

**Step 1.** On row 1, work a row of cables, beginning at center front with an up cable.

**Step 2.** Beginning at center front with an up cable just under Row 1, work four-step trellises between Rows 1 and 2.

Repeat this pattern on the bottom two rows of smocking, with the cables on the bottom row and beginning with down cables at center front on row 7, working the trellises up to row 6 and back down again.

The hearts, diamonds and flowerettes will be worked from the graph.

**Simple Hearts**

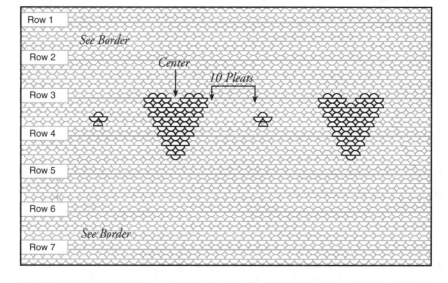

**Simple Diamonds**

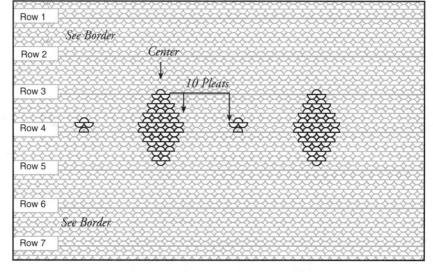

# Heirloom Sewing

## for

## Jill

# General Dress Directions
## Sizes 2-16

Please read all directions, both general and specific, before beginning the dress of your choosing. The general directions give the neck, sleeve, placket and sash finishes. The specific directions list each dress and give fabric and lace requirements along with detailed instructions on special embellishments techniques.

### General Fabric Requirements

| Dress without collar | Without a hem allowance | With a 4" hem allowance |
|---|---|---|
| 2 - 4 | 1 3/4 yds. | 2 yds. |
| 6 - 8 | 2 1/3 yds. | 2 1/2 yds. |
| 10 - 12 | 2 3/4 yds. | 2 7/8 yds. |
| 14 - 16 | 2 7/8 yds. | 3 yds. |

### Collar

Round and Pointed Collar Variation
    Sizes 2 - 6 - 1/2 yd., Sizes 8 - 16 - 5/8 yd.
Peter Pan Collar Variation
    All sizes - 1/4 yd.
Large Square Collar Variation
    All sizes - 1/3 yd.
Small Round Collar Variation
    All sizes - 1/3 yd.

### Sleeve Band Chart

These suggested measurements are cutting measurements for the cuffs including seam allowances. The width of the cuffs will be listed in the specific directions.

| Sizes | Measurement |
|---|---|
| 2 | 7 5/8" |
| 4 | 8 1/4" |
| 6 | 8 3/4" |
| 8 | 9 3/4" |
| 10 | 10 1/8" |
| 12 | 10 1/2" |
| 14 | 10 7/8" |
| 16 | 11 1/4" |

### Skirt Chart

These suggested measurements are cutting measurements for the skirt front length and the skirt back length including seam allowances. Adjust the length as needed to fit the child. The widths of the skirt front and skirt back are 45" each, all sizes, unless otherwise indicated in the specific dress directions. The circumference of the skirt when finished will be approximately 90". If a hem is desired, add 4 1/4" to the length measurements.

Cut 2 Panels 45" wide by:

| Size | Waisted Skirt Without Hem | Mid-Yoke Skirt Without Hem | High-Yoke Skirt Without Hem |
|---|---|---|---|
| 2 | 12 3/4" | 14 3/4" | 18 1/2" |
| 4 | 15 1/4" | 17 1/4" | 21 3/4" |
| 6 | 18 3/4" | 20 3/4" | 25 3/4" |
| 8 | 24 1/4" | 26 1/4" | 32" |
| 10 | 25 1/2" | 27 1/2" | 33 3/4" |
| 12 | 27 3/4" | 29 3/4" | 36 1/4" |
| 14 | 29" | 31" | 38" |
| 16 | 30 1/2" | 32 1/2" | 39 1/2" |

(If hem is desired, add 4 1/2" to skirt.)

### I. Cutting

1.  Refer to the specific directions on each dress for any embellishment that may need to be done before cutting out the bodice front. Cut out the bodice front on the fold.
2.  Cut out two bodice backs from the selvage. Mark the facing fold lines along the backs.
3.  Refer to the specific instructions before cutting out the sleeves. Some sleeve treatments are added before the sleeves are cut. Cut out the sleeves.
4.  Refer to the specific directions for each dress before cutting out the skirt. Cut out a skirt front and a skirt back as directed in the specific directions.
5.  Collar (optional) - The collars will be cut and constructed according to the specific directions under each dress.

### II. Neck Finishes
#### A. Bias Facing

1.  Measure around the neck with the back facings folded to the inside of the dress. Cut a bias strip 1" wide by the length around the neck.
2.  Fold the bias strip in half lengthwise, with the long cut edges even. Press.
3.  With the back facings folded to the outside of the bodice, place the cut edges of the bias strip to the cut edge of the neck. Trim the ends of the bias so that the folds of the back bodice extend 1/8" beyond the edges of the bias facing. Stitch the bias strip facing in place using a 1/4" seam. Trim the seam to 1/8". Place clips along the seam allowance (fig. 1). Fold the facing completely to the inside of the dress, folding the back folds to the inside of the dress.
4.  Stitch the facing in place by hand or machine (fig. 2).

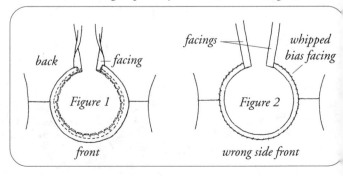

Figure 1 — back, facing, front

Figure 2 — facings, whipped bias facing, wrong side front

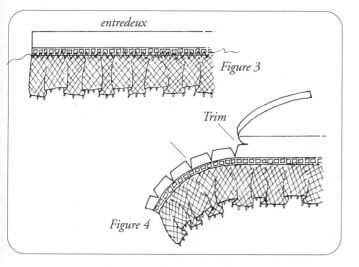

*entredeux*

*Figure 3*

*Trim*

*Figure 4*

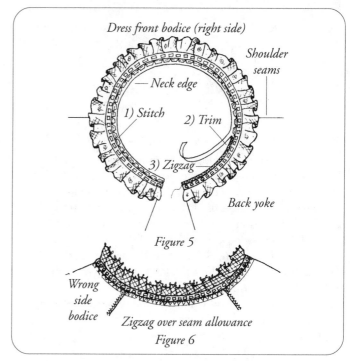

Dress front bodice (right side)

Shoulder seams

— Neck edge

1) Stitch    2) Trim

3) Zigzag

Back yoke

*Figure 5*

Wrong side bodice

Zigzag over seam allowance

*Figure 6*

## B. Entredeux and Gathered Edging Lace

1. Cut a strip of entredeux the length around the neck with the back facings extended.

2. Cut a piece of edging lace two times this length. Gather the lace to fit the entredeux strip.

3. Trim away one side of the entredeux and attach the gathered edging lace to the trimmed entredeux using the technique "entredeux to gathered lace" (fig. 3).

4. If the fabric edge remaining on the entredeux is not already $1/4$", trim to $1/4$". Clip this fabric so that is will curve along the neck edge of the dress (fig. 4). Place this strip to the neck of the dress with the back placket extended, right sides together. Attach the entredeux/gathered lace strip to the neck of the dress using the technique "entredeux to fabric" (fig. 5).

5. Using a tiny zigzag, tack the seam allowance to the dress. This stitching will keep the entredeux/gathered lace standing up at the neck (fig. 6).

## C. Bias Binding

1. Trim $1/4$" from the neck of the bodice (fig. 7).

2. Measure around the neck with the back facings folded to the inside of the dress. Cut a bias strip $1^1/2$" wide by the length around the neck plus 1".

3. Fold the bias strip in half lengthwise, with the long cut edges even. Press.

4. With the back facing folded to the inside of the bodice, place the cut edges of the bias to the cut edge of the neck. Stitch in place using a $1/4$" seam (fig. 8).

5. Trim the ends of the bias strip to extend $1/4$" beyond the folded edges of the back bodice.

6. Pull the binding away from the dress. Fold the $1/4$" extensions to the inside of the neck. Fold the binding over the seam allowance, enclosing the seam allowance. The binding should fit tightly against the seam allowance. Pin. Stitch the binding to the dress by hand or machine (fig. 9).

## D. Attaching a Collar

1. Place the front and backs right sides together and stitch the shoulder seams with a $1/4$" seam.

2. Place the wrong side of the collar to the right side of the neck of the bodice. Pin in place (fig. 10). Fold the bodice back facing on the fold line to the right side of the bodice (collar will be between the back and the facing) (fig. 11).

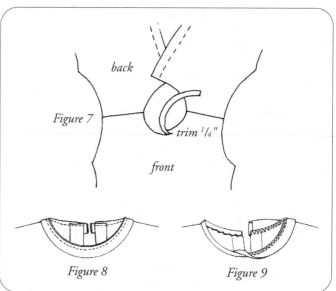

back

*Figure 7*

trim $1/4$"

front

*Figure 8*    *Figure 9*

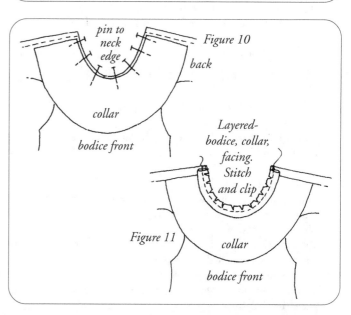

pin to neck edge

*Figure 10*

back

collar

bodice front

Layered-bodice, collar, facing. Stitch and clip

*Figure 11*

collar

bodice front

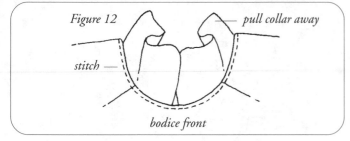

Figure 12

pull collar away

stitch

bodice front

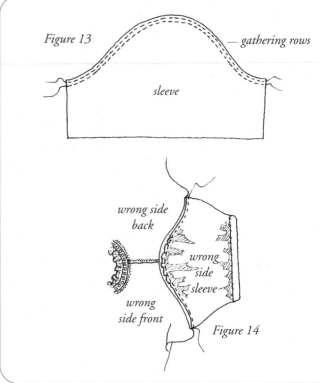

Figure 13 — gathering rows

sleeve

wrong side back

wrong side sleeve

wrong side front

Figure 14

3. Cut a bias strip 1" wide by neck measurement. Fold the bias strip in half and press. Place the cut edges of the strip to the neck of the collar/bodice. The bias strip starts and stops $1/2$" from the back edge (fig. 11). Cut off any excess bias.

4. Stitch the bias strip to the neck edge using a $1/4$" seam, starting at the fold lines on the back edges of the bodice (fig. 11).

5. Trim the seam to $1/8$". Clip the neck edge and understitch the bias band. Understitching is done by stitching through the bias band and the trimmed seams.

6. Holding the collar away from the bodice, stitch the facing to the bodice (fig. 12).

## III. Sleeves to Armholes

1. Refer to the specific directions for the dress being constructed to embellish the sleeves.

2. Run two gathering rows in the top of the sleeve at $1/8$" and $3/8$" from the edge (fig. 13).

3. Pull up the gathers in the top of the sleeve to fit the arm opening of the bodice. The gathers should fall about 3" to $3^1/2$" on each side of the shoulder seam. Stitch the sleeves to the arm opening, with right sides together (fig. 14).

## IV. Sleeve Finishes

### A. Bias Band

1. Cut two bias strips $1^1/2$" wide by the length on the sleeve band chart. Fold the bias in half and press.

2. Run two gathering rows in the bottom of each sleeve at $1/8$" and $1/4$". Gather the bottom of the sleeve to fit the binding. Place the right side of the bias strip to the right side of the sleeve and stitch using a $1/4$" seam allowance (fig. 15).

3. Fold the remaining edge of the bias strip to the wrong side of the sleeve $1/4$" (fig. 16).

4. Stitch the folded edge just over the seam allowance on the inside of the sleeve creating a $1/4$" bias binding (fig. 16).

### B. Bias Band with Piping

1. Cut two bias strips $1^1/2$" wide by the length on the sleeve band chart. Fold bias in half and press.

2. Place the raw edge of the piping to the raw edge of the sleeve bands, right sides together, and baste the piping in place with a zipper foot or cording foot with a $1/4$" seam allowance (fig. 17).

3. Run two gathering rows in the bottom of each sleeve at $1/8$" and $1/4$". Gather the bottom of the sleeve to fit the binding. Place the right side of the bias strip to the right side of the sleeve with the piping sandwiched between sleeve and band and stitch using a $1/4$" seam allowance (fig. 15).

4. Fold the remaining edge of the bias strip to the wrong side of the sleeve $1/4$" (fig. 16).

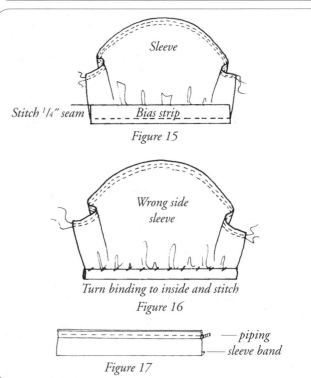

Sleeve

Stitch $1/4$" seam | Bias strip

Figure 15

Wrong side sleeve

Turn binding to inside and stitch

Figure 16

— piping
— sleeve band

Figure 17

5. Stitch the folded edge just over the seam allowance on the inside of the sleeve creating a $1/4$" bias binding.

### C. Sleeve Band

1. Cut two strips of fabric by the cuff width and length measurement given in the sleeve band chart for your dress size

2. Run two rows of gathering threads at $1/8$" and $3/8$" in the bottom edge of sleeve.

3. Pull up the gathers on the bottom of the sleeve to fit the band. Stitch the band to the sleeve, right sides together, using a $1/4$"

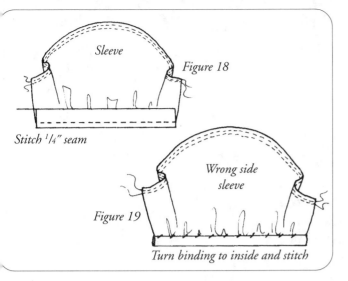

Figure 18

*Sleeve*

Stitch ¹/₄" seam

*Wrong side sleeve*

Figure 19

*Turn binding to inside and stitch*

seam (fig. 18). Fold the lower edge of the band to the inside ¹/₄". Place the folded edge just over the seam line on the inside of the sleeve(fig. 19). Hand or machine stitch in place.

## V. Placket

1. Cut a 5" slit down the center back of the skirt for the back placket (fig. 20).
2. Cut a strip of fabric from the selvage 11" by ³/₄".
3. Pull the slit in the skirt apart to form a "V". Place right side of the strip to right side of the skirt slit, cut edge to cut edge. The stitching will be made from the wrong side with the skirt on top and the placket strip on the bottom. The placket strip will be straight and the skirt will form a "V" with the point of the "V" ¹/₄" from the edge of the placket. Stitch, using a ¹/₄ seam. It is important to catch a few fibers in the seam at the point of the "V" (fig. 21).
4. Press the seam toward the selvage edge of the placket strip. Turn the selvage edge to the inside of the dress, enclosing the seam allowance. Stitch in place by hand or machine (fig. 22).
5. On the inside of the placket, stitch the placket at an angle from the lower inside edge to the folded edges (fig. 23).
6. The back of the dress will lap left over right. Fold the left side of the placket to the inside of the skirt and pin. Leave the right back placket open.

## VI. Sash

1. Cut the two sash pieces to the following measurements: Size 2-6 = 5" by 33" and Size 8-16 = 5" by 38".
2. Fold the sash in half lengthwise, right sides together, and stitch the long sides together.
3. Stitch an angle on one edge of the sash. Trim the seam allowance at the angle to ¹/₄" (fig. 24).
4. Turn the sash to the right side and press (fig. 25).
5. Place a pleat in the unfinished edge of the sash until this end measures 1¹/₄". Pin the sash directly above the piping on the back bodices matching the raw edges (fig. 26).

## VII. Darts

Refer to the dart on the bodice patterns and stitch in place.

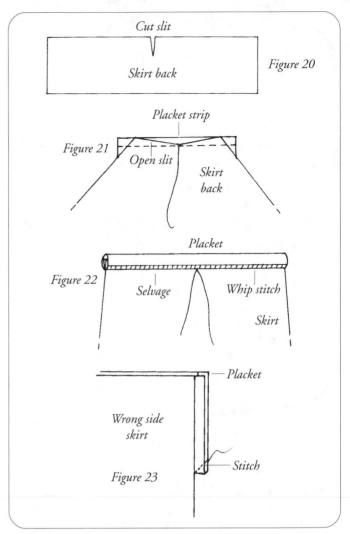

Cut slit

*Skirt back*

Figure 20

*Placket strip*

Figure 21

Open slit

*Skirt back*

*Placket*

Figure 22

*Selvage*

*Whip stitch*

*Skirt*

*Placket*

*Wrong side skirt*

Figure 23

*Stitch*

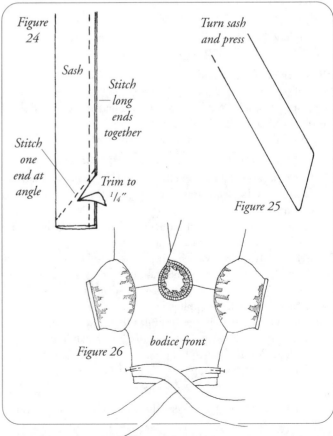

Figure 24

*Sash*

*Stitch long ends together*

*Stitch one end at angle*

Trim to ¹/₄"

Turn sash and press

Figure 25

*bodice front*

Figure 26

# Robin's Egg Australian Madeira Dress

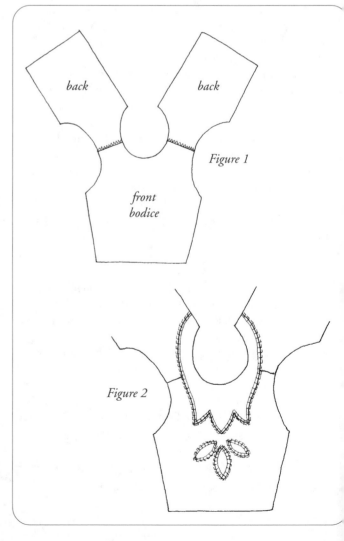

*Simplicity is the keyword when thinking of making this white tailored "older girl pleasing" batiste dress. The beautiful Australian Madeira appliqués are found around the neckline, on the sleeves, on the bodice of the dress and around the hem. Robin's egg blue is used on the white dress for the neckline, the sleeves and the hem. Robins' egg blue piping peeks from the waistline. Three petals of Australian Madeira Appliqué are found on the center front of the dress and on each sleeve. These beautiful petals are also used at the top of the Australian Madeira border on the hemline.*

## Fabric Requirements

|  | Sizes 2-6 | Sizes 8-10 | Sizes 12-16 |
|---|---|---|---|
| White Nelona 45" | $1^3/_4$ yds | $2^1/_4$ yds | $2^3/_4$ yds |
| Robin's Egg Blue Nelona 45" | $1^1/_4$ yd | $1^1/_4$ yd | $1^1/_4$ yd |
| Pink Swiss Batiste | $^1/_8$ yd | $^1/_8$ yd | $^1/_8$ yd |
| Yellow Swiss Batiste | $^1/_8$ yd | $^1/_8$ yd | $^1/_8$ yd |
| Cording | 1 yd | 1 yd | 1 yd |
| Buttons $^1/_2$" | 4 | 4 | 5 |

Embroidery floss to match robin's egg blue, pink, and yellow

## Pattern Pieces

All pattern pieces are found in the pattern envelope.
Waisted bodice front, waisted bodice back, puffed sleeve.
Templates: Australian Madeira appliqué for bodice, sleeve and skirt.
Australian Madeira Appliqué techniques: pages 349-353.
All seams $^1/_4$". Finish seams with a zigzag stitch or a serger.

## Cutting and Bodice Construction

1. Cut from white fabric the following: one front bodice on the fold, two bodice backs from the selvage and two sleeves on dress cutting line.
2. Sew the shoulder seams of the bodice, right sides together, using a $^1/_4$" seam allowance (fig. 1).
2. Refer to "Australian Madeira Applique Neck Finish" and finish the neck using robin's egg blue fabric for the Madeira applique design (fig. 2). Refer to "Australian Madeira Applique - Corded Accents" to stitch the applique in place.
3. Trace the petal designs on the pink and yellow fabrics.
4. Create the petals using the technique "Australian Madeira Applique Motifs." Stitch the petals in place referring to "Australian Madeira Applique - Corded Accents."

## Sleeves

1. Cut out two strips of robin's egg blue fabric 5" by the sleeve width.

*back*  *back*

*Figure 1*

*front bodice*

*Figure 2*

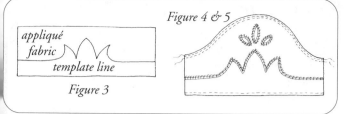

*Figure 4 & 5*

applique
fabric

template line

*Figure 3*

2. Trace the sleeve template on to the robin's egg blue fabric (fig. 3).

3. Refer to the technique "Australian Madeira Appliqué Hem Directions" and attach the appliqué to the bottom of each sleeve. Stitch using the technique "Australian Madeira Applique - Corded Accents."

4. Trace the petal designs on the pink and yellow fabrics. Create the petals using the technique "Australian Madeira Appliqué Motifs" Stitch the petals in place referring to "Australian Madeira Applique - Corded Accent" (fig. 4).

5. Run gathering threads in the top and bottom of sleeves at $^3/_8$" and $^1/_8$" (fig. 5).

6. Refer to the General Dress Directions, IV. Sleeve Finishes, A. Bias Band and finish the bottom of the sleeves with a bias band (p. 214).

7. Insert the sleeves into the armholes referring to the General Dress Directions, III. Sleeves to Armholes.

## Skirt

1. Refer to the General Dress Directions, skirt chart (p. 212) and cut two skirt pieces by the length and width given on the chart. Mark the center front and center back of the skirt pieces. Sew the side seams with a $^1/_4$" seam and finish the seams with a zigzag or serger.

2. Cut out two strips of robin's egg blue fabric 7 $^3/_4$" long by the skirt width. Sew these two strips together to form a circle. Make sure the circumference of the robin's egg blue circle and the circumference of the skirt are the same. Trace the Australia Madeira skirt template on the top edge of the robin's egg blue circle (fig. 6).

3. Refer to the technique "Australian Madeira Appliqué Hem Directions" and attach the appliqué the bottom of skirt. Stitch the applique to the skirt using the technique for "Australian Madeira Applique - Corded Accents."

4. Trace the petal designs on the pink and yellow fabrics (there will be 4 sets of petals). Create the petals using the technique "Australian Madeira Applique Motifs." Position the petals above the appliqué design and stitch the petals in place referring to "Australian Madeira Applique - Corded Accents." (fig. 7).

## Finishing the Garment

1. With right sides together, match the sleeve band, underarm seam and the bottom of the bodice, sew the side seams (fig. 8). Measure around the bottom of the bodice and make a piece of piping to this measurement from the robin's egg blue fabric. Refer to "Making Piping" if needed. Attach the piping to the bottom of the bodice with a $^1/_4$" seam (fig. 9).

2. Refer to the General Dress Directions (p. 215), V. Placket and stitch a placket in the skirt center back.

3. Run two rows of gathering stitches in the top of the skirt at $^1/_8$" and $^3/_8$".

4. Place the bodice to the skirt with right sides together. Pull up the gathers of the skirt to fit the bodice matching the center fronts and side seams. The center back openings will come to the fold line on the left and right backs. Wrap the back facings around the skirt center

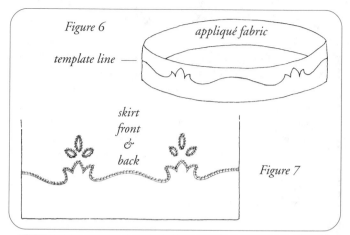

*Figure 6*

applique fabric

template line

skirt
front
&
back

*Figure 7*

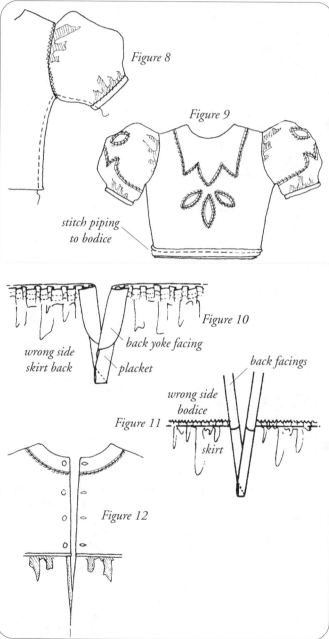

*Figure 8*

*Figure 9*

stitch piping
to bodice

*Figure 10*

back yoke facing

wrong side
skirt back

placket

back facings

wrong side
bodice

*Figure 11*

skirt

*Figure 12*

back openings. Sew the bodice to the skirt (fig. 10).

5. Pull the bodice away from the skirt, folding the back facings to the inside of the bodice (fig. 11).

6. Close the dress with buttons and buttonholes along each side of the back bodice (fig. 12).

# Cecil's Royal Diamond Dress

*Exquisitely designed with wonderful lace shaping and "cutting and pasting" techniques is this royal dress, named because it is indeed fit for a royal occasion. Quite honestly, I think this would be the world's prettiest communion or confirmation dress. Enjoy using your mitering, curving and straight lace shaping skills. If you have dresser scarves, shadow worked placemats, table runners or vintage napkins, this is the dress for you to keep them forever inside the diamonds. If you don't have any of these items, you can certainly enjoy putting machine embroidery on organdy pieces and inserting them into the diamonds. On our dress each diamond has a little "snippet" of different white, green, blue, yellow and pink shadow work embroidery taken from a table runner. Eyelet fabric would also be beautiful to use as the inset pieces. The front of the dress features a diamond in the center front with a pretty ruffle beneath. Three tucks are found on either side of the straight lace which reminds me of a Victorian blouse from 1900. Beading is shaped around the neckline with gathered lace attached at the top. The sleeves are beyond wonderful with mitered tucks, straight tucks, a lace diamond with the shadow work embroidery inside the diamond, and beading plus gathered lace with ribbon threaded through the beading. The bottom of the sleeve has entredeux and gathered lace. Six strands of embroidery floss are woven through the entredeux.*

*The glorious skirt has ten panels with two sizes of diamonds alternating in the center of the panels. The bottom of the dress has v shaped French insertion with a wonderfully wide ruffle featuring three pintucks and straight French lace on the bottom. The pink organza sash is attached into the waistline in the front making it one of those wonderful sashes which won't ride up or wander. What a great idea! The back closes with buttons and buttonholes.*

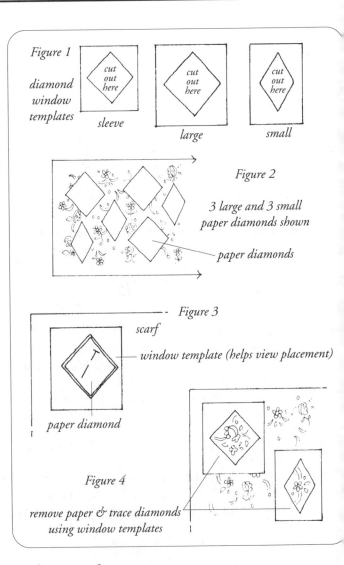

## Fabric Requirements

|  | Sizes 2-6 | Sizes 8-10 | Sizes 12-16 |
|---|---|---|---|
| White batiste 45" | $2^1/_2$ yds | 3 yds | 3 yds |
| $^5/_8$" Lace Insertion | 18 yds | $19^1/_2$ yds | 21 yds |
| $^3/_4$" Lace Edging | $3^1/_2$ yds | $3^1/_2$ yds | $3^5/_8$ yds |
| $1^1/_4$" Lace Edging for Skirts | 5 $^5/_8$ yds | 5 $^3/_4$ yds | 6 yds |
| $^5/_8$" Beading | $1^2/_3$ yds | 2 yds | 2 yds |
| Entredeux | $^3/_4$ yd | $^3/_4$ yd | $^3/_4$ yd |
| Organdy (optional) | $^1/_3$ yd | $^1/_3$ yd | $^1/_3$ yd |
| 4" Ribbon | 3 yd | 3 yd | 3 yd |
| 4 mm Silk Ribbon | 5 yds | 5 yds | 5 yds |
| Buttons $^1/_2$" | 4 | 4 | 5 |

2 Embroidered Dresser Scarves with 16 designs or eyelet fabric for center of diamonds.

2mm silk ribbon for sleeve entredeux; 1 yd all sizes

All seams $^1/_4$". Finish seams with a zigzag stitch or a serger.

## Pattern Pieces

All pattern pieces are found in the pattern envelope. Waisted bodice front, waisted bodice back, front bodice ruffle, puffed dress sleeve. Diamond and lace insertion template for the front bodice, inner sleeve template, large and small diamond template, sleeve diamond template, V template for skirt, lace insertion template for back bodice.

## Insertion Lace Diamonds

1. Trace and cut out one large, one small and one sleeve diamond window template (fig.1). Use these to trace onto paper, 5 large diamonds, 2 sleeve diamonds and 6 small diamonds. Cut out the diamonds. Position the diamonds on the dresser scarves to locate the designs that will be used (fig. 2). Use the window templates to determine placement and pin a paper diamond in each window as you go (fig. 3). If the designs will not fit the templates, the templates may be altered. Five large and five small diamonds are used on the skirt; these would be the easiest to change, if needed. Then go back and trace on the scarves where the paper diamonds are pinned with a wash-out marker using the window templates (fig.4).

*Figure 1*

diamond window templates

cut out here — sleeve

cut out here — large

cut out here — small

*Figure 2*

*3 large and 3 small paper diamonds shown*

paper diamonds

*Figure 3*

scarf

window template (helps view placement)

paper diamond

*Figure 4*

*remove paper & trace diamonds using window templates*

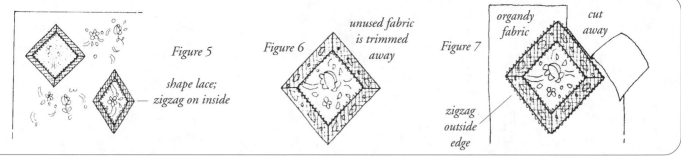

Figure 5

shape lace;
— zigzag on inside

Figure 6

unused fabric
is trimmed
away

Figure 7

organdy
fabric

cut
away

zigzag
outside
edge

2. Shape the lace insertion around the diamonds referring to lace shaping techniques. Stitch the lace on the inside of the diamond to the scarf fabric (fig.5).

3. Cut out the lace diamonds. Trim the scarf fabric from behind the lace (fig. 6).

4. To underline the lace motif diamond, position the lace diamonds on the organdy, stitch around outside of diamond with a small zigzag stitch and cut out on outer edge of lace (fig.7). This step stabilizes the diamond piece.

## Bodice

1. To construct the bodice front, cut a piece of fabric 18" by 16", 2 pieces 15" by 9", and one front bodice ruffle.

2. Trace the lace insertion template onto the front bodice ruffle. Shape the lace insertions on the template line. Stitch the lace to fabric on the top edge of the lace insertion. Cut fabric from behind the lace insertion. Measure the outer edge of the lace insertion and cut a piece of lace edging twice this length and gather to fit the bottom of the lace insertion. Stitch the gathered lace to the lace insertions with a small zigzag stitch referring to the technique "lace to lace" (fig. 8). Run two rows of gathering stitches in the top edge of the ruffle.

3. On the 18" by 16" piece of fabric trace the diamond and lace insertion template.

4. Position one of the small diamond lace motifs onto the traced diamond. Shape lace insertion on the template lines (fig. 9).

5. Position the ruffle below the diamond and under the lace insertions on each side. Gather the ruffle to fit under the diamond lace. Place the side edges of ruffle under the lace insertion.

6. Stitch the diamond down on the outer edge of lace. Stitch the lace insertion on the sides in place by stitching on the inside edge of the lace with a small zigzag. Do not stitch the outer side of the lace insertion (fig. 9).

7. Trim the fabric from behind the diamond and lace insertions being careful not to cut diamond lining fabric (fig. 9).

8. On the strips that are 10" by 6", make 3 pintucks starting $5/8$" from one long edge spacing the tucks $1/4$" apart. Do this on each strip (fig 10). Press.

9. Position the tucked strips under the lace insertion overlapping the insertion $1/8$" on the top of the fabric. Stitch the lace to the fabric with a small zigzag stitch. Trim the fabric from behind the lace (fig. 11).

10. Fold the constructed front in half and cut out a bodice front. The top of the diamond should be 1" from the neck edge in the center front (fig. 12).

11. Bodice back: cut two pieces 18" by 16", and two pieces 15" by 9" for the side panels.

12. To construct the bodice back pintucked piece on the strips that are 15" by 9", make 3 pintucks starting $5/8$" from one long edge spacing the tucks $1/4$" apart. Do this on each strip (fig. 10). Press.

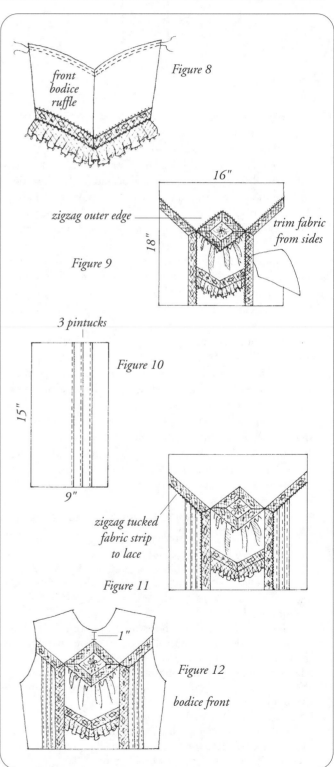

front
bodice
ruffle

Figure 8

16"

zigzag outer edge

18"

trim fabric
from sides

Figure 9

3 pintucks

Figure 10

15"

9"

zigzag tucked
fabric strip
to lace

Figure 11

1"

Figure 12

bodice front

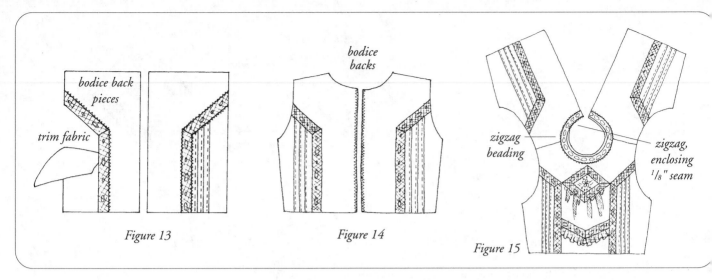

bodice back pieces

trim fabric

*Figure 13*

bodice backs

*Figure 14*

zigzag beading

zigzag, enclosing 1/8" seam

*Figure 15*

13. To construct the bodice back on the 18" by 16" piece of fabric trace the lace insertion template. The template will need to be reversed on one side to get a left and right back. Shape the lace insertion on the template lines. Stitch the inside edge of the lace with a small zigzag stitch. Trim from behind the lace insertion.

14. Position the tucked strip under the lace insertion overlapping the insertion 1/8" on the top of the fabric. Stitch the lace to the fabric with a small zigzag stitch. Trim the fabric from behind the lace (fig. 13).

15. Position the back bodice pattern onto the block and cut out a left and right back. Remember that the pattern will have to be flipped over to cut one side (fig. 14).

16. Finish back edge of fabric with a serger or and small turned back hem (fig. 14).

17. Stitch the shoulder seams with right sides together with a 1/4" seam (fig. 15).

18. Trim 1/8" from around the neck. Shape the lace beading around the neck edge leaving the 1/8 inch seam on the edge. Stitch the lace beading to the neck edge with a small zigzag on the inside and a larger zigzag on the neck to enclose the seam allowance (fig. 15). Weave the ribbon through the beading.

19. Measure around the neck edge and cut a piece of lace edging twice this length. Gather the lace to fit around the neck edge. Stitch the lace edging to the lace beading with a small zigzag stitch (fig. 16).

20. Press under the back facings and finish the lace edging (fig. 17).

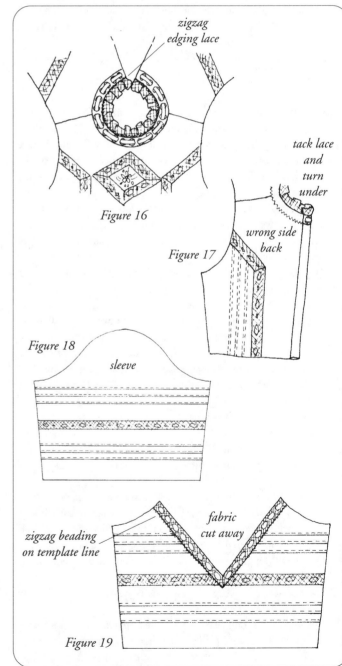

zigzag edging lace

*Figure 16*

tack lace and turn under

wrong side back

*Figure 17*

*Figure 18*

sleeve

zigzag beading on template line

fabric cut away

*Figure 19*

### Sleeves

1. Cut out two sleeves 2" (sizes 2-4) or 3" (sizes 6-16) longer than the sleeve pattern and two blocks of fabric 13" by 13". Measure up 1" (sizes 2-4) or 2" (sizes 6-16) from the bottom of the sleeve and make a pintuck. Make two more pintucks each 1/4" from the previous tuck.

2. Lace insertion is placed 1/4" above the last pintuck. Stitch the lace insertion down with a small zigzag stitch on each side. Cut the fabric from behind the lace.

3. Make three more pintucks, starting the first 1/4" from the top of the lace insertion and then spacing them 1/4" apart, aligning it as shown on the sleeve template (fig. 18).

4. Trace the "sleeve V template" onto each sleeve.

5. Shape the lace beading on the template line. Stitch the bottom of the lace beading to the sleeve with a small zigzag stitch. Trim the fabric from behind the lace beading (fig. 19).

6. Trace the inner sleeve template onto the 12" by 12" blocks.

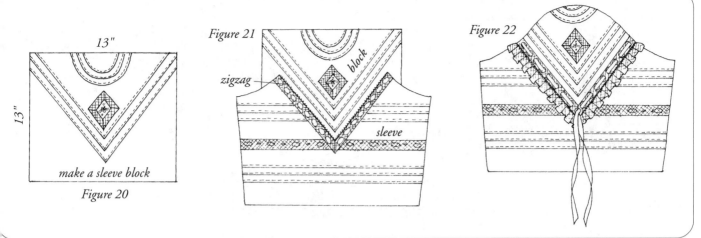

13"

13"

*make a sleeve block*

Figure 20

Figure 21

zigzag

block

sleeve

Figure 22

Position diamond/motif onto the sleeve block and stitch in place with a small zigzag stitch. Cut the fabric from behind the diamond. Stitch pintucks on the lines from the template (fig. 20).

Position the sleeves on top of the 13" by 13" blocks and stitch the inside edge of the lace beading with a small zigzag stitch (fig. 21). Trim the extra fabric from behind the lace beading. Position the sleeve on top of sleeve pattern and trace the top of the sleeve on the fabric. Cut out the top of the sleeve (fig. 22).

0. Gather a 36" strip of $^3/_4$" lace edging to fit around the outer edge of lace beading. Stitch in place with a small zigzag stitch.

1. Cut 4 pieces of ribbon 18" long. Weave ribbon through the beading starting at top and letting the ends hang loose at the point of the V. The ribbons will be tied in a bow at the point (fig. 22).

2. Run gathering threads in the top and bottom of the sleeve at $^1/_8$" and $^3/_8$". Refer to the sleeve band chart and cut two pieces of entredeux to this length. Cut two pieces of lace edging twice the sleeve band length. Trim one edge of the entredeux, gather the lace edging to fit and stitch the edging to the entredeux with a small zigzag stitch. Refer to the technique "gathered lace to entredeux" (fig. 23).

3. Gather the bottom of the sleeve to fit the entredeux/edging and stitch the band to the sleeve. Refer to the technique "entredeux to gathered fabric" (fig. 24).

4. Thread silk ribbon into a 26 tapestry needle and run ribbon through the entredeux.

## Skirt

Refer to the General Dress Directions, Skirt Chart and and cut the skirt, front and back, $3^1/_2$" shorter than the chart measurement and a width of 40". Mark the center front and center back.

Make marks all the way down the skirt front and back every 8"(fig. 25).

Sew the lace insertions on each line, centering the lace over the line. Stitch on both sides of the lace insertion with a small zigzag stitch. Cut fabric from behind the lace insertion (fig. 26).

Sew the side seams. Place the lace insertion over the seams. Stitch the insertion on both sides and cut the fabric from behind the lace (fig. 27).

Trace the V template on the bottom of the skirt (fig. 28). Shape the lace insertion on the bottom V's. Stitch the top edge of the lace to the fabric with a small zigzag stitch and trim the fabric from behind the lace. Place the diamond/motif in each panel

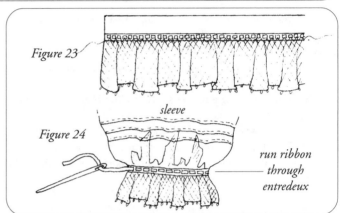

Figure 23

sleeve

Figure 24

run ribbon through entredeux

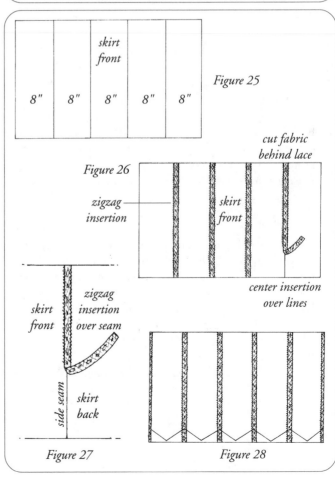

skirt front

8"    8"    8"    8"    8"

Figure 25

cut fabric behind lace

Figure 26

zigzag insertion

skirt front

center insertion over lines

zigzag insertion over seam

skirt front

side seam

skirt back

Figure 27

Figure 28

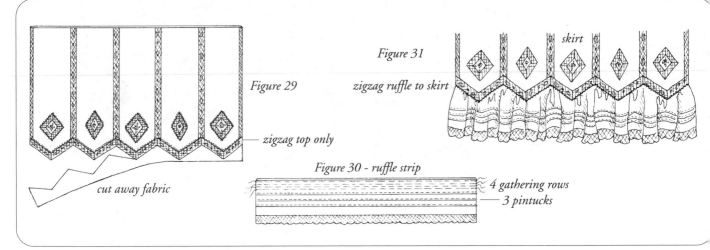

Figure 29

zigzag top only

cut away fabric

Figure 31

skirt

zigzag ruffle to skirt

Figure 30 - ruffle strip

4 gathering rows
3 pintucks

and stitch in place with a small zigzag then cut the fabric from behind the diamonds (fig. 29).

6.  Cut 4 ruffle strips 5¹/₂" by 40". Stitch ruffle strips together to form a circle. Attach 1¹/₄" lace edging to the bottom of the ruffle using the technique "lace to fabric."

7.  Stitch three rows of pintucks starting 1" up from the top of the lace and then 1¹/₄" apart (fig. 30).

8.  Run four rows of gathering threads at ¹/₄", ³/₄", 1¹/₂", and 2¹/₄" (fig. 29). Gather the ruffle to fit the bottom of the skirt.

9.  Pin the ruffle to the skirt by laying the skirt on top of the ruffle and pinning the points in place.

10  Stitch the outer edge of the lace insertion to the ruffle with a small zigzag stitch. Trim the excess fabric from behind the lace insertion (fig. 31).

## Finishing Garment

1.  Referring to the General Dress Directions, III. Sleeves to Armholes and insert sleeve (p. 214).

2.  Sew the side seams of the bodice and sleeves by matching the lace edging on the sleeves, underarm seams, and waist line (fig. 32).

3.  Fold the ribbon in half in the center and pin to the bottom edge of the front bodice ¹/₈" inside the seam line, bring out of the seam allowance at the side seam (fig. 33).

4.  Referring to the General Dress Directions. V. Plackets; put a packet in the center back (p. 215).

5.  Run gathering threads in the top of the skirt at ¹/₈" and ³/₈".

6.  Place the bodice to the skirt, right sides together. Pull up the gathers of the skirt to fit the bodice. The center back openings will come to the fold line on the left and right backs. Wrap the back facings around the skirt center back openings. Sew the bodice to the skirt (fig. 34).

7.  Pull the bodice away from the skirt, folding the back facings to the inside of the bodice (fig. 35).

8.  Close the dress with buttons and buttonholes along each side of the back bodice (fig. 36).

9.  Run floss through the entredeux on the bottom of the sleeves.

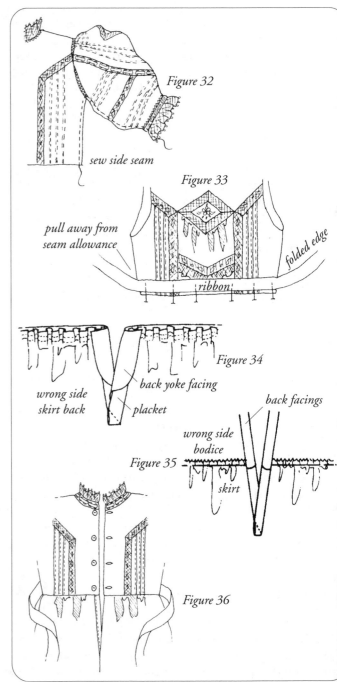

Figure 32

sew side seam

Figure 33

pull away from seam allowance

folded edge

ribbon

Figure 34

wrong side skirt back

back yoke facing

placket

back facings

wrong side bodice

Figure 35

skirt

Figure 36

# White and Pink Madeira Dress

Using a wonderful, new technique for EASY Madeira appliqué with wash away basting thread, this dress is a cinch to make and it is ever so pleasing for the girls who want a more tailored look. The Madeira trim travels around the faux bolero on the front of the dress, around the angel cap over the puffed sleeves and around the bottom of the skirt. The bodice of the dress features three rows of white French insertion, two rows of beading and a row of entredeux on either side of the fancy band down the front. Tiny feather stitching follows the outline of the Madeira treatment. The same feather stitching follows the outline on the sleeves and the skirt. Tiny bullion daisies with satin stitched leaves are scattered on the front and on the sleeves of the dress. The center portion of each sleeve has the same lace/entredeux treatment as the front of the dress. Tiny self piping is found at the waistline of the dress. Pink ribbons are stitched at the sides for a beautiful tied bow in the back, which closes with buttons and buttonholes.

## Fabric Requirements

|  | Sizes 2-6 | Sizes 8-10 | Sizes 12-16 |
|---|---|---|---|
| White Nelona Batiste | 2$^1$/$_2$ yds | 3 yds | 3 $^3$/$_8$ yds |
| Pink Nelona Batiste | 1 yd | 1$^1$/$_4$ yds | 1$^1$/$_8$ yds |
| $^1$/$_4$" Lace Insertion | 3 yds | 3$^1$/$_2$ yds | 4 yds |
| $^1$/$_2$" Lace Beading | 2 yds | 2$^1$/$_2$ yds | 2 $^3$/$_4$ yds |
| Entredeux | 2 yds | 2$^1$/$_2$ yds | 2 $^3$/$_4$ yds |
| $^1$/$_8$" Ribbon | 2 yds | 2$^1$/$_2$ yds | 2 $^3$/$_4$ yds |
| 1$^1$/$_2$" Ribbon | 2 yds | 2 yds | 2 yds |
| Cording | $^1$/$_2$ yd | $^1$/$_2$ yd | $^1$/$_2$ yd |
| Buttons $^1$/$_2$" | 4 | 4 | 5 |

Water Soluble Stabilizer
Wash A-way basting thread
Pink and Green Embroidery Floss
White and Pink Thread
Madeira Appliqué Directions - pages 340-348.

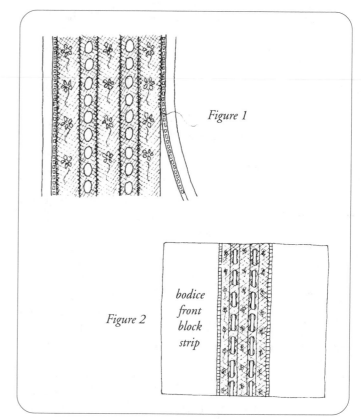

*Figure 1*

*Figure 2*

bodice front block strip

## Pattern Pieces

All pattern pieces and templates are found in the pattern envelope.
Waisted bodice front, waisted bodice back, puffed sleeve, sleeve overlay and front bodice overlay.
Templates: Madeira appliqué skirt template, sleeve overlay template and bodice overlay template

All seams $^1$/$_4$". Finish seams with a zigzag stitch or serger.

## Bodice

1. Cut two back bodices from white fabric on the selvage. Cut a square of white fabric for the front bodice the total width of the pattern and 1" longer. Fold this fabric in the center indicating the center front. Cut 3 strips of lace insertion, 2 strips of beading and 2 strips of entredeux 1" longer than the front bodice pattern.
2. Make the center lace band by sewing lace insertion, lace beading, lace insertion, lace beading, lace insertion using the technique "lace to lace." When the lace panel is complete, sew entredeux on each side using the technique "lace to entredeux" (fig. 1).
3. Cut the front bodice fabric in half along the fold, sew these fabric strips on each side of the lace panel using the technique "entredeux to flat fabric." Weave ribbon through the beading (fig. 2). Center and trace the entire front bodice on the created fabric and stitch

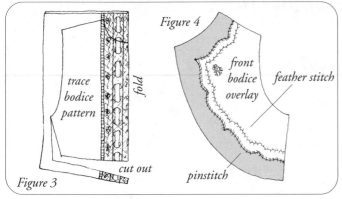

Figure 4

front bodice overlay

feather stitch

trace bodice pattern

fold

cut out

pinstitch

Figure 3

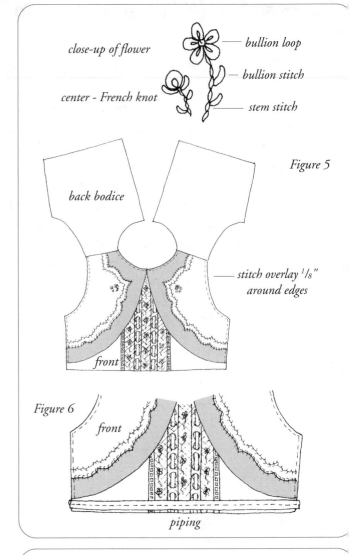

close-up of flower

center - French knot

bullion loop

bullion stitch

stem stitch

Figure 5

back bodice

stitch overlay ¹/₈" around edges

front

Figure 6

front

piping

just inside the traced lines. Cut out the bodice front (fig. 3).

4. Cut two front bodice overlays from the white fabric. Cut two front overlays from the pink fabric. Refer to "Magic Madeira Appliqué - Other Magic Madeira Appliqué Borders" (p. 344) and complete the Madeira appliqué border along the front overlay pieces (fig. 4).

5. Stitch a decorative feather stitch a foot's width away from the Madeira appliqué. Embroider the flower by hand using a bullion loop for the flower petals and bud, a French knot for the flower center and a stem stitch for the stem. Refer to the finished drawing for placement (fig. 4).

6. Position the completed overlays on the right side of the bodice front. Stitch in place ¹/₈" from outer edge to secure (fig. 5).

7. Sew the front bodice to the back bodice, right sides together at the shoulders using a ¹/₄" seam allowance (fig. 5).

8. Refer to the General Dress Directions, II. Neck Finishes, A. Bias Facing and finish the neck edge with a bias facing (p. 212).

9. Measure across the bodice front and make piping to fit the lower edge of the front bodice. Refer to technique "Making Piping" if needed. Attach the piping ¹/₄" from bottom edge of front bodice (fig. 6).

## Sleeves

1. Cut out two rectangles of fabric large enough for the sleeves. To prepare center lace panel for sleeves, measure the height of sleeves and multiply by two. Cut 3 strips of lace insertion, 2 strips of lace beading and 2 strips of entredeux. Construct the lace panel referring to "Bodice: Step 2." Weave ribbon through the lace beading (refer to fig. 1). Cut the lace band in half.

2. Fold sleeve fabric rectangles in half and cut along the fold. Sew fabric strips on each side of the lace panel. Refer to the technique "entredeux to flat fabric" (refer to fig. 2). Fold the created fabric in half and cut out two sleeves on dress cutting line (fig. 7).

3. Cut two sleeve overlays from white fabric. Transfer the Madeira appliqué template from the overlay pattern to two pieces of pink fabric. Refer to "Magic Madeira Appliqué - Other Magic Madeira Appliqué Borders." Complete the appliqué border stitching it in place with a pin stitch.

4. Stitch a decorative feather stitch ¹/₄" from the appliqué. Embroider the flower (refer to Bodice - step 5) in the center of the sleeve overlay with the center of the flower ¹/₂" above the feather stitching (fig. 8).

5. Lay the overlay on top of the sleeve, matching the top edges and stitch the top edges together ¹/₈" from the edge. Run gathering threads in the top and bottom of each sleeve at ¹/₈" and ³/₈" (fig. 8).

6. Refer to the sleeve band chart for the measurement for the bias band. Refer to the General Dress Directions, IV. Sleeve Finishes, A. Bias Band and finish the sleeve with a bias band (p. 214).

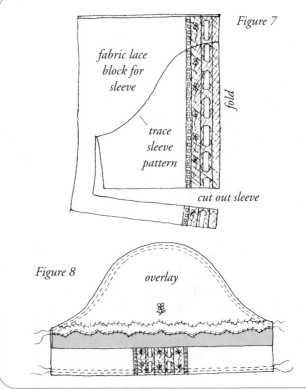

Figure 7

fabric lace block for sleeve

fold

trace sleeve pattern

cut out sleeve

Figure 8

overlay

Insert the sleeves into the armhole referring to the General
Dress Directions, III. Sleeves to Armholes (p. 214).

## Skirt

Refer to the Magic Madeira Appliqué Hems (pg. 342). Cut two
skirts the length and width given on the skirt measurement chart.
Cut out 2 strips of pink fabric 5 ¾" wide by skirt width.
Transfer the hem template to the border fabric as stated in the
Magic Madeira Appliqué Hem directions. Complete the appliqué
hem stitching it in place with a pin stitch.
Stitch a feather stitch ¼" above the finish appliqué (fig. 9).

## Finishing the Garment

Cut the 1½" ribbon in half for the sash. Put a small fold in one
end of ribbon and attach it to the bodice back ¼" from the
bottom side edge.
Sew the side seam matching the sleeve band, edge of sleeve overlay,
underarm seam and bottom of bodice (fig. 10).
Referring to the General Dress Directions, V. Plackets, put a
placket in the center back of the skirt.
Run two rows of gathering stitches in the top of the skirt at ⅛"
and ⅜".
Place the bodice to the skirt, right sides together. Pull up the
gathers of the skirt to fit the bodice. The center back openings
will come to the fold line on the left and right backs. Wrap the
back facings around the skirt center back openings. Sew the
bodice to the skirt.
Pull the bodice away from the skirt, folding the back facings to
the inside of the bodice.
Close the dress with buttons and buttonholes along each side of
the back bodice (fig. 11).

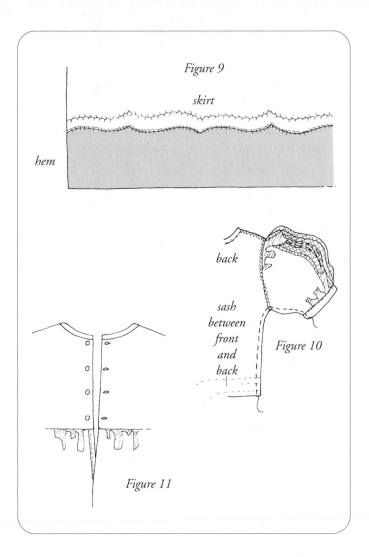

Figure 9

skirt

hem

back

sash
between
front
and
back

Figure 10

Figure 11

# Silk French Waterfall Dress

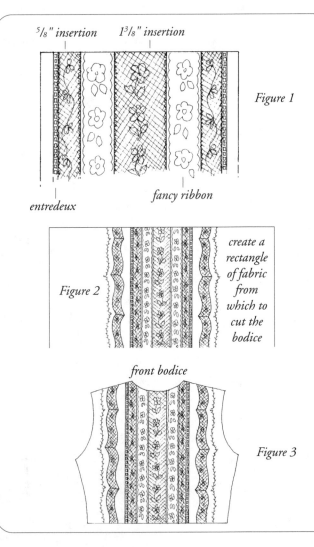

*French waterfall refers to scalloped laces running vertically on a garment. The bodice of this white silk dupioni dress has French insertions, decorative ribbon, entredeux and machine feather stitching in pink. The neckline is finished with white entredeux and gathered French edging. The sleeves have the same materials as the bodice and they are gathered at the bottom with entredeux. There is a very interesting cuff with three folded tucks plus some more white Swiss entredeux at the bottom of each cuff. The wide edging on the bottom of this cuff is really two pieces of white French lace insertion zigzagged to a piece of white French edging. The sash around the waistline is stitched into the dress and it also has three folded tucks. Satin ribbon is stitched in at the side seams and ties the dress in the back. The skirt has beautiful scalloped lace insertion above the hem and there are two rows of machine feather stitching in pink—one above the lace and one below.*

## Fabric Requirements

| | Sizes 2-6 | Sizes 8-10 | Sizes 12-16 |
|---|---|---|---|
| Silk Duponi 45" | $2^1/8$ yds | $2^5/8$ yds | $3^1/8$ yds |
| $5/8$" Lace Insertion | $11^1/2$ yds | $13^3/4$ yds | $13^3/4$ yds |
| $1^3/8$" Lace Insertion | $1/2$ yd | $1/2$ yd | $1/2$ yd |
| $7/8$" Lace Edging | 2 yds | $2^1/3$ yds | $2^1/3$ yds |
| 1" Fancy Ribbon | $1^1/2$ yds | 2 yds | 2 yds |
| Entredeux | $3^1/2$ yds | $4^5/8$ yds | $4^5/8$ yds |
| $1^1/2$" Satin Ribbon | 2 yds | 2 yds | 2 yds |
| Buttons $1/2$" | 4 | 4 | 5 |
| Decorative Embroidery Thread | | | |

## Pattern Pieces

All pattern pieces and templates are found in the pattern envelope.
Waisted bodice front, waisted bodice back, puffed sleeve.
Template: scalloped template for bodice and sleeve, and scalloped template for skirt.
All seams $1/4$". Finish all seam allowances with a zigzag or serger.

## Bodice

1. Cut one piece of $1^3/8$" lace insertion, 2 pieces of fancy ribbon, 2 pieces of $5/8$" lace insertion, and 2 pieces of entredeux 1" longer than the length of the pattern piece from the shoulder to the waist. The center panel is formed with $1^3/8$" lace insertion, fancy ribbon on each side of center lace, $5/8$" lace insertion on each side of fancy ribbon, and entredeux on outer edge of lace insertion. Sew panel together using the technique "lace to lace" and "lace to entredeux" (fig. 1).

2. Cut two panels from the silk 1" longer than the length of the pattern piece from the the shoulder to the waist and half the total width of the bodice pattern. Stitch the fabric strips on each side of the lace panel. Trace scallops for the insertion and embroidery using the scallop template for the bodice. Shape the $5/8$" lace insertion on the template lines. Stitch in place with a small zigzag on each side of the lace insertion. Stitch a decorative feather stitch on the stitch template lines (fig. 2). Cut the fabric from behind the lace insertion.

3. Fold the front panel in half to find the center front. Place the bodice front on the panel and cut out (fig. 3).

*5/8" insertion*  *1³/8" insertion*

*Figure 1*

*entredeux*  *fancy ribbon*

*Figure 2*

*create a rectangle of fabric from which to cut the bodice*

*front bodice*

*Figure 3*

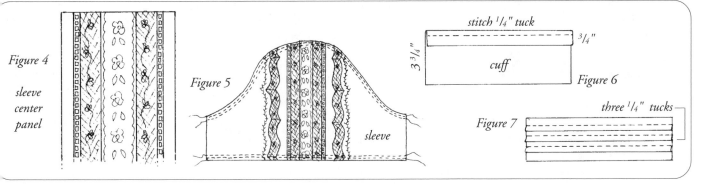

Figure 4

sleeve center panel

Figure 5

sleeve

stitch ¼" tuck

3¾"

¾"

cuff

Figure 6

three ¼" tucks

Figure 7

## Sleeves

Cut 2 pieces of fancy ribbon, 4 pieces of lace insertion, and 4 pieces of entredeux 1" longer than the center sleeve pattern. The center panel of the sleeves is created with the fancy ribbon in the center with lace insertion on each side of the ribbon and entredeux on the outside of the lace insertion. Sew panel together using the technique "lace to lace" and "lace to entredeux" (fig. 4).

Cut four panels from the silk 1" longer than the center sleeve pattern and half the entire sleeve width. Stitch the fabric pieces to each side of the lace pieces. Trace the scallops for the insertion and embroidery onto the panel pieces. Shape the lace insertion on the template lines. Stitch in place with a small zigzag on each side of the lace insertion. Stitch a decorative feather stitch on the stitch template lines (see fig. 2). Cut the fabric from behind the lace insertion.

Lay the sleeve pattern on the created fabric and cut out the sleeves on the dress cutting line (fig. 5).

Run gathering threads in the top and bottom of the sleeves at ⅛" and ⅜" (fig. 5).

Refer to the sleeve band chart (p. 212) for length and cut two strips of fabric for the cuff 3¾" by the sleeve band length and four pieces of entreduex to the sleeve band length.

Make three ¼" tucks in the sleeve cuff fabric. Began the first tuck by folding ¾" to the inside and stitching ¼" from the folded edge (fig. 6). From the stitching line of the last tuck, make another fold ¾" away and stitch ¼" from the folded edge. Make one more tuck in the same manner (fig. 7).

Attach the entredeux to the outside edges of the tucked strip with a ¼" seam allowance. Refer to technique "entredeux to flat fabric." Prepare the lace edging by cutting four pieces of lace insertion and two pieces of lace edging twice the sleeve band measurement. Stitch lace insertion to lace insertion then to the lace edging. Refer to the technique "lace to lace" (fig. 8). Gather the insertion/insertion/edging lace to fit the bottom sleeve band entredeux. Attach the gathered lace to the entredeux using the technique "gathered lace to entredeux" (fig. 8).

Tucks on the sleeves should be pressed toward the lace edging. Gather the bottom of the sleeve to fit the top sleeve band entredeux. Stitch the sleeve to the band. Refer to the technique "entredeux to gathered lace" (fig. 9).

## Skirt

Refer to the General Dress Directions, Skirt Chart (p. 212) and add 5" to the length and cut out a skirt front and back. Mark the center front and back.

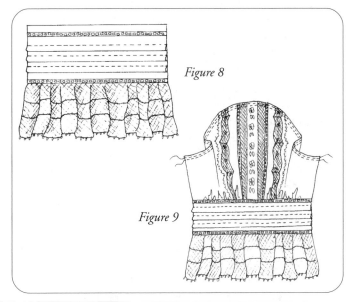

Figure 8

Figure 9

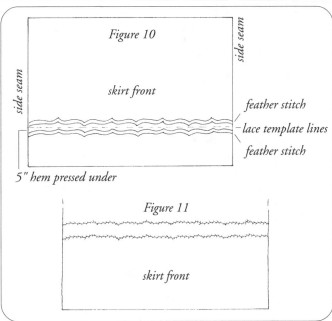

Figure 10

skirt front

side seam

side seam

feather stitch

lace template lines

feather stitch

5" hem pressed under

Figure 11

skirt front

2. Sew the side seams and finish the seams. Turn up a 5" hem in the bottom of the skirt and press in place. Trace the scallop template for skirt onto the bottom of the skirt with the edge of the hem between the lace template lines (fig. 10).

3. Unfold the hem and do machine feather stitch on the template lines (fig. 11).

4. Refold the hem and machine baste in place. Shape the lace insertion on the template lines. Stitch the bottom edge of the

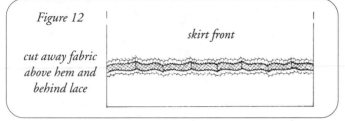

Figure 12

cut away fabric
above hem and
behind lace

skirt front

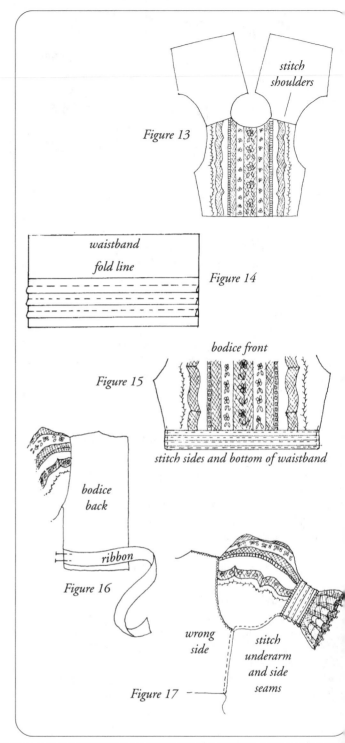

Figure 13

stitch
shoulders

waistband
fold line

Figure 14

bodice front

Figure 15

stitch sides and bottom of waistband

bodice
back

ribbon

Figure 16

wrong
side

stitch
underarm
and side
seams

Figure 17

lace insertion to the skirt with a small zigzag stitch. Cut the hem above the stitching line away.

5. Stitch the top edge of the lace insertion to the fabric with a small zigzag stitch. Cut the fabric from behind the lace insertion (fig. 12).

6. Refer to the General Dress Directions, V. Plackets and put a placket in the center back (p. 215).

7. Run gathering threads in the top of the skirt at $^1/_8$" and $^3/_8$".

## Finishing Garment

1. Cut out two bodice backs from the silk on the selvage. Mark the back fold line. Placing the bodice front and backs right sides together, sew the shoulder seams (fig. 13).

2. Finish the neck edge referring to the General Dress Directions, II. Neck Finishes, B. Entredeux and Gathered Lace.

3. Insert the sleeves into the armholes referring to the General Dress Directions, III. Sleeves to Armhole (p. 214).

4. The front waist band is made by measuring across the bottom of the front bodice, cut a piece of fabric by this length and 5" wide. The first tuck is made by folding back $^3/_4$" and stitching a $^1/_4$" tuck. From the stitching line of the last tuck make another fold $^3/_4$" away and stitch $^1/_4$" from the folded edge. Make one more tuck in the same manner (fig. 14).

5. Fold band in half with wrong sides together and press. Press the tucks toward the raw edge of the band. Pin on the bottom of the bodice front with the tucks to the outside and raw edges matching. Stitch in place on the bottom and sides of bodice (fig. 15).

6. Cut the $1^1/_2$" ribbon in half and stitch in place on bottom of the back bodice side where indicated on the pattern (fig. 16).

7. Stitch the side seams of the bodice and sleeve matching lace edging, sleeve band, underarms seam and the bottom of bodice (fig. 17).

8. Place the bodice to the skirt, right sides together. Pull up the gathers of the skirt to fit the bodice. The center back openings will come to the fold line on the left and right backs. Wrap the back facings around the skirt center back openings. Sew the bodice to the skirt (fig. 18).

9. Pull the bodice away from the skirt, folding the back facings to the inside of the bodice (fig. 19).

10. Close the dress with buttons and buttonholes along each side of the back bodice (fig. 20).

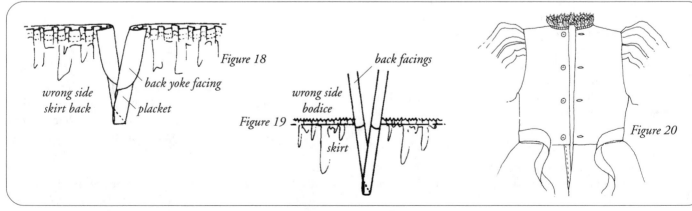

Figure 18

wrong side
skirt back

back yoke facing

placket

back facings

wrong side
bodice

Figure 19

skirt

Figure 20

# Blue Silk Ribbon Embroidered Dress

*J*apanese ribbon stitch, French knots, loop stitches, feather stitches, and lazy daisy stitches by hand have been mingled to finish this awesome round collar dress of blue silk dupioni. Combining beautiful colors of lavender, gold, dark blue, several shades of purple, pink and green silk ribbon is ravishing on this ice blue silk dupioni. Touches of the same colors in silver, green and gold have been stitched with traditional embroidery floss. Certainly some people would prefer to use a delicate circle of machine embroidery or silk ribbon embroidery by machine. The puffed sleeves have a tailored cuff which is embellished beautifully and simply with self piping around the top of the sleeve cuff, the bottom of the collar and the waistline. The back closes with buttons and buttonholes.

## Fabric Requirements

|  | Sizes 2-6 | Sizes 8-10 | Sizes 12-16 |
|---|---|---|---|
| Silk Duponi 45" | 2 ³/₄ yds | 3¹/₄ yds | 3 ⁵/₈ yds |
| Cording for piping | 1 yd | 1 yd | 1 yd |
| Buttons ¹/₂" | 4 | 4 | 5 |

Silk Ribbon YLI colors: 7mm: 7125, 7126, 53, 7084, 7022, 145, 82,120, 85, 22, 20; 4mm: 20; 2mm: 20
Silk Floss YLI colors: 21, 24, 819

## Pattern Pieces

All pattern pieces and templates are found in the pattern envelope. Waisted bodice front, waisted bodice back, puffed sleeve, round collar. Template: Silk ribbon collar template.
All seams ¹/₄". Finish seams with a zigzag stitch or serger.

## Collar

1. Cut out a block of fabric large enough for a collar and trace the collar onto the block of fabric. Trace the embroidery design onto the collar. Embroider collar. Directions for the silk ribbon embroidery begin on page 401 (fig. 1).
2. Cut out the collar with the embroidery and cut out one more matching silk collar for the lining. Measure around the outer edge of the collar and make enough piping to go around the collar. Directions for making piping are found on page 384.
3. Attach the piping to the outer edge of the right side of the collar with a ¹/₄" seam (fig. 2). Place the embroidered outer collar and collar lining right sides together with the piping sandwiched in between. Sew the collars together using the piping seam line as a guide (fig. 3). Trim the corners and turn the collar right side out (fig. 4).

## Bodice

1. Cut out a bodice front on the fold and two bodice backs on the selvage.
2. Sew front to back at the shoulder seam with right sides together.
3. Fit the collar to neck edge (fig. 4). Refer to the General Dress Directions, II. Neck Finishes, A. Bias Facing and finish the neck edge (p. 212).

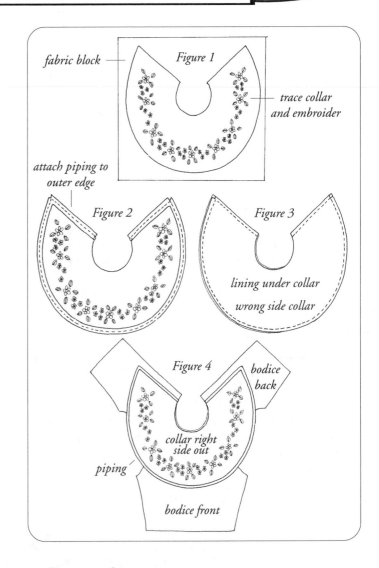

fabric block — Figure 1 — trace collar and embroider

attach piping to outer edge

Figure 2

Figure 3
lining under collar
wrong side collar

Figure 4
bodice back
collar right side out
piping
bodice front

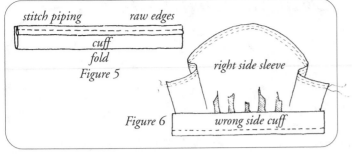

stitch piping      raw edges

cuff

fold

*Figure 5*

right side sleeve

*Figure 6*      wrong side cuff

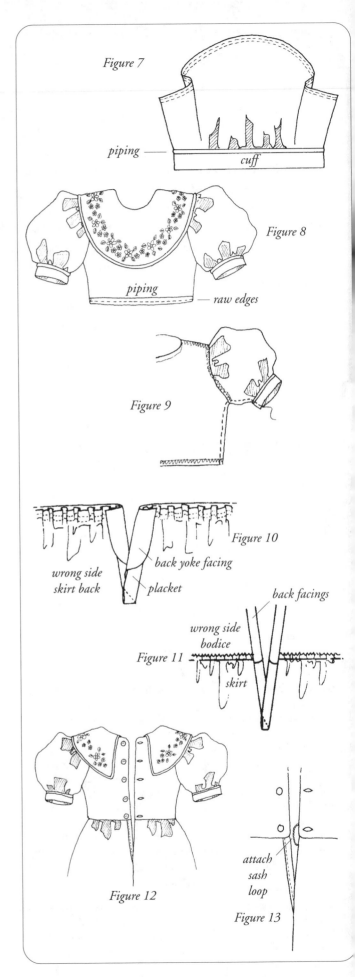

*Figure 7*

piping      cuff

*Figure 8*

piping      raw edges

*Figure 9*

wrong side skirt back    back yoke facing    placket    *Figure 10*

back facings

wrong side bodice

*Figure 11*    skirt

*Figure 12*

attach sash loop

*Figure 13*

## Sleeves

1. Cut out two sleeves on dress cutting line. Refer to the General Dress Directions, Sleeve Band Chart (p. 212) for a cuff length and cut two cuffs 3" by the chart length. Run gathers in the top and bottom of each sleeve at $1/8$" and $3/8$".

2. Make piping for each cuff. Fold the cuff in half with the wrong sides together matching the raw edges.

3. Sew the piping to the cuff matching the raw edges of the piping with the raw edges of the cuff (fig. 5).

4. Gather the bottom of the sleeves to fit the cuff. Pin the cuff to the bottom of the sleeve with the right side of sleeve to the piped side of the cuff. The piping will be sandwiched between the cuff and sleeve. Stitch in place using the stitching line of the piping as a guide (fig. 6). Turn the cuff away from the sleeve and press (fig. 7).

5. Insert the sleeves into the armholes referring to the General Dress Directions, III. Sleeves to Armholes (p. 214).

## Skirt

1. Refer to the General Dress Directions, Skirt Chart and add $4 1/4$" to the length for a hem and cut a skirt back and front. Mark the center back and center front.

2. Refer to General Dress Directions, V. Placket; and put a placket in the center back (p. 215).

3. Sew the side seams of the skirt. Turn under $1/4$" to the wrong side on the bottom of the the hem. Turn up a 4" hem and stitch in place by hand or machine.

## Finishing Garment

1. Measure across the bottom of the front bodice and make a piece of piping to fit across the bottom. Refer to the technique, "Making Piping." Attach the piping to the bottom of the front bodice with a $1/4$" seam matching the raw edges (fig. 8).

2. Refer to the General Dress Directions, VI. Sash and make a sash and attach it to the bodice back.

3. Matching the sleeve band, underarms seam and bottom of the bodice, sew the side seams (fig. 9).

4. Run two rows of gathering stitches in the top of the skirt at $1/8$" and $3/8$".

5. Place the bodice to the skirt with right sides together. Pull up the gathers of the skirt to fit the bodice. The center back openings will come to the fold line on the left and right backs. Wrap the back facings around the skirt center back openings. Sew the bodice to the skirt using the piping seam as a stitching guie. (fig. 10).

6. Pull the bodice away from the skirt, folding the back facings to the inside of the bodice (fig. 11).

7. Close the dress with buttons and buttonholes along each side of the back bodice (fig. 12).

8. Make a sash loop at the center back at waist (fig. 13). Refer to General Directions: Sash Loop (p. 288).

# Lace Waves Overskirt Dress

*What a magnificent way of using traditional heirloom fabric and laces in combination with artistic machine embroidery! The dress is baby blue Swiss batiste and the over treatments are white Swiss batiste. All of the white French laces are attached with machine pin stitching. There is an over bodice treatment, an over sleeve flounce, sometimes called an angel sleeve, and an overskirt. Beautiful machine embroidery designs in pale green and pale blue embellish all three sections. The lace shaping resembles ocean waves. Gathered white French edging is found at the bottom of each segment of wave lace shaping. The bottom lace edging has been made wider by adding a piece of insertion zig zagged to the edging before it was gathered. The sleeves are finished with Swiss entredeux, beading, entredeux and a gathered lace edging composed of the insertion and edging zig zagged together. The back of the dress closes with buttons and buttonholes. Blue organdy is used for the sash.*

## Fabric Requirements

| | Sizes 2-6 | Sizes 8-10 | Sizes 12-16 |
|---|---|---|---|
| Blue Batiste 45" | $1^3/_4$ yds | $2^1/_4$ yds | $2^5/_8$ yds |
| White Batiste 45" | $1^3/_4$ yds | $2^1/_4$ yds | $2^5/_8$ yds |
| $^5/_8$" Lace Insertion | 26 yds | 27 yds | 28 yds |
| $^3/_4$" Lace Edging | 18 yds | 19 yds | 20 yds |
| Beading | $^5/_8$ yds | $^3/_4$ yds | $^3/_4$ yds |
| Entredeux | $1^1/_8$ yds | $1^1/_4$ yds | $1^3/_8$ yds |
| Organdy Sash 45" | $^1/_3$ yd | $^1/_3$ yd | $^1/_3$ yd |
| Buttons $^1/_2$" | 4 | 4 | 5 |

$^1/_4$" Ribbon sleeves & sash - 2 yards for all sizes
Embroidery Thread

## Pattern Pieces

All pattern pieces and templates are found in the pattern envelope. Waisted front bodice, waisted back bodice, short puffed dress sleeve, sleeve overlay, bodice front overlay and bodice back overlay. Templates: Skirt scallop template, overskirt lace shaping template, sleeve template, front overlay template, back overlay template. All seams $^1/_4$". Finish seams with a zigzag stitch or serger.

## Bodice

1. From the blue batiste cut out a bodice front on the fold and two backs on the selvage edge. Sew the front bodice to the back bodice at the shoulder seams with right sides together and a $^1/_4$" seam. Sew the side seams with right sides together (fig. 1).

2. From the white batiste cut out a bodice front on the fold and two bodice backs. Trace the lace template guide onto the front and back bodices to create the overlays (fig. 2).

3. Shape the lace onto the overlay fabric. Stitch the lace to the fabric with a pinstitch or zigzag on the inside edge of lace insertion. Do not stitch the bottom edge of lace. Trim fabric from behind the lace (fig. 3).

4. Sew the side seams of overlay with right sides together matching the lace on the bottom edge.

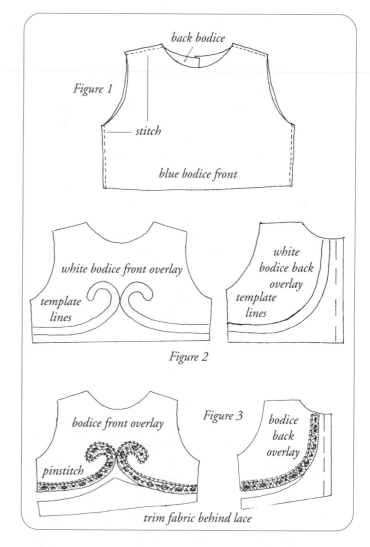

*back bodice*

*Figure 1*

*stitch*

*blue bodice front*

*white bodice front overlay*

*template lines*

*white bodice back overlay*

*template lines*

*Figure 2*

*bodice front overlay*

*pinstitch*

*Figure 3*

*bodice back overlay*

*trim fabric behind lace*

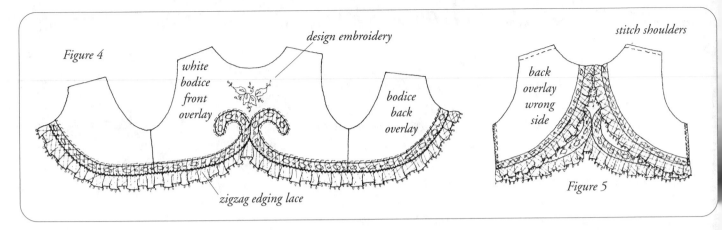

Figure 4

white bodice front overlay

design embroidery

bodice back overlay

zigzag edging lace

stitch shoulders

back overlay wrong side

Figure 5

5.  Measure around the outer lace edge of the bodice overlay. Cut a piece of lace edging twice this length. Gather the strip of lace edging to fit around the outer edge of the lace and stitch the lace edging to the lace insertions. Refer to the technique "lace to lace" (fig. 4). Zigzag the laces together at the center front, if needed.
6.  Stitch the embroidery on the center front by hand or machine (fig. 4).
7.  Sew the shoulder seams of the bodice overlay with right sides together using a ¹⁄₄" seam allowance (fig. 5).
8.  Place the bodice overlay over the bodice matching the neck edges and the armhole edges (fig. 6).
9.  Finish the neck edge with a bias facing referring to the General Dress Directions, II. Neck Finishes, A. Bias Facing (p. 212).

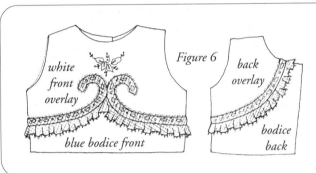

white front overlay

Figure 6

back overlay

bodice back

blue bodice front

### Sleeves

1.  From the blue batiste, cut two sleeves on dress cutting line. From the white batiste, cut two sleeves.
2.  Trace the lace template onto the sleeves to create the overlays (fig. 7).
3.  Repeat steps 3, 5 and 6 from the bodice construction to construct the sleeve overlay. Refer to the drawing (fig. 8).
4.  Embroider the design in the center of the sleeve overlay (fig. 9).
5.  Run two rows of gathering threads at ¹⁄₈" and ³⁄₈" in the bottom of the sleeve (fig. 10).
6.  Refer to the sleeve band chart (p. 212) for your dress size and cut 4 pieces of entredeux and 2 piece of beading to this length.
7.  Trim one side of the entredeux and attach the entredeux to each side of the beading. Refer to the technique "lace to entredeux" (fig. 11).
8.  Cut two pieces of insertion and two pieces of edging twice the sleeve band measurement. Attach the insertion and the edging with a small zigzag stitch to form two strips. Refer to the technique "lace to lace" (fig. 11).

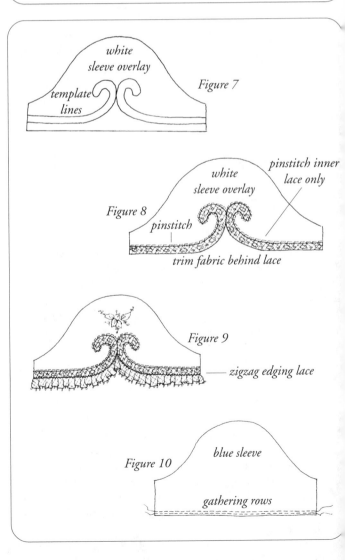

white sleeve overlay

template lines

Figure 7

pinstitch inner lace only

white sleeve overlay

Figure 8

pinstitch

trim fabric behind lace

Figure 9

zigzag edging lace

blue sleeve

Figure 10

gathering rows

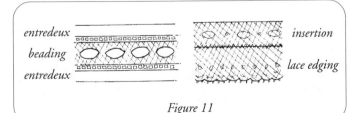

entredeux

beading

entredeux

insertion

lace edging

Figure 11

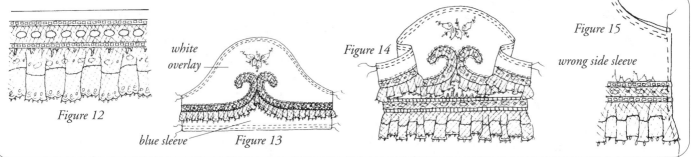

Figure 12

white
overlay

blue sleeve   Figure 13

Figure 14

Figure 15

wrong side sleeve

9. Gather the insertion/edging strip to fit the bottom of the beading and entredeux. Attach the gathered lace to the entredeux beading strip. Refer to the technique "gathered lace to entredeux" (fig. 12).

10. Place the sleeve overlay on top of the sleeve matching the top edges of the sleeve and overlay (fig. 13).

11. Run two rows of gathering threads in the top edge of the sleeve/overlay at $^1/_8$" and $^3/_8$" (fig. 13).

12. Gather the bottom of the sleeve to fit the entredeux beading strip and attach the sleeve to the beading strip. Refer to the technique "entredeux to gathered fabric" (fig. 14).

13. Sew the underarm seam matching the laces (fig. 15).

14. Gather the sleeve to fit the armhole. Fit the sleeve into the armhole, right sides together. Stitch in place (fig. 16).

Figure 16

neck

stitch sleeve
in armhole    sleeve

wrong
side bodice

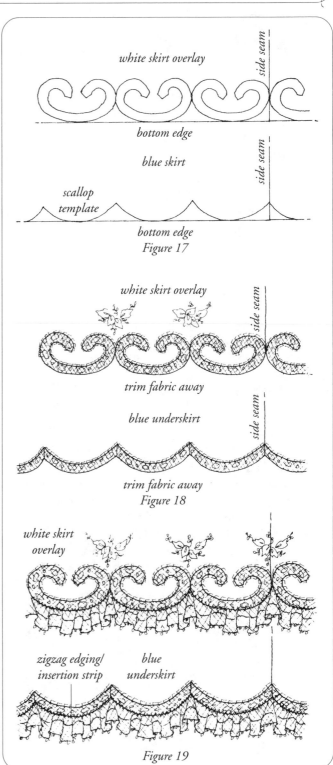

white skirt overlay

side seam

bottom edge

blue skirt

side seam

scallop
template

bottom edge
Figure 17

white skirt overlay

side seam

trim fabric away

blue underskirt

side seam

trim fabric away
Figure 18

white skirt
overlay

zigzag edging/        blue
insertion strip      underskirt

Figure 19

### Skirt

1. Refer to the General Dress Directions, Skirt Chart (p. 212) and cut a front and back from the blue batiste for the underskirt. Cut a skirt front and skirt back 3" shorter than the length on the skirt chart from white batiste for the overskirt.

2. Mark the center fronts and backs of skirts. Sew one side seam in both the under and the over skirt.

3. Trace twelve total scallop designs onto the bottom of the blue batiste, starting with a scallop on each side of the side seam. Trace twelve total lace shaping designs on the bottom of the white batiste (fig. 17), starting with a lace design on each side of the center seam.

4. Shape lace insertion on the bottom of the blue and white batiste. Stitch the top edge of the lace to the fabric with a pinstitch or zigzag. Refer to the drawing for lace shaping on the overskirt to determine where to stitch on lace. Cut fabric from behind the lace insertion (fig. 18).

5. Stitch the machine or hand embroidery on the overskirt. Center the embroidery as seen in the drawing (fig. 18).

6. To make the lace edging/insertion, cut two pieces of insertion and two pieces of edging 180" long. Stitch insertion to edging with a small zigzag stitch. Refer to the technique "lace to lace" (fig. 11).

7. Gather each edging/insertion strips to fit the bottom of the overskirt and underskirt. Sew the edging to the bottom of each skirt with a small zigzag stitch. Refer to the technique "lace to lace" (fig. 19).

8. Sew the remaining side seam, and do machine embroidery over the seam (fig. 19).

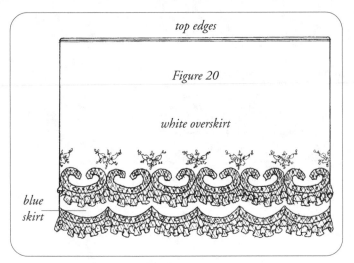

top edges

Figure 20

white overskirt

blue skirt

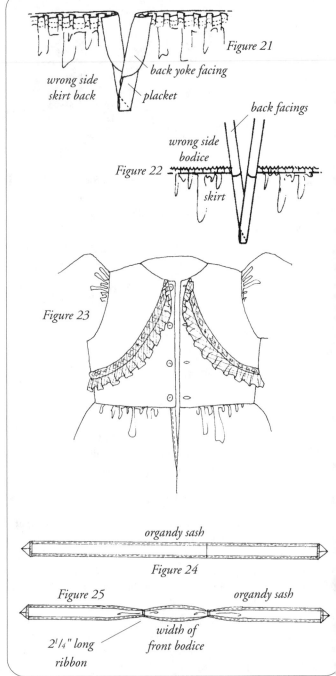

Figure 21

wrong side skirt back

back yoke facing

placket

back facings

wrong side bodice

Figure 22

skirt

Figure 23

organdy sash

Figure 24

Figure 25

organdy sash

$2^{1}/_{4}$" long ribbon

width of front bodice

9. Place overskirt on top of underskirt matching top edges, side seams, center fronts and center backs (fig. 20). Baste together at the top edge.

10. Referring to the General Dress Directions, V. Plackets and put a placket in the center back, treating the two skirts as one.

## Finishing Garment

1. Run two rows of gathering stitches in the top of the skirts, treating them as one, at $^{1}/_{8}$" and $^{3}/_{8}$".

2. Place the bodice to the skirt, with right sides together. Pull up the gathers of the skirt to fit the bodice. The center back openings will come to the fold line on the left and right backs. Wrap the back facings around the skirt center back openings. Sew the bodice to the skirt (fig. 21).

3. Pull the bodice away from the skirt, folding the back facings to the inside of the bodice (fig. 22).

4. Close the dress with buttons and buttonholes along each side of the back bodice (fig. 23).

5. To make the sash, cut one strip of organdy 43" by 5" and one strip 30" by 5". Sew the strips together on one 5" end, finish the seam. Hem the long sides of sash with a shirt tail hem. Fold ends of sash in half with right sides together, matching hemmed edges. Sew ends and finish the seams. Flip the seam to wrong side, this will form a triangle on the ends of the sash pieces (fig. 24). At the seam where the two sash pieces were sewn together, run gathering threads and gather to $1^{3}/_{4}$". Cut two pieces of ribbon $2^{1}/_{4}$" long and turn under $^{1}/_{4}$" on each end. Place one piece of ribbon behind the gathers and stitch the ribbon behind the gathers to stabilize. Measure across the front bodice. Take this measurement and measure down from gathers on sash toward the longer sash end and run gathering threads, gather to $1^{3}/_{4}$" and stabilize behind with other ribbon piece (fig. 25).

6. Make belt loops and place at the side seams and the center back.

7. Run ribbon through the beading on the sleeve.

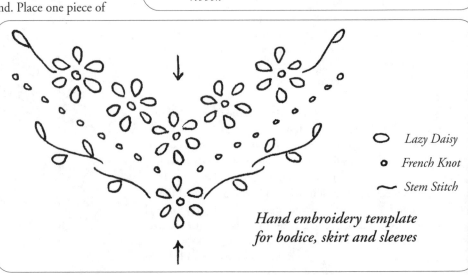

○ Lazy Daisy

• French Knot

～ Stem Stitch

*Hand embroidery template for bodice, skirt and sleeves*

# Morgan's Embroidery Masterpiece

*Peach silk dupioni forms the palette for this masterpiece of machine work. White English netting lace graces the front and back bodice overlays, the angel sleeves and the bottom of each sleeve. English netting is also used on the underskirt. Three tabs with peach machine embroidery travel across the shoulders on top of the English angel sleeves which fall delicately over the peach dupioni puffed sleeves. The bottom of the sleeves are finished with white entredeux, beading, entredeux and gathered English netting edging. Entredeux and gathered French white lace finish the neckline; this same entredeux and gathered lace edging strip is found going over the shoulder area; a peach silk ribbon rosette with tiny peach pearls stitched in the middle are on the front and back edges of the bodice. Self piping is at the waistline. The skirt has rectangular tabs with gorgeous machine embroidery on each tab. The underskirt has a bottom ruffle of dupioni trimmed with English netting and French lace on the bottom. The skirt has self piping around the waistline and the dress closes with buttons and buttonholes.*

## Fabric Requirements

|  | Sizes 2-6 | Sizes 8-10 | Sizes 12-16 |
|---|---|---|---|
| Silk Fabric 45" | $2^3/_4$ yds | $3^1/_4$ yds | $3^3/_4$ yds |
| Batiste 45" (skirt lining) | $^3/_4$ yd | 1 yd | $1^1/_3$ yds |
| " English Netting Edging | 8 yds | $8^1/_8$ yds | $8^1/_3$ yds |
| $_4$" Lace Edging | 7 yds | $7^1/_4$ yds | $7^1/_3$ yds |
| Beading | $^5/_8$ yd | $^3/_4$ yd | $^3/_4$ yd |
| Entredeux | 2 yds | $2^1/_2$ yds | $2^5/_8$ yds |
| " Satin Ribbon | 2 yds | 2 yds | 2 yds |
| mm Peach Silk Ribbon | 4 yds | 4 yds | 4 yds |
| Buttons $^1/_2$" | 4 | 4 | 5 |
| Silk organza | $^1/_3$ yd | $^1/_3$ yd | $^1/_3$ yd |
| Cording | $^1/_2$ yd | $^1/_2$ yd | $^1/_2$ yd |
| Seed beads |  |  |  |
| Decorative embroidery thread |  |  |  |

## Pattern Pieces

All pattern pieces are found in the pattern envelope. Bodice front, bodice back, puffed sleeve, shoulder epilets (found at end of directions) Masterpiece skirt template (found in pattern envelope). This dress has been embroidered using a sewing machine. A hand embroidery template is provided as an alternative. This dress is also beautiful without embroidery. The machine embroidery card used on this dress is Pfaff Embroidery Card 49, design #3.

All seams $^1/_4$". Finish seams with a zigzag stitch or serger.

## Bodice

1. From the silk fabric cut out a front bodice on the fold and two backs on the selvage. Measure $1^1/_4$" from the arm opening at the shoulder. Draw a line from this point parallel to the center front and center back. Measure $1^1/_4$" from the side edge of the arm opening. Draw a line from this point straight across to the center front and back. This creates the netting template (fig. 1a). Trace the netting template lines on the front and backs.

2. Place the netting edging on the front and backs following the template lines. Secure in place with a small zigzag stitch. Trim away the excess netting at the neck, shoulders, and sides (fig. 1b).

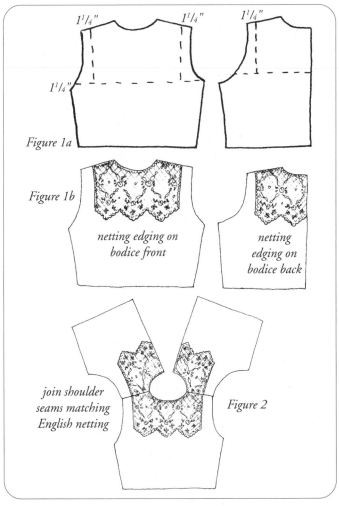

Figure 1a

Figure 1b

*netting edging on bodice front*

*netting edging on bodice back*

*join shoulder seams matching English netting*

Figure 2

3. Place the backs to the front at the shoulder seams with the right sides together and sew the shoulder seams with a $^1/_4$" seam (fig. 2).

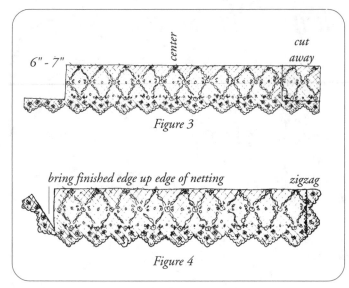

Figure 3

*bring finished edge up edge of netting*     *zigzag*

Figure 4

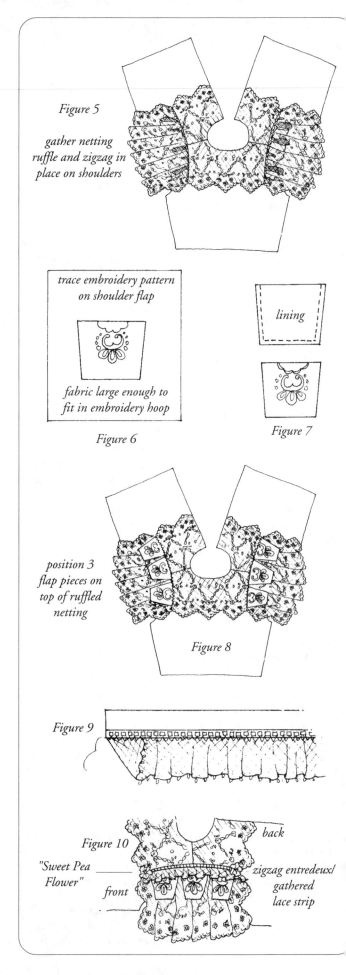

Figure 5

gather netting ruffle and zigzag in place on shoulders

*trace embroidery pattern on shoulder flap*

*lining*

*fabric large enough to fit in embroidery hoop*

Figure 6

Figure 7

position 3 flap pieces on top of ruffled netting

Figure 8

Figure 9

Figure 10

"Sweet Pea Flower"

back

front

zigzag entredeux/ gathered lace strip

4. Netting for the ruffle over the sleeve is made by cutting two pieces of the netting edging 30" long for sizes 2-6 and 34" long for sizes 8-16. Mark the center of each strip. Measure 6"-7" on each end. Trim netting just above the edging finish (between $^1/_4$" and $^1/_2$" depending on the scallop edge) from the outer edge to the last mark on both sides. This edging will be turned up the side of the netting to finish the edge of the netting (fig. 3). Place the finished edge to the unfinished edge of the netting and stitch in place with a small zigzag stitch (fig. 4).

5. Run gathering threads in the top edge of the netting for the ruffle at $^1/_8$" and $^3/_8$". Gather the ruffle to fit over the shoulder next to the netting from step 2. Zigzag in place (fig. 5).

6. Trace the embroidery pattern for the shoulder epilets (found at the end of these directions) on a piece of silk fabric large enough to fit into an embroidery hoop. Place the flap pattern piece on top of the design and trace around the pattern piece for the epilet. Repeat 5 more times. Work the embroidery on the 6 pieces either by hand or machine (fig. 6). Cut out.

7. Cut out 6 additional epilet pieces for the lining. Stitch the lining to the embroidered pieces with the right sides together. Trim the excess fabric, turn to the right side and press (fig. 7).

8. Position the epilet pieces on top of the ruffled netting(top edges of the epilet pieces may slightly overlap). Stitch in place with a zigzag stitch (fig. 8).

9. Measure across the shoulder where the netting is attached. Cut two pieces of entredeux to this measurement. Trim the fabric from one side of the entredeux. Cut two pieces of edging lace twice this measurement. Gather the edging lace to fit the entredeux. Fold the lace ends at an angle so that the raw edges of the lace are even with the bottom of the entredeux. Stitch the gathered lace and entredeux together with a small zigzag stitch. Refer to technique, gathered lace to entredeux (fig. 9).

10. Trim the fabric from the other side of the entredeux/lace edging strips. Position the entredeux/lace edging strip on the bodice so that it covers the stitching where the netting ruffle and the individual pieces were attached. Secure in place with a small zigzag stitch (fig. 10).

12. Make 4 small flowers from the 7mm silk ribbon (refer to the embroidery technique "Sweet Pea" p. 407). Secure in place at the ends of the entredeux in the front and back with 3 small seed beads in the center (see finished drawing).

13. Measure across the bottom of the front bodice and make fabric piping to go across the bottom of the bodice front. (Refer to "making piping.") Stitch to the bottom of the bodice front ¼" from the edge (fig. 11).

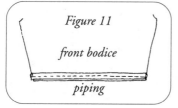

Figure 11

front bodice

piping

## Sash

1. Cut two strips of silk organza 5" by 45". The selvage edges will be left on organza.
2. Put a narrow hem in each long side of the strips.
3. On one end of each strip fold the selvage edge to the hemmed edge and stitch together using the hemmed stitch as a guide (fig. 12).
4. Fold the straight selvage end of the sash in ⅓ and attach to the back bodice at the side ¼" from the bottom edge (fig. 13).

## Sleeves

1. From the peach silk, cut out two sleeves on dress cutting line.
2. Run two rows of gathering threads at ⅛" and ⅜" in the bottom of the sleeve.
3. Refer to the General Dress Directions, Sleeve Band Chart (p. 212) for your dress size and cut 4 pieces of entredeux and 2 pieces of beading to this length.
4. Trim one side of the entredeux and attach the entredeux to each side of the beading. Refer to the technique "lace to entredeux."
5. Cut two pieces of the netting edging twice the sleeve band measurement. Run two rows of gathering stitches in the top edge of netting at ⅛ and ⅜".
6. Gather the edging to fit the bottom of the beading entredeux. Attach the gathered edging to the entredeux beading strip. Refer to the technique "entredeux to gathered fabric" (fig. 14).
7. Gather the bottom of the sleeve to fit the entredeux/beading/netting strip and attach the sleeve to the beading strip (fig. 15).

## Over Skirt

1. Refer to the General Dress Directions, Skirt Chart (p. 212), subtract 3" from the skirt length and cut a silk skirt front and back. Mark the center front and back.
2. Trace the Masterpiece skirt template lines ¼" above the lower edge of the skirt front and back with one design on each side of the center. Work the embroidery designs (hand embroidery template can be found at the end of these directions), centered on each panel, on the front and back skirt, so that the lower edge of the design is 1¼" from the bottom of the skirt template (fig. 16).
3. Stitch along the template lines on the front and back skirts so that the lines can be seen from the wrong side (fig. 17).

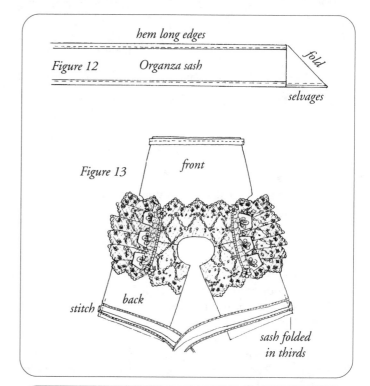

hem long edges

Figure 12    Organza sash

fold

selvages

Figure 13

front

back

stitch

sash folded in thirds

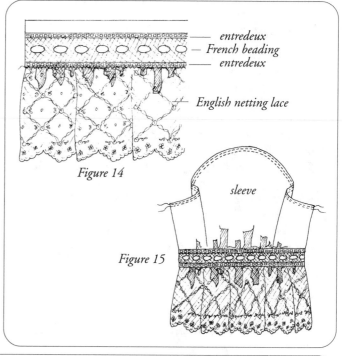

entredeux

French beading

entredeux

English netting lace

Figure 14

sleeve

Figure 15

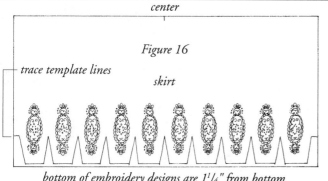

center

Figure 16

skirt

trace template lines

bottom of embroidery designs are 1¼" from bottom of traced skirt template lines

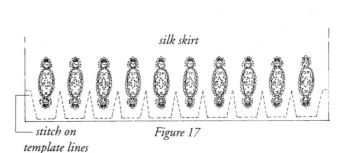

silk skirt

stitch on template lines

Figure 17

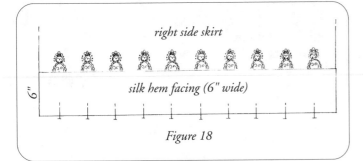

right side skirt

silk hem facing (6" wide)

6"

*Figure 18*

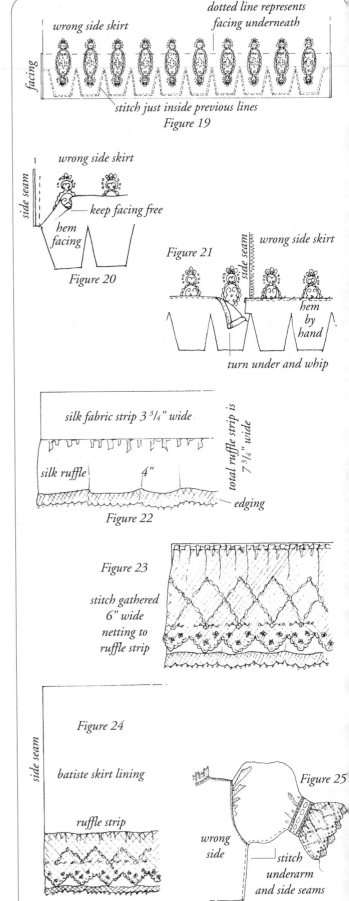

wrong side skirt — dotted line represents facing underneath

facing

stitch just inside previous lines
*Figure 19*

wrong side skirt

side seam

keep facing free

hem facing

*Figure 20*

*Figure 21*

side seam

wrong side skirt

hem by hand

turn under and whip

silk fabric strip 3 ¼" wide

silk ruffle    4"

total ruffle strip is 7 ¾" wide

edging

*Figure 22*

*Figure 23*

stitch gathered 6" wide netting to ruffle strip

*Figure 24*

side seam

batiste skirt lining

ruffle strip

wrong side

*Figure 25*

stitch underarm and side seams

4. Cut two strips of silk fabric 6" by the skirt width for the skirt hem facing. Place the facing on the right side of the skirt with the lower edges even. Pin (fig. 18). Stitch from the wrong side of the skirt just inside the previously stitched template lines (fig. 19).

5. Trim ¼" from the stitching. Clip the points and corners. Turn the facing to the wrong side and press well.

6. Stitch the front skirt to the back skirt at the side seams. Be careful not to catch the facing in the seams (fig. 20).

7. Finish the top edge of the hem facing by turning under ¼" to the wrong side and stitch in place.

8. Pin the hem in place. At the side seams tuck one hem facing under the other, turn under ¼" on the side of other hem facing and whip in place by hand. Hem the skirt by hand (fig. 21).

## Underskirt

1. Cut three strips 45" long by 4" wide for bottom ruffle from the silk. Sew the strips together to form one long strip. Attach ¾" lace edging to one long side. Run two rows of gathering threads in the top edge of the ruffle at ⅛" and ⅜".

2. Cut two strips 45" long by 3 ¼" wide from the silk. Sew together to form one long strip. Gather the ruffle strip to fit the bottom of the 3 ¼" strip. Sew together with a ¼" seam (fig. 22).

3. Cut a strip of netting edging 4⅓ yds. Run gathering threads in the top edge at ⅛" and ⅜". Gather to fit the top of the strip to which the ruffle was sewn. Stitch in place (fig. 23).

4. Cut two skirt pieces from the lining fabric by the skirt length minus 7½". Sew one side seam of the skirt lining.

5. Sew the netting/fabric strip to the bottom of the skirt lining with a ¼" seam.

6. Sew the other side of skirt lining seam matching netting ruffle and lace edged ruffle (fig. 24).

## Finishing Garment

1. Finish neck edge referring to General Dress Directions, II. Neck Finishes, B. Entredeux and Gathered Lace (p. 213).

2. Insert the sleeves into the armholes referring to the General Dress Directions, III. Sleeves to Armhole.

3. Matching the side seams of the bodice with the right sides together sew the side seam with a ¼" seam (fig. 25).

4. Place underskirt under the top skirt matching the center front center back and side seams. These will be treated as one.

5. Referring to the General Dress Directions, V. Plackets, put a placket in the center back, treating the two skirts as one.

6. Run two rows of gathering stitches in the top of the skirts, treating them as one, at ⅛" and ⅜".

7. Place the bodice to the skirt, right sides together. Pull up the gathers of the skirt to fit the bodice. The center back openings

will come to the fold line on the left and right backs. Wrap the back facings around the skirt center back openings. Sew the bodice to the skirt with a $1/4$" seam (fig. 26).

8. Pull the bodice away from the skirt, folding the back facings to the inside of the bodice (fig. 27).

9. Close the dress with buttons and buttonholes along each side of the back bodice (fig. 28). Run ribbon through the beading in the sleeves and tie into bows. (See finished drawing.)

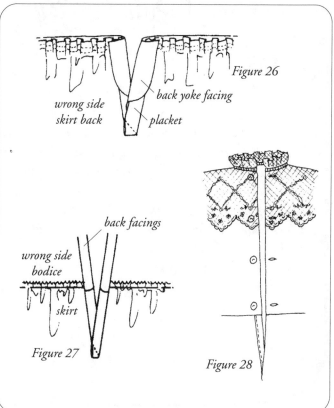

*wrong side skirt back*  
*back yoke facing*  
*placket*  
*Figure 26*

*back facings*  
*wrong side bodice*  
*skirt*  
*Figure 27*

*Figure 28*

## Embroidery Design

## Shoulder Epilets

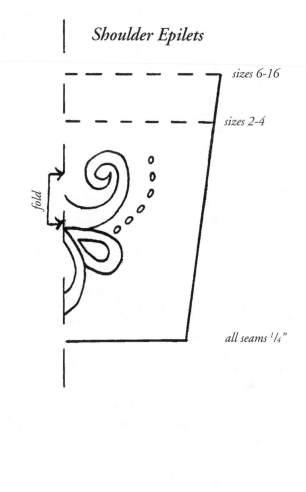

*sizes 6-16*

*sizes 2-4*

*fold*

*all seams $1/4$"*

〜〜 *Satin Stitch*

◦ *French Knot*

⬭ *Lazy Daisy*

〜 *Stem Stitch*

# Sarah Joy's Snowman Dress

*W*hat a wonderful way to celebrate the holidays with a red Christmas plaid silk dupioni dress with a fabulous machine embroidered snowman scalloped collar! This dress can be made very quickly which is a necessity for many of us especially those of us with 10 grandchildren. The white silk dupioni collar has plaid piping around the neckline and around the bottom of the collar; beautiful wide heavy lace edging has been slightly gathered and attached at the bottom of the collar. Using a precious Christmas machine embroidery disc, three snowpeople, two Christmas trees and two wreaths on the back finish this happy dress. A wide red satin sash is found at the waistline.

## Fabric Requirements

|  | Sizes 2-6 | Sizes 8-10 | Sizes 12-16 |
|---|---|---|---|
| Plaid Silk 45" (dress) | 2 yds | 2$\frac{1}{2}$ yds | 3 yds |
| White Silk 45" (collar) | $\frac{1}{2}$ yd | $\frac{1}{2}$ yd | 5/8 yd |
| 1$\frac{3}{4}$" Lace Edging | 2$\frac{1}{8}$ yds | 2$\frac{1}{4}$ yds | 2$\frac{1}{2}$ yds |
| 1$\frac{1}{2}$" Ribbon | 2 yds | 2$\frac{1}{2}$ yds | 2$\frac{1}{2}$ yds |
| Cord for Piping | 2 yds | 2 yds | 2$\frac{1}{2}$ yds |
| $\frac{3}{8}$" Covered Buttons | 4 | 4 | 5 |

Embroidery Floss for belt loops
Machine Embroidery Thread for Designs
All seams are $\frac{1}{4}$". Finish seams with a zigzag stitch or a serger.

## Pattern Pieces

All pattern pieces are found in the pattern envelope.
Waisted front bodice, waisted back bodice, puffed sleeve, scallop round dress collar

## Cutting Out

Cut out one front bodice on the fold, two back bodices on the selvage, two puffed sleeves on dress cutting line, two sleeve bands 2$\frac{1}{2}$" by sleeve band length (length is on sleeve band chart), one scalloped round dress collars on the fold, trace one scallop collar on fabric to be embroidered. Refer to the skirt measurement chart and add 3$\frac{1}{2}$" to the skirt length, cut two skirts by this measurements, cut bias strips for piping, one $\frac{3}{4}$" by 12" strip for placket from the selvage, cut a bias strip 1" wide by 18" for attaching collar.

## Construction

1. Select designs for the collar and work the embroidery on the collar (fig. 1). Cut out the collar.
2. Make piping to go around the collar and neck edge from the plaid. Refer to techniques on Making Piping.
3. Trim the piping to $\frac{1}{4}$" seam allowance. Sew the piping to the outer edge of the embroidered collar matching the raw edges of collar and piping, clipping the piping where needed to fit around the scallops (fig. 2).

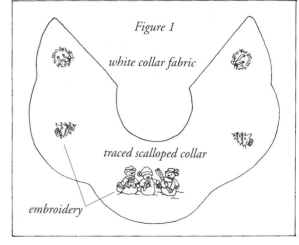

Figure 1
white collar fabric
traced scalloped collar
embroidery

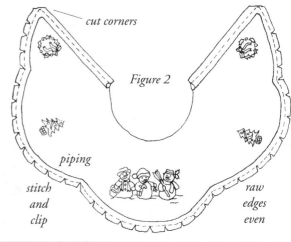

cut corners
Figure 2
piping
stitch
and
clip
raw
edges
even

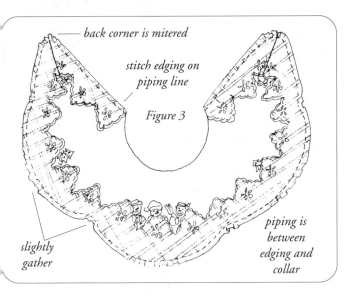

back corner is mitered

stitch edging on
piping line

*Figure 3*

slightly
gather

piping is
between
edging and
collar

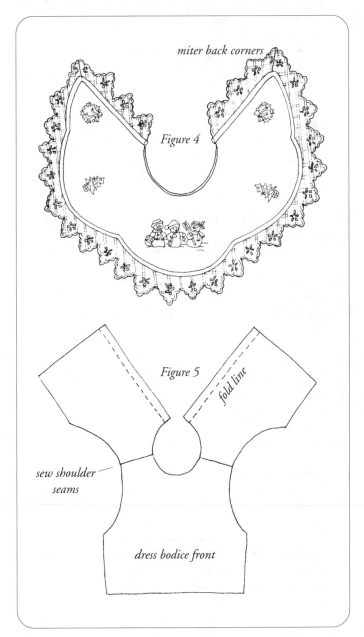

miter back corners

*Figure 4*

*Figure 5*

fold line

sew shoulder
seams

dress bodice front

4. Attach the lace edging to the seam where the piping was attached. Miter the back corners of the lace and slightly gather the lace around the scalloped edge to make the lace lay flat (fig. 3).
5. Place the collars with the right sides together and sew around the outer edge using the stitching line for piping as a guide. Trim and clip seam. Turn right side out and press (fig. 4).
6. Place backs to fronts with right sides together and sew the shoulder seams (fig. 5).
7. Fit the collar to the neck edge. Shape piping around the neck edge folding the edges into the seam line at the back fold lines. Fold the bodice back facing on the fold line to the right side of the bodice (collar will be between the back and the facing) (fig. 6).
8. Cut a bias strip 1" wide by the neck measurement. Fold the bias strip in half and press. Place the cut edges of the strip to the neck of the collar/bodice. Bias strip starts and stops $1/2$" from the back edge. Cut off any excess bias.
9. Stitch the bias strip to the neck edge using a $1/4$" seam, starting at the fold lines on the back edges of the bodice (fig. 7).
10. Trim the seam to $1/8$". Clip the neck edge and understitch the bias band. Understitching is done by stitching through the bias band and trimmed seam (fig. 8).

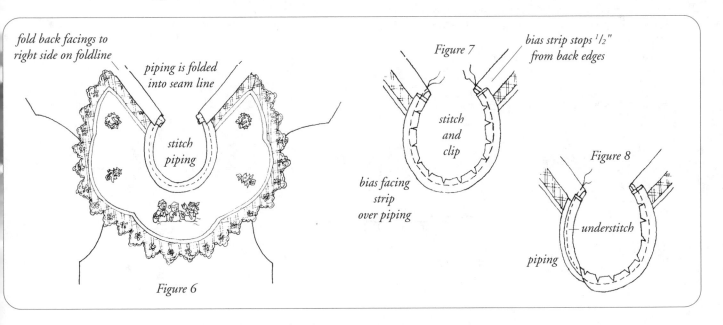

fold back facings to
right side on foldline

piping is folded
into seam line

stitch
piping

*Figure 6*

*Figure 7*

bias strip stops $1/2$"
from back edges

stitch
and
clip

bias facing
strip
over piping

*Figure 8*

understitch

piping

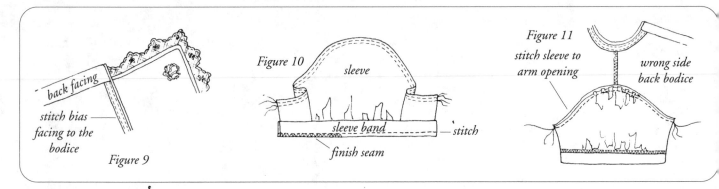

_back facing_

_stitch bias facing to the bodice_

Figure 9

Figure 10

_sleeve_

_sleeve band_ — _stitch_

_finish seam_

Figure 11
_stitch sleeve to arm opening_

_wrong side back bodice_

11. Holding the collar away from the bodice, stitch the facing to the bodice (fig. 9).
12. Run gathering threads in the top and bottom of each sleeve at $^1/_8$" and $^3/_8$".
13. Fold the sleeve band in half with the wrong sides together. Gather the bottom of the sleeve to fit the sleeve band. Place the right side of the sleeve band to the right side of the sleeve and stitch using a $^1/_4$" seam allowance. Finish seam (fig. 10). Press the sleeve band down.
14. Gather the top of the sleeve to fit the arm opening of the bodice. Stitch the sleeves to the arm opening with right sides together (fig. 11).
15. With right sides together sew the side seams of the bodice and sleeve (fig. 12).
16. Put a placket in the skirt center back referring to the General Dress Directions, V. Plackets.
17. Sew side seams of skirt. Finish bottom edge of skirt with a serged edge or turn under $^1/_4$" and stitch (fig. 13).
18. Run two rows of gathering threads in the top edge of skirt at $^1/_8$" and $^3/_8$" (fig. 13).
19. Place the bodice to the skirt, right sides together. Pull up the gathers of the skirt to fit the bodice. The center back openings will come to the fold line on the left and right backs. Wrap the back facings around the skirt center back openings. Sew the bodice to the skirt (fig. 14).
20. Pull the bodice away from the skirt, folding the back facings to the inside of the bodice (fig. 15).
21. Hand crochet belt loops at side seams to hold ribbon belt (fig. 16).
22. Close the dress with buttons and buttonholes along each side of the back bodice (fig. 16).
23. Hem the bottom of the skirt with a $3^1/_2$" hem.

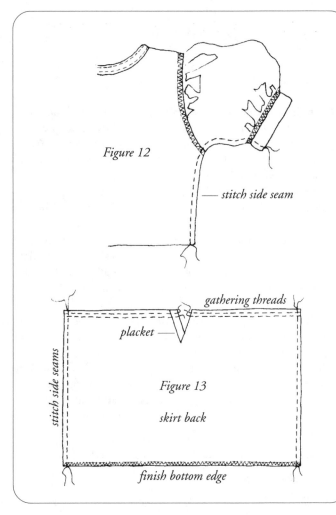

Figure 12

_stitch side seam_

_gathering threads_

_placket_

_stitch side seams_

Figure 13

_skirt back_

_finish bottom edge_

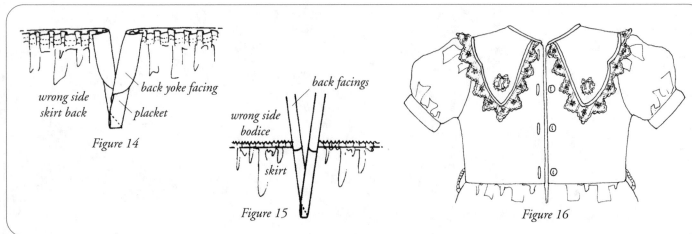

_wrong side skirt back_

_back yoke facing_

_placket_

Figure 14

_back facings_

_wrong side bodice_

_skirt_

Figure 15

Figure 16

# Black Ribbon Tabbed Dress

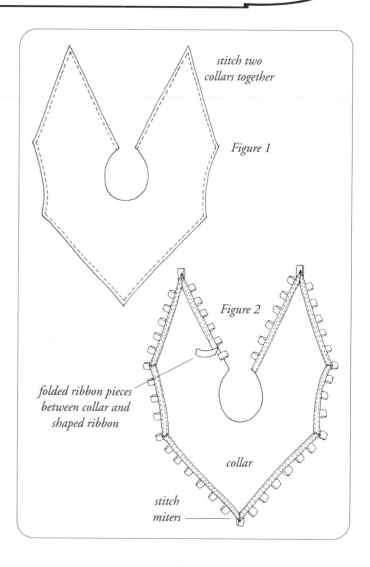

*The inspiration for this dark and elegant girl's corduroy dress came from a circa 1880 skirt purchased in Massachusetts. The dark brown corduroy printed collar features black grosgrain ribbon mitered and curved in two rows. Folded ribbon pieces are on the outside of the collar. The sleeves have this same ribbon/folded ribbon treatment. Self piping is found at the waistline. The skirt has strips of one inch ribbon stitched around with folded tabs spaced at intervals underneath the ribbon. There is a really pretty back-buttoned tailored belt with ribbon all the way around the fabric. The dress closes with buttons and buttonholes.*

## Fabric Requirements

|  | Sizes 2-6 | Sizes 8-10 | Sizes 12-16 |
|---|---|---|---|
| Fabric 45" | 2 $^7/_8$ yds | 3$^1/_4$ yds | 3 $^3/_4$ yds |
| 3/8" Ribbon | 7 $^3/_4$ yds | 7 $^7/_8$ yds | 8$^1/_2$ yds |
| 1" Ribbon | 10 yds | 10 yds | 10 yds |
| Cording | $^1/_2$ yd | $^1/_2$ yd | $^1/_2$ yd |
| $^1/_2$" Buttons | 6 | 6 | 7 |

All seams are $^1/_4$". Finish seams with a zigzag stitch or serger.

## Pattern Pieces

All pattern pieces are found in the pattern envelope.
Waisted bodice front, Waisted bodice back, V dress collar, puffed sleeve

## Cut Out

One bodice front on the fold, two bodice backs on the selvage, two collars, two short dress sleeves, two sleeve bands 2$^1/_2$" by length on sleeve band chart, skirt front and skirt back allowing for a 4" hem, bias band for neck facing, two belts 3$^1/_4$" by 9 ". Refer to the General Dress Directions for Sleeve Band Chart and Skirt Chart.

## Construction

1. Place the collar with right sides together and stitch around the collar (fig. 1). Trim and clip seam. Turn the collar right side out and press.
2. Embellish the collar with $^3/_8$" ribbon. Shape the ribbon on the outer edge of the collar mitering the ribbon at the points and corners. Make sure that the ribbon covers the outer edge of the collar. Cut 47 pieces of $^3/_8$" ribbon each being 1$^1/_4$" long. Fold these pieces in half. Slip a piece of the folded ribbon at each point and each corner between the shaped ribbon and collar. Space other pieces of ribbon $^3/_4$" apart all around collar's edge, slipping the folded ribbon between the shaped ribbon and the collar. Spacing may have to be adjusted on different size collars between points and corners. Stitch the ribbon to the collar on both sides of the ribbon. Stitch miters of ribbon (fig. 2).

*stitch two collars together*

*Figure 1*

*Figure 2*

*folded ribbon pieces between collar and shaped ribbon*

*collar*

*stitch miters*

3. Shape a second row of ribbon ³/₈" inside of the first row of ribbon. Miter the ribbon at points and corners. Stitch the ribbon to the collar on both sides of the ribbon (fig. 3).

4. Stitch the front to the back at the shoulders. Refer to the General Dress Directions, II. Neck Finishes, D. Attaching a Collar and attach the collar to bodice.

5. Refer to the General Dress Directions, IV. Sleeve Finishes, C. Sleeve Band and put the band on the bottom of sleeve.

6. Embellish the sleeve band with ³/₈" ribbon. Shape the ³/₈" ribbon on the bottom of the sleeve cuff. Cut 9 to 11 (depending on size dress) pieces of ³/₈" ribbon each being 1¹/₄" long. Fold these pieces in half. Space the pieces of ribbon on the bottom of the sleeve cuff spacing pieces ³/₄" apart. Slip the ribbon pieces under the ribbon on the bottom of the cuff. Stitch the ribbon in place on both sides of the ribbon (fig. 4).

7. Place a second piece of ribbon at the top edge of the cuff. Stitch in place on both sides of the ribbon (fig. 5).

8. Refer to the General Dress Directions, III. Sleeves to Armholes and insert the sleeves to the armholes.

9. Fold the belt pieces with right sides together. Stitch the belt together on one long side and one short side. Turn right side out and press.

10. Shape ³/₈" ribbon around the edge of the belt mitering the ribbon at the corners. Stitch ribbon to belt on both sides of ribbon. Stitch miters in place (fig. 6).

*Figure 6*　　*belt*

11. Place the belts ¹/₄" above the cut edge of the bodice on the side back bodice (fig. 7). The belt may need to be adjusted for dress size. The belt should overlap about 4" in the center back. Pin in place.

12. Make piping to go across the bottom of the front bodice. Stitch to the bottom of the bodice front matching raw edges of piping and bodice with a ¹/₄" seam (fig. 8).

13. Place right sides of the bodice together at the sides matching the bottom of bodice, underarm seams, and cuffs. Sew side bodice and sleeve seam (fig. 9).

14. Refer to the General Dress Directions, V. Placket and put a placket in the center skirt back.

15. Sew the side seams of the skirt.

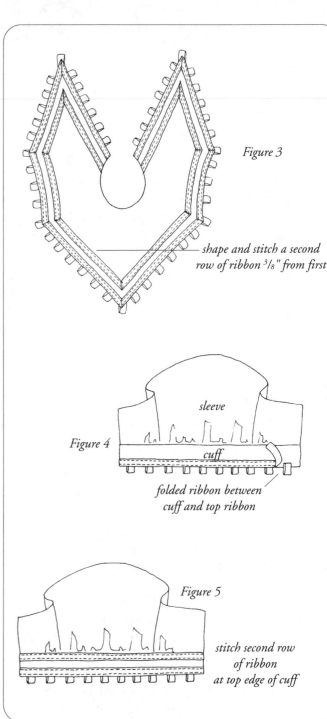

*Figure 3*

shape and stitch a second
row of ribbon ³/₈" from first

*Figure 4*　*sleeve*　*cuff*

folded ribbon between
cuff and top ribbon

*Figure 5*

stitch second row
of ribbon
at top edge of cuff

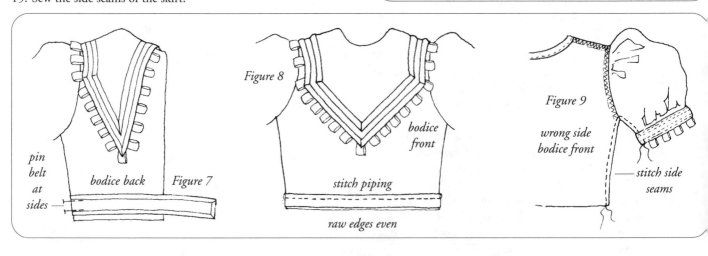

pin
belt
at
sides

*bodice back*　*Figure 7*

*Figure 8*

*bodice
front*

*stitch piping*

*raw edges even*

*Figure 9*

*wrong side
bodice front*

stitch side
seams

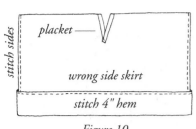

placket

stitch sides

wrong side skirt

stitch 4" hem

*Figure 10*

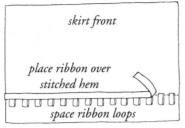

skirt front

place ribbon over
stitched hem

space ribbon loops

*Figure 11*

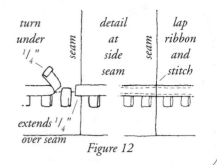

turn under ¹/₄"

extends ¹/₄" over seam

seam

detail at side seam

seam

lap ribbon and stitch

*Figure 12*

16. Finish the bottom edge of the skirt and turn up a 4" hem. Stitch hem in place on the machine (fig. 10).

17. Place 1" ribbon around the bottom of the skirt using the stitched hem line as a guide.

18. Cut 64 to 72 piece of 1" ribbon each 2¹/₂" long. Fold the ribbon pieces in half. Place the folded ribbon pieces under the bottom edge of the ribbon on the bottom of the skirt spacing each 1¹/₂" apart (fig. 11). Extend the ribbon ¹/₄" over one side seam at the beginning and fold under ¹/₄" at the other end and lap the ribbon at the side seam (fig. 12). Stitch the ribbon in place on the top and bottom edges of the ribbon.

19. Place a second piece of ribbon around the skirt 2¹/₄" above the top edge of the previous ribbon. Place the folded ribbon pieces under the bottom edge of the ribbon spacing each 1¹/₂" apart. Stitch the ribbon in place on the top and bottom edges of ribbon (fig. 13).

20. Run two rows of gathering stitches in the top of the skirt at ¹/₈" and ³/₈" (fig. 13).

21. Place the bodice to the skirt, right sides together. Pull up the gathers of the skirt to fit the bodice. The center back openings will come to the fold line on the left and right backs. Wrap the back facings around the skirt center back openings. Sew the bodice to the skirt (fig. 14).

22. Pull the bodice away from the skirt, folding the back facings to the inside of the bodice (fig. 15).

23. Close the dress with buttons and buttonholes along each side of the back bodice (fig. 16).

24. Lap the belt in the back and mark placement for buttonholes. Make buttonholes in belt. Mark placement for button and sew on buttons (fig. 16).

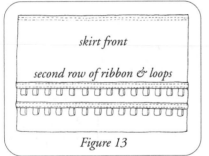

skirt front

second row of ribbon & loops

*Figure 13*

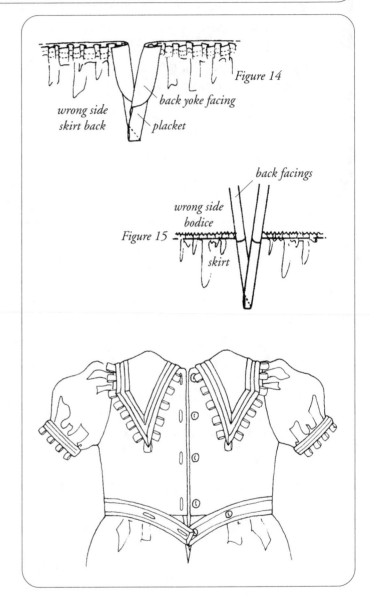

*Figure 14*

wrong side skirt back

back yoke facing

placket

back facings

wrong side bodice

*Figure 15*

skirt

# Anna's Cream Nightie

*Easy to make and comfortable to wear this nightie should be a favorite for wearing at home as well as at a spend the night party. The front and back yokes of this nightie are made with a piece of Swiss edging with Swiss beading at the bottom. The skirts are gathered with a large placket down both sides and the underarms tie with ribbons. The shoulder straps on this gown are fabric tubes; however ribbon would make great straps also. Bias tape has been stitched behind the beading area to form a casing for the ribbon to run through.*

## Fabric Requirements

| Fabric | Size 2 | Size 4 | Size 6 | Size 8 |
|---|---|---|---|---|
| Long Length | $1^1/2$ yds. | $1^3/4$ yds. | 2 yds. | $2^1/8$ yds. |
| Tea Length | 1 yd. | $1^1/4$ yds. | $1^5/8$ yds. | $1^3/4$ yds. |
| $^1/2$" Beading | 24" | 28" | 31" | 33" |
| $2^1/4$" Swiss Edging | 22" | 26" | 29" | 31" |
| $^1/4$" Ribbon | $2^1/2$ yds. | $2^1/2$ yds. | $2^1/2$ yds. | $2^1/2$ yds. |
| $^1/2$" Double Fold Bias Tape 1 yd. (all sizes) | | | | |

## Cutting

1. Cut one skirt front and and one skirt back 42" wide by the following lengths: (measurements include a $2^1/2$" hem allowance)

| Size | 2 | 4 | 6 | 8 |
|---|---|---|---|---|
| Skirt Front & Back | | | | |
| Long Length | $25^1/2$" | 29" | 35" | $37^1/2$" |
| Tea Length | 17" | $20^1/2$" | $27^1/2$" | 31" |

2. Cut two straps $1^3/4$" wide by the following length:

| Size | 2 | 4 | 6 | 8 |
|---|---|---|---|---|
| | 9" | 12" | 13" | 14" |

## Skirt

1. Place the skirt pieces right sides together. Starting at the lower edge of the skirt, sew the side seams using a $^3/4$" seam allowance, stopping 5" from the top edge. Press the seam open and finish the seam edges with a zigzag or serger. Pin the seam allowance folds in place at the top of the skirt pieces. Stitch a bar tack at the top of the open seam (fig. 1).

2. Run two rows of gathering threads on the top edge of the skirts front and back at $^1/8$" and $^3/8$", remember that the seams are pressed open.

3. Make the straps by folding the strip with right sides together and sewing the long side with a $^1/4$" seam. Turn the strap right

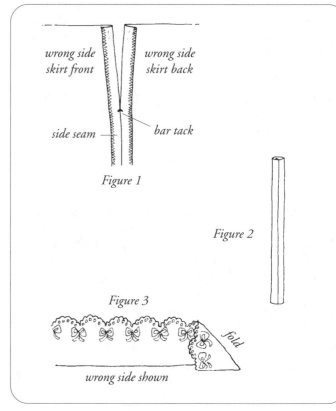

*wrong side skirt front*  
*wrong side skirt back*  
*side seam*  
*bar tack*  
*Figure 1*

*Figure 2*

*Figure 3*  
*wrong side shown*  
*fold*

side out and press so that the seam is in the center (fig. 2).

4. Refer to the measurements found under the fabric requirement for Swiss edging and beading. Cut each piece in half. Cut piece of double fold bias tape to the length of each beading piece.

5. The outer edges of the Swiss edging are finished by folding each short edge to the back at an angle with the edge extended $^1/4$" a the bottom (fig. 3).

6. Gather the skirts to fit the Swiss edging. With right sides together attach the skirt to the Swiss edging using a $^1/_4$" seam. Press the seam toward the Swiss edging (fig. 4).

7. Fold under $^1/_2$" on each end of the beading strip. Place the beading on the Swiss edging with the bottom edge of the beading along the seam. Stitch with a small zigzag stitch on both the top and bottom of the beading (fig. 5).

8. Fold the yokes to find the center front and center back. Place the straps 2" to $2^1/_2$" on each side of the center back and 2" to $2^1/_2$" on each side of the center front. Place the straps in place and adjust the length to fit the child or refer to the strap length given under cutting. Secure the straps in place by stitching at the bottom edge of the beading and bar tacking the strap to the Swiss edging at the top (fig. 6).

9. Fold $^1/_2$" to wrong side on each end of the bias tape. Place the bias tape over the seam allowance . Stitch in place with a straight stitch on both long sides. Do not sew the ends (fig. 7).

10. Cut the ribbon in half and weave through the beading leaving the ends evenly hanging for the side ties (fig. 8). Center each piece of ribbon in the beading and using small zigzag stitch, stitch the ribbon to the beading in the center. This stitching will secure the ribbon, keeping the ribbon centered.

11. Finish the bottom edge of the skirt with a serger or turn $^1/_4$" to the wrong side and stitch. Turn up the hem $2^1/_4$" to $2^1/_2$" and stitch in place with a straight stitch or hem by hand.

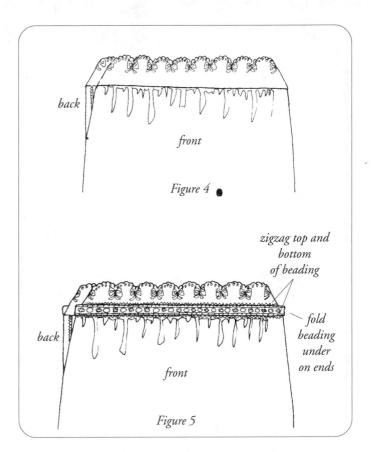

back

front

*Figure 4*

zigzag top and bottom of beading

back

front

fold beading under on ends

*Figure 5*

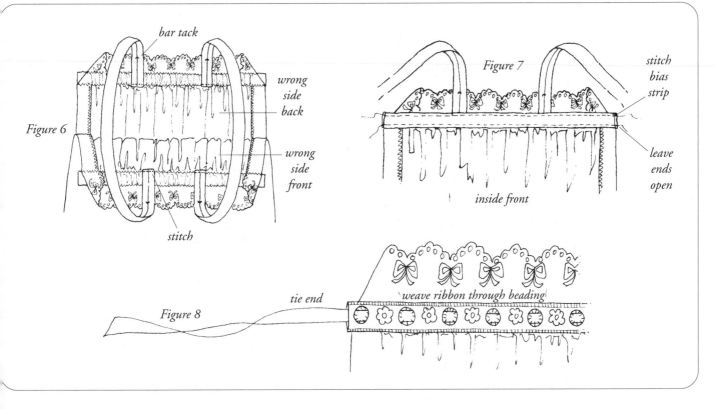

bar tack

wrong side back

wrong side front

*Figure 6*

stitch

*Figure 7*

stitch bias strip

leave ends open

inside front

weave ribbon through beading

tie end

*Figure 8*

# Emma's Peach Nightie

*S*uper easy to make and super fun to wear is this peach nightie. The front is composed of eyelet embroidered beading and eyelet embroidered edging; the lace edging is used to stabilize the front portion on the inside of the gown. Self fabric straps are used over the shoulders and two pieces of white ribbon tie on each side for trim only. Elastic gathered in the fullness for this gown and it is so easy to make and comfortable to wear. Ribbon is run behind the eyelet beading to look as if it is threaded through the beading. The nightie has a simple machine hem at the bottom.

## Fabric Requirements

| Fabric | Size 2 | Size 4 | Size 6 | Size 8 |
|---|---|---|---|---|
| Long Length | $1^1/_2$ yds. | $1^3/_4$ yds. | 2 yds. | $2^1/_8$ yds. |
| Tea Length | 1 yd. | $1^1/_4$ yds. | $1^5/_8$ yds. | $1^3/_4$ yds. |
| $^7/_8$” Eyelet beading | $10^1/_4$” | $12^1/_2$” | 14” | 15” |
| $^7/_8$” Eyelet edging | $10^1/_4$” | $12^1/_2$” | 14” | 15” |
| $^7/_8$” Lace edging or | $10^1/_4$” | $12^1/_2$” | 14” | 15” |
| ribbon (used for lining front bodice) | | | | |
| $^3/_8$” Ribbon | 2 yds. | 2 yds. | 2yds. | 2yds. |
| $^3/_8$” Elastic | $10^1/_4$” | $12^1/_2$” | 14” | 15” |

## Cutting

1. Cut one skirt front and and one skirt back 36” wide by the following lengths: (measurements include a $2^1/_2$” hem allowance)

| Size | 2 | 4 | 6 | 8 |
|---|---|---|---|---|
| Skirt Front | | | | |
| Long Length | 24” | $27^1/_2$” | $33^1/_2$” | 36” |
| Tea Length | $15^1/_2$” | 19” | 26” | $29^1/_2$” |
| Skirt Back | | | | |
| Long Length | $25^1/_2$” | 29” | 35” | $37^1/_2$” |
| Tea Length | 17” | $20^1/_2$” | $27^1/_2$” | 31” |

2. Cut two straps $1^3/_4$” wide by the following length:

| Size | 2 | 4 | 6 | 8 |
|---|---|---|---|---|
| | 9” | 12” | 13” | 14” |

## Back

1. Turn under $^1/_4$” at the top edge of the back. Press. Turn down $^5/_8$” to the wrong side of the back top edge and stitch at the bottom edge of the fold to form a casing (fig. 1).

2. Make the straps by folding the strip with right sides together and sewing with a $^1/_4$” seam along the long side. Turn right side out and press so that the seam is in the center (fig. 2).

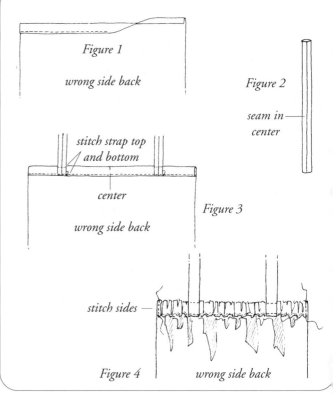

Figure 1

wrong side back

Figure 2

seam in center

stitch strap top and bottom

center

wrong side back

Figure 3

stitch sides

Figure 4   wrong side back

3. Attach the straps to the back about 5” to $5^1/_2$” from the center back on each side. Fold under $^1/_4$” at the bottom edge of the strap and stitch in place at the top and bottom of the casing (fig 3). Do not stitch through the casing.

4. Insert the elastic into the casing. Stitch the elastic in place at each side (fig. 4).

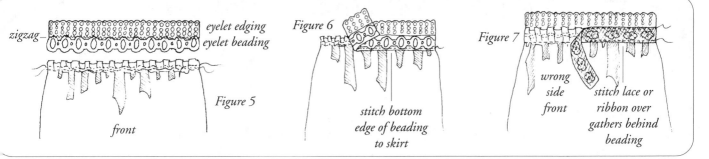

*zigzag* — eyelet edging / eyelet beading

*front*

**Figure 5**

**Figure 6** — stitch bottom edge of beading to skirt

**Figure 7** — wrong side front / stitch lace or ribbon over gathers behind beading

## Front

Stitch the eyelet edging and eyelet beading together with a small zigzag stitch. Refer to the technique "lace to lace" (fig. 5).

Run two rows of gathering threads in the top edge of the front skirt at $1/8$" and $3/8$". Gather the skirt to fit the beading strip (fig. 5).

Lay the beading/eyelet strip on top of the skirt front with the beading overlapping the gathering lines. Stitch the skirt to the beading strip at the bottom edge of the beading (fig. 6).

Cover the unfinished edge of the gathered skirt top with a piece of lace edging or a ribbon strip. Stitch the lace or ribbon at the top and bottom edges of the beading making sure that the top, unfinished edge of skirt is enclosed behind the lace or ribbon (fig. 7).

Cut a piece of ribbon to fit the beading and weave the ribbon through the beading.

Cut the remaining ribbon in half. Fold each piece of ribbon in half and attach the ribbon folds at the side edges of the beading (fig. 8).

## Finishing

Sew the side seams matching the top edge of beading/lace and top edge of the casing. Sew the sides together with a $1/4$" seam. Finish the seam with a zigzag or serger (fig. 9).

If the skirt front and back are uneven at the bottom, trim the longer to meet the shorter. Finish the bottom edge of the skirt with a serger or turn $1/4$" to the wrong side and stitch.

Turn up the hem $2^1/4$" to $2^1/2$" and stitch in place with a straight stitch or hem by hand.

Attached the straps to the front 2" to 3" on each side of the center. Turn strap edge under $1/4$" and stitch in place behind the beading (fig. 10).

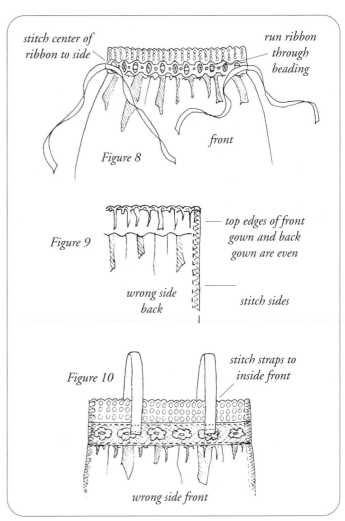

*stitch center of ribbon to side* / *run ribbon through beading*

*front*

**Figure 8**

**Figure 9** — top edges of front gown and back gown are even / *wrong side back* / stitch sides

**Figure 10** — stitch straps to inside front / *wrong side front*

# Rebekah's Butterfly Linen Dress

*Made of ecru linen and cotton blend this dress captures my imagination for any age girl for the summer months. With sleeves it certainly could be worn for any season. My granddaughter Rebekah loves butterflies so it reminds me of Rebekah. The machine scallops around the collar are done in variegated machine embroidery; the colors of the butterflies, the flowers and the trims are wonderfully bright; variegated blue, orange, green, pink, yellow and red. The hem is stitched in with machine scallops in the pink variegated thread also; notice how the satin stitched blue flower dips into the hem. There is pink piping around the waistline and the sash is ecru linen. Perky pink buttons are used to button the back.*

## Fabric Requirements

|  | Sizes 2-6 | Sizes 8-10 | Sizes 12-16 |
|---|---|---|---|
| Linen 45" | $2^1/_3$ yds | $2^3/_4$ yds | $3^1/_4$ yds |
| Buttons $^1/_2$" | 4 | 4 | 4 |

Purchased piping or 1/8 yd of fabric to cover piping in contracting color

Thread for Machine Embroidery (bright primary colors were used on the photographed dress)

## Pattern Pieces

All pattern pieces are found in the pattern envelope. Mid-waisted front bodice, mid-waisted back bodice, scalloped collar front, embroidery/cutwork template for the skirt and collar included in directions.

All seams $^1/_4$". Finish seams with a zigzag stitch or serger.

## Cutting

Two mid-waisted bodice fronts on the fold, four mid-waisted bodice backs on the selvage, add 3-1/3" to the mid-waisted skirt measurement for the hem and cut one skirt front and one skirt back, a block of fabric large enough to trace the collar, two strips of fabric for the sash for sizes 2-6 (5" by 33") for sizes 8-16 (5" by 38").

## Collar

1. Trace the collar onto the fabric block.
2. Complete the cutwork design on the corner of the collar referring to the directions on cutwork. Finish the outer edge of collar with a machine scallop. Note where the scallops need to stop at the top edge of the collar (fig. 1). Trim scallop edge and cut out the collar.

## Bodice

1. Place the collar on one bodice front with the wrong side of the collar to right side of the bodice. Baste the collar in place at the neck and shoulder edges; note where the last scallop will fall (fig. 2).

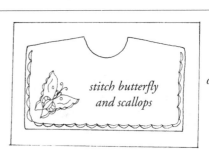

stitch butterfly and scallops

trace collar on fabric block

*Figure 1*

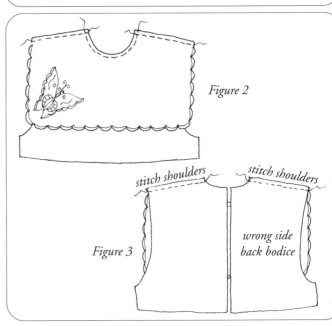

*Figure 2*

stitch shoulders    stitch shoulders

*Figure 3*

wrong side back bodice

2. Place the backs to the front with the right sides together matchin[g] the shoulder seams and sew the shoulder seams (fig. 3).

- Place the bodice front lining and the bodice back linings together at the shoulder and stitch. Lay both bodice pieces out flat (fig. 4).
- Fold the collar towards the center and pin in place. Place the front/back bodice and the front/back bodice lining together matching all edges with right sides together (fig. 5).
- Stitch around the neck curve and both armhole curves leaving the lower edges and the side seams of both the fronts and backs unstitched. Be very careful not to catch the collar in the stitching of the armholes (fig. 5). Trim and clip the curves on both the armholes and the neckline.
- Reach through the shoulder on top of the collar and pull the backs through the shoulder "tubes" and out the lower edge of the fronts.
- Press the neckline and the armhole seams well (fig. 6).

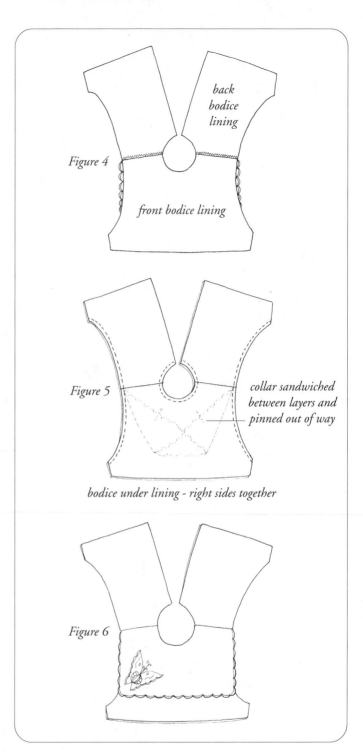

Figure 4

back bodice lining

front bodice lining

Figure 5

collar sandwiched between layers and pinned out of way

bodice under lining - right sides together

Figure 6

## Skirt

- Sew the side seams of the skirt. Finish the bottom of the skirt with a serger or overcast stitch.
- Turn up a $3^1/_2$" hem and baste in place.
- Trace the skirt butterfly template onto the skirt front. Refer to the technique on cutwork and embroider the design onto the skirt front.
- Using a decorative machine scallop, stitch the hem in place leaving the hem unstitched where the flower design goes into the hem (fig. 7).

## Finishing Dress

- Refer to the General Dress Directions, VI. Sash and make a sash and attach to the bodice back.
- Matching the underarm seam and the bottom of the front and back bodices and the front and back bodice linings, sew the side seams (fig. 8). Turn the lining to the wrong side and press. Measure around the bottom of the bodice and make a piece of covered piping to fit around the bottom from the contrasting fabric. Refer to the technique, Piping. Attach the piping to the bottom of the bodice treating the bodice and lining as one (fig. 9). Finish the back edge of the bodice treating the bodice and lining as one.
- Refer to the General Dress Directions, V. Plackets and put a placket in the center back.
- Run two rows of gathering stitches in the top of the skirt at $^1/_8$" and $^3/_8$".
- Place the bodice to the skirt with the right sides together. Pull up the gathers of the skirt to fit the bodice. The center back placket openings will come to the fold line on the left and right bodice

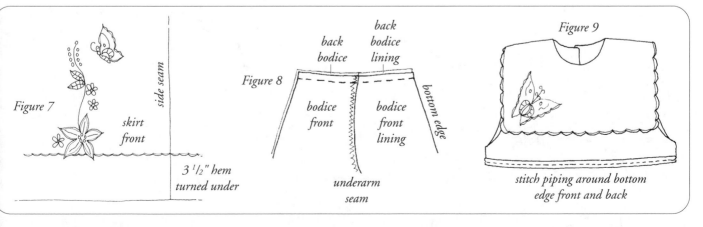

Figure 7

side seam

skirt front

$3^1/_2$" hem turned under

Figure 8

back bodice

back bodice lining

bodice front

bodice front lining

bottom edge

underarm seam

Figure 9

stitch piping around bottom edge front and back

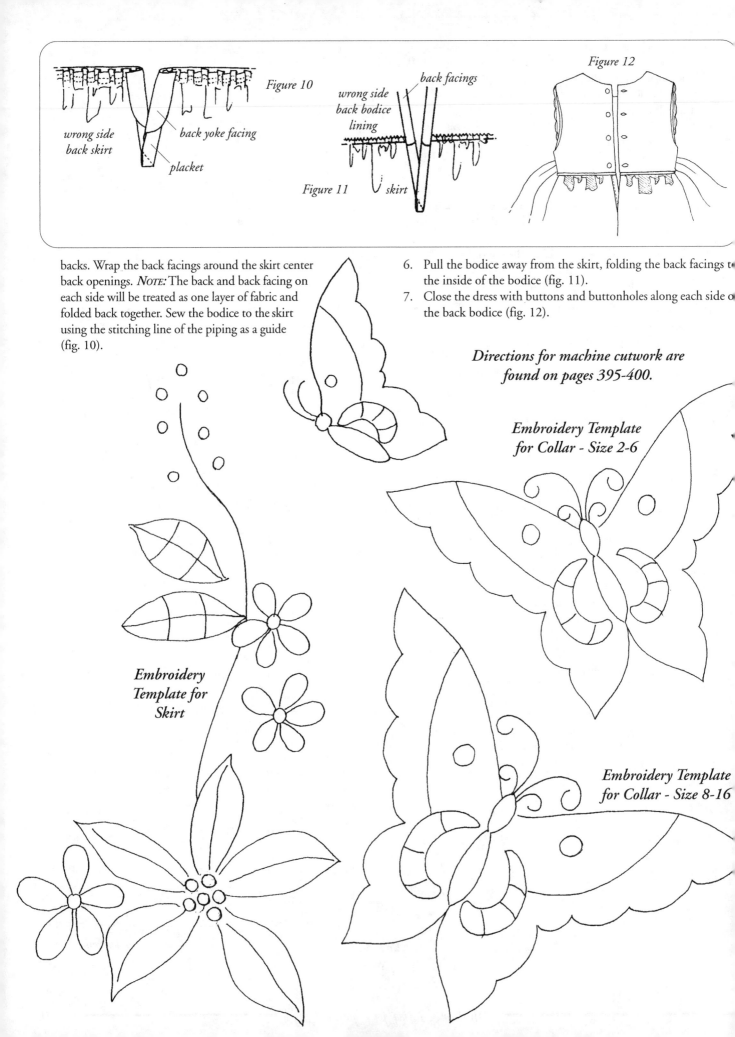

*Figure 10*

wrong side
back skirt

back yoke facing

placket

*Figure 11*

wrong side
back bodice
lining

back facings

skirt

*Figure 12*

backs. Wrap the back facings around the skirt center back openings. *Note:* The back and back facing on each side will be treated as one layer of fabric and folded back together. Sew the bodice to the skirt using the stitching line of the piping as a guide (fig. 10).

6. Pull the bodice away from the skirt, folding the back facings t the inside of the bodice (fig. 11).
7. Close the dress with buttons and buttonholes along each side o the back bodice (fig. 12).

*Directions for machine cutwork are found on pages 395-400.*

*Embroidery Template
for Collar - Size 2-6*

*Embroidery
Template for
Skirt*

*Embroidery Template
for Collar - Size 8-16*

# Pink Heart Dress

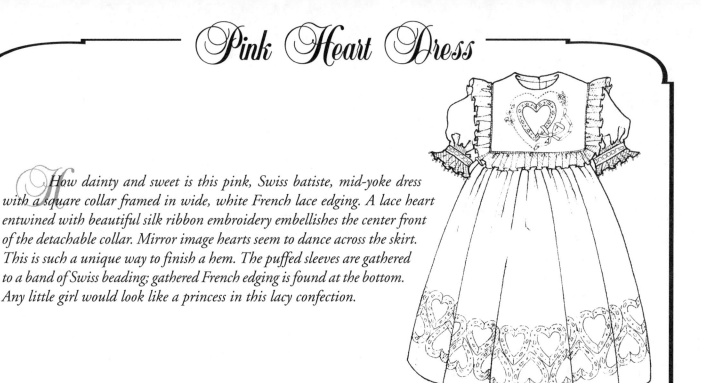

*H*ow dainty and sweet is this pink, Swiss batiste, mid-yoke dress with a square collar framed in wide, white French lace edging. A lace heart entwined with beautiful silk ribbon embroidery embellishes the center front of the detachable collar. Mirror image hearts seem to dance across the skirt. This is such a unique way to finish a hem. The puffed sleeves are gathered to a band of Swiss beading; gathered French edging is found at the bottom. Any little girl would look like a princess in this lacy confection.

## Fabric Requirements

|  | Sizes 2-6 | Sizes 8-10 | Sizes 12-16 |
|---|---|---|---|
| Fabric 45" | $2^1/_8$ yds | $2^5/_8$ yds | $3^1/_4$ yds |
| /8" Lace Insertion | $18^1/_2$ yds | $18^1/_2$ yds | $18^1/_2$ yds |
| 7/8" Lace Edging | $5^1/_4$ yds | $5^2/_3$ yds | $5^3/_4$ yds |
| Entredeux | $1^3/_4$ yds | $1^3/_4$ yds | 2 yds |
| Swiss Beading (sleeves) | $5/_8$ yd | $3/_4$ yd | $3/_4$ yd |
| /8" Ribbon for sleeves | 2 yds | 2 yds | 2 yds |
| /2" Buttons | 7 | 7 | 7 |

Silk Ribbon - 4mm for flowers and 7mm for large leaves and Beverley Bow. Select colors that are comparable to the fabric.
Embroidery Floss - green

## Pattern Pieces

All pattern pieces are found in the pattern envelope.
Detachable square collar front, detachable square collar back, mid-waisted front, mid-waisted back, puffed sleeve, lace heart collar template, heart skirt template.
All seams $1/_4$". Finish seams with zigzag stitch or serger.

## Cutting

One detachable square collar on the fold, two detachable square collar backs on the selvage, bias band $1^1/_4$" wide by the neck measurement to finish the neck edge of collar, bias band $1^1/_4$" wide by the neck measurement to finish the neck of the dress, mid-waisted bodice front on the fold, mid-waisted bodice back on the selvage, two dress sleeves on dress cutting line, refer to the Shirt Measurement Chart in the General Dress Directions for mid-waisted adding $3^1/_2$" to the length for the hem cut out a skirt front and a skirt back, a strip of fabric from the selvage 11" by $3/_4$" for the placket.

## Collar

. Center the lace heart template in the center of the collar front. Trace the lace template line and the embroidery design onto the collar (fig. 1).
. Shape the lace insertion on the collar, refer to the technique

**Figure 1**

collar front

work embroidery

shape lace and pinstitch

**Figure 2**

fold back facing to wrong side

wrong side back collar

section on lace shaping. Stitch in place with a small zigzag or pinstitch. Trim the fabric from behind the lace insertion.

3. Do the embroidery around the lace heart by hand or by machine. Refer to the technique section on hand and ribbon embroidery (fig. 1).

4. Press the back facing to the wrong side on the collar back (fig. 2).

5. Place the collar front to the collar backs with the right sides

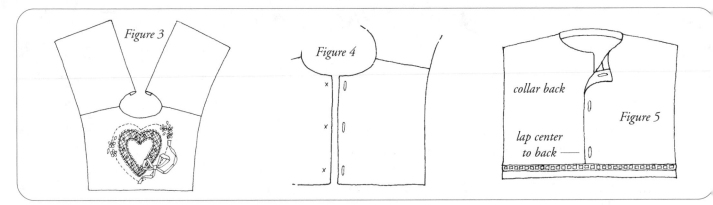

together and sew the shoulder seams (fig. 3).

6. Finish the neck edge with a bias facing referring to the General Dress Directions, II. Neck Finishes, A. Bias Facing.

7. Space 3 buttonholes down the collar back. Work the buttonholes and mark the placement for the buttons (fig. 4).

8. Lap the center back of the collar as it will be when buttoned. Cut a strip of entredeux the length of the bottom edge of the collar back. Sew the entredeux to the bottom of the collar using the technique, entredeux to flat fabric (fig. 5).

9. Cut a strip of entredeux the length of the bottom edge of the collar front. Sew the entredeux to the bottom of the collar front using the technique, entredeux to flat fabric (fig. 6).

10. Cut two pieces of entredeux long enough for the sides of the collar. Sew the entredeux to the sides of the collar using the technique, entredeux to flat fabric. Overlap the entredeux at the corners (fig. 6).

11. Trim the outer fabric edge from the entredeux. Measure around the outer edge of the collar. Cut a piece of edging lace twice this measurement. Gather the edging lace to fit around the collar. Attach the gathered lace edging to the entredeux using the technique, Gathered Lace to Entredeux starting at the back corner. Join lace edging at a corner with a small zig zag stitch (fig. 7).

12. Sew buttons on the collar back (fig. 7).

## *Dress Construction*

1. Press the back folds in the bodice backs. Place the backs to the front at the shoulder seams and stitch the shoulder seams (fig. 8).

2. Finish the neck edge with a bias facing referring to the General Dress Directions, II. Neck Finishes, A. Bias Facing.

3. Cut two strips of Swiss beading to the measurement given on the cuff chart. Cut two pieces of edging lace twice the length of the beading.

4. Gather the edging lace to fit the beading. Stitch the edging to the beading using the technique entredeux to gathered lace (fig. 9).

5. Gather the bottom of the sleeve to fit the beading/edging lace band. Stitch the band to the sleeve, right sides together, using the technique entredeux to gathered fabric (fig. 10).

6. Insert the sleeves into the armhole referring to the General Dress Directions, III. Sleeves to Armholes (fig. 11).

7. Sew the side seam matching the bottom of the sleeve, underarm

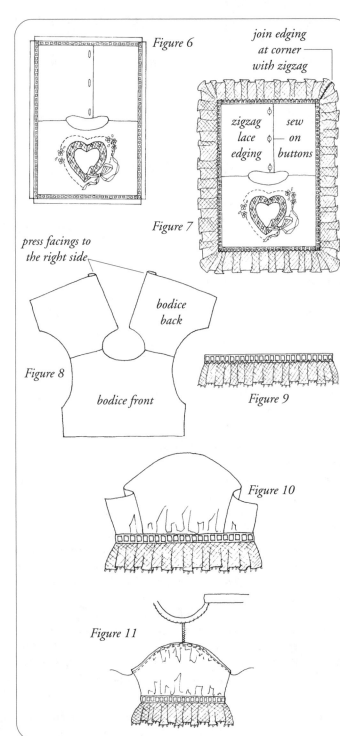

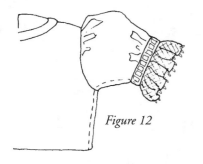

Figure 12

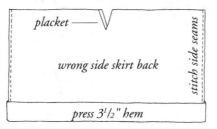

placket — wrong side skirt back — stitch side seams

press 3¹/₂" hem

Figure 13

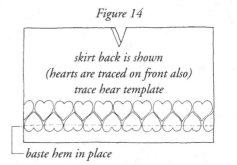

Figure 14

skirt back is shown
(hearts are traced on front also)
trace hear template

— baste hem in place

seam and bottom of bodice (fig. 12).

. Referring to the General Dress Directions, V. Plackets, put a placket in the center back of the skirt.

. Sew the skirt side seams. Press up a 3¹/₂" hem in the bottom of the skirt to the wrong side (fig. 13).

0. Place the skirt heart template on the bottom of the skirt and trace the lace hearts placement on the skirt (fig. 14).

1. Baste the hem in place with a basting stitch (fig. 14).

2. Shape lace hearts on the template lines. Stitch the lace hearts to the skirt with a small zig zag stitch (fig. 15).

3. Trim excess hem from the inside of the hearts close to the zig zag stitch (fig. 16).

4. Run two rows of gathering stitches in the top of the skirt at 1/8" and ³/₈" (fig. 16).

5. Place the bodice to the skirt, right sides together. Pull up the gathers of the skirt to fit the bodice. The center back openings will come to the fold line on the left and right backs. Wrap the back facings around the skirt center back openings. Sew the bodice to the skirt (fig. 17).

6. Pull the bodice away from the skirt, folding the back facings to the inside of the bodice (fig. 18).

7. Close the dress with buttons and buttonholes along each side of the back bodice (fig. 19).

8. Cut ribbon in half and run ribbon through the Swiss beading on the sleeves and tie a bow (fig. 19).

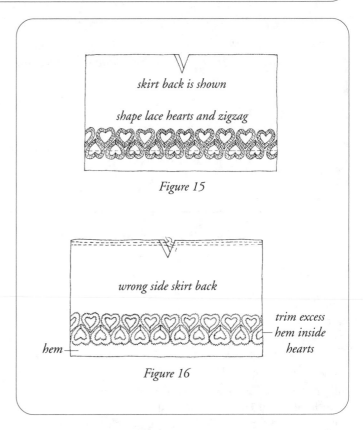

skirt back is shown

shape lace hearts and zigzag

Figure 15

wrong side skirt back

hem — — trim excess hem inside hearts

Figure 16

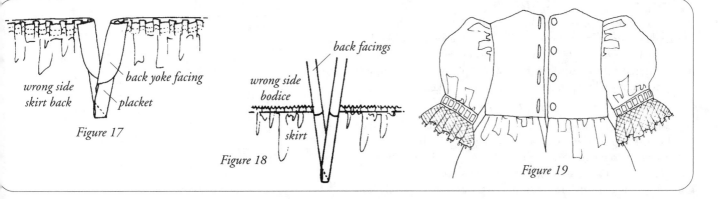

wrong side skirt back — back yoke facing — placket

Figure 17

wrong side bodice — back facings — skirt

Figure 18

Figure 19

# Button-on Skirt

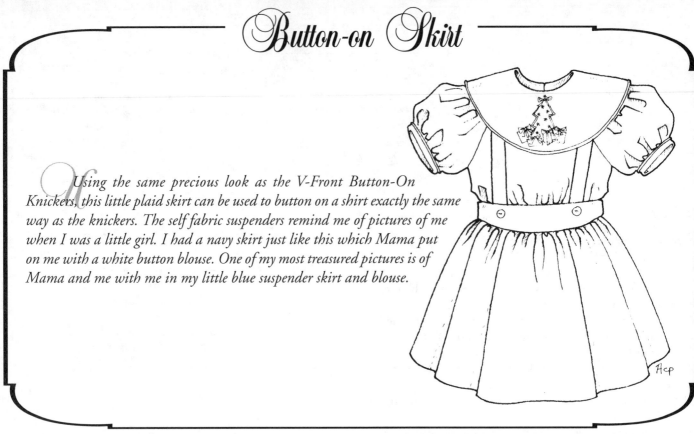

*Using the same precious look as the V-Front Button-On Knickers, this little plaid skirt can be used to button on a shirt exactly the same way as the knickers. The self fabric suspenders remind me of pictures of me when I was a little girl. I had a navy skirt just like this which Mama put on me with a white button blouse. One of my most treasured pictures is of Mama and me with me in my little blue suspender skirt and blouse.*

## Fabric Requirements

|  | Sizes 2 | Sizes 4-6 | Sizes 8 |
|---|---|---|---|
| Fabric 45" | 1 yd. | 1 1/3 yds. | 1 1/2 yds. |

1/2 yd. of 3/4 elastic
four 1/2" buttons
thread
wash-out marker
Optional: Piping

## Pattern Pieces

All pattern pieces are found in the pattern envelope.
Skirt front, skirt back, skirt waistband
All seams 1/4". Seams finished with zigzag stitch or serger.

## Cutting

One skirt front, one skirt back, one skirt waistband. Optional: suspenders - cut two fabric strips 2 1/2" wide by the following lengths: Size 8 to 30", Size 6 to 28", sizes 4 to 26" and sizes 2 to 25". Mark the indicated fold lines, dots, buttonhole placement and other markings on the fabric pieces with a wash-out marker.

## Construction

1. Turn in 1/4" on the edge of the upper extensions of the back and front skirt pieces. Stitch close to the edge (fig. 1). Turn the back extension to the inside along the fold line and pin (fig. 2).
2. Place the front and back skirts with right sides together at the side seams and stitch from the dot to the bottom edge. Clip to the dot at the extension (fig. 3). Finish the side seam and press.
3. With the extensions right sides together, stitch across the bottom edge of the extension from the dot to the outside edge (fig. 4).
4. Fold the front extension toward the front of the skirt, pressing at the front fold line (fig. 5). Pin the front fold in place.
5. Place gathering rows along the top edge of the skirts front at 1/8" and 3/8" from the edge. Gather the front to fit the waistband.

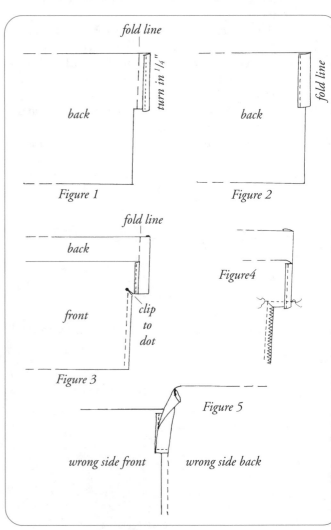

fold line

*back*    turn in 1/4"

*Figure 1*

fold line

*back*

*Figure 2*

fold line

*back*

*front*    clip to dot

*Figure 3*

*Figure 4*

*Figure 5*

*wrong side front*    *wrong side back*

6. Piping Option: Make a piece of piping (refer to "Making Piping") 1" longer than the measurement of the short sides plus one "v" side. Stitch the piping to the right side of the waistband starting at the fold, clipping the corners, and continuing to the opposite fold (fig. 6).

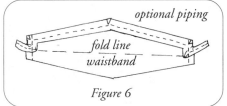

*optional piping*

*fold line*
*waistband*

Figure 6

7. Place the waistband with right sides together to the skirt front, with the fold line of the extensions of the skirt meeting the seam allowance of the band. Stitch, pivoting at the point in the center (fig. 7).

8. Trim the seam and the corners. Turn the waistband up and press the seam toward the band. Turn under ¹/₄" to the wrong side on the other side of the waistband. Fold the waistband in half along the fold line, right sides together. Stitch the ends, being careful not to catch the skirt in the seam (fig. 8).

9. Trim the seams and turn the waistband right side out and to the inside. Hand whip the edge of the band to the inside at the seam line. Work the buttonholes in the front waistband at the markings (fig. 9).

10. Turn in ¹/₄" along the top edge of the back of the skirt. Fold the casing to the inside along the fold line, wrong sides together, making sure that the top front of the skirt and the top back are even. Stitch close to the top and bottom long edges.

11. Cut a piece of elastic to the following measurement:
    Size 2        6" to 6¹/₂"
    Size 4        7" to 8"
    Size 6        9" to 10"
    Size 8        11" to 12"
    Run the elastic through the casing, leaving ¹/₂" free from elastic at each end. Secure with several rows of straight stitching. Sew buttons on the back extensions opposite the buttonholes (fig. 10).

12. Optional: Suspenders. Fold each suspender in half lengthwise. Stitch along the long side using a ¹/₄" seam. Turn each suspender to the right side, press. Finish the short ends of the suspenders by turning the cut edges to the inside and hand or machine stitch in place. Hand whip the backs of the suspenders to the inside of the back waistband. The suspenders can crisscross in the back (fig. 11).

13. Try the skirt on the child. Mark and sew the buttons on the front ends of the suspenders. Note: If you are pairing this skirt with a shirt with buttons at the waistline, buttonholes instead of buttons will need to be worked at the ends of each suspender.

14. Turn under ¹/₄" on the bottom of the skirt. Hem skirt to desired length.

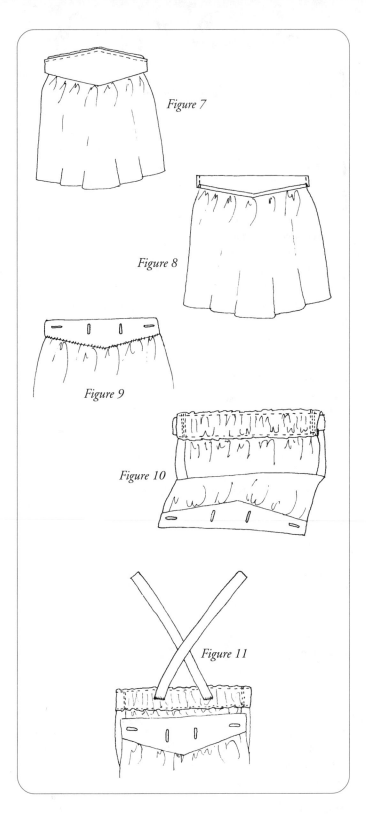

Figure 7

Figure 8

Figure 9

Figure 10

Figure 11

# Bradley's Madeira Appliqué Dress

*What a masterpiece dress made of white linen with Madeira appliqué treatments on the bodice, the sleeves and the skirt done in pale blue linen. The Windowpane Madeira appliqué motif on the front is of blue. There are wonderful insets of mitered lace in the center of each windowpane as well as French knots and lazy daisies of blue silk ribbon embroidery. The lace shaping uses white French lace and follows the shape of the Madeira design on the front. More blue silk ribbon embroidery embellishes the points of the white French lace insertion. The lined Peter Pan collar has Swiss entredeux around the outside edge with gathered white French lace edging around the collar. A beautiful blue Madeira treatment is found on the sleeves; blue linen piping is used in the front bodice where the gathered skirt joins the bodice. The puffed sleeve has Swiss entredeux at the bottom, white French beading, Swiss entredeux and a wide gathered white lace edging. White satin ribbon is used for the sash. The blue Madeira treatment on the bottom of the skirt has scallops on the bottom and the top. More windowpane treatments similar to the ones on the bodice are found on the skirt. White French edging is mitered to follow the shape of the blue Madeira linen skirt.*

*The underskirt of the dress has a wide ruffle with wide French lace attached to the bottom of the ruffle. The back of the dress closes with buttons and buttonholes.*

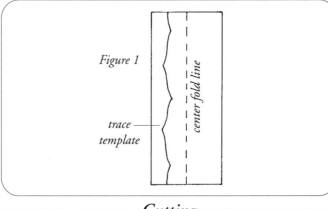

## Fabric Requirements

|  | Sizes 2-4 | Sizes 6-8 | Sizes10-12 | Sizes 14-16 |
|---|---|---|---|---|
| White Linen | 1³/₄ yds | 2¹/₂ yds | 2 ⁵/₈ yds | 3 yds |
| Colored Linen | ³/₄ yd | ³/₄ yd | ³/₄ yd | 1 yd |
| Swiss Batiste (underskirt) | 1¹/₄ yds | 1⁵/₈ yds | 1⁷/₈ yds | 2 yds |
| ³/₄" Lace Insertion | 6 yds | 6 yds | 6 yds | 6 yds |
| 1" Lace Edging (collar) | 1 yd | 1¹/₂ yds | 1³/₄ yds | 1³/₄ yds |
| 3/4" Lace Edging (motifs) | 3 yds | 3 yds | 3 yds | 3 yds |
| 3" Lace Edging | 5 yds | 6¹/₃ yds | 6¹/₃ yds | 6¹/₃ yds |
| 2" Lace Edging sleeve lace for size 2 and 4 | 1¹/₃ yds |  |  |  |
| Beading | ¹/₂ yd | ⁵/₈ yd | ²/₃ yd | ²/₃ yd |
| Entredeux | 2 yds | 2¹/₄ yds | 2¹/₂ yds | 2¹/₂ yds |
| 4mm Silk Ribbon (#126) | 10 yds | 10 yds | 10 yds | 10 yds |
| 2" Ribbon | 2¹/₄ yds | 2¹/₄yds | 2¹/₄ yds | 2¹/₄ yds |
| 1/2" Buttons | 4 | 4 | 5 | 5 |
| Cording (for piping) | ¹/₂ yd | ¹/₂ yd | ¹/₂ yd | ¹/₂ yd |
| Water Soluble Stabilizer | 1 yd. | 1 yd | 1 yd | 1 yd |

Wash A-way basting thread
#100 universal needle
white light-weight thread

## Pattern Pieces

All pattern pieces are found in the pattern envelope. Waisted bodice front, waisted bodice back, puffed dress sleeve, Peter Pan collar Templates: Bradley's Madeira dress skirt template, Bradley's Madeira dress sleeve template and Bradley's Madeira dress bodice template. All seams ¹/₄". Seams finished with zigzag stitch or serger.

*Figure 1*

*trace template*

*center fold line*

## Cutting

Cut two back bodices from white fabric on the selvage. Cut a squar[e] of white fabric for the front bodice the total width of the pattern an[d] 1" longer. Fold this fabric in the center and mark indicating th[e] center front. Cut two sleeves. Cut two skirt pieces referring to th[e] General Dress Directions, Skirt Chart. Cut four Peter Pan colla[r] with 1" removed from the outer edge to account for the 1" lac[e] edging added to the collar. Cut two underskirt pieces from Swis[s] batiste 7¹/₄" shorter than the skirt pieces. Cut four underskirt ruff[le] pieces from Swiss batiste 5" by 42". Cut one bias neck facing 1[ ] wide by the neck measurement.

## Bodice

*Refer to the "Magic Madeira Appliqué" section pages 339 to 348 for easy Madeira appliqué directions.*

1. Cut a piece of blue fabric 1" longer than the pattern piece an[d] 5" wide for the Madeira border on the center front of the bodic[e]. Refer to the template for the size you are creating. Fold the fabri[c] in half to measure 2¹/₂". Open the fabric and trace the Madeir[a] appliqué bodice template on half of the blue linen fabric piec[e] (fig. 1).

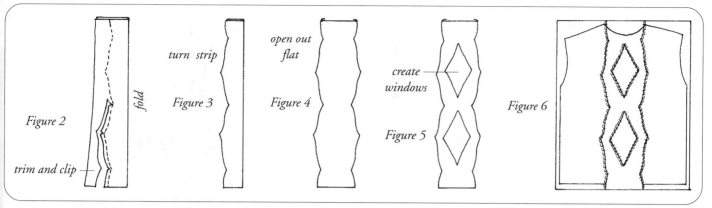

turn strip

Figure 3

open out flat

Figure 4

create windows

Figure 5

Figure 6

fold

Figure 2

trim and clip

2.  Re-fold the fabric in half and stitch along the template lines with wash-away basting thread. Trim the fabric ⅛" to ¼" from the edge, clipping the curves and corners as needed (fig. 2). Turn the strip to the right side through the top or bottom opening (fig. 3). Using a point turner, make sure the edges are turned thoroughly. Starch and press until dry. Because wash-away thread was used, pull the layers apart along the outer edge. If they can not be easily pulled apart, re-starch and press until dry. The starch is used to dissolve the wash-away thread. Lay flat and press keeping the outer edge folded to the back of the fabric (fig. 4).

3.  Trace the Madeira appliqué windows from the bodice template on the Madeira piece. Create the windows referring to "Magic Madeira Appliqué Windows"(fig. 5).

4.  Trace the bodice pattern on the bodice fabric rectangle cut earlier. Center the Madeira piece along the center of the bodice, referring to the bodice template for the neck edge placement line.

5.  Stitch the outer edges and window edges to the bodice rectangle using a #100 universal needle and a pinstitch (fig. 6).

6.  Refer to "Creating Diamond Lace Motifs" pg. 357 and create 14 lace diamond motifs. Place a motif inside each Madeira appliqué window on the bodice and zigzag in place. The remaining motifs will be for the skirt.

7.  Trace the bodice lace template on the bodice rectangle. Shape lace insertion along the template lines. Referring to the lace shaping directions. Stitch in place using a #100 universal needle and a pinstitch (fig. 7).

8.  Stitch silk ribbon lazy daisies and French knots as indicated on the bodice template. Do not stitch the flowers in the center of the lace motifs until the fabric has been cut from behind the lace (fig. 8).

9.  Cut out the bodice and trim the fabric from behind the lace motifs and the lace zigzags (fig. 9). Stitch the flowers in the center of the motifs (fig. 10).

10.  Attach the front bodice to the back bodice at the shoulders using a ¼" seam (fig. 11a).

11.  Stitch the collar pieces together along the outer edge using a ¼" seam. Trim the seam to ⅛" (fig. 11b). Turn each collar to the right side and press.

12.  Trim one fabric edge from the entredeux and clip the other fabric edge. Butt the trimmed edge to the collar edge and stitch in place with

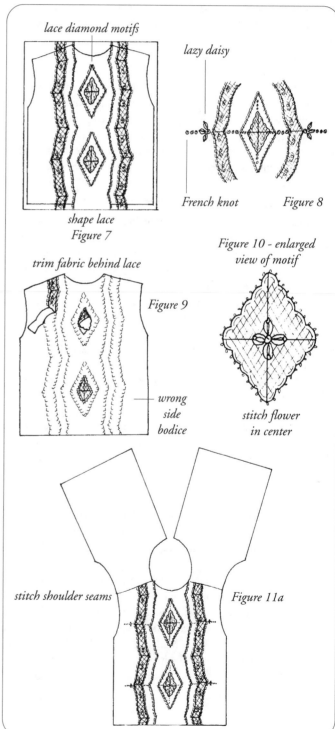

lace diamond motifs

lazy daisy

shape lace
Figure 7

French knot          Figure 8

Figure 10 - enlarged view of motif

trim fabric behind lace

Figure 9

wrong side bodice

stitch flower in center

stitch shoulder seams

Figure 11a

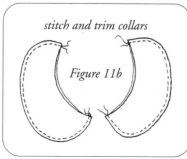

stitch and trim collars

Figure 11b

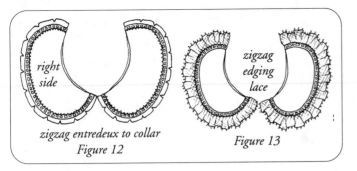

*right side*

*zigzag entredeux to collar*
Figure 12

*zigzag edging lace*

Figure 13

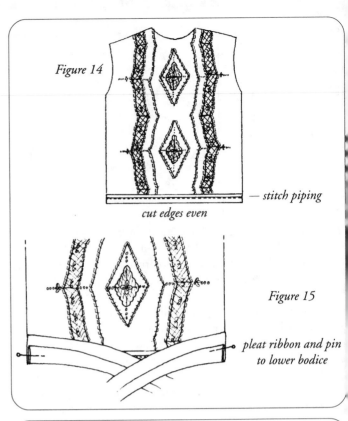

Figure 14

*cut edges even*

— *stitch piping*

Figure 15

*pleat ribbon and pin to lower bodice*

a zigzag (fig. 12). Using a tapestry needle, weave silk ribbon through the holes of the entredeux.

13. Cut the 1" edging in half, gather to fit the outer edge of the collars and stitch using the technique "entredeux to gathered lace" (fig. 13).

14. Finish the neck edge referring to the General Dress Directions, II. Neck Finishes, A. Bias Facing.

15. Create a piece of piping with the blue linen the length of the front waist. Stitch the piping to the lower edge of the front bodice with the cut edges of the piping to the cut edge of the bodice (fig. 14).

16. Cut the ribbon in half, pleat and pin to each side of the bodice front starting at the cord of the piping (fig. 15). Set aside.

## Sleeves

1. Trace the sleeve template on each sleeve. Cut a strip of blue fabric 5¹/₂" wide and 1" longer than the length of the sleeve. Complete the sleeve embellishment refer to the bodice - steps 1 to 9 (fig. 16).

2. Cut four pieces of entredeux and two pieces of lace beading to the length given on the Sleeve Band Length given in the general dress directions. Stitch the entredeux on each side of the lace beading using the technique "entredeux to lace". This creates two sleeve bands.

3. Cut two piece of lace edging (2" wide for size 2 and 4, 3" wide all other sizes) to the following measurement: Sizes 2-4 = 24" and 6-16 = 30". Gather each piece to fit the sleeve band. Attach using the technique "entredeux to gathered lace"(fig. 17).

4. Run two gathering rows in the top and bottom of each sleeve. Gather the bottom of the sleeve to fit the sleeve band. Stitch the bands to the sleeves using the technique "entredeux to gathered fabric" (fig. 18). Set sleeves aside.

## Skirt

1. Cut two pieces of blue linen 8¹/₂" wide by 45". Trace the Madeira appliqué skirt template on the wrong side of one blue piece matching the center of the template with the center of the fabric (fig. 19).

2. Refer to "Magic Madeira Appliqué Hems" (pages 340-341) and create the Madeira border for the hem. Do not stitch the hem in place until the Madeira windows are created. Transfer the Madeira window templates to the hem border fabric. Create the windows referring to "Magic Madeira Appliqué Windows" (fig. 20).

3. Stitch the side seams of the hem border to form one continuous hem piece. Stitch the side seam of the skirt so

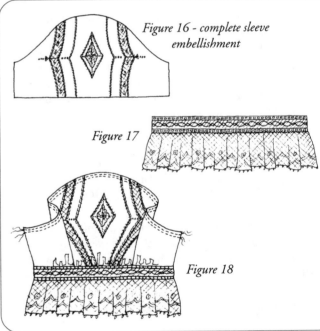

*Figure 16 - complete sleeve embellishment*

Figure 17

Figure 18

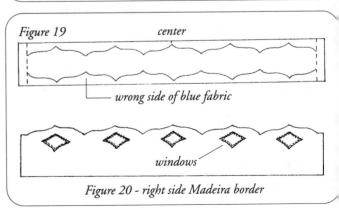

Figure 19          *center*

*wrong side of blue fabric*

*windows*

*Figure 20 - right side Madeira border*

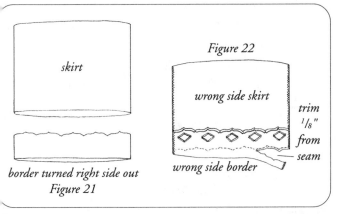

skirt

*Figure 22*

wrong side skirt

trim
¹/₈"
from
seam

wrong side border

*border turned right side out*
*Figure 21*

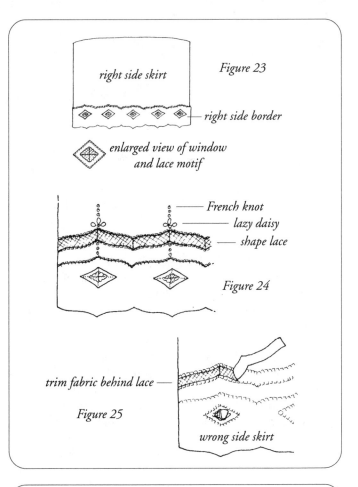

right side skirt

*Figure 23*

right side border

enlarged view of window
and lace motif

French knot
lazy daisy
shape lace

*Figure 24*

trim fabric behind lace

*Figure 25*

wrong side skirt

that the border and the skirt are the same measurement (fig. 21). Cut the underskirt pieces the same width as the skirt pieces. Set underskirt pieces aside.

- Place the right side of the hem border to the wrong side of the lower edge of the skirt, with the lower points of the hem border touching the edge of the skirt. Stitch in place along the lower edge of the hem border. Trim the skirt to the hem border fabric (fig. 22). Clip the curves and points. Flip the hem border to the right side of the skirt. Press well along the lower edge. Stitch the upper edge of the Madeira appliqué hem in place and the inside edges of the windows using a #100 universal needle and a pinstitch. Stitch a lace motif in the center of each Madeira window (fig. 23).
- Trace the skirt lace template on the skirt. Shape lace insertion along the template lines. Referring to the lace shaping directions. Stitch in place using a #100 universal needle and a pinstitch (fig. 24).
- Stitch silk ribbon lazy daisies and French knots as indicated on the template. Do not stitch the flowers in the center of the lace motifs until the fabric has been cut from behind the lace (fig. 24).
- Trim the fabric from behind the lace motifs and the lace zigzags (fig. 25). Stitch the flowers in the center of the motifs (See fig. 10).

## Underskirt

- Stitch one side seam of the underskirt in place (fig. 26).
- Stitch the four ruffle strips together to form one long strip.
- Attach the 3" edging lace to one long edge of the ruffle using the technique "lace to fabric" (fig. 27).
- Run two gathering rows in the top edge of the ruffle at ¹/₈" and ¹/₄" (fig. 27). Gather the ruffle to fit the underskirt. Stitch in place using a ¹/₄" seam (fig. 28). Overcast the seam allowance with a zigzag or serger.
- Stitch the second side seam in place (fig. 29).

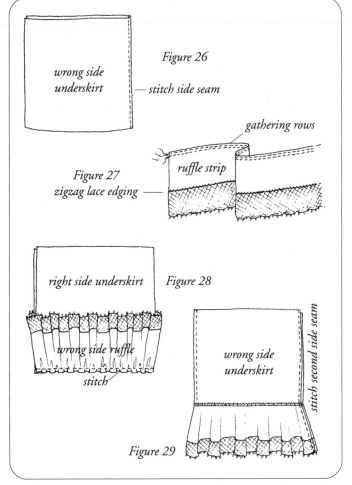

wrong side underskirt

*Figure 26*

stitch side seam

gathering rows

*Figure 27*
zigzag lace edging

ruffle strip

right side underskirt

*Figure 28*

wrong side ruffle

stitch

wrong side underskirt

stitch second side seam

*Figure 29*

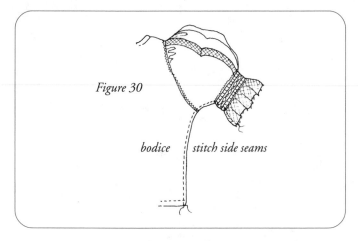

*Figure 30*

bodice | stitch side seams

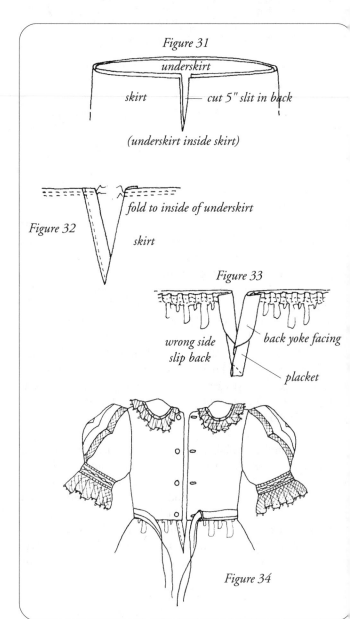

*Figure 31*

underskirt

skirt — cut 5" slit in back

(underskirt inside skirt)

*Figure 32*

fold to inside of underskirt

skirt

*Figure 33*

wrong side
slip back

back yoke facing

placket

*Figure 34*

## Constructing the Dress

1. Attach the sleeves to bodice referring to the General Dress Directions, III. Sleeves to Armholes.

2. With right sides together, sew the sides of the bodice in place (fig. 30).

3. Place the right side of the underskirt to the wrong side of the skirt, matching the top cut edges. Cut a 5" slit in the center back of both the skirt and the underskirt (fig. 31). Place a continuos lap placket in the center back of the of the dress treating the underskirt and skirt as one layer. Refer to the general dress directions - V. Continuous Lap Placket. Fold one side of the placket to the inside of the slip. Run two gathering rows at $^1/_8$" and $^1/_4$" (fig. 32). Gather the skirt/underskirt to fit the bodice with the edges of the placket to the fold line of the back bodice. Wrap the back facings around the skirt/underskirt opening (fig. 33). Stitch in place along the piping of the front bodice and using a $^1/_4$" seam along the back bodice. Overcast the seam allowance with a zigzag or serger.

4. Place buttons and buttonholes along the back bodice to close the dress.

5. A sash loop is optional but will help keep the bow from sagging. Refer to Basic Smocked Yoke Directions, XVI. Finishing the dress, B. Sash loop (p. 288) (fig. 34).

# Basic Smocked Yoke Dress

  To have a wonderfully fitting yoke dress pattern was a plan from the beginning of this book. We love smocking and I would be willing to bet many of you do! When Joanna was little I loved both bishop dresses as well as yoke dresses. Our granddaughters have worn both and have loved both. When the girls get older they tend to prefer the yoke dresses and our elementary school age girls still love wearing smocked yoke dresses to church. Since Bradley prefers dresses over pants she loves to wear them to school.

  I believe you will love our smocking plates designed especially for this book. I believe you will love the wonderfully fitting yoke dress pattern included in this book with its many variations. From years of experience sewing and designing for girls, we have learned that children come in many sizes. We have included sizes 2-16 for you in this yoke dress pattern. To describe the different versions in this book, I would like to take each dress featured in the photography and tell a little about the design and special sewing details.

## Christmas Tree Plaid Dress

When Joanna saw this dress she said, "You have to keep that dress for Cecil to wear when she is old enough." Using a red cotton Christmas plaid fabric, this dress has the most adorable smocking with a Christmas tree in the middle, packages on either side and two wreaths above the packages. The short puffed sleeves are finished with a tailored bias binding. There is plaid self piping at the top and bottom of the smocked piece of white fabric. I love the way the packages are "tied" with metallic embroidery thread, regular embroidery thread, and silk ribbon. The swags on the Christmas tree are red and gold beads threaded alternately. The balls on the tree are red and gold embroidered French knots and the gold star at the top is gold metallic thread. The white collar of the dress is piped with plaid piping. The dress closes in the back with buttons and buttonholes.

## The Tiny Tennis Blue Gingham Dress

Royal blue and white gingham fabric is the perfect setting for this adorable tennis shoe smocking design plate. Smocked on white fabric this smocked inset is piped with whipped piping in white and red. This whipped piping is used on the white collar as well as at the top and bottom of the smocking. This version is sleeveless and has a self fabric sash. The dress closes in the back with buttons and buttonholes.

*P.S. These tennis shoes would be as cute on an outfit for a little boy!*

## Let's Go Dutch Dress

This dress with its happy, fun filled fabrics and adorable smocking design plate just winks at me. The fabric is a heavy blue broadcloth; the ruffled collar is lined in pink stripes as are the ruffles over the sleeves. Both the ruffles over the sleeves and the ruffled collar are piped on the outside edge. A bias binding attaches the collar to the dress. There is a lot of back smocking on this adorable plate with its tulips and windmill. Perky polka dotted bows are stitched on each side of the plate to make this dress just too cute. The back closes with buttons and buttonholes.

## Bike Ride Dress

On a bicycle built for two Daisy and her friend are having so much fun. This adorable plate has a little boy in a straw hat and a little girl riding along. This has to be a turn of the century plate because of his straw hat, blue bow tie and her black boots. Such fun. The three balloons float behind and the wonderful cloud is in front. Choosing the perfect fabric for this yoke dress was easy. The precious blue and white gingham sets off perfectly the blue clouds and the clothing of the children. The Peter Pan collar is white and piped in the blue gingham. The cuffs are simple and sweet. Blue gingham piping is in the waistline seam and at the top of the smocked piece. The back closes with buttons and buttonholes.

## Pretty in Pinks Dress

Made of a heavy broadcloth, almost like poplin, this dress is sweet beyond sweet. The front bodice features two sets of two folded tucks; the neckline is finished with entredeux and gathered lace. The sleeves also have these two sets of two folded tucks with the gathered lace rolled and whipped to the edge of the sleeve. The sleeve is gathered with elastic. The smocking plate is mostly smocked white on white with two colors of pink for the bows and little blue flowers with green leaves finishing the look. The dress has a self sash and the back closes with buttons and buttonholes. The skirt also has two sets of two folded tucks. Piping is used at the top of the smocked skirt. What a beautiful way for a little girl to look for any occasion.

## Cupid's Hearts Dress

What a precious dress in poly/cotton broadcloth for easy upkeep and loads of wear! The round collar in white is piped in white. It perfectly frames the adorable cupid plate with the two angels holding a heart. Tiny hearts in pink and red outline the whole plate. There is a plain cuff on the dress the back closes with buttonholes and buttons. There is white piping at the top of the smocking design plate.

# Basic Smocked Yoke Dress

*High Yoke Dress Front (no smocking)*          *High Yoke Dress Back*

*Note: Yardages are listed individually for dress, sash and collar.*

## I. Fabric and Lace Requirements for the Dress ONLY

| Size | Fabric |
|------|--------|
| 2 | 2 yds. |
| 4 | $2^1/_4$ yds. |
| 6 | $2^1/_2$ yds. |
| 8 | 3 yds. |
| 10 | $3^1/_4$ yds. |
| 12 | $3^1/_2$ yds. |
| 14-16 | $3^5/_8$ yds. |

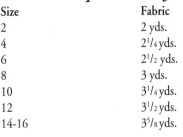

*Smocked*

## Sleeves

For smocked sleeve or elastic sleeve, add $1^1/_2$" to the length of the puffed dress sleeve.
For all sizes: $1^1/_4$ yds. of $^5/_8$" wide lace edging for smocked sleeves and sleeves with elastic

### Yardage for Fabric Sash

Sizes 2-6 - $^1/_4$ yd; Sizes 8-16 - $^1/_3$ yd

## II. Fabric and Trim Requirements for the Collars

*Use the flat trim measurements for piping, entredeux, flat lace and tatting.*
*To use gathered lace, double the amount needed for flat trim.*

*Dress Back with Sash*

| Collar Types | Sizes | Fabric | Flat Trim |
|--------------|-------|--------|-----------|
| Scalloped Round & Square | 2 - 4 | $^1/_3$ yd. | $1^1/_4$ yds. |
| | 6 | $^3/_8$ yd. | $1^3/_8$ yds. |
| | 8 - 10 | $^1/_2$ yd. | $1^1/_2$ yds. |
| | 12 - 16 | $^1/_2$ yd. | $1^3/_4$ yds. |
| Pointed | 2 | $^3/_8$ yd. | $1^1/_2$ yds. |
| | 4 | $^1/_2$ yd. | $1^1/_2$ yds. |
| | 6 | $^1/_2$ yd. | $1^3/_4$ yds. |
| | 8 - 10 | $^5/_8$ yd. | $2^1/_4$ yds. |
| | 12 - 16 | $^5/_8$ yd. | $2^3/_8$ yds. |
| Peter Pan | 2 - 6 | $^1/_4$ yd. | 1 yd. |
| | 8 - 16 | $^1/_4$ yd. | $1^1/_4$ yds. |

Embroidered Edging for Smocked or Ruffled Collars

Sizes 2 - 6:  $1^1/_4$ yds. of edging, $3^1/_2$" to 4" wide

Sizes 8 - 16:  $1^1/_2$ yds. of edging, $4^1/_2$" to 5" wide

Notions: purchased or self-made piping, buttons, 1 yd. of $^1/_4$" elastic (optional for sleeves), thread, floss and ribbon for embroidery and smocking, double-sided wash-away basting tape, washout marking pen

# General Yoke Dress Directions

**Important:** Read through all of the instructions before beginning to cut and sew, because there are many variations and options to be considered. Any sleeve and collar variation may be used for any dress, therefore no specific pattern pieces have been listed with the smocking plates.

## I. General Directions

All pattern pieces are found in the pattern envelope.

*All seams are $^1/_4$" unless otherwise noted. Overcast the seam allowances using a zigzag or serger, or make French seams.*

### A. Layout and Cutting

(Refer to the Layout Guide)

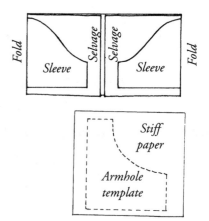

1. Follow the layout guide to cut two front yokes on the fold, two waisted bodice backs or short back yokes on the fold, and two sleeves on the fold. Collars will be cut later. It may be necessary to adjust the waisted back bodice length if the smocking rows given for a specific graph are fewer or more than the suggested number for the skirt (**refer to the chart in part B of this section for suggested number of smocking rows**). Make changes to the back bodice as follows:

   a. If the plate calls for fewer smocking rows, shorten the back bodice by about $^3/_8$" for each omitted row.

   b. If the plate calls for more smocking rows, lengthen the back bodice by about $^3/_8$" for each additional row. Be sure to check that the new back waistline will not extend lower than the child's natural waistline.

2. Sashes are optional, to be used with the waisted back bodice only.

3. Bias strips will be cut for smocked, ruffled or detached collars and bound sleeves only, or for piping. Add the amounts of piping needed for each section (yokes, collar, sleeves) to determine the total amount of bias that will be required.

4. Cut a front and a back skirt piece to the measurements given in the chart. Since a 45" wide skirt is not wide enough to smock for larger sizes, side panels will be added to sizes 8 - 16 after smocking is completed. Measurements for the side panels are included in the skirt chart. Skirt length may be adjusted by using a deeper or narrower hem, or by adding to or subtracting from the cut length of the skirt pieces. If cutting lengths are adjusted, be sure to change the front and back skirt pieces by equal amounts.

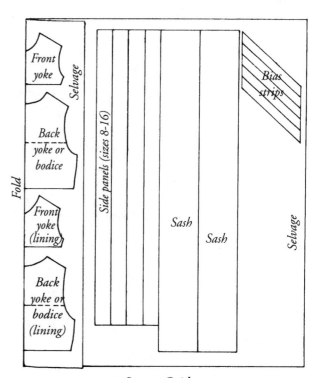

**Layout Guide**

## Cutting Lengths and Widths for Skirt Pieces

For larger sizes, the numbers in parentheses indicate the width to cut the two side panels for each smocked skirt section, and the length is the same as the main skirt piece for that size.

*A 4" hem allowance and ¹/₄" waistline seam allowance are included in the given measurements.*

NOTE: 2-6 skirt width 40" - 45"; 8 - 16 45" (side panels may be needed)

| size | yoke front and high back yoke | waisted back bodice | mid-waist back bodice |
|------|-------------------------------|---------------------|-----------------------|
| 2 | 22¹/₂" | 16 ³/₄" | 18 ³/₄" |
| 4 | 25 ³/₄" | 19¹/₄" | 21¹/₄" |
| 6 | 29 ³/₄" | 22³/₄" | 24 ³/₄" |
| 8 | 36" (2) | 28¹/₄" | 30¹/₄" |
| 10 | 37 ³/₄" (2 ³/₈) | 29¹/₂" | 31¹/₂" |
| 12 | 40¹/₄" (2 ³/₈) | 31³/₄" | 33 ³/₄" |
| 14 | 42" (2 ³/₈) | 32" | 34" |
| 16 | 43¹/₂" (2 ³/₈) | 34¹/₂" | 36¹/₂" |

## B. Charts for Pleating and Tie-off Measurements

### Suggested Number of Pleating Rows

| Size | # of Pleated Rows | # of Smocked Rows |
|------|-------------------|-------------------|
| 2 | 8 - 13 | 6 - 11 |
| 4 | 10 - 16 | 8 - 14 |
| 6 - 8 | 12 - 19 | 10 - 17 |
| 10 | 14 - 21 | 12 - 19 |
| 12 - 16 | 14 - 23 | 12 - 21 |

### Tie-off Width, cut edge to cut edge

| Size | Front |
|------|-------|
| 2 | 13¹/₂" |
| 4 | 14" |
| 6 | 14 ³/₄" |
| 8* | 12¹/₂" |
| 10* | 13" |
| 12* | 13¹/₂" |
| 14* | 13 ⁷/₈" |
| 16* | 14¹/₂" |

\* - Side panels will add width to these sizes after the smocking is completed.

## C. Construction Sequence

1. Prepare and smock the skirt front (sections II and III).

2. Attach the skirt to the front yoke to complete the dress front (section IV).

3. Prepare the skirt back and apply the placket (section V).

4. Attach the skirt back to the high back yoke or waisted bodice, and attach optional sashes (section VI).

5. Sew the dress back to the front, right sides together, at the shoulder seams (section VII).

6. Adapt the collar pattern if necessary (section VIII.B).

7. Embellish and construct the collar (section VIII.C, sections IX and X).

8. Attach the collar to the dress, or finish the collar and neck edge for a detachable collar (section XI).

9. Hand -whip the lining in place (section XI).

10. Construct the sleeves (section XII) and attach the sleeves to the dress (section XIII).

11. Sew the side seams (section XIV).

12. Turn up the hem, or make and attach a fancy band (section XV).

13. Finish the dress by adding buttonholes and buttons, and a sash loop (section XVI).

## II. Preparing the Skirt Front

*To add side panels to the skirt for sizes 8 - 16, refer to the Special Note at the end of this section before pleating the skirt piece.*

1. Fold the skirt piece in half and mark the center front with a washable pen or a small thread loop. Roll the skirt piece on a dowel and pleat the number of rows required for the smocking design (refer to the chart in section I.B). The first pleating thread should be ¹/₄" from the top edge of the fabric. If the number of rows for the graph is different from the number suggested for the skirt, the waisted back bodice must be adjusted so that the waistline seam will meet the bottom smocked row of the front skirt (refer to the instructions given in section I.A step 1) .

2. Remove the pleating threads from the ¹/₄" seam allowance at each <u>side</u> of the skirt piece. Tie-off the skirt piece to the measurements given in the chart (section I.B) (**fig. 1**).

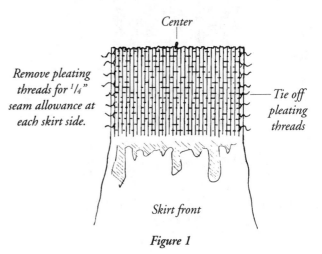

Center

Remove pleating threads for ¹/₄" seam allowance at each skirt side.

Tie off pleating threads

Skirt front

*Figure 1*

3. Steam and block the tied-off pleats. Let the fabric dry completely before smocking

4. Use the armhole template guide to mark the armhole curves. Do not cut out the armholes (**fig. 2**).

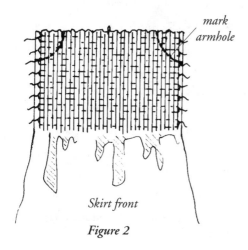

*mark armhole*

*Skirt front*

**Figure 2**

— *Special Note* —

### Adding Side Panels to Larger Sizes

*In order to have enough fullness in the pleats for sizes 8 - 16, side panels must be added to the skirt piece. The following modifications to the instructions in sections II and III will be necessary:*

1. *Pleat the center skirt piece as directed, and tie-off to the given measurement. Do not draw the armholes. The skirt will be smocked all the way across, since there are no armholes at this point.*

2. *After smocking, attach the extra pieces to each side of the center piece with a ¹/₄" seam, using a zipper foot to stitch close to the pleats (fig. a).*

3. *Use the template to draw armholes on the side panels. Stay-stitching is not necessary (fig. a).*

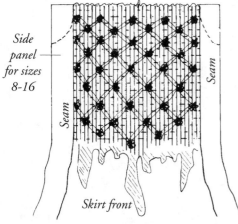

*Side panel for sizes 8-16*

*Seam*

*Seam*

*Skirt front*

**Figure A**

## III. Smocking the Skirt Front

1. Remember that the top and bottom pleating rows are the stabilizer rows. They are not part of the smocking design. The top row may be smocked with cables or stem stitch, on the right or wrong side, to make construction easier.

2. Refer to the individual graphs for specific smocking instructions. Refer to the Special Note found earlier on this page for smocking sizes 8 - 16. For sizes 2 - 6, stop the smocking at the armhole guide lines (**fig. 1**).

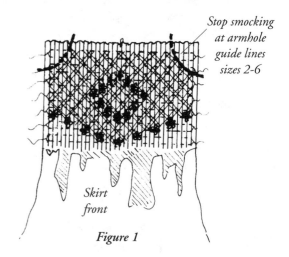

*Stop smocking at armhole guide lines sizes 2-6*

*Skirt front*

**Figure 1**

3. Refer to the graphs and stitch keys for embroidery placement.

4. Stay-stitch along the armhole guide lines with a tiny zigzag or straight stitch to hold the pleats (**fig. 2**).

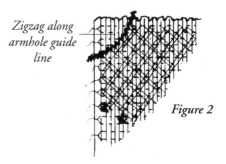

*Zigzag along armhole guide line*

**Figure 2**

5. Re-block the smocking if needed before constructing the dress.

6. Do not remove the pleating threads until the dress is constructed.

## IV. Assembling the Dress Front

1. Cut out the armholes on the skirt front piece, being careful not to cut through the stay-stitching, and do not cut off the knots of the smocking.

2. For a piped yoke:

    a. Cut a piece of piping the length of the bottom edge of the front yoke pattern.

    b. To attach the piping, place double-sided wash-away basting tape along the seam allowance of purchased or self-made piping. Stick the piping to the smocked skirt piece, just above the top row of smocking (the seam allowance is 1/2"). Be sure to keep the piping straight (**fig. 1**).

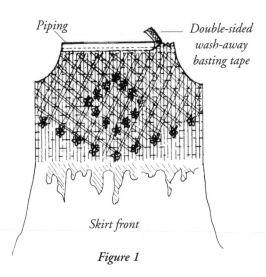

*Figure 1*

    c. Place one front yoke piece to the skirt piece, right sides together, and pin in place (**fig. 2**).

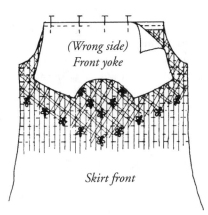

*Figure 2*

    d. Use a zipper foot or cording foot to stitch through all the layers, close to the piping (refer to fig. 2).

    e. Press the seam toward the yoke, exposing the piping (**fig. 3**).

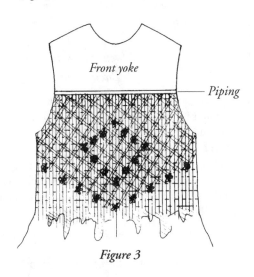

*Figure 3*

3. If a smocked panel is used, refer to the technique section "Add Fabric Panels to the Sides of the Smocked Panel."

**Bike Ride Smocked Dress**

## V. Preparing the Skirt Back

*If the dress back will be smocked, refer to the Special Note at the end of this section before completing section A below.*

### A. Applying a Placket and Piping to a High Back Yoke

1. For an unsmocked back skirt, trace and cut out the armholes ( if the skirt will be smocked, refer to the Special Note at the end of this section). Fold the back skirt piece in half and make a light crease along the center back. Cut a 4" slit along the crease at the top of the skirt. Run two rows of gathering stitches, 1/4" and 1/2" from the top edges of the back skirt piece, stopping the stitches 1/4" from the slit and the side edges (**fig. 1**).

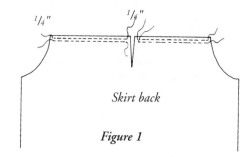

*Figure 1*

2. Cut two pieces of piping, each 1" longer than the bottom edge of the back yoke pattern (**fig. 2** ).

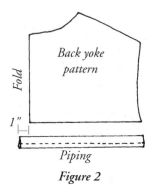

*Figure 2*

3. Pull the gathering threads (or pleating threads) out of the way and place the piping to the right side of the skirt piece, with the stitching of the piping lined up on the 1/2" seam allowance of the skirt. Pin the piping in place for 2"on each side of the slit, but do not stitch (**fig. 3**).

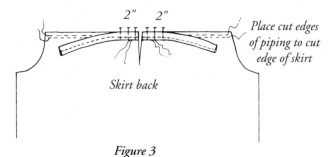

*Figure 3*

4. Cut a piece of fabric for the placket, 1" x 8" with one long side on the selvage. Open the slit in the skirt out to form a straight line and place the raw edge of the slit along the long cut edge of the placket piece, right sides together. There will be a small "V" shape at the bottom of the slit, this is normal. Use a 1/4" seam to stitch the skirt to the placket, with the skirt on top. The ends of the piping will be caught in the seam. *Do not* catch the gathering threads in the seam. The seam will catch only a few threads of the skirt slit at the "V" (**fig. 4**).

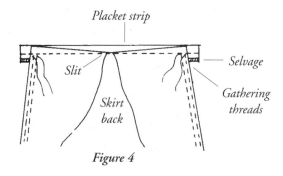

*Figure 4*

5. Press the seam toward the placket piece. Fold the selvage edge of the placket to the inside and whip the selvage edge to the stitching line (**fig. 5**).

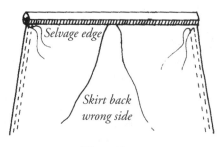

*Figure 5*

6. On the wrong side of the skirt piece, fold the placket in half so that the top edges of the skirt meet. Stitch a small dart across the bottom of the placket on the inside, being careful not to catch the skirt in the stitching (**fig. 6**).

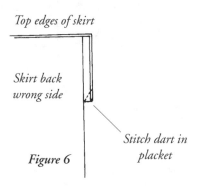

*Figure 6*

7. Fold the right placket to the inside and leave the left placket extended. The finished dress will lap right over left (**fig. 7**).

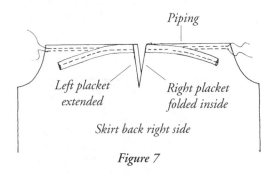

*Piping*

*Left placket extended*   *Right placket folded inside*

*Skirt back right side*

**Figure 7**

8. Pull up the gathering threads or adjust the smocking to make the skirt fit the yokes, matching the edges of the placket to the back fold line (**fig. 8**).

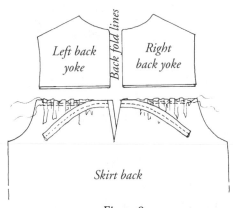

*Left back yoke*   *Back fold lines*   *Right back yoke*

*Skirt back*

**Figure 8**

9. Apply washout basting tape to the side of the piping seam allowance that will be against the skirt. Stick the piping to the skirt, matching the stitching line of the piping to the $1/2$" seam allowance. Use a zipper foot to baste close to the piping (**fig. 9**).

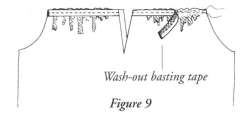

*Wash-out basting tape*

**Figure 9**

## B. Applying a Placket to an Unpiped High Back Yoke or Waisted Back Bodice

1. For an unsmocked high-yoke skirt, trace and cut out the armholes.

2. Fold the back skirt piece in half and make a light crease along the center back. Cut a 4" slit along the crease at the top of the skirt. Run two rows of gathering stitches, $1/4$" and $1/2$" from the top edges of the back skirt piece, stopping the stitches $1/4$" from the slit (refer to fig. 1 in part A of this section).

3. Cut a piece of fabric for the placket, 1" x 8" with one long side on the selvage. Open the slit out to form a straight line and place the raw edge of the slit along the long cut edge of the placket piece, right sides together. There will be a small "V" shape at the bottom of the slit, this is normal. Use a $1/4$" seam to stitch the skirt to the placket, with the skirt on top. The seam will catch only a few threads of the skirt slit at the "V" (refer to fig. 4 in part A of this section).

4. Press the seam toward the placket piece. Fold the selvage edge of the placket to the inside and whip the selvage edge to the stitching line (refer to fig. 5 in part A of this section).

5. On the wrong side of the skirt piece, fold the placket in half so that the top edges of the skirt meet. Stitch a small dart across the bottom of the placket on the inside, being careful not to catch the skirt in the stitching (refer to fig. 6 in part A of this section).

6. Fold the right placket to the inside and leave the left placket extended. The finished dress will lap right over left (**fig. 10**).

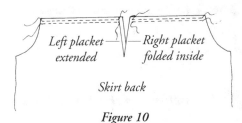

*Left placket extended*   *Right placket folded inside*

*Skirt back*

**Figure 10**

7. Pull up the gathering threads to make the skirt fit the bodice, matching the edges of the placket to the back fold line (**fig. 11**).

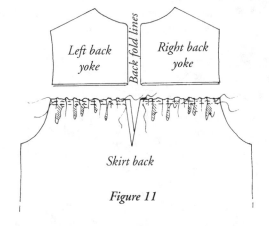

*Left back yoke*   *Back fold lines*   *Right back yoke*

*Skirt back*

**Figure 11**

## Smocked Back Skirt

*If the dress back will be smocked, use the high back yoke option with piping. It will be necessary to make the following modifications to the instructions given in section V.A:*

1.  *For sizes 8 - 16, refer to the Special Note at the end of section II, then continue with these instructions.*

2.  *After cutting the placket slit (section V.A, step 1), pleat the top of the skirt with the same number of rows as the skirt front. Be sure that the second edge of the placket slit goes into the pleater straight.*

3.  *After pleating, separate the edges of the slit, pull some slack into the pleating threads and cut them to allow the slit to open. Remove the pleating threads from ¹/₄" at the slit edges and the sides (**fig. a**).*

Remove pleating threads

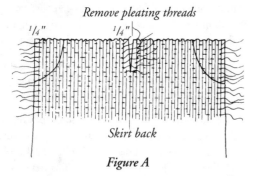

¹/₄"    ¹/₄"

Skirt back

**Figure A**

4.  *Apply the placket as directed in section V.A, steps 2 - 7. Line up the corded edge of the piping just above the top row of smocking.*

5.  *Pull up the pleating threads and tie-off to the measurements given in the chart (section I.B). Mark the armholes for sizes 2 - 6. Smock according to the directions in section III.*

6.  *Continue with section V.A, step 9, placing the piping just above the top row of smocking.*

# VI. Assembling the Dress Back

## A. Bodice to Skirt

1.  Press a crease in the bodice back pieces along the foldline. This creates a lining for each bodice piece. Make sure that one piece is the right bodice and the other is the left bodice. Mark the pieces so that the bodice section will not be confused with the lining section (**fig. 1**).

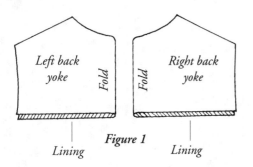

Left back yoke    Fold    Fold    Right back yoke

**Figure 1**

Lining    Lining

2.  Pin one bodice section to the skirt, right sides together. The crease in the bodice will meet the edge of the placket (remember that the right placket is folded to the inside, the crease will meet the foldline). Adjust the skirt gathers to fit the bodice and baste the bodice to the skirt (**fig. 2**).

Crease in bodice meets edge of right placket

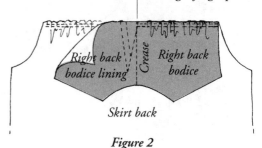

Right back bodice lining    Crease    Right back bodice

Skirt back

**Figure 2**

3.  Stitch in place with a ¹/₄" seam. If piping is used, the seam should be stitched close to the piping with a zipper foot. Trim the seam and press the bodice up (**fig. 3**).

Lining folded in

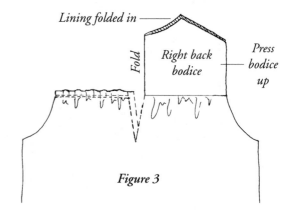

Fold    Right back bodice    Press bodice up

**Figure 3**

4.  Repeat steps 1 - 3 for the remaining bodice piece.

**High Yoke Dress Back**

## B. Sashes for Waisted Back Bodice

1. Cut sash pieces to the following sizes:

   Sizes 2 - 6:   4¹/₂" by 36"

   Sizes 8 - 16:   5¹/₂" by 45"

2. Stitch ¹/₈" from the edge on each long side, using a short straight stitch. Press the long edges to the wrong side along the stitching lines. Press another ¹/₈" on each long side to create a ¹/₈" double hem. Also press ¹/₄" along one short end (**fig. 4**).

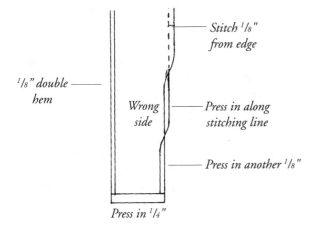

¹/₈" double hem

Stitch ¹/₈" from edge

Wrong side

Press in along stitching line

Press in another ¹/₈"

Press in ¹/₄"

*Figure 4*

3. Stitch the hem on one long side only. Fold and press the stitched corner of the pressed short end to meet the opposite unhemmed long edge, forming a triangular pocket at the end of the sash (**fig. 5**).

4. If you would like to add a touch of embroidery to the sash, open out the triangular fold and stitch a small flower on the right side of the sash, positioned so that the folded triangle will hide the back of the embroidery (**fig. 6**).

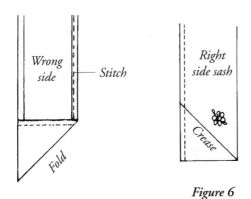

Wrong side

Stitch

Fold

*Figure 5*

Right side sash

Crease

*Figure 6*

5. Refold the triangular piece. Hem the remaining long edge, stitching through the folded end. Tack the center of the open pocket edge in place with invisible stitches (**fig. 7**).

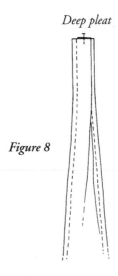

Wrong side

Tack

Hem through folded end

*Figure 7*

6. Fold a deep pleat at the unhemmed end of the sash, so that the long edges almost fold over each other (**fig. 8**).

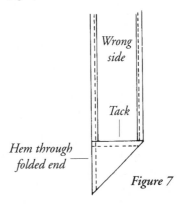

Deep pleat

*Figure 8*

7. Place the raw ends of the sash pieces at the sides of the bodice back, with the bottom edge of the sash overlapping the waistline seam by ¹/₄". Baste the sash pieces in place (**fig. 9**).

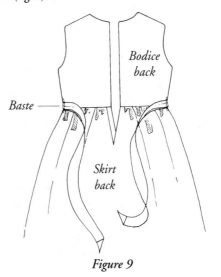

Bodice back

Baste

Skirt back

*Figure 9*

## VII. Shoulder Seams

1. Open out the back bodice linings. Pin the dress front to the dress back at the shoulder seams, right sides together. Stitch the seams. Do not stitch the lining in this seam (**fig. 1**).

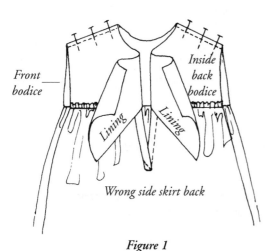

*Figure 1*

2. With right sides together, stitch the remaining front yoke piece to the bodice back lining sections at the shoulder seams. Press all of the shoulder seams open (**fig. 2**).

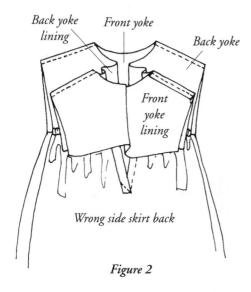

*Figure 2*

## VIII. Peter Pan and Flat Collar Variations and Construction

### A. Variations

There are several collar variations presented here. Smocked or ruffled collars are described, as well as shaped flat collars: Round, Square, Pointed and Scalloped. The trimming methods described are embroidery, piping, piping with gathered lace, entredeux with flat lace or tatting and entredeux

with gathered lace. The pattern piece for each collar will show which trim method it was designed to use. There is also a section explaining how to adapt a pattern for different trims.

After the pattern is adapted (if necessary) for the chosen trims, refer to the section describing that particular trim. Application of that trim to the various collar types will be discussed.

### B. Adapting Collar Patterns for Different Trims

When adapting a pattern for trims, adjustments will be made to only those edges where the trim is applied. The neck seam will not be changed on any pattern. The trim may not extend up the center back edges of some shaped collars; in that case, the center back edge will not be adjusted. For some large flat collars, the width of the trim will not affect the look of the collar enough to make any adjustment necessary. In all cases, the seam allowance will remain the same as indicated on the pattern.

In figures 1 - 4, the solid line is the original cutting line, and the dotted line is the new cutting line.

1. If a collar is designed for no trim and trim will be added, subtract the finished width of the trim from only the outer edge of the pattern piece. The change may be as little as $^1/_8$" for baby piping, or as much as $^5/_8$" for entredeux and lace edging. Do not change the neck seam (**fig. 1**).

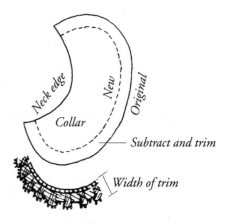

*Figure 1*

2. If the collar is designed for trim (the size will be specified on the pattern), a different size trim may be used by making the following adjustments:

a. To apply narrower trim, measure the difference in the two trim sizes and add that amount to the outer edge of the collar pattern, do not change the neck (**fig. 2**).

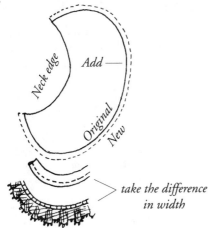

*Figure 2*

b. To apply wider trim, measure the difference in the two trim sizes and subtract that amount from the outer edge of the collar pattern, do not change the neck (**fig. 3**).

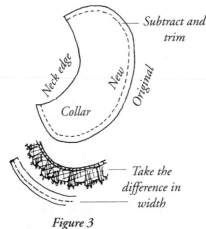

*Figure 3*

3. If the collar is designed for trim and the trim will be omitted, add the width of the trim to the outer edge of the collar pattern, do not change the neck (**fig. 4**).

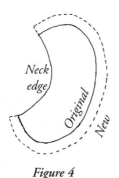

*Figure 4*

## C. General Instructions for Peter Pan or Flat Collar Construction

Some trim applications will be done before construction and some will be applied after construction. The specific instructions for each trim method will refer to this construction section at the right time.

1. Place the collar pieces with right sides together and stitch around the outer edge with a short straight stitch, leaving the neck seam open (**fig. 5**).

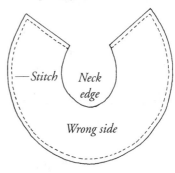

*Figure 5*

2. Set the machine for a tiny zigzag and stitch again, just outside the previous stitching. Trim the seam close to the zigzag (**fig. 6**).

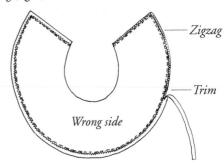

*Figure 6*

3. Trim diagonally across outside corners (square and pointed collars, and the back edge of the round collar) and clip into inside points (scalloped collars). Be careful not to clip into the stitches. If the seam is very small, it may not be necessary to clip around curves (round, pointed and scalloped collars) (**fig. 7**).

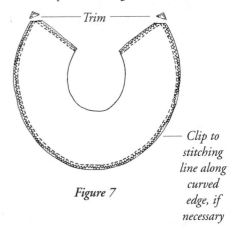

*Figure 7*

4. Turn the collar to the right side and press the edges well. Baste the neck edges together (**fig. 8**).

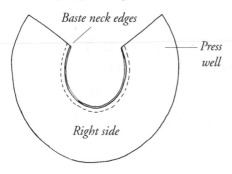

Figure 8

# IX. Collar Embellishment for Peter Pan and Flat Collars

## A. Embroidery

1. Embroidery should be the first embellishment added to a collar. When adding embroidery to a plain collar, be sure that the design fits in the required space with a little space between the design and the seam line. Allow a little extra room at the neck edge to allow for the fold of the collar to the outside (**fig. 1**).

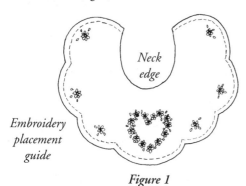

Figure 1

2. Trace the pattern onto fabric that is at least 1" larger than the pattern on all sides and stay-stitch around the collar outline, but do not cut out the collar. This prevents the collar from stretching as the embroidery work is done, and it also allows more room to work close to the seam lines (**fig. 2**).

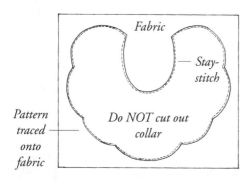

Figure 2

3. Refer to general embroidery instructions for information on design transfer, hoops, supplies and stitching.

4. Embroidered pieces should be pressed facedown on a padded surface.

5. Cut out the collar pieces and refer to the specific instructions in section IX for any other trims to be added, then construct the collar according to section VIII.C.

## B. Baby Piping

1. Pattern Adjustments:

   a. To add baby piping to a plain collar, refer to section VIII.B, step 1.

   b. To use baby piping on a collar designed for wider trim, refer to section VIII.B, step 2a.

   c. To omit piping, refer to section VIII.B, step 3.

2. Cut the collars from the fabric.

3. Trim the seam allowance of the piping to ¹/₄". Clip the seam allowance of the piping so that it will lay smoothly around the collar curves (**fig. 4**).

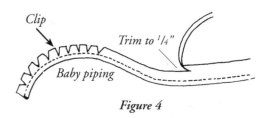

Figure 4

4. Place the piping around the outer edge of the collar piece. The raw edge of the piping should meet the raw edge of the collar. If the piping does not lay flat, add more clips or make the clips a little deeper, but do not cut through the stitching. Be sure that there is a clip where the piping goes around a corner (square or pointed collars, back edge of round collars) or into a point (scalloped collars) (**fig. 5**).

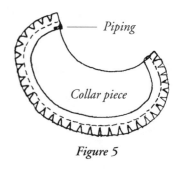

Figure 5

5. Use a cording foot or zipper foot to baste the piping in place, with the stitches close to the cord of the piping (**fig. 6**).

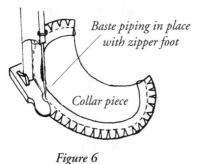

Figure 6

6. Refer to section VIII.C to construct the collar. Use a zipper foot and work with the piped pieces on top so that you can stitch right on top of the previous stitching line.

## C. Baby Piping with Gathered Lace

1. Pattern adjustments:

   a. To add gathered lace and piping to a plain collar, refer to section VIII.B, step 1. The actual width of the lace will be used as the finished width, because this method does not take up a seam allowance in the lace. Since the piping will overlap the lace, no other adjustments are needed.

   b. To add gathered lace to a collar already designed for baby piping, refer to section VIII.B, step 2b. Subtract ⅛" from the actual lace width and use this number as the difference.

2. Apply baby piping and construct the collar as directed in section IX.C.

3. Gather the lace by pulling the top thread of the heading. Adjust the gathers evenly.

4. Working on the wrong side of the collar, place the right side of the lace heading over the piping and whip the lace to the under collar (**fig. 7**).

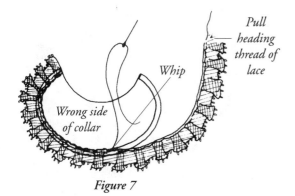

Figure 7

## D. Entredeux with Lace

1. Pattern Adjustments:

   a. To add entredeux and lace to a plain collar, refer to section VIII.B, step 1 and use the combined widths of the lace and trimmed entredeux as the finished width.

   b. To change the width of the trim on a collar designed for a specific size trim, refer to section VIII.B, step 2.

2. Construct the collar according to section VIII.C.

3. Trim the batiste border from one side of the entredeux. Clip the other border of the entredeux so that it will lie smoothly around curves and corners.

4. Place the collar on a pinning board and shape the entredeux around the outer edge of the collar. Pin the entredeux in place and steam to shape it. For corners (square or pointed collars, back edge of round collars) or points (scalloped collars), the entredeux may be cut and overlapped by one hole to give sharp points (**fig. 8**).

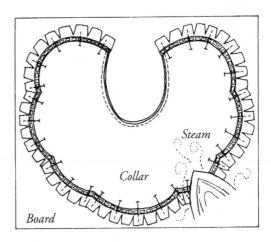

Figure 8

5. After the entredeux has dried completely, butt it to the edge of the collar and hand-whip or zigzag it in place. If a zigzag is used, make sure that the needle goes into each hole of the entredeux. Trim the remaining border from the edge of the entredeux (**fig. 9**).

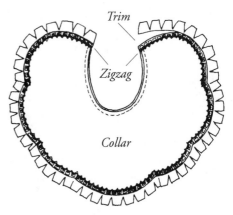

Figure 9

6. To shape flat lace around curves (round, pointed and scalloped collars):

   a. Place the collar on a pinning board and butt the lace to the edge of the entredeux, following the shape of the collar.

   b. To go around curves, pin the outer edge of the lace flat, then use a pin to pull the heading thread just enough to make the heading lie flat around the curve. Steam the lace to shape it, then let it dry completely before attaching it to the entredeux (refer to step 9 in this section) (**fig. 10**).

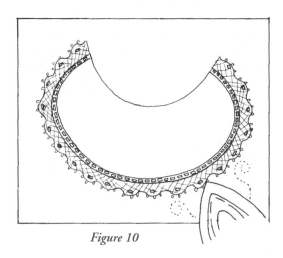

*Figure 10*

7. To miter flat lace around corners and points (square, pointed and scalloped collars):

   a. Use a wash-out pencil to draw a line to bisect and extend beyond each corner or point that will be mitered (**fig. 11**).

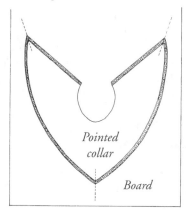

*Pointed collar*

*Board*

*Figure 11*

b. Butt the lace heading to the entredeux and pin, following the collar shape until a corner or point is reached. Place pins through the lace at both points where the bisecting line crosses the lace edges (**fig. 12**).

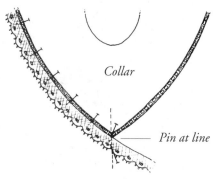

*Collar*

*Pin at line*

*Figure 12*

c. Fold the lace back on itself, in the direction it just came from. Remove the pin at the wide edge of the miter and replace it on the line, through both layers of lace (**fig. 13**).

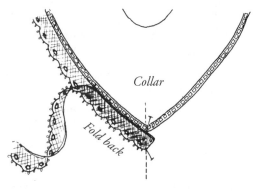

*Collar*

*Fold back*

*Figure 13*

d. Flip the lace open and re-pin the miter, then continue down the next section of the collar (**fig. 14**).

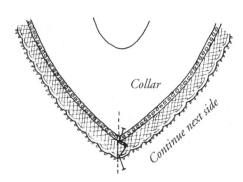

*Collar*

*Continue next side*

*Figure 14*

e.  Refer to step 9 in this section to attach the lace.

8.  To gather lace, pull the gathering threads in the lace heading and adjust the gathers evenly. When going around an outside corner, readjust the gathers so that there is a little extra fullness at the corner. When going into an inside point, readjust the gathers so that there is a little less fullness (**fig. 15**).

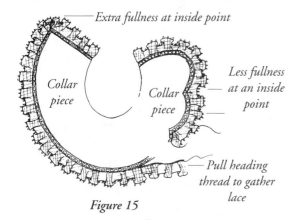

Extra fullness at inside point

Collar piece

Collar piece

Less fullness at an inside point

Pull heading thread to gather lace

**Figure 15**

9.  To attach the lace, butt the edge of the lace heading to the entredeux and whip by hand or zigzag, making sure that the needle goes into every hole of the entredeux (**fig. 16**).

Zigzag

Collar

**Figure 16**

## X. Smocked or Ruffled Collars

1.  Cut a piece of embroidered Swiss edging to the following sizes, with one long side along the decorative edge:

Sizes 2 - 6: 40" long and $3^1/_2$" to 4" wide

Sizes 8 - 16: 50" long and $4^1/_2$ to 5" wide

### Piped Ruffle Option

a.  Cut two fabric strips to the following measurements: sizes 2 to 6 = $2^3/_4$" by 36", sizes 8 to 10 = 3" by 39", and sizes 12 to 16 = $3^1/_4$". This will be one outer ruffle piece and one lining piece. Note: The lining piece can be cut from contrasting fabric, if desired.

b.  Create the ruffle referring to Section XIII-B, "Sleeveless Option With Angel Ruffle", step 2 to 4.

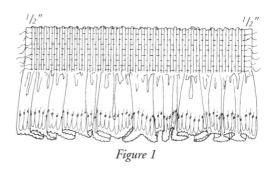

2.  For a ruffled collar, run two gathering rows, $1/_8$" and $1/_4$" from the top edge of the edging, stopping the stitching $1/_2$" from the ends. Refer to step 6 of this section to hem the ends.

3.  For a smocked collar, roll the edging onto a dowel and pleat the required rows called for on the graph. Remember to pleat two extra rows, to be used as holding rows. The first pleating row should be $1/_4$" from the top edge of the collar. Remove the pleating threads from $1/_2$" at each edge, to create seam allowances (**fig. 1**).

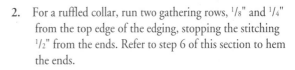

$1/_2$"                    $1/_2$"

**Figure 1**

4.  Shape and block the collar, using steam to set the pleats. Let the collar dry completely before smocking (**fig. 2**).

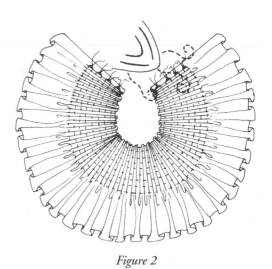

**Figure 2**

5.  Smock the top holding row with a stem stitch; this replaces backsmocking and will make construction easier. Smock the collar according to the specific instructions with the graph. Re-block after smocking, if necessary.

**6.** Turn under ¹/₄" and then ¹/₄" again at the collar back edges, to form a hem. Stitch the folded edge of the hem to the back side of the collar (**fig. 3**).

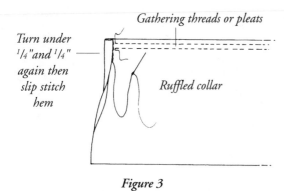

*Turn under ¹/₄"and ¹/₄" again then slip stitch hem*

*Gathering threads or pleats*

*Ruffled collar*

*Figure 3*

# XI. Completing the Collar and Neck Edge

## A. Attaching Peter Pan and Wide Flat Collars to the Dress

**1.** Push the yoke lining out of the way and pin the completed collar to the neck edge of the dress, matching the center fronts and center backs. The wrong side of the collar will be against the right side of the dress. The center back edges of all collars should meet the center back line of the dress back. The two sections of Peter Pan collars should just meet each other at the center front as they cross the ¹/₄" seam allowance line. Baste the collar in place (**fig. 1**).

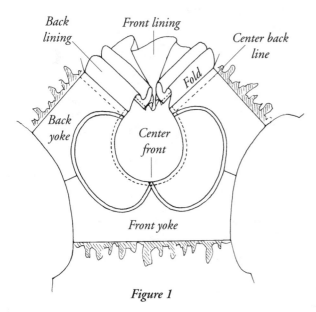

*Back lining*

*Front lining*

*Center back line*

*Fold*

*Back yoke*

*Center front*

*Front yoke*

*Figure 1*

**2.** Fold the lining over the bodice (right sides will be together, with the collar in between the layers) and pin along the neck edge. Make sure that center fronts and shoulder seams are matched, and the back edge is turned to the outside along the fold. Stitch through all layers with a ¹/₄" seam (**fig. 2**).

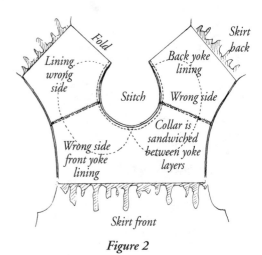

*Fold*

*Lining wrong side*

*Skirt back*

*Back yoke lining*

*Stitch*

*Wrong side*

*Collar is sandwiched between yoke layers*

*Wrong side front yoke lining*

*Skirt front*

*Figure 2*

**3.** Trim and clip the neck seam. Turn the lining to the inside and press well.

**4.** Turn under the ¹/₄" seam allowance at the bottom lining edges and whip the lining to the waistline seams of the dress back and the dress front (**fig. 3**).

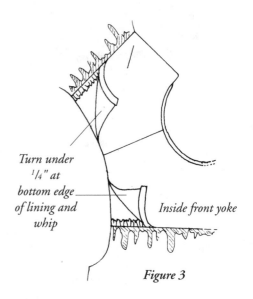

*Turn under ¹/₄" at bottom edge of lining and whip*

*Inside front yoke*

*Figure 3*

## B. Attaching Smocked or Ruffled Collars to the Dress

1. Fold the bodice lining to the wrong side of the dress, wrong sides together, matching the center fronts and shoulder seams. Baste the two layers together along the neck edge (**fig. 4**).

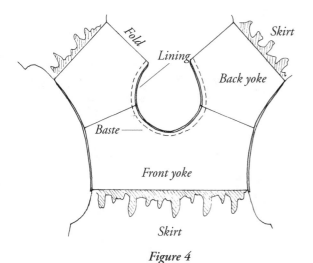

*Figure 4*

2. Pin the completed collar to the dress at the neck edge, with the center fronts matched. The left back collar edge should stop 1" from the back fold. The right back collar edge should meet the back fold. Adjust the pleats or gathers to fit. The wrong side of the collar will be against the right side of the dress. Baste the collar to the dress (**fig. 5**).

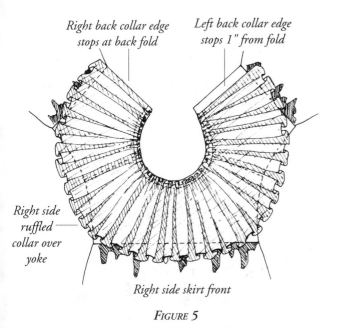

FIGURE 5

3. Cut a bias strip 2" wide and ¹/₂" longer than the neck edge of the dress.

4. Fold the bias strip with wrong sides together and long edges meeting. Press the folded strip (**fig. 6**).

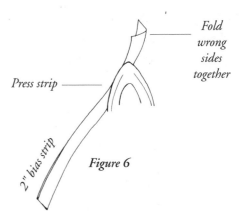

*Figure 6*

5. Place the raw edges of the bias strip even with the raw neck edge of the dress. Let the bias strip extend ¹/₄" past the folded back edges of the dress. Stitch the bias strip in place with a ¹/₂" seam. Trim the seam to a neat ¹/₄" (**fig. 7**).

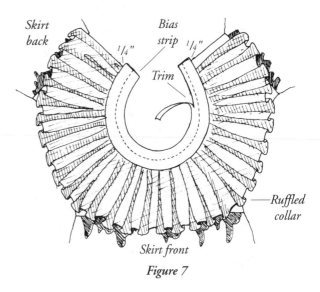

*Figure 7*

6. Press the seam toward the bias strip. Fold the two ¹/₄" back extensions to the inside (**fig. 8**).

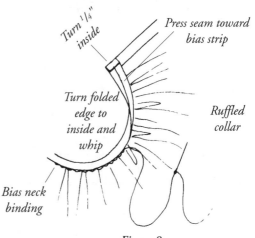

*Figure 8*

7. Turn the folded edge of the bias strip to the inside to meet the stitching line, and whip the bias strip to the seam by hand (refer to fig. 8).

8. Turn under the $^{1}/_{4}$" seam allowance at the bottom lining edges and whip the lining to the waistline seams of the dress back and the dress front (refer to fig. 3 in part A of this section ).

## XII. Sleeve Construction

### Sleeve Band Measurements

Use the following measurements for cutting elastic or bias binding, or for tying-off smocked sleeves:

| Size | Each Sleeve |
|------|-------------|
| 2 | $8^{1}/_{4}$" |
| 4 | $9^{1}/_{4}$" |
| 6 | $9^{7}/_{8}$" |
| 8 | $10^{1}/_{4}$" |
| 10 | $10^{1}/_{2}$" |
| 12 | $10^{3}/_{4}$" |
| 14 | 11" |
| 16 | 11" |

### A. Smocked Sleeves

*Add $1^{1}/_{2}$" to the length of the sleeve pattern*

1. Mark the center top and bottom of the sleeve before pleating. Roll the sleeves onto a dowel and pleat the required number of rows. Remember to pleat two extra rows to be used as stabilizer rows. Let the bottom edge of the sleeve run through the pleater groove that is two away from the last threaded needle, or as directed in the instructions for a specific sleeve. Leave long pleating threads so that the sleeve can be flattened after pleating.

2. Flatten the sleeve and finish the bottom edge with lace:

   a. Place a piece of flat edging along the bottom edge of the sleeve, right sides together. The heading of the lace should be $^{1}/_{8}$" from the raw edge of the sleeve (**fig. 1**).

*Use the technique "Lace to Flat Fabric"*

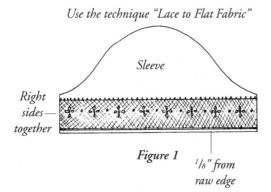

Right sides together

Sleeve

*Figure 1*

$^{1}/_{8}$" from raw edge

b. Set the machine for a zigzag stitch. The stitch should be wide enough that the left "zig" goes over the heading of the lace and the right "zag" goes all the way off the edge of the fabric. (**fig. 2**).

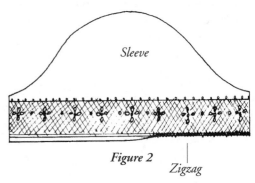

Sleeve

*Figure 2*

Zigzag

c. Press the lace open.

3. Remove the pleating threads from 1" of fabric at each side of the sleeve and run two gathering rows across the top of the sleeve, $^{1}/_{8}$" and $^{1}/_{4}$" from the edge (**fig. 3**).

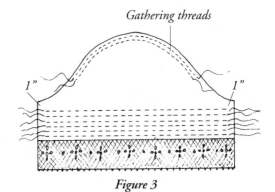

Gathering threads

1"    1"

*Figure 3*

4. Pull up the pleats and tie-off to the measurements in the chart, from cut edge to cut edge. Steam the pleats and let dry completely before smocking.

5. Smock the sleeves according to the chosen graph. If the sleeves are too loose after smocking, they may be backsmocked, or a ribbon of the correct length may be hand-whipped to the back side of the smocking (**fig. 4**).

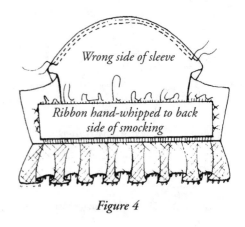

*Wrong side of sleeve*

*Ribbon hand-whipped to back side of smocking*

*Figure 4*

6. Refer to section XIII to attach the sleeves to the dress.

## B. Sleeves with Bias Binding

For this sleeve option, cut the puffed sleeve along the "girl's dress sleeve cutting line."

1. Run two gathering rows across the top and bottom of the sleeves, ⅛" and ¼" from the edges (**fig. 5**).

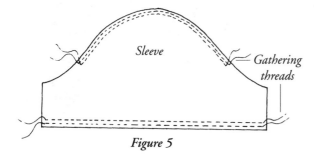

*Figure 5*

2. Cut two bias strips 1⅝" wide by the measurement given in the chart, or measure the child's arm and add ½". Fold the bias strips with wrong sides together and long edges meeting. Press the folded strips (**fig. 6**).

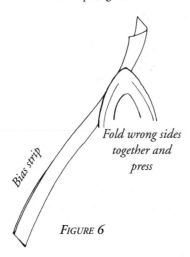

*Figure 6*

3. Place the raw edges of the bias strips even with the bottom edge of the sleeves. Pull up the gathers to make the bottom of the sleeves fit the bias strips, stopping the gathers 1" from each edge. Pin and stitch the bias strips in place with a ¼" seam. Trim the seam to a neat ⅛" (**fig. 7**).

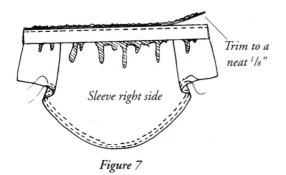

*Figure 7*

4. Press the seam toward the bias strip and attach the sleeves to the dress (refer to section XIII). Sew the side seams of the dress (refer to section XIV).

5. Turn the folded edge of the bias strips to the inside of the sleeves, letting the edges meet the stitching lines that attached the bindings. Whip the bindings to the seam by hand (**fig. 8**).

*Figure 8*

## C. Elastic in the Sleeves

*Add 1½" to the length of the puffed sleeve (girl's dress cutting line)*

1. Mark the elastic placement line on the wrong side of the sleeves with a washable pen or pencil, 1½" from the bottom edge (**fig. 9**).

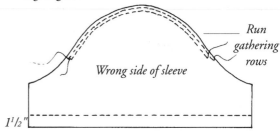

*FIGURE 9*

2. Attach flat edging to the bottom edge of the sleeve according to section XII.A, step 2.

3. Cut a piece of elastic to the size of the upper arm of the child plus ¼". Use the lengths given in the chart if the child is not available to be measured. Lay the elastic over the placement line and straight stitch down the middle of the elastic at one edge of the sleeve for ⅝" (**fig. 10**).

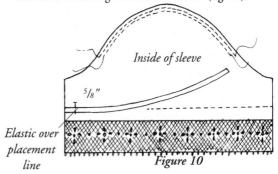

*Figure 10*

5. Raise the needle and set the machine for a zigzag stitch wide enough to clear both edges of the elastic. Stretch the elastic along the placement line and zigzag over it to within ⁵/₈" of the other edge of the sleeve. Set the machine back to a straight stitch and stitch down the middle of the elastic to the edge of the sleeve (**fig. 11**).

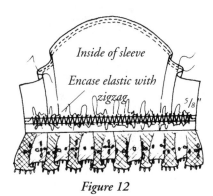

*Inside of sleeve*

*Encase elastic with zigzag*

⁵/₈"

**Figure 12**

## XIII. Attaching the Sleeves to the Dress

1. Baste the bodice and the lining together at the armhole edge (**fig. 1**).

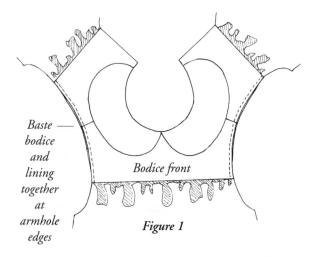

*Baste bodice and lining together at armhole edges*

*Bodice front*

**Figure 1**

2. Pull up the gathers at the top of the sleeves to fit the armhole. Pin the sleeves to the dress, matching the center of the sleeve top edge to the shoulder seam of the dress. Adjust the gathers to stop at the yoke line in front and in the back. If a sleeve cap ruffle and yoke overlay are used, the bottom edge of the ruffle should meet the bottom edge of the overlay (**fig. 2**).

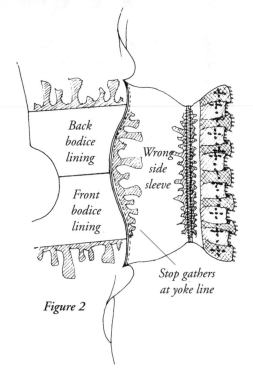

*Back bodice lining*

*Front bodice lining*

*Wrong side sleeve*

*Stop gathers at yoke line*

**Figure 2**

3. Stitch the sleeves in place with a ¹/₄" seam. Remove the extra gathering thread and pleating threads.

### XIII-A - Sleeveless Option

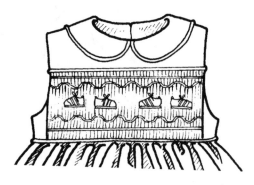

1. Cut a bias strip longer than the circumference of the sleeve opening and 1" wide.

2. Fold the strip in half, long sides together and press (**fig. 1**).

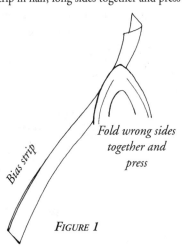

*Bias strip*

*Fold wrong sides together and press*

**FIGURE 1**

3. Place the cut edges of the folded bias strip to the arm opening. Stitch in place using a $^1/_4$" seam (**fig. 2**).

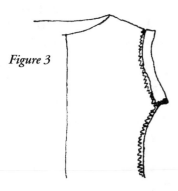

*Figure 2*

Attach folded bias strip to arm opening

4. With the strip pressed away from the arm opening, sew up the side seam (**fig. 3.**).

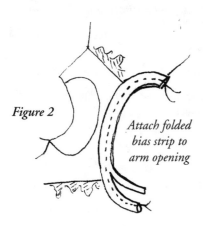

*Figure 3*

5. Turn the bias strip to the inside of the arm opening and stitch in place by hand or machine (**fig. 4**). This creates a bias facing.

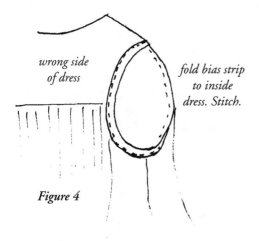

*wrong side of dress*

*fold bias strip to inside dress. Stitch.*

*Figure 4*

## XIII-B - Sleeveless Option with Angel Ruffle

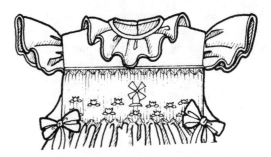

1. Cut four fabric strips $3^1/_2$" wide to the following measurements: sizes 2 to 6 = 19", sizes 8 to 10 = 21" and sizes 12 to 16 = 22". This will be two outer ruffle pieces and two lining pieces. Note: The two lining pieces can be cut from contrasting fabric if desired.

2. Cut the corners from each end to look like figure 1.

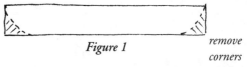

*Figure 1*

*remove corners*

3. Make and attach piping to the curved edge on the right side of the two outer pieces. Place the lining pieces to the right side of the piped pieces. The piping will be between the outer and lining pieces. Stitch just inside the piping seam line (**fig. 2**). Clip the curves, turn to the right side and press.

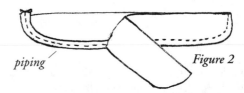

*piping*

*Figure 2*

4. Run two gathering rows along the straight side of the ruffle at $^1/_8$" and $^1/_4$" (**fig. 3**) .

*Figure 3*

5. Gather the to fit the top part of the arm opening. The gathers should fall about $2^1/_2$" to 3" on each side of the shoulder seam. Baste in place using a $^1/_4$" seam (**fig. 4**). With the ruffle to the right side of the bodice, attach a bias facing as described in "Sleeveless Option", steps 1 to 5.

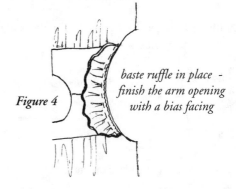

*Figure 4*

*baste ruffle in place - finish the arm opening with a bias facing*

# XIV. Side Seams

1. Pin the side seams from the bottom of the sleeves all the way to the bottom edge of the dress. The sleeve seams should meet at the bottom edge and the underarm seam. The bottom edge of the smocking should meet the back waist seam if a waisted back bodice is used. If sashes are used, they will be sewn into the seam (**fig. 1**).

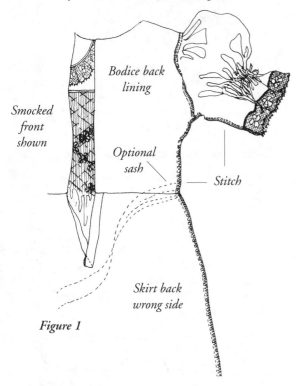

*Bodice back lining*

*Smocked front shown*

*Optional sash*

*Stitch*

*Skirt back wrong side*

**Figure 1**

2. Stitch with a ¹/₄" seam, treating the bodice and lining as one layer. Press the seams toward the dress back.

# XV. Hems

## A. Turned-up Hem

1. Press ¹/₄" to the wrong side around the bottom edge of the dress (**fig. 1**).

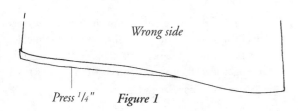

*Wrong side*

*Press ¹/₄"*     **Figure 1**

2. Press the hem to the wrong side of the dress at the hem line and pin or baste (**fig. 2**).

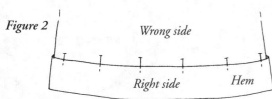

**Figure 2**     *Wrong side*

*Right side*     *Hem*

3. Slip-stitch or blind-hem side dress.

# XVI. Finishing the Dress

## A. Buttonholes and Buttons

*Beauty pins may be used in place of buttons and buttonholes. Beauty pins are available from Martha Pullen Company.*

1. Mark buttonhole placement on the right back bodice.

2. Place stabilizer under the buttonhole marks and work buttonholes.

3. Attach buttons to the back left bodice.

## B. Sash Loop

*A sash loop is optional, but it will help keep the bow from sagging.*

1. Thread a hand needle with a double strand of thread and knot the end. At the center back waist, attach the thread to the inside of the right back bodice with a knot.

2. Bring the needle to the right side of the garment and take a small stitch to create a loop in the thread, but do not pull the loop tight. Holding the needle in the left hand, reach through the loop with the right index finger and pull a loop of the needle thread through the first loop (**fig. 1**).

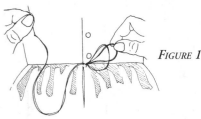

**FIGURE 1**

3. Pull on the second loop to tighten the first loop down close to the fabric. Use the right hand to pull a new loop through and tighten down the previous loop (**fig. 2**).

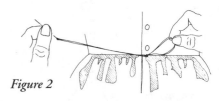

**Figure 2**

4. When the chain is long enough to make a loop that the sash will pass through, pull the needle through the last loop and tighten it into a knot (**fig. 3**).

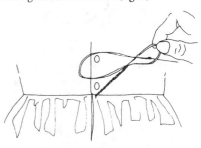

**Figure 3**

5. Insert the needle through the fabric to the wrong side and tie off with a secure knot.

# Smocking Directions & Duplicate Stitch Graphs

# Duplicate Stitch Graphs

One of my all time favorite stitched "things" to do for children is duplicate stitch. How I remember the days when Judy DeRosier made a new duplicate stitched sweater for Gina to model in nearly every issue of Sew Beautiful magazine. To celebrate an occasion with a sweater is just as special as doing names and cross stitch designs on little girls lingerie. Joanna loved her duplicate stitch sweaters and I think you will love these which Laura Jenkins Thompson has donated for you, the readers of this book. By the way, I used to cross stitch all of her panties. Today, underwear embellishment is so much easier with embroidery machines!

Duplicate stitch is fast, easy and perfect to use when you have a little smocked dress or suit and you want just that extra touch to finish it off. Duplicate stitch is sweet when you want the individualized "special handmade touch" and you don't have time to smock a whole dress or suit. It is so cute to duplicate stitch a sweater to go with a little appliqué design on a simple dress or jumper. We have such cute duplicate stitch designs and most of them are simple to make and can be done very quickly.

For back to school for boys and girls the pencil is precious. Choose those happy fun buttons available at any fabric store and you have a showstopper "outfit" to wear. For little boys stitch airplanes, gingerbread men, apples, hot air balloons, Easter eggs, chickens, slippers, school slates, football bears, ice cream cones or footballs.

Little girls would love lots of the same designs but we have also included bows and bubbles for them. Embellish with ribbons, buttons and lots of love for a special "handmade" garment which was basically purchased. Little touches of gathered lace around the collar and down the front make little girls' sweaters very delicate and sweet. I love duplicate stitch on button up sweaters as well as pull over sweaters and you will not believe the prices on duplicate stitch sweaters at the expensive department stores.

One of the nice things about hand work of any kind is that you can put it into a baggie and stitch a few stitches while waiting for car pool riders to get out of school, riding on the airplane (like me), watching TV at night when your husband just loves watching football or the nature channel, or sitting with a friend at the hospital. I have a true confession. Once, I decided to see if I could put in several smocking stitches at a red light. I did. When I told Joe, he said, "Martha do not ever do that again. You will cause a wreck and how will you ever explain that you were sewing and driving at the same time?" I didn't ever do that again since I am one of those "seat belt, two hands on the steering wheel at all times kinds of people." All of those sitting times are the perfect time to duplicate stitch, remove store bought buttons and sew on those happy buttons to complete sweater which will bring smiles and giggles when you make your presentation to your favorite Jack or Jill.

# Cardigans For Kids (Of All Ages)
## By
### Laura Jenkins Thompson

The Duplicate Stitch craze is sweeping the nation. Here is a new group of classic designs for cardigans based on popular novelty buttons. Carefully designed to exactly match each button in shape and color, these quick and easy graphs may be used for both children or adults, boys and girls, and for every season of the year.

## GENERAL INSTRUCTIONS

- Use a large tapestry needle. Appropriate sizes are # 18 (larger) to # 22 (smaller). It should have a very blunt tip.
- Use regular DMC embroidery floss. The sweaters pictured require 6 strands of floss. (Larger gauges may require 12 strands of floss to cover the original sweater stitch). Purchase at least 2 skeins of floss of each color. One skein may be sufficient for details and more than 2 skeins may be needed for larger areas.
- One square on a graph is one duplicate stitch. One stitch looks like a "V".
- To determine placement of any design, count actual sweater stitches to center each design. The number of stitches in each design has been given for each graph.

- The designs pictured are all stitched on purchased children's sweaters with a gauge of 9.5 x 11 stitches per inch. The designs may be worked on sweaters with larger gauges. Keep in mind these designs will be larger if the sweater gauge is larger. Count the actual stitches to be sure the design will fit.
- Some sweaters may require larger buttonholes to be made on the sewing machine for the novelty buttons to fit properly.
- Complete instructions, basic tips, stitching hints, and 10 other embroidery designs for purchased sweaters are available in *The Duplicate Stitch Made Easy* by Laura Jenkins Thompson.

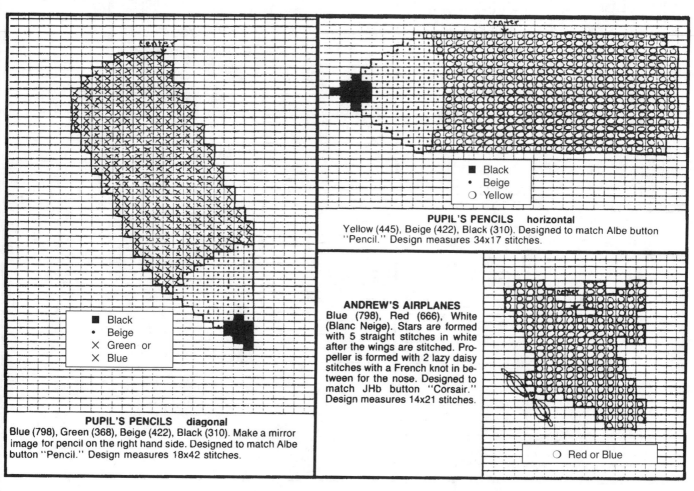

■ Black
• Beige
○ Yellow

**PUPIL'S PENCILS   horizontal**
Yellow (445), Beige (422), Black (310). Designed to match Albe button "Pencil." Design measures 34x17 stitches.

**ANDREW'S AIRPLANES**
Blue (798), Red (666), White (Blanc Neige). Stars are formed with 5 straight stitches in white after the wings are stitched. Propeller is formed with 2 lazy daisy stitches with a French knot in between for the nose. Designed to match JHb button "Corsair." Design measures 14x21 stitches.

○ Red or Blue

■ Black
• Beige
✕ Green or
✕ Blue

**PUPIL'S PENCILS   diagonal**
Blue (798), Green (368), Beige (422), Black (310). Make a mirror image for pencil on the right hand side. Designed to match Albe button "Pencil." Design measures 18x42 stitches.

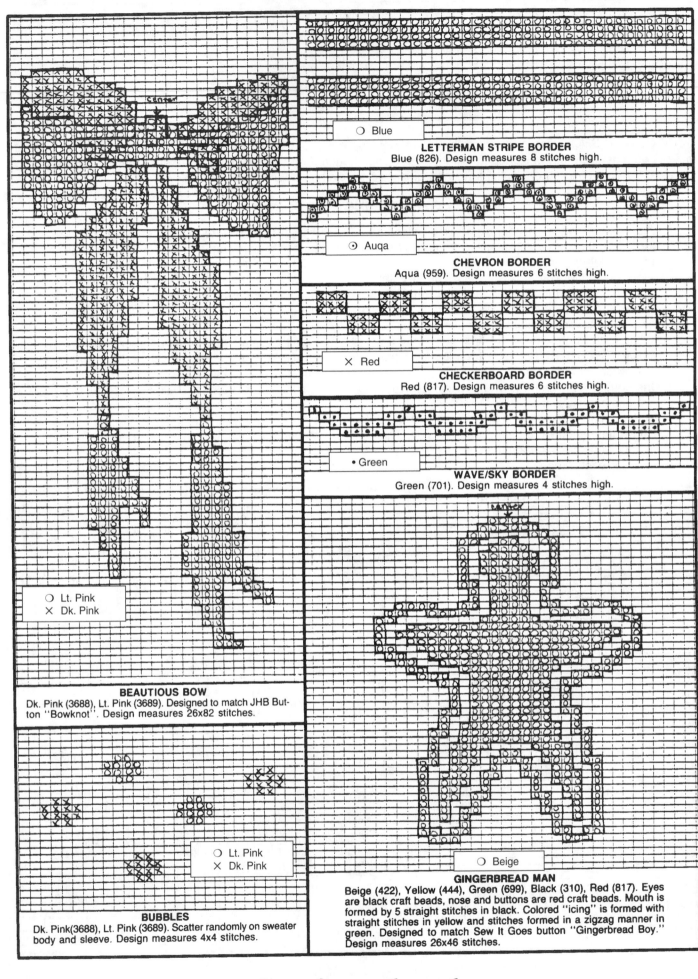

○ Blue

### LETTERMAN STRIPE BORDER
Blue (826). Design measures 8 stitches high.

⊙ Auqa

### CHEVRON BORDER
Aqua (959). Design measures 6 stitches high.

✕ Red

### CHECKERBOARD BORDER
Red (817). Design measures 6 stitches high.

• Green

### WAVE/SKY BORDER
Green (701). Design measures 4 stitches high.

○ Lt. Pink
✕ Dk. Pink

### BEAUTIOUS BOW
Dk. Pink (3688), Lt. Pink (3689). Designed to match JHB Button "Bowknot". Design measures 26x82 stitches.

○ Lt. Pink
✕ Dk. Pink

### BUBBLES
Dk. Pink(3688), Lt. Pink (3689). Scatter randomly on sweater body and sleeve. Design measures 4x4 stitches.

○ Beige

### GINGERBREAD MAN
Beige (422), Yellow (444), Green (699), Black (310), Red (817). Eyes are black craft beads, nose and buttons are red craft beads. Mouth is formed by 5 straight stitches in black. Colored "icing" is formed with straight stitches in yellow and stitches formed in a zigzag manner in green. Designed to match Sew It Goes button "Gingerbread Boy." Design measures 26x46 stitches.

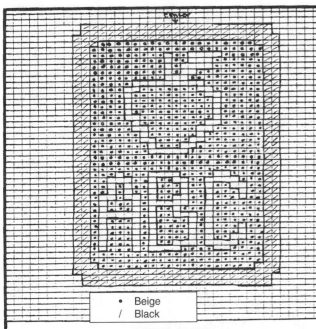

| | |
|---|---|
| • | Beige |
| / | Black |

### SCHOOL SLATE
Black (310), Beige (422). "Chalk Drawing" is formed by the background of the white sweater not stitched. Designed to match Albe button "Slate Board." Design measures 25x46 stitches.

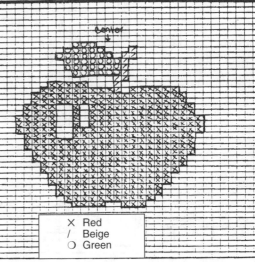

| | |
|---|---|
| X | Red |
| / | Beige |
| O | Green |

### APPLE FOR THE TEACHER
Red (666), Beige (422), Green (367). Glimmer on apple is formed by the background of the white sweater not stitched. Design measures 23x29 stitches.

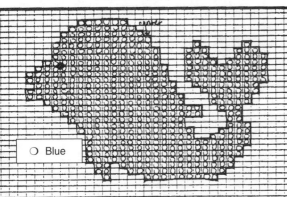

| | |
|---|---|
| O | Blue |

### FLIPPER AND FRIEND
Blue (797), Green (701). Make a mirror image for left dolphin. Eye is formed with 6 strands of white and 3 strands of blue floss in a French knot. Designed to match JHB button "Flipper." Design measures 29x28 stitches.

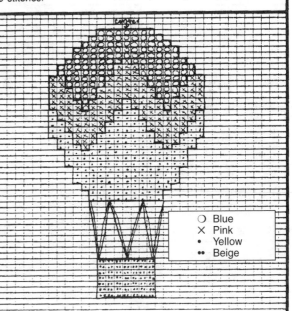

| | |
|---|---|
| O | Blue |
| X | Pink |
| • | Yellow |
| •• | Beige |

### HOT AIR BALOONS
Blue (809), Pink (3326), Yellow (445), Beige (422). Ropes are formed by long straight stitches in beige. Designed to match Albe button "Hot Air Balloon." Design measures 19x47 stitches.

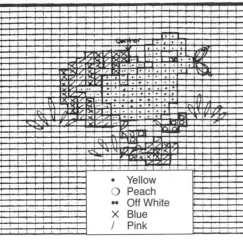

| | |
|---|---|
| • | Yellow |
| O | Peach |
| •• | Off White |
| X | Blue |
| / | Pink |

### CAPITAL CHICK
Yellow (445), Peach (352), Green (703), Blue (809), Pink (3326), Off White (822). Eye is one "V" stitch. Beak is formed by 2 lazy daisy stitches. Grass is formed by groups of straight stitches in green. Designed to match Capital Imports Swiss embroidered edging. Design measures 24x23 stitches.

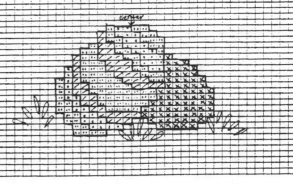

### EASTER EGGS
Yellow (445), Green (703), Blue (809), Pink (3326), Off White (822). Green dots are French knots. Blue chevron is formed with straight stitches. Grass is formed by groups of straight stitches in green. (Refer to photo for placement) Designed to match Albe Button "Easter Egg." Design measures 28x20 stitches.

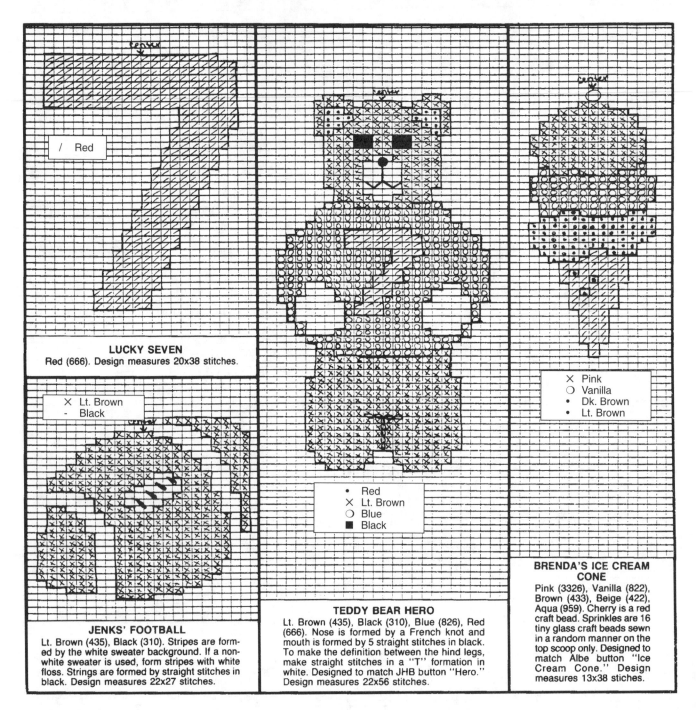

**LUCKY SEVEN**
Red (666). Design measures 20x38 stitches.

/ Red

X Lt. Brown
- Black

**JENKS' FOOTBALL**
Lt. Brown (435), Black (310). Stripes are formed by the white sweater background. If a non-white sweater is used, form stripes with white floss. Strings are formed by straight stitches in black. Design measures 22x27 stitches.

• Red
X Lt. Brown
O Blue
■ Black

**TEDDY BEAR HERO**
Lt. Brown (435), Black (310), Blue (826), Red (666). Nose is formed by a French knot and mouth is formed by 5 straight stitches in black. To make the definition between the hind legs, make straight stitches in a ''T'' formation in white. Designed to match JHB button ''Hero.'' Design measures 22x56 stitches.

X Pink
O Vanilla
• Dk. Brown
• Lt. Brown

**BRENDA'S ICE CREAM CONE**
Pink (3326), Vanilla (822), Brown (433), Beige (422), Aqua (959). Cherry is a red craft bead. Sprinkles are 16 tiny glass craft beads sewn in a random manner on the top scoop only. Designed to match Albe button ''Ice Cream Cone.'' Design measures 13x38 stiches.

*Laura Jenkins Thompson is an award winning and internationally known needlework designer, teacher and author. Since 1985 she has been teaching classes for national, regional and local needlework organizations from coast to coast in the areas of smocking, construction, embroidery and fine machine sewing. Laura is a favorite instructor at Martha Pullen's School of Art Fashion, and she has been writing articles for Sew Beautiful magazine since 1988. Besides having published numerous needlework books, patterns and designs. Laura is also the author and illustrator of Joseph's Charleston Adventure, a fictional hardback children's book, which has been named the "Official Children's Book of the City of Charleston."*

*Complete instructions on how to do the duplicate stitch are available in The Duplicate Stitch Made Easy by Laura Jenkins Thompson. Girls' (crew neck) and boys' (v-neck) cardigans are also available in sizes 12m-14 through Laura Jenkins Thompson Ltd.*

*For information on how to order the instruction booklet, children's sweaters, 24 design plates for duplicate stitch, and many other designs, patterns and products for heirloom sewing, smocking and embroidery, contact*
*Laura Jenkins Thompson*
*455 Rice Hope Drive*
*Mount Pleasant, SC 29464*
*Phone: 843-884-1780    Fax: 843-884-4208    e-mail: laurajt@awod.com*
*Please be sure to visit Laura's website: www.laurajenkinsthompson.com*

*For directions on pleating and smocking, refer to the book, "The Joy of Smocking."*
*This book can be purchased from Martha Pullen Company.*

## BABY BLUES

### DESIGNED BY LITTLE MEMORIES SMOCKING DESIGNS

* This straight yoke design is worked over 170 pleats as shown.

**GEOMETRIC DESIGN:** Use 3 strands of floss if working on a sheer to light weight fabric. Use 4 strands of floss if working on a medium to heavy weight fabric.

A. To center the entire design- find the center 2 pleats on Row 1. Begin with an up cable and cable 85 across. Turn the panel upside down and cable 84 across to complete the left side.

B. On Row 3- begin with an up cable and cable across.

C. On approx. Row $2^1/_3$, begin with a down cable- cable 1; trellis 1 up to Row 2; cable 3; trellis 1 back down. Repeat this design across.

D. Just beneath the cable stitching on Row $2^1/_3$, begin with an up cable- cable 1; trellis 1 down to just above the cable stitch on Row 3; cable 3; trellis 1 back up. Repeat this design across.

E. On approx. Row $3^1/_4$, begin with a down cable- cable 2; * trellis 4 down to Row 4; cable 1; trellis 4 back up; cable 3. Repeat design from * across.

F. On approx. Row $4^5/_8$, begin with a down cable- cable 1; trellis 1 up to approx. Row $4^1/_4$; cable 1; trellis 1 back down. Repeat design across.

G. Just beneath the cable stitching on Row $4^5/_8$, begin with an up cable- cable 1; trellis 1 down to Row 5; cable 1; trellis 1 back up. Repeat design across.

H. On approx. Row $6^1/_3$, begin with a down cable- cable 1; trellis 1 up to Row 6; cable 1; trellis 1 back down. Repeat design across.

I. Just beneath the cable stitching on Row $6^1/_3$, begin with an up cable- cable 1; trellis 1 down to just above Row 7; cable 1; trellis 1 back up. Repeat design across.

J. On Row 8- begin with a down cable and cable across.

K. Just above the cable stitching on Row 8, begin with an up cable- cable 2; * trellis 4 up to Row 7; cable 1; trellis 4 back down; cable 3. Repeat design from * across as shown.

L. Just beneath Row $8^1/_2$, begin with a down cable- cable 1; trellis 1 up to just below cable stitching on Row 8; cable 3; trellis 1 back down. Repeat design across.

M. Just beneath the cable stitching on Row $8^1/_2$, begin with an up cable- cable 1; trellis 1 down to Row 9; cable 3; trellis 1 back up.

N. On Row 10- begin with a down cable and cable across.

O. On Row $5^1/_2$, using 3 strands of white floss- count 5 pleats right from the first pleat on the left side and work the first lazy daisy stitch. Work lazy daisy stitches from left to right each one being stitched over the previous one as shown. Follow the diagram for exact placement.

**COLORS USED-** DMC: White & 3755.
**ANCHOR:** 2 & 140.

## BABY CARS

### DESIGNED ANGELA PULLEN

* This straight yoke design is worked over 170 pleats as shown.

**GEOMETRIC DESIGN:** Use 3 strands of floss if working on a sheer to light weight fabric. Use 4 strands of floss if working on a medium to heavy weight fabric.

* This design is worked over 154 pleats as shown. Each car requires 22 pleats, the truck requires 24 pleats, and the bus requires 30 pleats.

* Stitch count for figures are not given in the written instructions. Follow diagrams carefully for accurate stitch count and cable placement.

I. **BORDERS:** (4 strands)

A. Upper Border: To center the border design, find the center 2 pleats on Row 1. Begin with a down cable and cable 77 across. Turn the panel upside down and cable 76 across to complete the left side. Add 3 cable "picot" stitches just below Row 1 as shown.

B. Lower Border: On Row 4- Begin with a down cable and cable across. Again, add the cable "picot" stitches just below Row 4.

II. **BABY VEHICLES:** (4 strands)

A. Left Blue Car: To position, count 58 pleats left from the center valley on Row 3. Begin with a down cable. (Arrow denotes beginning cable stitch.) Stack upward to work the upper portion of the car. Note where all color changes and $^1/_2$ stitches occur. Then, stack downward to complete.

B. Hood Ornament: (2 strands) Using floss # 318, work 1 french knot wrapped 2 times for the hood ornament as shown.

C. Red Truck: Count 30 pleats left from the center valley on Row 3. Begin with a down cable. (Note: It is easier to add the red $^1/_2$ stitch after working the next row up.) Stack upward to work the upper portion of the truck, noting where color changes and $^1/_2$ stitches occur. Then, stack downward to complete.

D. Bus: Count 2 pleats right from the center valley on Row 2. Begin with a down cable and stack downward to complete the bus. Follow the diagram carefully, noting all color changes and where $^1/_2$ stitches occur.

E. Bus Lettering: (2 strands) Using floss # 3799, work small straight stitches to form the letters "b", "u", and "s" as shown on the diagram.

F. Right Green Car: Count 37 pleats right from the center valley on Row 3 and complete as the directions given in this section, Steps A and B.

G. Wheel Centers: (2 strands) Using white floss, work 1 french knot wrapped 2 times for the center of each wheel on all of the vehicles as shown.

III. **BACKSMOCKING:** (2 strands) Backsmock across Row 2 & 3.

**COLORS USED-** DMC: White, 725, 798, 828, 943, 666, 318 & 3799.
**ANCHOR:** 2, 305, 131, 9159, 188, 46, 399 & 236.

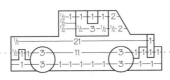

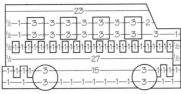

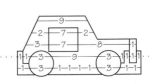

# BABY CHRISTMAS
## DESIGNED BY ANGELA PULLEN

* This design is worked over 180 pleats as shown. Each poinsettia requires 18 pleats and each Christmas tree requires 14 pleats.

* Stitch count for figures are not given in the written instructions. Follow diagrams carefully for accurate stitch count and cable placement.

I. **BORDERS:** (4 strands)
A. Upper Border: To center the border design, find the center 2 pleats on Row 1. Begin with an up cable and cable 90 across. Turn the panel upside down and cable 89 across to complete the left side.
B. Lower Border: On Row 4- begin with a down cable and cable across.

II. **POINSETTIAS:** (4 strands)
A. Flower # 1: To position, count 87 pleats left from the center valley on Row 3. Begin with a down cable. (Arrow denotes beginning cable stitch.) Stack downward to work the lower portion of the flower, noting color changes as they occur. Then, stack upward to complete.
B. Flower # 2: Count 47 pleats left from the center valley on Row 3 and complete as the directions given above.
C. Flower # 3: Count 7 pleats left from the center valley on Row 3 and complete as the directions given above. Flower # 4: Count 34 pleats right from the center valley on Row 3 and complete as the directions given above.
D. Flower # 5: Count 74 pleats right from the center valley on Row 3 and complete as the directions given above.

III. **CHRISTMAS TREE:** (4 strands)
A. Tree # 1: To position, count 67 pleats left from the center valley on Row 3. Begin with a down cable. (Arrow denotes beginning cable stitch.) Stack upward to work the entire tree. Add 1 satin stitch at the bottom for the trunk as shown.
B. Tree # 2: Count 27 pleats left from the center valley on Row 3 and complete as the directions given above.
C. Tree # 3: Count 14 pleats right from the center valley on Row 3 and complete as the directions given above.
D. Tree # 4: Count 54 pleats right from the center valley on Row 3 and complete as the directions given above.

IV. **BACKSMOCKING:** (2 strands) Backsmock across Rows 2 & 3.
**COLORS USED-** DMC: 563, 319, 321, 726 & 801.
**ANCHOR:** 208, 218, 9046, 295 & 359.

### SPACING GUIDE

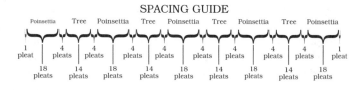

Poinsettia  Tree  Poinsettia  Tree  Poinsettia  Tree  Poinsettia  Tree  Poinsettia

| 1 pleat | 4 pleats | 4 pleats | 4 pleats | 4 pleats | 4 pleats | 4 pleats | 4 pleats | 4 pleats | 1 pleat |

18 pleats  14 pleats  18 pleats  14 pleats  18 pleats  14 pleats  18 pleats  14 pleats  18 pleats

## BATTER'S UP
### DESIGNED BY LITTLE MEMORIES SMOCKING DESIGNS

* This design is worked over 164 pleats as shown. Each set of bats require 50 pleats.

* Stitch count for figures are not given in the written instructions.

---

Follow diagrams carefully for accurate stitch count and cable placement.

I. **BORDERS:** ( 4 strands)
A. Upper Borders: To center the border design, find the center 2 pleats on approx Row $1^2/_3$. Begin with an up cable- cable 5;* trellis 2 down to Row 2; cable 1; trellis 1 up to approx Row $1^3/_4$; cable 5; trellis 1 down to Row 2; cable 1; trellis 2 back up to Row $1^2/_3$; cable 9. Repeat design from * across right side of panel. Turn panel upside down- cable 4; * trellis 2 up to Row 2; cable 1; trellis 1 back down to Row $1^3/_4$; cable 5; trellis 1 back up to Row 2; cable 1; trellis 2 back down to Row $1^2/_3$; cable 9. Repeat design from * to complete the left side. On Row 3- cable 1; trellis 1 down to Row $3^1/_4$; cable 5; trellis 1 back up to Row 3; cable 1; trellis 2 down to Row $3^1/_3$; cable 9; trellis 2 back up to Row 3. Repeat design across.
B. Lower Borders: On Row 10- cable 1; trellis 1 up to Row $9^3/_4$; cable 5; trellis 1 down to Row 10; cable 1; trellis 2 up to Row $9^2/_3$; cable 9; trellis 2 back down to Row 10. Repeat design across. On Row 11, work design as instructions given above for Row 3.
C. Baseballs: (4 strands) See diagram for exact placement and stack baseballs between Rows 2 and 3 and Rows 10 and 11 as shown.
D. Baseball's Seams: (1 strand) Using floss # 321, work 2 curved straight stitches anchored twice for seam details in each ball. See diagram for exact placement.

II. **BASEBALL BATS:** ( 4 strands)
A. Left Set of Bats: To position, count 62 pleats left from the center valley on Row 5. Begin with a down cable. (Arrow denotes beginning cable stitch.) Stack upward to work the upper portion of the left bat. Then, stack downward to the *. Note where all $^1/_2$ stitches occur. ( HINT: It is easier to work the upper part of each bat separately and connect the two together on the row where the * is shown on the diagram.) On the row where the * is, stack across, forming the first row of the right bat. Stack upwards to work the upper portion of the right bat, again noting where all $^1/_2$ stitches occur. Then, stack downward to complete the lower portion of each bat.
B. Right Set of Bats: Count 13 pleats right from the center valley on Row 5 and complete as directions given above.
C. Bat Handles: (4 strands) Using floss # 3072, work small diagonal straight stitches for the handle details as shown.
D. Bat Handle Ends: (4 strands) Using the same color floss as upper portion of each bat, work 3 trellis stitches as shown.

III. **BACKSMOCKING:** (2 strands) Backsmock across Row 4, 5, 6, 7, 8 & 9.
**COLORS USED-** DMC: White, 321, 700, 435, 434 & 3072.
**ANCHOR:** 2, 9046, 228, 1046, 310 & 847.

## SPACING GUIDE

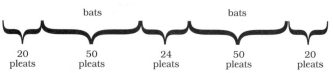

bats                    bats

| 20 pleats | 50 pleats | 24 pleats | 50 pleats | 20 pleats |

## BIKE RIDE
### DESIGNED BY ANGELA PULLEN

* This design is worked over 172 pleats as shown. The boy and girl on the bike require 88 pleats.

* Stitch count for figures are not given in the written instructions. Follow diagrams carefully for accurate stitch count and cable placement.

**I. BORDERS:** (4 strands)

A. Upper Border: To center the entire design, find the center 2 pleats on Row 1. Begin with an up cable and cable 86 across. Turn the panel upside down and cable 85 across to complete the left side.

B. Lower Border: On Row 10- begin with an up cable- cable 3; trellis 3 down to Row 10$\frac{1}{2}$; cable 3; trellis 3 back up to Row 10. Repeat this design across.

**II. BOY AND GIRL ON THE BIKE:** (4 strands)

A. Boy/ Girl/ Bike: On Row 9- begin with a down cable. (Arrow denotes beginning cable stitch.) Cable across the entire row noting color changes as they occur, to work the road outline and the bottom of the bike tires. Stack upward to Row 7 to work the lower portion of the bike, boy and girl. Follow the diagram carefully for all color changes, where $\frac{1}{2}$ stitches occur, and where pleats are being skipped. Then, continue stacking upward to complete the figures as shown.

B. Boy's Bow Tie: (2 strands) Using floss # 3755, work 2 lazy daisy stitches for the bow loops as shown.

C. Boy's Shoe String Bow: (2 strands) Using floss # 3799, work 2 lazy daisy stitches for the string loops.

D. Girl's Shoe Buttons: (2 strands) Using white floss, work 1 french knot wrapped 2 times for each button.

E. Bike Wheel and Gear Details: (2 strands) Using floss # 3799, work 1 french knot wrapped 2 times for each knob on the bike as shown on the diagram.

**III. SUN AND CLOUD:** (4 strands)

A. Sun/ Cloud: To position, count 41 pleats right from the center valley on Row 4. Begin with a down cable. (Arrow denotes beginning cable stitch.) Stack downward to work the lower portion of the sun and cloud, noting where color changes and $\frac{1}{2}$ stitches occur. Then, stack upward to complete.

**IV. BALLOONS:** (4 strands)

A. Balloon # 1: Count 69 pleats left from the center valley on Row 6. Begin with an up cable. (Arrow denotes beginning cable stitch.) Stack upward to complete the figure. Work 2 satin stitches for the balloon's end.

B. Balloon # 2: Count 71 pleats left from the center valley on Row 4 and complete as directions given above.

C. Balloon # 3: Count 57 pleats left from the center valley on Row 4 and complete as directions given above.

D. Balloon Strings: (1 strand) Using floss # 3799, work 3 very long, loose straight stitches from the end of each balloon down to just below the girl's hand. See the diagram for exact placement. Anchor each stitch 4 times to secure the strings into position. Work 1 bow at the base of each balloon with 2 lazy daisy stitches and another bow at the girls hand as shown.

**V. BACKSMOCKING:** (2 strands) Backsmock across Row 2, 3, 4, 5, 6, 7 & 8.

**COLORS USED-** DMC: White, 350, 414, 415, 435, 422, 676, 726, 754, 775, 911, 3755 & 3799.

**ANCHOR:** 2, 11, 235, 398, 1046, 943, 891, 295, 1012, 128, 205, 140 & 236

## SPACING GUIDE
### Girl/Boy/Bike

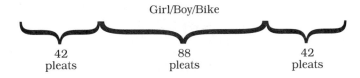

| 42 pleats | 88 pleats | 42 pleats |

## CAROUSEL
### DESIGNED BY ANGELA PULLEN

* This design is worked over 168 pleats as shown. The carousel horse requires 51 pleats and the star poles require 26 pleats each.

* Stitch count for figures are not given in the written instructions. Follow diagrams carefully for accurate stitch count and cable placement.

**I. BORDERS:** (4 strands)

A. Lower Border: To center the entire design, find the center 2 pleats on Row 8. Begin with a down cable and cable 84 across the right side noting color changes as they occur. Turn the panel upside down and cable 83 across to complete the left side. Stack downward to complete the bottom border. NOTE: Do not work the poles at this time.

B. Upper Border: Stack the upper border between Row 1$\frac{1}{3}$ and Row 2 as shown. Add 3 step cable flowerettes. See diagram for exact placement.

**II. CAROUSEL HORSE:** (4 strands)

A. Horse/ Pole: To center, count 23 pleats left from the center valley on Row 5. Begin with an up cable. (Arrow denotes beginning cable stitch.) Stack downward to work lower portion of the horse and pole, meeting the cable stitches previously stitched at the top of the base on the lower border. Note where all color changes and $\frac{1}{2}$ stitches occur. Then, stack upward to complete the horse and pole, once again meeting the cable stitches previously stitched at the bottom of the upper border.

B. Horse's Eye: (4 strands) Work 1 straight stitch for the eye.

C. Reins: (2 strands) Using floss #666, work 3 straight stitches to form the reins as shown. Anchor the longest stitch going from the saddle to under the horse's neck once to position and secure. Using 3 strands of floss # 726, work 1 french knot wrapped 2 times to connect the straight stitches together under the horse's neck. Work another french knot using floss # 3790 for the saddle horn. See the diagram for exact placement.

D. Lower Saddle Detail: (1 strand) Using floss # 666, work 2 small diagonal stitches as shown on the diagram.

**III. STAR POLES:** (4 strands)

A. Left Pole: Count 55 pleats left from the center valley on Row 5. Begin with an up cable. (Arrow denotes beginning cable stitch.) Stack downward to work lower portion of the star and the pole, once again meeting the cable stitches at the top of the base on the lower border. Note where all color changes and $\frac{1}{2}$ stitches occur. Then, stack upward to complete, meeting the cable stitches on the upper border.

B. Right Pole: Count 42 pleats right from the center valley on Row

5 and complete as directions given above.

C. Star Centers: (2 strands) Using floss # 726, work 5 lazy daisy stitches to form the flower. Using 3 strands of floss # 726, work 1 french knot wrapped 2 times for the center. See diagram for exact placement.

**IV. BACKSMOCKING:** (2 strands) Backsmock across Row 3, 4, 5, 6 & 7.
**COLORS USED**- DMC: 666, 825, 726, 3790, 3781, 3799 & 740.
**ANCHOR:** 46, 162, 295, 393, 1050, 236 & 316.

## SPACING GUIDE

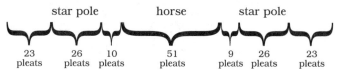

| star pole | | | horse | | star pole | |
|---|---|---|---|---|---|---|
| 23 pleats | 26 pleats | 10 pleats | 51 pleats | 9 pleats | 26 pleats | 23 pleats |

---

## *CHRISTMAS TREE*
### DESIGNED BY ANGELA PULLEN

* This design is worked over 168 pleats as shown. The Christmas tree requires 22 pleats and each wreath requires 28 pleats.

* The following specialty items are needed for this design:
  Red ribbon floss
  DMC # 5282 gold metallic floss
  YLI # 99 blue 4 mm silk ribbon
  YLI # 61 green 4 mm silk ribbon
  Red and gold glass Mill Head seed beads

* Stitch count for figures are not given in the written instructions. Follow diagrams carefully for accurate stitch count and cable placement.

### I. BORDERS: (4 strands)
A. Upper Border: To center the border design, find the center 2 pleats on Row 1. Begin with an up cable and cable 84 across. Turn the panel upside down and cable 83 across to complete the left side.
B. Lower Border: On Row 10, begin with an up cable and cable across.

### II. CHRISTMAS TREE: (4 strands)
A. Tree: To position, count 10 pleats left from the center valley on Row 7. Begin with an up cable. (Arrow denotes beginning cable stitch.) Stack downward to work the lower portion of the tree. Then, stack upward to complete.
B. Star Tree Top: (3 strands) Using the gold metallic floss, work 3 straight stitches to form the star.
C. Tree Ornaments: (3 strands) Using floss # 321 and #726, work 1 french knot wrapped 2 times for each ornament as shown on the diagram.
D. Bead Garland: String beads onto a strong thread, and attach to the tree. See diagram for exact placement.

### III. CHRISTMAS WREATHS: (4 strands)
A. Left Wreath: To position, count 60 pleats left from the center valley on Row 5. Begin with a down cable and stack downward and counter clockwise to work the lower portion of the wreath. Then, stack upward to complete.
B. Right Wreath: Count 33 pleats right from the center valley on Row 5 and complete as directions given above.

C. Ribbon Bow Trim: Using red ribbon floss, work 5 long diagonal straight stitches for trimming around the wreath. Work 8 lazy daisy stitches to form the bow. Work 1 french knot for the center of the bow as shown.
D. Wreath Ornaments: See diagram for exact placement and complete as directions given in Section II, Step C.

### IV. CHRISTMAS PRESENTS: (4 strands)
A. Present # 1: Count 71 pleats left from the center valley on Row 8. Begin with an up cable and stack downward to work lower portion of the present. Note where $^1/_2$ stitches occur. Then, stack upward to complete.
B. Present # 1 Details: (3 strands) Using gold metallic floss, work 2 straight stitches across the present and work 3 lazy daisy stitches for the bow.
C. Present # 2: Count 56 pleats left from the center valley on Row 8. Begin with an up cable and stack downward to complete the present, noting where $^1/_2$ stitches occur.
D. Present # 2 Details: Using blue silk ribbon, work 2 straight stitches across the present and work 2 lazy daisy stitches for the bow.
E. Present # 3: Count 37 pleats left from the center valley on Row 8 and complete as directions given in this section, Step A.
F. Present # 3 Details: Using green silk ribbon, complete as directions given in this section, Step B.
G. Present # 4: Count 22 pleats left from the center valley on Row 8 and complete as directions given in this section, Step C.
H. Present # 4 Details: Using red ribbon floss, complete as directions given in this section, Step B.
I. Present # 5: Count 15 pleats right from the center valley on Row 8 and complete as directions given in this section, Step C.
J. Present # 5 Details: (3 strands) Using gold metallic floss, complete as directions given in this section, Step B.
K. Present # 6: Count 26 pleats right from the center valley on Row 8 and complete as directions given in this section, Step A.
  L. Present # 6 Details: Using red ribbon floss, complete as directions given in this section, Step B.
M. Present # 7: Count 41 pleats right from the center valley on Row 8 and complete as directions given in this section, Step C.
N. Present # 7 Details: Using green silk ribbon, complete as directions given in this section, Step D.
O. Present # 8: Count 60 pleats right from the center valley on Row 8 and complete as directions given in this section, Step A.
P. Present # 8 Details: Using blue silk ribbon, complete as directions given in Step B.

**IV. BACKSMOCKING:** (2 strands) Backsmock across Row 2, 3, 4, 5, 6, 7, 8 & 9.
**COLORS USED**- DMC: 321, 420, 726, 796, 943, & 3818.
**ANCHOR:** 9046, 374, 295, 133, 188 & 923.

## SPACING GUIDE

| | wreath | | | | wreath | |
|---|---|---|---|---|---|---|
| 24 pleats | 28 pleats | 64 pleats | | | 28 pleats | 24 pleats |

| present | present | present | present | Christmas Tree | present | present | present | present |
|---|---|---|---|---|---|---|---|---|
| 13 pleats | 3 pleats | 3 pleats | 3 pleats | 3 pleats | 3 pleats | 3 pleats | 3 pleats | 3 pleats | 13 pleats |
| 12 pleats | 16 pleats | 12 pleats | 8 pleats | 22 pleats | 8 pleats | 12 pleats | 16 pleats | 12 pleats |

## CUPID'S HEARTS
### DESIGNED BY ANGELA PULLEN

* This design is worked over 182 pleats as shown. The cupids holding the heart require 100 pleats.

* 8 mm white silk ribbon is used in this design.

* Stitch count for figures are not given in the written instructions. Follow diagrams carefully for accurate stitch count and cable placement.

I. **BORDERS:** (4 strands)

A. Upper Border: To center the heart border, count 91 pleats left from the center valley on Row 1. Begin with an up cable. (Arrow denotes beginning cable stitch.) Cable across Row 1 as shown, noting color changes as they occur. Stack downward to complete the lower portion of the hearts. Then, stack upward to complete.

B. Lower Border: On Row 8- begin with an up cable and work the heart border as directions given above.

II. **CUPIDS HOLDING THE HEART:** (4 strands)

A. Cupids/ Heart: To position, count 42 pleats left from the center valley on Row 4. Begin with an up cable. (Arrow denotes beginning cable stitch.) Work across the entire row including the heart and the right cupid. Follow the diagram carefully for stitch placement and where color changes occur. Stack downward to work lower portion of the entire figure. Then, stack upward to complete the cupids and the heart again, noting color changes and where 1/2 stitches occur.

B. Cupid's Eyes and Mouth: (3 strands) Using floss # 334, work 1 small straight stitch for each eye. Using floss # 309, work 1 straight stitch for the mouth as shown.

C. Add a silk ribbon bow on the heart.

III. **BACKSMOCKING:** (2 strands) Backsmock across Row 2, 3, 4, 5, 6 & 7.

**COLORS USED-** DMC: 962, 309, 776, 415, 318, 800, 334, 948, 754 & 307.

**ANCHOR:** 75, 42, 24, 398, 399, 144, 977, 1011, 1012 & 289.

## SPACING GUIDE
### cupid/heart/cupid

41 pleats      100 pleats      41 pleats

## FLOWERS AND BUTTERFLIES
### DESIGNED BY ANGELA PULLEN

* This design is worked over 182 pleats as shown. Each butterfly and flower requires 18 pleats.

* Stitch count for figures are not given in the written instructions. Follow diagrams carefully for accurate stitch count and cable placement.

I. **BORDERS:** (4 strands)

A. Upper Border: To center the border design, find the center 2 pleats on Row 1. Begin with an up cable and cable 91 across.

Turn the panel upside down and cable 90 across to complete the left side. Just above Row 1, work 2 step cable stitches across as shown on the diagram.

B. Lower Borders: On Row 5- begin with an up cable and cable across. Again, add 2 step cable stitches above Row 5 as shown. On Row 4- stem stitch across the row. (The thread goes below or under the needle when working a stem stitch.)

II. **BUTTERFLIES:** (4 strands)

A. Butterfly # 1: To position, count 83 pleats left from the center valley on Row 3. Begin with a down cable. (Arrow denotes beginning cable stitch.) Stack upward to work the upper portion of the butterfly. Then, stack downward to complete its wings.

B. Butterfly # 2: Count 31 pleats left form the center valley on Row 3 and complete as the direction given above.

C. Butterfly # 3: Count 21 pleats right from the center valley on Row 3 and complete as the directions given above.

D. Butterfly # 4: Count 75 pleats right from the center valley on Row 3 and complete as the directions given above.

E. Antennas: (2 strands) Using floss # 3799, work 1 diagonal straight stitch for each antenna as shown.

F. Antenna and Wing Details: (2 strands) Using floss # 3799, work 1 french knot wrapped 2 times each at the top of the antennas and on the lower wings as shown.

III. **FLOWERS:** (4 strands)\par

A. Flower # 1: To position, count 61 pleats left from the center valley on Row 3. Begin with an up cable. (Arrow denotes beginning cable stitch.) Stack upward to work the upper portion of the flower, noting color changes as they occur. Then, stack downward to complete.

B. Flower # 2: Count 9 pleats left from the center valley on Row 3 and complete as the diections given above.

C. Flower # 3: Count 44 pleats right from the center valley on Row 3 and complete as the directions given above.

IV. **BACKSMOCKING:** (2 strands) Backsmock across Row 2 & 3.

**COLORS USED-** DMC: 3810, 3746, 3799, 352, 351 & 726.

**ANCHOR:** 168, 1030, 236, 9, 10 & 295.

### SPACING GUIDE

Butterfly   Flower   Butterfly   Flower   Butterfly   Flower   Butterfly

4 pleats   18 pleats   8 pleats   18 pleats   8 pleats   18 pleats   8 pleats   18 pleats   8 pleats   18 pleats   8 pleats   18 pleats   8 pleats   18 pleats   4 pleats

## LET'S GO DUTCH
### DESIGNED BY LITTLE MEMORIES SMOCKING DESIGNS

* This design is worked over 162 pleats as shown. The windmill requires 32 pleats. Stitch count for figures are not given in the written instructions. Follow diagrams carefully for accurate stitch count and cable placement.

I. **BORDERS:** (4 strands)

A. UPPER BORDER: To center border design, find the center 2 pleats on Row 1- cable 1; trellis 3 down to Row 1 1/2; cable 1; trellis 3 back up to Row 1. Repeat design across right side of the panel. Turn the panel upside down- trellis 3 up to Row 1 1/2; cable 1; trellis 3 back down to Row 1. Repeat design across to complete left side of the panel.

B. LOWER BORDER: On Row 10- cable 1; trellis 3 up to Row 9 1/2; cable 1; trellis 3 back down to Row 10 and repeat the design across.

## II. WINDMILL: (4 strands)

A. Windmill/ Ground: To position, count 16 pleats left from the center valley on Row 5. Begin with an up cable. (Arrow denotes beginning cable stitch.) Stack downward to work the lower portion of the windmill and the ground. Note where color changes and ½ stitches occur. Then, stack upward to complete.

## III. TULIPS: (4 strands)

A. Tulip # 1: To position, count 65 pleats left from the center valley on Row 7. Begin with an up cable and stack upward to work the flower. Note where the satin stitches are worked to form the stem.

B. Tulip # 2: Count 25 pleats left from the center valley on Row 7 and complete as the directions given above.

C. Tulip # 3: Count 16 pleats right from the center valley on Row 7 and complete as the directions given above.

D. Tulip # 4: Count 56 pleats right from the center valley on Row 7 and complete as the directions given above.

E. Tulip # 5: Count 45 pleats left from the center valley on Row 8 and complete as direction given above.

F. Tulip # 6: Count 5 pleats left from the center valley on Row 8 and complete as the directions given above.

G. Tulip # 7: Count 36 pleats right from the center valley on Row 8 and complete as directions given above.

H. Tulip # 8: Count 65 pleats left from the center valley on Row 9 and complete as directions given above.

I. Tulip # 9: Count 25 pleats left from the center valley on Row 9 and complete as the directions given above.

J. Tulip # 10: Count 16 pleats right from the center valley on Row 9 and complete as the directions given above.

K. Tulip # 11: Count 56 pleats right from the center valley on Row 9 and complete as the directions given above.

## IV. BACKSMOCKING: (2 strands) Backsmock across Row 2, 3, 4, 5, 6, 7, 8 & 9.

**COLORS USED-** DMC: White, 809, 912, 961, 435 & 414.
**ANCHOR:** 2, 130, 209, 76, 1046 & 235.

## SPACING GUIDE

windmill

| 64 pleats | 32 pleats | 64 pleats |

## PREHISTORIC PLAY

* This design is worked over 166 pleats as shown. The triceratop requires 46 pleats. The brontosaurus requires 39 pleats and the tyrannosaurus rex requires 41 pleats.

* Stitch count for figures are not given in the written instructions. Follow the diagrams carefully for accurate stitch count and cable placement.

## I. BORDERS: (4 strands)

A. Upper Border: To center the border design, find the center 2 pleats on Row 1. Begin with an up cable and cable 83 across. Turn the panel upside down and cable 82 across to complete the left side. Just above cabled Row 1, work 3 cable "picot" stitches across as shown.

B. Lower Border: On Row 9- begin with a down cable and cable across. Add cable "picot" stitches below cabled Row 9 as shown.

C. Ground Outline: After all figures have been completed, go back and stitch the ground outline between Rows 5 & 7 connecting each dinosaur with the outline.

D. Flowers: Work 3 cable flowerettes for each flower as shown after all figures have been completed.

## II. LEFT TRICERATOP: (4 strands)

A. Triceratop: To position, count 67 pleats left from the center valley on Row 5. Begin with a down cable. (Arrow denotes beginning cable stitch.) Stack downward to work the lower portion of the dinosaur. Note all color changes. Then, stack upward to complete.

B. Triceratop's Eye: (3 strands) Work 2 horizontal straight stitches to outline the eye as shown.

C. Triceratop's Body Details: (3 strands) Using floss # 958, work 1 french knot wrapped 2 times for each small spot as shown.

D. Triceratop's Tail: (3 strands) Using floss # 958, work 1 loose straight stitch to form the tail. See the diagram for exact placement. Work 1 french knot, wrapped 2 times each, at the top and bottom of the straight stitch to secure. Using floss # 743, work 4 small straight stitches to form the end of the tail.

## III. CENTER BRONTOSAURUS: (4 strands)

A. Brontosaurus: Count 18 pleats left from the center valley on Row 6. Begin with a down cable. (Arrow denotes beginning cable stitch.) Stack downward to work the lower portion of the dinosaur including the ground outline between its legs. Watch for color changes and where ½ stitches occur. Then, stack upward to complete.

B. Brontosaurus's Eye: (3 strands) Work 1 french knot wrapped 2 times for the eye as shown.

C. Brontosaurus's Mouth: (3 strands) Work 1 straight stitch for the mouth outline.

## IV. RIGHT TYRANNOSAURUS REX: (4 strands)

A. Tyrannosaurus: Count 40 pleats right from the center valley on Row 6. Begin with an up cable. (Arrow denotes beginning cable stitch.) Stack downward to work the lower portion of the dinosaur. Note color changes as they occur. Then, stack upward to complete.

B. Tyrannosaurus's Eye: (3 strands) Work 1 french knot wrapped 2 times for the eye as shown.

C. Tyrannosaurus's Mouth: (3 strands) Work 1 straight stitch for the mouth outline.

D. Tyrannosaurus's Body Details: (3 strands) Using floss # 3760, work 1 french knot wrapped 2 times for each small spot as shown.

## V. CLOUDS: (4 strands)

A. CLOUD # 1: To position, count 69 pleats left from the center valley on Row 2. (Arrow denotes beginning cable stitch.) Begin with a down cable and stack upward to complete the upper portion of the cloud. Then, stack downward to complete.

B. CLOUD # 2: Count 26 pleats left from the center valley on Row 2 and complete as directions given above.

C. CLOUD # 3: Count 62 pleats right from the center valley on Row 2. Begin with an up cable and complete as directions given above.

## VI. BACKSMOCKING: (2 strands) Backsmock across Row 2, 3, 4, 5, 6, 7 & 8.

**COLORS USED-** DMC: White, 310, 519, 518, 3760, 743, 958, 209, 602 & 954.
**ANCHOR:** 2, 403, 1038, 1039, 169, 302, 187, 109, 63 & 203.

## PRETTY IN PINK
### DESIGNED BY LITTLE MEMORIES SMOCKING DESIGNS

* This design is worked over 158 pleats as shown.

* Stitch count for the bow design is not given in the written instructions. Follow diagrams carefully for accurate stitch count and cable placement.

I. **GEOMETRIC DESIGN:** (3 strands if using very light weight or sheer fabric or 4 strands if using a medium to heavier weight fabric.)

A. To center the entire design, find the center 2 pleats just below the pleating thread on Row 1. Begin with an up cable- cable 1; trellis 2 down to Row 1 1/2; cable 1; trellis 2 back up just below Row 1; cable 1. Repeat this design across the right side of the panel. Turn the panel upside down- trellis 2 up to Row 1 1/2; cable 1; trellis 2 back down just below Row 1; cable 1. Repeat this design across to complete the left side.

B. Just above the pleating thread on Row 2- cable 1; trellis 2 up; cable 1 (meeting the down cable stitched on Row 1 1/2); trellis 2 back down to just above the pleating thread on Row 2. Repeat this design across as shown.

C. Just beneath the cable stitch on Row 2- cable 1; trellis 2 down to Row 2 1/2; cable 1; trellis 2 back up and repeat this design across.

D. Just above the pleating thread on Row 3, repeat the design as directions given in Step B.

E. Just beneath the cable stitch on Row 3, repeat the design as directions given in Step C.

F. Just above the pleating thread on Row 4, repeat the design as directions given in Step B.

G. Just below the cable stitch on Row 4, repeat the design given in Step C.

H. Just above the pleating thread on Row 5, repeat the design as directions given in Step B.

I. Just below the cable stitch on Row 5- cable 1; trellis 1 down to approx Row 5 1/3; cable 3; trellis 2 back up. Repeat this design across.

J. Just beneath the cable stitches on Row 5 1/3, begin with an up cable and cable 3. Then, begin with another up cable and cable 5. Repeat this across as shown.

K. Just above the cable stitch on Row 1, begin with a down cable- cable 1; trellis 1 up approx. a third of a row up; cable 3; trellis 1 back down and repeat this design across.

L. Just above the stitching worked in Step K, begin with a down cable and cable 3. Then, begin with another down cable and cable 5. Repeat this design across.

M. On Row 9, begin with an up cable and repeat the design as directions given in Step J.

N. On Row 8 1/2, begin with an up cable- cable 1; trellis 1 down to just above cable stitches on Row 9; cable 3; trellis 1 back up to Row 8 1/2.

II. **BOWS AND FLOWERS:** (4 strands)
A. Bows: To center the bow design, count 15 pleats left from the

center valley on Row 7. Begin with a down cable. (Arrow denotes beginning cable stitch.) Stack upward to work the upper portion of the center bow, watching for all color changes as they occur. Then, stack downward to complete. Continue working to the right to complete the right bow. Then, turn the panel upside down and work the left bow as shown.

B. FLOWERS: See diagram for exact placement and work as shown.

C. Leaves: (3 strands) Using floss # 563, work 1 lazy daisy stitch for each leaf.

III. **BACKSMOCKING:** (2 strands) Backsmock across Row 6, 7 & 8.
**COLORS USED**- DMC: White, 3689, 3326, 3688, 341 & 563.
**ANCHOR:** 2, 49, 36, 66, 117 & 208.

## SANTA'S RIDE
### DESIGNED BY ANGELA PULLEN

* This design is worked over 158 pleats as shown.

* Stitch count for the bow design is not given in the written instructions. Follow diagrams carefully for accurate stitch count and cable placement.

I. **BORDERS:** (4 strands)
A. Lower Border: To center the entire design, find the center 2 pleats on Row 9. Begin with down cable and cable 93 across the right side. Turn the panel upside down and cable 92 to complete the left side. Then, stack upward from Row 9 to work the tree border.

B. Stars: After all of the figures have been stitched, form each star in white metallic thread by working 1 straight stitch over 2 pleats as shown on the diagram.

II. **SANTA AND HIS SLEIGH:** (4 strands)
A. Santa/ Sleigh: To position, count 78 pleats left from the center valley on Row 5. Begin with an up cable. (Arrow denotes beginning cable stitch.) Stack upward to work the upper portion of the sleigh and Santa. Note all color changes as they occur. Then, stack downward to complete.

B. Star Tree Top: (1 strand) Using floss # 726, work 3 small straight stitches as shown to form the star.

C. Bow on Santa's Pack: (3 strands) Using floss # 413, work 2 lazy daisy stitches for the bow loops and 2 straight stitches for the bow ends. See diagram for exact placement.

D. Pom on Santa's Hat: (3 strands) Using white floss, work 1 french knot wrapped 2 times for pom.

E. Santa's Hand: Using floss # 945, work 2 outline stitches to form the hand.

III. **REINDEER:** (4 strands)
A. Reindeer # 1: To position, count 40 pleats left from the center valley on Row 5. Begin with a down cable. (Arrow denotes beginning cable stitch.) Stack downward to work the lower portion of the reindeer. Note color changes as they occur. Then, stack upward to complete the figure.

B. Reindeer # 2: Count 8 pleats left from the center valley on Row 5 and complete as directions given above.

C. Reindeer # 3: Count 29 pleats right from the center valley on Row 4. Begin with a down cable and complete as directions given above.

D. Reindeer # 4: Count 57 pleats right from the center valley on Row 4. Begin with a down cable and complete as directions given above.

E. Reindeer's Eyes and Noses: (3 strands) Using floss # 413, work 1 french knot wrapped 2 times for each eye and nose with the exception of reindeer # 4's nose- use floss # 321 instead.

F. Reins: (2 strands) Using floss # 321, work 4 long loose straight stitches and anchor 1 time for each stitch to position and secure.

## IV. BACKSMOCKING: (2 strands) Backsmock across Row 1, 2, 3, 4, 5, 6, 7 & 8.
COLORS USED- DMC: White, 909, 321, 420, 436, 712, 726, 413 & 945.
ANCHOR: 2, 923, 9046, 374, 1045, 926, 295, 401 & 881.

### SPACING GUIDE

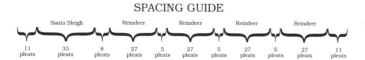

| Santa Sleigh | | Reindeer | | Reindeer | | Reindeer | | Reindeer | |
| 11 pleats | 33 pleats | 8 pleats | 27 pleats | 5 pleats | 27 pleats | 5 pleats | 27 pleats | 5 pleats | 27 pleats | 11 pleats |

## TINY TENNIES
### DESIGNED BY LITTLE MEMORIES SMOCKING DESIGNS

* This design is worked over 168 pleats as shown. Each tennis shoe requires 26 pleats.

* Stitch count for figures are not given in the written instructions. Follow diagrams carefully for accurate stitch count and cable placement.

### I. BORDERS: ( 4 strands)
A. Upper Borders: To center border design, find the center two pleats on Row 2. Begin with a down cable- cable 4;* trellis 3 down to Row 2½; cable 7; trellis 3 back up to Row 2; cable 7. Repeat design from * across right side of the panel. Turn the panel upside down- cable 3;* trellis 3 back up to Row 2½; cable 7; trellis 3 back down to Row 2; cable 7. Repeat this design from * across to complete left side of the panel. Using floss # 797, outline stitch across Row 1 as shown. (Remember, the thread goes above or over the needle when working an outline stitch.)

B. Lower Borders: On Row 8- cable 7; trellis 3 up to Row 7½; cable 7; trellis 3 back down to Row 8 and repeat design across. Using floss # 797, outline stitch across Row 9.

### II. TENNIS SHOES: (4 strands)
A. Shoe # 1: To position, count 70 pleats left from the center valley on Row 5. Begin with a down cable. (Arrow denotes beginning cable stitch.) Stack downward to work lower portion of the shoe. Note color changes and where ½ stitches occur. Then, stack upward to complete the figure.

B. Shoe # 2: Count 34 pleats left from the center valley on Row 5. Begin with a down cable and complete as directions given above.

C. Shoe # 3: Count 11 pleats right from the center valley on Row 5. Begin with a down cable and complete as directions given above.

D. Shoe # 4: Count 47 pleats right from the center valley on Row 5. Begin with a down cable and complete as directions given above.

E. Shoe Laces and Bows: (4 strands) Using floss # 666, work 2 small diagonal straight stitches for laces in the shoes. Work 2 lazy daisy stitches for the bow loops as shown.

### III. BACKSMOCKING: (2 strands) Backsmock across Rows 3, 4, 5, 6, & 7.
COLORS USED- DMC: White, 797, 791, 415, & 666.
ANCHOR: 2, 132, 178, 398 & 46.

### SPACING GUIDE

| tennis shoe | | tennis shoe | | tennis shoe | | tennis shoe | |
| 13 pleats | 26 pleats | 10 pleats | 26 pleats | 18 pleats | 26 pleats | 10 pleats | 26 pleats | 13 pleats |

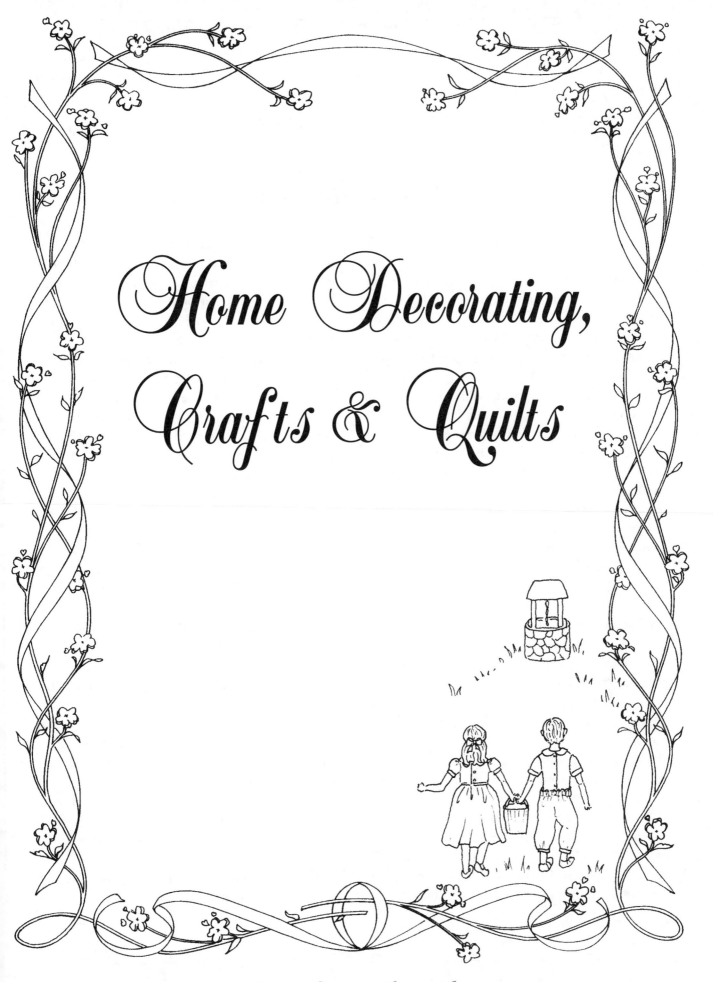

# Home Decorating,
# Crafts & Quilts

# Quilts, Home Decorating & Crafts
## - an Introduction

Clothing is not the only thing sewers can enjoy making for their children and grandchildren. Home decorating projects which are quick and easy are very exciting when making memories for our little ones. This section is going to be fun for you to use if you enjoy this type of sewing and who doesn't? Baby gifts can cost a fortune and not be very personal in addition to costing a fortune. We have several projects for unique baby gifts including the Prince and Princess Sleeps Here door decorations. Also the cutwork bunny would be especially nice for a new baby or for a birthday present for anyone on your list. If you have a star athlete or a budding ballerina, the book ends should be their absolutely favorite presents. I really believe these book ends would be the perfect present for the mother or father of these children also. What mother or grandmother would not like the fan pillow with photo transfers of her favorite Jack or Jill permanently resting on her bed? Enjoy these projects for your home.

Quilts have been a universal way to preserve family memories and to make something which will be treasured for generations to come. Joanna has the quilt which Joe's mother, Emma Pullen, had made for her before she was born. Mom had been a wonderful needle woman in her younger years but her eyesight was failing when we announced that a baby was on the way. She ordered a beautiful kit for a Peter Rabbit quilt and had a quilter make this special quilt for my baby shower. Joanna always had her quilt at the foot of her bed when she was a little girl; this quilt is on the foot of her guest bedroom right now and she will always remember that Gramps gave her this hand made quilt before she was born. My dear friend, Dr. Cornelia Anderson, made Joanna and Chase a complete Noah's Ark bedroom linen ensemble before

Cecil was born. The quilt has an original poem stitched in as well as all of the Martha Pullen Noah's Ark embroidery card designs. This quilt will be treasured by me, Joanna and Cecil forever and I believe by Cecil's children and grandchildren. What a glorious sewing gift to make for a child - a quilt.

We have four quilts for you in this book. One of the quilts, constructed by Louise Baird, is a reproduction of an antique quilt. The appliqué quilt, purchased in Lebanon, Ohio is adorable for children, not just babies. We commissioned Angela Cataldo Pullen to design an alphabet quilt perfect for children of all ages. Since this is a Jack and Jill book, we had Angela design a Sunbonnet Jack and Jill Quilt for you using the beloved theme of sunbonnet children. Our Sunbonnet Jack and Jill children are holding calico balloons on a wonderful day in the flower garden. Charlotte Gallaher designed and contributed her precious soccer quilt, Brandon's Quilt, featuring photo transfers and pure joy of Brandon's years in soccer. Of course you could adapt this to whatever sport your Jack or Jill loves. For many children, sports are absolutely the focal point of extra curricular activities; you can capture these memories in a quilt which I believe will be treasured forever.

All of our quilts and home decorating and craft projects are machine made or glued! For today's busy lifestyles, I think this is exciting for most of us. If you own a machine which embroiders you could substitute machine embroidery for the appliquéd designs on both the alphabet quilt and the antique reproduction quilt. Please enjoy our quilting, home decorating and crafting section we have loved preparing for you. I think you will find these projects to be elegant and fun to make.

# Memory Fan Pillow

*Made of lavender silk dupioni this precious pillow has photos, using fabric photo transfer methods, in the center of three of the portions of the fan. The inside of the fan sections is filled with white English lace netting connected with white American faggoting. Notice the beautiful little English lace points which spill out onto the beautiful scalloped lavender pillow. White tatting surrounds the scallops of the pillow and a beautiful silk ribbon bow (fru fru) is stitched at the bottom of the white lace fan. Purchased pink and green trim surrounds the pictures of the three children. I am so sentimental that a gift like this would be my very favorite under the Christmas tree or for Mother's Day. I cannot think of any mother or grandmother who would not love this fan pillow to keep on her bed or in her favorite chair in any room of the house.*

## Supplies

- 1/3 yard silk dupioni
- Two pieces of batting 12" by 20"
- Polyfil
- 7/8 yard 3/8" wide tatted edging
- 2/3 yard 8" wide scalloped netting lace
- 1 1/2 yards faggoting
- 3/4 yard decorative braided trim (we chose one that resembled roses)
- Photo transfer paper
- 5 yards 4mm silk ribbon for ribbon rossette
- Thread to match silk
- Lightweight thread to match faggoting and lace
- Wash-out marker

## Pattern Pieces

Fan template, triangular lace template, and oval template for photo transfers are found in the pattern envelope.

## Cutting

Two pieces of silk dupioni using the fan template and two pieces of batting using the fan template.

## Construction

NOTE: All seams are 1/2"

1. Refer to the instructions for photo transfer to create three photographs the size of the oval template. Lay photos aside.
2. Trace the triangular lace template onto the netting lace 5 times across the piece with a wash-out marker. Cut out the netting triangles.
3. Trim away the fabric edge from each side of the faggoting. Place the wrong side of the faggoting to the right side of the lace with the outside edges even. Stitch with a narrow zigzag along the side of the faggoting nearest the fan shape of the lace (fig. 1). Trim away the excess lace from behind the faggoting.

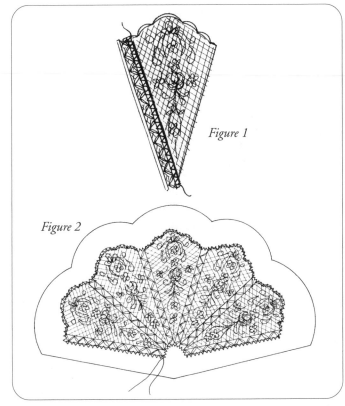

Figure 1

Figure 2

4. Continue placing the faggoting onto the lace, stitching on the inside edge and trimming away the excess lace.
5. Attach the five fan shaped lace pieces together beginning and ending with faggoting.
6. Center the lace/faggoting fan shape onto one of the silk pieces. Stitch with a narrow zigzag around the outside of the faggoting and around the edge of the lace edging (fig. 2).

7. Trim the photo transfers to the size of the oval template. Place the oval photo transfers onto the lace according to the drawing. Zigzag around the edge of each photo.

8. Place the braided trim around each photo transfer and stitch into place to cover up the zigzag.

9. On a flat surface, layer one piece of batting, the pillow top which you constructed above right side up, the pillow back right side down and the other piece of batting. Stitch around the pillow through all layers using a $^1/_2$" seam. Leave approximately 4" open along one of the lower straight edges through which to turn and stuff the pillow (fig. 3). Clip the seam allowance.

10. Turn the pillow right side out and press. Pin along the stitching line well and stitch with a straight stitch through all layers.

11. Butt the tatted edging up to the finished scalloped edge of the pillow. Zigzag with a small stitch just catching the fabric edge. If you prefer, you may stitch this trim on by hand (fig. 4).

12. Refer to the directions for making a ribbon rosette. Create a ribbon reosette with the silk ribbon.

13. Attach the ribbon rosette at the point of the lace fan shape where the faggoting meets.

14. Stuff the pillow through the opening.

15. Stitch the opening of the pillow closed by hand or machine.

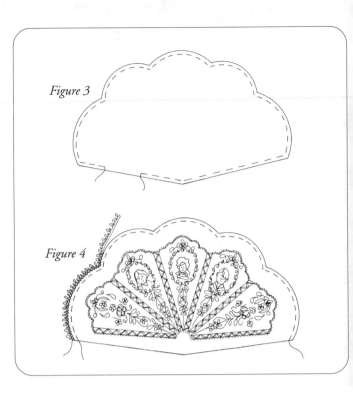

Figure 3

Figure 4

# Baseball Bookends

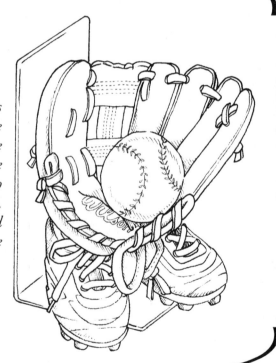

Absolutely the perfect gift for your little league baseball player is this bookend. It is also a wonderful way to preserve memories when little feet have long outgrown the first pair of cleats. I think this gift might be just the perfect father's day present for Dad or Granddaddy after the shoes are not in use anymore! You know how sentimental all of us tend to be about our little one's activities. Anyway, use a regular metal book end, glue the shoes, the glove and the very used and worn ball together and you have the all time perfect gift. You might want to tuck a little picture of the favorite baseball player in this book end also.

## Supplies

One set of black metal bookends (back vertical end 6" by 8") with cork on the bottom
One pair of baseball cleats (small)
1 baseball glove (small)
1 baseball
Some ribbon or rawhide to match the glove to tie it to the bookend
Glue (Tacky craft glue for gluing to metal)

## Directions

Refer to the finished drawing for placement of items.

1. Arrange the shoes on the bookend and glue down.

2. When the glue has dried, place the glove on top of the shoes and tie and glue them to the bookend.

3. Glue the baseball in place in the glove.

# Ballet Bookends

*Oh my do these bookends bring back memories to me of 15 years of driving to dance lessons with Joanna! Dance recitals, ballet shoes, tutus, and pink in general are precious to me. Once again this is the perfect gift for a little girl or for a mother or grandmother to remember those happy times with dance. Using a purchased metal bookend, this treasure is constructed using two books the same size covered in pink wrapping paper. The metal book end is covered with pink silk dupioni. After the books have been glued to the covered book ends, white tulle has been glued along with the well worn ballet shoes. White tulle is inserted into each ballet shoe and a little pink gossamer ribbon has been glued into the whole creation. I am going to search for a little pair of well worn pink ballet shoes and make one of these for myself and for Joanna and Chase's little girl, Cecil. Since I was a dancer and a dance teacher in the past, I might just make one with my own memories of my Mama driving me to dance lessons all of my life.*

## Supplies

One set of metal bookends (vertical end 6" by 8") with cork on the bottom

1 pair of small ballet slippers (pink or peach is nice with white tulle)

1 yard of tulle (if you have a small tutu, you could use that instead)

2 books approximately 1³/₈" thick (can be purchased at a second hand book store)

1 yard sheer ribbon to coordinate with the ballet slippers

Gift wrap or fabric to cover the books

Enough coordinating fabric to cover the bookend

Glue

## Directions

1. Cover the books with the paper or fabric.
2. Cut a piece of fabric 1" wider than the width of the bookend from the selvage edge and long enough to go up the back, down the front and across the bottom with ¹/₂" extra to tuck under at the bottom.
3. Glue the selvage edge at the bottom back of the bookend with ¹/₂" extending on each side. Fold the ¹/₂" on each side around the metal bookend. Glue in place. Fold the fabric down at the top of the bookend, folding under the ¹/₂" and cover the outside of the bookend down to the bend in the metal. Clip the ¹/₂" fold of fabric at the bend. Glue the remaining fabric on the bottom of the bookend and glue the ¹/₂" of fabric to the underside of the bookend (fig. 1). shows how the fabric will be folded to fit the metal bookend.
4. Glue the books to the bookend base.
5. Cut two strips of tulle 10" by the width of the tulle.
6. Stitch a gathering stitch 6" from the edge along the longest side of the tulle. Repeat with the other strip.
7. Pull up the gathers to measure 15" or so.
8. Fold along the gathers and topstitch. This helps to make the gathered strips a little more manageable (fig. 2).
9. Arrange on top of the books and on top of each other to create

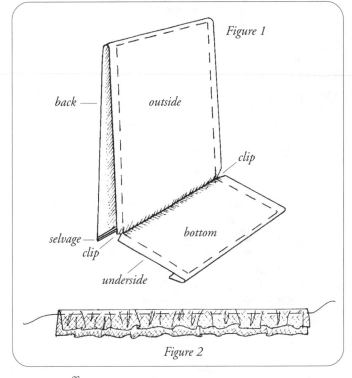

Figure 1

back — outside

clip

selvage — clip

bottom

underside

Figure 2

a tutu effect.
10. Cut 2 squares about 24" each from the leftover tulle.
11. Place one square in each shoe as if you were putting a hankie in a pocket with the points sticking up.
12. Arrange the shoes on top of the tutu.
13. Glue the tutu and shoes down when you are pleased with the placement. **REMEMBER:** Most bookends are viewed from the side and not from the front.
14. Tuck the ribbon around the shoes twisting and twirling as you wish. Glue in place.

# "A Star Sleeps Here" Door Decoration

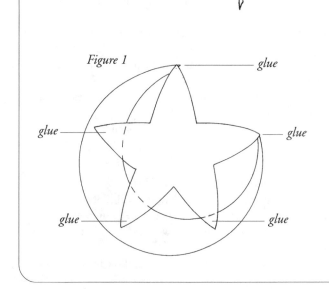

What a special and inexpensive way to recognize a star of any kind. This happy door hanger for a bedroom could be used for any special occasion from a behavior improvement to a special report card or to any other time when your precious ones should be called a star. Of course, I believe all children are stars everyday so you might want to make one just for general purposes! Using thick cardboard a moon has been cut in white and an ecru star has been cut also. Magic markers are all you need to print "A Star Sleeps Here" and to outline the outside of the star in red. Red ribbon is glued on to make the door hanger. Memories are made of this kind of recognition. This would also be a wonderful project for your children or grandchildren to make for grandmother or grandfather who is in assisted living or a nursing home. This is one of those universally fabulous projects which costs almost nothing and says, "I love you" to anyone you present it to.

## Supplies

Two 9-inch square pieces of mat board
1 yard of ⅛" narrow red ribbon
Exacto knife
Permanent red pen
Glue

## Pattern Pieces

Star Template and Moon Template are found in the pattern envelope.

## Directions

1. Cut out the star and moon using an exacto knife with a new blade.
2. Trace the letters onto the star.
3. Write over the tracing with a permanent red pen.
4. Outline the outer edges of the star with red.
5. Place the star on the moon as shown.
6. Glue the star into place on the moon (fig. 1).
7. Glue the ribbon to the back creating a hanger.

Figure 1

# "The Princess Sleeps Here" Door Decoration

*Using wonderful machine embroidery and machine embroidered letters, this is the perfect baby gift. Made of peach silk dupioni, the pillow has ecru edging gathered around the edge. The words "The Princess Sleeps Here" are stitched with a beautiful machine alphabet in dark green. The flowers are green, white, lavender and peach. A purchased tassel hangs from the bottom and a thread from the tassel makes the door hanger. A little gift like this would be adorable for a baby gift and would not cost a fortune to make. To make this gift absolutely perfect, embroider the child's name and birthday on the back of the pillow.*

## Supplies

Two 9" by 7" pieces of peach silk (If you will be doing machine embroidery, be sure to cut the pieces large enough to fit your hoop)
One piece of 9" by 7" tear-away stabilizer (optional)
1 yard of ¹/₂" lace edging
One long silky tassel (peach)
1¹/₄ yards of narrow cord to match the tassel
Sulky Threads for Embroidery:

| | |
|---|---|
| 1174 Dk. Pine Green | 12115 Vari-Pine Greens |
| 1001 Bright White | 1015 Med. Peach |
| 1021 Maple | 2122 Vari-Baby Pinks |

Thread to match silk dupioni
Small amount of polyfil
Princess Door Hanger Template is found in the pattern envelope.

## Directions

1. Place the stabilizer behind the silk and place both into your machine hoop. Embroider the wording on one piece of silk as shown. Choose a machine embroidery floral design and stitch in place above the lettering. Our door hanging was embroidered on a Pfaff sewing machine using cards 10 and 41. If your machine does not have embroidery capabilities you may choose to hand embroider the door hanger using the optional design given. Be sure to keep the embroideries at least ¹/₂" inside the raw edge of the fabric.
2. Cut out a front and back from the silk centering the embroidery on the hanger front.
3. Stitch right sides together with a ¹/₄" seam leaving an opening for turning (fig. 1). Turn right sides out. Stuff lightly with polyfil. Pin opening closed.
4. Fold the cord in half and mark with a pin. Pin this center at the lower point of the "pillow." Stitch the cord around one side of the outer edge using a narrow zigzag and an edge stitch foot if available. Stop at the center top (fig. 2). Repeat with the other side.
5. Tie a knot at the top where the cords meet, then tie a small bow.

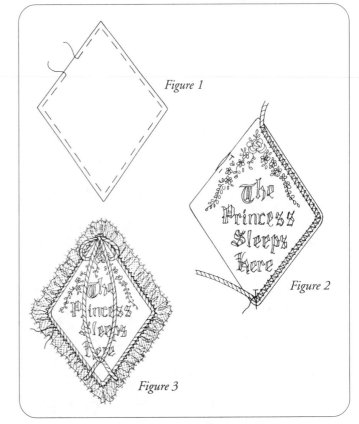

*Figure 1*

*Figure 2*

*Figure 3*

Put a dab of glue or seam sealant on the knot so it can't come undone. Go up about 8 inches and tie another knot. Knot each of the tails where you would like and cut off the excess cord.

6. Gather the lace by pulling the top thread in the heading and stitch it to the cord with a narrow zigzag (fig. 3).
7. Stitch the tassel at the lower point of the hanger and flip the top tassel cord over to make it look like a bow. Stitch the cord in place.

# "The Prince Sleeps Here" Door Decoration

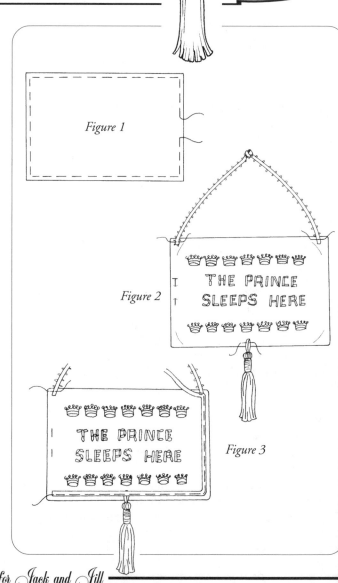

𝒯his beautiful door decoration has the words "The Prince Sleeps Here" machine embroidered in gold; tiny little crowns, also in gold, are embroidered at the top and bottom of the pillow. Gold braid is used around the front of the pillow and for the hangar. A purchased gold tassel hangs from the bottom. For those of us who have an embroidery machine, this is such a personal and inexpensive way to welcome a new baby. Of course the color scheme could coordinate with the baby's nursery theme as well as the embroidered figures on the top and the bottom of this precious gift.

## Supplies

Two pieces of 6" by 8" silk (If you will be doing machine embroidery, be sure to cut the pieces large enough to fit your hoop)
One piece of 6" by 8" stabilizer (optional) Tear-away stabilizer may need to be larger to fit your hoop
1$\frac{1}{8}$ yards of gold braid trim
1 gold tassel
7004 dark gold Sulky thread
Polyfil
"The Prince Sleeps Here" template is found in the pattern envelope.

## Directions

1. Mark the center of the fabric. Place the stabilizer behind the silk and place both into your machine hoop. Embroider the lettering on one piece of silk as shown. Choose a decorative machine embroidery design and stitch in place above and below the lettering. If your machine does not have embroidery capabilities you may choose to hand embroider the door hanger using the optional design given. Be sure to keep the embroideries at least $\frac{1}{2}$" inside the raw edge of the fabric.

2. Remove the stabilizer and place the silk pieces right sides together and stitch with a $\frac{1}{4}$" seam leaving an opening for turning (fig. 1). Turn right sides out. Stuff lightly with polyfil. Pin opening closed.

3. Cut 13" off the gold braid. Tie a loose knot in the middle. Place the ends on each top corner and baste (fig. 2). Hold up to make sure it hangs straight. If it doesn't move the knot in whatever direction it takes to make it hang properly.

4. Pin the tassel in the middle of the lower edge. Baste (fig. 2). Starting at the lower edge, stitch the braid down using whatever stitch works best with the braid you have, hiding the ends of the top hanger cord under the braid (fig. 3). Use seam sealant on all cut edges of the braid.

5. If your tassel has a long loop on the top, pull it through to the back and glue down cutting off the excess.

*Figure 1*

*Figure 2*

*Figure 3*

# Cutwork Flower Calico Bunny

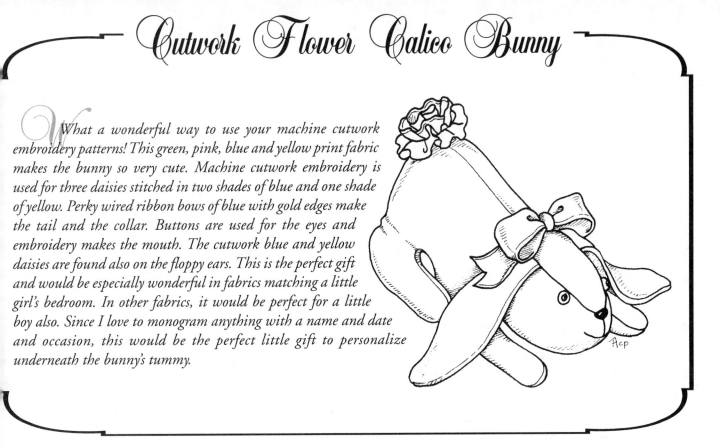

What a wonderful way to use your machine cutwork embroidery patterns! This green, pink, blue and yellow print fabric makes the bunny so very cute. Machine cutwork embroidery is used for three daisies stitched in two shades of blue and one shade of yellow. Perky wired ribbon bows of blue with gold edges make the tail and the collar. Buttons are used for the eyes and embroidery makes the mouth. The cutwork blue and yellow daisies are found also on the floppy ears. This is the perfect gift and would be especially wonderful in fabrics matching a little girl's bedroom. In other fabrics, it would be perfect for a little boy also. Since I love to monogram anything with a name and date and occasion, this would be the perfect little gift to personalize underneath the bunny's tummy.

## Supplies

⅜ yd of floral fabric (a tightly woven fabric works best)
¼ yd coordinating solid fabric for lining beneath the cutwork
½ yd fusible fleece
Purchased eyes and nose
Two yards of wire edged ribbon
Thread to match fabric
Two spools of Sulky thread - colors to coordinate with print
1 spool of yellow Sulk thread
Brown embroidery thread for mouth
Polyfill stuffing
Wash-out marker

## Pattern Pieces

Bunny body, lower head, head side, ear, head top, and under body are found in the pattern envelope.

## Embroidery and Cutting

1. Outline all pattern pieces on the fabric with a wash-out marker.
2. Trace the cutwork design onto each piece. Refer to the section on Cutwork and complete the cutwork on two of the ear pieces and both body pieces.
3. Back the cutwork piece with the coordinating solid fabric.
4. After embroidering and before cutting, fuse fusible fleece to the wrong side of the fabric (don't put fleece on the ear pieces). Stitch just inside the drawn lines of the cutwork pieces with backing to hold the two layers together. Redraw the cutting lines if needed and cut out your pattern pieces.

## Construction

1. Place the ears right sides together and stitch around the ear with a ¼" seam leaving the bottom open for turning. Turn and press. Repeat to complete the other ear. Baste the ears to the side head pieces between the marks, the wrong side of the ear will be

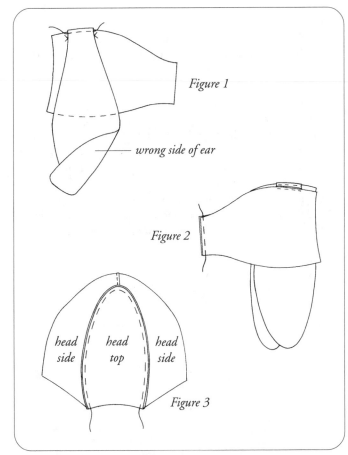

*Figure 1*

*wrong side of ear*

*Figure 2*

*head side*    *head top*    *head side*

*Figure 3*

to the right side of the fabric on the side head piece (fig. 1).
2. Place the head sides with right sides together and stitch the center front together with a ¼" seam (fig. 2). With right sides together stitch the head top to the head sides (fig. 3). With right sides

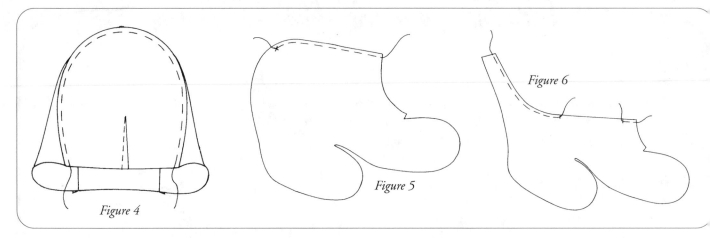

Figure 4

Figure 5

Figure 6

together stitch the dart in the lower head with a ¹/₄" seam. Stitch the lower head to the head sides (fig. 4).

3.  Place the bunny body right sides together and stitch the body sections together along the center back seam from the neck to the X with a ¹/₄" seam (fig. 5). Place the under body sections together along the under seam and stitch leaving the opening between the marks for stuffing and turning (fig. 6). With right sides together stitch the under body to the body starting at the neck base, around the paws and up to the center back on each side. Clip to the stitching at the inner corners (fig. 7). Turn right side out.

4.  Snap glue or sew the eyes and nose in place, refer to the finished drawing for placement. Embroider the bunnies' mouth by hand with embroidery floss.

5.  Stitch the head to the body, matching the center seams and making sure the head is pointed up in the right direction (fig. 8). Be careful not to catch the ears in the stitching.

6.  Turn the rabbit right side out.

7.  Stuff the rabbit and hand stitch closed.

8.  Make a flower tail using a 27" piece of the wire edge ribbon. Pull the wire on one edge to gather the ribbon. Gather the ribbon to measure 7". Fold one edge diagonally and wrap the ribbon around the folded edge. Hand sew it together along the gathers as you wrap it. Fold the raw edge diagonally so it is on the bottom and catch it in your stitching. Hand sew the tail to the rabbit.

9.  Tie the remaining ribbon around the bunny's neck and shape the wires to form a pretty bow. Trim off the excess ribbon.

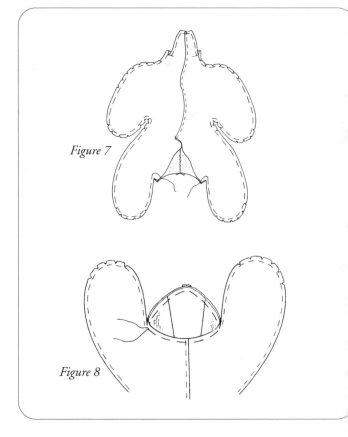

Figure 7

Figure 8

# Embroidered Teddy Bear

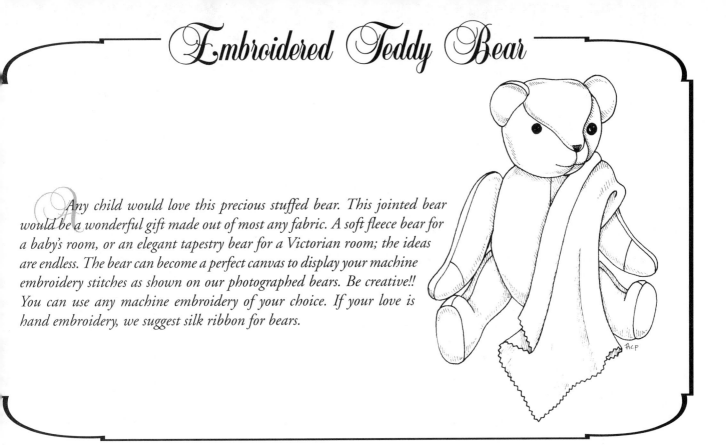

*Any child would love this precious stuffed bear. This jointed bear would be a wonderful gift made out of most any fabric. A soft fleece bear for a baby's room, or an elegant tapestry bear for a Victorian room; the ideas are endless. The bear can become a perfect canvas to display your machine embroidery stitches as shown on our photographed bears. Be creative!! You can use any machine embroidery of your choice. If your love is hand embroidery, we suggest silk ribbon for bears.*

## Supplies

¾ yd fabric (a tightly woven fabric works best)
Thread to match
½ yd fusible fleece
Bear eyes
sets of 35 mm Safety Lock Doll and Bear Joints
Tear-away stabilizer or Solvy for embroidery
Temporary spray adhesive (optional)
Machine embroidery supplies
Open toe foot
Polyfill stuffing
Wash-out marker
Ribbon or doily to tie around your Bear's neck
Large doll needle

## Pattern Pieces

Outer arm, inner arm, hand, ear, foot pad, leg, side head, head gusset and bear body are found in the pattern envelope. Pay special attention to the instructions on the pattern pieces when tracing the pattern pieces. All seam are ¼".

## Embroidery, Cutting, Fusing

1. Cut out the pattern pieces and trace them onto the fabric. When doing this, make sure the pattern pieces are positioned on the fabric so that the fabric will fit in the hoop to do embroideries or to highlight a particular part of the print on the fabric. When tracing the pattern, pay special attention to the instructions on the pattern pieces. Some of the pieces are cut once and then reversed to cut the second so that there will be a right and left side.

2. If the fabric to be embroidered will not fit in the hoop, temporary spray adhesive may be used to adhere the stabilizer to the fabric. The bear can take a long time to make if a lot of embroideries and decorative stitches are used or a shorter time if less stitches are used.

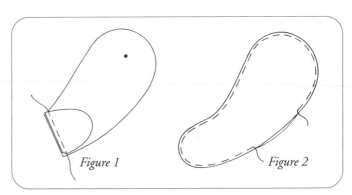

Figure 1                    Figure 2

3. Complete the embroidery referring to your machine instructions. The embroidery on both bears was done on a Viking sewing machine using Viking embroidery designs.

4. To prepare the fabric for cutting, first remove the stabilizer. Retrace the pattern pieces if needed (if the embroideries turned out different that what was expected the pattern pieces may need to be repositioned at this time). When everything is traced properly, fuse the fusible fleece to the wrong side of the fabric.

5. Transfer all markings from the pattern pieces to the fabric. This is a very important step!

6. Iron a second layer of fusible fleece to the areas where the joints will be. A circle the size of a quarter will do, or just use the pattern piece.

7. Cut out all pattern pieces.

## Construction

1. To construct the arm, sew the hand to the inner arm with right sides together using a ¼" seam (fig. 1). With right sides together, sew the inner and outer arm together leaving an opening for turning and stuffing (fig. 2). Turn right side out. Place a small snip at the inner arm joint placement mark.

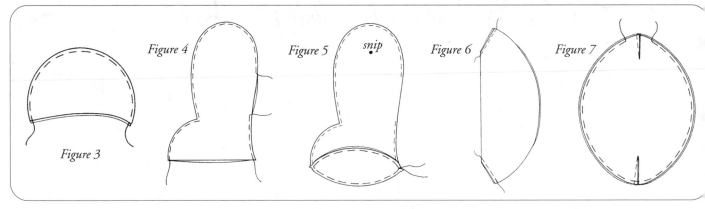

*Figure 4*  *Figure 5*  snip  *Figure 6*  *Figure 7*

*Figure 3*

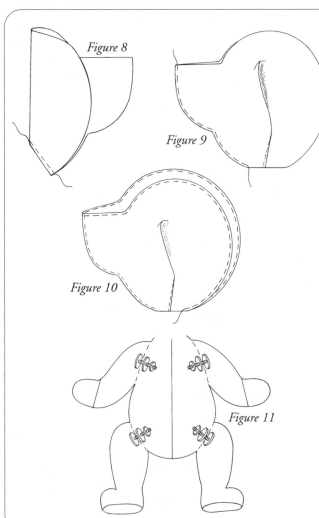

*Figure 8*

*Figure 9*

*Figure 10*

*Figure 11*

2.  Place the ears right sides together and stitch around the ear with a ¹/₄" seam leaving the bottom of the ear open (fig. 3). Turn. Whip the bottom edge of each ear closed by hand.

3.  Place right sides of the legs together. Stitch around the leg leaving the bottom of the leg open and an opening on the side of the leg for stuffing (fig. 4). Sew the foot pad to the bottom of each leg. Place a small snip on the inner leg at the joint placement mark (fig. 5).

4.  Stitch darts in the bear body using a ¹/₄" seam (fig. 6). Make a small snip at the arm joint circles and the leg joint circles. With right sides together stitch the body pieces together leaving a 3" opening in the top (fig. 7). Turn right side out.

5.  Stitch darts in the bear side head using a ¹/₄" seam (fig. 8). Stitch the chin in place from the nose to 1" before the dart (fig. 9). Sew the gusset to the head (fig. 10). There will be a hole in the bottom of the head to join the head to the body. Turn right side out. Insert the eyes in place.

6.  Insert the joints in the proper places and connect the body parts (fig. 11).

7.  Stuff the bear and hand sew the openings closed.

8.  Stitch the ears to the head. Stitch the nose.

9.  Position the head on the body and whip stitch the head in place.

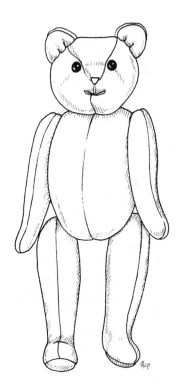

# Antique Reproduction Appliqué Quilt

In Lebanon, Ohio I purchased a baby quilt which was so torn up and worn out, it was put in a big basket of "things" which I believe the dealer thought would never sell. The original quilt was baby blue on the outside and on the major dividing sashing, with small pink squares in the middle sections and white background squares for the appliqué. The appliqué pieces were torn off or there were big holes in some of the sections including parts of the quilt. All of the appliqué stitching on the original quilt was done with black thread; we chose black thread for our appliqué also. You could certainly use other colors to match your fabrics if you do not want the black outlining to be so prominent.

Sweet designs captured my imagination and I purchased this quilt with the full intentions of taking it straight to Louise Baird for reproduction into something you would love to make for either your little girl or little boy. In her masterful way, Louise "redesigned" this quilt in bright colors which are very pleasing for boys and girls and which would go past the baby pink and baby blue stage. Since this book was indeed not a baby book, she redesigned the quilt to fit many different stages of life for a boy or girl. The sashing around the quilt is red cotton; the sashing within the quilt is royal blue; the background fabrics for each block is off white cotton and the quilt is backed in the same royal blue as the outside binding. I love the flannel rabbit, fruit square, birthday cake, dancing girl, teddy bear, happy snowman, ice cream cone, milk bottle and glass, duck, chick coming out of the egg, butterfly, and little girl holding a rattle. Actually these are such precious appliqués, they would be beautiful used on clothing, pillows or other home decorating items. Describing each block will be my pleasure; however, you can use whatever fabrics you have in your stash to make these appliqué. That is what we used.

## Bunny Block

This adorable bunny is made of a white flannel fabric. The appliqué thread around the bunny is black. The whiskers are done using a triple motion straight stitch also in black thread. Pink eyes are appliquéd; the center of the eyes were drawn on with black permanent marking pen. The bunny's nose is a piece of black ultrasuede straight stitched down.

## Pear and Apple Block

Bright red cotton fabric is used for the apple, yellow fabric for the pear and green fabric for the leaf. Black thread is used for the appliqué stitching around the fruit, for the stems of both the pear and the apple and the veins in the leaf.

## Birthday Cake Block

Silver lame is used for the cake stand with the icing on the cake being hot pink. The cake is pale pink and the candle is yellow with a darker yellow flame. The thread color for all of the appliqué is black.

## Dancing Girl Block

Yellow printed calico makes the dress; the pinafore and pantaloons are white dotted Swiss. The flesh is a pale pink with the eyes, nose and mouth appliquéd in black thread. Her hair is dark brown; her kerchief is blue. Her shoes are black as is the thread for all of the appliqué.

## Little Brown Bear Block

Brown fabric is used for the bear; all of the stitched details are in black thread as it was on the antique quilt. A medium blue bow is tied around the bear's neck. The thread for all the stitching including the outline is black.

## Happy Snowman

What a cheerful fellow with white velveteen used for the body. The broomstick is brown and the top of the broom is yellow. His plaid scarf is made of red, yellow and black and his hat is black broadcloth. All of the appliqué stitching as well as the decorative face stitching is done in black thread.

## Ice Cream Cone

This ice cream cone, as on the antique quilt, is strawberry and uses pink fabric. The cone portion is medium brown, similar to the actual color of an ice cream cone. All of the decorative stitching is done in black.

## Milk Bottle and Glass Block

How well I remember glass bottles of milk and glasses which were actually shaped like this one. The fabric for the underlining of "milk" in the bottle and the glass is white broadcloth. The over fabric is a shiny, translucent white fabric. The glass and bottle actually look as if the milk is in them. The stitching on the underpieces of white is done in white stitching. The outline stitching is in black. The straw is white satin stitching in the width of an actual straw.

## Duck Block

This is such a happy bright yellow duck with orange feet and bill. Cotton is the fabric and the stitching around the duck is black. The eye brows and eyes are black also.

## Chick Coming Out of the Egg Block

This baby chick is made of pale yellow cotton with a bright yellow for the bill. The eggs are of a white cotton; all stitching is done in black.

## Butterfly Block

Yellow, purple and pink are the colors for the butterfly's wings; the body of the butterfly is black. All of the fabrics are cotton. The stitching is done in black.

## Little Girl Holding a Rattle

Absolutely adorable is this little girl dressed in a red gingham dress. Her flesh is in a flesh colored cotton; her shoes are black cotton. Her rattle is purple and her hair is brown. There is a red scalloped collar on her dress and in her hair is a red bow. The stitching details on her face are done in black thread as is all of the appliqué.

# Antique Quilt

## Supplies

Black Machine embroidery thread (Sulky 40 weight used)
1³/₄ yard of 45" wide off-white cotton fabric
1²/₃ yard of red cotton fabric (If you don't mind piecing the outside red border of the quilt, you could get by with ¹/₂ yard of red fabric)
2¹/₄ yard of blue cotton fabric
Scraps of different fabrics for appliqué
Fusing agent, such as Steam-A-Seam 2 or Wonder Under
Permanent marking pen
Tear away stabilizer
Black lightweight sewing thread for the bobbin for doing the appliqué such as Sulky Bobbin thread or Mettler 60 weight cotton thread
Open-toe appliqué foot
Size 70/10 to 80/12 sharp needle
Crib size low loft batting
Invisible thread
Ruler, rotary cutter and mat
Walking foot or free motion quilting foot (optional)
¹/₄" quilting or ¹/₄" seam foot (optional)
Safety pins, quilt tack gun or needle and sewing thread for basting

## Appliqué Templates

Antique Quilt Templates (12) are found in the pattern envelope.

## Cutting

1. Cut twelve 14" squares of off-white fabric (fig. 1).
2. From the blue fabric cut one piece 45" by 60" for the quilt backing and 17 rectangles 2¹/₂" by 11" (fig. 2).
3. From the red fabric cut four strips 3¹/₄" by 54" and six 2¹/₂" squares (fig. 3).
4. The remainder of the fabric can be used for appliquéing the quilt squares.

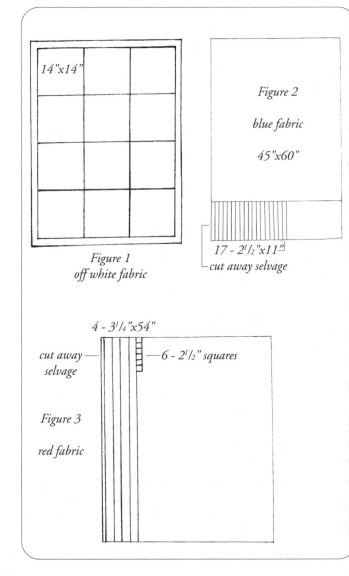

14"x14"

Figure 1
off white fabric

Figure 2

blue fabric

45"x60"

17 - 2¹/₂"x11"
cut away selvage

4 - 3¹/₄"x54"

cut away
selvage

6 - 2¹/₂" squares

Figure 3

red fabric

## Directions

NOTE: Refer to the appliqué section to complete appliqués

- Fold each of the twelve squares of fabric from step 1 cutting into fourths and finger press to mark the vertical and horizontal centers.
- Trace the designs onto the paper side of the fusible web with a permanent, fine line black marker. Cut out, leaving a little paper around each design. Remember to reverse the designs if you want them to appear as they do on the quilt drawing.
- Adhere the fusible web to the wrong side of the appliqué fabrics following the manufacturer's directions. Cut out each appliqué piece on the lines.
- Fuse the cut out shapes to each square lining up the center marks with creases in the squares. You may layer the appliqué pieces on top of each other as long as the fabric beneath doesn't show through the top fabric unless you wish to achieve this effect.
- Set up the machine for appliqué by inserting the sharp needle, placing the open-toe appliqué foot on the machine and black machine embroidery thread in the needle. Use black lightweight or embroidery thread in the bobbin. Set the satin stitch width to 2 mm. Black thread is used for all of the appliqué.
- Refer to the Appliqué Technique Satin Stitch Maneuvers and complete the satin stitch appliqué. Remember to always stitch background to foreground. Place the tear away stabilizer under the fabric before satin stitching. Each block is stitched separately.
- Remove the tear away stabilizer when the satin stitching is complete. Press each square.
- Cut each square to measure 11" by 11", keeping the vertical and horizontal centers as marked in step 1 above.

## Construction

NOTE: All seams are ¹/₄" unless otherwise indicated. Always press the seams to one side, usually toward the darker fabric. During quilt construction, when seams meet, the seams should be pressed in opposite directions to prevent too much bulk at the seam line.

- Lay the pieces out on a table or the floor to arrange placement of the squares. Depending on the color of the fabrics you used to appliqué, you may wish to rearrange the squares. Stitch a blue rectangle from "step 2, Cutting" to the bottom of nine of the completed appliqué squares. Also, stitch a red 2¹/₂" square of fabric from "step 3, Cutting" to the end of six of the 2¹/₂" by 11" strips. Add the last three appliquéd squares and three blue strips below the others (fig. 4).
- Sew the squares together as shown (fig. 5). You will now have three vertical panels consisting of four appliquéd squares divided by a blue strip. Between each vertical panel you will have a strip consisting of four blue strips connected by a red square.
- Stitch the vertical panels together to create the quilt top (fig. 6).
- On each side of the quilt top, add one of the 3¹/₄" by 54" strips from "step 3, Cutting." Trim away the excess strip at the bottom of the quilt top (fig 7).
- Stitch the remaining two red strips from "step 3, Cutting" to the top and bottom of the quilt top. Cut away the excess strip as shown in figure 8.
- Press the quilt top and the quilt backing. Place the quilt backing on a large flat surface with the wrong side up. Fold into quarters and mark the centers on each of the four sides.
- Place the quilt batting on top of the backing.
- Place the wrong side of the quilt top to the batting centering the

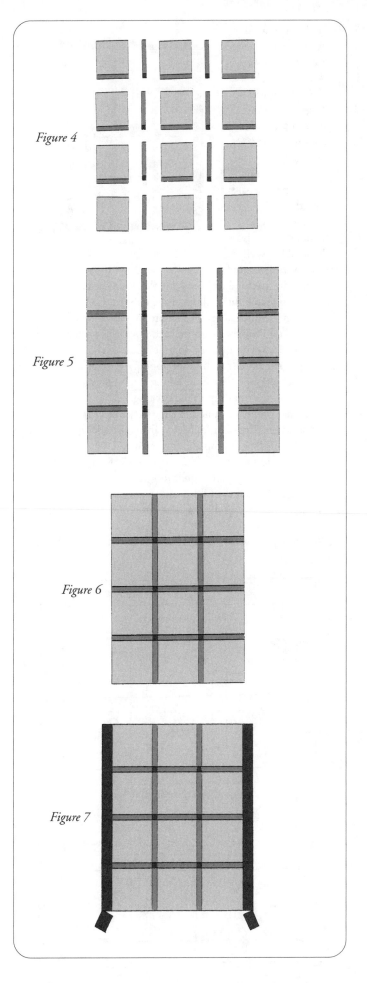

Figure 4

Figure 5

Figure 6

Figure 7

quilt top according to the marks made in step 6 above. The backing and the batting will be larger than the quilt top (fig. 9).

9. Baste all layers together using the safety pins, quilt tack gun or needle and thread. Temporary adhesive may also be used between the layers instead of pins.

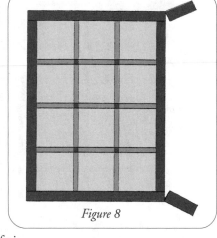

Figure 8

10. Set up the machine with invisible thread in the needle and blue thread to match the backing in the bobbin.

11. Stitch in the ditch along all straight lines using the walking foot or a $^1/_4$" quilting foot with the feed dogs up or a free motion quilting foot with the feed dogs down.

12. Straight stitch quilt around the appliqué designs in each block. All stitching should be done taking care to prevent pleats or puckers in the quilt top or the backing.

13. Place the completed quilt on a large flat surface. Trim the batting to match the edge of the quilt top. Trim the backing to 1" beyond the edge of the quilt top and the batting.

14. On each side, fold the backing so that the cut edge of the backing meets the cut edge of the quilt top (fig. 10).

15. Fold again so that the folded edge meets the $^1/_4$" seam line. Straight stitch using the machine or you may wish to stitch by hand (fig. 10).

16. Repeat steps 14 and 15 for the top and bottom of the quilt (fig. 11)

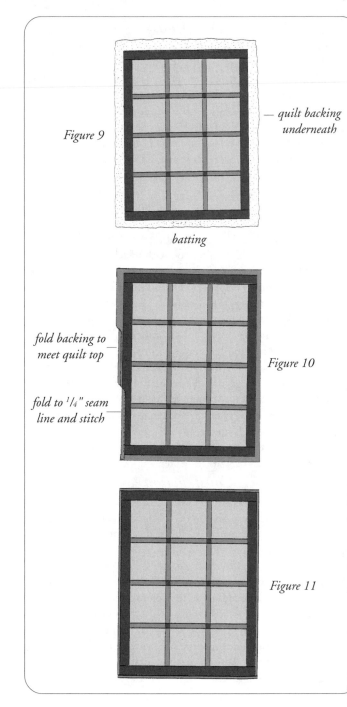

Figure 9

— *quilt backing underneath*

*batting*

*fold backing to meet quilt top*

*fold to $^1/_4$" seam line and stitch*

Figure 10

Figure 11

# Alphabet Quilt

When I think of boys and girls I automatically think of alphabet books and learning the alphabet. How well I remember the plastic letters of the alphabet which were lovingly stuck to the refrigerator during our children's alphabet learning days. How well I remember my Mama's reading A is for apple books to me when I was a child; I read those same books to all of our children. How could we possibly include several quilts for boys and girls without one of them being an alphabet quilt? Being a school teacher I can think of all kinds of games one could play looking for the elephant, the house, the insect or the donut as well as looking for the E, the Q, the S and so on. Our children loved bright colors; this quilt is done in bright colors. The basic background of the quilt is white; the sashings and bindings are bright red. The back of the quilt is white. There are flowers in the upper right and lower left hand corners. The "A is for Apple" is in the upper left corner and the "Z is for Zebra" is in the lower right corner. The quilt is made of 100% cotton quilting fabric; the batting is polyester low loft batting. The decorative threads are Sulky 40 weight rayon thread with a little sulky metallic thread in several places. Have fun making this quilt for your favorite boy or girl. I believe it will be treasured for many generations to come.

### A square
The A square has a red apple with a green leaf, a brown stem, and brown lettering.

### B square
The B square has a brown baseball bat with red grip tape around the bottom. Underneath the bat is a white baseball with red accent stitching.

### C square
The C square has a cream colored cow with brown spots and a six stringed brown tail. The cow lettering is in purple. There are three flowers around the quilt. On the left side there is a purple flower. On the right there is a red flower, and on the bottom middle there is a yellow flower. Each flower has a green stem with a few strands of green grass thread.

### D square
The D square has a brown donut with pink icing and pink lettering. There are blue, yellow, red, and green speckles on the pink icing.

### E square
The E square has a gray elephant with gray lettering. The elephant has a black round eye and a white tusk.

### F square
The F square has a blue flower with green leaves and a green stem. The flower's center is yellow along with yellow lettering.

### G square
The G square has a cream colored goat with a black eye. There is a yellow, pink, and blue flower surrounded by several strands of green grass. The lettering is in yellow.

### H square
The H square has a red house with a black roof outline, a maroon colored chimney, a circular silver window, and a brown door along with a brown fence. There is a half circle of green grass with red, yellow, blue, and, purple flowers on the grass. The lettering is outlined in red.

### I square
The I square has a red insect with a black head, black antennas, and a black speckled head. The insect is sitting on a green leaf with a green stem. The lettering is in green.

### J square
The J square has three silver jacks along with a silver ball. The lettering is in green.

### K square
The K square has a large purple kite along with a smaller blue kite. The strand on both kites is a cream color. The purple kite has a green, blue, yellow, and peach bow attached to the cream strand. The blue kite has a red, blue, and orange bow attached to its cream strand

### L square
The L square has a light pink heart along with a dark pink outline. The words BE MINE are in the center of the light pink heart. The lettering is in light pink.

### M square
The M square has a gray mouse with a black eye and a black nose. The inside of the mouse's ear is light pink. The gray mouse is eating a piece of light yellow cheese with dark yellow speckles. The lettering is in black.

### N square
The N square has a silver needle with blue thread through it. The lettering is in blue to match the thread.

### O square
The O square has a gray owl with a white tummy and white eyes with black dots in the center of the white eyes. The owl is on a brown stem with green leaves. The lettering for the word owl is brown and the hoo hoo is gray.

### P square
The P square is a silver plane with white clouds outlined in silver. There are two black birds. One bird is above the plane and the other is below the plane. The lettering is in baby blue.

### Q square
The Q square is a light purple quilt with dark purple squares. The quilt is outlined in light yellow. Inside the dark purple quilt squares are light purple hearts.

### R square
The R square is a colorful rainbow with a big yellow sun. The rainbow colors include red, orange, yellow, green, blue, and purple. The clouds underneath the rainbow are white with a silver outline. The lettering is in dark blue.

### S square
The S square is a cream colored snail with a brown shell. The snail has a brown eye and the lettering is in gold.

### T square
The T square has a dark green turtle with a light green shell. The turtle has a black eye and the lettering is in green.

### U square
The U square has a dark blue umbrella with a light blue lining. The umbrella handle is silver with a brown grip. The raindrops that surround the umbrella are metallic white. The lettering of the U square is in brown.

### V square
The V square is a dark brown violin. The fingerboard is cream colored with dark brown strings and tuning pegs. The bow is dark gray, and the lettering is also dark gray.

### W square
The W square is a dark gray whale with a white and black eye. The scallops of water below the whale are light blue as well as the three light blue threads of water coming out of the whale's head.

### X square
The X square is a white xylophone outlined in metallic silver. The mallets are cream and brown The lettering of the X square is in red.

### Y square
The Y square is a metallic silver mirror trimmed in light brown. The lettering of the word you and the letter Y are in black.

### Z square
The Z square is a black zebra with metallic silver spots. There is a white cloud outlined in silver with a yellow sun peaking through the cloud. The lettering is in yellow.

# Alphabet Quilt

## Supplies

3¹⁄₃ yards of white Victorian batiste for squares and backing
2 yards of red fabric for strips and binding
45" by 60" quilt batting
Assorted scrap fabrics for appliqué
2 yards of paper backed fusible web
2 yards of tear away stabilizer
Machine embroidery threads to match the appliqué fabrics
Wash-out fabric marker
Permanent marker
Optional: ruler, rotary cutter and mat
NOTE: Wash and press all of the fabrics to be used in the quilt.

All seam allowances are ¹⁄₄".

NOTE: Accuracy in cutting and stitching the ¹⁄₄" seam allowance is very important! Measure the quilt top before cutting the white strips in steps 19 and 22. Adjust measurement if necessary.

## Templates

Templates for the quilt squares A - Z and the Zigzag template are found in the pattern envelope.

## Directions

1. Wash, dry and press all of the fabrics to be used in the quilt. A light coating of spray starch can be used.
2. Cut 28 blocks 7" square from the white Victorian. Fold each square to mark the vertical and horizontal center of each block.
3. Trace the appliqué pieces onto the paper side of the fusible web. Remember to reverse the template if you want the square to be identical to the finished drawing. Example: If you do not reverse the template the elephant will be facing the other direction. However, the A B C's will need to be reversed to read correctly.
4. Cut out roughly around the appliqué pieces (not directly on the lines).
5. Apply the fusible web with the drawn designs to the wrong side of the fabrics to be used in the appliqué. Cut out each piece o the lines. Keep the pieces for the different blocks separate.
6. Place the white fabric block on top of the template matching th vertical and horizontal centers.
7. Remove the paper backing from the appliqué piece
8. Place the white fabric block on top of the template matching the center
9. Remove the paper from the pieces of only one block at a time
10. Fuse the pieces to the white square. NOTE: Always fuse the piec background to foreground. When a piece is in front of anothe piece as you work background to foreground, the top piece shoul cover up a bit of the under piece.
11. Satin stitch appliqué the designs to the squares. Place a tear awa stabilizer under the stitching.

## Special Block Instructions

"B Block" - The stitching lines on the baseball are stitched with feather stitch.

"C Block" - The 5-petal flowers are stitched using a football shape satin stitch. If you do not have a preprogrammed stitch for you machine you may increase and decrease the width of the stitch t create the football shape. Use different colors for each flower. Th stems and grass are stitched in green with a narrow satin stitch. Th eyes and nostrils of the cow are stitched with a tiny satin dot. Th tail is made by using a triple straight stitch and a 1.5 length.

"D Block" - The dots on the "icing" of the donut are made by stitchir tiny satin   stitch dots in various colors.

"E Block" - The elephant's eye is made by using an oval or tiny footba shape. The hoofs are made by widening the satin stitch at the fron edge of each foot.

"G Block" - The 4-petal flowers are stitched in the same way as thos for Block C. A center satin stitch dot is added in the middle of eac flower. This may also be achieved by increasing and decreasing th width if you do not have a suitable stitch on your machine.

"H Block" - The "fluffy" flowers are made by stitching a wide ba tack with the length at 0. Continuing making bar tack petals aroun the flower. When you have the desired number of bar tacks, stitch tiny circle in the center of each flower to secure. On the back of th square, clip the bobbin threads of the bar tack. Using a large blun tipped needle or a skewer, pull the threads on the front of the squa until the clipped bobbin threads pull to the front at the end of eac petal. Remove the bobbin threads from the ends of the "petals". Th threads will fray around the center of each flower.

"I Block" - The spots on the ladybug are made with a tiny sati stitched dot.

"J Block" - The dots at the ends of the jacks are made with a sati stitched dot.

"K Block" - The "bow ties" on the kite tail of the small kite are mad with a satin stitch triangle.

"M Block" - The eye, nose and holes of the cheese are made wi satin stitch dots.

"N Block" - The needle is made by gradually increasing the width of the satin stitch towards the top of the needle.

"P Block" - The dots at the ends of the wings of the birds are made with a sating stitch dot.

"Q Block" - The hearts on the quilt are made using a preprogrammed heart shape.

"S and T Block" - The eyes are stitch using a tiny satin stitch dot.

"U Block" - The raindrops are satin stitched teardrop shapes.

"V Block" - The strings of the violin are made with a triple straight stitch.

"W Block" - The black portion of the whale's eye is made with a "football" shaped satin stitch.

"Z Block" - The stripes on the zebra are made with satin stitching increasing and decreasing the width. The rays of the sun are made using a triple straight stitch.

12. Stitch all letters and words using a satin stitch with a width of 1 mm.
13. Remove all of the tear away stabilizer from behind the squares. Press all squares right side down on a towel.
14. Cut strips of red fabric 1¼" by the width of the red fabric.
15. From the long strips, cut 18 that are 7" x 1¼".
    Stitch the 7" strips to the right hand side of blocks B, C, D, F, G, H, J, K, L, N, O, P, R, S, T, V, W and X. Press the seam flat and then toward the red fabric (fig. 1).
16. Stitch the blocks together to make four horizontal rows as follows: First row - B, C, D, E; Second row - F, G, H, I; Third row - J, K, L, M; Fourth row - N, O, P, Q; Fifth row - R, S, T, U; Sixth row - V, W, X, Y. Press the seams toward the red fabric. (fig. 2).
17. Stitch a 1¼" wide by 28¾" long strip to the bottom edge of rows 1 through 5. Press the seams flat and then toward the red fabric (fig. 3).
18. Stitch the six horizontal rows together to form the center of the quilt. Add a 1¼" wide red strip to each side of the center of the quilt (fig. 4).
19. Cut 2 strips of white fabric 7" x 43¼" long. Stitch one to each long side of the panel using a ¼" seam allowance (fig. 4). Press the seams toward red fabric.
20. Stitch a 1¼" wide red strip to the top and bottom of the panel. Press the seams toward the red fabric (fig. 4).
21. Add a 1¼" x 7" red strip to the right side of the "A" block and one of the corner flower blocks (fig. 5). Add a 1¼" x 7" red strip to the left side of the "Z" block and one of the corner flower blocks (fig. 6). Press the seams toward the red fabric.
22. Cut 2 strips of white background fabric 7" x 28 ¾". Stitch the red strip of the "A" block to one short end and the red strip of the flower block (the one with the red strip on the left side of the block) to the other short end. Repeat with the other strip and the remaining flower block and the "Z" block (fig. 7). Press the seam toward the red fabric. These strips should equal the width of the quilt. Measure your quilt to make certain that these measurements will fit EXACTLY.
23. Stitch these strips to the top and bottom of the quilt top (see finished drawing). Press the seams toward the red fabric.

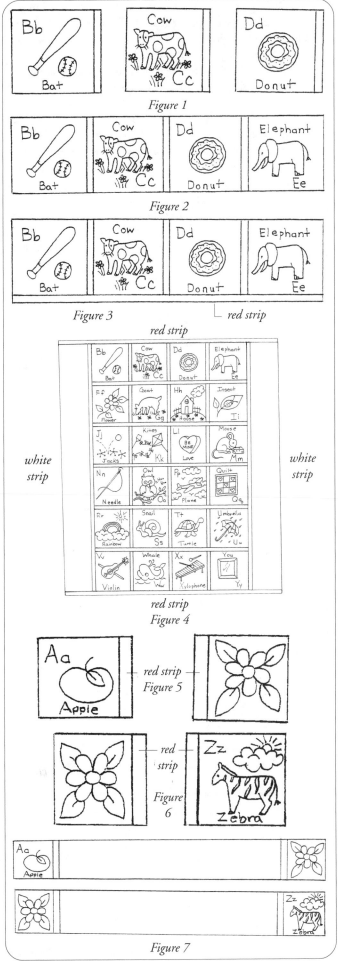

Figure 1

Figure 2

Figure 3    red strip

red strip

white strip

white strip

red strip

Figure 4

red strip
Figure 5

red strip

Figure 6

Figure 7

24. Trace the Zigzag Template onto the white panels added in steps 19 and 22 placing the raw edge of the fabric even with the line indicated. Adjust placement if necessary. Continue the zigzag pattern across the panel (see finished drawing).

25. Place the stabilizer behind the panel and satin stitch along the drawn zigzag shape. Remove the stabilizer and press well.

26. Place the quilt top on a flat surface and measure. Cut a piece of white Victorian for the quilt backing ¹/₂" larger than the quilt top. Also, cut a piece of quilt batting ¹/₂" larger than the quilt top.

27. Sandwich the batting between the quilt top and the quilt backing. Pin securely with large safety pins or use a quilt tacking gun to secure the layers together.

28. Pin well around the outside edge of the layers. Stitch the layers together ¹/₄" from the raw edge of the **quilt top - not the batting.**

29. Using a walking foot or quilting foot, straight stitch in the ditch on each side of the red strips between the squares. Stitch across the red strip which overlaps the one beneath.

30. Straight stitch on each side of the zigzag shape on all four sides of the quilt.

31. Place the quilt on a flat surface and measure around the outside edges. Cut enough bias 2¹/₂" wide from the red fabric to go around the quilt adding several inches for each mitered corner. Connect the bias strips where necessary with a diagonal seam.

32. Fold the bias in half and press. Place the raw edges of the bias strip even with the raw edge of the **quilt top - not the batting.** Pin well.

33. Stitch the bias to the outer edge of the quilt using the stitching line from step 28 as a guide mitering all four corners.

34. Trim the backing and batting even with quilt top.

35. Fold the bias over the batting and the backing. Slip stitch the fold of the bias to the stitching line on the back of the quilt.

*Zigzag Template for ABC Quilt*

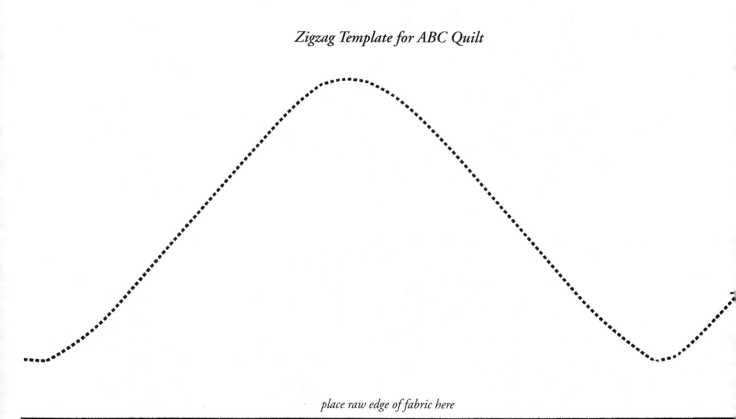

*place raw edge of fabric here*

# Brandon's Quilt

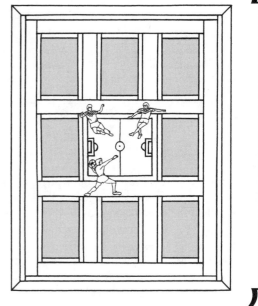

Charlotte Gallaher designed and made this quilt for her nephew, Brandon. Celebrating his love of soccer and his dedication to the sport, Charlotte chose pictures of him with his soccer ball through the years to transfer onto fabric and then to use in the quilt squares. The base of the quilt front is a navy and royal blue fabric. The sashing is made of yellow stars on a blue background. There is another sashing piece of red and blue with stars in-between. The middle of the quilt has a green soccer field with three players in action shots done in appliqué. Yellow fabric outlines each photo transfer picture of Brandon. The lining of the quilt is done in a soccer fabric and there is a soccer ball done in appliqué. Charlotte put a happy birthday message, Brandon's full name and from "Aunt Charlotte Gallaher" in portions of the soccer ball appliqué. This quilt is really a treasure if you have a beloved child who loves soccer. If your child participates in another sport this quilt idea can be easily adapted to another sport. Please look at this wonderful quilt on the photographed pages of this book to see Brandon's photos on the quilt.

## Supplies

Enough white or ivory cotton fabric to cut eight squares 6" by 8". Yardage will vary depending on the width of the fabric.
15" square of white fabric for soccer ball on the back of the quilt
Scraps of black fabric for sections on the soccer ball
$^1/_4$ yard of fabric A - gold fabric
1 yard of fabric B - shaded blue fabric
1 yard of fabric C - red/blue/gold print
$^1/_2$ yard of fabric D - green fabric
1 yard of fabric E - dark blue with gold stars
2 yards of fabric F - blue fabric with soccer balls
Small pieces of fabric in flesh, blue, white and gold for appliqué
Thread to match the fabric for quilting
Invisible thread
Sulky threads in colors to match the appliqué fabrics
Black Sulky thread
Tear-away stabilizer
Wash-out Marker
Safety pins, quilt tack gun or needle and sewing thread for basting
Fusible web
15" square of fusible batting
Batting for quilt
All seam allowances are $^1/_4$".

## Templates

Soccer Field template, Soccer Players templates (3) and Soccer Ball template are found in the pattern envelope.

## Cutting

1. Cut the white or ivory fabric into eight squares 6" by 8". Lay aside.
2. From fabric A (gold fabric) cut sixteen strips $1^1/_2$" wide by 5" long. Label and lay aside. Also cut sixteen strips $1^1/_2$" wide by $9^1/_4$" from fabric A. Label and lay aside.
3. From fabric B (shaded blue fabric) cut four pieces $3^1/_2$" by $9^1/_4$". Also cut four pieces $3^1/_3$" by $25^1/_2$" and two pieces $3^1/_2$" by $38^3/_4$". Label all pieces and lay aside.

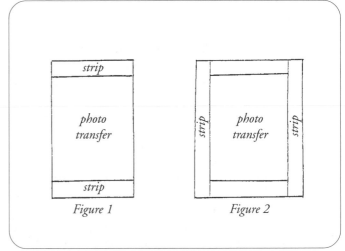

Figure 1        Figure 2

4. From fabric C (red/blue/gold print) cut bias strips $2^1/_2$" wide that when sewn together will be a continuos strip $4^1/_2$ yards long. Lay aside.
5. From fabric D (green fabric) cut a rectangle 18" by 15". Lay aside.
6. From fabric E (blue with yellow stars) cut strips $2^1/_4$" wide that when sewn together will be a continuos strip approximately $4^3/_4$ yards long. Repeat to create a second strip approximately $4^3/_4$ yards long.

## Directions

1. Follow the package instructions for transferring the photos and transfer the photos to the eight squares of fabric cut out in "step 1 - Cutting." Trim the fabric squares to measure 5" by $7^1/_4$" centering the photo image.
2. Sew the 5" long strips from "step 2 - Cutting" to the top and bottom of each photo transfer (fig. 1). Press the seams towards the picture on each piece.
3. Sew the $9^1/_4$" from "step 2 - Cutting" to the sides of each picture. Press the seams toward the strips (fig. 2).

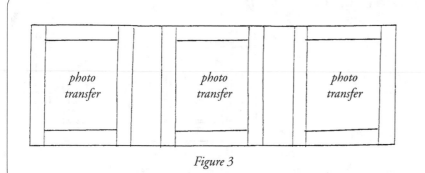

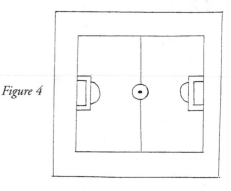

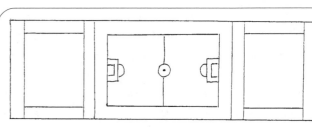

Figure 3

Figure 4

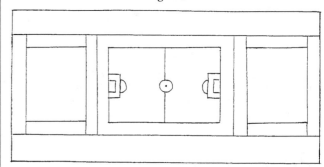

Figure 5

Figure 6

Figure 7

Figure 8

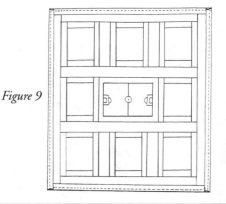

Figure 9

4. Stitch one $3^{1}/_{2}$ by $9^{1}/_{4}$" pieces from "step 3 - Cutting" between two of the pictures on the side edges. Press the seam toward the strip. Join the second picture to the third picture with another $3^{1}/_{2}$" by $9^{1}/_{4}$" piece forming the top row of pictures (fig. 3). In the same manner assemble the bottom row of pictures using the remaining $3^{1}/_{2}$" by $9^{1}/_{4}$" pieces.

5. Using a wash-out marker trace or draw the soccer field design lines onto the center of the 18" by 15" piece from "step 4 - Cutting" (fig. 4). Stitch along the traced lines with white Sulky thread using a narrow satin stitch (width 1.5). Use tear-away stabilizer underneath the stitching. Tear away the stabilizer after stitching and press the rectangle well.

6. Trace the soccer figures to the paper side of the fusible web. Fuse the traced figures onto a skin-colored fabric. In the same manner, trace the shirt, pants, socks and soccer ball onto fusible web and then to the appropriate color fabric. Iron on the "clothes" to the figures. Set aside.

7. Trim the soccer field rectangle from step 5 to measure $9^{1}/_{4}$" by 13".

8. Sew the two remaining photo transfers to each side of the soccer field rectangle (fig. 5).

9. Sew a $3^{1}/_{2}$" by $25^{1}/_{2}$" piece from "step 3 - Cutting" to the top and bottom of the pictures/soccer field row. Press the seams toward the strips (fig. 6). Attach the other two 3-picture panels above and below the center panel. Attach the remaining two $3^{1}/_{2}$" by $25^{1}/_{2}$" to the top and bottom of the panel (fig. 7).

10. Place the soccer figures onto the center fabric piece referring to the finished drawing. Iron the figures into place. Using the appropriate Sulky thread colors, stitch the uniforms, socks, shoes and soccer ball using appliqué techniques.

11. Sew the two $3^{1}/_{2}$" by $38^{3}/_{4}$" strips from "step 3 - Cutting" to each side of the panel (fig. 8).

12. Attach the $2^{1}/_{2}$" wide bias strips together to create at least $4^{1}/_{2}$ yards of bias. Fold the strips in half, wrong sides together, having the raw edges even. Press. Pin to the right side of the quilt with the raw edges of the quilt and the bias even. Stitch the strip to the top and bottom first and then down each side. Baste the folded bias to the quilt at $^{1}/_{4}$" from the raw edges (fig. 9).

13. Cut a piece of batting 6" to 7" larger on all sides than the quilt top.

14. Measure the piece of batting cut in step 13 and cut a backing for the quilt from fabric F (blue with soccer balls) the same size as the batting.

15. Place the backing on a large flat surface with the wrong side up. Center the batting over the backing and place the quilt top right side up on top of the batting. The batting will extend 6" to 7" beyond the quilt top.

16. Pin, baste or use a quilt tacking gun to secure the layers together in several places.

17. Using invisible thread in the needle and thread to match the quilt backing in the bobbin, quilt through all layers by stitching in the ditch with a straight stitch along the seam lines and the outlines of the soccer players.

18. Stitch the $2^{1}/_{4}$" strips of fabric E from "step 6 - Cutting" together until you have enough to go around the entire quilt top and miter each corner (approximately $4^{3}/_{4}$ yards).

19. Place the fabric strip from step 18 right sides together to the quilt sandwiching the bias strip in between (fig. 10).

20. Miter the corners, folding the strip away from the quilt to assure a pretty miter. Pin the layers together. If you prefer not to miter the outside border, sew the border across the top and bottom and then down each side as done in steps 9 and 11.

21. Stitch all layers together using the basting seam from step 12 as a guide (fig. 10).

22. Press the border away from the quilt and the bias strip towards the quilt. Press the miters well.

23. On the back of the quilt, trim only the backing away $^{1}/_{4}$" from the seam line stitched in step 22 (fig. 11).

24. Trim the batting even with the outermost edge of the quilt top (fig. 12).

25. Stitch the remaining $2^{1}/_{4}$" strips together to make one continuous strip approximately $4^{3}/_{4}$ yards long. Press under $^{1}/_{4}$" along one long side.

26. Place the strips right sides together to the border on the quilt top finishing the corners as in step 21 above.

27. Stitch together with a $^{1}/_{4}$" seam through the two layers of fabric and the layer of batting.

28. Turn the border to the back of the quilt and hand stitch to the seam line created in step 22 above.

29. Hand stitch all miters to secure.

30. Enlarge a picture of a soccer ball on a copier to the size you desire for the back of the quilt.

31. Trace the ball's lines onto white fabric. Appliqué black fabric sections to the "black" areas of the ball using fusible web.

32. Iron fusible batting to the back and straight stitch $^{1}/_{4}$" from the edge around outside of the soccer ball. Trim the batting and fabric close to the straight stitch. Zigzag (width - 1.5) over the straight stitch letting the outside swing of the zigzag fall just beyond the raw edge of the fabric. Satin stitch over the outline of the sections of the soccer ball. Slip stitch the soccer ball in a corner on the back of the quilt.

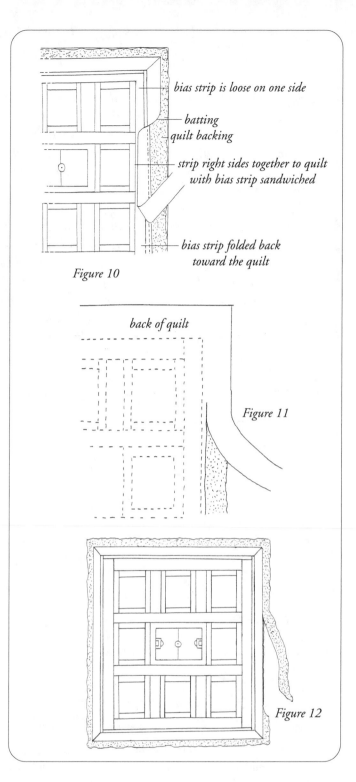

*bias strip is loose on one side*

*batting*
*quilt backing*

*strip right sides together to quilt with bias strip sandwiched*

*bias strip folded back toward the quilt*

*Figure 10*

*back of quilt*

*Figure 11*

*Figure 12*

# Sunbonnet Jack & Jill Quilt

What would a child's quilt collection be without a sunbonnet variety? The sashing of this quilt is blue, the binding is pink and the back of the quilt is white. Using various colors of solid cotton fabrics as well as printed calico fabrics, these three children are holding balloons on a wonderful afternoon. I think the time of year is early spring because of all the wonderful calico flowers blooming underneath their feet on the quilt. There is a green strip of fabric representing the grass and the rest of the quilt background is white. One of the sunbonnet girls is wearing calicos in red, navy and ecru. The hands of all the children are beige flesh colored. The girls' shoes are brown; the boy's are black. Our little man is wearing red, and gold and the other little Jill is wearing shades of lavender, lavender stripe and a lavender hat. The flowers are in all shades of blue, pink, purple, beige and gold. Nearly every color is represented in the balloons and the strings of the balloons are done in a medium goldish beige. The quilt is primarily appliquéd with a little machine embroidery and triple stitching for the embellishment. The quilt is backed in white.

## Supplies

2¼ yds. of white fabric for background and backing
³⁄₈ yd. green fabric for the ground
1½ yds. of blue fabric for border
½ yd. pink fabric for binding
Scraps of fabrics for the appliqué
White sewing thread
Pink sewing thread to match the binding fabric
Machine embroidery threads to match the appliqué fabrics
Temporary adhesive spray (Optional) (KK2000)
Tear-away stabilizer
Regular sewing foot
Open toe appliqué foot
Paper backed fusible web
Permanent marker such as an ultra fine Sharpie
Wash-out marker
Ruler

## Templates

Sunbonnet "Jack and Jill" Quilt template is found in the pattern envelope.

## Directions

1. Wash, dry and press all of the fabrics to be used in the quilt. Do not use fabric softener.
2. Cut white background "sky" fabric 30" long and 27" wide. Mark the vertical center (fig. 1).
3. Cut green "ground" fabric 13" long by 27" wide. Mark the vertical center (fig. 2).
4. Trace the "ground line" onto a strip of tear-away stabilizer. Mark the vertical center.
5. Place the strip of stabilizer with the traced line along the upper edge of the green fabric, matching the vertical center marks. Straight stitch along the line through the stabilizer using a short stitch length (about 1.5 mm) (fig. 3).
6. Carefully tear the stabilizer away. Turn under and press above the stitched line, clipping as necessary to obtain a flat edge (fig. 4).

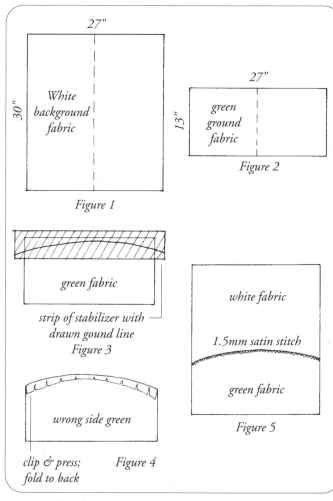

Figure 1

White background fabric

27"

30"

Figure 2

green ground fabric

27"

13"

Figure 3

green fabric

strip of stabilizer with drawn gound line

Figure 4

wrong side green

clip & press; fold to back

Figure 5

white fabric

1.5mm satin stitch

green fabric

7. Place the folded edge of the ground fabric along the lower edge of the white fabric and satin stitch on the fold using a 1.5 mm stitch width. Trim the white and green fabric on the wrong side, leaving a ¼" seam allowance (fig. 5).

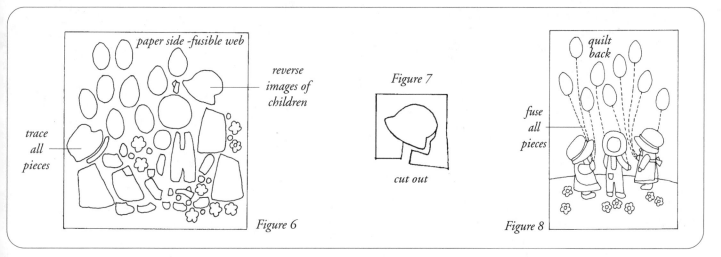

paper side -fusible web

reverse images of children

trace all pieces

*Figure 6*

*Figure 7*

cut out

quilt back

fuse all pieces

*Figure 8*

8. To duplicate this appliqué design, reverse the images. Trace all of the appliqué shapes onto the paper side of the fusible web. Roughly cut out all of the pieces (fig. 6).

9. Fuse the web to the wrong side of the chosen appliqué fabrics. Cut out the pieces on the traced line (fig. 7).

10. Fuse the pieces to the quilt background following the placement on the template. Fuse from the background to the foreground (fig. 8).

11. Trace the balloon strings, flower stems and leaves on the quilt background with a wash-out marker.

12. Stitch the balloon strings using a triple straight stitch, narrow open zigzag or a "lightening" stitch (fig. 8).

13. Satin stitch appliqué all of the shapes to the background, using matching embroidery thread for each piece. Refer to the appliqué instructions as needed. Use a stabilizer under the background fabric where satin stitching is done. Always stitch background to foreground. Do not stitch the flowers at this time (fig. 9).

14. Use a medium width open zigzag stitch for the stems, W = 2, L = .5-1. Start at the bottom of the stem working toward the flower. When a leaf is reached, pivot so that the traced leaf is in front of the foot (fig. 10a). Change the machine settings for a satin stitch length, the width will be adjusted as the leaf is stitched. While stitching toward the tip of the leaf, increase and decrease the width to match the traced leaf. Pivot 180° with the needle fabric (fig. 10b).

15. Stitch back to the stem increasing and decreasing the stitch width to cover the first stitching. This creates a padded satin stitch. A programmed decorative stitch that resembles a leaf can be used. Added stabilizer may be needed for the wide satin stitching (fig. 11).

16. Appliqué the centers onto the flowers and the flowers in place on the quilt top.

17. Match the ground line of the quilt top to the ground line on the template. Cut the quilt top 27" wide by 37$^1/_2$" long. Place a mark on the edges of the center rectangle at the vertical and horizontal centers.

18. From the blue fabric, cut 6 pieces 7" x 45" (or the width of the fabric). Using a diagonal seam, stitch 2 of the pieces together two times to create two long pieces (fig. 12). Leave the other pieces 45" wide. Mark the center of each of the pieces. The two longer pieces are for the sides of the center rectangle.

19. Pin one of the blue borders to the center rectangle, matching the center marks. The side pieces will be longer than the center rectangle.

20. Use a $^1/_4$" seam allowance and begin stitching $^1/_4$" from the edge. Use a straight stitch. Stop stitching $^1/_4$" before the end of the

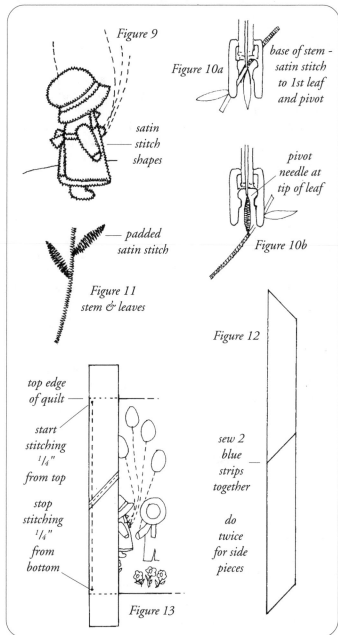

*Figure 9*

satin stitch shapes

*Figure 10a*

base of stem - satin stitch to 1st leaf and pivot

pivot needle at tip of leaf

*Figure 10b*

padded satin stitch

*Figure 11*
stem & leaves

*Figure 12*

sew 2 blue strips together

do twice for side pieces

top edge of quilt

start stitching $^1/_4$" from top

stop stitching $^1/_4$" from bottom

*Figure 13*

quilt top. It is VERY important to begin and end the stitching $^1/_4$" from the end (fig. 13). Press the seam flat and the press the seam allowance to the blue border.

21. Pin, stitch and press the blue border to each remaining side of the rectangle, stitching the same as in step 18. Make certain that the stitching at the corners does not catch the previously stitched border (fig. 14).

22. Place the top on a flat surface, wrong side up, overlapping the borders. At each corner, one border will overlap the other border at a 90° angle. Using a wash-out marker and ruler, draw a line from the raw edges of the border to the seam line. Repeat for each corner (fig. 15).

23. Fold one corner diagonally, matching the edges of the blue borders and the seam line. Pin and stitch on the drawn line, stopping at the seam (fig. 16). Trim the excess border fabric to ¹/₄". Press the seam open (fig. 17). Repeat for each corner.

24. Measure the quilt top with the blue border attached. Cut a backing piece of white fabric to this size and press. Mark the vertical and horizontal centers. Cut a piece of batting the same size as the backing.

25. Place the backing, wrong side up on a flat surface. Tape the backing to the surface, making certain there are no wrinkles or puckers. Spray lightly with a temporary spray adhesive (fig. 18).

26. Place the batting on the backing. The spray adhesive will adhere the batting to the backing without pins or other basting. Spray the batting lightly with a temporary spray adhesive (fig. 18).

27. Center the quilt top on the batting. The spray adhesive will adhere the quilt top to the batting without pins or other basting. Make certain that there are no wrinkles or puckers between all of the layers. Pinning or basting stitches can be added as desired (fig. 19). If you do not use temporary spray adhesive, you will need to pin the layers together.

28. Place invisible thread in the needle and white sewing thread in the bobbin. Quilt all of the layers together, straight stitching on one side of the all of the satin stitching as well as the balloon strings, flower stems and leaves. This stitching can be done free motion with a darning or quilting foot or with the feed dogs up using a walking foot or other foot. When quilting, take care to prevent any puckers or pleats from forming on the back side (fig. 20).

29. Square up the quilt by cutting the backing and batting even with the top.

30. Cut pieces of bias binding 3¹/₂" wide. Stitch the pieces together to form a length of bias 12" longer than the circumference of the quilt. Fold the binding in half to measure 1³/₄" in width and press (fig. 21).

31. Pin the folded binding to the right side of the quilt, matching the raw edges. Start the binding along one of the sides. Stitch using a ¹/₂" seam allowance, starting about 1" form the cut end of the strip. Stop stitching at the miter line, backstitch. Fold a ¹/₂"

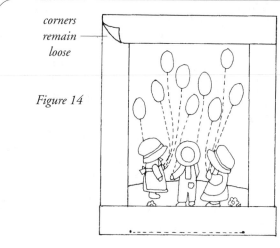

corners remain loose

*Figure 14*

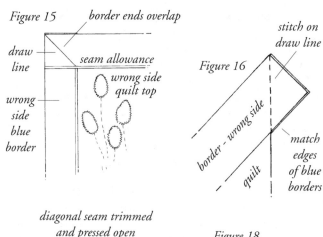

*Figure 15*    border ends overlap

draw line

seam allowance

*wrong side quilt top*

wrong side blue border

*Figure 16*    stitch on draw line

border - wrong side

quilt

match edges of blue borders

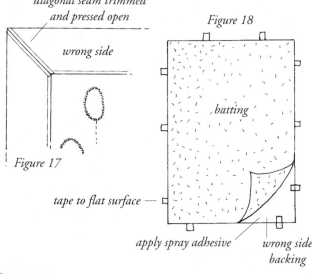

diagonal seam trimmed and pressed open

*wrong side*

*Figure 17*

*Figure 18*

*batting*

tape to flat surface

apply spray adhesive    wrong side backing

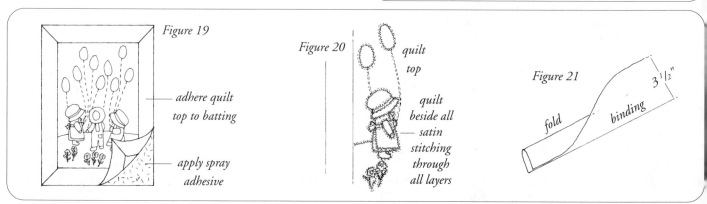

*Figure 19*

adhere quilt top to batting

apply spray adhesive

*Figure 20*    quilt top

quilt beside all satin stitching through all layers

*Figure 21*    3¹/₂"

fold    binding

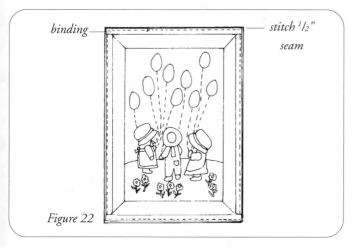

Figure 22

binding ——— stitch ¹/₂" seam

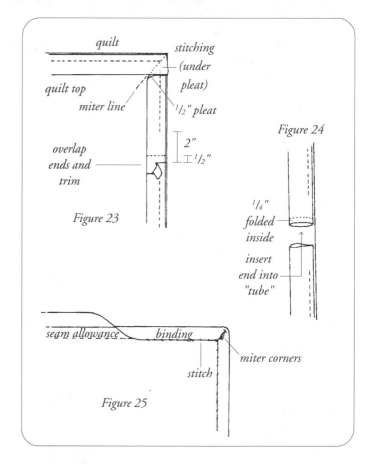

quilt
stitching (under pleat)
quilt top
miter line
¹/₂" pleat

overlap ends and trim

2"
¹/₂"

Figure 23

Figure 24

¹/₄" folded inside

insert end into "tube"

seam allowance ——— binding
miter corners
stitch

Figure 25

pleat in the binding at the corner, begin stitching along the second side of the binding, starting at the miter line. Continue stitching the binding to the quilt placing ¹/₂" pleats at the corners. Stop stitching about 2" from the beginning (fig. 22). Overlap the beginning and the end ¹/₂" and trim away any excess (fig. 23). Fold one edge of the binding to the inside ¹/₄". Place the straight end into the folded end and (fig. 24) finish stitching the binding to the quilt

32. Fold the binding, enclosing the seam allowance. The folded edge of the binding should be placed just past the seam line. At the corners the binding will be folded into a miter. Stitch the binding in place with a straight machine stitch or by hand (fig. 25).

# New Techniques

# Pinless Lace Shaping

What fun it is to present for the very first time a completely new method of lace shaping. I believe pinless lace shaping should be done after the "sticking pins into a lace shaping board" method has been mastered and used many times. Pinless lace shaping means just that-shaping lace without first pinning it into place into a board, starching and pressing, removing it from the board, placing a few pins in to hold the lace to the fabric, and stitching.

To make pinless lace shaping, you must draw your shapes onto the fabric with a wash-out fabric marker or Dixon pencil. For miters, such as diamonds, bottoms of hearts, or scallops you still must draw on the miter lines just as you do for pinned lace shaping. You still need stabilizer even when you are doing the straight stitching. You can either pin the stabilizer to your fabric with the drawn templates or you can use KK2000 to "glue" them down. KK2000 is a temporary spray adhesive which is fabulous.

Then, using a straight stitch, stitch the outside of the lace shape all the way around the shape until you come to the ending place. There you need to go ahead and shape the miter or turn under the lace if you are making lace circles, before making your final attachment straight stitch. Go back to your miter points and using a wooden skewer or some other pointed object and fold in your miters, press, and pin.

It is optional at this point after you have straight stitched the outside and pressed in the miters whether you straight stitch the inside of the lace shapes. I do not think it is necessary; however, you might prefer to. It is now time to decorative stitch with a pinstitch or wing needle entredeux or any other decorative attachment stitch that you think is beautiful, the outside of the lace shape as well as the inside. After you stitch the lace shape, cut away (very carefully) the inside fabric from behind the lace.

Using a #60 or #70 universal needle (regular sewing needle) zigzag over the miters after the fabric has been cut away from behind the lace shape. You can either leave the little "lace dart" in the garment or you can trim it away. That question has been asked of me so many times when I am teaching and my pat answer about the folded miter part (after it has been zigzagged down) is either way is correct. Possibly it is a little prettier to cut away the miter; probably it is a little stronger to leave the miter in place. In my antique clothing the miter is always there because they did not have a zigzag sewing machine to stabilize the stitching. Even if the miter were stitched down, by hand, the miter fold was always left in the garment. In today's heirloom designing world, I know designers who always zigzag and leave the dart and those who zigzag and trim it away. The question I believe you should always ask when sewing anything is "What makes me happy and what do I think is best?" You are the designer and the only one who can make your decision.

# Pinless Lace Diamonds

## Directions

1. Trace the diamond template and miter lines on the fabric using a wash-out marker (fig. 1).
2. Place stabilizer under the fabric and pin in place about 2" from each point of the diamond. Temporary spray adhesive can be used to hold the stabilizer in place.
3. Starting at the lower point of the diamond, place the outside heading of the lace along the template lines allowing a 1" tab of lace to extend beyond the lower point (fig. 2).
4. Stitch the lace in place using a straight stitch (L = 1.5 to 2.0) along the template line starting at point "A". Continue basting the outer edge of the lace along the template lines stopping at each point of the diamond with the needle in the fabric to pivot. Continue in this manner (fig. 2).
5. Stop stitching between point "D" and "A" with the needle in the fabric (fig. 2).
6. To miter the lower point, lay the lace along the template line crisscrossing the beginning and ending lace pieces at point "A" (fig. 3).
7. Using a pin or sishkabob stick to help get the proper angle, fold the top piece of lace under along the miter line. The tab of the top piece of lace will lay exactly on top of the lower lace tab. Hold the miter in place with a pin or shishkabob stick (fig. 4).
8. Continue stitching to point "A" (fig. 4). Remove the lace diamond from the machine.
9. Trim the tabs of lace even with the edge of the lace diamond (fig. 5).
10. Using a shishkabob stick push the excess lace at points "B", "C", and "D" to the underside of the lace diamond creating a miter (fig. 6). Pin to hold in place. Starch and press if desired. Optional: stitch the inside edge of the lace in place (fig. 7).
11. Stitch the inside edge and outside edge of the lace diamond using one of the following stitches: a small tight zigzag (L=2.0 to 2.5, W=.5 to 1), a wing or large needle pinstitch, a wing or large needle entredeux stitch or a decorative satin stitch (fig. 8).
12. Remove the stabilizer from the fabric and carefully trim the fabric from behind the lace as close to the stitching as possible (fig. 9).
13. Zigzag (L=1, W=1.5) along the fold of the lace at each miter. Trim the excess lace from behind the miters (fig. 10).

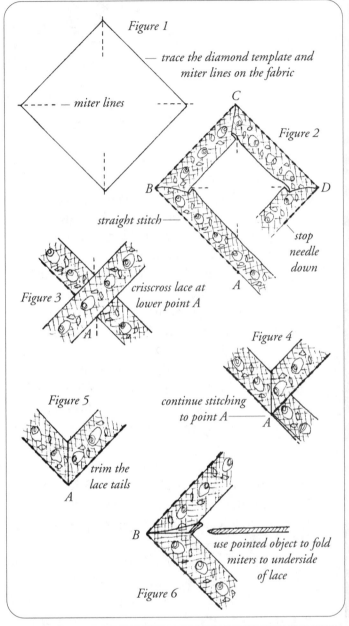

Figure 1

— trace the diamond template and miter lines on the fabric

— miter lines

Figure 2

straight stitch —

stop needle down

Figure 3

crisscross lace at lower point A

Figure 4

continue stitching to point A —

Figure 5

trim the lace tails

use pointed object to fold miters to underside of lace

Figure 6

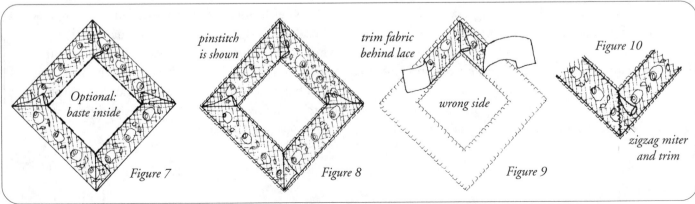

Optional: baste inside

Figure 7

pinstitch is shown

Figure 8

trim fabric behind lace

wrong side

Figure 9

Figure 10

zigzag miter and trim

# Pinless Lace Scallops

Since scallops require putting lace all the way around the skirt, I suggest you read completely the pinned method of making a scalloped skirt before going to the pinless method. My suggestion to make a pinless lace scalloped skirt would be to trace all of the scallops on the skirt front and back before beginning the lace shaping. Stitch the lace along the bottom of the scallop the first time around. Stop and shape the miter at each point, pin the miter in place in the fabric and begin stitching the next scallop. After stitching all of the bottom of the lace scallops into place and after you have pinned the miters into place through the fabric and/or the stabilizer, it is time to pull the heading thread of the lace at the side point of each scallop to pull the top of the lace curves flat against the fabric. Pull each scallop separately.

After the scallops are shaped flat and pressed, it is time to stitch the top of the scallops, then the bottom of the scallops with your decorative wing needle entredeux or pinstitch or just zigzag. Notice I said the top of the scallops are to be decoratively stitched first. Please read on for my reasoning. Since you will probably want to add gathered lace to the bottom of a skirt, you have the choice of stitching the gathered lace to the bottom of the skirt before you cut away the straight fabric which is still attached, or you can cut the fabric away before you zigzag the gathered lace to the bottom of the skirt. This is only if you are going to zigzag the gathered lace to the bottom of the skirt.

If you are going to use wing needle entredeux to attach your gathered lace, you HAVE to do this step before cutting away the fabric from the bottom of the skirt. If you are going to use a wing needle to attach the skirt, then you will use wing needle entedeux and stitch the top of the scallops first before finishing the bottom with wing needle entredeux and gathered lace.

## Directions

1. Trace the scallop template and miter lines on the fabric using a wash-out marker. The lace will be shaped with the lower edge of the lace along the template line (fig. 1).
2. Place stabilizer under the fabric and pin in place about 2" away from the template lines.
3. Starting with a tab of lace extending beyond the miter line of the scallop, place the lower heading of the lace along the template line (fig. 2).
4. Stitch the lace in place using a straight stitch (L = 1.5 to 2.0) along the template line starting on a miter line. Continue stitching the outer edge of the lace along the template line stopping 1" from the next miter line with the needle in the fabric (fig. 2).
5. Place the lace along the template line at the miter line, use a pin or sishkabob stick to help get the proper angle and fold the lace back on itself at the miter line. This creates a dart. Hold the dart or miter in place with a shishkabob stick or pin (fig. 3).
6. Continue shaping the lace along the template line and continue stitching the lace along the template line. Stop needle down 1" from the next miter line (fig. 4).
7. Repeat steps 5 and 6 until the scallops are complete. If the scallops are continuous as they would be along the hem of a skirt, where the beginning scallop meets the ending scallop

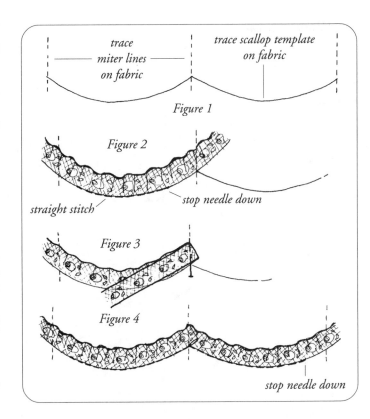

trace miter lines on fabric

trace scallop template on fabric

*Figure 1*

*Figure 2*

straight stitch

stop needle down

*Figure 3*

*Figure 4*

stop needle down

allow the pieces to crisscross at the miter (fig. 5). Fold the top piece of lace along the miter line, the tab of the top piece of lace will lay exactly on top of the lower lace tab. Hold the miter in place with a pin or sishkabob stick. Stitch in place (fig. 6).

8. Remove from the machine. If the scallops are continuous, trim the tabs of lace even with the edge of the lace scallop at the beginning and ending scallop (fig. 7).

9. Pin the lace to the fabric/stabilizer at each point. Pull the very top thread along the inside heading of the lace causing the lace to lay flat against the fabric (fig. 8). Starch lightly and press. Optional: straight stitch along the inside edge of the lace (fig. 8).

10. Stitch the inside edge and outside edge of the lace scallop to the fabric using one of the following stitches:  a small tight zigzag (L=2.0 to 2.5, W=.5 to 1), a wing or large needle pinstitch, a wing or large needle entredeux stitch or a decorative satin stitch (fig. 9).

11. Remove the stabilizer from the fabric and carefully trim the fabric from behind the lace as close to the stitching as possible (fig. 10).

12. Zigzag (L=1, W=1.5) along the fold of the lace at each miter. Trim the excess lace from behind the miters (fig. 11).

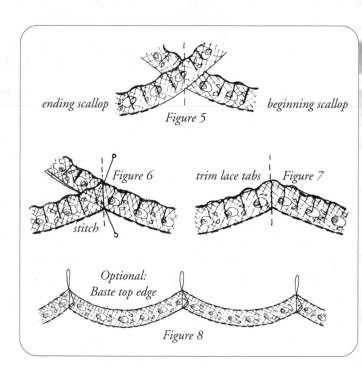

ending scallop    Figure 5    beginning scallop

Figure 6    trim lace tabs    Figure 7

stitch

Optional:
Baste top edge

Figure 8

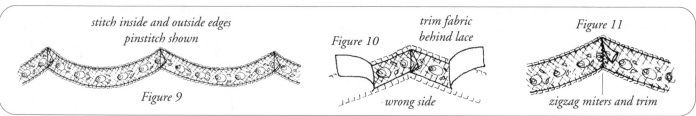

stitch inside and outside edges
pinstitch shown

Figure 9

trim fabric
behind lace

Figure 10    wrong side

Figure 11

zigzag miters and trim

*We have given you three different sizes of scalloped templates below if you would like to use them.*

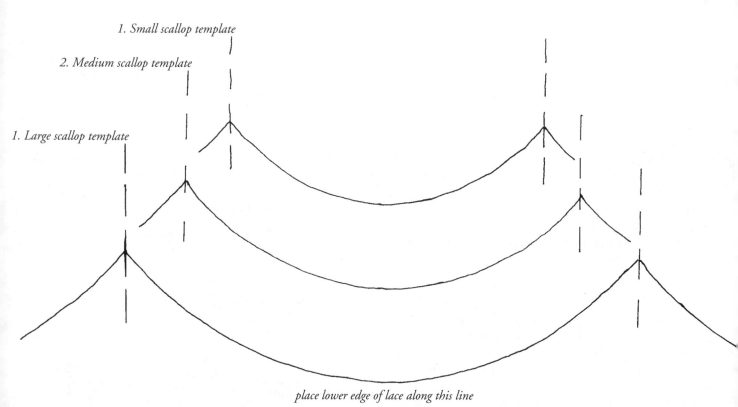

*1. Small scallop template*

*2. Medium scallop template*

*1. Large scallop template*

*place lower edge of lace along this line*

# Pinless Lace Circles

## Directions

1. Trace the circle template on the fabric using a wash-out marker. The lace will be shaped inside the circle with the outer edge of the lace along the template line (fig. 1).
2. Place stabilizer under the fabric and pin in place about 2" away from the template lines.
3. Place the outer heading of the lace along the template line.
4. Stitch the lace in place using a straight stitch (L = 1.5 to 2.0) along the template line starting at the cut edge of the lace. Continue stitching the outer edge of the lace along the template line stopping 1" from the beginning with the needle in the fabric (fig. 2).
5. Place the lace along the template line allowing the ending lace to overlap the beginning lace about $^1/_2$" (fig. 3). Trim away any extra lace. Fold the top piece of lace under $^1/_4$" and continue stitching the lace to the template line (fig. 4).
6. Remove the lace circle from the machine.
7. Pull the very top thread along the inside heading of the lace causing the lace to lay flat against the fabric. Starch lightly and press. Optional: straight stitch along the inside edge of the lace circle (fig. 5).
8. Stitch the inside edge and outside edge of the lace circle to the fabric using one of the following stitches: a small tight zigzag (L=2.0 to 2.5, W=.5 to 1), a wing or large needle pinstitch, a wing or large needle entredeux stitch or a decorative satin stitch (fig. 6).
9. Remove the stabilizer from the fabric and carefully trim the fabric from behind the lace as close to the stitching as possible (fig. 7).
10. Zigzag (L=1, W=1.5) along the fold of the lace. Trim the excess lace from behind the fold (fig. 8)

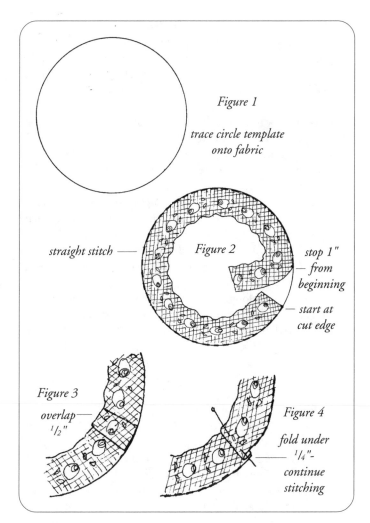

Figure 1

trace circle template onto fabric

straight stitch

Figure 2

stop 1" from beginning

start at cut edge

Figure 3

overlap $^1/_2$"

Figure 4

fold under $^1/_4$"- continue stitching

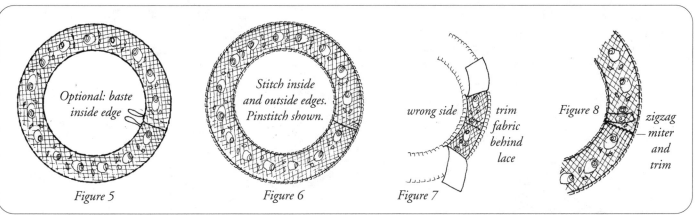

Optional: baste inside edge

Figure 5

Stitch inside and outside edges. Pinstitch shown.

Figure 6

wrong side

trim fabric behind lace

Figure 7

Figure 8

zigzag miter and trim

# Pinless Lace Bows

## Directions

1. Trace the bow template on the fabric using a wash-out marker. The lace bow will be shaped inside the bow template. It can be shaped in three pieces (two loops and the knot) or in two pieces (the loops in one piece and the knot). The outer edge of the lace will be placed along the template line (fig. 1).

2. Place tear away stabilizer under the fabric and pin in place about 2" away from the template lines.

3. Place the outer heading of the lace along the template line of one bow loop starting the lace in the center of the bow template (fig. 2).

4. Stitch the lace in place using a straight stitch (L = 1.5 to 2.0) along the template line starting just inside the knot template lines. Continue stitching the outer edge of the lace along the template line. The lace may overlap as they get closer to the knot. Continue stitching until one loop is stitched in place (fig. 2).

5. For the second loop, either continue with the same piece of lace or use a separate piece. Stitch the second loop in place as it is shaped along the template line (fig. 3).

6. Remove the fabric with the lace bow loops from the machine.

7. Pull the very top thread along the inside heading of the lace causing the lace to lay flat against the fabric. Starch lightly and press. Optional: straight stitch along the inside edge of the lace bow loops (fig. 4).

8. Cut a piece of lace ¹/₂" longer than the bow knot. Fold the cut ends of the lace under ¹/₂" (fig. 5). Place the lace knot along the template line. Straight stitch around the knot (fig. 6).

9. Stitch the inside edge and outside edge of the lace bow and the bow knot to the fabric using one of the following stitches: a small tight zigzag (L=2.0 to 2.5, W=.5 to 1), a wing or large needle pinstitch, a wing or large needle entredeux stitch or a decorative satin stitch (fig. 7).

10. Remove the stabilizer from the fabric and carefully trim the fabric from behind the lace and the lace ends behind the bow knot as close to the stitching as possible (fig. 8).

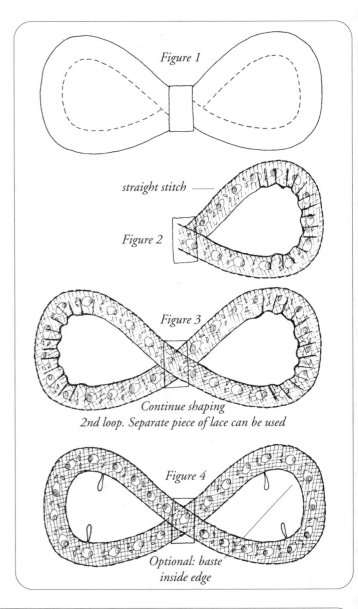

*Figure 1*

*straight stitch*

*Figure 2*

*Figure 3*

*Continue shaping
2nd loop. Separate piece of lace can be used*

*Figure 4*

*Optional: baste
inside edge*

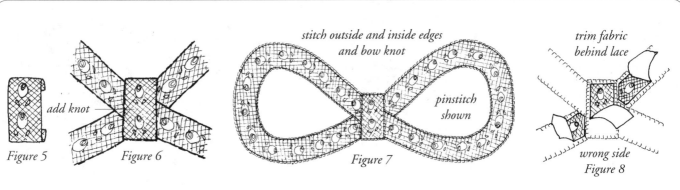

*add knot*

*Figure 5*

*Figure 6*

*stitch outside and inside edges
and bow knot*

*pinstitch
shown*

*Figure 7*

*trim fabric
behind lace*

*wrong side
Figure 8*

# Creating Pinless Circular Puffing

## Directions

1. Cut a strip of fabric 2" wide by three times the circumference of the circle. Several fabric strips may need to be stitched together to achieve the desired length. To stitch fabric strips together, use a small serged seam or a small straight seam overcast with a zigzag.

2. Using a gathering foot and a straight stitch (L= 3.0 to 4.0, adjust the length as needed remembering that a longer length makes more gathers and a shorter length makes less gathers) stitch each side of the strip $^3/_8$" from the cut edge. This will gather each side of the strip creating a strip of puffing (fig. 1).

3. Trim the seam allowance on each side down to $^1/_4$" (fig. 2).

4. Trace the circular template on the fabric.

5. Place the outer stitching line of the puffing strip on the template line and stitch in place along the outer stitching line of the puffing. This is peek-a-boo stitching because you lift the puffing, find the template line, place the puffing stitching line on the drawn line and stitch for about 2". Peek again, line up and stitch (fig. 3). Hold in place with a wooden skewer.

6. Allow the puffing strip to overlay by 1". Cut away any excess. Fold the top piece under $^1/_2$" and continue stitching. The circular strip will appear to be continuos (fig. 4).

7. For the inside of the puffing circle, press the puffing with your hand. I call this the "smush technique" (fig. 5).

8. Shape lace along the inside and outside edge of the circle hiding the stitching lines of the puffing with the headings of the lace. Refer to "Shaping Lace Circles" and "Dancing in the Dark Lace Shaping" for shaping lace along the outer edge of the puffing. **Note:** If the inside of the circle is not exactly circular try this. Center a plate or saucer on the puffing. Make sure the plate or saucer covers the inside stitching line of the puffing. Trace around the plate with a wash-out marker. Use the traced line for shaping the inside lace (fig. 6).

9. Stitch both edges of lace to fabric. Trim the fabric from behind the lace (fig. 7).

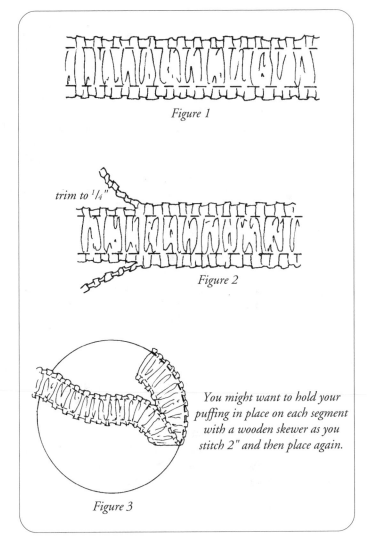

*Figure 1*

*trim to $^1/_4$"*

*Figure 2*

*Figure 3*

You might want to hold your puffing in place on each segment with a wooden skewer as you stitch 2" and then place again.

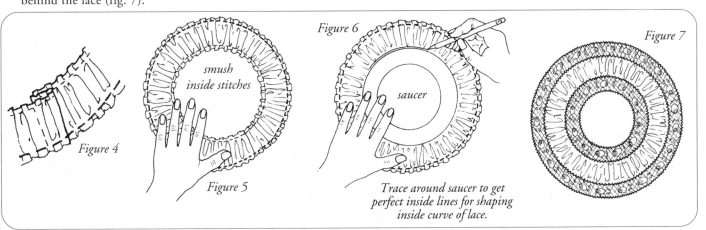

*Figure 4*

smush inside stitches

*Figure 5*

*Figure 6*

saucer

Trace around saucer to get perfect inside lines for shaping inside curve of lace.

*Figure 7*

# Dancing in the Dark Lace Shaping

## Directions

Sometimes the template used or design needed requires a different placement for the lace. If lace is being shaped on the outer edge of circular puffing, the inside edge of the lace must hide the stitching line of the puffing and therefore the *inside* edge of the lace must be used as a guide for stitching the *outer* edge of the lace to the fabric.

1. After the circular puffing is stitched in place (fig. 1)(refer to Creating Pinless Circular Puffing), place the inside edge of the lace along the outer stitching line of the puffing. Stitch the outer edge of the lace in place using a straight stitch (L = 1.5 to 2.0) starting at the cut edge of the lace (fig. 2). I call this "dancing in the dark" because you are not stitching on a template line, you must use the inside edge of the lace against the stitching line to guide you, while stitching the outer edge.

2. Continue placing the inside edge of the lace along the stitching line of the puffing while stitching the outer edge of the lace. Stop the end of the lace 1" from the beginning with the needle in the fabric (fig. 3). Use a wooden skerwer to hold the outside of the lace.

3. Allow the ending lace to overlap the beginning lace about 1/2". Trim away any extra lace. Fold the top piece of lace under 1/4" and continue stitching the lace along the outer edge (fig. 4).

4. Remove the lace circle from the machine.

5. Pull the very top thread along the inside heading of the lace causing the lace to lay flat against the fabric hiding the stitching line of the puffing. Starch lightly and press. Optional: straight stitch along the inside edge of the lace circle (fig. 5).

6. Stitch the inside edge and outside edge of the lace circle to the fabric using one of the following stitches: a small tight zigzag (L=2.0 to 2.5, W=.5 to 1), a wing or large needle pinstitch, a wing or large needle entredeux stitch or a decorative satin stitch (fig. 6).

7. For the inside lace of the puffing circle, place the outer edge of the lace along the inside stitching line of the puffing. This would not be "dancing in the dark" because you are actually stitching on the template line (the inside gathering stitch). Refer to the technique for "Pinless Lace Circles" to complete the inside lace insertion (fig. 7).

8. Remove the stabilizer from the fabric and carefully trim the fabric from behind the lace as close to the stitching as possible (fig. 8).

9. Zigzag (L=1, W=1.5) along the fold of the lace. Trim the excess lace from behind the fold (fig. 9).

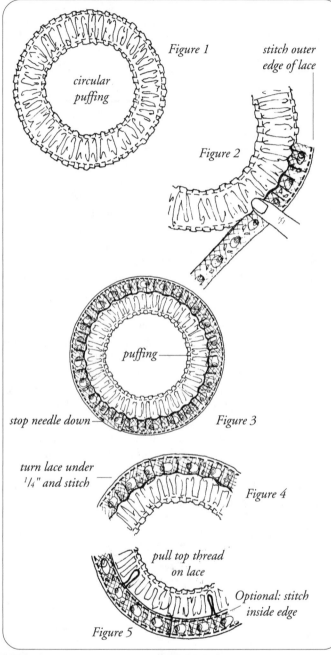

Figure 1

circular puffing

stitch outer edge of lace

Figure 2

puffing

stop needle down

Figure 3

turn lace under 1/4" and stitch

Figure 4

pull top thread on lace

Optional: stitch inside edge

Figure 5

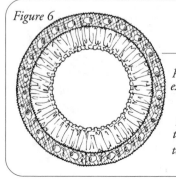

Figure 6

If your inside puffing circle is not exactly, round, place a saucer in the puffing circle and trace a round shape to use. Refer back to page 337.

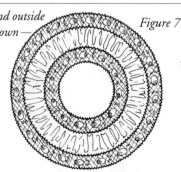

stitch lace - inside and outside edges; zigzag shown

Figure 7

wrong side

trim excess lace
Figure 9

trim fabric behind lace    Figure 8

# Magic Madeira Technique
### (Wash Away Basting Thread Technique)

This completely revolutionary method of making gorgeous Madeira Appliqué hems, borders, collars or motifs is so very easy. Madeira borders and hems are very tailored and wonderful on clothing for boys and girls as well as women. Using Madeira borders on pillows or other linens for the home is absolutely the most expensive look one could hope to get. You will love this new and very easy method using wash away basting thread which we have illustrated in this book on these pages.

The cover garments illustrate most elegantly how to use Madeira borders on both the little boy suit with the Madeira panel down the front with the Madeira Appliqué Windows on the front. The dress has the most beautiful double sided Madeira border on the skirt as well as the beautiful Madeira panel down the front. On the dress, we have used lace diamond motifs in the center of each section. All of these directions are contained in this new technique section of the book. These techniques are truly new and we believe you will adore how easy Madeira has become. Presenting these techniques for you almost reminds me of the joy we had in bringing you the fold back miter methods for the very first time. We love developing new techniques which make your sewing easier. This is always one of our main goals at Martha Pullen Company.

### Hints for Using Wash Away Basting Thread (and for storing )
When you thread either your thread or bobbin with wash away basting thread, be sure to REMOVE this thread from your machine after you stitch the portion where you use it. I also suggest storing your wash away basting thread in a glass jar or in a plastic baggie clearly marked, "wash away basting thread." First, you do not want humidity to get to your thread. Second, you do not ever want to use this thread mistakenly as real thread. If you choose to put your wash away thread in your bobbin rather in your top thread carrier, please, please mark this bobbin carefully with finger nail polish or some permanent marker before putting it into a plastic bag for further use.

### Using Universal or Wing Needles for Pinstitching and Hemstitching
Many people prefer using a #110 universal needle over the #100 wing needle for pinstitching. My suggestion to you would be to try both and see which look you prefer. Both are gorgeous. If your machine does not have a pinstitch setting, then by all means just use a #60 or #70 universal needle and a tiny zigzag to attach your Madeira borders. I think it is advisable to use stabilizer underneath any large needle stitching. If you would like to try your fabrics to see if stabilizer is or is not necessary, it is simple to do. I usually use a tear away stabilizer underneath any type of wing needle or #110 universal entredeux or pin stitching. With enough spray starch and on certain types of fabrics, stabilizer might not be necessary. Your decision is the only correct one.

# Magic Madeira Appliqué Hem
## with a Shaped Hemline

*The dress has a fabulous Madeira hem with lace diamond motifs in each border shape. We have included two methods of transferring the template to the border fabric. The first is with a wash-out fabric marker or pencil. My favorite is to use a Dixon pencil which has a sharp clear point. The second method is using an iron-on tear away stabilizer to transfer the Madeira border design to the Madeira fabric.*

## Supplies

Skirt fabric
Madeira appliqué border fabric
Wash-out fabric marker or pencil
Iron-on Tear Away stabilizer (Sulky Totally Stable™)(method B)
Wash-away basting thread (YLI, Wash-A-Way™ thread)
Point turner or wooden skewer
Starch
#110 universal or #100 wing needle
#60 or #70 universal needle

## — I. Preparing the Skirt and Border Fabric —

1. Cut two strips of fabric for the Madeira appliqué border the width given in the pattern directions or the width of the fabric and 1" longer than the length of the template.
2. Cut two skirt pieces the width given in the pattern directions or the width of the fabric.

## — II. Transferring the Template to the Border Fabric —

Transfer the Madeira appliqué border template using one of the following methods:

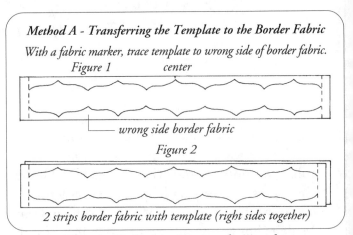

*Method A - Transferring the Template to the Border Fabric*
With a fabric marker, trace template to wrong side of border fabric.
Figure 1     center
*wrong side border fabric*
Figure 2
*2 strips border fabric with template (right sides together)*

### Transfer Method A - Tracing the Template

1. Using a fabric marker, transfer the Madeira appliqué template to the wrong side of <u>one piece of the border fabric</u> in the following manner: starting the template in the center of the fabric, ¹/₄" from the lower cut edge, trace the template repeat on each side of the center or as the template indicates. Continue tracing the design alternating sides until the desired width is complete or until there is no more room for an additional repeat. Mark the side seams at the end of the last template repeat on each end (fig. 1).
2. Place the second border strip of fabric to the first, right sides together (fig. 2).

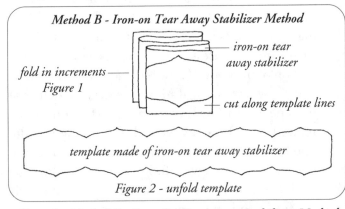

*Method B - Iron-on Tear Away Stabilizer Method*
*iron-on tear away stabilizer*
*fold in increments*
*Figure 1*
*cut along template lines*
*template made of iron-on tear away stabilizer*
*Figure 2 - unfold template*

### Transfer Method B - Iron-On Tear Away Stabilizer Method

1. Cut a strip or piece of iron-on tear-away stabilizer, slightly longer than the Madeira appliqué border and the width of the fabric. For example: if the width of the fabric is 45" and the length of the template is 4", cut the stabilizer 45" by 5".
2. Measure the template repeat and fold the stabilizer in increments of the template repeat. For example: if the template repeat is 4", fold the stabilizer in 4" increments. Trim off any extra stabilizer on the end. Trace the template repeat on the folded stabilizer (fig. 1) and cut along the template lines. Unfold the template. The template is ready to iron on (fig. 2).

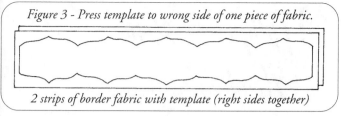

*Figure 3 - Press template to wrong side of one piece of fabric.*

*2 strips of border fabric with template (right sides together)*

3. Center the template on the wrong side of the border fabric and press the template in place (fig. 3).
4. Place the second strip of border fabric to the first, right sides together (fig. 3). Pin in place.

## III. Stitching Madeira Magic

1. Thread the needle and/or the bobbin with **wash-away basting thread**.
2. With the two layers of skirt border fabric right sides together, stitch along the <u>upper traced template line</u> (method A) or stitch along the upper cut edge of the stabilizer (method B). <u>Do not stitch</u> along the lower template line. Remove the stabilizer if method B is used (fig. 1).
3. Trim the excess fabric ¹/₈" to ¹/₄" above the stitching line. Clip the points (fig. 2). Turn the border fabrics to the right side, using a point turner or wooden skewer to "punch out" all points. Press well (fig. 3).
4. Starch heavily, spraying most of the starch along the seam line. Press to dry and pull apart (fig. 4). If the piece is difficult to pull apart starch again along the seam line. Press dry and try pulling apart again. The border fabric must be dry before pulling apart. Now, the upper edge of the border is turned under and ready to stitch. You might want to use a press cloth of fabric as you spray starch (wetting the seam) and press completely dry. This spray starch wets the wash away basting thread so it dissolves.

## IV. Attaching the Madeira Appliqué Border to the Shirt

1. **Remove the wash-away thread from the machine** and thread the machine with lightweight sewing thread. Stitch the sides of the border fabric in place so that the design lines are continuous. Measure the circumference of the border. Stitch the sides of the skirt in place so that the circumference of the skirt is the same as the border (fig. 1).
2. Place the right side of the border fabric to the wrong side of the skirt, matching the side seams. Pin.
3. Stitch the border to the skirt along the template lines. Trim the excess fabric ¹/₈" to ¹/₄" below the stitching line. Clip points and curves as necessary (fig. 2).
4. Flip the border to the right side of the skirt. If needed, use a point turner or wooden skewer to "punch out" all points. Press well. Pin in place. Starch and press.
5. Using a wing needle or 110 universal needle and a pinstitch (L=2.5, W=2.0), stitch the upper edge of the border to the skirt. Stabilizer may be required under the base fabric. If your machine does not have a pinstitch, a regular needle and a tiny zigzag (L=1.5, W=1.5) can be used to stitch the upper edge of the border in place (fig. 3).

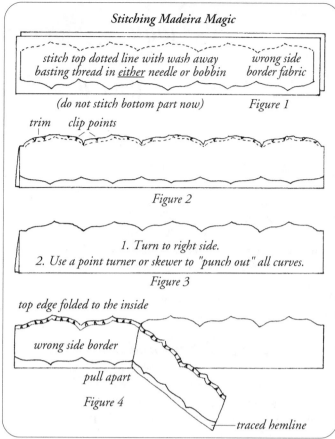

**Stitching Madeira Magic**

*stitch top dotted line with wash away basting thread in either needle or bobbin*   *wrong side border fabric*

*(do not stitch bottom part now)*   *Figure 1*

*trim*   *clip points*

*Figure 2*

1. Turn to right side.
2. Use a point turner or skewer to "punch out" all curves.

*Figure 3*

*top edge folded to the inside*

*wrong side border*

*pull apart*

*Figure 4*

*traced hemline*

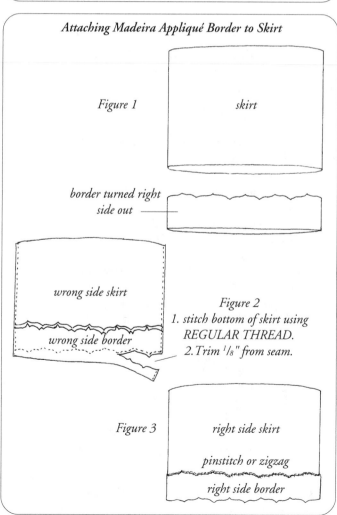

**Attaching Madeira Appliqué Border to Skirt**

*Figure 1*   *skirt*

*border turned right side out*

*wrong side skirt*

*wrong side border*

*Figure 2*
1. stitch bottom of skirt using REGULAR THREAD.
2. Trim ¹/₈" from seam.

*Figure 3*   *right side skirt*

*pinstitch or zigzag*

*right side border*

# Magic Madeira Appliqué Hem with a Staight Hemline

## Supplies

Skirt fabric
Madeira appliqué border fabric
Wash-out fabric marker or pencil
Iron-on Tear Away stabilizer (Sulky Totally Stable™)(method B)
Wash-away basting thread (YLI, Wash-A-Way™ thread)
Point turner or wooden skewer
Starch
#110 universal or #100 wing needle
#60 or #70 universal needle

## I. Preparing the Skirt and Border Fabric

1. Cut two strips of fabric for the Madeira appliqué border the width given in the pattern directions or the width of the fabric and 1" longer than the length of the template.
2. Cut two skirt pieces the width given in the pattern directions or the width of the fabric.

## II. Transferring the Template to the Hem Border Fabric

Transfer the Madeira appliqué border template to the wrong side of one strip of hem border fabric using a wash-out marker (fig. 1).

## III. Stitching Madeira Magic

1. Place the two hem border strips of fabric, right sides together (fig. 2).
2. Thread the needle and/or the bobbin with **wash-away basting thread**.
3. With the two layers of skirt border fabric right sides together, stitch along the traced template line. Do not stitch along the lower edge (fig. 1).
4. Trim the excess fabric ¹/₈" to ¹/₄" above the stitching line. Clip the points (fig. 2). Turn the border fabrics to the right side, using a point turner or wooden skewer to "punch out" all points. Press well (fig. 3).
5. Starch, spraying most of the starch along the seam line. Press to dry and pull apart (fig. 4). If the piece is difficult to pull apart starch again along the seam line. Press dry and try pulling apart again. The border fabric must be dry before pulling apart (fig. 5). Now, the upper edge of the border is turned under and ready to stitch.

## IV. Attaching the Madeira Appliqué Border to the Skirt

1. **Remove the wash-away thread from the machine** and thread the machine with lightweight sewing thread. Stitch the sides of the border fabric in place so that the design lines are

White and Pink
Madeira Dress

---

*Transferring the Template to the Hem Border Fabric*

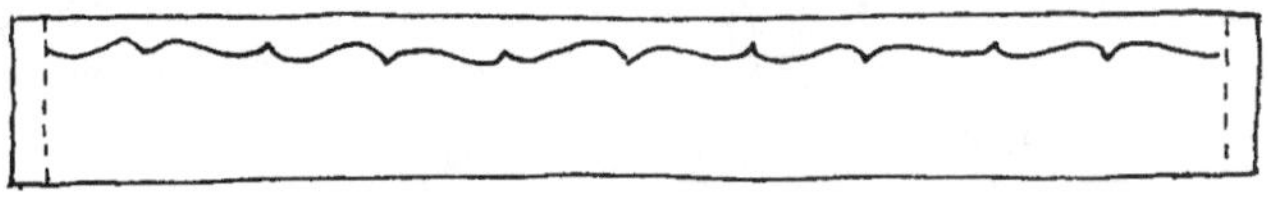

*Figure 1*

---

*Stitching Madeira Magic*

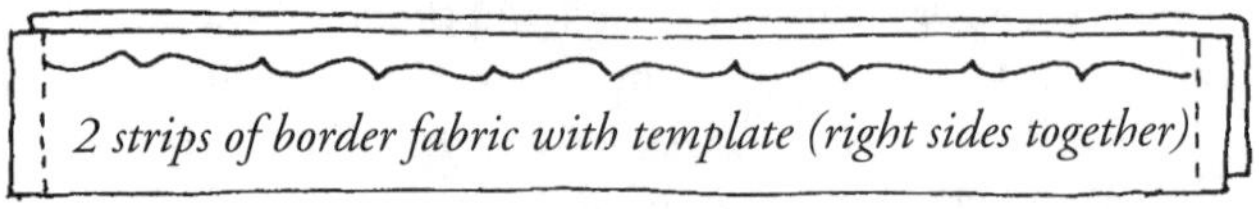

*2 strips of border fabric with template (right sides together)*

*Figure 2*

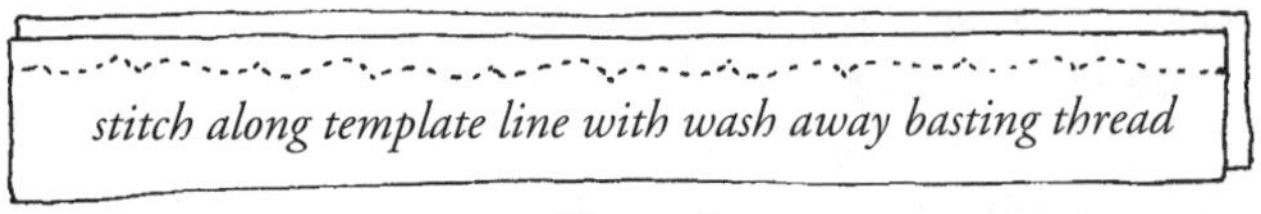

*stitch along template line with wash away basting thread*

*Figure 3*

*trim and clip points*

*Figure 4*

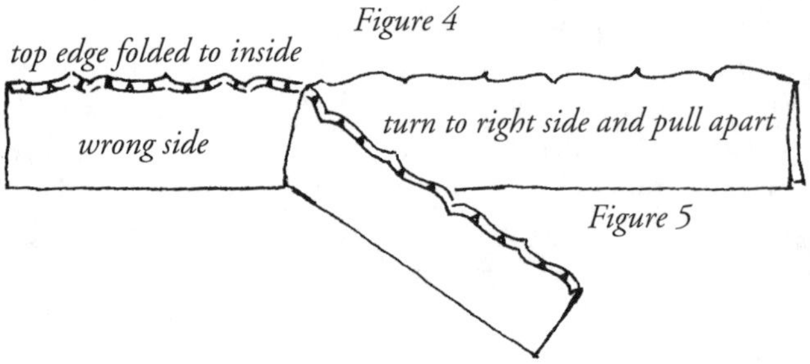

top edge folded to inside

wrong side

turn to right side and pull apart

*Figure 5*

continuous. Measure the circumference of the border. Stitch the sides of the skirt in place so that the circumference of the skirt is the same as the border (fig. 6).

2. Place the right side of the border fabric to the wrong side of the skirt, matching the side seams. Pin.

3. Straight stitch the border to the skirt $1/4$" from the lower edge (fig. 7).

4. Flip the border to the right side of the skirt. Press well. Pin in place. Starch and press.

5. Using a wing needle or 110 universal needle and a pinstitch (L=2.5, W=2.0), stitch the upper edges of the border to the skirt. Stabilizer may be required under the base fabric. If your machine does not have a pinstitch, a regular needle and a tiny zigzag (L=1.5, W=1.5) can be used to stitch the upper edge of the border in place (fig. 8).

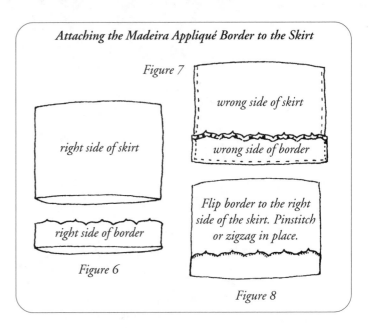

**Attaching the Madeira Appliqué Border to the Skirt**

Figure 7

right side of skirt

wrong side of skirt

wrong side of border

right side of border

Figure 6

Flip border to the right side of the skirt. Pinstitch or zigzag in place.

Figure 8

# Magic Madeira Appliqué Collars

## Supplies

Collar fabric
Madeira appliqué collar border fabric
Wash-out fabric marker or pencil
Wash-away basting thread (YLI, Wash-A-Way™ thread)
Point turner or wooden skewer
Starch
#110 universal or #100 wing needle
#60 or #70 universal needle

## Directions

1. Cut a rectangle of fabric for the collar and an identical rectangle of fabric for the Madeira appliqué collar border. Starch and press both pieces.

2. Cut the collar from the base fabric and put aside.

3. Fold the Madeira border fabric in half, right sides together, along the center front. Trace half the Madeira appliqué border template and the cutting line on the wrong side of the border fabric (fig. 1).

4. Thread the needle and/ or the bobbin with wash-away basting thread.

5. With the border fabric folded in half, stitch the two layers together along the upper traced line of the template (fig. 2).

6. Trim the excess fabric $1/8$" to $1/4$" above the stitching line. Clip the points (fig. 3). Cut along the collar

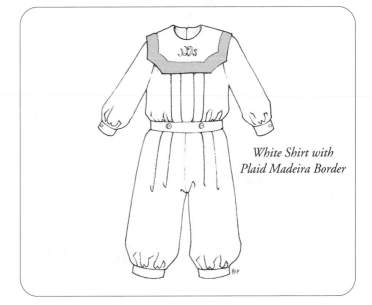

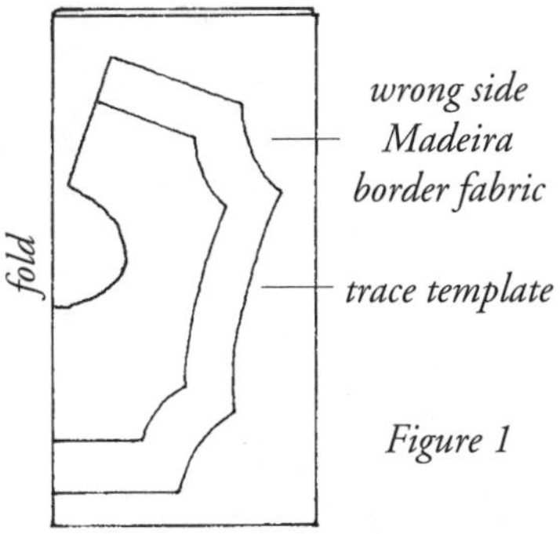

*White Shirt with Plaid Madeira Border*

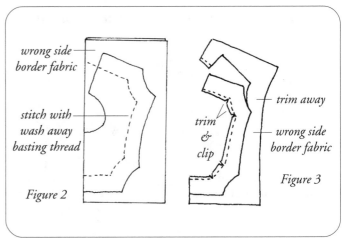

fold

wrong side Madeira border fabric

trace template

Figure 1

wrong side border fabric

stitch with wash away basting thread

Figure 2

trim & clip

trim away

wrong side border fabric

Figure 3

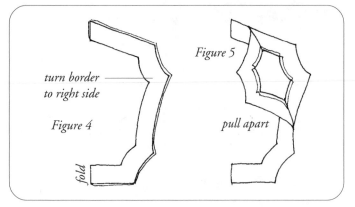

*turn border to right side*

*Figure 5*

*Figure 4*

*fold*

*pull apart*

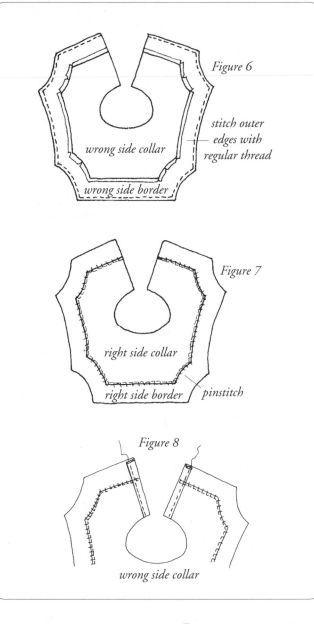

*Figure 6*

*wrong side collar*

*stitch outer edges with regular thread*

*wrong side border*

*Figure 7*

*right side collar*

*right side border*  *pinstitch*

*Figure 8*

*wrong side collar*

cutting line. Turn the border to the right side, using a point turner or wooden skewer to "punch out" all points. Press well (fig. 4).

7. Starch, spraying most of the starch along the seam line. Press to dry and pull apart (fig. 5). If the piece is difficult to pull apart starch again along the seam line. Press dry and try pulling apart again. The wash-away thread must have been wet enough to "melt" but the border piece can not be pulled apart until it is pressed dry. Remember, the border fabric must be dry before pulling apart. Now, the inside edge of the template is turned under and ready to stitch.

8. **Remove the wash-away thread from the machine** and thread the machine with lightweight sewing thread.

9. Place the right side of the border to the wrong side of the collar, matching the edges. Pin. Stitch the border to the collar along the outer edges using a ¹/₄" seam allowance. Clip the curves and corners (fig. 6).

10. Flip the border to the right side of the collar, using a point turner or wooden skewer to "punch out" all points. Pin in place. Starch and press.

11. Using a wing needle or 110 universal needle and a pinstitch (L=2.5, W=2.0), stitch the inner edges of the border to the collar. Stabilizer may be needed under the base fabric. If your machine does not have a pinstitch, a regular needle and a tiny zigzag (L=1.5, W=1.5) can be used to stitch the inside edge of the border in place (fig. 7).

# Other Magic Madeira Appliqué Borders

## Sleeves, Overlays, Cuffs, Jackets, Vests, etc.

### Supplies

Base fabric for garment
Madeira appliqué border fabric
Wash-out fabric marker or pencil
Wash-away basting thread (YLI, Wash-A-Way™ thread)
Point turner or wooden skewer
Starch
#110 universal or #100 wing needle
#60 or #70 universal needle

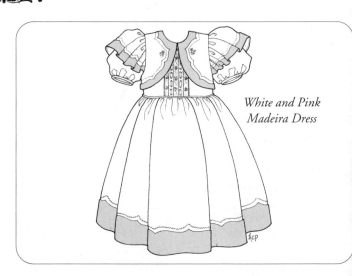

*White and Pink Madeira Dress*

## Directions

1. Cut the pattern pieces from the base fabric (fig. 1a -sleeve border), (fig. 1b - bodice overlay as seen in the White and Pink Madeira Dress) that are to have Madeira appliqué borders. Starch and press.

2. Cut pieces of border fabric slightly larger than the finished border (fig. 2a and 2b).

3. Using a fabric marker, trace the border template on the border fabric as described below:

### A. Creating Two Mirror Image Pieces
*(for two sleeves or right and left vest fronts)*

You will be creating two mirror image border pieces by tracing the template on the wrong side of only one border piece, placing the second piece to the first right sides together. The traced template piece will need to be on top.

### B. Creating Only One Piece
*(for a vest back or one piece curtain)*

If only one border piece is needed, fold the piece in the center and trace the template on the wrong side of half the border fabric. The two halves will be mirror images of each other. With the border folded in half, right sides together and the traced template piece on top, it will be ready to stitch.

4. Thread the needle and/or the bobbin with **wash-away basting thread**.

5. With the two layers of border fabric together, stitch along the inside or upper traced line of the border template. Do not stitch the lower or outer template lines (fig. 3a and 3b).

6. Trim the excess fabric ⅛" to ¼" above the stitching line. Cut along the outer or lower cutting line. Clip the points (fig. 4a. and 4b.). Turn the border fabrics to the right side, using a point turner or wooden skewer to "punch out" all points. Press well (fig. 5a and 5b).

7. Starch, spraying most of the starch along the seam line. Press to dry and pull apart (fig. 6a and 6b) If the piece is difficult to pull apart starch again along the seam line. Press dry and try pulling apart again. The border fabric must be dry before pulling apart. Now, the upper edges of the border are turned under and ready to stitch.

8. **Remove the wash-away thread from the machine** and thread the machine with lightweight sewing thread.

9. If the border has side seams or shoulder seams stitch the seams in place. Repeat for the base fabric pieces. Make sure the identical seams are taken in the border fabric and base fabric so that they fit together correctly.

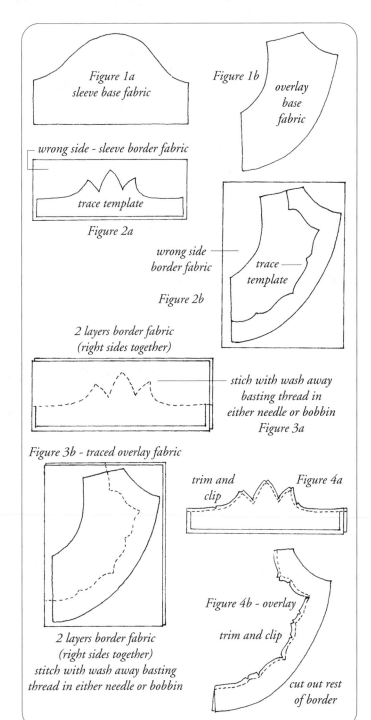

Figure 1a
sleeve base fabric

Figure 1b
overlay base fabric

wrong side - sleeve border fabric

trace template

Figure 2a

wrong side border fabric

trace template

Figure 2b

2 layers border fabric
(right sides together)

stich with wash away basting thread in either needle or bobbin
Figure 3a

Figure 3b - traced overlay fabric

trim and clip    Figure 4a

Figure 4b - overlay
trim and clip

cut out rest of border

2 layers border fabric
(right sides together)
stitch with wash away basting
thread in either needle or bobbin

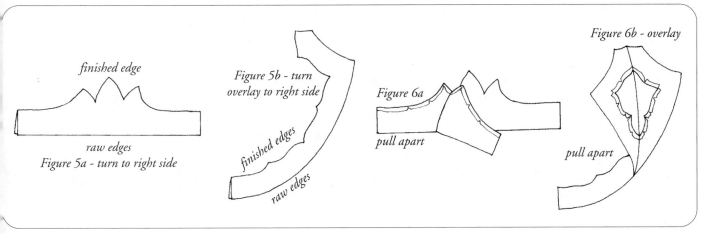

finished edge

Figure 5b - turn overlay to right side

finished edges

raw edges

raw edges
Figure 5a - turn to right side

Figure 6a

pull apart

Figure 6b - overlay

pull apart

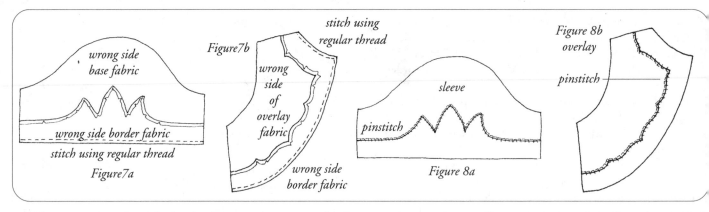

*wrong side base fabric*

*wrong side border fabric*

*stitch using regular thread*

**Figure 7a**

*Figure 7b*

*wrong side of overlay fabric*

*stitch using regular thread*

*wrong side border fabric*

*sleeve*

*pinstitch*

**Figure 8a**

*Figure 8b overlay*

*pinstitch*

10. Place the right side of the border fabric to the wrong side of the base fabric, matching the seams. Pin.

11. Stitch the border to the base using a $^{1}/_{4}$" seam (fig. 7a and 7b).

12. Flip the border to the right side of the skirt. If needed, use a point turner or wooden skewer to "punch out" all points. Press well. Pin in place. Starch and press.

13. Using a wing needle or 110 universal needle and a pinstitch (L=2.5, W=2.0), stitch the upper edges of the border to the sleeve (fig. 8a and 8b). Stabilizer may be needed under the base fabric. If your machine does not have a pinstitch, a regular needle and a tiny zigzag (L=1.5, W=1.5) can be used to stitch the upper edge of the border in place.

# Magic Madeira Motifs

## Supplies

Base fabric for garment
Madeira appliqué motif fabric
Wash-out fabric marker or pencil
Water soluble stabilizer
Point turner or wooden skewer
Starch
#110 universal or #100 wing needle
#60 or #70 universal needle

*Robin's Egg Madeira Dress*

## Directions

1. Trace the Madeira appliqué motif to the wrong side of the motif fabric (fig. 1).

2. Place a piece of water soluble stabilizer to the right side of the traced motif. Pin (fig. 2).

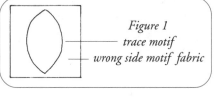

*Figure 1*
*trace motif*
*wrong side motif fabric*

3. Stitch the two layers together along the template lines with a short straight stitch (fig. 2). Trim the seam allowance to $^{1}/_{4}$" or $^{1}/_{8}$". Clip the corners and curves (fig. 3).

4. Cut an "x" in the stabilizer (fig. 3), and turn the motif to the right side using the stabilizer or scrap fabric as a facing. Use a point turner or wooden skewer to "punch out" all points.

5. Starch and press well from the right side. Remove the excess stabilizer.

6. Place the motif in the desired location, pin. Stitch the motif in place using a wing needle or 110 universal needle and a pinstitch (L=2.5, W=2.0) (fig. 5). Stabilizer may be needed under the base fabric. If your machine does not have a pinstitch, a regular needle and a tiny zigzag (L=1.5, W=1.5) can be used to stitch the motif in place.

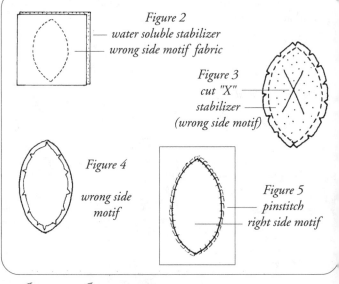

*Figure 2*
*water soluble stabilizer*
*wrong side motif fabric*

*Figure 3*
*cut "X" stabilizer (wrong side motif)*

*Figure 4*
*wrong side motif*

*Figure 5*
*pinstitch right side motif*

# Magic Madeira Appliqué Two Sided Panel

## Supplies

Base fabric for garment
Madeira appliqué panel fabric
Wash-out fabric marker or pencil
Water soluble stabilizer
Wash-away basting thread (YLI, Wash-A-Way™ thread)
Point turner or wooden skewer
Starch
#110 universal or #100 wing needle
#60 or #70 universal needle

## Directions

1. Cut a piece of panel fabric longer and wider than the panel.
2. Fold the fabric in half and crease the fold. Open the fabric and trace the Madeira appliqué panel template on half of the fabric piece on the wrong side (fig. 1).
3. Re-fold the fabric in half, right sides together, traced side on top.
4. Thread the needle and/or the bobbin with **wash-away basting thread**.
5. With the two layers of panel fabric together, stitch along the traced line of the template (fig. 2).
6. Trim the excess fabric 1/8" to 1/4" from the stitching line. Clip the points (fig. 2).
7. Turn the strip to the right side through the top or bottom opening (fig. 3). Using a point turner, make sure the edges are turned thoroughly.
8. Starch, spraying most of the starch along the seam line. Press to dry and pull apart. If the piece is difficult to pull apart starch again along the seam line. Press dry and try pulling apart again. The panel fabric must be dry before pulling apart. Now, the edges of the panel are turned under and ready to stitch. Lay flat and press keeping the outer edge folded to the back of the fabric (fig. 4).
9. **Remove the wash-away thread from the machine** and thread the machine with lightweight sewing thread.
10. Place the panel on the base fabric (bodice, sleeve, etc.) and pin in place.
11. Stitch each side of the panel to the base fabric using a wing needle or 110 universal needle and a pinstitch (L=2.5, W=2.0) (fig. 5). Stabilizer may be needed under the base fabric. If your machine does not have a pinstitch, a regular needle and a tiny zigzag (L=1.5, W=1.5) can be used to stitch the sides of the panel in place.

*Logan's Madeira Shirt*

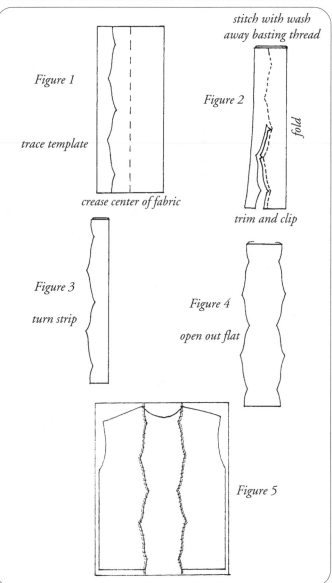

*Figure 1*

*trace template*

*crease center of fabric*

*stitch with wash away basting thread*

*Figure 2*

*fold*

*trim and clip*

*Figure 3*

*turn strip*

*Figure 4*

*open out flat*

*Figure 5*

# Madeira Appliqué Windows

## Supplies

Base fabric for garment
Madeira appliqué panel fabric
Wash-out fabric marker or pencil
Water soluble stabilizer
Point turner or wooden skewer
Starch
#110 universal or #100 wing needle
#60 or #70 universal needle

## Directions

*The Madeira appliqué window is created before
the border is attached to the base fabric.*

1. Create the Madeira appliqué border as described for hems, collars and other borders. Do not attach the border to the base fabric. (A hemline is shown in figures 1-4.)

2. Transfer the template lines of the "window" in the desired location or as the template indicates on the right side of the Madeira appliqué border (fig. 1).

3. Place a piece of water soluble stabilizer on top of the window template lines. Stitch along the lines. Trim $^1/_8$" to the inside from the stitching lines, creating an opening. Clip the corners and curves, if needed (fig. 2).

4. Pull the water soluble stabilizer through the opening to the wrong side. Press. Now the edges of the "window" are folded to the wrong side of the border. Pull or trim away any excess water soluble stabilizer (fig. 3).

5. Place the right side of the border to the wrong side of the collar, hem or other base fabric, matching the edge of the border with the edge of the base. Pin. Stitch the border to the base along the outer edges using a $^1/_4$" seam allowance. Clip curves and corners. (See Magic Madeira Appliqué Hems - fig. 2)

6. Flip the border to the right side of the garment, using a point turner or wooden skewer to "punch out" all points. Pin in place. Starch and press.

7. Using a wing needle or 110 universal needle and a pinstitch (L=2.5, W=2.0), stitch the inside edges of the border to the base (fig. 4) (Also see Magic Madeira Appliqué Hems - fig. 3). If your machine does not have a pinstitch, a regular needle and a tiny zigzag (L=1.5, W=1.5) can be used to stitch the inside edge of the border in place.

8. Using the same stitch as in step 7, stitch along the edges of the window opening.

*Bradley's Madeira
Appliqué Dress*

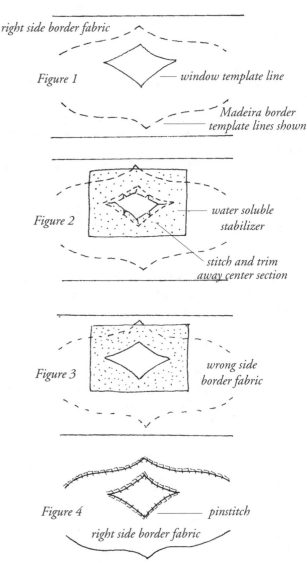

*right side border fabric*

**Figure 1** — *window template line*

*Madeira border
template lines shown*

**Figure 2** — *water soluble
stabilizer*

*stitch and trim
away center section*

**Figure 3** — *wrong side
border fabric*

**Figure 4** — *pinstitch*

*right side border fabric*

# Australian Madeira Appliqué

One of the Australian Madeira Appliqué Techniques presented is the original one taught by Lynne Holyoake at our Martha Pullen School of Art Fashion here in Huntsville. This technique 1. stitches the bottom applique piece to the bottom of the hem, 2. turns up the Madeira piece to the right side of the dress, 3. stitches (tiny zig zag) the Madeira shape such as scallops and points through the Madeira piece and the skirt, 4. trims the excess Madeira from the outside of the stitching and 5. stitches with the wing needle decorative stitch over the stitching just done through the skirt and the Maderia piece. You really have to be careful not to cut the dress fabric when you are cutting away the excess Madeira fabric.

The second Australian Madeira Appliqué Technique lets you 1. straight stitch the design, 2. zig zag the design, 3. cut out the design—all before you 4. stitch the straight bottom of the Madeira piece to the bottom of the skirt and 5. stitch the final wing needle decorative stitching attaching the Madeira shaped top line of the border to the dress skirt.

## Australian Madeira Appliqué Hems

There are two different ways Australian Madeira appliqué can be accomplished but the look is the same. Both methods, I and II, are given in the Australian Madeira Hem directions. Try both and see which one you like the best. The illustrations for the hem are given for both a straight hemline indicated by the "a" illustrations (fig. a) and a shaped hemline are indicated by the "b" illustrations (fig. b).

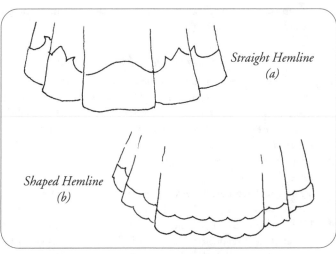

Straight Hemline
(a)

Shaped Hemline
(b)

### Supplies

Skirt fabric
Madeira appliqué hem fabric
Washout marking pen or pencil
Lightweight thread to match the base or appliqué fabric
70/10 universal needle
120/20 universal needle or 100 to 120 wing needle
Open-toe appliqué foot (optional)
Light-weight stabilizer
Trimming or appliqué scissors
Spray starch
Optional: KK2000 or other temporary spray adhesive

### Method I

1. Cut the skirt pieces as stated in the dress directions. Cut the appliqué hem fabric as stated in the dress directions. Stitch the side seams of the skirt. Stitch the side seams of the appliqué hem fabric. Make sure the circumference of the skirt and the circumference of the appliqué hem are the same (fig. 1).

2. Spray starch the base and appliqué fabric several times for easier handling.

3. Trace the hemline design on the wrong side of the appliqué fabric with the washout pen (fig. 1a - straight hemline will not need a template for the lower edge, fig. 1b - shaped hemline template).

4. Place the right side of the appliqué band to the wrong side of the skirt. Stitch the band to the skirt using a ¼" seam for a straight hemline (fig. 2a). Note: if the hemline is shaped, stitch along the template lines and trim the seam allowance to ⅛", clipping the corners and curves as needed (fig. 2b).

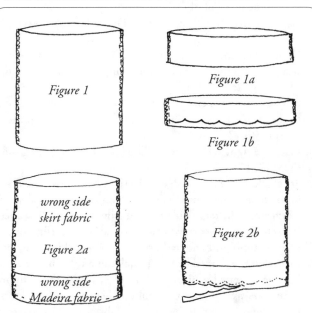

Figure 1

Figure 1a

Figure 1b

wrong side skirt fabric

Figure 2a

wrong side Madeira fabric

Figure 2b

5. Flip the appliqué band to the right side of the skirt (fig. 3a and 3b). Note: for a shaped hem, use a point turner on the shaped hem to punch out any points or curves (fig. 3b).

6. Trace the upper template to the appliqué band on the right side. Pin the upper edge of the band in place or use the temporary spray adhesive to hold the appliqué hem band to the base fabric.

7. Using a small zigzag (L=1.5, W=1.5), stitch the top of the hem to the skirt along the template lines.

8. Carefully trim the excess hem fabric above the stitching (fig. 3a and 3b).

9. Place tear-away stabilizer under the base fabric. Pin in place or use the temporary spray adhesive to hold in place.

10. Place the 120/20 universal needle or the wing needle in the machine.

11. Choose the pinstitch, appliqué stitch, blanket stitch or zigzag. Adjust the stitch width and length so that the width of the stitch covers the previous stitching and the cut edge of the fabric (fig. 4).

12. Position the fabric under the needle so that the straight part of the stitch is on the base fabric and the "fingers" of the stitch go into the appliqué fabric (fig. 4a and 4 b).

13. Carefully remove the stabilizer.

14. Rinse to remove all of the markings and excess starch. Press. Complete the hem referring to the Australian Madeira Appliqué Motif Directions, step 9-15 (fig. 4).

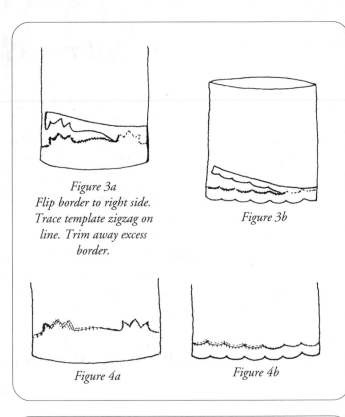

Figure 3a
Flip border to right side. Trace template zigzag on line. Trim away excess border.

Figure 3b

Figure 4a

Figure 4b

## Method II

1. Cut the skirt pieces as stated in the dress directions. Cut the appliqué hem fabric as stated in the dress directions. Stitch the side seams of the skirt. Stitch the side seams of the appliqué hem fabric. Make sure the circumference of the skirt and the circumference of the appliqué hem are the same (fig. 1).

2. Spray starch the base and appliqué fabric several times for easier handling.

3. Trace the design on the wrong side of the appliqué fabric with the washout pen (fig. 1a and 1 b).

4. Using a 70/10 universal needle and an open-toe appliqué foot, if available, thread the machine with the lightweight thread in the needle and bobbin.

5. Using a short, straight stitch (L=1.5), stitch along the template lines.

6. Choose a narrow open zigzag (L=1, W=1). Stitch on top of the straight stitching, straddling the straight stitch with the zigzag stitch (fig. 2a and 2b).

7. Carefully trim the excess appliqué fabric from the hem as close to the stitching as possible using the trimming or appliqué scissors (fig. 3a and 3b).

8. Place the right side of the appliqué band to the wrong side of the skirt. Pin.

9. Stitch along the lower edge of the skirt/band using a $1/4$" seam for a straight hemline (fig. 4a) or if the hemline is shaped, stitch along the template lines and trim the seam allowance to $1/8$", clipping the corners and curves as needed (fig. 4b).

10. Flip the appliqué band to the right side of the skirt. Use a point turner on the shaped hem to punch out any points or curves.

11. Pin the upper edge of the hem in place or use the temporary spray adhesive to hold the appliqué hem to the base fabric.

12. Place the stabilizer under the base fabric. Pin in place or use

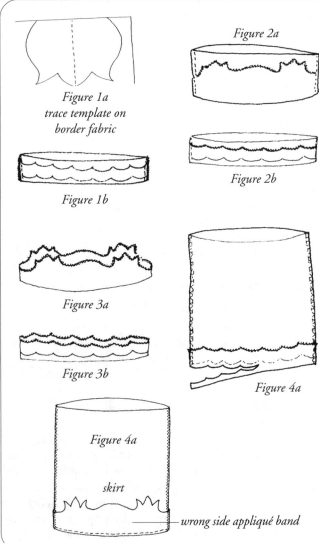

Figure 1a
trace template on border fabric

Figure 2a

Figure 1b

Figure 2b

Figure 3a

Figure 3b

Figure 4

Figure 4a

skirt

wrong side appliqué band

the temporary spray adhesive to hold in place.

13. Place the 120/20 universal needle or the wing needle in the machine.
14. Choose the pinstitch, appliqué stitch, blanket stitch or zigzag. Adjust the stitch width and length so that the width of the stitch covers the previous stitching and the cut edge of the fabric.
15. Position the fabric under the needle so that the straight part of the stitch is on the base fabric and the "fingers" of the stitch go into the appliqué fabric (fig. 5a and 5b).
16. Carefully remove the stabilizer.
17. Rinse to remove all of the markings and excess starch. Press.

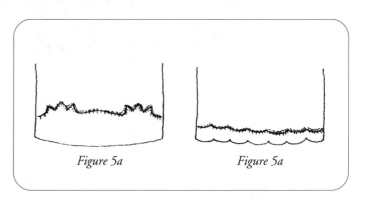

*Figure 5a*   *Figure 5a*

# Australian Madeira Appliqué Corded Accents

## Supplies

2 fabrics, one for the base fabric and one for the appliqué
Washout marking pen or pencil
Lightweight thread to match the base or appliqué fabric
70/10 universal needle
120/20 universal needle or 100 to 120 wing needle
Open-toe appliqué foot (optional)
Light-weight stabilizer
Trimming or appliqué scissors
Spray starch
Optional: KK2000 or other temporary spray adhesive
Floss the match or contrast with the appliqué

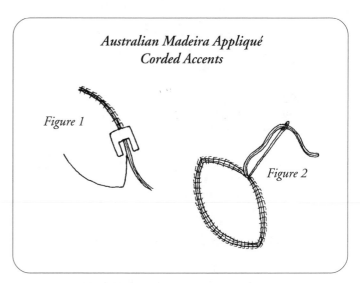

*Australian Madeira Appliqué Corded Accents*

*Figure 1*

*Figure 2*

## Australian Madeira Appliqué Corded Accents Directions

1. Follow steps for Australian Madeira Appliqué - Motif, Hems or Neck Finish. Before the decorative edge of the appliqué is stitched to the base fabric, place six strands of embroidery floss covering the cut edge of the appliqué. Stitch catching the floss in the pinstitch, appliqué stitch, blanket stitch or zigzag (fig. 1).

2. Thread the ends of the floss through a tapestry needle and take to the back of the fabric (fig. 2). Tie the ends to secure.

# Australian Madeira Appliqué Motifs

*Robin's Egg
Madeira Dress*

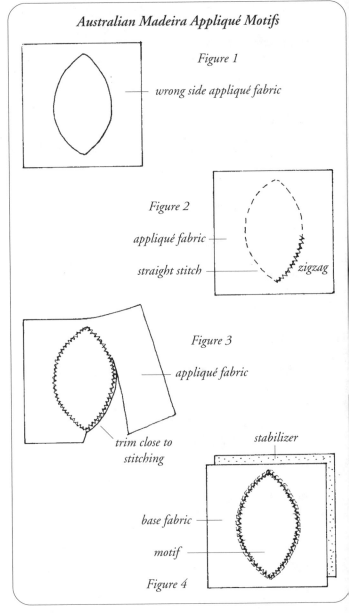

*Figure 1*

*wrong side appliqué fabric*

*Figure 2*

*appliqué fabric*

*straight stitch*

*zigzag*

*Figure 3*

*appliqué fabric*

*trim close to stitching*

*stabilizer*

*base fabric*

*motif*

*Figure 4*

## Supplies

2 fabrics, one for the base fabric and one for the appliqué
Wash-out marking pen or pencil
Lightweight thread to match the base or appliqué fabric
70/10 universal needle
120/20 universal needle or 100 to 110 wing needle
Open-toe appliqué foot (optional)
Lightweight tear-away stabilizer
Trimming or appliqué scissors
Spray starch
Optional: KK2000 or other temporary spray adhesive

## Australian Madeira Appliqué
## Motif Directions

1. Spray starch the base and appliqué fabric several times for easier handling.
2. Trace the design on the wrong side of the appliqué fabric with the washout pen (fig. 1).
3. Using a 70/10 universal needle and an open-toe appliqué foot, if available.
4. Thread the machine with the lightweight thread in the needle and bobbin.
5. Using a short, straight stitch (L=1.5), stitch along the template lines (see fig. 2).
6. Choose a narrow open zigzag (L=1, W=1). Stitch on top of the straight stitching, straddling the straight stitch with the zigzag stitch (fig. 2).
7. Carefully trim the excess appliqué fabric from the outer edge of the motif as close to the stitching as possible using the trimming or appliqué scissors (fig. 3).
8. Place the wrong side of the appliqué on the right side of the base fabric in the correct position (fig. 4).
9. Pin in place or use the temporary spray adhesive to hold the appliqué and the base together.

10. Place the stabilizer under the base fabric. Pin in place or use the temporary spray adhesive to hold in place.
11. Place the 120/20 universal needle or the wing needle in the machine.
12. Choose the pinstitch, appliqué stitch, blanket stitch or zigzag. Adjust the stitch width and length so that the width of the stitch covers the previous stitching and the cut edge of the fabric (fig. 4).
13. Position the fabric under the needle so that the straight part of the stitch is on the base fabric and the "fingers" of the stitch go into the appliqué fabric (fig. 4).
14. Carefully remove the stabilizer.
15. Rinse to remove all of the markings and excess starch. Press.

# Australian Madeira Appliqué Neck Finish

## Supplies

Dress or shirt bodice
Madeira appliqué fabric
Wash-out marking pen or pencil
Lightweight thread to match the base or appliqué fabric
70/10 universal needle
120/20 universal needle or 100 to 110 wing needle
Open-toe appliqué foot (optional)
Lightweight tear-away stabilizer
Trimming or appliqué scissors
Spray starch
Optional: KK2000 or other temporary spray adhesive
Paper to create the template

## Australian Madeira Appliqué Neck Finish Directions

1. Sew the shoulder seams of the bodice in place (fig. 1).
2. Creating the neck template:
   a. Fold the bodice in half along the center front matching the back edges. Create the Madeira Appliqué Neck template by placing the folded bodice on a piece of paper. Trace the center front, neck opening, arm opening at the shoulder and back edge on the paper. Mark shoulder seams at neck and armhole (fig. 2). Remove the bodice.
   b. Place a mark half way between the neck edge and arm opening. Measure from the neck opening to the mark. Continue placing marks this distance from the neck edge center front to center back to form a semi-circle (for example, on a size 8, the shoulder measurement is $4^1/_2$". Half of $4^1/_2$" is $2^1/_4$". Place mark $2^1/_4$" from the neck edge to form a semi-circle). Place the "petal" template along the circle front, joining the lines of the circle and trace (fig. 3a). Cut out the template along the template lines (fig. 3b).
3. Place the template on a folded piece of Madeira appliqué fabric. Cut a rectangle of fabric larger than the template (fig. 3c). Trace the entire template on the fabric (fig. 4).
4. Follow the Australian Madeira Appliqué Motif Directions, Step 1-7 (fig. 5).
5. Place the right side of the appliqué to the wrong side of the bodice matching the center fronts and neck edges. Pin.
6. Stitch along the neck using a $^1/_4$" seam; clip the curves as needed (fig. 6).
7. Flip the appliqué band to the right side of the bodice.
8. Complete the appliqué referring to the Australian Madeira Appliqué Motif Directions, step 9-15 (fig. 7).

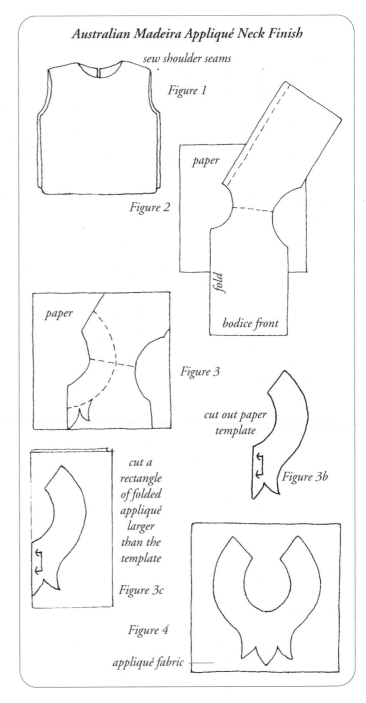

### Australian Madeira Appliqué Neck Finish

sew shoulder seams

Figure 1

paper

Figure 2

paper

fold

bodice front

Figure 3

cut out paper template

Figure 3b

cut a rectangle of folded appliqué larger than the template

Figure 3c

Figure 4

appliqué fabric

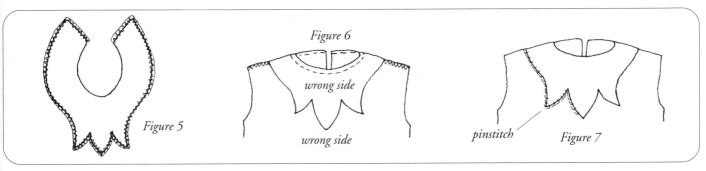

Figure 5

Figure 6

wrong side

wrong side

pinstitch

Figure 7

# Creating Tiny Gathering Foot Puffing

## Directions

1. The puffing strip should be at least two times the length of the desired puffing strip length. It is best to create a strip that is too long for the project than to end up 2" too short. The excess can be removed on each end.

2. If two 45" length strips are needed, cut one in half and stitch each half to the end of the remaining long strip. This will prevent a seam from falling directly in the center of your collar or project. Mark the center of the puffing strip before it is gathered. Quarter points may also be marked if needed.

3. Keep the seams of the strips as tiny as possible. A very small French seam or a serged seam works well to reduce bulk.

4. The puffing strip may be pressed but do not starch it before gathering.

5. The speed of the sewing needs to be very slow for making tiny puffing. Select the slow speed option on your machine if one is available. This will keep the stitching speed consistently slow.

6. The puffing strip should be $1^3/_4$" to 2" wide to allow enough seam allowance and prevent the gathering foot from riding on the first row of stitching. The strip will be gathered with a $^1/_2$" seam allowance on each side using a stitch length of 4. Stitch with the right side of the fabric up.

7. Adjustments may be made to the stitch length to make the puffing looser or fuller. Remember, a longer stitch length will give more gathers and a shorter stitch length will give less gathers. Do not let the strings of the fabric wrap around the foot of the machine. This will cause the fabric to back up behind the foot causing an uneven seam allowance, as well as uneven gathers. Leave the thread tails long in case adjustments are needed.

8. Stitch one side of the puffing.

9. Turn the strip around to stitch the second side of the puffing strip. The fabric will again be right side up.

10. Carefully flatten the gathered fabric to the left of the gathering foot as it is being gathered so that the fabric is as smooth as possible when it goes underneath the foot. **Do not** apply pressure or try to feed the fabric. The feeding must remain constant.

11. Align the puffing gathers by gripping each side of the strip at the gathering rows and wiggle the fabric up and down while pulling slightly on the puffing. This will straighten the puffing.

12. The puffing strip is now complete and ready to insert into a garment or project.

13. Trim seam allowance very close if desired.

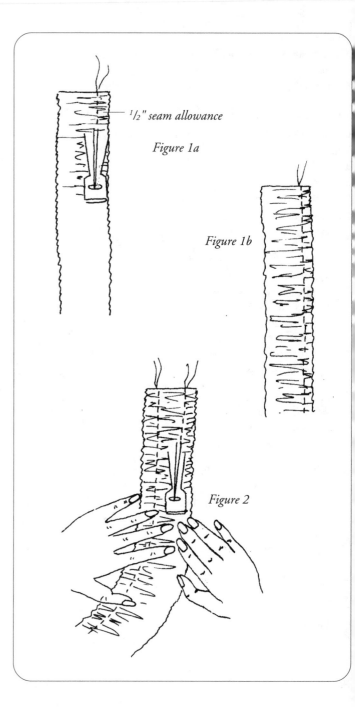

$^1/_2$" seam allowance

Figure 1a

Figure 1b

Figure 2

# Don't Distort Your Smocking
## Add Fabric Panels to the Sides of Smocked Panels

### Directions

1. Measure the width at the bottom of the yoke. This will be measurement A (fig. 1).
2. Measure the width of the shirt, blouse or bodice under the arm opening. This will be measurement B (fig. 2).
3. Block the smocked panel to the width of measurement A or smaller. It should not be larger than measurment A.
4. After blocking the smocked panel, measure the smocked insert. This is measurement C (fig. 3).
5. Subtract measurement C from measurement B. This gives you measurement D, the total amount of fabric to be added to the smocked panel for this pattern.
6. Add 2" to measurement D, divide this measurment in half (measurment E). Cut two pieces of fabric to measurment E by the length of the smocked panel (fig. 4).
7. NOTE: Piping can be added to the smocked panel before the fabric panels are added to each side or piping can be added to the smocked panel after the fabric panels are added.
8. Stitch the fabric panels on each side of the smocked panel creating a new panel (fig. 5).
9. Center the yoke along the top of the new panel and stitch in place (fig. 6).
10. For a shirt or blouse: Using the shirt or blouse pattern as a guide, cut a rectangle of fabric the width of the new panel and longer than needed to fit the pattern piece (fig. 7).
    For a yoke dress: Cut the front skirt to the length desired plus a hem. Gather the top of the gathered skirt at 1/8" and 1/4" leaving 1" flat on each side.
11. Stitch the skirt or fabric rectangle to the lower edge of the new panel.
12. Using the pattern piece, cut out the armholes and any excess along the sides and bottom (fig. 8 - shirt or blouse, fig. 9 - dress).

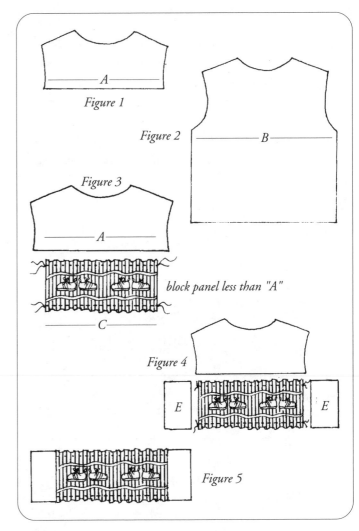

Figure 1

Figure 2

Figure 3

block panel less than "A"

Figure 4

Figure 5

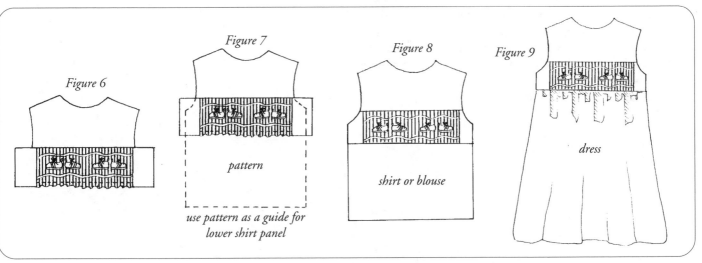

Figure 6

Figure 7

pattern

use pattern as a guide for lower shirt panel

Figure 8

shirt or blouse

Figure 9

dress

# Adding Smocked Panels: The Easy Way

*I*nserting a smocked panel to a sweatshirt, a pillow top or even a picture is quick and easy using this method. This method is also great to use to add narrow smocked strips to blouse or jacket cuffs, lapels of dresses or boy shirt lapels like the lapel shirts featured in this book. Putting a smocked panel on the front of a Bible cover would make a perfect gift for a child or relative.

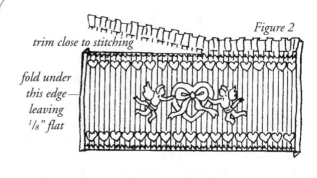
Figure 2
trim close to stitching
fold under this edge— leaving ¹/₈" flat

## Directions

cover edges with ribbon    miter corners
Figure 3

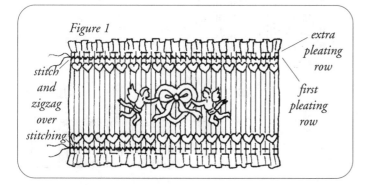
Figure 1
stitch and zigzag over stitching
extra pleating row
first pleating row

Figure 4

1. After smocking, block the smocking to the desired width. Straight stitch between the first and last rows of smocking and the first and last holding rows of the pleating. Zigzag (L=2, W=2) on top of the stitching line (fig. 1). Trim along the edge of the zigzag (fig. 2). Turn the short cut edges of the smocking strip under, leaving ¹/₈" flat.
2. Place the smocking on the garment in the desired location.
3. Baste in place along all four sides.
4. Cover the edges of the smocking with ribbon, mitering the corners (fig. 3) or add ribbon to each side and then across the top and bottom (fig. 4).
5. Stitch the ribbon in place along each edge (fig. 5).

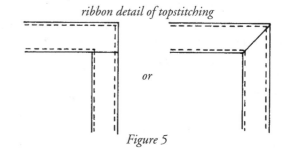
ribbon detail of topstitching
or
Figure 5

# Making Lace Diamond Motifs

Bradley's Madeira
Appliqué Dress

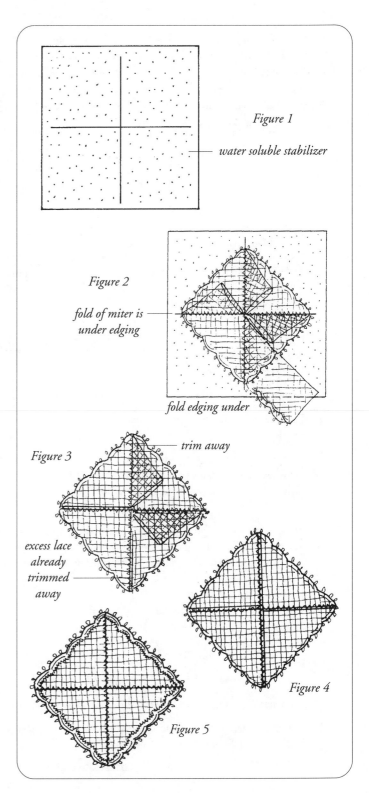

Figure 1

water soluble stabilizer

Figure 2

fold of miter is
under edging

fold edging under

Figure 3

trim away

excess lace
already
trimmed
away

Figure 4

Figure 5

## Materials Needed

Water Soluble Stabilizer
Lace Edging ($^1/_2$" to $^3/_4$")
   Note: Wider edging will produce larger motifs.
Lightweight Sewing Thread
Wash-out Fabric Marker

## Directions

1. Cut a piece of water soluble stabilizer 4" square.
2. Using a new wash-out fabric marker draw a vertical and horizontal line (+) in the center of the stabilizer (fig. 1).
3. Place the water soluble stabilizer on a lace shaping board. Miter edging lace along the drawn lines where heading meets in the center, creating a lace diamond. Refer to "Lace Shaping - Diamonds."
4. Zigzag along each fold of the miter (fig. 2).
5. Pull or trim the water soluble stabilizer from behind the lace.
6. Trim the excess lace from each miter (fig. 3) creating a diamond motif (fig. 4).
7. Place the diamond in the desired location. Pin in place and zigzag just inside the scalloped edge of the lace (fig. 5).

# Shadow Appliqué The Easy Way

## Supplies

- ✿ Fabric for the appliqué
- ✿ Top fabric which should be sheer
- ✿ Background fabric
- ✿ Fusible Web or Temporary spray adhesive
- ✿ Machine embroidery thread
- ✿ Lightweight bobbin thread
- ✿ Wing needle
- ✿ Fabric marker
- ✿ Appliqué foot, regular or open toe
- ✿ Spray starch
- ✿ Tear away stabilizer (optional)

## Method I

1. Trace the design on the paper side of the fusible web. Reverse (mirror image) the design if necessary (**fig. 1**).

2. Fuse the design to the RIGHT side of the appliqué fabric and cut out the design (**fig. 2**).

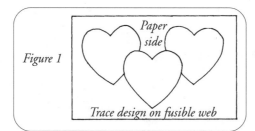

*Figure 1*
Paper side

*Trace design on fusible web*

3. Spray starch the top fabric several times to stiffen for easier handling.

4. Fuse the design in the correct position to the wrong side of the top sheer fabric (**fig. 3**).

5. Set up the machine for a pinstitch, using a wing needle, machine embroidery thread in the needle and a lightweight cotton thread in the bobbin. Loosen the top thread slightly. Use a regular or open-toe appliqué foot.

6. Stitch around the design using the pinstitch. Stitch with the right side up and always stitch background to foreground. The straight part of the pinstitch should be on the top fabric NEXT to the outer edge of the appliqué with the "fingers" of the pinstitch going INTO the design. A stabilizer may be used under the fabric if necessary to prevent tunneling (**fig. 4**).

## Method II

1. Spray starch the appliqué and the top fabric several times to stiffen the fabrics.

2. Trace the design on the appliqué fabric with a fabric marker (**fig. 1**). Trace the design in the correct position on the top fabric (**fig. 2**).

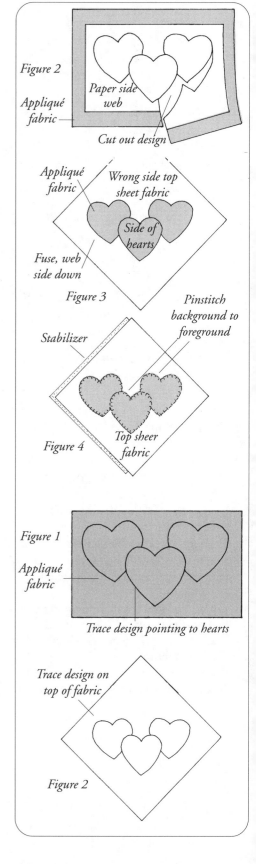

*Figure 2*
Appliqué fabric —
Paper side web
*Cut out design*

Appliqué fabric
Wrong side top sheet fabric
Side of hearts
Fuse, web side down
*Figure 3*

Stabilizer
Pinstitch background to foreground
*Figure 4*
Top sheer fabric

*Figure 1*
Appliqué fabric
*Trace design pointing to hearts*

*Trace design on top of fabric*
*Figure 2*

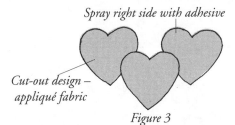

Spray right side with adhesive

Cut-out design – appliqué fabric

Figure 3

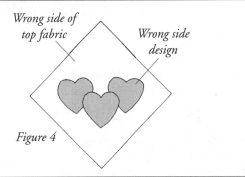

Wrong side of top fabric

Wrong side design

Figure 4

3. Cut out the design from the appliqué fabric.

4. Spray the right side of the cut out appliqué design with a temporary spray adhesive. Follow the directions on the product for correct use (**fig. 3**).

5. Position the cut out design on the wrong side of the top fabric, matching the cut edges of the appliqué with the traced design. Press with your hand so that no

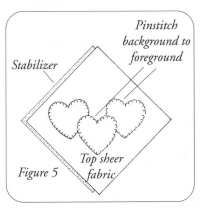

Stabilizer

Pinstitch background to foreground

Top sheer fabric

Figure 5

wrinkles form in the appliqué or top fabric. The design can be repositioned as necessary, but handle as little as possible so that the edges of the appliqué do not fray or stretch (**fig. 4**).

6. Set up the machine for a pinstitch, using a wing needle, machine embroidery thread in the needle and a lightweight cotton thread in the bobbin. Loosen the top thread slightly. Use a regular or open-toe appliqué foot.

7. Stitch around the design using the pinstitch. Stitch with the right side up and always stitch background to foreground. The straight part of the pinstitch should be on the top fabric NEXT to the outer edge of the appliqué with the "fingers" of the pin stitch going INTO the design. A stabilizer may be used under the fabric if necessary to prevent tunneling (**fig. 5**).

# Double Needle Fancywork

Twin needles can be used for decorative stitching as well as pintucks. The width adjustment for the decorative and satin stitches cannot be as wide as when using a single needle.

## Supplies

❀ Twin needle
❀ Machine embroidery threads
❀ White bobbin thread
❀ Wash-out marker
❀ Stabilizer

## Directions

1. Insert the twin needle into the machine. Thread both needles with machine embroidery thread following the directions in the machine manual for twin needle sewing.

2. Adjust the width so that neither needle will not strike the throat plate at the widest part of the stitch. Turn the fly wheel by hand for the complete pattern cycle to insure that the needles will not strike the needle plate. Some machines have a twin needle button that restricts the width of stitches. Engage this function if available.

3. Adjust the length of the stitch to match the width.

4. Place a stabilizer under the fabric.

5. Almost any stitch can be used for this decorative stitching, so play on a scrap of stabilized fabric, adjusting the width and length as desired, always remembering that the width is restricted by the width between the needles. The different widths between the needles create different effects. With a narrow width twin needle such as a 1.7 mm needle, a space may be left unstitched between the edges of the stitches created by the two needles. This gives the effect of three separate colors.

The following are decorative stitches with a single needle and the same stitch with a double needle:

Scallop - single needle (**fig. 1a**)      Scallop - double needle (**fig. 1b**)
Straight stitch scallop - single needle (**fig. 2a**)
Straight stitch scallop - double needle (**fig. 2b**)
Other decorative stitches using a double needle (**fig. 3**)

Single scallop

Figure 1a

Double needle scallop

Figure 1b

Straight stitch scallop

Figure 2a

Straight stitch double needle scallop

Figure 2b

Some other double needle decorative stitches

Figure 3

# Lace and Ribbon Weaving

1. Cut a piece of fusible interfacing larger than the desired woven area or pattern piece. Trace the pattern piece on the interfacing with a washout marker or pencil.

2. Place the fusible interfacing, fusible side up, on the ironing board or lace shaping board. Cut lace and/or ribbon strips to the length of the interfacing. Center the strips on top of the interfacing with the edges touching but not overlapping. Pin the top of the strips in place. Place a piece of wash away basting tape 1/8" away from the outer strips. The paper backing of the wash away basting tape will be removed as the sticky surface is needed (fig. 1).

3. Cut strips of ribbon or lace to the width of the interfacing. Start weaving the strips. As the pieces are woven, use the sticky tape on each side to hold the strip in place. Continue working until the pattern outline is covered (fig. 1).

4. Lay a press cloth on the woven strips. Press lightly to secure strips. Turn up-side-down and press on the interfacing side to make sure all pieces are fused.

5. Re-trace the pattern on the woven piece. Stitch just inside the traced lines. Cut out (fig. 2).

6. Optional: For extra stability stitch along the strips with clear, nylon thread or add machine decorative stitches with colored thread as desired.

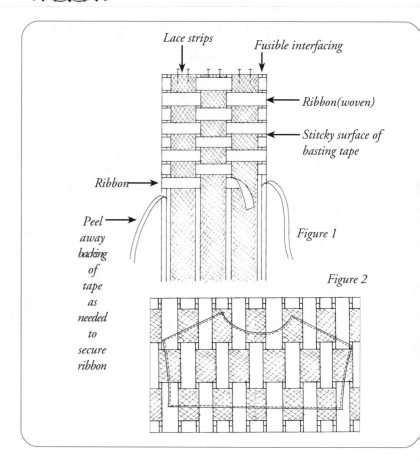

Lace strips
Fusible interfacing
Ribbon(woven)
Stitcky surface of basting tape
Ribbon
Peel away backing of tape as needed to secure ribbon
*Figure 1*

*Figure 2*

# Ribbon to Lace

## Supplies

✿ Ribbon
✿ Insertion lace
✿ Lightweight machine embroidery thread to match the ribbon and/or lace

## Directions

1. Spray starch the lace being careful not to stretch the lace.
2. Butt the edge of the lace to the edge of the ribbon (**fig. 1**).
3. Zigzag with a wide enough stitch to catch the heading of both and with a length of .5 mm to 1 mm (**fig. 2**).

### Note

Care must be taken not to stretch the lace as it is stitched to the ribbon. The ribbon is stable and will not stretch, but the lace stretches easily.

A walking foot can be used if available to keep the lace from stretching. Also reduce the pressure on the presser foot if that is an option.

The heading of the lace can be placed on top of the heading of the ribbon for stitching. Use a straight stitch or narrow open zigzag to stitch together, taking care to keep the lace in the same place on the ribbon (**fig. 3**). ❂

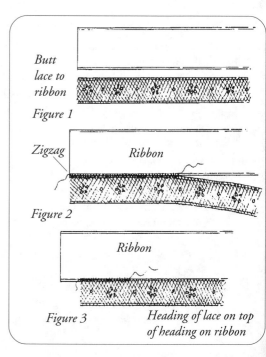

Butt lace to ribbon
*Figure 1*

Zigzag
Ribbon
*Figure 2*

Ribbon
*Figure 3*
*Heading of lace on top of heading on ribbon*

# Corded Satin Stitch

A corded satin stitch can be used in any type of appliqué, but looks especially beautiful on shadow appliqué. It gives the effect of a narrow, padded or raised satin stitch.

## Supplies

❋ Machine embroidery thread for the needle and bobbin
❋ Small cord, gimp or other fiber to be stitched over
❋ #70 or #80 sewing machine needle to match the fabric being stitched
❋ Wash-out marker

## Directions

1. Trace the design to be satin stitched onto the fabric with a wash-out marker.

2. Place a tear-away or paper stabilizer under the design area (**fig. 1**).

3. Use colored machine embroidery thread in the needle and a matching color or white machine embroidery thread in the bobbin.

4. Loosen the top tension to the "buttonhole" setting or decrease the tension by two to three numbers. Loosening the top tension so that the bobbin tension is stronger than the top will give a smoother appearance to the satin stitch.

5. On a scrap of fabric, test the thread tension with a satin stitch using a stabilizer under the fabric. Adjust the stitch length so that it is short enough to completely cover the cord but continue feeding under the foot. Adjust the stitch width so that it just wide enough to cover the cord. A wider stitch will not give the raised look.

6. Practice stitching over the cord. Guide the fabric with the left hand while holding the cord taught in front of the needle. Hold the cord up off the fabric a little (**see fig. 4**).

7. Once the thread tension, stitch width and length are adjusted, the satin stitch over the cord is smooth and even and the cord is always covered, the project can be started.

8. Place the beginning of the design line under the needle. Take one complete stitch to bring the bobbin thread to the top side. Take several very short straight stitches to tie on the threads. Trim the thread tails (**fig. 2**).

9. Place one end of the cord over the beginning of the design line, leaving several inches before beginning to stitch. Adjust the width and length as in the practice piece (**fig. 3**).

10. Stitch around the design with the cord laying over the design lines. Hold the cord with the right hand, slightly off of the fabric, taught (but do not pull) and in front of the needle (**fig. 4**).

11. When stitching around curves, pivot with the needle on the outer edge of the curve so that gaps will not be formed in the stitches (**fig. 5**). When turning corners, pivot with the needle on the inside so that the cord can be pulled around the needle to form the corner. Once the corner is anchored, stitch the same as for a curve (**fig. 6**).

12. At the end of the design, change back to a straight stitch, then take several tiny straight stitches, along the side of the satin stitches so that they will not be visible. Pivot 180 degrees if necessary to stitch along the edge of the satin stitch. Clip the thread tails close to the fabric. Leave several inches of cord (**fig. 7**).

13. Use a large eyed needle to pull the cord ends to the back (**fig. 8**).

14. From the back side, carefully tear away the stabilizer.

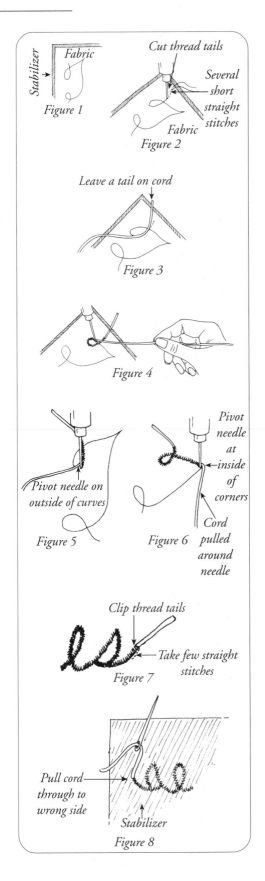

Figure 1

Figure 2

Cut thread tails

Several short straight stitches

Fabric

Stabilizer

Fabric

Leave a tail on cord

Figure 3

Figure 4

Pivot needle on outside of curves

Figure 5

Pivot needle at inside of corners

Figure 6

Cord pulled around needle

Clip thread tails

Take few straight stitches

Figure 7

Pull cord through to wrong side

Stabilizer

Figure 8

# Classic Techniques

# Beginning French Sewing Techniques

## Lace to Lace

Butt together and zigzag.

Suggested machine settings: Width 2$^1$/$_2$, length 1.

## Lace to Fabric

Place right sides together.

Fabric extends $^1$/$_8$" from lace.

Zigzag off the edge and over the heading of the lace.

Suggested Machine Settings: Width 3$^1$/$_2$, Length $^1$/$_2$ to 1
    (almost a satin stitch).

## Lace to Entredeux

Trim batiste from one side of the entredeux.

Butt lace to entredeux and zigzag.

Suggested Machine Settings: Width 2$^1$/$_2$, Length 1$^1$/$_2$.

## Gathered Lace to Entredeux

Trim one side of the entredeux.

Gather lace by pulling heading thread.

Butt together and zigzag.

Suggested Machine Settings: Width 2$^1$/$_2$, Length 1$^1$/$_2$.

## Entredeux to Flat Fabric

Place fabric to entredeux, right sides together.

Stitch in the ditch with a regular straight stitch.

Trim seam allowance to $^1$/$_8$".

Zigzag over the seam allowance.

Suggested Machine Settings: Width 2$^1$/$_2$, Length 1$^1$/$_2$.

## Entredeux to Gathered Fabric

Gather fabric using two gathering rows.

Place gathered fabric to entredeux, right sides together.

Stitch in the ditch with a regular straight stitch.

Stitch again $^1$/$_{16}$" away from the first stitching.

Trim seam allowance to $^1$/$_8$".

Zigzag over the seam allowance.

Suggested Machine Settings: Width 2$^1$/$_2$, Length 1$^1$/$_2$.

## Optional: Top Stitch (to be used after Entredeux to Flat or Gathered Fabric)

Turn seam down, away from the lace, entredeux, etc.

Tack in place using a zigzag.

Suggested Machine Settings: Width 1$^1$/$_2$, Length 1$^1$/$_2$.

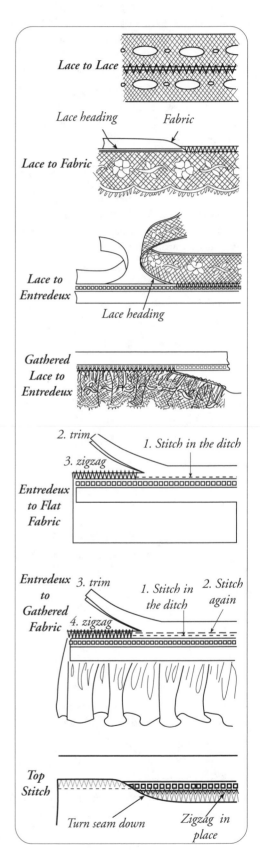

## Cutting Fabric From Behind Lace
## That Has Been Shaped and Zigzagged

I absolutely love two pairs of Fiskars Scissors for the tricky job of cutting fabric from behind lace that has been shaped and stitched on. The first is Fiskars 9491, blunt tip 5" scissors. They look much like kindergarten scissors because of the blunt tips; however, they are very sharp. They cut fabric away from behind laces with ease. By the way, both of the scissors mentioned in this section are made for either right handed or left handed people.

The second pair that I really love for this task is the Fiskars 9808 curved blade craft scissors. The curved blades are very easy to use when working in tricky, small areas of lace shaping. Fiskars are crafted out of permanent stainless steel and are precision ground and hardened for a sharp, long lasting edge.

## Repairing Lace Holes Which
## You Didn't Mean To Cut!

Trimming fabric away from behind stitched-down lace can be difficult. It is not uncommon to slip, thus cutting a hole in your lace work. How do you repair this lace with the least visible repair? It is really quite simple.

1. Look at the pattern in the lace where you have cut the hole. Is it in a flower, in a dot series, or in the netting part of the lace (fig. 1)?

2. After you identify the pattern where the hole was cut, cut another piece of lace $^1/_4$" longer than each side of the hole in the lace.

3. On the bottom side of the lace in the garment, place the lace patch (fig. 2).

4. Match the design of the patch with the design of the lace around the hole where it was cut.

5. Zigzag around the cut edges of the lace hole, trying to catch the edges of the hole in your zigzag (fig 3).

6. Now, you have a patched and zigzagged pattern.

7. Trim away the leftover ends underneath the lace you have just patched (fig. 3).

8. If you cut really close to the fabric, place a piece of organdy or netting behind the lace and fabric slice and zigzag all together to repair.

## Piecing Lace Not Long Enough For Your Needs

From my sewing experience, sometimes you will need a longer piece of lace than you have. Perhaps you cut the lace incorrectly or bought less than you needed and had to go back for more. Whatever the reason, if you need to make a lace strip longer, it is easy to do.

1. Match your pattern with two strips that will be joined later (figs. 1 and 3).

2. Is your pattern a definite flower? Is it a definite diamond or some other pattern that is relatively large?

3. If you have a definite design in the pattern, you can join pieces by zigzagging around that design and then down through the heading of the lace (fig. 2).

4. If your pattern is tiny, you can zigzag at an angle joining the two pieces (fig. 2). Trim away excess laces close to the zigzagged seam (fig. 4).

5. Forget that you have patched laces and complete the dress. If you discover that the lace is too short before you begin stitching, you can plan to place the pieced section in an inconspicuous place.

6. If you were already into making the garment when you discovered the short lace, simply join the laces and continue stitching as if nothing had happened.

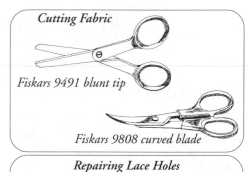

**Cutting Fabric**

*Fiskars 9491 blunt tip*

*Fiskars 9808 curved blade*

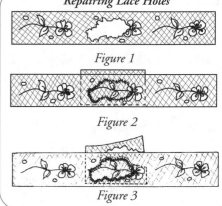

**Repairing Lace Holes**

*Figure 1*

*Figure 2*

*Figure 3*

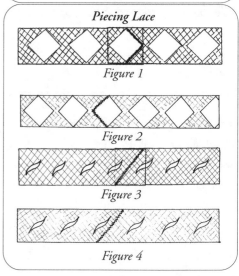

**Piecing Lace**

*Figure 1*

*Figure 2*

*Figure 3*

*Figure 4*

## If Your Fancy Band Is
## Too Short

Not to worry; cut down the width of your skirt. Always make your skirt adapt to your lace shapes, not the lace shapes to your skirt.

## Making Diamonds, Hearts,
## Tear-Drops, Or Circles Fit
## Skirt Bottom

How do you make sure that you engineer your diamonds, hearts, teardrops, or circles to exactly fit the width skirt that you are planning? The good news is that you don't. Make your shapes any size that you want. Stitch them onto your skirt, beginning at the side seam. Work from this seam out to both sides. When you get your lace shapes stitched out to both sides, you will reach a point where another shape will not fit. Then, simply trim off excess fabric from the side of the skirt. Sew the other side seam and your lace shapes will fit perfectly every time.

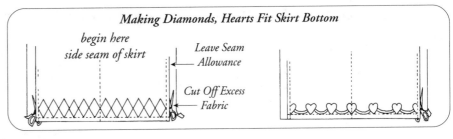

*Making Diamonds, Hearts Fit Skirt Bottom*

*begin here*
*side seam of skirt*

*Leave Seam*
*Allowance*

*Cut Off Excess*
*Fabric*

# Machine Entredeux

## Making Entredeux (Or Hemstitching) On Today's Computer Sewing Machines

About eight years ago I was conned into purchasing a 1905 hemstitching machine for $1500. I was told that it had a perfect stitch and that stitch (about 2 inches) was demonstrated to me by the traveling salesman. I was very happy to finally have one of those wonderful machines. Guess how long that wonderful machine lasted before it broke down? I stitched about 10 inches more which looked great; at that point, the stitching was awful. I called several repairmen. It never made a decent hemstitch again.

The good news to follow this sad story is that today's new computer machines do an excellent job of making hemstitching and they work! I am going to give our favorite settings for our favorite sewing machines. Before you buy a new sewing machine, if you love heirloom sewing, please go try out each of these machines and see if you love these stitches as much as we do.

## Using A Stabilizer and Wing Needle or Large Needle for Hemstitching Or Pinstitching

Before you do any hemstitching or any decorative work with a wing needle which involves lots of stitching on these wonderful machines, first let me tell you that **you must use a stabilizer!** Many people prefer using a #110 universal needle over the #100 wing needle for pinstitching. My suggestion to you would be to try both and see which look you prefer. Both are gorgeous. If your machine does not have a pinstitch setting, then by all means just use a #60 or #70 universal needle and a tiny zigzag to attach your Madeira borders. I think it is advisable to use stabilizer underneath any large needle stitching. If you would like to try your fabrics to see if stabilizer is or is not necessary, it is simple to do. I usually use a tear away stabilizer underneath any type of wing needle or #110 universal entredeux or pin stitching. With enough spray starch and on certain types of fabrics, stabilizer might not be necessary. Your decision is the only correct one.

## Preparing Fabric Before Beginning Hemstitching or Pinstitching

Stiffen fabric with spray starch before lace shaping or decorative stitching with the hemstitches and wing needles. Use a hair dryer to dry the lace before you iron it if you have spray starched it too much. Also, if you wet your fabrics and laces too much with spray starch, place a piece of fabric on top of your work, and dry iron it dry. Hemstitching works best on natural fibers such as linen, cotton, cotton batiste, silk or cotton organdy. I don't advise

hemstitching a fabric with a high polyester content. Polyester has a memory. If you punch a hole in polyester, it remembers the original positioning of the fibers, and the hole wants to close up.

## Threads To Use For Pinstitching Or Hemstitching

Use all cotton thread, 50, 60, 70 or 80 weight. If you have a thread breaking problem, you can also use a high quality polyester thread or a cotton covered polyester thread, like the Coats and Clark for machine lingerie and embroidery. Personally, I like to press needle down on all of the entredeux and pin stitch settings.

## Pinstitching Or Point de Paris Stitch With A Sewing Machine

The pin stitch is another lovely "entredeux look" on my favorite machines. It is a little more delicate. Pin stitch looks similar to a ladder with **one of the long sides of the ladder missing**. Imagine the ladder rungs being fingers which reach over into the actual lace piece to grab the lace. The side of the ladder, the long side, will be stitched on the fabric right along side of the outside of the heading of the lace. The fingers reach into the lace to grab it. You need to look on all of the pinstitch settings given below and realize that you have to use reverse image on one of the sides of lace so that the fingers will grab into the lace while the straight side goes on the outside of the lace heading.

*Pinstitch*

*Mirror Image*
*Pinstitch*

### Bernina 180 E

Pinstitch
-100 wing needle or 100 universal
-Stitch #330 as is or L=3,W=2

Entredeux
-100 wing or 100 universal
-Stitch #701 as is or L=3, W=2.5

### Pfaff 7570

Pinstitch
-100 wing or 100 universal
-Stitch #112, tension 3, twin needle button, L=3, W=4

Entredeux
-100 wing or 100 universal
-Stitch #132, L=5, W=3.5
-Stitch #113, L=2, W=4
-Stitch #114, L=2.5, W=3.5
-Stitch #115, L=3, W=3.5

### Viking Husqvarna, Designer I and 1+

Pinstitch
-100 wing needle or 100 universal
-Stitch D6, L=2.5 to 3, W=2 to 2.5

Entredeux
-100 wing needle or 100 universal
-Stitch D7 (as is)

### Elna CE20

Pinstitch
-100 wing needle or 100 universal
-Stitch #149, L=2.5, W=2.5

Entredeux
-100 wing needle or 100 universal
-Stitch #36, L=1.5, W=2.5

### Singer XL - 1000

Pinstitch
-100 wing needle or 100 universal
-Screen #6, Stitch #7
-Medium or Small (width changes with the length)

Entredeux
-100 wing needle or 100 universal
-Screen #6, Stitch #8
-Medium or Small (width changes with the length)

### Janome 9000

Pinstitch
-100 wing needle or 100 universal
-Stitch #26, L=2.5, W=2.0 to 3.0

Entredeux
-100 wing needle or 100 universal
-Stitch #39, L=1.5, W=3.5

### Brother

Pinstitch
-100 wing needle or 100 universal
-Screen #4, Stitch #8, L=2.5, W=2.0 ot 2.5

Entredeux
-100 wing needle or 100 universal
-Screen #4, Stitch #9, L=2.5, W=3

### Baby Lock, Esanté

Choose Decorative Stitch - Heirloom
Pinstitch
-100 wing needle or 100 universal
-Stitch #4 (as is)

Entredeux
-100 wing needle or 100 universal
-Stitch #5 (as is)

## *— Attaching Shaped Lace To The Garment With Machine Entredeux Or Pinstitching And A Wing Needle*

Probably my favorite place to use the machine entredeux/wing needle hemstitching is to attach shaped laces to a garment. Simply shape your laces in the desired shapes such as hearts, diamonds, ovals, loops, circles, or bows, and stitch the stitch. In addition to stitching this gorgeous decorative stitch, it also attaches the shaped lace to the garment (fig. 1). Always use stabilizer when using this type of heavy hemstitching.

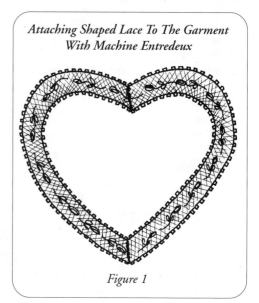

*Attaching Shaped Lace To The Garment With Machine Entredeux*

*Figure 1*

# Puffing Method I

## Gathering The Puffing Using The Gathering Foot On Your Machine

Two years ago, I wouldn't have told you that this was the easiest method of applying puffing into a round portrait collar. The reason being I didn't know how to make perfect puffing using the gathering foot for the sewing machine. I thought you used the edge of the gathering foot to guide the fabric underneath the gathering foot. This left about a $1/4$" seam allowance. It also made the gathers not perfect in some places with little "humps" and unevenness on some portions. Therefore, I wasn't happy with puffing made on the gathering foot. To make perfect gathering, you had to move the fabric over so that you would have at least a $1/2$" seam allowance. There are two sides to the feed dogs; when you use the side of the gathering foot, then the fabric only catches on one side of the feed dogs. It works like magic to move your fabric over and guide it along one of the guide lines on the sewing machine. If your machine doesn't have these lines, simply put a piece of tape down to make a proper guide line.

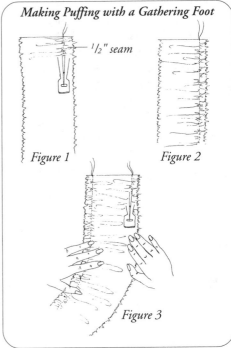

*Making Puffing with a Gathering Foot*

*$1/2$" seam*

*Figure 1*      *Figure 2*

*Figure 3*

## Making Puffing with a Gathering Foot

1.  The speed of the sewing needs to be consistent. Sew either fast or slow but do not sew fast then slow then fast again. For the beginner, touch the "sew slow" button (if available on your machine). This will help to keep a constant speed.

2.  The puffing strip should be gathered with a $1/2$ seam allowance, with an approximate-straight stitch length of 4, right side up (fig. 1). Remember that you can adjust your stitch length to make your puffing looser or fuller. Do not let the strings of the fabric wrap around the foot of the machine. This will cause to fabric to back up behind the foot causing an uneven seam allowance, as well as uneven gathers. You can use a $1^1/2$ to to 1 or 2 to 1 fullness of fabric (fig. 2).

3.  Begin gathering the second side of the strip, right side up. This row of gathering will be made from the bottom of the strip to the top of the strip. In other words, bi-directional sewing (first side sewn from the top to the bottom, second side sewn from the bottom to the top) is allowed. Gently unfold the ruffle with the left hand allowing flat fabric to feed under the foot. Do not apply any pressure to the fabric (fig. 3). The feeding must remain constant. The puffing strip in now complete.

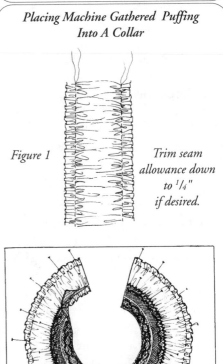

*Placing Machine Gathered Puffing Into A Collar*

*Figure 1*      *Trim seam allowance down to $1/4$" if desired.*

*Figure 2*

## Placing Machine Gathered Puffing Into A Collar

1.  Cut your strips of fabric.

2.  Gather both sides of the puffing, running the fabric under the gathering foot. Be sure you have at least a $1/2$" seam allowance. You can trim your seams down to $1/4$" now if you want to.

3.  You, of course, have two raw edges when you gather puffing with the gathering foot (fig. 1).

4.  Shape the puffing around the fabric board below the row of lace (or rows of lace) that you have already shaped into the rounded shape. Place the pins into the board through the outside edge of the puffing. Place the pins right into the place where the gathering row runs in the fabric (fig. 2).

5. Pull the raw edge of the machine puffed strip up underneath the finished edge of the curved lace, so that your zigzagging to attach the puffing will be on the machine gathering line. Put the rounded lace edge on top of the puffing. Pin the bottom edge of the puffing first so you can "arrange" the top fullness underneath the curved lace edge which is already in place (the top piece of lace) (see fig. 2).

6. It will be necessary to "sort of" arrange the machine gathered puffing, especially on the top edge which will be gathered the fullest on your collar, and pin it where you want it since the machine gathering thread doesn't give too much. After you have pinned and poked the gathering into place where it looks pretty on the top and the bottom, flat pin it to the tissue paper and zigzag the puffing strip to the lace, stitching right on top of the lace.

NOTE: You will have an unfinished fabric edge underneath the place where you stitched the lace to the puffing. That is okay. After you have zigzagged the puffing to the lace, then trim away the excess fabric underneath the lace edge. Be careful, of course, when you trim this excess fabric, not to accidentally cut the lace.

7. If you have a machine entredeux/wing needle option on your sewing machine, you can stitch this beautiful stitch in place of the zigzagging. Since the fabric is gathered underneath the lace, you will have to be very careful stitching to get a pretty stitch.

8. Shape another piece of lace around the bottom of this puffing, bringing the inside piece of curved lace exactly to fit on top of the gathering line in the puffing. Once again, you will have unfinished fabric underneath the place where you will zigzag the lace to the puffing collar. After zigzagging the lace to the puffing collar, trim the excess fabric away.

9. Continue curving the rest of the laces to make the collar as wide as you want it to be.

# Puffing Method II

## — Gathering the Puffing with Two Gathering Rows —

1. The puffing strip should be at least two times the length of the desired puffing strip length. It is best to create a strip that is too long for the project than to end up 2" too short. The excess can be removed on each end.

2. If two 45" length strips are needed, cut one in half and stitch each half to the end of the remaining long strip. This will prevent a seam from falling directly in the center of your collar or project. Mark the center of the puffing strip before it is gathered. Quarter points may also be marked if needed.

3. Keep the seams of the strips as tiny as possible. A very small French seam or a serged seam works well to reduce bulk.

4. The puffing strip may be pressed but do not starch it before gathering.

5. Keep the speed of the machine consistent when gathering the strip. The slow speed option may be selected if available.

6. The strip of fabric should be cut 1" wider than the finished puffing desired in the garment or project. The puffing will have a $1/2$" seam allowance on each side.

7. Set the machine to a stitch length of 3.5 to 4 and loosen the top tension slightly. The strip will be stitched with the right side of the fabric up.

8. Run two rows of machine gathering along one side of the strip placing one row $1/2$" from the raw edge and the other $1/4$" from the raw edge.

9. Repeat for the other side of the strip.

10. Pull up the gathers so that the strip is tightly gathered.

11. Align the puffing gathers by gripping each side of the strip at the gathering rows and wiggle the fabric up and down while pulling slightly on the puffing. This will straighten the puffing.

12. The gathers may now be loosened to the desired fullness.

13. The puffing strip is now complete and ready to insert into a garment or project.

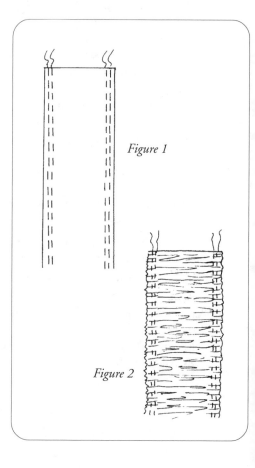

Figure 1

Figure 2

# Basic Pintucking

## Double Needles

Double needles come in different sizes. The first number on the double needle is the distance between the needles. The second number on the needle is the actual size of the needle. The chart below shows some of the double needle sizes. The size needle that you choose will depend on the weight of the fabric that you are pintucking (fig. 1).

*Figure 1*

Let me relate a little more information for any of you who haven't used the double needles yet. Some people have said to me, "Martha, I only have a place for one needle in my sewing machine." That is correct and on most sewing machines, you probably still can use a double needle. The double needle has only one stem which goes into the needle slot; the double needles join on a little bar below the needle slot. You use two spools of thread when you thread the double needles. If you don't have two spools of thread of the fine thread which you use for pintucking, then run an extra bobbin and use it as another spool of thread. For most shaped pintucking on heirloom garments, I prefer either the 1.6/70, the 1.6/80 or the 2.0/80 size needle.

a. 1.6/70 - Light Weight

b. 1.6/80 - Light Weight    e. 3.0/90 - Medium Weight

c. 2.0/80 - Light Weight    f. 4.0/100 - Heavy Weight

d. 2.5/80 - Light Weight

*Figure 2*

## Pintuck Feet

Pintuck feet are easy to use and they shave hours off pintucking time when you are making straight pintucks. They enable you to space straight pintucks perfectly. I might add here that some people also prefer a pintuck foot when making curved and angled pintucks. You can also use a regular zigzag sewing foot for pintucks. Pintuck feet correspond to the needle used with that pintuck foot; the needle used corresponds to the weight of fabric. The bottom of these feet have a certain number of grooves 3, 5, 7, or 9. The width of the groove matches the width between the two needles. When making straight pintucks, use a pintuck foot of your choice. The grooves enable one to make those pintucks as close or as far away as the distance on the foot allows (fig. 2).

## Preparing Fabric For Pintucking

Do I spray starch the fabric before I pintuck it? I usually do not spray starch fabric before pintucking it. Always press all-cotton fabric. A polyester/cotton blend won't need to be pressed unless it is very wrinkled. Tucks tend to lay flatter if you stiffen fabric with spray starch first; that is why I don't advise spray starching the fabric first in most cases. Pintuck a small piece of your chosen fabric with starch and one without starch, then make your own decision.

## Straight Pintucking With A Pintuck Foot

Some of my favorite places for straight pintucks are on high yoke bodices of a dress and along the sleeves. On blouses, straight pintucks are lovely running vertically on the front and back of the blouse, and so slenderizing! One of the prettiest treatments of straight pintucks on blouses is stitching about three to five pintucks right down the center back of the blouse. Tuck a little shaped bow or heart on the center back of the blouse; stitch several tiny pintucks and top them off with a lace shape in the center back. Horizontally placed straight pintucks are lovely running across the back yoke of a tailored blouse. Tucks are always pretty running around the cuff of a blouse. I love pintucks just about anywhere.

1. Insert your double needle. Thread machine with two spools of thread. Thread one spool at a time (including the needle). This will help keep the threads from becoming twisted while stitching the tucks. This would be a good time to look in the guide book which came with your sewing machine for directions on using pintuck feet and double needles. Some sewing machines have a special way of threading for use with double needles.

2. The first tuck must be straight. To make this first tuck straight, do one of three things: (a.) Pull a thread all the way across the fabric and follow along that pulled line. (b.) Using a measuring stick, mark a straight line along the fabric. Stitch on that line. (c.) Fold the fabric in half and press that fold. Stitch along that folded line.

3. Place the fabric under the foot for the first tuck and straight stitch the desired length of pintuck. (Length=1 to $2^1/2$; Needle position is center) (fig. 1).

4. Place your first tuck into one of the grooves in your pintuck foot. The space between each pintuck depends on the placement of the first pintuck (fig. 2).

5. Continue pintucking by placing the last pintuck made into a groove in the foot.

## Straight Pintucking Without A Pintuck Foot

1. Use a double needle. Use your regular zigzag foot.

2. Thread your double needles.

3. Draw the first line of pintucking. Pintuck along that line. At this point you can use the edge of your presser foot as a guide (fig. 3).

NOTE: You might find a "generic" pintuck foot for your particular brand of machine.

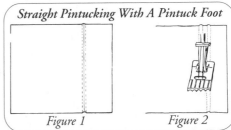

*Straight Pintucking With A Pintuck Foot*

*Figure 1*      *Figure 2*

*Straight Pintucking Without A Pintuck Foot*

*Figure 3*

## Corded Pintucks

Cords make pintucks more prominent. Use Mettler gimp or #8 pearl cotton. Cording comes in handy when pintucks are being shaped. When pintucking across a bias with a double needle, you may get some distortion. The cord acts as a filler and will keep the fabric from distorting. Sometimes you might choose to use cording in order to add color to your pintucks. If you asked me, "Martha, do you usually cord pintucks?," my answer would be "no." However, just because I don't usually cord pintucks, doesn't mean that you won't prefer to cord them.

Some machines have a little device which sits in the base of the machine and sticks up just a little bit. That device tends to make the pintucks stand up a little more for a higher raised effect. Some people really like this feature.

1. If your machine has a hole in the throat plate, run the cord up through that hole and it will be properly placed without another thought (fig. 1).

2. If your machine does not have a hole in the throat plate, put the gimp or pearl cotton underneath the fabric, lining it up with the pintuck groove. Once you get the cording lined up under the proper groove, it will follow along for the whole pintuck (fig. 2).

3. You can stitch pintucks without a pintuck foot at all. Some sewing machines have a foot with a little hole right in the middle of the foot underneath the foot. That is a perfectly proper place to place the cord for shadow pintucks. Remember, if you use a regular foot for pintucking, you must use the side of the foot for guiding your next pintuck.

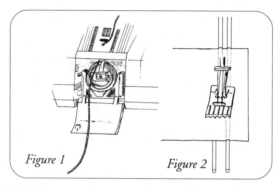

Figure 1                    Figure 2

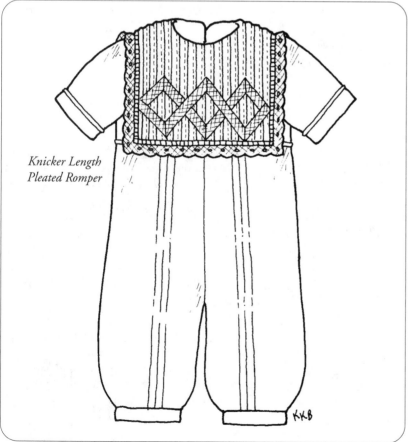

*Knicker Length Pleated Romper*

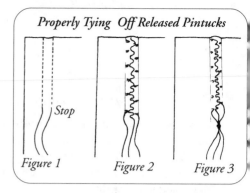

*Properly Tying Off Released Pintucks*

*Stop*

Figure 1            Figure 2            Figure 3

## Shaping Curves And Angles With Pintucks

Pintucks are inexpensive to make. They add texture and dimension without adding cost to the dress. They're rarely found on store-bought clothing. One of my favorite things in the whole world to do is to follow lace shapes with pintucks or decorative stitches on my machine for an enchanting finish. Or you may simply use your template and pintuck the shape instead of using lace. For threads, use white-on-white, ecru-on-ecru, or any pastel color on white or ecru.

The effect of shaped pintucks is so fabulous and so interesting. Virtually everyone is afraid that they don't know how to make those fabulous pintucks that transform a garment into a pintuck fantasy. It is so easy that I just can't wait to share with you the tricks. I promise, nobody in my schools all over the world ever believes me when I tell them this easy way. Then, everybody, virtually everybody, has done these curved and angled pintucks with absolute perfection. They usually say, "This is really magic!"

The big question here is, "What foot do I use for scalloped pintucks?" For straight pintucks, I use a pintuck foot with the grooves. That foot is fine for curved or scalloped pintucks also, but you can also use either the regular zigzag foot or the clear appliqué foot, which is plastic and allows easy "see through" of the turning points. Try your pintuck foot, your regular sewing foot, and your clear appliqué foot to see which one you like the best. Like all aspects of heirloom sewing, the "best" foot is really your personal preference. Listed below are my absolute recommendations for curved and angled pintucks.

## Martha's General Rules Of Curving
## And Angling Pintucks

1. Use a regular zigzag foot, or a pintuck foot (fig. 1).

2. Either draw on your pintuck shape, or zigzag your lace insertion to the garment. You can either draw on pintuck shapes or follow your lace shaping. My favorite way to make lots of pintucks is to follow lace shaping which has already been stitched to the garment.

3. Using a ruler, draw straight lines with a fabric marker or washable pencil, bisecting each point where you will have to turn around with your pintuck. In other words, draw a line at all angles where you will have to turn your pintuck in order to keep stitching. This is the most important point to make with curved and angled pintucks. When you are going around curves, this bi-secting line is not necessary since you don't stop and pivot when you are turning curves. Everywhere you have to stop and pivot, these straight lines must be drawn (fig. 2).

4. Use a 1.6 or a 2.0 double needle. Any wider doesn't curve or turn well!

5. Set your machine for straight sewing, L=1.5. Notice this is a very short stitch. When you turn angles, this short stitch is necessary for pretty turns.

6. Press "Needle Down" on your sewing machine if your machine has this feature. This means that when you stop sewing at any time, your needle will remain in the fabric.

7. Stitch, using either the first line you drew or following around the lace shaping which you have already stitched to your garment. The edge of your presser foot will guide along the outside of the lace shape. When you go around curves, turn your fabric and keep stitching. Do not pick up your foot and pivot, this makes the curves jumpy, not smooth (fig. 3).

8. When you come to a pivot point, let your foot continue to travel until you can look into the hole of the foot, and see that your double needles have straddled the line you drew on the fabric. Remember your needles are in the fabric (fig. 4).

9. Sometimes, the needles won't exactly straddle the line exactly the way they straddled the line on the last turn around. Lift the presser foot. (Remember, you needles are still in the fabric.) Turn your fabric where the edge of the presser foot properly begins in a new direction following your lace insertion lace shaping or your drawn line, lower the presser foot, and begin sewing again (fig. 5).

10. Wait A Minute! Most of you are now thinking, "Martha, You Are Crazy. There are two major problems with what you just said. You said to leave the double needles in the fabric, lift the presser foot , turn the fabric, lower the presser foot and begin sewing again. If I do that I will probably break my double needles, and there will be a big wad or hump of fabric where I twisted the fabric to turn around to go in a new direction. That will never work!" I know you are thinking these two things because everybody does. Neither one of these things will happen! It is really just like MAGIC. TRY THIS TECHNIQUE AND SEE WHAT I AM SAYING. Ladies all over the world absolutely adore this method and nobody believes how easy it is.

11. After you get your first row of double needle pintucks, then you can use the edge of your regular zigzag sewing machine foot, guiding along the just stitched pintuck row as the guide point for more rows. The only thing you have to remember, is to make long enough lines to bisect each angle that you are going to turn. You must have these turn-around lines drawn so you can know where to stop sewing, leave the needles in the fabric, turn around, and begin stitching again. These lines are the real key.

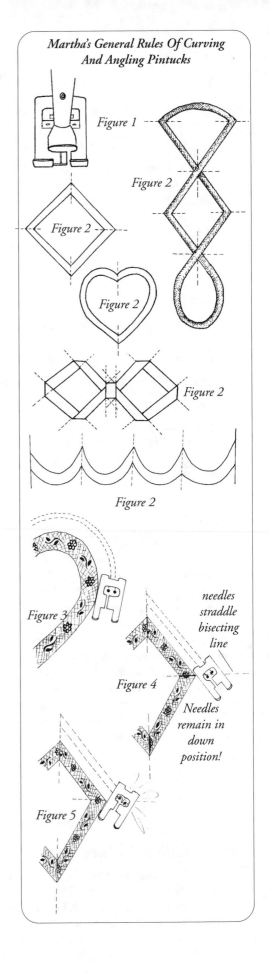

*Martha's General Rules Of Curving*
*And Angling Pintucks*

Figure 1

Figure 2

Figure 2

Figure 2

Figure 2

Figure 2

Figure 3

Figure 4

needles
straddle
bisecting
line

*Needles
remain in
down
position!*

Figure 5

# Lace Shaping Techniques

## General Lace Shaping Supplies

- ❀ Fabric to apply lace shape
- ❀ Lace (usually insertion lace)
- ❀ Glass head pins
- ❀ Spray starch
- ❀ Lightweight sewing thread

- ❀ Lace shaping board or covered cardboard
- ❀ Washout marker or washout pencil
- ❀ Wing needle (optional)
- ❀ Stabilizer (If a wing needle stitch is used)

## Using Glass Head Pins

Purchasing GLASS HEAD PINS is one of the first and most critical steps to lace shaping. All types of lace shaping must be pinned in place, starched lightly and pressed. The iron is placed directly on top of the pins. Since plastic head pins melt onto your fabric and ruin your project, obviously they won't do. Metal pins such as the iris pins with the skinny little metal heads won't melt; however, when you pin hundreds of these little pins into the lace shaping board, your finger will have a hole poked into it. Please purchase glass head pins and throw away your plastic head pins. Glass head pins can be purchased by the box or by the card. For dress projects, as many 100 pins might be needed for each section of lace shaping. So, make sure to purchase enough.

## Shape 'N Press (Lace Shaping Board)

I used fabric boards (covered cardboard) until the June Taylor's Shape 'N Press board became available. It is truly wonderful. This board measures 24" by 18" and has permanent lace shaping templates drawn right on the board. I never have to hunt for another lace shaping template again. Here is how I use it. I place my skirt, collar, pillow top or other project on top of the board with the desired template positioned correctly (I can see the template through the fabric), shape the lace along the template lines pinning into the board, spray starch lightly, re-pin the lace just to the fabric. Now I can move the fabric, correctly positioning the template, and start the process again. I also use the flip side of the board. It has a blocking guide for bishops and round collars (sizes newborn to adult).

*Shape 'N Press Board*

## Making A Lace Shaping Board or Fabric Board

If a lace shaping board is not available, a fabric board can be made from cardboard (cake boards, pizza boards or a cut up box) covered with fabric or paper. A child's bulletin board or a fabric covered ceiling tile will work. Just staple or pin fabric or white typing paper or butcher paper over the board before you begin lace shaping. Just remember you must be able to pin into the board, use a bit of stray starch and iron on it.

## Tracing the Template

Trace the template on the fabric with a wash out marker. It is simpler to draw your shapes on fabric by making dots about one half inch apart than it is to draw a solid line. This also means less pencil or marker to get out of the fabric when your lace shaping is finished. Mark all angles with miter lines (a line dividing the angle in half). Sometimes it is helpful to make the solid lines at the angles and miter lines (**fig. 1**). Hint: If you do not want to draw the template on the fabric, trace the template on stabilizer or paper with a permanent marker. Place the template under the fabric. Because the fabric is "see-through" the lines can be seen clearly. Shape the lace along the template lines. Complete the design as stated in the lace shaping directions. Remember to remove the template paper before stitching so that the permanent pen lines are not caught in the stitching.

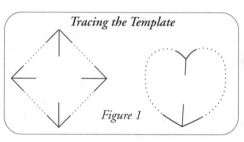

*Tracing the Template*

*Figure 1*

## Shish Kabob Sticks

I first learned about using wooden shish kabob sticks from some of the technical school sewing teachers in Australia. By the way, where does one get these wooden shish kabob sticks? At the grocery store! If you can only find the long ones, just break them in half to measure 5" or 6" long and use the end with the point to push and to hold laces (or other items) as they go into the sewing machine. These sticks are used instead of the usual long pin or worse still, seam ripper that I have used so often. Using this stick is a safety technique as well as an efficient technique.

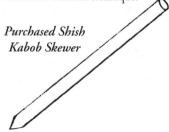

*Purchased Shish Kabob Skewer*

# Shaping Lace Diamonds

Lace diamonds can be used almost anywhere on heirloom garments. They are especially pretty at the point of a collar, on the skirt of a dress, at angles on the bodice of a garment, or all the way around a collar. The easiest way to make lace diamonds is to work on a fabric board with a diamond guide. You can make your diamonds as large or as small as you desire. I think you are really going to love this easy method of making diamonds with the fold back miter.

## Making Lace Diamonds

### Materials Needed
* Spray starch, iron, pins, fabric board
* Lace insertion
* Diamond guide

1. Draw the diamond guide or template (fig. 1).

2. Tear both skirt pieces. French seam or serge one side only of the skirt.

3. Working from the center seam you just made, draw diamonds all the way around the skirt. This way you can make any sized diamonds you want without worrying if they will fit the skirt perfectly. When you get all the way around both sides of the skirt you will have the same amount of skirt left over on both sides.

4. Simply trim the excess skirt away. Later you will French seam or serge the skirt on the other side to complete your skirt. This is the easy way to make any type of lace shaping on any skirt and it will always fit perfectly (fig. 2).

5. The guide or template, which you have just drawn, will be the outside of the diamond. Draw lines going into the diamond, bisecting each angle where the lace will be mitered. This is very important, since one of your critical pins will be placed exactly on this line. These bisecting lines need to be drawn about 2 inches long coming in from the angles of the diamonds (fig. 3). If you are making a diamond skirt, it is easier to draw your diamond larger and make your diamond shaping on the inside of the diamond. That way, the outside points of your diamond can touch when you are drawing all of your diamonds on the skirt.

6. As I said earlier, you can shape the laces for diamonds on either the outside or the inside of the template. I actually think it is easier to shape your laces on the inside of the template.

7. Place your skirt with the drawn diamonds on a fabric board.

8. Place the lace flat and guiding it along the inside of the drawn template, put a pin at point A and one at point B where the bisecting line goes to the inside (fig. 4a). The pin goes through both the lace and the fabric into the fabric board.

9. Guiding the edge of the lace along the drawn template line, place another pin into the fabric board through the lace (and the fabric skirt) at point C and another one at point D on the bisecting line (fig. 4b).

10. Fold back the lace right on top of itself. Remove the pin from the fabric board at point D, replacing it this time to go through both layers of lace rather than just one. Of course, the pin will not only go through both layers of lace but also through the skirt and into fabric board (fig. 5).

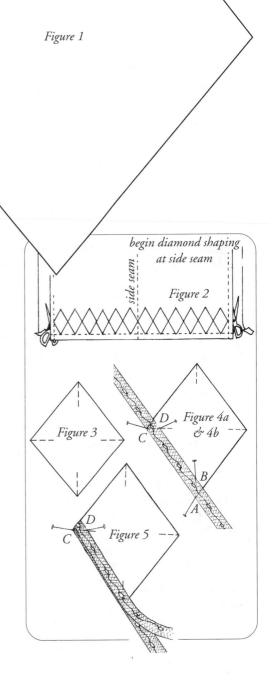

*Figure 1*

*begin diamond shaping at side seam*

*side seam*

*Figure 2*

*Figure 3*

*Figure 4a & 4b*

*Figure 5*

11. Take the lace piece and bring it around to once again follow the outside line. You magically have a folded miter already in place (see fig. 6).

12. Guiding further, with the edge of the lace along the inside of the drawn template line, place another pin into the fabric board through the lace at point E and another at point F on the bisecting line (fig. 6).

13. Fold the lace right back on top of itself. Remove the pin at point F, replacing it this time to go through both layers of lace rather than just one (fig. 7).

14. Take the lace piece and bring it around to once again follow the outside line. You magically have a folded miter already in place (fig. 8).

15. Guiding further, with the edge of the lace along the inside of the drawn template line, place another pin into the lace at point G and another pin at point H on the bisecting line.

16. Fold the lace right back on top of itself. Remove the pin at point H, replace it this time to go through both layers of lace rather than just one.

17. Take the lace piece and bring it around to once again follow the outside line. You magically have a folded miter already in place (fig. 9).

18. At the bottom of the lace diamond, let the laces cross at the bottom. Remove the pin at point B and replace it into the fabric board through both pieces of lace. Remove the pin completely at point A (fig. 10).

19. Taking the top piece of lace, and leaving in the pin at point B only, fold the lace under and back so that it lies on top of the other piece of lace. You now have a folded in miter for the bottom of the lace.

20. Put a pin in, now, at point B (fig. 11). Of course you are going to have to cut away this long tail of lace. I think the best time to do that is before you begin your final stitching to attach the diamonds to the garment. It is perfectly alright to leave those tails of lace until your final stitching is done and then trim them.

21. You are now ready to spray starch and press the whole diamond shape. After spray starching and pressing the diamonds to the skirt, remove the pins from the fabric board and flat pin the lace shape to the skirt bottom. You are now ready to zigzag the diamond or machine entredeux stitch the diamond to the garment. Suggested zigzag settings are Width=2 to 3, Length=1 to 1¹/₂.

## Finishing The Bottom Of The Skirt

These techniques are for finishing the bottom of a Diamond Skirt, a Heart Skirt, a Bow Skirt, or any other lace shaped skirt where the figures travel all the way around the bottom touching each other.

## Method One

### Using Plain Zigzag To Attach Diamonds (Or Other Shapes) To The Skirt

1. First, zigzag across the top of the diamond pattern, stitching from point A to point B, again to point A and finish the entire skirt (fig. 12). Your lace is now attached to the skirt all the way across the skirt on the top. If your fabric and diamonds have been spray starched well, you don't have to use a stabilizer when zigzagging these lace shapes to the fabric. The stitch width will be wide enough to cover the heading of the lace and go off onto the fabric on the other side. The length will be from ¹/₂" to 1", depending on the look that you prefer.

2. Zigzag all of the diamonds on the skirt, on the inside of the diamonds only (fig. 13).

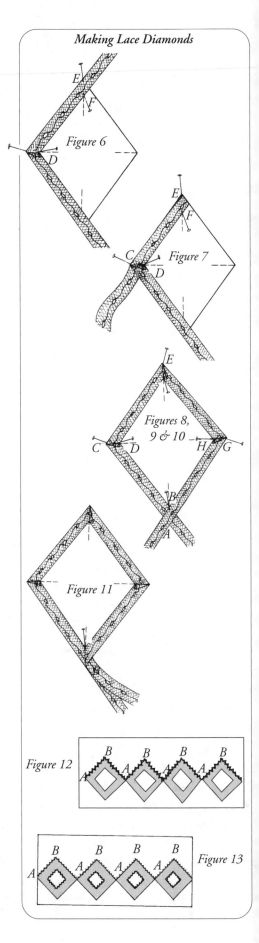

*Making Lace Diamonds*

*Figure 6*

*Figure 7*

*Figures 8, 9 & 10*

*Figure 11*

*Figure 12*

*Figure 13*

3. You are now ready to trim away the fabric of the skirt from behind the diamonds. Trim the fabric carefully from behind the lace shapes. The rest of the skirt fabric will now fall away leaving a diamond shaped bottom of the skirt (fig. 14a). The lace will also be seen through the top of the diamonds. Zigzag over the fold at each miter. Trim away the excess lace from the back (fig. 14b).

4. If you are going to just gather lace and attach it at this point, then gather the lace and zigzag it to the bottom of the lace shapes, being careful to put extra fullness in the points of the diamonds (fig. 15). If your lace isn't wide enough to be pretty, then zigzag a couple of pieces of insertion or edging to your edging to make it wider (fig. 16).

5. If you are going to put entredeux on the bottom of the shapes before attaching gathered lace to finish it, follow the instructions for attaching entredeux to the bottom of a scalloped skirt given earlier in this lace shaping section. Work with short pieces of entredeux stitching from the inside points of the diamonds to the lower points of the diamonds on the skirt.

## Finishing The Bottom Of The Skirt Method Two

### Using A Wing Needle Machine Entredeux Stitch To Attach Diamonds (Or Other Lace Shapes) To The Skirt

1. If you are going to use the wing needle/entredeux stitch on your sewing machine to attach your diamonds or other lace shapes to the skirt, use the entredeux stitch for attaching all of the lace shapes to the skirt. Remember you must use a stabilizer when using the entredeux stitch/wing needle on any machine.

2. Place your stabilizer underneath the skirt, behind the shapes to be stitched. You can use small pieces of stabilizer which are placed underneath only a few shapes rather than having to have a long piece of stabilizer. Just be sure that you have stabilizer underneath these lace shapes before you begin your entredeux/wing needle stitching.

3. First, stitch the top side of the diamonds entredeux stitching from point A to point B all the way around the skirt. (fig. 17).

4. Secondly, stitch the inside of the diamonds using the entredeux stitch (fig. 18). Do not cut any fabric away at this point. Remember to continue using stabilizer for all entredeux/wing needle stitching.

5. You are now ready to gather your lace edging and machine entredeux it to the bottom of the skirt, joining the bottom portions of the diamonds at the same time you attach the gathered lace edging. If your machine has an edge joining or edge stitching foot with a center blade for guiding, this is a great place for using it.

6. Gather only a few inches of lace edging at a time. Butt the gathered lace edging to the flat bottom sides of the diamonds.

7. Machine entredeux right between the gathered lace edging and the flat side of the diamond. Remember, you are stitching through your laces (which are butted together, not overlapped), the fabric of the skirt and the stabilizer (fig. 19). Put a little extra lace gathered fullness at the upper and lower points of the diamonds.

8. After you have stitched your machine entredeux all the way around the bottom of the skirt, you have attached the gathered lace edging to the bottom of the skirt with your entredeux stitch.

9. Trim the fabric from behind the lace diamonds. Trim the fabric from underneath the gathered lace edging on the bottom of the skirt (fig. 20).

10. Either zigzag your folded miters in the angles of the diamonds or simply leave them folded in. I prefer to zigzag them (fig. 21). You also have the choice of cutting away the little folded back portions of the miters or leaving them for strength.

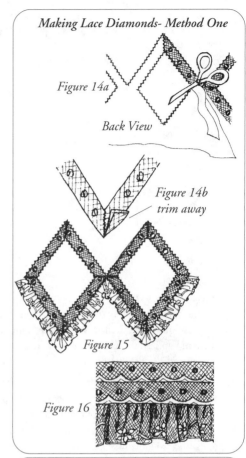

**Making Lace Diamonds- Method One**

*Figure 14a*

*Back View*

*Figure 14b*
trim away

*Figure 15*

*Figure 16*

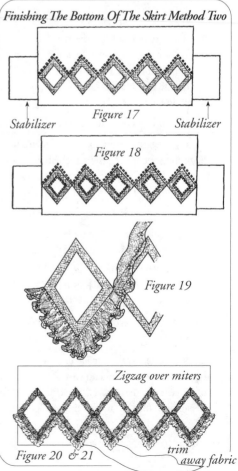

**Finishing The Bottom Of The Skirt Method Two**

*Figure 17*

Stabilizer          Stabilizer

*Figure 18*

*Figure 19*

*Zigzag over miters*

*Figure 20 & 21*          trim away fabric

# Shaping Flip-Flopped Lace Bows

*Figure 1*

I make lace bows using a technique called "flip-flopping" lace — a relatively unsophisticated name for such a lovely trim. I first saw this technique on an antique teddy I bought at a local antique store. It had the most elegant flip-flopped lace bow. Upon careful examination, I noticed the lace was simply folded over at the corners, then continued down forming the outline of the bow. The corners were somewhat square. Certainly it was easier than mitering or pulling a thread and curving. I found it not only looked easier, it was easier.

Follow the instructions for making a flip-flopped bow, using a bow template. This technique works just as well for lace angles up and down on a skirt. You can flip-flop any angle that traditionally would be mitered. It can be used to go around a square collar, around diamonds, and around any shape with an angle rather than a curve.

## Flip-Flopping Lace

1. Trace the template onto the fabric exactly where you want to place bows (fig. 1). Remember, the easy way to put bows around a skirt is to fold the fabric to make equal divisions of the skirt. If you want a bow skirt which has bows all the way around, follow the directions for starting at the side to make the bows in the directions given for a diamond skirt.

2. Draw your bows on your garment or on a skirt where you want this lace shape.

3. Place your garment on your fabric board before you begin making your bow shapes. Beginning above the inside of one bow (above E), place the lace along the angle. The template is the inside guide line of the bow (fig. 2).

4. At the first angle (B), simply fold the lace so that it will follow along the next line (B-C) (fig. 3). This is called flip-flopping the lace.

5. Place pins sticking through the lace, the fabric, and into the shaping board. I like to place pins on both the inside edges and the outside edges. Remember to place your pins so that they lie as flat as possible.

6. The lines go as follows: A-B, B-C, C-D, D-A, E-F, F-G, G-H, H-E. Tuck your lace end under E, which is also where the first raw edge will end (fig. 4).

7. Cut a short bow tab of lace that is long enough to go around the whole tie area of the bow (fig. 4). This will be the bow tie!

8. Tuck in this lace tab to make the center of the bow (fig. 5). Another way to attach this bow tie is to simply fold down a tab at the top and the bottom and place it right on top of the center of the bow. That is actually easier than tucking it under. Since you are going to zigzag all the way around the bow "tie" it really won't matter whether it is tucked in or not.

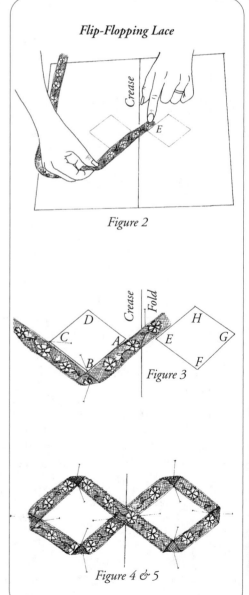

*Flip-Flopping Lace*

*Figure 2*

*Figure 3*

*Figure 4 & 5*

9. Spray starch and press the bow, that is shaped with the pins still in the board, with its bow tie in place (fig. 6). Remove pins from the board and pin the bow flat to the skirt or other garment. You are now ready to attach the shaped bow to the garment.

10. This illustration gives you ideas for making a bow two ways. First, the "A" side of the bow has just the garment fabric peeking through the center of the bow. Second, the "B" side of the bow illustrates what the bow will look like if you put a pintucked strip in the center. Both are beautiful (fig. 7).

11. If you prefer the bow to look like side (A), which has the fabric of the garment showing through the middle of the bow, follow these steps for completing the bow. Zigzag totally around the outside of the bow. Then, zigzag around the inside portions of both sides of the bow. Finally, zigzag around the finished bow "tie" portion (fig. 8). The bows will be attached to the dress.

12. If you prefer the bow to look like side (B), which will have pintucks (or anything else you choose) inside, follow the directions in this section. (These directions are when you have bows on areas other than the bottom of a skirt or sleeve or collar. If you have bows at the bottom of anything, then you have to follow the skirt directions given in the diamond skirt section.)

13. Zigzag the outside only of the bows all the way around. Notice that your bow "tie" will be partially stitched since part of it is on the outside edges.

14. I suggest pintucking a larger piece of fabric and cutting small sections which are somewhat larger than the insides of the bows (fig. 9).

15. Cut away fabric from behind both center sections of the bow. I lovingly tell my students that now they can place their whole fists inside the holes in the centers of this bow.

16. Place the pintucked section behind the center of the lace bows. Zigzag around the inside of the bows, which will now attach the pintucked section. From the back, trim away the excess pintucked section. You now have pintucks in the center of each side of the bow (fig. 10).

17. Go back and stitch the sides of the bow "tie" down. After you have zigzagged all the way around your bow "tie," you can trim away excess laces which crossed underneath the tie. This gives the bow tie a little neater look.

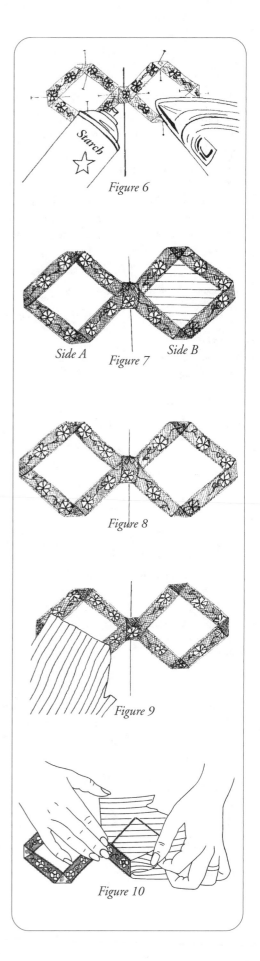

Figure 6

Side A    Figure 7    Side B

Figure 8

Figure 9

Figure 10

# Tied Lace Bows

This method of bow shaping I saw for the first time years ago in Australia. It is beautiful and each bow will be a little different which makes it a very interesting variation of the flip-flopped bow. Your options on shaping the bow part of this cute bow are as follows:

1. You can flip-flop the bow
2. You can curve the bow and pull a string to make it round
3. You can flip-flop one side and curve the other side. Bows can be made of lace insertion, lace edging, or lace beading. If you make your tied lace bow of lace edging, be sure to put the scalloped side of the lace edging for the outside of the bow and leave the string to pull on the inside.

## Materials Needed

❀ 1 yard to 1¼ yards lace insertion, edging or beading for one bow

## Directions

1. Tie the lace into a bow, leaving equal streamers on either side of the bow (fig. 1).
2. Using a lace board, shape the bow onto the garment, using either the flip-flopped method or the pulled thread curved method.

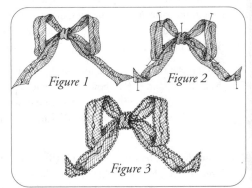

*Figure 1*    *Figure 2*

*Figure 3*

3. Shape the streamers of the bow using either the flip-flopped method or the pulled thread method (fig. 2).
4. Shape the ends of the streamer into an angle (fig. 2).
5. Zigzag or machine entredeux stitch the shaped bow and streamers to the garment (fig. 3).

# Hearts-Fold Back Miter Method

## Curving Lace

Since many heirloom sewers are also incurable romantics, it's no wonder hearts are a popular lace shape. Hearts are the ultimate design for a wedding dress, wedding attendants' clothing, or on a ring bearer's pillow. As with the other lace shaping discussed in this chapter, begin with a template when making hearts. When using our heart template, we like to shape our laces inside the heart design. Of course, shaping along the outside of the heart design is permitted also, so do whatever is easiest for you.

1. Draw a template in the shape of a heart. Make this as large or as small as you want. If you want equal hearts around the bottom of a skirt, fold the skirt into equal sections, and design the heart template to fit into one section of the skirt when using your chosen width of lace insertion.

2. Draw on your hearts all the way around the skirt if you are using several hearts. As always, when shaping lace, draw the hearts onto the fabric where you will be stitching the laces.

3. Draw a 2" bisecting line at the top into the center and at the bottom of the heart into the center (fig. 1).

NOTE: I would like to refresh your memory on lace shaping along the bottom of a skirt at this time. You make your hearts (or whatever else you wish to make) above the skirt while the skirt still has a straight bottom. Later after stitching your hearts (or whatever else) to the skirt, you cut away to make the shaped skirt bottom.

4. Lay the fabric with the hearts drawn on top, on top of the fabric board. As always, pin the lace shaping through the lace, the fabric and into the fabric board.

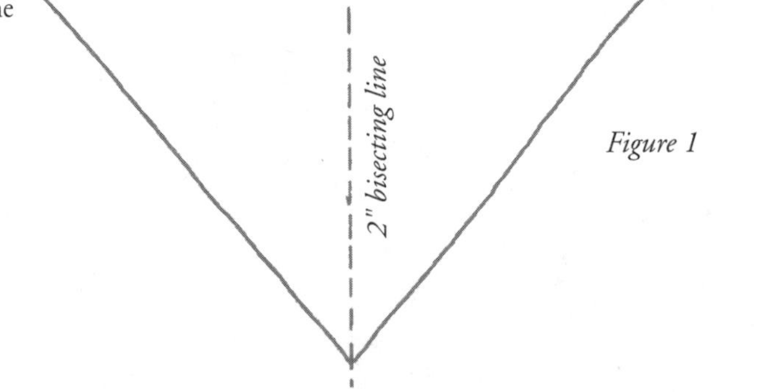

2" bisecting line

*Figure 1*

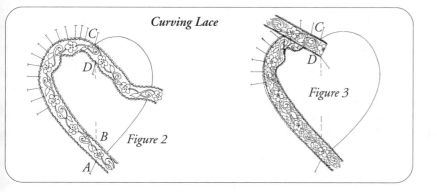

*Figure 2*

*Figure 3*

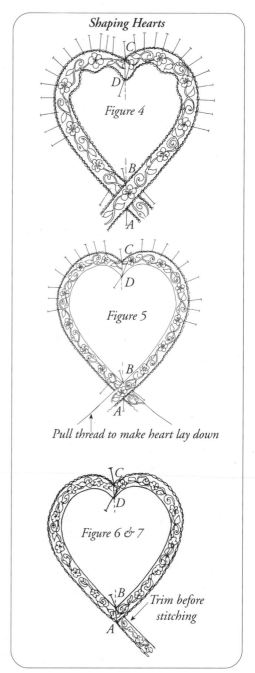

*Figure 4*

*Figure 5*

Pull thread to make heart lay down

*Figure 6 & 7*

Trim before stitching

5. Cut one piece of lace which will be large enough to go all the way around one heart with about 4" extra. Before you begin shaping the lace, leave about 2" of lace on the outside of the bottom line.

6. Place a pin at point A. Beginning at the bottom of the heart, pin the lace on the inside of the heart template. The pins will actually be on the outside of the lace insertion; however, you are shaping your laces on the inside of your drawn heart template.

7. Work around the heart to point C, placing pins at ¹/₂" intervals. Notice that the outside will be pinned rather tightly and the inside will be curvy. Note: One of our students who was a math teacher told me years ago while I was teaching this lace shaping, a very important fact. She said, "Martha did you know that a curved line is just a bunch of straight lines placed in a funny way?" She said this as I was trying to explain that it was pretty easy to get the straight lace pinned into a curve. Since I remembered as little about my math classes as possible, I am sure that I didn't know this fact. It makes it a lot easier to explain taking that straight lace and making a curve out of it to know that fact.

8. After finishing pinning around to the center of the heart, place another pin at point D (fig. 2).

9. Lay the lace back on itself, curving it into the curve that you just pinned (fig. 3). Remove the pin from point C and repin it, this time pinning through both layers of lace.

10. Wrap the lace to the other side and begin pinning around the other side of the heart. Where you took the lace back on itself and repinned, there will be a miter which appears just like magic. This is the new fold back miter which is just as wonderful on hearts as it is on diamonds and scalloped skirts.

11. Pin the second side of the lace just like you pinned the first one. At the bottom of the heart, lay the laces one over the other and put a pin at point B (fig. 4).

12. It is now time to pull the threads to make the curvy insides of the heart lay flat and become heart shaped. You can pull threads either from the bottom of the heart or threads from the center of each side of the heart. I prefer to pull the threads from the bottom of the heart. Pull the threads and watch the heart lay down flat and pretty. (fig. 5). After teaching literally hundreds of students to make hearts, I think it is better to pull the thread from the bottom of the heart. You don't need to help the fullness lay down; simply pull the thread. On other lace shaped curves such as a scalloped skirt, loops, or ovals, you have to pull from the inside curve.

13. Spray starch and press the curves into place.

14. To make your magic miter at the bottom of the heart, remove the pin from point A, fold back the lace so it lays on the other piece of lace, and repin point A. You now have a folded back miter which completes the easy mitering on the heart (fig. 6). You are now ready to pin the hearts flat onto the garment and remove the shaping from the fabric board.

15. You can trim these bottom "tails" of lace away before you attach the heart to the garment or after you attach the heart to the garment. It probably looks better to trim them before you stitch (fig. 7). Remove fabric with shaped lace from board. Pin in just a few places and stich fabric to lace.

16. You can attach the hearts just to the fabric or you can choose to put something else such as pintucks inside the hearts. If you have hearts which touch going all the way around a skirt, then follow the directions for zigzagging which are in the diamond section.

17. If you have one heart on a collar or bodice of a dress, then zigzag the outside first. If you choose to put something on the inside of each heart, cut away the fabric from behind the shape after zigzagging it to the garment. Then, put whatever you want to insert in the heart behind the heart shape and zigzag around the center or inside of

the heart. Refer to the directions on inserting pintucks or something else in the center of a lace shape in the flip-flopped bow section.

18. You can certainly use the entredeux/wing needle stitching for a beautiful look for attaching the hearts. Follow the directions for machine entredeux on the lace shaped skirt found in the diamond section of this lace shaping chapter.

19. After you cut away the fabric from behind the hearts, go back and zigzag over each mitered point (fig. 8). You then have the choice of either leaving the folded over section or of cutting it away. Personally, I usually leave the section because of the strength it adds to the miters. The choice is yours.

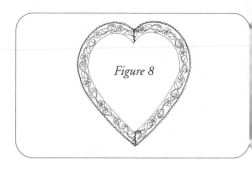

*Figure 8*

# Scalloped Skirt

I have always loved scalloped skirts. The first one that I ever saw intimidated me so much that I didn't even try to make one for several years after that. The methods which I am presenting to you in this section are so easy that I think you won't be afraid to try making one of my favorite garments. Scalloping lace can be a very simple way to finish the bottom of a smocked dress or can be a very elaborate way to put row after row of lace scallops with curved pintucks in between those scallops. Plain or very elaborate - this is one of my favorite things in French sewing by machine. Enjoy!

## Preparing The Skirt For Lace Scallops

Before I give you the steps below, which is one great way to prepare scallops on a skirt, let me share with you that you can also follow the instructions found under the beginning lace techniques for scallops as well as diamonds, hearts, teardrops or circles. These instructions are so that you can use any size scallop that you want to for any width skirt. How do you do that? Stitch or serge up one side seam of your whole skirt before placing the scallops.

1. Pull a thread and cut or tear your skirt. I usually put 88 inches in my skirt, two 44-inch widths - one for the front and one for the back. Make the skirt length the proper one for your garment. Sew one side seam.

2. Trace one scallop on each side of the side seam. Continue tracing until you are almost at the edge of the fabric. Leave a seam allowance beyond the last scallops and trim away the excess (fig. 1).

3. Now you are ready to shape the lace along the template lines.

## Pinning The Lace Insertion To The Skirt Portion On The Fabric Board

1. Cut enough lace insertion to go around all of the scallops on the skirt. Allow at least 16 inches more than you measured. You can later use the excess lace insertion in another area of the dress. If you do not have a piece of insertion this long, remember to piece your laces so that the pieced section will go into the miter at the top of the scallop.

2. Pin the lace insertion to the skirt (one scallop at a time only) by poking pins all the way into the fabric board, through the bottom lace heading and the fabric of the skirt. Notice on (figure 2) that the bottom of the lace is straight with the pins poked into the board. The top of the lace is rather "curvy" because it hasn't been shaped to lie flat yet.

3. As you take the lace into the top of the first scallop, carefully place a pin into the lace and the board at points C and D. Pinning the D point is very important. That is why you drew the line bisecting the top of each scallop (fig. 2). Pin the B point at exactly the place where the flat lace crosses the line you drew to bisect the scallop.

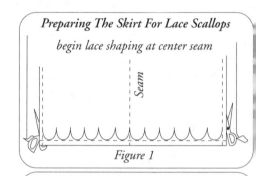

*Preparing The Skirt For Lace Scallops*

*begin lace shaping at center seam*

Seam

*Figure 1*

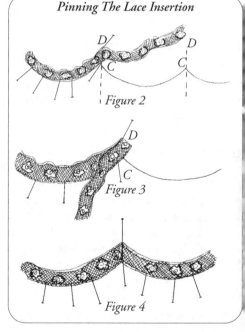

***Pinning The Lace Insertion***

D  C  D  C

*Figure 2*

D  C

*Figure 3*

*Figure 4*

4. Fold back the whole piece of lace onto the other side (fig. 3). Remove the pin at C and repin it to go through both layers of lace. Leave the pin at point D just as it is.

5. Then fold over the lace to place the next section of the lace to travel into the next part of the scallop (fig.4).

NOTE: If a little bit of that folded point is exposed after you place the lace into the next scallop, just push it underneath the miter until the miter looks perfect (fig. 5). I call this "mushing" the miter into place.

6. To shape the excess fullness of the top of the scallop, simply pull a gathering thread at the center point of each scallop until the lace becomes flat and pretty (fig. 6).

7. Place a pin in the lace loop you just pulled until you spray starch and press the scallop flat. Remember, it is easier to pull the very top thread of the lace, the one which makes a prominent scallop on the top of the lace. If you break that thread, go in and pull another one. Many laces have as many as 4 or 5 total threads which you can pull. Don't worry about that little pulled thread; when you zigzag the lace to the skirt or entredeux stitch it to the skirt, simply trim away that little pulled thread. The heaviness of the zigzag or the entredeux stitch will secure the lace to the skirt.

8. Spray starch and press each scallop and miter after you finish shaping them.

9. After finishing with the section of scallops you have room for on that one board, pin the laces flat to the skirt and begin another section of your skirt (fig 7). You have the choice here of either zigzagging each section of the skirt as you complete it, or waiting until you finish the whole skirt. Remove the skirt from the board.

10. If you choose to use a decorative stitch on your sewing machine (entredeux stitch with a wing needle) you will need to stitch with some sort of stabilizer underneath the skirt. Stitch 'n Tear is an excellent one. Some use tissue paper, others prefer wax paper or adding machine paper. As long as you are stitching using a wing needle and heavy decorative stitching, you really need a stabilizer.

11. If you have an entredeux stitch on your sewing machine, you can stitch entredeux at both the top and bottom of this scalloped skirt (fig. 8). There are two methods of doing this.

## Method Number One

1. After you finish your entredeux/wing needle stitching on both the top and the bottom of the scalloped skirt, trim away the fabric from behind the lace scallop.

2. Carefully trim the fabric from the bottom of the skirt also, leaving just a "hair" of seam allowance (fig. 9).

3. You are now ready to zigzag over the folded in miters (fig. 10). Use a regular needle for this zigzag.

4. Now zigzag the gathered laces to the bottom of this machine created entredeux.

## Method Number Two

1. Machine entredeux the top only of the scallop (fig. 11a). Don't cut anything away.

2. Butt your gathered lace edging, a few inches at a time, to the shaped bottom of the lace scallop. Machine entredeux stitch in between the flat scalloped lace and the gathered edging lace, thus attaching both laces at the same time you are stitching in the machine entredeux (fig. 11b). Be sure you put more fullness at the points of the scallop.

3. After the gathered lace edging is completely stitched to the bottom of the skirt with your machine entredeux, cut away the bottom of the skirt fabric as closely to the stitching as possible (fig. 12).

4. Zigzag over your folded in miters (fig. 12a).

5. If you are going to attach the lace to the fabric with just a plain zigzag stitch, you might try (Width=1$\frac{1}{2}$ to 2, Length=1 to 1$\frac{1}{2}$). You want the zigzag to be wide enough to completely go over the heading of the laces and short enough to be strong. If you are zigzagging the laces to the skirt, zigzag the top only of the lace scallops (see fig. 13).

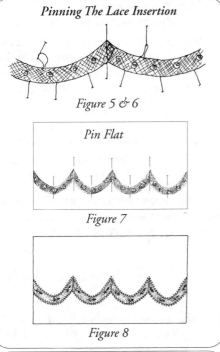

*Pinning The Lace Insertion*

*Figure 5 & 6*

*Pin Flat*

*Figure 7*

*Figure 8*

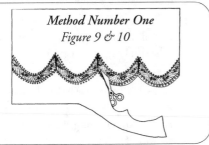

*Method Number One*
*Figure 9 & 10*

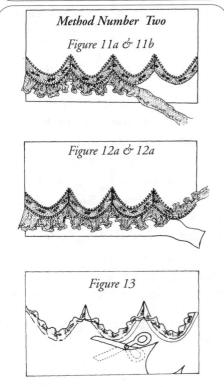

*Method Number Two*

*Figure 11a & 11b*

*Figure 12a & 12a*

*Figure 13*

6. After you zigzag the top only of this skirt, carefully trim away the bottom portion of the fabric skirt, trimming all the way up to the stitches (fig. 13).

7. Now you have a scalloped skirt. Later you might want to add entredeux to the bottom of the scalloped skirt. It is perfectly alright just to add gathered laces to this lace scallop without either entredeux or machine stitched entredeux. Just treat the bottom of this lace scallop as a finished edge; gather your lace edging and zigzag to the bottom of the lace (see fig. 14).

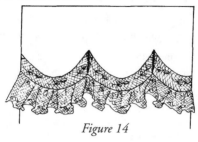

Figure 14

## Finishing The Center Of The Miter

### After Attaching It To The Skirt and Trimming Away The Fabric From Behind the Scallops

I always zigzag down the center of this folded miter. You can leave the folded lace portion in the miter to make the miter stronger or you can trim away the folded portion after you have zigzagged over the miter center (fig. 14).

## Sewing Hand-Gathered French Lace To Entredeux Edge

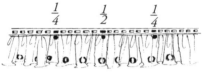

### Sewing Hand-Gathered French Lace To Entredeux Edge

Figure 15

$\frac{1}{4}$  $\frac{1}{2}$  $\frac{1}{4}$

Figure 16

1. Gather the lace by hand by pulling the thread in the heading of the lace. I use the scalloped outside thread of the heading first since I think it gathers better than the inside threads. Distribute gathers evenly.

2. Trim the side of the entredeux to which the gathered lace is to be attached. Side by side, right sides up, zigzag the gathered lace to the trimmed entredeux (Width=1½; Length=2) (fig. 15).

3. Using a wooden shish kabob stick, push the gathers evenly into the sewing machine as you zigzag. You can also use a pick or long pin of some sort to push the gathers evenly into the sewing machine.

HINT: To help distribute the gathers evenly fold the entredeux in half and half again. Mark these points with a fabric marker. Before the lace is gathered, fold it in half and half again. Mark the folds with a fabric marker. Now gather the lace and match the marks on the entredeux and the marks on the lace (fig. 16).

# French Seam

1. Place the fabric pieces with wrong sides together.

2. Stitch a row of tiny zigzag stitches (L 1.0, W 1.0) ³⁄₁₆" outside the seam line (see fig. 1).

3. Press the seam flat and trim away the seam allowance outside the zigzags (fig. 1).

4. Open out the fabric and press the seam to one side.

5. Fold the fabric along the seam line with right sides together, encasing the zigzag stitching (fig. 2).

6. Stitch a ³⁄₁₆" seam, enclosing the zigzag stitching (fig. 3).

7. Press the seam to one side.

NOTE: A serged, rolled edge may be used for the first seam, when the fabric pieces are wrong sides together. No trimming will be needed, as the serger cuts off the excess seam allowance. If a pintuck foot is available, use it to stitch the second seam for either the zigzag or serger method. Place the tiny folded seam into a groove of the foot so that the needle will stitch right along beside the little roll of fabric (fig. 4).

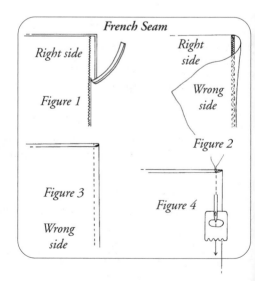

French Seam

Right side

Right side

Wrong side

Figure 1

Figure 2

Figure 3

Wrong side

Figure 4

# Extra-Stable Lace Finishing

## Extra-Stable Lace Finish for Fabric Edges

1. If the lace is being attached to a straight edge of fabric, pin the heading of the lace to the right side, ¹/₄" or more from the cut edge, with the right side of the lace facing up and the outside edge of the lace extending over the edge of the fabric. Using a short straight stitch, stitch the heading to the fabric (fig. 1).

2. If the lace is being attached to a curved edge, shape the lace around the curve as you would for lace shaping; refer to "Lace Shaping" found on page 40. Pull up the threads in the lace heading if necessary. Continue pinning and stitching the lace as directed in Step 1 above (fig. 2).

3. Press the seam allowance away from the lace, toward the wrong side of the fabric (fig. 3). If the edge is curved or pointed, you may need to clip the seam allowance in order to press flat (fig. 4).

4. On the right side, use a short, narrow zigzag to stitch over the lace heading, catching the fold of the pressed seam allowance (fig. 5).

5. On the wrong side, trim the seam allowance close to the zigzag (fig. 6).

NOTE: Extra-Stable Lace Finish for Fabric Edges can be used for lace shaping (figs. 7 & 8).

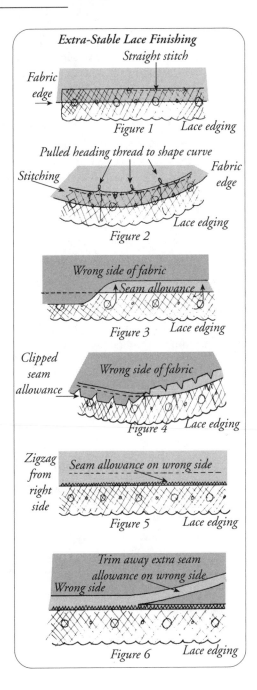

### Extra-Stable Lace Finishing

Figure 1

Figure 2

Figure 3

Figure 4

Figure 5

Figure 6

### Extra-Stable Lace Finish for Fabric Edges

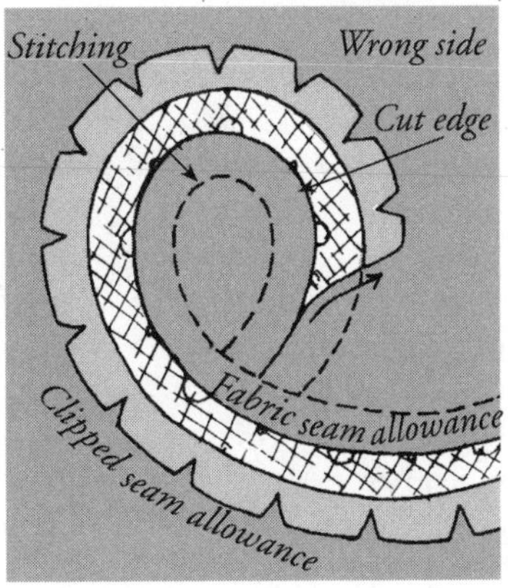

Figure 7

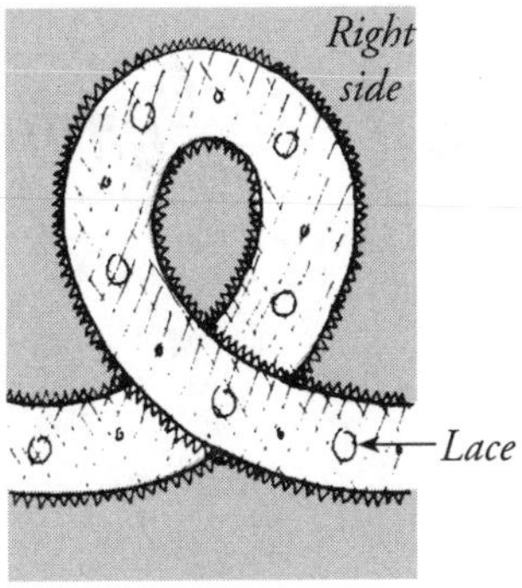

Figure 8

# Making Piping

If self-made piping will be used, measure all of the places it will be applied and use these instructions for making it:

Cut a bias strip 1¼" wide by the length needed. Bias may be pieced so that the piping will be made in one long strip. Place tiny cording along the center of the strip on the wrong side and fold the fabric over the cording, meeting the long edges of the fabric. Use a zipper foot or pintuck foot to stitch close to the cording (fig. a).

*Bias strip*

*Cord*　*Stitch*

*Figure a*

# Double Piping

## Directions

1. Create two pieces of piping.
2. Place one piece of piping on top of the other piece with the cords of the piping side by side.
3. Stitch the two piping pieces together along the stitching line of the top piece of piping creating double piping.

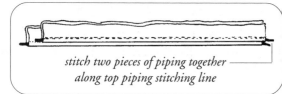

*stitch two pieces of piping together along top piping stitching line*

# Striped Piping

## Supplies

Several different colored strips of fabric 2¼" by 45".
Small cord, gimp or pearl cotton, sports yarn

## Directions

1. Sew strips together using a ¼" seam off-setting the top edge of each strip 2" (fig. 1).
2. Starch and press the seam allowances open.
3. Cut bias strips 1¼" wide from the created fabric (see fig. 1). Attach these strips together to achieve the desired length for piping. Fold the fabric strip in half lengthwise. Place the cord in the fold of the fabric strip, covering the cord.

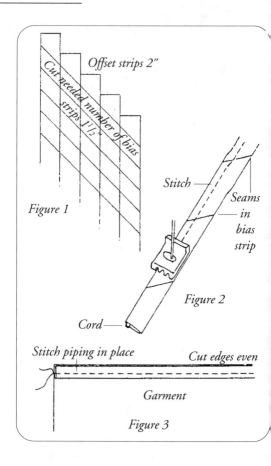

*Offset strips 2"*

*Cut needed number of bias strips 1½"*

*Figure 1*

*Stitch*

*Seams in bias strip*

*Figure 2*

*Cord*

*Stitch piping in place*　*Cut edges even*

*Garment*

*Figure 3*

# Attaching Piping

## Directions

1. Using a pintuck foot (or any foot with a small groove in the bottom) place the covered cord in the groove of the foot. A zipper foot can also be used. Stitch close to the cord (about 1/16" away) creating piping (fig. 2). Trim the seam allowance of the piping to the seam allowance in the garment or project.
2. Place the piping to the project or garment with the cut edges even. Stitch in place along the straight stitch line (fig. 3).

# Appliqué

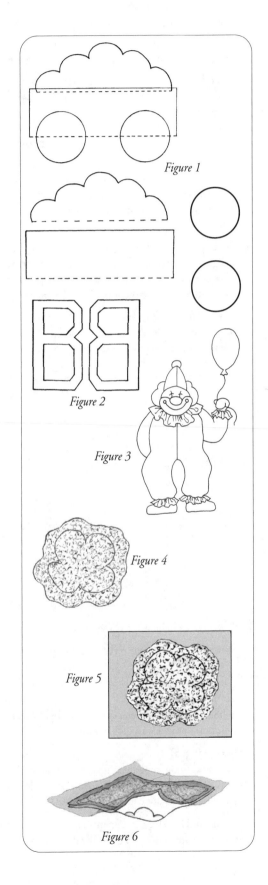

Figure 1

Figure 2

Figure 3

Figure 4

Figure 5

Figure 6

## Using The Patterns

Each appliqué design can be dissected into smaller pieces. Some of the appliqué pieces may extend under other appliqué pieces. Some appliqué designs are drawn with a dotted line extending from the appliquéd piece. This shows that the fabric extension is under another piece. When dissecting these designs, watch for these dotted lines. When you are tracing your pattern which will later be used for cutting out your appliqué fabric, include the dotted extension as a part of your pattern.

For example, on a coal car of the train, the coal pattern piece extends under the body of the car and the body of the car extends under the wheels (**fig. 1**). This is the appliqué design. Here are the dissected pieces.

Some appliqué patterns have a definite right and left side (**fig. 2**). For example, letters of the alphabet ( B, E, R), or a clown holding balloons with his left hand (**fig. 3**). Other patterns do not, such as the letter A (uppercase) or O. Keep this in mind when following the directions below.

## 1. Tracing Pattern On Bonding Agent

If Wonder Under™ or another paper-backed bonding agent is used, **trace each individual pattern piece on paper backing**, with a permanent fine-tip marker. Since the pattern is placed on the wrong side of the fabric, and if it has a definite right and wrong side, the pattern should be traced in reverse. Any design traced exactly as it is featured in this book will appear in reverse on the project.

Take the clown appliqué as an example. If the clown were holding balloons in his left hand and that is how you want it to look on the garment, the design would need to be traced in reverse. If the balloons on the completed project need to be in the clown's right hand, trace as is. All samples in this book were traced in reverse first.

### Tracing A Pattern In Reverse Image

1. Photocopy or trace the design from this book.

2. Hold the design to a window with the design facing outside.

3. Trace the design on the back of the paper.

4. This newly traced design is your reverse image.

## 2. Roughly Cut Pattern

Roughly cut out pattern pieces to separate, leaving about $^1/_4$ inch to $^1/_2$ inch around pattern lines. **Do not cut** pattern on cutting lines at this time (**fig. 4**).

## 3. Fusing

Follow the bonding agent instructions and fuse to the wrong side of a square of appliqué fabric. Be sure the bonding agent does not extend past the edges of the fabric to be appliquéd (**fig. 5**).

## 4. Cutting Out Appliqué

Cut out appliqué pieces along cutting lines. Remember to use the dotted extensions where indicated as the cutting lines.

* Fine Fuse™ or Stitch Witchery™ (**fig. 6**)

a. An appliqué pressing sheet is required. Plastic coated freezer paper or lightweight iron-on stabilizer is also needed.

**b.** Trace pattern pieces onto paper side of freezer paper or stabilizer with a fine-tip permanent marker. Since the pattern is placed on the right side of the fabric the pattern should be traced as is, no reversal is necessary.

**c.** Press to right side of appliqué fabric.

**d.** Fuse bonding agent to wrong side of fabric using the pressing sheet between bonding agent and iron. Iron according to manufacturer's instructions.

**e.** Peel off pressing sheet. Cut out pattern pieces along lines traced on the stabilizer. There will be paper on the right side and the bonding agent on the wrong side of each piece.

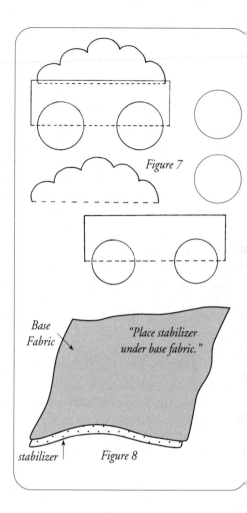

*Figure 7*

*Base Fabric*

*"Place stabilizer under base fabric."*

*stabilizer*

*Figure 8*

### 5. Placing Appliqué Pieces

**a.** Place pattern pieces on base fabric in desired position, fitting pieces together as you would a puzzle. Remember when putting the pieces together, the background pieces may extend under foreground pieces (designated by dotted lines). This will help you to see how the final design will look, as well as decipher where each piece will be fused (**fig. 7**).

**b.** Slide appliqué to the side, away from placement of design. While looking at the total design, remove paper backing from first piece to be fused. If paper is difficult to remove try scratching an X or a line in the paper backing with a straight pin or needle. This will help release the paper from the appliqué piece.

**c.** Fuse in position. Repeat in order for other pieces. Fusing order instructions are given for each design. **Note:** The background pieces are fused first, layering perspectively to the foreground to complete the fusing of the design.

### 6. Stabilizer

Place stabilizer under base fabric in the area of the appliqué (**fig. 8**).

### 7. Stitching

Satin stitch each piece, background to foreground. Satin stitch maneuvers, including straight lines, curves, corners, and points will be discussed in the section, *Stitch Maneuvers.*

# *Appliqué Stitch Maneuvers*

### General Directions

1. Never start stitching at a corner or point; start at a straight side or curve.

2. Preferably, the appliqué piece should be positioned so that the left swing of the needle (zig) stitches on the appliqué piece and the right swing of the needle (zag) stitches off the appliqué piece (**fig. 1**). **All stitch maneuver directions are given with appliqué piece positioned on the left needle swing unless otherwise indicated.** Sometimes the appliqué piece should be placed on the right needle swing (**fig. 2**). Appliqué piece position is provided in such maneuvers.

3 **Tie-On (fig. 3).** Using a short straight stitch, take one complete stitch on the fabric right next to the appliqué. Pull gently on the top thread, bringing the bobbin thread to the top side of the fabric. Place threads under and behind foot. Take several straight stitches on base fabric just off appliqué.

4. Set the machine for a zigzag, medium width and satin or buttonhole length. Slightly loosen the top tension to allow the thread to "wrap" to the wrong side. If "needle

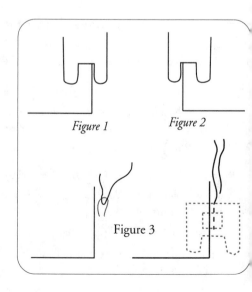

*Figure 1*

*Figure 2*

*Figure 3*

down" is available on your machine, it will be helpful in satin stitching and pivoting. Reposition appliqué so that zigzag stitches are placed mostly on the appliqué but extend completely off the edge of the appliqué. This will stitch the appliqué piece on in a neat fashion encasing the raw edges of the appliqué. If the entire stitch is taken on the appliqué, fuzzy may occur on the edge of the appliqué piece. If you don't stitch enough on the appliqué fabric, the appliqué may pull from the stitching.

5. Take all stitches perpendicular to the edge of the appliqué.

6. Stitch individual pieces and detail lines (that identify arms, legs, flower petals, etc.), working background to foreground.

7. Do not push or pull but simply guide the fabric through the machine. Let the machine do the work. A gentle nudge may be required when crossing over previous stitching.

8. **Tie-Off (fig. 4).** Change to a short straight stitch, reposition appliqué, and take several straight stitches just beside the satin stitch.

9. Cut threads very close to the stitching.

10. Complete design using steps 1-8 on this page.

11. With a water-soluble marker, transfer any straight stitch detail not previously satin stitched (eyes, mouth, hair, nose, glasses). These will be stitched using free-motion embroidery or hand embroidery.

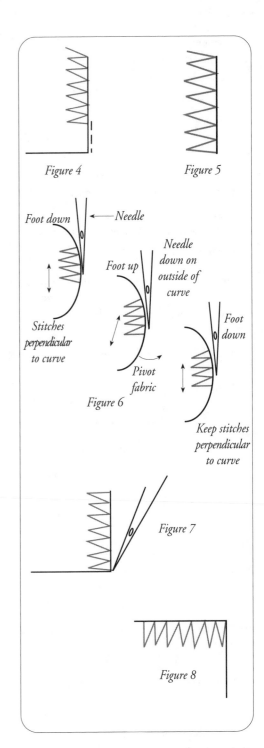

Figure 4          Figure 5

Foot down — Needle

Foot up

Needle down on outside of curve

Foot down

Stitches perpendicular to curve

Pivot fabric

Figure 6

Keep stitches perpendicular to curve

Figure 7

Figure 8

### Straight Lines

Follow steps in General Directions (**fig. 5**).

### Curves
#### Outside and Inside

1. Zigzag along the appliqué as described in steps 1 - 7 of the *General Directions*. While stitching along a curve, the stitching will fail to be perpendicular to the appliqué, therefore pivoting is required. There is more area to cover along the outside edge of the curve, so the pivot must be taken with the needle down at this outside edge (**fig. 6**).

2. To pivot on a curve, leave the needle in the **outside edge of the curve** (not specifically on the zig or the zag). Raise the foot and pivot very slightly, keeping the stitches perpendicular to the edge of the appliqué. It is better to pivot too often than not often enough. If the needle is left in the inside edge of the curve while pivoting, a V will occur in the stitching.

**Note:** When stitching around a curve, the tendency is to force the stitching without pivoting. This will cause the appliqué edge to be wavy, therefore pivoting is very important!

**Pivoting Rule For Curves:** To pivot on an outside curve, the needle is left in the fabric right next to the appliqué piece. To pivot on an inside curve the needle is left in the appliqué piece itself.

### Corners
#### Block Corners

Any zigzag sewing machine will accomplish this very simple method of turning corners.

#### Outside Block Corner
##### Method 1

1. Zigzag along the appliqué as described in steps 1 - 7 of the *General Directions*.

2. Stitch down first side to corner, stopping with the needle down at the point of the corner (**fig. 7**).

3. Pivot 90° (**fig. 8**). Walk the machine by using the fly wheel to take the first stitch that should be placed in the edge of the previous stitching.

4. Continue stitching along the second side (**fig. 9**). Some machines may need a little push to begin satin stitching the second side at the corner. To keep the machine from bogging down at this point, push gently by placing fingers along the sides of the foot to help move the stitching over the previous satin stitch at the corner.

### Outside Block Corner
#### Method 2

1. Zigzag along the appliqué as described in steps 1 - 7 of *General Directions*.

2. Stitch down first side to corner, stopping with the needle down on the left swing [not on the point of the corner (zag) but on the other side (zig)] (**fig. 10**).

3. Pivot 90°. Raise needle out of fabric, raise presser foot, and reposition so that the needle pierces the same hole of the last stitch before the pivot (**fig. 11**). Lower foot.

4. Continue stitching.

### Inside Block Corner
#### Method 1

1. Bisect corner using a water-soluble marker (**fig. 12**).

2. With appliqué on left needle swing, zigzag along the appliqué as described in steps 1 - 7 of the General Directions. Continue stitching until the left needle swing hits the drawn line (**fig. 13**).

3. With needle in fabric, raise foot, pivot 90°, walk the machine by using the fly wheel to take the first stitch that should be placed in the edge of the previous stitching (**fig. 14**), lower foot and continue stitching along the second side.

4. Some machines may need a little push to begin satin stitching the second side at the corner. To keep the machine from bogging down at this point, push gently by placing fingers along the sides of the foot to help move the stitching over the previous satin stitch at the corner.

### Inside Block Corner
#### Method 2

1. Bisect corner using a water-soluble marker (See **fig. 12**).

2. With appliqué on left needle swing, zigzag along the appliqué as described in steps 1 - 7 of the General Directions.

3. Continue stitching until the left needle swing hits the drawn line (**fig. 15**).

4. On the next stitch, leave the needle down on the right swing (**fig. 16**). Raise foot, pivot 90°, lower foot, raise needle out of fabric, raise presser foot, and reposition so that the needle pierces the same hole of the last stitch before the pivot (**fig. 17**).

5. Continue stitching along the second side.

## *Mitered Corners*

Before beginning the maneuvers of miters and points it will be helpful to practice on stabilized scrap fabric, increasing and decreasing the stitch width with the right hand while guiding fabric with the left. Watch where the needle is stitching, not the stitch width knob or lever. Also practice this stitching method using right and left needle position, if available.

Mitering corners can be done if your machine has the capability of changing needle positions (right, left or both) and being able to change the stitch width while stitching in any of these needle positions. Note: Once the needle position is changed, it may stay in that position to continue stitching until the next maneuver (corner or point) is reached.

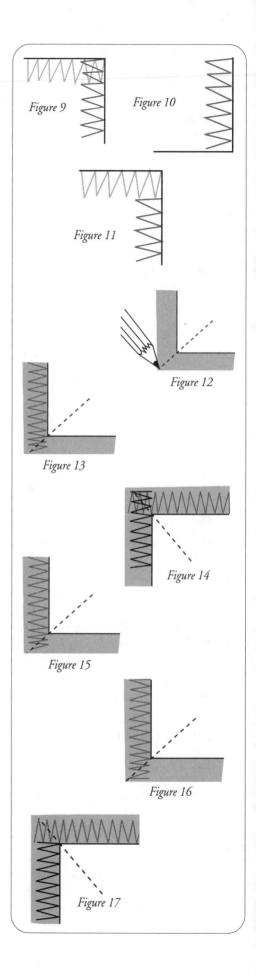

Figure 9    Figure 10

Figure 11

Figure 12

Figure 13

Figure 14

Figure 15

Figure 16

Figure 17

## Sewing Machines with Right and Left Needle Position
### Outside Corner

1. Place appliqué pieces on the left swing of the needle.

2. Zigzag along the appliqué as described in steps 1 - 7 of the General Directions.

3. Stitch down first side to corner, stopping with the needle down at the point of the corner (**fig 18**).

4. Pivot 90° (**fig. 19**). Lower the foot. Note the stitch width used.

5. Raise needle from fabric, change to right needle position and a 0 stitch width. Reposition so that the needle pierces the same hole of the last stitch before the pivot.

6. Guide the fabric with the left hand while gradually increasing stitch width with the right hand, stopping at the original width setting. Changing the width from 0 to the original width should be completed when the edge of the previous stitching of the first side is reached (**fig. 20**). It will be helpful to watch where your needle is stitching, not the stitch width knob or button.

### Inside Corner

1. Place the appliqué pieces on the left swing of the needle.

2. Bisect inside corner with water-soluble marker (**fig. 21**).

3. Zigzag along the appliqué as described in steps 1 - 7 of the General Directions.

4. Stitch down first side until the left swing of the needle intersects drawn line (**fig. 22**).

5. Leaving the needle down, raise the foot, pivot 90° (**fig. 23**), lower foot. Note the stitch width being used.

6. Raise needle from fabric. Change to left needle position and a 0 stitch width. Reposition so that the needle pierces the same hole of the last stitch before the pivot.

7. Guide the fabric with the left hand while gradually increasing stitch width with the right hand, stopping at the original width setting. Changing the width from 0 to the original width should be completed when the edge of the previous stitching of the first side is reached. It will be helpful to watch where your needle is stitching, not the stitch width knob or button (**fig. 24**).

## Sewing Machines with Right Needle Position Only–Outside Corner

Refer to Mitered Corners - Outside Corners.

### Inside Corner

1. Refer to Mitered Corners - Inside Corner. However, appliqué piece must be positioned on the right needle swing.

2. Stitch until the right swing of the needle intersects the drawn line leaving the needle down (**fig. 25**).

3. Raise the foot, pivot 90°, lower foot (**fig. 26**).

4. Note the stitch width being used. Raise needle from fabric. Change to right needle position and a 0 stitch width.

5. Reposition so that the needle pierces the same hole of the last stitch before the pivot.

6. Guide the fabric with the left hand while gradually increasing stitch width with the right hand, stopping at the original width setting. Changing the width from 0 to the original width should be completed when the edge of the previous stitching of the first side is reached (**fig. 27**). It will be helpful to watch where your needle is stitching, not the stitch width knob or button.

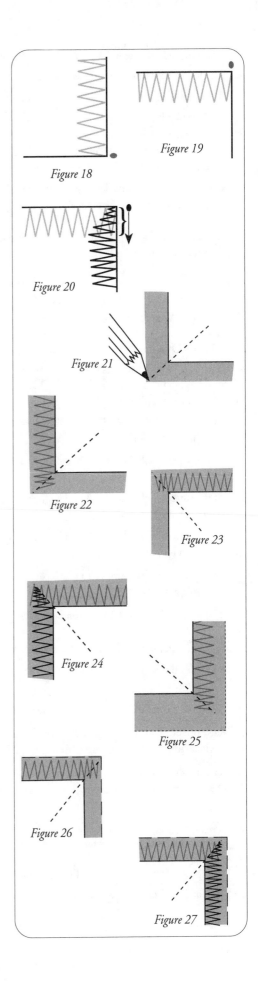

Figure 18

Figure 19

Figure 20

Figure 21

Figure 22

Figure 23

Figure 24

Figure 25

Figure 26

Figure 27

**Sewing Machines with Left Needle Position Only Outside Corner**

1. Appliqué piece must be positioned on the right needle swing.

2. Stitch down first side to corner, stopping with the needle down at the point of the corner (**fig. 28**).

3. Raise foot, pivot 90°, lower foot. Note the stitch width being used. Raise needle from fabric, change to left needle position and a 0 stitch width. Reposition so that the needle pierces the same hole of the last stitch before the pivot (**fig. 29**).

4. Guide the fabric with the left hand while gradually increasing stitch width with the right hand, stopping at the original width setting. Changing the width from 0 to the original width should be completed when the edge of the previous stitching of the first side is reached (**fig. 30**). It will be helpful to watch where your needle is stitching, not the stitch width knob or button.

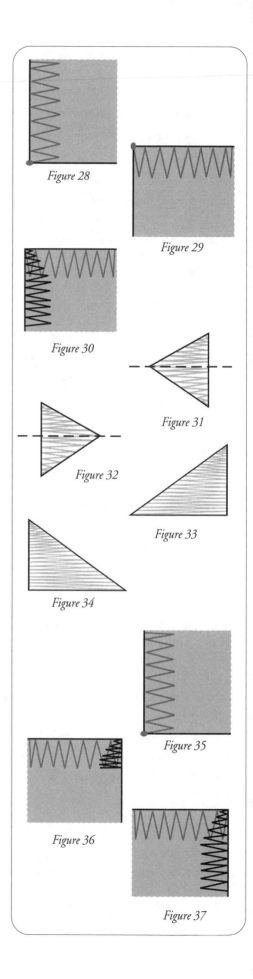

Figure 28

Figure 29

Figure 30

### Inside Corner

The inside corner directions are the same directions given under *Mitered Corners - Right and Left Needle Position - Inside Corners.*

### *Optional Decorative Stitch Used for Mitered Corners

There are several machines that have a solid triangle as a decorative stitch. All or part of this stitch can be used to miter a corner. On a stabilized scrap fabric, work one complete pattern starting at the beginning of the pattern.

- If the pattern looks like (**fig. 31**), only half of the pattern will be used and it is in right needle position.

- If the pattern looks like (**fig. 32**), only half of the pattern will be used and it is in left needle position.

- If the pattern looks like (**fig. 33**), it is stitching in a right needle position and the entire pattern is used.

- If the pattern looks like (**fig. 34**), it is stitching in left needle position and the entire pattern is used.

- If your machine has mirror image this pattern can be stitched in either right or left needle position.

Follow directions above for appropriate needle position through the pivot.

Figure 31

Figure 32

Figure 33

Figure 34

### *Directions For Built In Decorative Stitch Triangle*

1. Stitch down first side to corner stopping with the needle down at the point of the corner (**fig. 35**).

2. Raise foot, pivot 90°, lower foot. Note the stitch width and length being used.

3. Raise needle and engage decorative stitch matching the length and width of the original satin stitch. Stitch pattern through widest point (**fig. 36**).

4. Raise needle. Engage original satin stitch taking the first stitch by reentering the hole of last stitch. Continue (**fig. 37**).

Figure 35

Figure 36

Figure 37

### *Points*

All points are stitched in center needle position.

### Outside Point

1. Appliqué piece on left needle swing.

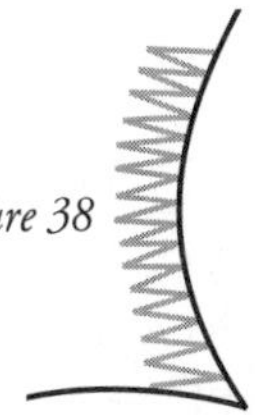

Figure 38

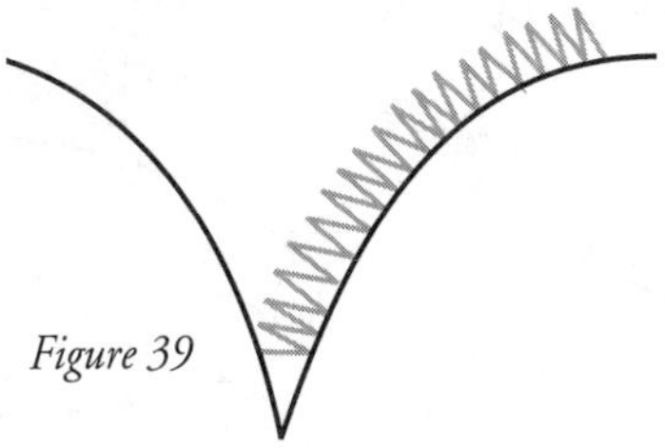

Figure 39

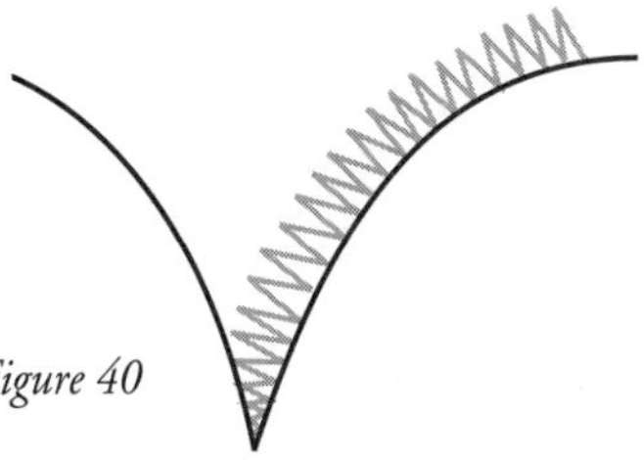

Figure 40

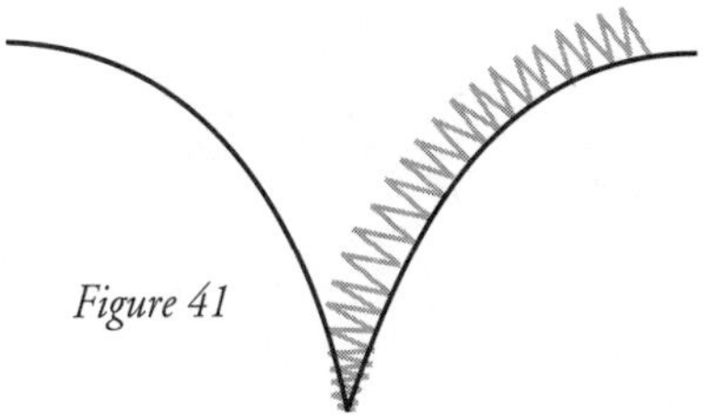

Figure 41

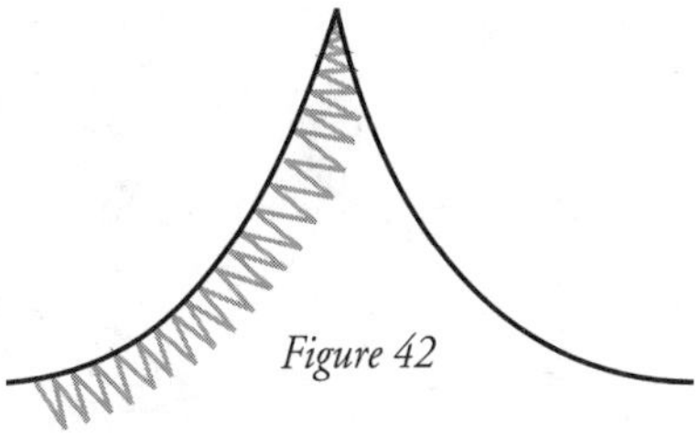

Figure 42

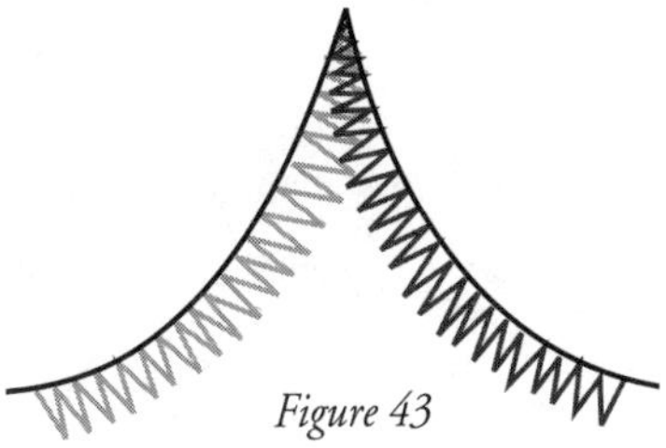

Figure 43

2. Zigzag along the appliqué as described in steps 1 - 7 of the General Directions. Zigzag toward point until needle is stitching off both sides of the appliqué piece. Leave needle down on left side (**fig. 38**).
3. Raise foot, pivot so that point is directly toward you (**fig. 39**).
4. Note stitch width. Continue stitching to the point guiding the fabric with your left hand, while decreasing stitch width with your right hand to cover appliqué piece.
   a. For a sharp point it will be necessary to take the stitch width down to 0 (**Fig. 40**).
   b. For a blunt point, taking the width to 0 is not necessary (**fig. 41**).
5. Lower needle, raise foot, pivot 180° (the point of the appliqué piece is pointed away from you) (**fig. 42**).
6. Lower foot, raise the needle and reposition so that the first stitch will reenter the hole of the last stitch.
7. Continue stitching away from the point, guiding the fabric with your left hand, while increasing the stitch width with your right hand to the original width. Continue stitching (**fig. 43**), pivoting as necessary to keep the satin stitches perpendicular to the appliqué edge.

### Inside Point

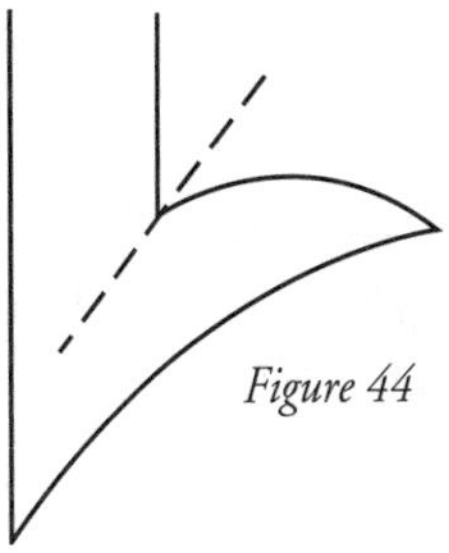

Figure 44

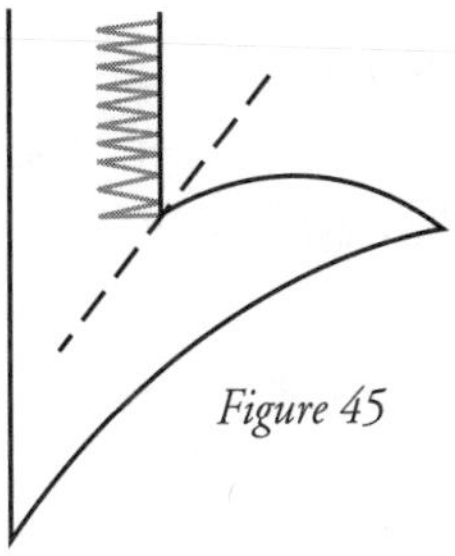

Figure 45

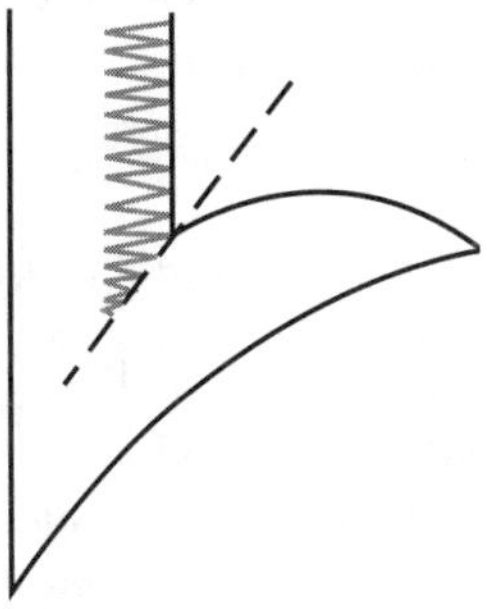

Figure 46

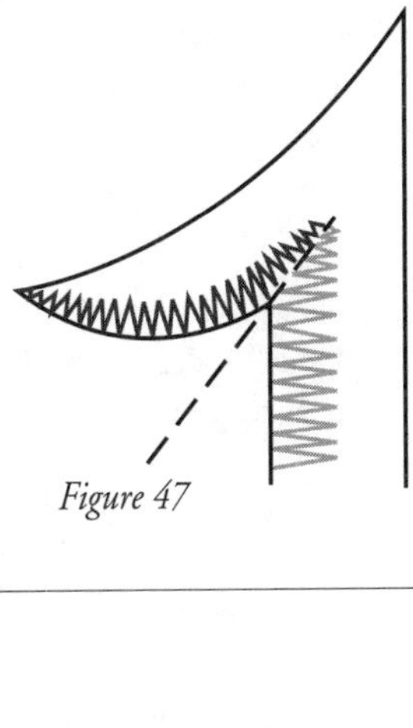

Figure 47

1. Appliqué piece on left needle swing.
2. Bisect the point using a water-soluble pen (**fig. 44**).
3. Zigzag along the appliqué as described in steps 1 - 7 of the General Directions. Continue stitching until the right swing of the needle is off the appliqué at the point (**fig. 45**).
4. Note original stitch width. Guide the fabric with your left hand, so that the right needle swing hits the bisected line as you decrease stitch width gradually to 0 (**fig. 46**).
5. With the needle down, raise the foot, pivot approximately 180° positioning unstitched edge of appliqué under the foot. Lower the foot and continue stitching as you gradually increase the stitch width to the original width keeping the right needle swing butted up against the edge of the previous stitching. Continue stitching (**fig. 47**), pivoting as necessary to keep the satin stitches perpendicular to the appliqué edge.

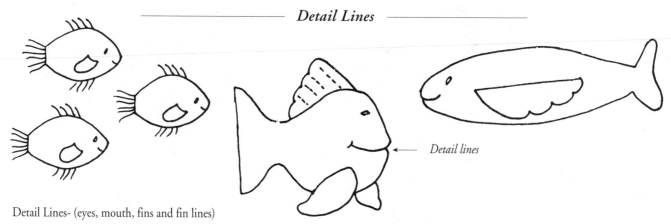

Detail Lines- (eyes, mouth, fins and fin lines)

After completing appliqué, stitch detail lines using straight stitches, zigzag stitches or decorative stitches. Detail lines can also be stitched by hand. ✳

# Shadow Appliqué

Different colored fabrics can be applied to the wrong side of a sheer fabric to give a shadow effect. This simple technique can be applied to collars, blouse fronts, cuffs, and skirt hems. An open zigzag, blanket stitch or other decorative stitch can be used to apply the colored fabrics to the base fabrics.

## Supplies

✳ Sheer Base Fabric (blouse, collar, etc.)

✳ Bright or Dark Appliqué Fabric

✳ Open Toe Appliqué Foot

✳ Machine Embroidery Thread

✳ Size 70 to 80 Needle

✳ 6" to 8" Hoop (Wooden machine embroidery or spring tension)

✳ Marking Pens or Pencils, Water or Air Soluble

✳ Small, Sharp Pointed Scissors

✳ Appliqué Scissors

## Shadow Appliqué Fabrics

### 1. Base Fabric

The base fabric should be a sheer fabric so that the fabric appliqué will show through from the wrong side. If a fabric other than white is used, experiment to see how it will change the color of the appliqué fabric. The appliqué will show more distinctly after it is lined.

### 2. Appliqué Fabric

The appliqué color should be bright enough to show through base fabric. Some colors will look "muddy" under the base fabric. Always test appearance of color by placing a single layer of appliqué fabric between two layers of the base fabric.

## General Shadow Appliqué
### Directions

1. To determine the size of base fabric to be shadow appliquéd, consider the position of the appliqué. The fabric should extend beyond the appliqué design in all directions, so that it may be placed in the hoop. For example, when doing shadow appliqué on a pocket edge, even though the pocket pattern itself is small, you must start with a piece of fabric large enough to fit in the hoop (**fig. 1**). Another example would be when placing shadow appliqué near the edge of a collar, the base fabric must be large enough to contain the whole collar pattern plus enough fabric on the edges to hold in the hoop (**fig. 2**).

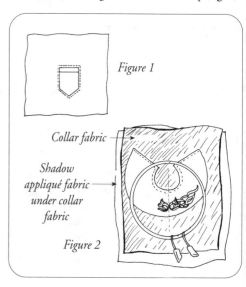

*Figure 1*

*Collar fabric*

*Shadow appliqué fabric under collar fabric*

*Figure 2*

2. Press and starch the pretreated fabric to remove all of the wrinkles and give the fabric some body. Several applications of starch can be used.

3. Trace the pattern piece (cutting lines, seam lines and center front line and all other necessary markings) (**fig. 3**). Trace the design, within the pattern stitching lines, to the

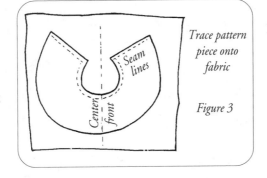

Trace pattern piece onto fabric

Figure 3

base fabric in the desired position (**fig. 4**). When tracing, especially the design for the appliqué, maintain as fine a line as possible since you will be stitching ON this line. A washable marking pencil with a sharp point is helpful. To trace the design, place the base fabric in a hoop large enough to encompass the design. This will help to hold the fabric flat and keep it from shifting while tracing. Don't pull fabric too tight in hoop.

4. To determine the thread color to use, place a piece of each of the appliqué fabrics between two layers of base fabric. Match the thread to the color that shows through the base fabric. It will be lighter than the actual appliqué fabric. Use this color for the top thread. White or base fabric color thread can be used in the bobbin throughout the project.

The upper thread tension should be loosened so that the bobbin thread will pull the top thread to the wrong side. It should not be so loose that the bobbin thread forms a straight line on the wrong side. Test to make correct adjustments.

5. Decide what stitch to use to attach the appliqué fabric to the base fabric. There are several choices.

   a. A narrow open zig zag can be used, a stitch width of about 1 mm and a length of 1 mm (**fig. 5**). This is not a satin stitch, but a short, narrow zig zag stitch.

   b. A pin stitch or blanket stitch can also be used if your machine has this capability (**fig. 6**). The pin stitch generally has a heavier look than the blanket stitch. The stitch width should be narrowed to about 1 mm and the length may also need to be adjusted. Test on a sample to make adjustments.

6. With machine shadow appliqué, the appliqué fabric is placed to the wrong side of the base fabric and you must work from foreground to background (opposite from regular machine appliqué). Place both fabrics in a hoop, layered with the right side of the appliqué fabric to the wrong side of the base fabric. When learning to do shadow appliqué by machine, have the appliqué fabric large enough to be placed in the hoop with the base fabric. As you become more accustomed to this technique it is not necessary to place the fabrics in a hoop (**fig. 7**). When the stitching is done, care should be taken to keep the appliqué fabric from shifting or wrinkles being stitched in. Pin in place if necessary or use a touch of water soluble glue stick to hold the fabric in place. Spray starching the appliqué fabric again will help it to remain flat.

Decide on the starting point, generally not a corner or a point. Pull up bobbin thread and tie on by taking several tiny straight stitches on the drawn line of the appliqué pattern. Stitch on design line to completely enclose area in that color (**fig. 8**). When using the pin stitch or blanket stitch, the straight part of the stitch should be on the design line and the "fingers" part or "ladder steps" of the stitch should be INTO the appliqué (**fig. 9**). You may need to engage "mirror image" if your machine has this capability or stitch in the opposite direction to place the stitch correctly.

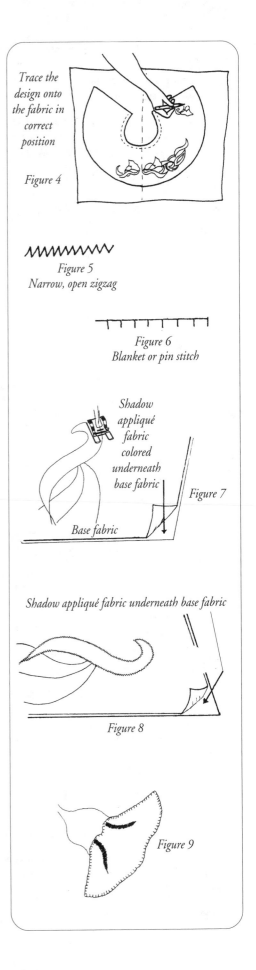

Trace the design onto the fabric in correct position

Figure 4

Figure 5
Narrow, open zigzag

Figure 6
Blanket or pin stitch

Shadow appliqué fabric colored underneath base fabric

Base fabric

Figure 7

Shadow appliqué fabric underneath base fabric

Figure 8

Figure 9

6. Trim the <u>appliqué</u> fabric close to the stitching lines, being careful not to cut the stitches (**fig. 10**). If both the base fabric and the appliqué fabric are in the hoop, remove the hoop, and re-hoop just the base fabric. Trimming will be easier if the base fabric remains in the hoop.

7. Working foreground to background, place the next color to be appliquéd under the base fabric as above and stitch. For areas that touch each other, the stitching must be done on BOTH sides of the appliqué (**fig. 11**) Allow the regular zigzag stitches to just touch each other (not overlap) or the straight part of the pin or blanket stitch to be beside each other (**fig. 12**).

8. Continue in this manner until all of the appliqué pieces are attached and trimmed.

9. Wash fabric to remove all of the markings.

10. Press with the right side down on a towel. ✷

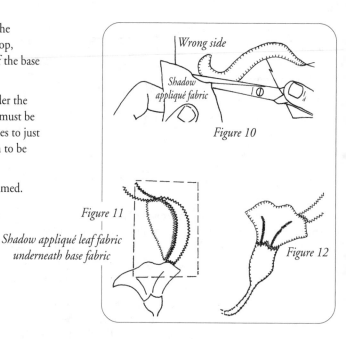

*Figure 10*

*Figure 11*

*Shadow appliqué leaf fabric underneath base fabric*

*Figure 12*

# Puffy or Padded Appliqué

This appliqué design will give a three-dimensional affect. Balloons and clown bodies are the perfect designs for this technique. Reverse Appliqué Stitching techniques combined with batting for a puffy effect, make up Puffy Appliqué.

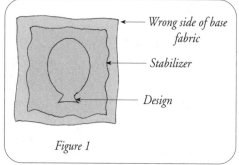

← *Wrong side of base fabric*

← *Stabilizer*

← *Design*

*Figure 1*

## — *Directions* —

1. Trace the entire design onto the stabilizer. Place the stabilizer in position on the wrong side of the base (or garment) fabric (**fig. 1**). Remember to work background to foreground.

2. Place batting, next, on right side of base (or garment) fabric.

3. Place the wrong side of the appliqué fabric on top of the batting (**fig. 2**).

4. Stitch (width = 1, length = 1) along the pattern lines drawn on the stabilizer. Right side of the appliqué fabric will be next to the feed dogs. In other words, you are stitching on the wrong side of the garment.

5. Trim excess batting and appliqué fabric with appliqué scissors, close to the stitching on the right side (**fig. 3**).

6. Continue this process, one piece at a time until the design is finished.

7. If regular fabrics are used, re-stitch each pattern piece on right side as described in section, Stitch Maneuvers, on page 170 (**fig. 4**). If the fabric does not ravel, as in tricot-backed lamé, you are finished.

8. Remove stabilizer on the wrong side. ✷

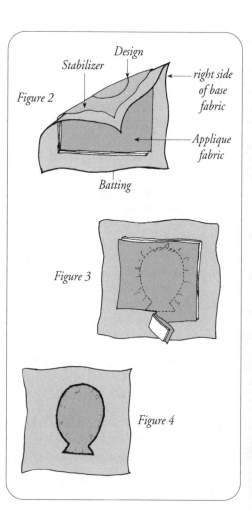

*Design*

*Stabilizer*

← *right side of base fabric*

*Figure 2*

← *Applique fabric*

*Batting*

*Figure 3*

*Figure 4*

Cutwork is a type of embroidery in which an area of fabric is cut away and the edges are bound with a satin stitch. Using the sewing machine to first reinforce an area to be cut away, trimming the fabric and then satin stitching the edge makes it quick and easy. Cutwork can be used on collars, cuffs, blouse fronts and skirt hems. If you have a machine with built-in embroidery, many pretty cutwork design can be stitched automatically.

## General Supplies

- ✳ Darning foot, open darning foot or darning spring
- ✳ Machine embroidery hoop (wooden or spring)
- ✳ Needles (#70 to #90)
- ✳ Light weight or machine embroidery thread
- ✳ Stabilizer (water soluble, tear away, or liquid)

- ✳ Water soluble pen or pencil
- ✳ Small, sharp pointed scissors
- ✳ Extra fine permanent marker
- ✳ White water soluble pen
- ✳ Bobbin case (optional)
- ✳ Open toe appliqué foot
- ✳ Interfacing
- ✳ Appliqué Scissors

## Stabilizers

Water soluable stabilizer (WSS) is preferred since it can be washed away without putting stress on the stitches or bars when it is removed. It will not leave any residue or stiffness when removed completely. Use 2 to 4 layers, depending on body of base fabric and the heaviness and width of the stitches.

## Fabric Used for Cutwork

The most often used fabric for cutwork is linen or linen-like fabrics. The fabric should not be too loosely woven and should have enough body to support the stitches. More than one layer of fabric can be used to add body. The fabric can be interfaced with a lightweight fusible interfacing prior to any stitching. If the fabric for a collar is interfaced, back it with another layer of fabric. The fabric should be pretreated before any marking or stitching is done due to shrinkage and to remove finish from the factory.

## General Cutwork Directions

### Fabric Preparation

1. To determine the size of fabric for the cutwork, consider the position of the cutwork. The fabric should extend beyond the cutwork design in all directions so that it may be placed in the hoop. For example, when doing cutwork on a pocket edge, even though the pocket pattern itself is small, you must start with a piece of fabric large enough to fit in a hoop (fig. 1). Another example would be when placing cutwork on the edge of a sleeve, the fabric must be large enough to contain the whole cutwork design plus enough fabric on the edges to be held in the hoop (fig. 2).

2. Press and starch the pretreated fabric to remove all of the wrinkles and give the fabric some body. Several applications of starch can be used.

3. Interface the fabric if needed.

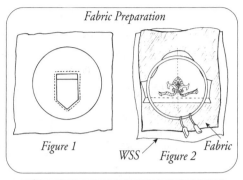

*Fabric Preparation*

*Figure 1*

*WSS* *Figure 2* *Fabric*

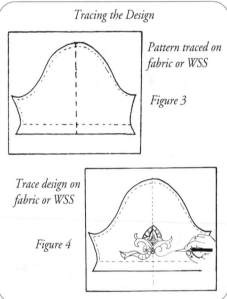

*Tracing the Design*

*Pattern traced on fabric or WSS*

*Figure 3*

*Trace design on fabric or WSS*

*Figure 4*

## Tracing the Design

There are two ways to trace the pattern piece and design onto the fabric:

1. See-through fabric: Place the pattern under the fabric. Trace the pattern onto the fabric using a water or air soluable pen (fig. 3). Use of a light box, if available, is helpful. Follow manufacturers' instructions for the marking pen or pencil. Sometimes heat from an iron may set these marks, so always test first!

2. Opaque fabric (cannot see through): When using a dark colored or opaque fabric the design must be traced onto a layer of WSS. The WSS is then placed on top of the fabric in the desired position (fig. 4). Use the Pigma pen when tracing a design to be placed on a light colored opaque fabric. Use the white washable marker to trace the design to be placed on top of a dark fabric.

3. Mark the cutting and seam lines.

4. Mark the center front or any other important marking lines.

5. DO NOT CUT OUT AT THIS TIME (fig. 5).

6. Mark all areas to be cut out with an "X" (fig. 6).

7. Richelieu bar placement can also be marked with a line extending beyond the area to be cut away (fig. 7). Richelieu bars connect both sides of an open area, helping to stabilize the area. Bars are not necessary for small cut away areas.

a.  Straight Richeleiu Bars:

These bars should be no longer than about ¹/₂ inch long. When the bar is too long, it will not stabilize the area adequately. These bars can be straight across, connecting one side of the opening to the opposite side (fig. 8) For an open area that has one side larger than another, as a half circle, the bars can be placed at angles to form an open "V" or "V's" (fig. 9). Use as many bars as necessary to stabilize the open area (fig. 10).

b.  Divided Richelieu Bars:

A wider width open area may be too wide for a straight bar. In this case, a DI-VIDED bar will be formed to look like a "Y" (fig. 11). For a large open area, the space must be stabilized with bars of any shape connected to each other AND the sides of the open area (fig. 12).

## Placing the Fabric in a Hoop

1. For machine embroidery, the fabric is placed in the hoop opposite from hand embroidery. The right side of the fabric will be facing up, the wrong side is down toward the bed of the machine (fig. 13). Stabilizer should be added under the two layers.

2. When the pattern is traced onto the WSS, pin or baste the WSS in position on top of the fabric.

3. Place one to three layers of WSS to wrong side of the fabric.

4. When the design size is larger than the hoop, baste all layers together so that the pattern, the fabric and the WSS under the fabric will not shift when changing the hoop position (fig. 14).

## Preparing the Sewing Machine for Cutwork

### Thread and Tension

Thread machine with matching machine embroidery thread in top and bobbin. The tension is balanced at this time.

## Cutwork with an Appliqué Foot

1. Place open toe appliqué foot on machine.

2. With a straight stitch, length of 1 to 1.5 mm, stitch around all areas to be cut away. Stitching over ALL of the lines in the design (not just areas to be cut away) will add a padding under the final satin stitch (fig. 15). This straight stitch will prevent stretching when the fabric is cut away from the design.

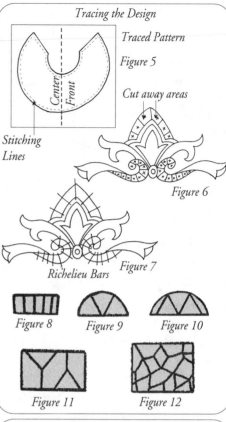

Tracing the Design

Traced Pattern
Figure 5

Center Front

Stitching Lines

Cut away areas

Figure 6

Figure 7

Richelieu Bars

Figure 8    Figure 9    Figure 10

Figure 11    Figure 12

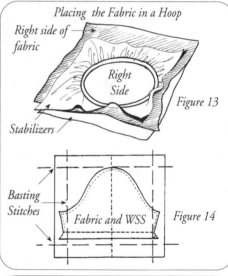

Placing the Fabric in a Hoop

Right side of fabric

Right Side

Figure 13

Stabilizers

Basting Stitches

Fabric and WSS    Figure 14

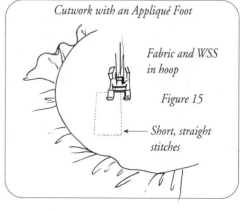

Cutwork with an Appliqué Foot

Fabric and WSS in hoop

Figure 15

Short, straight stitches

3. Stitch over the straight stitch with a short narrow zig zag, width of 0.5 to 1 mm and length of 1 mm (fig. 16). This is not a satin stitch. Stitch all of the design lines that are in the hoop. You can move the hoop to complete all of the design lines before cutting any area away. The zigzag stitch will help prevent the fabric from pulling away from the stitches when the areas are cut away.

4. With the fabric still in the hoop, trim the fabric close to the stitching from the appropriate areas leaving the lower layer(s) of WSS in place (fig. 17). The lower, uncut layers of WSS will prevent distortion of the cut away areas. If the design is on the top layer of WSS, this will be cut away also. Use sharp, small pointed scissors to cut away, being careful not to cut the stitches. Appliqué scissors are very useful.

5. LOOK AT THE DESIGN. The Richelieu bars and the satin stitches to cover the bars and raw edges are worked background to foreground. Place design back under the needle at the appropriate starting point.

6. Set up the sewing machine for a satin stitch: Loosen the top thread tension so that the bobbin thread will pull the top thread to the back for a smoother stitch on the right side. Set stitch length at satin stitch. The stitch width will be adjusted during the stitching.

7. Richelieu bars are completed before the final satin stitching is done.

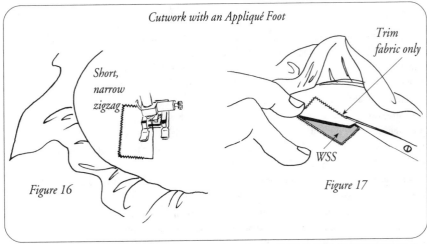

Cutwork with an Appliqué Foot

Short, narrow zigzag

Trim fabric only

WSS

Figure 16

Figure 17

## Straight Richelieu Bars

1. Pull up bobbin thread near first bar, place both upper and lower threads under and behind the foot (fig. 18). Take three to six short straight stitches (satin stitch length) to TIE-ON (this is done each time you start a new area), ending at first bar placement (fig. 19). Cut thread ends close to the first stitch.

2. Lift foot and move fabric across the opening so that needle will pierce opposite side beyond the previous zigzag stitch (fig. 20). Lower foot and take one stitch. This is a "WALK" stitch over the opening. You have not actually "stitched" through the opening, but just moved the thread over it. You can see two separate threads, the top and the bobbin thread. Repeat at least two more times so that there will be three walked stitches over the opening (6 threads) (fig. 21). These walked stitches will form the base for the bars. More or fewer walk stitches can be taken to make a thicker or narrower finished bar.

3. Change the stitch width to cover the walked stitches (1 to 2 mm), usually a little narrower than the final satin stitching will be. This width will be determined by the number of walked stitches. Satin stitch over the walked stitches only within the opening (fig. 22) being certain all walk threads are caught in the satin stitch and covered completely.

4. Straight stitch on the fabric to the next bar within the same opening. Repeat as above. Finish all bars within this area (fig. 23).

You can finish all of the walk stitches within an area before satin stitching or finish each bar individually.

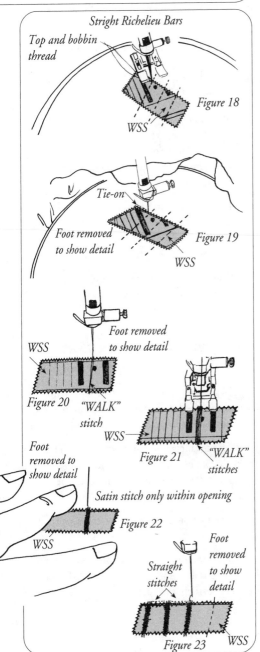

Stright Richelieu Bars

Top and bobbin thread

WSS

Figure 18

Tie-on

Foot removed to show detail

Figure 19

WSS

WSS

Foot removed to show detail

Figure 20

"WALK" stitch

WSS

Figure 21

"WALK" stitches

Foot removed to show detail

Satin stitch only within opening

Figure 22

WSS

Straight stitches

Foot removed to show detail

Figure 23

WSS

## Divided Richelieu Bars

For a bar that is shaped like a "Y", begin at the upper left leg of the "Y". After tying on, move (WALK) from the tie-on stitch to the desired place on WSS within the opening (where the left and right legs of the "Y" join). Take a stitch IN the WSS (fig. 24). This will be the first SEGMENT of the bar. Walk to the top of the right leg of the "Y". Take a stitch into the fabric (fig. 25)(another segment). Walk back to the end of the first segment, take a stitch (fig. 26). You now have TWO walked stitches in this segment. Walk to the opposite side of the opening, creating the last segment of the "Y" bar (fig. 27). Take a stitch into the fabric just beyond the zigzag stitching. Walk to intersection in the WSS, take a stitch. Now two of the segments have two walked stitches (four threads). At this point, you can walk in any direction to increase the walk stitches in the segments and you can satin stitch one segment (if it has six threads) before ALL of the segments have six threads. You must finish the satin stitching at the fabric edge and not in the WSS (fig. 28). Sometimes it will be necessary to add an additional walked stitch so that the satin stitching will finish at the fabric edge and not in the WSS. The cut away area should have enough bars to support the opening.

For large open areas, make a network of walked stitches, connecting them to each other within the opening and to the fabric at the edges of the opening (fig. 29). All of these walked stitches MUST be connected to another segment or to the fabric at the edge of the opening. If they are not connected, when the WSS is rinsed away it will fall apart.

1.  Satin stitch: After all of the bars are completed, adjust the stitch width so that it will be wide enough to cover the previous stitching (straight and zigzag stitch) AND the raw edges of the opening. The most commonly used is a stitch width of 2 mm or less. Satin stitch to cover the raw edges (fig. 30).

2.  After all the necessary stitching is done and before moving to another area you must TIE-OFF the threads. Change stitch width to zero (satin stitch length), reposition fabric so that needle will go back into same hole it just came out of, and take three to six stitches next to the satin stitches (fig. 31). These tie off stitches should be done on the fabric and not in the cut away opening.

3.  Remember to always work background to foreground. This may mean to satin stitch only a portion of an opening before going to another area (fig. 32).

## *Free Motion Cutwork using a Darning Foot or Darning Spring*

Machine cutwork can be done in free motion, that is, with the feed dogs lowered or covered and the darning foot or spring on the machine. When doing free motion work, **YOU** are the stitch length. You have to move the hoop to create a stitch length.

The advantages to doing cutwork with free motion are the hoop can be moved in any direction, not just front to back as with a foot on and more of the design can be encompassed in the hoop (larger hoop can be used and position will not need to change as frequently).

Free motion does require more practice and control than does cutwork with the foot.

The procedure of free motion cutwork is the same as with the appliqué foot. Everything is done the same except that **YOU** move the hoop to create the stitch length of the straight stitch, the open zigzag and the satin stitch zigzag.

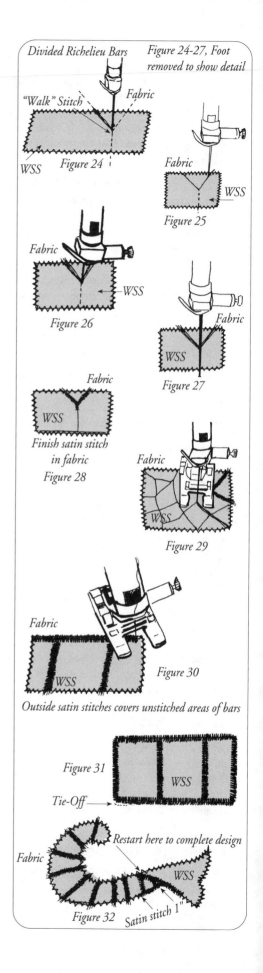

Divided Richelieu Bars    Figure 24-27, Foot removed to show detail

"Walk" Stitch    Fabric

WSS    Figure 24

Fabric    WSS    Figure 25

Fabric    WSS    Figure 26

Fabric    WSS    Figure 27

Fabric    WSS    Finish satin stitch in fabric    Figure 28

Fabric    WSS    Figure 29

Fabric    WSS    Figure 30

Outside satin stitches covers unstitched areas of bars

Figure 31    WSS    Tie-Off

Restart here to complete design    Fabric    WSS    Figure 32    Satin stitch 1"

## Optional Cutwork Techniques

The following techniques can be done with the applique foot or free motion stitching.

### Small Areas

Small areas can be cut away and then satin stitched without bars.

1. For a small area such as a tear drop, first straight stitch and then open zigzag.

2. Slit the fabric and the WSS in the opening down the middle with a "Y" at each end (fig. 33).

3. Satin stitch the opening, drawing in and encasing the raw edges as you stitch (fig. 34).

### Larger Areas

Larger areas without bars can be treated in a similar manner.

1. First straight stitch and then open zigzag.

2. Slit the fabric and the WSS in the opening down the middle with a "Y" at each end (fig. 35).

3. Fold fabric and WSS to wrong side andglue with a glue stick to hold in place (fig. 36).

4. Satin stitch as described to encase the previous stitching and the folded edge.

5. Trim any excess fabric and WSS from the wrong side close to the satin stitch (fig. 37).

### Larger Area with Bars

Larger areas with bars can be treated in a similar manner.

1. Straight stitch, open zigzag, and slit the fabric and the WSS as described above.

2. Fold fabric and WSS to wrong side and glue with a glue stick to hold in place (fig. 38).

3. Form the Richelieu bars as described previously.

4. Satin stitch to encase the previous stitching and the folded edge.

5. Trim any excess fabric and WSS from the wrong side close to the satin stitch.

### Corded Edge Cutwork

A cord can be encased in the finishing satin stitch if desired. This will add strength to the open area.

1. Lay the cord next to the raw edge of the opening (fig. 39).

2. Encase the cord when doing the satin stitch.

### Netting or Sheer Fabric for Support

A layer of netting or other sheer fabric can be placed behind the main fabric so that when an area is cut away, the netting or sheer fabric will support the opening. This will also eliminate the need for Richelieu bars in large cut away areas.

1. The netting or sheer fabric is placed to the wrong side of the base fabric before any stitching is done.

2. To facilitate cutting the base fabric away without cutting the netting or sheer fabric, place an extra layer of WSS **BETWEEN** the base fabric and the netting.

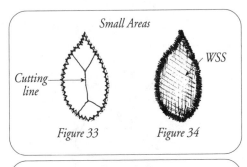

Small Areas

Cutting line

WSS

*Figure 33*    *Figure 34*

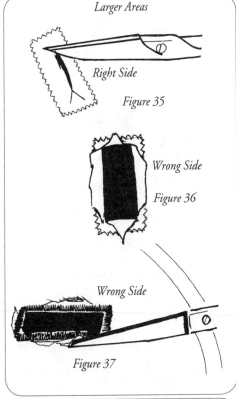

Larger Areas

Right Side

*Figure 35*

Wrong Side

*Figure 36*

Wrong Side

*Figure 37*

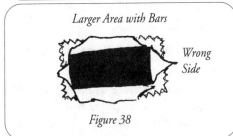

Larger Area with Bars

Wrong Side

*Figure 38*

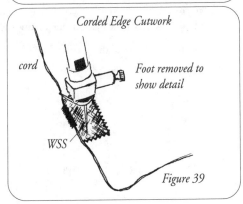

Corded Edge Cutwork

cord

Foot removed to show detail

WSS

*Figure 39*

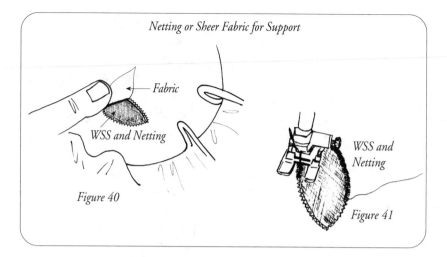

Figure 40

WSS and Netting

Figure 41

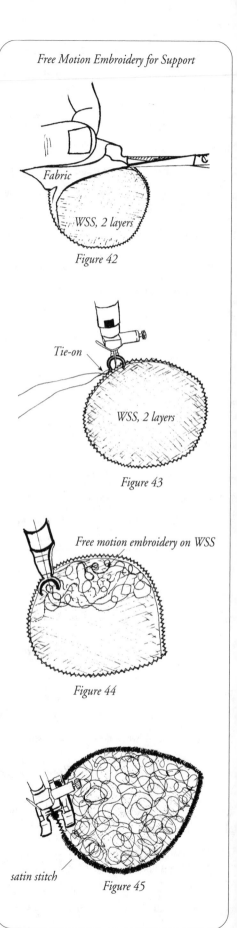

3. As the straight stitching and narrow open zigzag stitching are done the netting will be attached to the base fabric.

4. Cut away the base fabric from the openings on the right side of the fabric and the excess netting from the wrong side (fig. 40).

5. Finish with the final satin stitching to encase the raw edges (fig. 41).

## Free Motion Embroidery for Support

Straight stitch free motion embroidery can be used to fill a cut away area eliminating the need for bars to connect the edges. This is especially helpful for large cut away areas. Stitches will be placed in the open space and on top of the WSS.

1. Have at least two layers of WSS behind the base fabric.

2. Do the straight stitching and the narrow open zigzag as described above.

3. Cut away the base fabric from the opening being careful to leave the WSS (fig. 42).

4. Set up the machine for machine embroidery. Place the open darning foot or darning spring on the machine. Lower the feed dogs. Thread tension should be balanced or the top thread tension slightly loosened.

5. The fabric is in a hoop.

6. Pull up bobbin thread and tie-on at the edge of the open area (fig. 43).

7. Straight stitch on top of the WSS in the open space by running the machine at a steady moderate speed. These stitches should overlap each other AND pierce the edge of the base fabric often so that when the WSS is washed away, the stitches will hold together (fig. 44). This stitching can be rather dense or more open and airy.

8. After this stitching is done, replace the darning foot with the appliqué foot and raise the feed dogs. Reset the machine for a satin stitch.

9. Satin stitch the edges of the opening (fig. 45).

## Straight Stitch
### (silk ribbon or floss)

Simply bring the needle up from under the fabric (fig. 1) and insert it down into the fabric a short distance in front of where the needle came up (fig. 2). It is an in and out stitch. Remember to pull the ribbon loosely for nice full stitches.

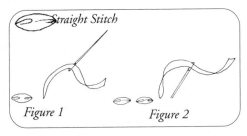

Straight Stitch

Figure 1          Figure 2

## Japanese Ribbon Stitch
### (silk ribbon)

Use any size ribbon. Bring the needle up from under the fabric, (fig. 1) loop it around and insert the needle down into the center of the ribbon a short distance in front of where the needle came up (fig. 2). Pull the ribbon so that the end curls in on itself loosely so that it does not disappear.

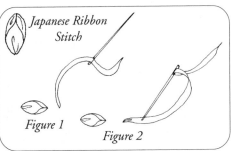

Japanese Ribbon Stitch

Figure 1          Figure 2

## Stem/Outline Stitch
### (silk ribbon or floss)

Worked from left to right, this stitch makes a line of slanting stitches. The thread is kept to the left and below the needle. Make small, even stitches. The needle is inserted just below the line to be followed, comes out to the left of the insertion point, and above the line, slightly.

1. Come up from behind at "a" and go down into the fabric again at "b" (see fig. 1). This is a little below the line. Come back up at "c" (fig. 1). This is a little above the line. Keep the thread below the needle.

2. Go back down into the fabric at "d" and come up a little above the line at "b" (fig. 2).

3. Continue working, always keeping the thread below the needle (fig. 3).

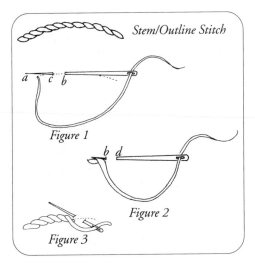

Stem/Outline Stitch

Figure 1

Figure 2

Figure 3

## French Knot
### (silk ribbon or floss)

The most asked question about French knots is "How many wraps?" The number of wraps will depend on the size of the knot desired, the type of thread or floss being used, and personal preference. Generally, use one strand of floss or 2mm silk ribbon with one to two wraps per knot. If a larger knot is needed, use more strands of floss or larger silk ribbon. Often times, French knots will not lay flat on the fabric. To eliminate this problem, once the needle has been reinserted in the fabric (fig. 3), slip the wrapped floss or ribbon gently down the needle until it rests against the fabric. Hold the wraps against the fabric and slowly pull the floss or ribbon through the wraps to the wrong side. This will cause the knot to be formed on the surface of the fabric and not float above it.

1. Bring the needle up through the fabric (fig. 1).

2. Hold the needle horizontally with one hand and wrap the ribbon around the needle with the other hand (fig. 2). If you are using a single strand of floss, one or two wraps will create a small knot. If you are making French knots with 2mm silk ribbon, the knot will be larger. As stated above, the size of the knot varies with the number of strands of floss or the width of the silk ribbon being used.

3. While holding the tail of the ribbon to prevent it from unwinding off the needle, bring the needle up into a vertical position and insert it into the fabric just slightly beside where the needle came out of the fabric (fig. 3). Pull the ribbon or floss gently through the fabric while holding the tail with the other hand.

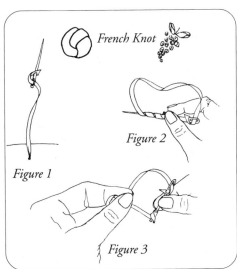

French Knot

Figure 1          Figure 2

Figure 3

## Lazy Daisy Stitch
### (silk ribbon or floss)

1. Bring the needle up through the center point if you are stitching a flower, and up just next to a vine or flower for leaves (fig. 1).

2. Insert the needle down into the same hole in which you came up. In the same stitch come through about ⅛″ to ⅜″ above that point (fig. 2). Wrap the ribbon behind the needle and pull the ribbon through, keeping the ribbon from twisting (fig. 3).

3. Insert the needle straight down into the same hole or very close to the same hole at the top of the loop (fig. 4). Notice in the side view of figure 4 that the needle goes down underneath the ribbon loop. The top view of figure 4 shows that the stitch is straight and will anchor the ribbon loop in place.

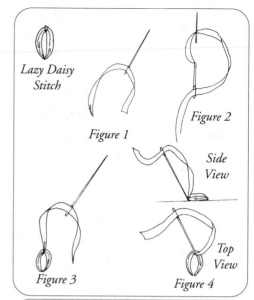

Lazy Daisy Stitch

Figure 1

Figure 2

Side View

Figure 3

Figure 4

Top View

## Feather Stitch
### (silk ribbon or floss)

1. Bring the needle up through the fabric at "A" (fig. 1). Insert the needle down about ¼″ to ⅜″ across from "A" and into the fabric at "B". In the same stitch bring the needle out of the fabric ¼″ to ⅜″ down and slightly to the right of center at "C" (fig. 2). With the ribbon behind the needle, pull the ribbon through (fig. 3). This stitch is much like the lazy daisy only the needle does not insert into the same hole in which it came up. Notice that the stitch is simply a triangle.

2. Now you will begin working your triangle from right to left, or left to right. "C" will now become "A" for your next stitch. Repeat the stitch as in step 1 (fig. 4).

3. Next time repeat the stitch on the other side (fig. 5). The trick is that "A" and "B" will always be straight across from each other and that "A", "B", and "C" will line up vertically (fig. 6).

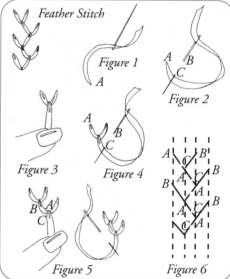

Feather Stitch

Figure 1

A  B
C

Figure 2

Figure 3

Figure 4

Figure 5

Figure 6

## Bullion Stitch
### (silk ribbon or floss) Use a 24 or 26 chenille needle.

1. Bring the needle up from under the fabric at point "A" and take a stitch down in "B" about ⅜″ to ¼″ away and come back up through "A" beside (not through) the floss. Do not pull the needle all the way through (fig. 1). Note: The distance from "A" to "B" will determine the length of the bullion.

2. Now, hold the end of the needle down with your thumb. This will pop the point of the needle up away from the fabric. Wrap the floss or floss coming from point "A" around the needle 5 to 6 times (fig. 2).

3. With your finger, push the wraps of floss to the bottom of the needle next to the fabric so that they are all lined up tight (fig. 3). With your other hand, place your finger under the fabric and your thumb on top of the bullion and gently pull the needle and floss through the wraps (fig. 4).

4. You almost have a bullion, but first you most lay the coils over to the opposite side and take up the slack floss (fig. 5). To do this, lay the bullion over and place your finger under the fabric and your thumb on top of the bullion and gently pull the floss until the slack is out (fig. 6). Insert the needle into the fabric at the end of the bullion (fig. 7) and tie off.

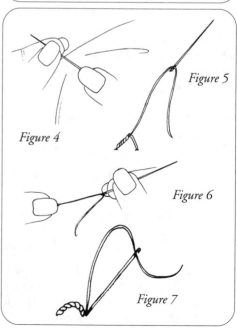

Figure 5

Figure 4

Figure 6

Figure 7

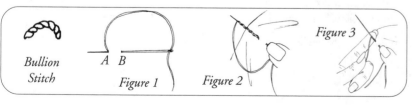

Bullion Stitch

A  B

Figure 1

Figure 2

Figure 3

## Chain Stitch
### (silk ribbon or floss)

This is a glorified lazy daisy stitch that works beautifully on smocking and adds dimension to silk ribbon embroidery. It is a great outline stitch for stems and vines when done with one or two strands of floss.

1. Bring the needle up through the fabric at A. Swing the floss or ribbon around in a loop and hold the loop with your thumb (fig. 1).

2. While holding the loop, insert the needle in at B and out through C in one stitch. Keep the needle and floss or ribbon going over the loop (fig. 2).

3. Instead of inserting the needle to the other side like a lazy daisy, you will make another loop and insert the needle down, right beside C where you last came up, this will become a new A. In the same stitch, bring the needle through B and pull (fig. 3). Keep the needle over the loop.

4. Continue looping and stitching in an "A, B" - "A, B" sequence.

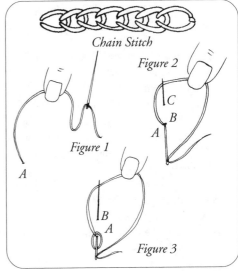

Chain Stitch

Figure 1

Figure 2

Figure 3

## Fly Stitch
### (silk ribbon or floss)

This stitch may be used for leaves at the base of flowers, it may be worked singly or in rows to give the appearance of ferns. This is an easy stitch to master and you will find many uses for it as fillers.

1. Come up at A. Insert the needle in the fabric at B, coming out of the fabric at C, making sure the loop of ribbon is below C (fig. 1). Keep the needle on top of the loop of ribbon.

2. The length of the anchor stitch is determined by the length of the stitch taken between C and D. The floss or ribbon comes out of the fabric at C and needle is inserted into the fabric at D. The longer the distance between D and D, the longer the anchor stitch. Gently pull the ribbon to the wrong side (fig. 2 & 3).

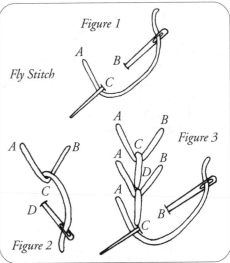

Fly Stitch

Figure 1

Figure 2

Figure 3

## Side Stitch Rose
### (silk ribbon)

This rose takes careful placement and looks particularly good in 4mm variegated ribbon. It is made up of side ribbon stitch petals; instead of piercing the ribbon in the middle, pierce on either the left or the right side of the ribbon, depending on which way you want the petal to turn.

1. Start with an upright stitch, piercing the ribbon on the right-hand side (fig. 1). This is petal 1. The petal will turn slightly to the right (fig. 2).

2. Place a second petal, slightly longer, to the right of petal 1, piercing on the left-hand side (fig. 3). This is petal 2.

3. Place a third petal, slightly shorter, to the left of petal 1, piercing the ribbon on the right-hand side. Place a fourth petal, the same length as the third, to the right of petal 2, piercing the ribbon on the left-hand side (fig. 4).

4. Place petals 5 and 6 at an angle on each side, piercing petal 5 on the right and petal 6 on the left (fig. 5).

5. Petals 7 and 8 drop below, leaving a small space below the top petals (fig. 6).

6. Work petals 9 and 10 from the base of petals 7 and 8 and over petals 1 and 2. The length of petals 9 and 10 will be 2/3 the length of petals 1 and 2. There will be a small gap in between petals 9 and 10 (fig. 7).

7. Petal 11 is placed between petals 9 and 10 and is slightly taller than petals 9 and 10 fig. 8).

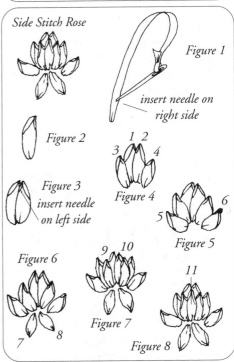

Side Stitch Rose

Figure 1

insert needle on right side

Figure 2

Figure 3
insert needle on left side

Figure 4

Figure 5

Figure 6

Figure 7

Figure 8

## Straight Stitch Rose
### (silk ribbon)

This is sometimes called a fish bone rose.

1. Start with a straight stitch. This will be the middle stitch of the flower (fig. 1).
2. Put a stitch at an angle to the left, crossing over the base of the middle stitch (fig. 2).
3. Put a stitch at an angle to the right, covering the base again and placing the bottom of the stitch slightly below the stitch done in step 2 (fig. 3).
4. Continue to work from side to side until the required size is achieved (fig. 4).
5. Add leaves by placing 3 shorter straight stitches at angles below the flower (fig. 5).
6. The more stitches used and the looser the tension will give greater fullness to the flower.
7. If you stop at step 3, this produces a lovely fat rosebud, especially if petal one is a dark color with a slightly lighter color for petals 2 & 3 (fig. 6). Using 7 mm ribbon for large flowers looks very nice.
8. A very pretty effect can be achieved if using 3 or 4 shades for the full rose — a little extra effort but definitely worth it.

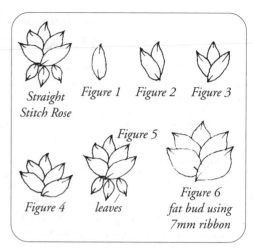

Straight Stitch Rose

Figure 1  Figure 2  Figure 3

Figure 4  Figure 5  leaves  Figure 6 fat bud using 7mm ribbon

## Chain Stitch Rose
### (silk ribbon or floss)

1. Work 3 French knots in a dark color close together to form a triangle (fig. 1).
2. Using a lighter color, work chain stitches (fig. 2) around the French knot (fig. 3).
3. Continue working around until the size desired is achieved (fig. 4).
4. For greater shading effects, change to another color after the first two rounds.

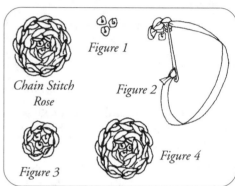

Chain Stitch Rose

Figure 1  Figure 2  Figure 3  Figure 4

## Tortured Fly Stitch
### (silk ribbon or floss)

This stitch is made very similar to the Fly Stitch. However, the stitches are not angled out as much and one side is much longer than the other giving the appearance of a fish hook.

1. Bring the needle to the front of the fabric at point A. Enter the needle at point B and out at C having the silk ribbon loop under the needle as it comes out at C (fig. 1).
2. Enter the needle at point D and out at E with the ribbon looped under the needle (fig. 2).
3. Continue this stitch alternating sides with the needle placement.
4. To finish the stitch, take the needle to the back of the work at F and tie off (fig. 3).

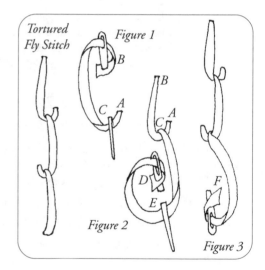

Tortured Fly Stitch

Figure 1  Figure 2  Figure 3

## Rosebud
### (silk ribbon with floss)

1. Stitch a straight stitch with 2mm silk ribbon (fig. 1).
2. Place a fly stitch at the lower point of the straight stitch with green DMC Flower thread or 2 strands of embroidery floss (fig. 2).
3. Work an extra straight stitch from the center of the rosebud to the base (fig. 3).

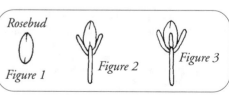

Rosebud

Figure 1  Figure 2  Figure 3

## Leaves
### (silk ribbon)

1. Work the leaves using a Japanese Ribbon Stitch (fig. 1).
2. Cluster the leaves in groups of two or three according to the template (fig. 2).

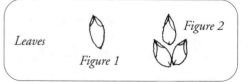

Leaves

Figure 1  Figure 2

## Lady Bird
### (silk ribbon with floss)

A little lady bird can look charming amongst a group of flowers.

1. Using red 4mm silk ribbon, work a ribbon stitch, piercing the silk ribbon on the right-hand side so it rolls to one side (fig. 1).
2. Work a second stitch to the right of the first stitch, piercing the ribbon on the left-hand side (fig. 2).
3. Using dark floss, work a large French knot for the head and slightly smaller ones for the body spots (fig. 3).
4. With the dark floss, work 2 pistol stitches for the antennae, and a straight stitch covering the join between the red stitches to mark the wings (fig. 4).

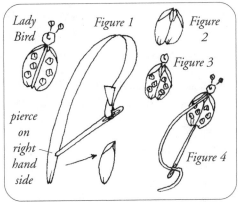

## Stems and Branches
### (silk ribbon and floss)

A silk ribbon and thread combination create nice flowing stems and branches for your flowers.

1. With 4mm green silk ribbon, work a ribbon stitch for the length of your stem (fig. 1).
2. When all embroidery is finished, take 2 strands of DMC floss or DMC Flower Thread and put long stitches down the center of the stems, taking a small back stitch approximately every half inch (fig. 2). Alternate from right to left as you stitch the length of the branch (fig. 3). This gives life to the stems and bridges the color jump between the sharp green of the leaves and the pale green of the stems.

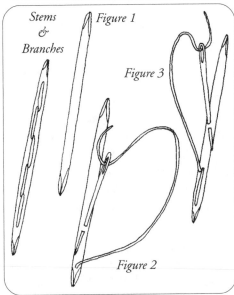

## Beverley Bow
### (silk ribbon and floss)

This lovely bow seams to dance its way over most things I do!

1. Allow approximately 16" of silk ribbon.
2. Make two loops in the ribbon holding one loop in each hand and having an equal amount of ribbon hanging below each loop (fig. 1).
3. Wrap one loop around the other and through the center. Pull the loops into a knot (fig. 2).
4. Place the bow in the desired spot and pin into place at the center knot.
5. Using pins, flip flop the ribbon to create a pretty bow (fig. 3). Do the same with the streamers of the bow. The more twists and turns, the more life it has (fig. 4).
6. If you don't like the shape reposition the pins until the desired bow shape is created.
7. When you have created the shape you like, stitch in place with French knots, using 2 strands of embroidery thread, or D. M. C. Flower thread (fig 5).

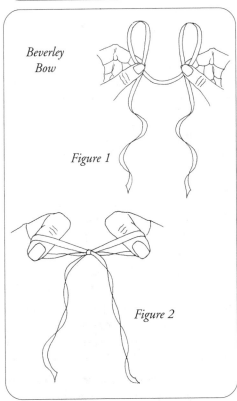

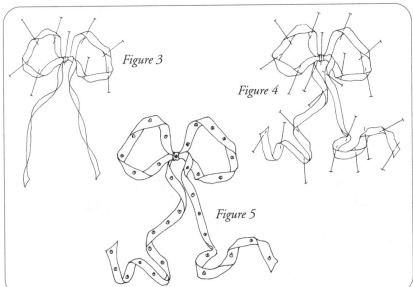

## Colonial Knot
### (silk ribbon or floss)

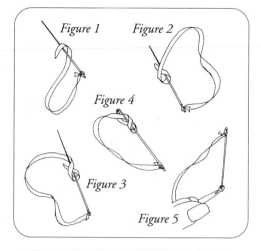

Figure 1  Figure 2

Figure 4

Figure 3

Figure 5

Basic knot stitches are used in a variety of ways. They can be the centers of daisies or the blossoms of hyacinths. Colonial knots make beautiful grape clusters on a vine or tiny rosettes in a bouquet. The colonial knot differs from the French knot in the method of wrapping the floss or ribbon around the needle. It will also make a larger knot than the French knot. If you want the colonial knot to be "fluffy", do not pull the ribbon tight. The knot will "sit tall" on top of the fabric.

1. Come up from beneath the fabric and wrap the needle under the ribbon one (fig. 1).
2. Next, wrap the ribbon over the needle once (fig. 2) and back under once (fig. 3). This makes a figure eight.
3. Insert the needle beside the original hole (fig. 4). While holding the needle vertically, pull the slack out of the ribbon so that the knot tightens around the needle (fig. 5). Continue holding the ribbon taut until the needle and ribbon have been pulled all the way through.

## Loop Stitch
### (silk ribbon)

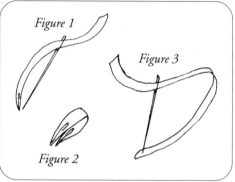

Figure 1

Figure 3

Figure 2

This stitch is to be made very loosely while keeping the ribbon straight. It can be used for daisies and bows or any where a loop look is needed. Experiment with different ribbon widths to achieve a variety of styles and uses.

**Straight Stitch Method:** Insert the needle up through the fabric and loop around away from you, inserting the needle just slightly beside where you came up (fig. 1).

1. Pull the ribbon straight (without twists) and loosely adjust the loop to the desired size (fig. 2).

**Japanese Stitch Method:** Insert the needle up through the fabric and this time loop it towards you, inserting the needle through the center of the ribbon just beside where the needle came up (fig. 3). Again, pull loosely while keeping the ribbon straight.

## Spider Web Rose
### (silk ribbon and floss)

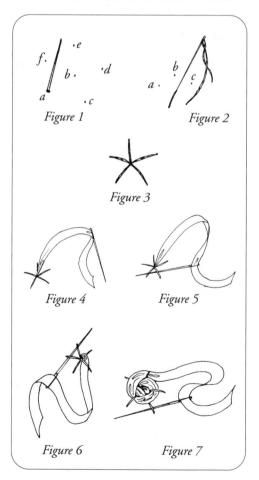

Figure 1

Figure 2

Figure 3

Figure 4

Figure 5

Figure 6

Figure 7

This rose is one of the prettiest and easiest of all the silk ribbon stitched roses. Use 13mm for large puffy roses, 7mm for medium roses and 4mm for small roses. The spokes or "legs" on the spider will be shorter for 4mm ribbon than for 7mm ribbon. You will gain a good judgement for this after you have stitches a few roses and played with the different sizes.

Begin with a five legged "spider, or five spokes, stitched with either a single strand or a double strand of embroidery floss. For larger roses use a double strand. It may be helpful to mark a center with five evenly spaced dots around it using a washout pen or pencil as you are learning to make this rose.

1. To stitch the spider, come up from the bottom of the fabric with your needle through dot "a" then down in the center dot "b" (fig. 1). Come up through "c" then down in "b" (fig. 2). Continue around; up in "d" down in "b", up in "e" down in "b" etc... until the spider is complete and tie off underneath (fig. 3).

2. Now, with your silk ribbon, insert the needle up through the center "b" (fig. 4). Slide the needle under a spoke or "spider leg" and pull ribbon through loosely (fig. 5).

3. Skipping over the next spoke, go under the third spoke (fig. 6) and begin weaving in a circle over and under every other spoke (fig. 7).

4. Continue weaving until the spokes are covered. Insert the needle underneath the last "petal" and pull through to the back.

You may stitch leaves first and then stitch the rose on top, or you may bring your needle up from underneath a "petal" and stitch leaves under the rose.

# Sweet Pea

Here is a dainty little flower to add to your floral bouquet. This one is so fun to make and can be made with several sizes of ribbon. Again, it is an individually handmade flower that is later stitched to the project. The stitching on this flower is covered by the stem.

Sizes 7mm and 13 mm ribbon are easiest to handle; however, for tiny projects, a 4mm works well and looks like a blossom. For very large projects, a 32mm will create a huge carnation looking flower. Use a 7mm green ribbon for the flower base and leaves. Since sweet peas actually grow on vines, you may want to stitch a wrapped stitch vine before adding your flowers. This flower is not limited to being just a sweet pea, it can also be a poppy on its' side or a carnation on its' side by simply adding a stem. It's up to you.

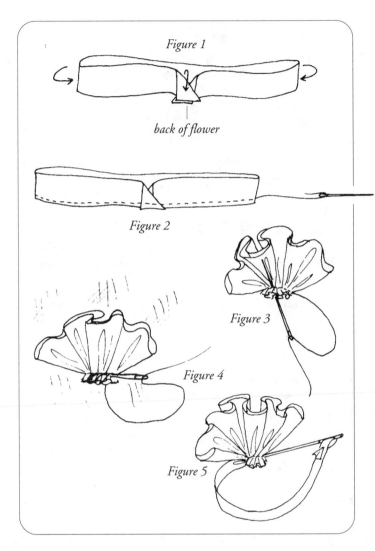

Figure 1

back of flower

Figure 2

Figure 3

Figure 4

Figure 5

1.  Thread a needle with matching sewing thread and knot the end. Cut a piece of 7mm ribbon about 7" long. Use less for 4mm and more for 13mm ribbon. Fold each end to the center and fold the raw edges down (fig. 1). Pin to secure.

2.  With tiny stitches, run a gathering stitch across the bottom through both layers (fig. 2). Pull the thread to gather the ribbon and take a couple of tack stitches to secure (fig. 3).

3.  Place on the fabric with the folded edges to the back and tack stitch to secure (fig. 4).

4.  Thread a 7mm green ribbon and make a straight stitch wrapping over the bottom of the flower to cover the tack stitches (fig. 5). This will also hold the sides of the flower up. Add leaves to complete.

# Ribbon Rosettes (Fru Fru)

## Ribbon Rosette

Ribbon rosettes are used to embellish children's dresses, doll dresses, craft projects, pillows and other home decorating projects. Ribbon rosettes are most commonly made from double-faced satin ribbon or silk ribbon. The width and length of the ribbon will vary according to the project. Commonly used ribbon widths are $1/16$", $1/8$" or $1/4$" while the lengths will vary from 18" to 5 yards.

1. Place dots on the ribbon evenly spaced apart, usually 1" to 2", leaving ribbon at each end un-dotted for the streamers. The directions for the project will give the length of the ribbon to be used and the dot spacing (**fig. 1**).

2. Thread a needle with a doubled thread and begin picking up the dots on the ribbon (**fig. 1**). Thread the dots onto the needle and pull them up tightly to form a rosette. Take a few stitches to secure the loops together (**fig. 2**).

3. Tack the rosette in place or pin in place using a small gold safety pin.

## Knotted Ribbon Rosette

1. Make dots on the ribbon as described in step 1 of Ribbon Rosettes. At every other dot, tie a knot in the ribbon (**see fig. 3**).

2. Thread a needle with a doubled thread and begin picking up the dots on the ribbon. Thread the dots onto the needle (**fig. 3**) and pull them up tightly to form a rosette. Take a few stitches to secure the loops together.

3. Tie knots in the streamers, if desired (**fig. 4**).

4. Tack the rosette in place or pin in place using a small gold safety pin.

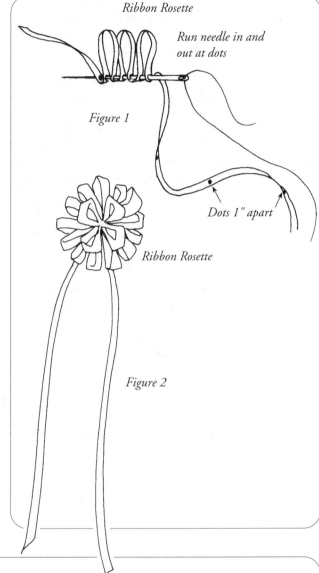

Ribbon Rosette

Run needle in and out at dots

*Figure 1*

Dots 1" apart

Ribbon Rosette

*Figure 2*

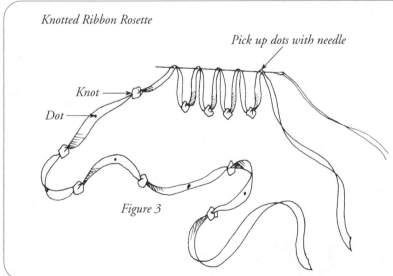

Knotted Ribbon Rosette

Pick up dots with needle

Knot

Dot

*Figure 3*

*Figure 4*

# Shadowwork Embroidery

---

*Whether stitching from the front or the back, appropriate needles and floss are a must to obtain satisfactory results in shadowwork. A #26 tapestry needle is excellent for shadowwork. The dull point is preferred by most people and the size of the needle creates an opening large enough to see for placement of the stitches. If a sharper point is desired, a #7 crewel will also give good results. Both DMC and Susan Bates are excellent choices of floss for shadowwork embroidery. In most cases, one strand of floss is used. Shadowwork may be done on a variety of fabrics. If the color of the floss may be detected through the weave of the fabric, then the fabric can be considered suitable for shadowwork. However, the heavier and tightly woven the fabric, the more suttle the color will be which shows through. The preferred fabric for shadowwork is batiste or other sheer fabrics.*

# Shadow Work Embroidery — From The Back

---

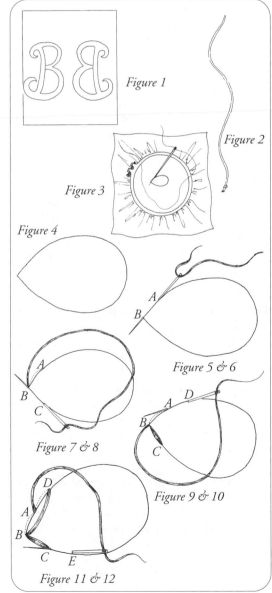

Figure 1

Figure 2

Figure 3

Figure 4

Figure 5 & 6

Figure 7 & 8

Figure 9 & 10

Figure 11 & 12

With this method, you embroider from the wrong side of the fabric. When the fabric is loaded into the hoop, the wrong side of the fabric will be facing out. The design is traced onto that side. The stitches, a closed herringbone, are rather like "sewing" with a bite taken out of the top of the design and a bite taken out of the bottom. I prefer this method more than working from the front, because it is easiest.

1.  Trace your design onto the wrong side of the fabric. If you are using an alphabet, be sure that the letters are properly reversed (**fig. 1**). An easy way to reverse letters or a design onto the wrong side of the fabric is to use a photocopy machine. Copy the design onto a clear plastic sheet like you would use for an overhead projector. This is called a transparency. Flip the transparency over. Run a copy on paper this time. It will be reversed properly.

2.  Insert the fabric into the embroidery hoop.

3.  Cut a piece of embroidery floss approximately 18 - 22 inches long (**fig. 2**). Remember to knot the cut end, although you will later cut that knot away.

4.  There are two ways of placing the loose end (the knotted end of the floss) while you stitch your shadow embroidery.

    a.  Lay the end of the floss (rather a long one) outside the embroidery hoop and close the hoop over it. This gives you plenty of floss to later weave into the completed design (**fig. 3**).

    b.  Bring your knot up through the circle of fabric as far away from your first stitch as possible.

    Note: Sometimes there is not enough embroidery floss "tail" to easily weave into the completed design.

    Following the illustrations given, using the leaf shape (**fig. 4**), begin your stitching.

5.  With the thread below the needle, bring the needle down at (A) (**fig 5**) and up at (B) (**fig. 6**). Pull through.

7.  Move down. Thread above the needle, put your needle down at (C) (**fig. 7**) and up at (B) (**fig. 8**). Move into the exact same hole as your needle made on the first bite at (B).

8.  With the thread below the needle, bring the needle down at (D) (**fig. 9**) and up at (A) (**fig. 10**).

9.  With the thread above the needle, bring the needle down at (E) (**fig. 11**) and up at (C) (**fig. 12**).

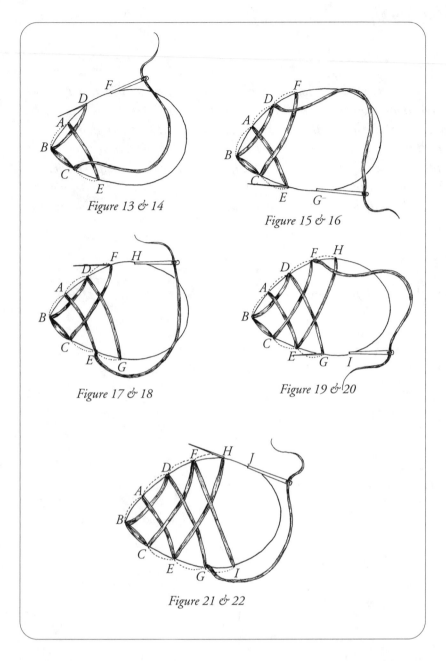

Figure 13 & 14

Figure 15 & 16

Figure 17 & 18

Figure 19 & 20

Figure 21 & 22

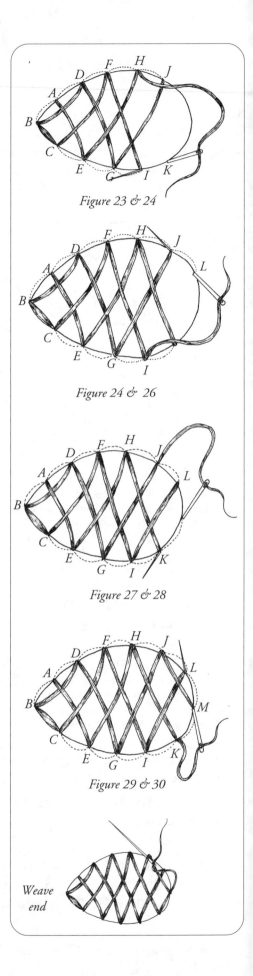

Figure 23 & 24

Figure 24 & 26

Figure 27 & 28

Figure 29 & 30

Weave end

10. When you come to a large curve, make your outside stitches (on the largest part of the curve) larger. Make the inside stitches closer together. You may find it necessary, sometimes, to go in one hole twice on the inside area. Finish the design according to (**figures 13 - 30**).

11. Keep turning your work so that the portion of the design you are currently working on is horizontally in front of you and so that you are working from left to right.

12. When you have finished your work, weave the tail of the thread through the stitching on the sides. As with most needlework, never knot your thread. Just weave it.

13. After you have finished with a design or with the amount of floss you have in your needle, weave that end into the design. Clip the knotted end which is either in the upper section of the fabric or held outside the embroidery hoop. Re-thread the needle with this end, and weave this end into the work as well.

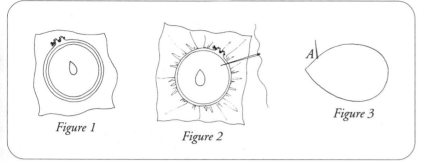

Figure 1

Figure 2

Figure 3

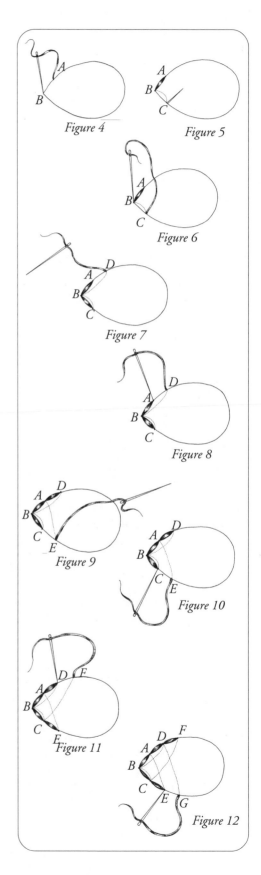

Figure 4

Figure 5

Figure 6

Figure 7

Figure 8

Figure 9

Figure 10

Figure 11

Figure 12

1. Trace the design you would like to shadowwork on the right side of the fabric (**fig. 1**).

2. Place the fabric into the embroidery hoop centering the design to be stitched. The right side of the fabric will be facing you.

3. Cut a piece of embroidery floss approximately 18 - 22 inches long. Separate the strands of floss. Thread one strand of floss through your favorite shadowwork needle. I suggest using a 10 sharp, 10 Crewels, or a 26 tapestry needle. Remember to knot the cut end of the floss, although you will later cut that knot away.

4. Securing the thread.

   **Method 1.** Place the knot on the wrong side of the fabric between the hoop and the fabric. Close the hoop (**fig. 2a**).

   **Method 2.** Place the needle in the right side of the fabric as far away from your first stitch as possible. The knot will end up on the right side of the fabric (**fig. 2b**).

   Either of these methods will put the needle/thread on the back side of the fabric. Note: This thread tail will need to be long enough to weave back through the stitching after the design is complete.

5. Bring the needle to the right side of the fabric at the beginning point (A) (**fig. 3**).

6. To make the first stitch, take the needle down at point (B) to the wrong side of the fabric (**fig. 4**).

7. Move to the other side of the design and bring the needle up at (C) (**fig. 5**) and back down at (B) (**fig. 6**). Pull gently.

8. Bring the needle up from the backside at (D) (**fig. 7**) and back down at (A) (**fig. 8**).

9. Move down to the other side and come up through (E) (**fig. 9**) and go back down at (C) (**fig. 10**).

10. Move to the other side and come up at (F) and back down at (D) (**fig. 11**).

12. Move to the other side and come up through (G) and down at (E) (**fig. 12**).

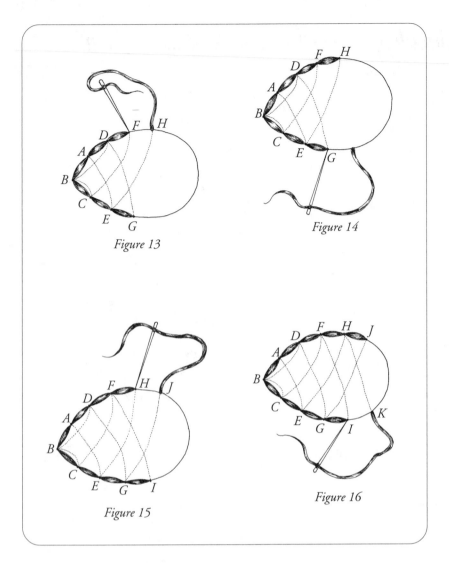

*Figure 13*

*Figure 14*

*Figure 15*

*Figure 16*

*Figure 17*

*Figure 18*

*Figure 19*

*Figure 20*

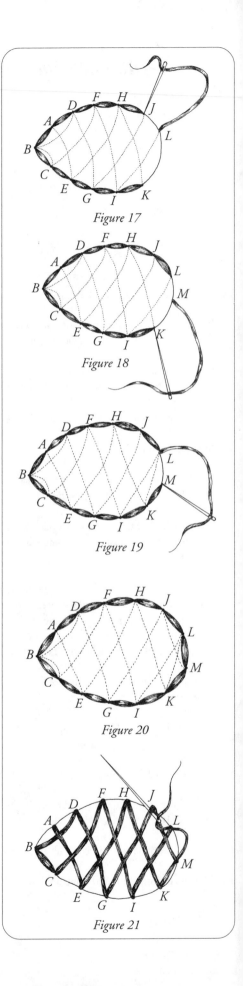

13. When you come to large curve, make your outside (on the largest part of the curve) larger. Make the inside stitches closer together. You may find it necessary to go in one hole twice on the inside area. Finish the design according to (**figures 13 - 20**).

14. After you have finished with a design or with the amount of floss you have in your needle, weave that end into the design. Clip the knotted end which is either in the upper section of the fabric or held outside the embroidery hoop. Rethread the needle with this end, and weave this end into the work as well (**fig. 21**).

*Figure 21*

1907 Romper .......................... 175
A Look Back ........................... 11
  Looking Back ........................ 86
    19th Century Clothing for Children 88
    Baby Clothing 1890 - 1919 ......... 91
    Baby Clothing 1919 - 1945 ......... 95
    Children's Fashions - 19th Century 93
    Girls' Fashions, 1919 - 1945 ....... 97
    Infant's Clothing - 19th Century ... 86
    Pink & Blue: The True Story ....... 100
    Sewing & Shopping-19th Century 99
    The Saga of Ready-made
      Baby Clothes ..................... 105
  Martha's Private Collection ......... 12
    Antique Clothing ................... 13
    Boy's Suits ........................ 25
    Patterns and Pages from the Past ... 34
    Vintage Photographs ................ 63
A Star Sleeps Here Door Decoration . 308
About the Author ...................... 416
Adding Smocked Panels:
  The Easy Way ........................ 356
Alphabet Quilt ........................ 319
Andrew's Airplanes-Duplicate
  Stitch Graph ........................ 291
Anna's Cream Nightie .................. 246
Antique Clothing ...................... 13
Antique Quilt ......................... 315
Apple for Teacher-Duplicate
  Stitch Graph ........................ 293
Appliqué .............................. 385
  Appliqué Stitch Maneuvers .......... 386
  Puffy or Padded Appliqué ........... 394
  Shadow Appliqué .................... 392
Appliqué Stitch Maneuvers ............ 386
Attaching Piping ...................... 384
Australian Madeira Appliqué .......... 349
Australian Madeira Appliqué Corded
  Accents ............................ 351
Australian Madeira Appliqué Hems .. 349
Australian Madeira Appliqué Motifs . 352
Australian Madeira Appliqué Neck
  Finish ............................. 353
Baby Blues - Smocking Plate .......... 295
Baby Cars - Smocking Plate ........... 295
Baby Christmas - Smocking Plate ..... 296
Baby Clothing 1890 - 1919 ............ 91
Baby Clothing 1919 - 1945 ............ 95
Ballet Bookends ...................... 307
Baseball Bookends .................... 306

Basic Pintucking ..................... 369
Basic Smocked Yoke Dress ............. 263
Batter's Up - Smocking Plate ......... 296
Beautious Bow - Duplicate Stitch
  Graph .............................. 292
Beginning French Sewing Techniques 363
Beverley Bow ......................... 405
Bib Knickers ......................... 203
Bike Ride - Smocking Plate ........... 296
Black Ribbon Tabbed Dress ............ 243
Blue Silk Ribbon Embroidered Dress 229
Boy's Suits - Antique ................ 25
Bradley's Madeira Appliqué Dress ..... 258
Brandon's Quilt ...................... 323
Brenda's Ice Cream Cone-Duplicate
  Stitch Graph ....................... 294
Bubble Gum Collar Shirt .............. 190
Bubbles - Duplicate Stitch Graph ..... 292
Bullion Stitch ....................... 402
Button-On Skirt ...................... 256
Button-On Suit Pants ................. 158
Campbell's Jabot Shirt ............... 114
Capital Chick - Duplicate Stitch
  Graph .............................. 293
Carousel - Smocking Plate ............ 297
Cat and Dog Collar Shirt ............. 192
Cecil's Royal Diamond Dress .......... 218
Chain Stitch ......................... 403
Chain Stitch Rose .................... 404
Checkerboard Border-Duplicate
  Stitch Graph ....................... 292
Chevron Border - Duplicate Stitch
  Graph .............................. 292
Children's Fashions - 19th Century ...... 93
Christmas Tree - Smocking Plate ....... 298
Christmas Tree Collar Shirt .......... 186
Christopher's Double Piping Shirt .... 111
Classic Techniques ................... 362
  Basic Pintucking ................... 369
    Corded Pintucks .................. 370
    Curving and Angling Pintucks ..... 371
  Beginning French Sewing Techniques 363
    Entredeux to Flat Fabric ......... 363
    Entredeux to Gathered Fabric ...... 363
    Gathered Lace to Entredeux ........ 363
    Lace to Entredeux ................ 363
    Lace to Fabric ................... 363
    Lace to Lace ..................... 363
    Top Stitch ....................... 363
  Lace Shaping Techniques ............ 372

    Shaping Lace Diamonds ............. 373
    Shaping Flip-Flopped Lace Bows . 376
    Tied Lace Bows ................... 378
    Hearts-Fold Back Miter Method .. 378
    Scalloped Skirt .................. 380
  Machine Entredeux ................. 365
  Puffing Method I .................. 367
  Puffing Method II ................. 368
Colonial Knot ........................ 406
Corded Pintucks ...................... 370
Corded Satin Stitch .................. 361
Creating Pinless Circular Puffing .... 337
Creating Tiny Gathering Foot
  Puffing ............................ 354
Cupid's Hearts - Smocking Plate ....... 299
Curving and Angling Pintucks ......... 371
Cutwork .............................. 395
Cutwork Flower Calico Bunny ........ 311
Dancing in the Dark Lace Shaping ... 338
David's Shirt ........................ 117
Don't Distort Your Smocking .......... 355
Double Needle Fancywork .............. 359
Double Piping ........................ 384
Duplicate Stitch Graphs .............. 289
  Andrew's Airplanes ................. 291
  Apple for the Teacher .............. 293
  Beautious Bow ...................... 292
  Brenda's Ice Cream Cone ............ 294
  Bubbles ............................ 292
  Capital Chick ...................... 293
  Checkerboard Border ................ 292
  Chevron Border ..................... 292
  Easter Eggs ........................ 293
  Flipper and Friend ................. 293
  Gingerbread Man .................... 292
  Hot Air Balloons ................... 293
  Jenks' Football .................... 294
  Letterman Stripe Border ............ 292
  Lucky Seven ........................ 294
  Pupil's Pencils .................... 291
  School Slate ....................... 293
  Teddy Bear Hero .................... 294
  Wave/Sky Border .................... 292
Easter Egg Collar Shirt .............. 188
Easter Eggs-Duplicate Stitch Graph .. 293
Ecru Batiste and Linen Shirt ......... 131
Embroidered Teddy Bear ............... 313
Embroidery Techniques ................ 401
  Beverley Bow ....................... 405
  Bullion Stitch ..................... 402

# Index

Chain Stitch .............................. 403
Chain Stitch Rose ...................... 404
Colonial Knot ........................... 406
Feather Stitch ........................... 402
Fly Stitch ................................. 403
French Knot .............................. 401
Japanese Ribbon Stitch ............... 401
Lady Bird ................................. 405
Lazy Daisy Stitch ...................... 402
Leaves ..................................... 404
Loop Stitch .............................. 406
Rosebud .................................. 404
Side Stitch Rose ....................... 403
Spider Web Rose ....................... 406
Stem/Outline Stitch .................. 401
Stems and Branches .................. 405
Straight Stitch .......................... 401
Straight Stitch Rose ................... 404
Tortured Fly Stitch .................... 404
Emma's Peach Nightie ................ 248
Entredeux to Flat Fabric ............. 363
Entredeux to Gathered Fabric ........ 363
Extra-Stable Lace Finishing .......... 383
Feather Stitch ........................... 402
Flipper and Friend-Duplicate Stitch
    Graph ................................. 293
Flowers and Butterflies -
    Smocking Plate ...................... 299
Fly Stitch ................................. 403
French Knot .............................. 401
French Seam .............................. 382
Front Buttoned Pants ................. 151
Fru Fru .................................... 408
Gathered Lace to Entredeux ......... 363
General Dress Directions ............. 212
General Shirt Directions .............. 194
General Smocked Shirt Directions .... 201
General Yoke Dress Directions ........ 268
Gingerbread Collar Shirt .............. 184
Gingerbread Man - Duplicate Stitch
    Graph ................................. 292
Gingham Linen Lapel Collar Shirt .... 140
Girls' Fashions, 1919 - 1945 .......... 97
Greyson's Shirt .......................... 143
Hearts-Fold Back Miter Method ....... 378
Heirloom Sewing for Jack ............. 107
    1907 Romper ........................ 175
    Button-On Suit Pants .............. 158
    Campbell's Jabot Shirt ............ 114
    Christopher's Double Piping Shirt . 111

David's Shirt ............................. 117
Ecru Batiste and Linen Shirt ......... 131
Front Buttoned Pants ................. 151
Gingham Linen Lapel Collar Shirt . 140
Greyson's Shirt .......................... 143
Knicker Length Pleated Romper .... 172
Logan's Madeira Appliqué Shirt ..... 146
Marshall's Scalloped Shirt ............ 108
One Piece Sailor Romper ............. 164
Pleated Front Knickers ................ 160
Sailor Collar with Tie ................. 149
Short Lined Pleated Romper ......... 168
Silk and Blue Linen Shirt ............ 134
Straight Front Knee Pants ............ 162
Tied Sailor Collar Shirt ............... 122
Tucked Panel Lapel Shirt ............. 128
V-Front Button-On Pants ............. 157
V-Waist Button-On Knickers ......... 154
Ward's Bias Trim Shirt ................ 119
White Linen Lapel Collar Shirt ...... 137
White Shirt with Plaid Madeira
    Border ................................ 125
Heirloom Sewing for Jack or Jill ....... 178
Million Different Variations Shirt .. 179
    Bubble Gum Collar Shirt ......... 190
    Cat and Dog Collar Shirt ......... 192
    Christmas Tree Collar Shirt ...... 186
    Easter Egg Collar Shirt ........... 188
    General Shirt Directions ......... 194
    Gingerbread Collar Shirt ......... 184
    Monogrammed Round Collar ...... 181
    Smocked Shirts .................... 196
    General Smocked Shirt Directions 201
Bib Knickers .......................... 203
    Simple Hearts ...................... 210
    Simple Diamonds .................. 210
Heirloom Sewing for Jill .............. 211
    General Dress Directions ......... 212
    Anna's Cream Nightie ............ 246
    Black Ribbon Tabbed Dress ...... 243
    Blue Silk Ribbon Embroidered Dress 229
    Bradley's Madeira Appliqué Dress .. 258
    Button-On Skirt .................... 256
    Cecil's Royal Diamond Dress ........ 218
    Emma's Peach Nightie ............ 248
    Lace Waves Overskirt Dress ...... 231
    Morgan's Embroidery Masterpiece . 235
    Pink Heart Dress ................... 253
    Rebekah's Butterfly Linen Dress ..... 250
    Robin's Egg Australian Madeira Dress 216

Sarah Joy's Snowman Dress ........... 240
Silk French Waterfall Dress ........... 226
White and Pink Madeira Dress ...... 223
Basic Smocked Yoke Dress ............. 263
    Yoke Dress Yardage Requirements .. 267
    General Yoke Dress Directions ....... 268
Madeira Applique-Straight Hemline . 342
Madeira Applique-Shaped Hemline .. 340
Home Decorating, Crafts & Quilts ... 303
    A Star Sleeps Here Door Decoration 308
    Alphabet Quilt ..................... 319
    Antique Quilt ...................... 315
    Ballet Bookends .................... 307
    Baseball Bookends ................. 306
    Brandon's Quilt .................... 323
    Cutwork Flower Calico Bunny ....... 311
    Embroidered Teddy Bear ........... 313
    Memory Fan Pillow ................. 305
    Sunbonnet Jack & Jill Quilt ......... 326
    The Prince Sleeps Here Door
        Decoration ...................... 310
    The Princess Sleeps Here Door
        Decoration ...................... 309
Hot Air Balloons - Duplicate Stitch
    Graph ................................. 293
Infant's Clothing in the 19th Century . 86
Japanese Ribbon Stitch ................. 401
Jenks' Football - Duplicate Stitch
    Graph ................................. 294
Knicker Length Pleated Romper ....... 172
Lace to Entredeux ....................... 363
Lace to Fabric ........................... 363
Lace to Lace ............................. 363
Lace Motifs .............................. 357
Lace and Ribbon Weaving ............. 360
Lace Shaping Techniques ............... 372
Lace Waves Overskirt Dress ........... 231
Lady Bird ................................. 405
Lazy Daisy Stitch ....................... 402
Leaves ..................................... 404
Let's Go Dutch - Smocking Plate ..... 299
Letterman Stripe Border-Duplicate
Stitch Graph ............................. 292
Logan's Madeira Appliqué Shirt ....... 146
Looking Back ............................. 86
Loop Stitch .............................. 406
Lucky Seven - Duplicate Stitch Graph 294
Machine Entredeux ..................... 365
Madeira Appliqué Windows ........... 348
Magic Madeira Appliqué Collars ...... 343

Magic Madeira Appliqué Two Sided
    Panel .................................... 347
Magic Madeira Motifs ..................... 346
Magic Madeira Technique .................. 339
Making Piping ............................. 384
    Attaching Piping ..................... 384
    Double Piping ........................ 384
    Striped Piping ....................... 384
Marshall's Scalloped Shirt ................ 108
Martha's Private Collection ............... 12
Memory Fan Pillow ......................... 305
Million Different Variations Shirt ..... 179
Monogrammed Round Collar .......... 181
Morgan's Embroidery Masterpiece .... 235
New Techniques ............................. 330
    Adding Smocked Panels:
    The Easy Way .......................... 356
    Australian Madeira Appliqué ......... 349
    Australian Madeira Appliqué Hems 349
    Australian Madeira Appliqué
        Corded Accents ................... 351
    Australian Madeira Appliqué Motifs 352
    Australian Madeira Appliqué Neck
        Finish ............................ 353
    Corded Satin Stitch .................. 361
    Creating Tiny Gathering Foot Puffing 354
    Don't Distort Your Smocking ......... 355
    Double Needle Fancywork ............. 359
    Making Lace Diamond Motifs ....... 357
    Lace and Ribbon Weaving............. 360
    Magic Madeira Technique ............. 339
        Magic Madeira Appliqué Hem with
            Shaped Hemline ................ 340
        Magic Madeira Appliqué Hem
            with a Straight Hemline....... 342
        Magic Madeira Appliqué Collars .. 343
        Other Magic Madeira Appliqué
            Borders ....................... 344
        Magic Madeira Motifs ............. 346
        Magic Madeira Appliqué Two
            Sided Panel ................... 347
        Madeira Appliqué Windows ...... 348
    Pinless Lace Shaping ................. 331
        Pinless Lace Diamonds ............ 332
        Pinless Lace Scallops ............ 333
        Pinless Lace Circles ............. 335
        Pinless Lace Bows ................ 336
        Creating Pinless Circular Puffing . 337
        Dancing in the Dark Lace Shaping . 338
    Shadow Appliqué The Easy Way .... 358

One Piece Sailor Romper ................. 164
Other Magic Madeira Appliqué
    Borders ............................... 344
Other Magic Madeira Appliqué
    Borders ............................... 344
Patterns and Pages from the Past ....... 34
Pink & Blue: The True Story ............ 100
Pink Heart Dress ......................... 253
Pinless Lace Bows ........................ 336
Pinless Lace Circles ..................... 335
Pinless Lace Diamonds ................... 332
Pinless Lace Scallops .................... 333
Pinless Lace Shaping ..................... 331
Pleated Front Knickers ................... 160
Prehistoric Play - Smocking Plate ...... 301
Pretty In Pink - Smocking Plate ........ 301
Puffing Method I .......................... 367
Puffing Method II ......................... 368
Puffy or Padded Appliqué ............... 394
Pupil's Pencils-Duplicate Stitch Graph . 291
Rebekah's Butterfly Linen Dress ........ 250
Ribbon Rosettes (Fru Fru) .............. 408
Ribbon to Lace ........................... 360
Robin's Egg Australian Madeira Dress .. 216
Rosebud .................................. 404
Sailor Collar with Tie ................... 149
Santa's Ride - Smocking Plate........... 301
Sarah Joy's Snowman Dress ............. 240
Sash Loop ................................ 288
Scalloped Skirt .......................... 380
School Slate-Duplicate Stitch Graph . 293
Sewing & Shopping - 19th Century .. 99
Shadow Appliqué ......................... 392
Shadow Appliqué The Easy Way ....... 358
Shadowwork Embroidery -
    From the Back ......................... 409
Shadowwork Embroidery -
    From the Front ........................ 411
Shaping Flip-Flopped Lace Bows ...... 376
Shaping Lace Diamonds ................. 373
Short Lined Pleated Romper ........... 168
Side Stitch Rose ......................... 403
Silk and Blue Linen Shirt ............... 134
Silk French Waterfall Dress ............. 226
Simple Diamonds - Smocking Plate .. 210
Simple Hearts - Smocking Plate ....... 210
Smocked Shirts .......................... 196
Smocking Directions & Duplicate
    Stitch Graphs ......................... 289

Smocking Plate Directions .............. 295
    Baby Blues ........................... C-36, 295
    Baby Cars ............................ C-37, 295
    Baby Christmas ...................... C-37, 296
    Batter's Up .......................... C-38, 296
    Bike Ride ............................ C-39, 296
    Carousel ............................. C-40, 297
    Christmas Tree ....................... C-41, 298
    Cupid's Hearts ....................... C-42, 299
    Flowers and Butterflies ............. C-43, 299
    Let's Go Dutch ....................... C-44, 299
    Prehistoric Play ..................... C-45, 300
    Pretty In Pink........................ C-46, 301
    Santa's Ride ......................... C-47, 301
    Simple Diamonds ..................... 210
    Simple Hearts ........................ 210
    Tiny Tennies ......................... C-48, 302
Spider Web Rose .......................... 406
Stem/Outline Stitch ...................... 401
Stems and Branches ...................... 405
Straight Front Knee Pants .............. 162
Straight Stitch .......................... 401
Straight Stitch Rose ..................... 404
Striped Piping ........................... 384
Sunbonnet Jack & Jill Quilt ............ 326
Sweet Pea ................................ 407
Teddy Bear Hero - Duplicate Stitch
    Graph ................................. 294
The Prince Sleeps Here Door
    Decoration ............................ 310
The Princess Sleeps Here Door
    Decoration ............................ 309
The Saga of Ready-made Baby Clothes  105
Tied Lace Bows ........................... 378
Tied Sailor Collar Shirt ................ 122
Tiny Tennies - Smocking Plate ......... 302
Top Stitch ............................... 363
Tortured Fly Stitch ...................... 404
Tucked Panel Lapel Shirt ............... 128
V-Front Button-On Pants ............... 157
V-Waist Button-On Knickers ........... 154
Vintage Photographs ...................... 63
Ward's Bias Trim Shirt .................. 119
Wave/Sky Border - Duplicate Stitch
    Graph ................................. 292
White and Pink Madeira Dress ......... 223
White Linen Lapel Collar Shirt ........ 137
White Shirt with Plaid Madeira
    Border ................................ 125
Yoke Dress Yardage Requirements ..... 267

# About
## Martha Campbell Pullen, Ph.D.

Martha Campbell Pullen didn't invent heirloom sewing — the art of joining laces to create fabric has survived for centuries — but she and her fabulous staff can take some of the credit for turning this age-old art into a hobby that's approaching "all the rage" proportions.

Martha personally learned how to smock and French sew by machine over 20 years ago when she was making clothes for her baby daughter. She realized if she could be drawn in so passionately, other women could be as well.

Today, she fronts her own heirloom sewing empire, which grew out of a tiny shop in Huntsville, Alabama. In 1981, two months after opening that shop, she began importing laces and fabrics to sell mail-order both wholesale and retail. Next, came Martha Pullen Heirloom Sewing Schools, which now attract more than 600 women to Huntsville twice a year. Their success prompted Pullen to venture out of her local market, conducting full scale Martha Pullen schools in Australia, England, Sweden, Canada, New Zealand and Texas. She has done mini-schools in almost every state in the United States.

An accomplished author, she has more than 25 books to her credit including three hardback manuals in excess of 400 pages. "You Can Make Money From Your Hobby," her most recent book has been published by Broadman and Holman, an arm of the Baptist Sunday School Board. It is available in Christian and mainstream bookstores nationally.

Adding to that list of successes, and probably the project of which she is most proud, is *Sew Beautiful*, a magazine she founded and began publishing over a decade ago. The publication focusing on heirloom and other classic sewing arts has an international following and distributes in excess of 90,000 copies bi-monthly. Four years ago, she began sharing her love of heirloom sewing with public television audiences around the country through her *Martha's Sewing Room* series.

To encourage heirloom sewn garments in cooler climates, Martha expanded the range of materials used from traditional batistes and other lightweight materials to wool challis, corduroys, flannels and home decorating fabrics. She has even come up with a name for these heirloom garments — love clothes.

"I call them 'love clothes' because I quickly realized that they are the special garments we make with love for the people we love," she explained. "With sewing, it almost seems that the love goes right from the machine or stitching needle into whatever we are making, especially where children are involved. It means so much more than just purchasing something ready made. Best of all, the classic, beautifully-sewn heirloom garments can carry that love from one generation to another."

Annually, Martha presents *Martha's Sewing Market* at the Arlington Convention Center in Arlington, Texas and in Orlando at the Tupperware Convention Center. Her consumer exhibitions feature top international sewing instructors, more than 50 free class choices per day, a vendor arena, fashion shows, and displays. All of these activities are available after paying a low admission fee.

"Sewing makes memories that are passed on from generation to generation through the actual garments but also through the stitches learned," said Martha, who is on the road promoting the art of sewing many weeks out of every year.

A native of Scottsboro, Alabama, Martha is an internationally-known lecturer and teacher in the heirloom sewing field. After graduating with a degree in speech and English from the University of Alabama, she taught those subjects at almost every level of middle school and high school. Later, her studies led to a Ph.D in educational administration and management from the University of Alabama.

She has been named Huntsville Madison County Chamber of Commerce Executive of the Year, the second woman in the history of the organization to receive this award. She has been a nominee for *Inc*, magazine's executive of the year. She is a member of Rotary International and Optimist International. She has served on the board of directors of the Smocking Arts Guild of America and has presented workshops in French sewing by machine throughout the United States, Australia, England, Canada, Sweden and New Zealand. She is the wife of Joe Ross Pullen, an implant dentist and president of her company, mother of five and grandmother to ten! An active member of her church, she also volunteers with the Southern Baptist International Mission Board.

To request a free Martha Pullen Company catalogue containing Martha Pullen products and publications, please write to:
Martha Pullen Company • 518 Madison Street • Huntsville, AL 35801 • (256) 533-9586 • Fax (256) 533-9630
1-800-547-4176 • website – www.marthapullenco.com • email – info@marthapullenco.com